Art Between Matter and Code

Bridging Classical Art and Digital Frontiers

Gianpiero Moioli

Apress®

Art Between Matter and Code: Bridging Classical Art and Digital Frontiers

Gianpiero Moioli
Milan, Italy

ISBN-13 (pbk): 979-8-8688-2375-6 ISBN-13 (electronic): 979-8-8688-2376-3
https://doi.org/10.1007/979-8-8688-2376-3

Managing Director, Apress Media LLC: Welmoed Spahr
Acquisitions Editor: Aditee Mirashi
Development Editor: James Markham
Editorial Assistant: Jacob Shmulewitz
Copy Editor: Kimberly Wimpsett

Cover designed by eStudioCalamar

Distributed to the book trade worldwide by Springer Science+Business Media New York, 1 New York Plaza, New York, NY 10004. Phone 1-800-SPRINGER, fax (201) 348-4505, e-mail orders-ny@springer-sbm.com, or visit www.springeronline.com. Apress Media, LLC is a Delaware LLC and the sole member (owner) is Springer Science + Business Media Finance Inc (SSBM Finance Inc). SSBM Finance Inc is a **Delaware** corporation.

For information on translations, please e-mail booktranslations@springernature.com; for reprint, paperback, or audio rights, please e-mail bookpermissions@springernature.com.

Apress titles may be purchased in bulk for academic, corporate, or promotional use. eBook versions and licenses are also available for most titles. For more information, reference our Print and eBook Bulk Sales web page at http://www.apress.com/bulk-sales.

Any source code or other supplementary material referenced by the author in this book is available to readers on GitHub. For more detailed information, please visit https://www.apress.com/gp/services/source-code.

If disposing of this product, please recycle the paper

To my professors and to my students, past and present,
for reminding me that art is always a shared process.

Table of Contents

About the Author

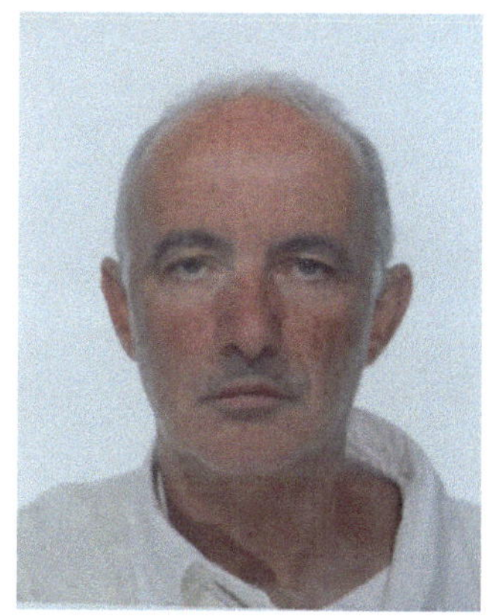

Gianpiero Moioli is a sculptor, architect, and professor of sculpture, virtual architecture, and history of contemporary architecture at the Brera Academy of Fine Arts in Milan. He has been a certified instructor (BFCT) with the Blender Foundation since 2008.

Gianpiero graduated with a degree (MA) in sculpture from the Brera Academy of Fine Arts in Milan and received his degree (MA) in architecture from the Polytechnic University of Milan. In 2008, he and Stefania Albertini created the Brera Academy Virtual Lab, a virtual sculpture and architecture laboratory at the Academy of Fine Arts of Brera. He started using Blender in 2004 and presented his first results with this open-source software in three Blender conferences in 2008, 2010, and 2011.

About the Technical Reviewer

Ms. Kritika is a dynamic and experienced interdisciplinary researcher. With a substantial portfolio of scholarly publications and keynote engagements, her insights have been widely recognized across various academic and industry platforms. In addition, she serves as a technical reviewer for academic conferences and journal reviewer for top journals.

Meet the Academic Editor

Zhiwen Zhou Postdoctoral Researcher from Jingdezhen Ceramic University, Jiangxi, China

Current Position: Xinjiang Normal University (with professorial remuneration)

Research Areas: Design Studies, Fine Arts, Ceramic Art Design and Theory

Academic Achievements:

- Published 10 papers, such as *Art & Design Research* CSSCI-indexed journals
- Principal investigator of a Jiangxi Provincial Postdoctoral Research Grant
- Participated in more than 17 national, provincial, and municipal research projects, contributing notably to the monograph writing and revision for the Major Project of the National Social Science Fund of China in Arts (Project No. 19ZD24)

International Engagements:

- Invited speaker at international art and design forums hosted by Swinburne University of Technology (Australia), Indonesia, University of Florence (Italy), Silpakorn University(Thailand), and Jingdezhen Ceramic University (China), among others

Exhibitions and Awards:

- Recipient of more than 20 awards in national art competitions and exhibitions across China

Acknowledgments

This book grew out of a long process of research, artistic practice, and reflection across different places, institutions, and encounters.

I would like to express my deep gratitude to my professors, whose creativity, and generosity have profoundly shaped my formation and thinking: Giancarlo Marchese, Tommaso Trini, Francesco Leonetti, Corrado Levi, Flaminio Gualdoni, and Maria Grazia Sandri.

I also wish to thank my students, past and present, whose curiosity and openness to experimentation continually renew my perspective on sculpture, technology, and contemporary artistic practice.

I am also grateful to Zhou Zhiwen, Spandana Chatterjee, Krishnan Sathyamurthy, Gryffin Winkler, and Ms. Kritika, for their invaluable support and collaboration throughout the development of this project.

Introduction

"Now I really make the little idea from clay, and I hold it in my hand. I can turn it, look at it from underneath, see it from one view, hold it against the sky, imagine it any size I like, and really be in control—almost like God creating something."[1]

Henry Moore

At the heart of this project lies my trajectory as an artist and professor of sculpture, virtual architecture, and video sculpture at the Brera Academy of Fine Arts. I did not set out to write an art history essay or a technical manual but rather a reflection on the evolution of sculpture—from Neoclassicism to Spatialism to the present—shaped by the profound transformations introduced by digital technologies.

As artist and educator, I have witnessed the convergence of art, science, and technology—an ongoing process that redefines the boundaries of form, space, and material. Over the past decade, my work has developed between physical and digital environments, transforming sculpture into a field where form merges with data, simulation, and interaction.

We are entering an era of AI-augmented creativity, where generative tools complement traditional software workflows and can even produce files directly in formats such as DOC, PDF, or BLEND. However, at the moment, specialized software is still required for complex production work such as 3D modeling, rendering, or fabrication.[2]

In this expanded context, creativity becomes the ability to imagine, direct, and orchestrate complex hybrid processes.

---

[1] This statement encapsulates Henry Moore's approach to thinking and working, as documented in *Henry Moore: Writings and Conversations*, ed. Alan Wilkinson (University of California Press, 2002).

[2] This concept describes the shift from using many separate programs step-by-step to working with unified systems that can generate complex results from a single command. This change affects not only artists but also designers, architects, and graphic professionals, transforming their role from executors to curators of possibilities.

This book is conceived as a hybrid, like my own sculptures: suspended between history and technology, between matter and code. The visual materials reflect this tension, juxtaposing classical works with virtual sculptures, diagrams, and conceptual images. Modeling, in my practice, is drawing in space, an action that translates thought into form, whether through physical tools or digital environments.

Today, sculpture functions as a dynamic system, responsive, and mutable. Process-driven approaches have become central: from initial sketches to virtual prototypes, the conceptual structure often constitutes the work itself. This creative path unfolds as a process where real and virtual intersect—generating new forms and perspectives.

Genesis of the Volume: A Dialogue between Traditional Techniques and New Technologies

From modeling and procedural generation to AI-driven transformations and 3D printing, this volume explores how artists can act as "world-builders" today.[3] This role—in different ways—also marked figures such as Picasso and Duchamp, who redefined the languages of art and opened new horizons.

In the same spirit, Philippe Starck has shown how design itself can transcend mere function to become a metaphor for dematerialization and invisibility, shaping new forms of everyday life. As he powerfully declared in his 2007 TED Talk: "We can say to our children: OK! Done! That was our story. That passed. Now you have a duty: invent a new story. Invent a new poetry. The only rule is, we have not to have any idea about the next story."[4]

In our time, the artist operates simultaneously as sculptor of virtual forms, coder, and storyteller. Through the interplay of matter and code, I seek to present a vision of art as a driving force of change rather than merely a response to it.

---

[3] "World-builders" recalls figures who reshaped our perception of reality: Columbus by redrawing the map of the globe, Einstein by altering space and time, Picasso by inventing Cubism, and Duchamp by redefining art through the readymade.

[4] Philippe Starck, *Design and Destiny*, TED Talk, Monterey, California, March 2007, transcript available at `https://www.ted.com/talks/philippe_starck_design_and_destiny?subtitle=en`

From Clay to Code

Before exploring digital sculpture, it is essential to recall its roots in the physical manipulation of matter—stone, bronze, wood, and especially clay and plaster. For centuries, sculpture was defined by direct engagement with space, gravity, and the tactile presence of form.

The uniqueness of these works lies in their materiality. Authenticity and ownership were inscribed in the object itself, its weight, its surface, and the traces of artistic intention embedded in matter. This grounding in the physical world offers a powerful counterpoint to today's dematerialized digital sculptures.

Antonio Canova exemplifies this tradition, with works that were monumental, allegorical, and rooted in classical ideals of beauty and virtue. Yet his practice also allows for contemporary reinterpretations. His pursuit of ideal form and his refined treatment of marble anticipate, on a conceptual level, certain concerns that later emerge in digital aesthetics, such as lightness and dematerialization.

In this light, Canova may be seen as a precursor to digital sculpture, anticipating themes of immateriality and the dissolution of boundaries between form and void.

Similarly, Henry Moore's process underscores the sculptural gesture as a total act of vision. Beginning with small clay maquettes, Moore retained full spatial control over the evolving form.[5] These hand-sized models, shaped and viewed from all angles, contained the potential of monumental works. His emphasis on the initial gesture as a conceptual whole finds a clear parallel in today's digital modeling, where a 3D object can be endlessly rotated, scaled, and refined in virtual space. However, this digital process is inherently reversible and immaterial, contrasting with the sculptor's immediate, physical commitment.

This lineage, from clay and marble to code, frames the tools of contemporary creation.[6]

---

[5] A vivid example is the Thames Television program *Fusion* (first broadcast in September 1971), filmed in the artist's studio and foundry and available on YouTube (*Sculptor - Henry Moore - Thames Television* `https://www.youtube.com/watch?v=LrRc3sT2vXo&t=12s`). Moore often emphasized how the maquette allowed him to see a form "from every angle simply by turning it in his hand," before enlarging it to monumental scale.

[6] Clay and marble here stand as symbolic poles of sculptural tradition—clay as immediacy and gesture, marble as permanence and ideal form—now extended into the immateriality of code.

From Material Objects to Virtual Realities

Moore's method resonates with the spirit of Part III of this book, where imagination escapes narrative constraints and explores energy, architecture, memory, and the unknown (see Figure 1).

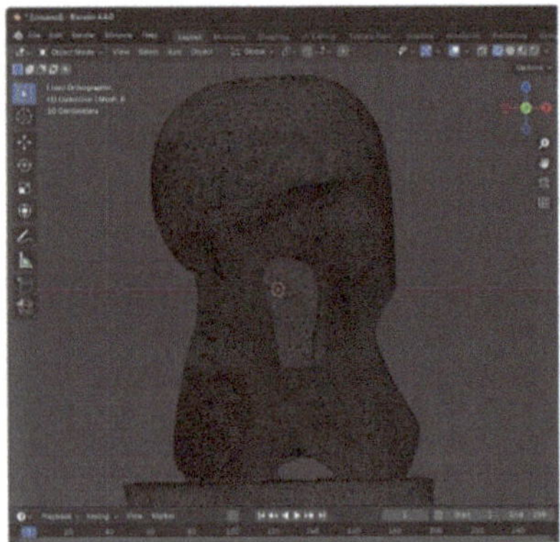

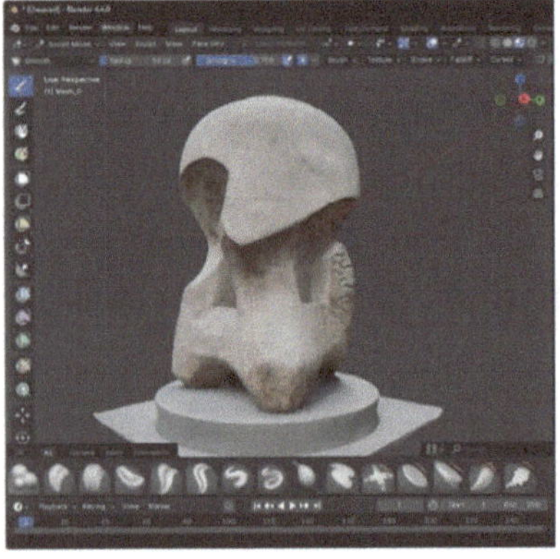

Figure 1. Henry Moore, Atom Piece, 1964–65, AGO.
Photo: By Just - Own work, Public Domain, CC0 1.0 Public Domain Nuclear Energy, University of Chicago – © Wikimedia Commons,
https://commons.wikimedia.org/w/index.php?curid=20426296
3D model: Atom Piece, by vr_me_candice. Sketchfab, CC BY 4.0,
https://skfb.ly/oMSRW

A striking example of this approach is *Atom Piece,* where Moore engages directly with the theme of energy, one of the core trajectories of Part III of this book.

Here, matter is no longer mass but threshold; form becomes spatial tension. Rather than representing a subject, the sculpture evokes invisible forces, internal pulses, and atomic pressure.

In this sense, *Atom Piece* anticipates a sculptural imagination beyond representation, one that explores symbolic configurations and fluid topologies, resonating with the dynamics of contemporary digital creation.[7]

A small gesture—whether in clay or code—can unfold into entire immersive worlds. This convergence defines a new sculptural imagination, reshaping not only form but also authorship, space, and perception.

The Tools of Contemporary Creation

Today's sculptural tools include virtual modeling environments like Blender, text-to-image synthesis such as Stable Diffusion, simulation software, and 3D printing platforms. These applications extend the reach of gesture into digital and immersive dimensions. Some key tools are open source (Blender, Stable Diffusion), while others have free tiers with paid professional versions (Unity, TouchDesigner), creating a mixed accessibility landscape.

They are not just instruments; they are conceptual interfaces where tradition and innovation converge. Creation becomes a continuum of gesture, simulation, and code. The artist's studio transforms into a generative environment, where traditional materials like clay meet digital data from 3D scanning or procedural generation. As a result, a form exists on multiple levels: as matter, the physical print or sculpture; as file, the parametric model or voxel data; and as experience, the immersive installation or VR interface.

A New Threshold

We begin at the intersection between the tangible and the virtual, between historical legacy and speculative invention.

This is the threshold where sculpture expands.

---

[7] For more on the history and context of this work, see the Henry Moore Foundation catalogue entry for Atom Piece (LH 526), or the Tate Collection notes on Atom Piece (Working Model for Nuclear Energy). `https://www.tate.org.uk/art/research-publications/henry-moore/henry-moore-om-ch-atom-piece-working-model-for-nuclear-energy-r1171996`. This connection aligns with my own thematic explorations, the first being *"Breath of Fire - Flames and Energy"*, where matter is similarly transformed by internal forces into dynamic, spatial expressions.

PART I

From Gesture to Code

This first part traces how sculpture moves from traditional practice into contemporary digital forms, arriving at a paradigm where creation oscillates between real and virtual, organic and algorithmic, natural and scientific.

In this dynamic interplay, the categories of materiality, form, and authorship are redefined.

The throughline is clear: technological mediation reshapes the artwork's very ontology.

What happens to matter, gesture, and form when they enter the virtual?

The roots of this question lie in the early avant-gardes and extend through Arte Povera, Conceptual Art, and Land and Environmental Art, which progressively opened art to expansive and immaterial processes. Paradoxically, the spread of virtual technologies has also produced a countermovement: digital tools return art to physicality, through 3D printing, augmented environments, and metaverse spaces. Sculpture becomes tangible again, even when born from code.

Grounded in the sculptural heritage of the Brera Academy—founded in 1776—and the broader Milanese scene, this book revisits pivotal figures and research that fuse tradition with innovation. From Canova's neoclassical clarity to the expressive force of the Lombard lineage and from Lucio Fontana's radical spatial ruptures to Studio Azzurro's immersive narratives, each step marks a decisive shift in how we conceive ideas, gestures, matter, and space.

Within this continuum, the tension between Apollonian order and Dionysian flux—once framed through sculpture and music—finds new life in the immaterial realms of code, data, and algorithmic form. This initial section establishes the conceptual framework for the current hybrid practices of sculpture, which are situated between historical heritage and technological innovation.

At the center stands the gesture, the principle that leads to code.

Fontana's cut was not a break but a passage: it opened a field beyond painting and objecthood—toward possibility.

That gesture reverberates today in digital environments, where sculpture is not carved but generated, animated by interaction, and open to transformation.

The four chapters that follow map this evolution across materials and tools, digital modeling, algorithmic processes, and the questions of identity and authenticity that accompany them.

CHAPTER 1

Ideas, Materials, Technologies, and Aesthetics (1776–Today)

The transition from traditional to digital art and sculpture is not a rupture but rather an ontological expansion of material, gesture, and authorship.

This chapter examines the evolving nature of artistic practice through the lens of technological innovation and material transformation, exploring how form, space, and meaning are redefined when sculptural gestures are transposed into digital environments.

Central to this transformation is the emergence of new artistic substances—data, algorithms, and virtual topologies—which, while replacing traditional media, preserve the essence of the generative and exploratory act of art and sculpture.

The chapter opens with a historical focus on sculpture from 1776 to the present.

It traces the changing interplay between the artist's idea, physical matter, and, in recent decades, digital code.

It highlights how these evolving forces have shaped sculptural aesthetics—from the neoclassical ideals of the Brera Academy to the hybrid, immaterial forms of contemporary digital experimentation, emphasizing the shift from permanence in matter to coded, mutable expressions of form.

This historical trajectory begins with the birth of Neoclassicism in the late 18th century, when Antonio Canova's mastery transformed marble into a language of timeless ideals—marking a foundational moment from which the Brera Academy's sculptural heritage would emerge.

G. Moioli, *Art Between Matter and Code*, https://doi.org/10.1007/979-8-8688-2376-3_1

1.1 Tradition and Break: From Neoclassicism to Spatialism and Beyond

At the entrance of the Brera Academy in Milan, Canova's *Napoleon as Mars the Peacemaker* stands both as a monument and a challenge (Figure 1-1).

Figure 1-1. Courtyard of Honour, Brera Academy, Milan.
Napoleon as Mars the Peacemaker by Antonio Canova (bronze cast, 1811) positioned centrally within the courtyard framed by a two-tiered Tuscan-Ionian portico.
Photo: Author's own photograph, © Gianpiero Moioli, 2025, licensed under CC BY 4.0

Cast in bronze, the sculpture embodies the neoclassical ideal of timeless beauty, harmony, and permanence. For generations, it has welcomed students and artists into a space shaped by discipline, tradition, and the study of art.

This is where my journey began.[1]

In the Cortile Napoleonico, Canova's sculpture does not simply inhabit the architectural space; it structures it.

The rational geometry of the courtyard becomes a frame for the absolute form of the sculpture, which serves both as axis and symbol of the academy's ideals.

The encounter between the neoclassical body and architectural void creates a silent dialogue: the statue monumentalizes time, while the courtyard monumentalizes space.

Like Fontana's gesture that cuts through the canvas to open up space through absence, Canova's figure opens it through presence, a classical form that shapes the void around it.

Canova stands as the silent root of Brera's neoclassical tradition, a legacy quietly unfolding through generations.[2]

Within the halls of Brera, where classical statuary and anatomical models once defined the foundations of artistic education, I began to reflect not only on how we shape matter but also on how the very meaning of matter has evolved.

Clay, plaster, bronze, marble, plastics: these were once the essential materials of modern sculpture.

They carried with them weight, resistance, transparency, ritual.

Today, new elements enter the artist's studio: files, code, energy, light, sound; each one challenging our understanding of volume, permanence, and authorship.

And yet the essential gesture endures: to give form to thought, to reveal a presence within absence.

From that very persistence arises the central question: **"What happens to matter, gesture, and form when they enter the virtual?"**

---

[1] The Cortile Napoleonico of the Brera Academy, designed in the early 19th century during Napoleonic reforms, houses the bronze *Napoleon as Mars the Peacemaker*, cast in Rome in 1811 by Francesco and Luigi Righetti from Canova's 1809 plaster model. The marble original (1803–1806) is at Apsley House, London. Installed in 1859, the bronze remains a powerful symbol of classical ideals and academic tradition.

[2] See: Valli, Francesca. "*Con nostro vantaggio e con vostro onore*: Canova e l'Accademia di Brera" In *Antonio Canova*. La cultura figurativa e letteraria dei grandi centri italiani. *Vol. 2: Milano, Firenze, Napoli*. Proceedings of the IV Settimana di Studi Canoviani. Bassano del Grappa, 2006.

1.1.1 Neoclassicism: The Idea in Material Form

Neoclassicism, whose roots reach back to the 1740s with the first excavations at Herculaneum and Pompeii and with Winckelmann's early writings, marked a conscious return to the classical ideals of perfection, proportion, and harmony. By the 1770s, however, the style had moved from theory and isolated experiments to become the fully dominant language of official art and architecture across much of Europe. In this respect, 1776 - the year in which the Accademia di Belle Arti di Brera was founded under Habsburg rule - serves as an excellent milestone. Antonio Canova (1757-1822), a leading figure of the movement, indirectly shaped the Brera Academy through his influence on its artistic and institutional reforms during the Napoleonic period (Figure 1-2).[3]

[3] Although Antonio Canova was never a professor at the Brera Academy, he became a central symbolic figure in its early years due to the strong alignment between his neoclassical ideals and the academic principles promoted by Brera after its foundation in 1776. During the Napoleonic period, his influence was echoed and reinforced by Giuseppe Bossi, a leading figure in Brera's institutional reforms and a close admirer of Canova's work. The installation of *Napoleon as Mars the Peacemaker* in the Academy's courtyard in 1859 further cemented Canova's symbolic presence, making his art an enduring point of reference for generations of students trained at Brera.

Figure 1-2. Antonio Canova, Psyche Revived by Cupid's Kiss, 1787–1793.
Marble, 155 × 168 cm, Louvre Museum, Paris.
Photo: Wikimedia Commons – © Jean-Pol GRANDMONT, Public Domain (placed in the public domain by the rights holder). `https://commons.wikimedia.org/wiki/File:0_Psych%C3%A9_ranim%C3%A9e_par_le_baiser_de_l'Amour_-_Canova_-_Louvre_1.JPG`

His sculptures, such as Psyche Revived by Cupid's Kiss (1787–1793),[4] translated the artist's vision of idealized beauty into marble.

The interplay here was direct: the artist's idea of classical perfection guided the choice and shaping of material, in a process entirely grounded in physical gesture and craft.

But Neoclassicism established a vision of art in which the concept preceded the object.

The artist's task was not merely to imitate nature but to distill it into pure, essential structures, forms that embodied reason, balance, and permanence.

[4] The sculpture "Psyche Revived by Cupid's Kiss" was completed in 1793, but the work period should be verified. The Hermitage version was completed 1787–1793, but the Louvre version has different dates (1787–1793 for the first version, 1800–1805 for the second).

In this sense, Neoclassicism laid the conceptual groundwork for the digital age: it elevated the mental project, the design, as something autonomous from physical execution.

This framework mirrors the logic of today's digital creation, in which the artwork is often conceived as a code, a model, a project, or a virtual prototype before becoming material.

Before exploring technologies, this chapter begins with a reconsideration of **traditional materials** and the **aesthetic, cultural, and symbolic meanings** they continue to carry, now echoed, transformed, or translated into the languages of the digital.

From this intersection, a new aesthetic emerges, grounded not in permanence but in transformation; not in physical weight but in flows of information.

It is an aesthetic that moves between the visible and the invisible, where gestures meet algorithms, and material becomes both real and speculative.

As traditional sculpture expands into digital territories, we may recall Nietzsche's vision of art as a tension between the Apollonian and the Dionysian.

In Nietzsche, the opposition between Apollonian sculpture and Dionysian music expressed a fundamental tension between control and chaos, form and flux.[5]

Today, this polarity extends to digital practices, from virtual modeling to procedural generation and AI. As the artist shifts from shaping matter to programming systems, creation becomes a dialogue between intention and unpredictability—a theme further explored in Chapter 3.

The boundary between the physical and the virtual is no longer a line to be crossed but a fluid zone in which the artwork exists simultaneously as substance and code, presence and process, object and algorithm.

The evolution from Canova to Fontana marks a profound transition not only in aesthetic ideals but also in the technical paradigms that underpin the sculptural process.

[5] See Friedrich Nietzsche, *The Birth of Tragedy* (1872), especially Chapters 1–3, where he contrasts the Apollonian, associated with sculpture, clarity, and form, with the Dionysian, linked to music, intoxication, and the dissolution of boundaries. This aesthetic dualism serves as a foundational lens for understanding creative tension in both classical and contemporary artistic practices.

Canova's work, although firmly anchored in a celebrative, monumental, and allegorical tradition, marks an early step toward digital sculpture and artistic design practices.[6]

His pursuit of proportion, mathematical order, and ideal beauty anticipates the algorithmic structures and generative logics that now define virtual and computational art.

Antonio Canova's neoclassicism embodied absolute control over material, rooted in proportional systems derived from antiquity.

His working method, centered on clay modeling, plaster molding, and meticulous marble carving, reflected a workflow aimed at maintaining precision and coherence from the first sketch to the final execution.

In Canova's practice, clay was not merely a preliminary step but a space of invention, where the sculptor's hand could rapidly capture emotions, gestures, and compositional possibilities in a tactile and expressive form.

The clay model functioned as a tactile sketch, capturing the immediacy of the first idea and allowing for intuitive experimentation.[7]

The plaster model served simultaneously as a prototype, archive, and, above all, the space of planning, retaining the trace of the original gesture while facilitating multiple translations into bronze or marble.

Today, digital modeling reactivates a similar structure: no longer bound to physical constraints yet still driven by the sculptor's need to mediate between idea and form.

In both traditional and digital practices, sculpture is not only the manipulation of matter, but the construction of meaning through systems, whether mechanical, analog, or digital, and through its evolving relationship with space.

---

[6] Canova's creative process typically began with rapid drawings, followed by small clay or terracotta models (*bozzetti*), which were refined into full-scale plaster casts. These were then used by skilled assistants to carve the final marble version under Canova's supervision, often using mechanical pointing devices to transfer proportions with extreme precision. This layered approach—drawing, modeling, measuring, and final execution—reveals a structured, iterative workflow that parallels the logic of contemporary digital prototyping and fabrication.

[7] See: *Canova: Sketching in Clay*, National Gallery of Art, Washington D.C. & Art Institute of Chicago, 2023–2024. The exhibition brought together more than 50 terracotta models by Canova, highlighting how clay functioned not only as a preparatory medium but as an autonomous space of invention and expressive gesture, preserving the immediacy of the artist's hand. `https://patrons.org.es/canova-sketching-in-clay/`

1.1.2 The Lombard Tradition: Expressive Materiality

By the 1830s, the Lombard tradition introduced a distinctive regional expressiveness, shifting sculptural focus from classical idealism toward emotional depth and local identity.

Sculptors such as Vincenzo Vela (1820–1891), Medardo Rosso (1858–1928), and Leonardo Bistolfi (1859–1933) emphasized tactile surfaces and subjective vision. Vela's dynamic forms gave substance to sentiment, while Rosso's wax and plaster experiments explored dissolution and ephemerality, transforming matter into a perceptual event rather than a static object.

In these cases, the sculptor's engagement with immediate, humble materials such as plaster and terracotta became even more central—no longer confined to preliminary stages, as in Canova's practice, but elevated to vehicles of direct expression and perception.

Bistolfi's monumental sculptures mark an important step in contemporary sculptural technique. His use of clay modeling and plaster casts was central as intermediate steps but also as autonomous artistic moment. The *Gipsoteca Leonardo Bistolfi* in Casale Monferrato preserves these passages, showcasing intimate and unfinished pieces that reveal the sculptor's processual intelligence.

Similarly, the Gipsoteca Canoviana in Possagno, expanded by Carlo Scarpa in 1957, presents an unparalleled collection of plaster casts from Antonio Canova's studio. In the *Ala Scarpa* white forms are staged in a luminous and contemplative environment, where every cast preserves the immediacy of Canova's gesture and the evolution of form (Figure 1-3).

***Figure 1-3. Gipsoteca Canoviana, Possagno**, Canova Plaster Cast Gallery, Possagno, extension by Carlo Scarpa, 1957. By seier+seier, CC BY 2.0, `https://commons.wikimedia.org/w/index.php?curid=33666844`*

Plaster casts are not mere reproductions: they preserve the immediacy of the gesture and the evolution of form.[8]

Brera's own Gipsoteca exemplifies this approach, where casts of classical sculpture coexist with isolated torsos, hands, and fragments, evoking a past always available for reinterpretation.

With Adolfo Wildt (1868–1931) and Arturo Martini (1889–1947), sculpture moved further from classical continuity, seeking instead spiritual abstraction and narrative mythology.

In Marino Marini (1901–1980), the body becomes archetype and tension, suspended between ancient totem and modern fracture. His *Cavalieri* are not heroes but vulnerable forms—marked by existential instability.

Through the works of Wildt, Martini, and Marini, sculpture unfolded into spiritual abstraction and existential tension.

[8] Vitruvius, in *De Architectura*, mentions *gypsus* (plaster) as a material used for stuccoes and ornamental work, emphasizing its ability to set quickly and its role in Roman wall decoration. The reference to the Latin root *gypsum* thus evokes this ancient tradition of a living, immediate, and malleable material—central to the sculptural gesture and its formative process.

All of these sculptors were deeply connected to Brera, Milan, and the broader Lombard cultural field, where the Gipsoteca functioned not only as a didactic environment but as a living archive of form and memory.

Despite bronze and marble remaining the official and most celebrated materials, for these artists **terracotta and plaster continued to be fundamental expressive media**—valued not merely as technical stages but for their immediacy, fragility, and capacity to record the sculptor's gesture in its most direct form.

In this context, clay modeling and plaster casting were to 19th and early 20th-century sculpture what digital modeling and scanning are to us today: not only preparatory tools but generative acts.

Just as clay and plaster once captured gesture and transition, digital meshes now embody the evolving interplay between idea, form, and material—expanding sculpture into new dimensions.

This continuity between gesture and material, planning and process, finds an echo in Lucio Fontana's early works. A student of Adolfo Wildt at the Brera Academy, Fontana initially explored terracotta, plaster, and ceramics, materials central to the Lombard tradition's expressive vocabulary.

Yet even in those early experiments, he reconfigured matter through a modernist, transgressive lens, revealing a growing desire to move beyond the object's physical constraints.

1.1.3 Spatialism: Ideas Beyond Physical Constraints

Lucio Fontana's Spatialism (1946–1968)[9] marked a radical break in the history of sculpture, prioritizing space, light, and gesture over traditional material concerns.

His *Concetti Spaziali*—the iconic slashed canvases—and his spatial environments employed minimal matter to evoke vast conceptual dimensions, transcending the artwork's physicality.

This trajectory culminated in the radical gesture of the cut: simple, precise, and philosophical. With it, **Fontana redefined painting and sculpture not as mass or volume but as a dynamic threshold between presence and absence, material and void.**

[9] Spatialism as a formal movement began with the "Manifesto Blanco" in 1946.

This conceptual threshold—the cut as both presence and absence—finds renewed relevance in the context of digital and procedural modeling.

Today, that gesture can be reinterpreted not through material incision but by generating space through code.

In contemporary digital practice, space is no longer carved but computed; the void is no longer opened by the artist's hand but modeled as a parametric aperture, infinitely adjustable and generatively unstable.

Contemporary artists interpret Fontana's cuts logic not by piercing the canvas but by constructing virtual interfaces where space, surface, gesture, and emptiness are algorithmically negotiated.

In Figure 1-4, we have attempted to interpret the concepts of Spatialism using AI. This is not a reproduction of Fontana's gesture but its translation into another register: the algorithmic cut.

Figure 1-4. Parametric thresholds: light as aperture.
Diptych of luminous openings exploring the transition from surface to space.
AI-generated image, © Gianpiero Moioli, 2025

Here, the void is not the physical absence of matter but a parametric field, a computational opening that can be expanded, reshaped, or endlessly recombined. The incision becomes a rule, a modular operation that organizes both surface and space in procedural terms.

By moving from incision to instruction, from the cut of the blade to the command of the algorithm, digital practice does not erase Fontana's radical gesture. It extends it.

It transforms the canvas into an interface, the cut into a variable, and space itself into a generative system.[10]

By replicating the *logic* of the cut, rather than its material execution, digital work extends Fontana's gesture in another register, a computational space where the void is neither sculpted nor symbolic but procedurally rendered.

It is precisely in this shift—from authored mark to generative structure—that we begin to glimpse the evolving nature of form, presence, and meaning in the post-material age.

Fontana's work laid a conceptual foundation for later explorations by valuing the idea over the material form, and gesture over mass.

In *Concetto Spaziale, Attese,* one or more vertical incisions disrupt a monochromatic canvas.[11]

These cuts are not destructive but generative: they open the surface to the dimension beyond, transforming the void into form.

To explore this legacy in a contemporary context, AI-generated reinterpretations of Fontana's works do not replicate the surface of his canvases but rather extend his incisions into new spatial, temporal, and virtual dimensions.

The cut does not become a mark but a logic: a modular operation that can be translated, scaled, and reactivated in procedural space, extending into space itself.

[10] Prompt used for generation: "A minimal, monochromatic surface with a pure saturated background color, interrupted by one or more precise vertical cuts. The incisions reveal a glowing luminous void beyond the surface. Abstract, high-resolution, museum documentation style, dramatic lighting, emphasis on presence and absence, threshold between matter and emptiness. Clean composition, centered object, contemporary art photography."

[11] This highly iconic series by Lucio Fontana, developed from 1958 onwards, is known as Concetto Spaziale, Attesa (singular, when featuring a single cut) or Concetto Spaziale, Attese (plural, for multiple cuts).

Through generative models, we can now project the gesture of *Concetto Spaziale* beyond the flat surface, unfolding it into immersive environments, architectural volumes, or dynamic simulations (Figure 1-5).[12]

Figure 1-5. Time vector: light as duration.
Diptych exploring luminous apertures in three-dimensional space.
AI-generated image, © Gianpiero Moioli, 2025

This is not a matter of stylistic reproduction but of conceptual continuity. Just as Fontana moved from the canvas to the *Ambienti Spaziali,*[13] opening the artwork into lived space, we now can experiment that same threshold into virtual realms.

[12] Prompt used for generation: "An immersive monochromatic minimal room where luminous slashes open three-dimensional voids in space. Beams of light extend from the cuts, projecting dynamic apertures into architectural volume. The space feels infinite and generative, with void and form continuously recomposed. Ultra-clean, immersive installation aesthetic, realistic lighting, wide-angle view, digital art environment."

[13] On Lucio Fontana's "Ambienti spaziali" (Spatial Environments), see Fondazione Lucio Fontana, official entry "Ambienti spaziali / Spatial Environments," which defines them as large-scale environmental works conceived for immersive experience—often in dialogue with existing architecture or designed for exhibitions—shifting the focus from object to space and from representation to event.

`https://www.fondazioneluciofontana.it/en/le-ambientazioni-1926-1968/`

We will return to this concept in section 1.4.1.

AI and virtuality expand Lucio Fontana's ideas of spatial environments into hybrid physical-digital ecologies, enabling new interpretations that deepen our understanding of his vision and language.

Rather than closing the work, these tools reopen it. They allow us to reimagine what lies beyond the cut, not merely as a visual element but as a structural, spatial, and ontological possibility.

This opens the door to a new sculptural paradigm: the void as a generative field of potential, and the incision as a vector of creation, continuously unfolding in virtual space.

From Canova to Fontana and now to AI and digital tools, sculpture reveals a continuum: from permanence to infinity, from material form to code.

Today, technologies such as 3D scanning, AI, and digital fabrication do not oppose this tradition; they extend it. They transform the plaster cast into a mesh, the studio into an interface, and the form into a process.

In doing so, they invite us to reimagine what it means to sculpt, not merely to shape matter but to design experience.

Fontana's radical gesture does not negate Canova; it responds to him. Where Canova gives form to myth, Fontana gives form to the void.

One sculpts matter into permanence; the other opens it toward infinity.

The contemporary artist exists between these two poles, navigating the space between tradition and experimentation, preservation and innovation, and the weight of the body and the weightlessness of data.

In this continuum, new tools like **3D modeling, procedural systems, and artificial intelligence** do not replace sculpture; they extend its language.

Just as Fontana expanded the concept of form into space, today we expand form into code, into simulation, into environments that are no longer carved but generated.

1.1.4 Brera: Narrated Space, Lived Space

Alongside Lucio Fontana's immaterial revolution, the Sculpture Department of the Brera Academy of Fine Arts saw the emergence of two fundamental figures during the postwar decades, particularly between the 1950s and 1970s: Giancarlo Marchese and Alik Cavaliere.

Both artists, students of Marino Marini, reinterpreted the Italian plastic tradition through highly personal and profoundly contemporary visions, expanding sculpture toward narrative and environmental dimensions.

Giancarlo Marchese conceived sculptural space as a site of mental presence, opening introspective thresholds rather than merely physical ones. His practice resonates with a poetics of silence, in which form becomes an inner trace—subtle, essential, and meditative.

By contrast, Alik Cavaliere constructed full-fledged poetic scenographies, populated by vegetal, surreal, and metaphysical structures. His works transform space into a journey, a narrative landscape, a philosophical reflection, where the viewer becomes an active participant in a theater of memory and transformation.

In both cases, sculpture becomes a narrative device, and space is no longer a passive container but an active agent of meaning: a field to inhabit, traverse, and question.

Their approaches anticipate contemporary practices of immersive installation and environmental storytelling, laying the conceptual foundations for an expanded aesthetics now renewed through digital worlds, augmented reality, and interactive environments.

1.1.4.1 Giancarlo Marchese: Space as a Threshold of Thought

The work of Giancarlo Marchese, developed between the 1970s and 2000s, stands out for its radical exploration of the **relationship between form, void, and perception**.

His use of glass, with its inherent transparency and reflective qualities, further transforms perception, creating a dynamic interplay of light and shadow that destabilizes the viewer's sense of space and invites a contemplative engagement with the work's ethereal boundaries (Figure 1-6).

Figure 1-6. Giancarlo Marchese, S.N. 274, Formal dialectic, 1993.
Glass, and cast iron 230 × 160 × 40 cm
Private collection, Milan

His sculpture does not aim to occupy space but to question it.

Using an essential language of raw materials—such as glass, metal, and stone—and measured signs, Marchese creates places of waiting and suspension: forms that do not impose meaning but invite an inward gaze.

His structures, often open and fragmentary, act as thresholds between the visible and the invisible, evoking thought rather than mass, trace rather than volume.

In this sense, his work ideally connects to Fontana's reflections but offers an intimate and meditative interpretation, where the sculptural gesture is reduced to the essential, allowing the silence of space to emerge.

An emblematic example is the work *Dialettica Formale* (1993), created in glass and cast iron, which encapsulates many of the central themes of Marchese's poetics.

Here, the frame, typically a marginal and decorative element, becomes the protagonist. Instead of enclosing an image, it opens onto transparent, undulating glass, traversed by reflections and distortions that shift with the light and the viewer's position.

It is an invitation to look beyond, to experience space as a mental field: unstable, never fully defined.

As is often the case in Marchese's work, meaning is not imposed but evoked: each fragment, each detail, opens to a possible inner narrative, in a balance between formal rigor and symbolic openness.

1.1.4.2 Alik Cavaliere: Ecological Narrative and Lived Space

In Alik Cavaliere's work, sculptural space becomes a narrative and poetic environment, an inner ecosystem crafted from humble materials and natural forms: roots, sprouts, metallic branches, rusted surfaces.

His installations, such as those visible at the Centro Artistico Alik Cavaliere—originally his studio—do not impose themselves as monuments but disperse within the space, almost seeking a quiet dialogue with time, memory, and fragility (Figure 1-7).

Figure 1-7. Alik Cavaliere. *...E ne ha così assoluta certezza, quanto se n'abbia l'istessa natura, 1966-67, bronze, steel, plastic, 261 x 137 x 95 cm. Private collection, Milan. A sculpture poised between organicity and abstraction, where the arboreal form dissolves into a spatial synthesis*

His sculpture is a story. Each fragment, each leaf, each bronze stem is an episode in a broader, elusive narrative where nature and culture intertwine.

The void between elements is an integral part of the work: a space to traverse, to inhabit. In this sense, Cavaliere anticipates an idea of immersive installation in which the visitor is called not only to observe but to walk, linger, and reflect.

His deeply ecological and humanistic poetics forms an ideal bridge between the sculpture of the late 20th century and contemporary practices of environmental storytelling, augmented reality, and relational art.

Like Marchese, Cavaliere constructs not objects but experiences, where the void, light, and material interplay evoke an inner dialogue with the environment.

1.1.4.3 Albertini and Moioli: Machines, Bubbles, and Narrative Space

In this perspective, Albertini and Moioli have continued the Brera tradition while developing it through new material and technological dimensions.[14]

Their practice develops as a dialogue between organic and rational forms, between material solidity and luminous transparency.

Since then, they have pursued a shared path that revolves around the interplay of **machine and bubble**: the machine as a rational and narrative device, rooted in industrial logic, and the bubble as a luminous, transparent form that embodies fragility, virtuality, and incorporeal vision.

This duality expands into the urban and architectural scale with works such as *Labirinto Verticale* (2000), a monumental steel structure in Ulsan (South Korea), which transforms sculpture into an inhabitable and symbolic space, mediating between geometry, material presence, and collective narration (Figure 1-8).

[14] *Albertini e Moioli. La macchina per fare le bolle, la circumfolgore e altri congegni*, curated by Paolo Campiglio, Silvana Editoriale, Milan 2008.

Figure 1-8. Albertini and Moioli, Labirinto Verticale, 2000.
Steel and iron, 530 (h) × 250 × 250 cm. Dongchon Stadium, Ulsan Metropolitan City, South Korea

Albertini and Moioli's research thus turns sculpture into a narrative and relational machine, suspended between body and light, memory and imagination, matter and virtuality.

As professors at Brera and former students of its historic masters, they extend the Academy's sculptural tradition while projecting it into new technological and narrative horizons.

In their practice, the sculptural object becomes at once a device, a story, and a space to inhabit.

At this point, however, I must speak in the first person: that vision—where machines, bubbles, and environments unfolded as open narratives—also marked my own path. Together with Stefania Albertini, we explored not only material and luminous environments but also the early dimensions of immateriality and virtual worlds as will be further explored in Chapter 9.[15] From that shared start, I have since continued to develop these themes more directly through Blender and digital environments, which have gradually taken shape in the reflections and practices that are recounted in this book.

1.1.4.4 Art as Narrative: Sculptural Space and the Creation of Worlds

The work of Lucio Fontana, Giancarlo Marchese, and Alik Cavaliere reveals a profound transformation in sculptural language: **from formal act to narrative gesture, from object to device of imagination.**

In different ways, these artists contributed to shifting the very center of sculpture toward the construction of spaces where narratives can unfold.

Fontana opens breaches in reality; Marchese evokes silence and inner thresholds; Cavaliere populates environments with fragments of nature and memory.

This perspective anticipates what we now call environmental or immersive storytelling, where the artwork does not communicate a fixed message but rather invites the viewer to construct their own path, their own interpretation.

Art thus becomes a tool to found worlds, to expand the imaginary, and to articulate alternative visions of reality and unreality.

It is an art that engages with literature, myth, and fantasy, while also resonating with contemporary languages such as augmented reality, interactive narration, and digital simulation.

From within the environment of Brera, through the legacy of Fontana, Marchese, and Cavaliere, emerges a conception of the artwork as an expanded narrative space, where art and storytelling converge to generate new modes of thought and new ways of inhabiting the world.

In continuity with this lineage, the collaborative work of Albertini and Moioli further developed sculpture as a relational and narrative machine, opening it toward immateriality and early virtual explorations.

[15] From that shared start, Stefania Albertini and I also explored the early dimensions of virtuality. Over time, our paths diverged: hers toward material experimentations and luminous and design-oriented elements, mine toward the immateriality of code and digital worlds (§1.5).

This perspective is further explored in my writings on storytelling and contemporary art, such as *Prolegomeni al Manifesto del Pop Management 6.0* (Moioli 2024) and in recent reflections published in China Weixin (Moioli 2024).[16]

1.1.5 Studio Azzurro: Immersion, Narrative, and Digital Environment

Another cornerstone in the evolution toward virtual and technology-based art within the Milanese art scene—particularly that of the Brera Academy—is represented by Studio Azzurro.

Founded in Milan in 1982, Studio Azzurro is among the most influential Italian collectives operating at the crossroads of art, technology, and narrative installation. Their pioneering approach to **video, interactive environments**, and **immersive storytelling** has consistently challenged the boundary between artwork and viewer, expanding the concept of sculpture into a **dynamic, sensorial, and experiential space**.

Works such as *Stanze* (1985), *Il giardino delle cose* (1992), and *Tavoli* (1995) seamlessly integrate moving images, soundscapes, and responsive sensors, giving rise to performative environments that actively engage the viewer (Figure 1-9).

[16] See: Moioli, Gianpiero. "*Prolegomeni al Manifesto del Pop Management 6.0 - Storytelling Pop*." *Nova100 - Il Sole 24 Ore*, 28 Nov. 2024, `https://marcominghetti.nova100.ilsole24ore.com/2024/11/28/prolegomeni-al-manifesto-del-pop-management-60-storytelling-pop-opinion-piece-di-gianpiero-moioli/`. and Moioli, Gianpiero. "Journey through Alternate Worlds," 2024, `https://mp.weixin.qq.com/s/HxZWXc1cMjAnFMnY8oatpQ`

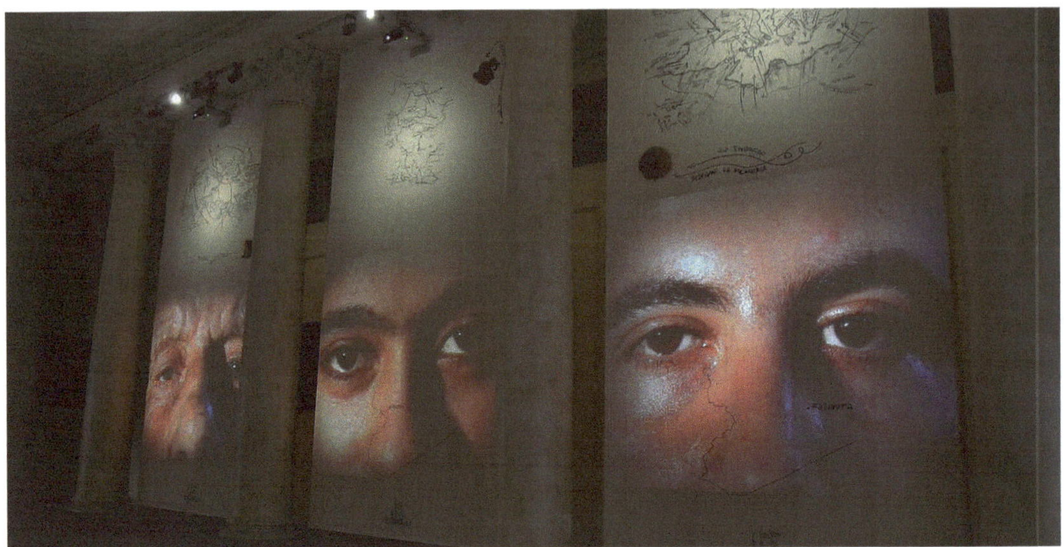

Figure 1-9. Studio Azzurro, video-environmental installation, Palazzo Reale, Milan, 2016.
The work invites the viewer to interact with projected images within an immersive, responsive space, transforming perception into narrative.
Photo by Simona Denise Deiana. Used under Creative Commons license CC BY-SA 4.0.
https://creativecommons.org/licenses/by-sa/4.0

Their research can be understood as a conceptual continuation of Fontana's spatial explorations, where gesture becomes presence, and presence unfolds into narrative.

This trajectory found a significant moment of public presentation in the exhibition *Immagini sensibili*, held at Palazzo Reale in Milan in 2016.[17] The show offered an immersive and participatory experience, involving both specialized and general audiences, and illustrating how the viewer could become an active participant within the installation space.

Rather than merely showcasing completed works, the exhibition foregrounded the relational and performative nature of Studio Azzurro's art, emphasizing its capacity to generate meaning through interaction, spatial dramaturgy, and temporal unfolding. The installations did not impose narratives but suggested paths, inviting visitors to

[17] Simona Denise Deiana, "Studio Azzurro a Milano, la magia della videoarte [Studio Azzurro in Milan: The Magic of Video Art]," *LifeGate*, May 3, 2016.

https://www.lifegate.it/studio-azzurro-milano-la-magia-della-videoarte

co-construct the experience through movement, gesture, and perception. In this way, *Immagini sensibili* reaffirmed the group's commitment to a **nonlinear, open-ended narrative model**, in which the artwork becomes an **environment to inhabit and explore**, rather than an object to contemplate.

Their practice, discussed in section 1.4.3, remains a touchstone for understanding how today's digital artists continue to explore the convergence of narrative and spatial immersion.

1.1.6 Toward Immaterial Space: From Fontana to Studio Azzurro

Lucio Fontana enacted a radical break with classical sculptural tradition. His *Concetti Spaziali* do not merely represent a new form; they propose a new way of conceiving space.

By cutting through the surface, Fontana transforms the void into active matter and space into perceptual experience, inaugurating a vision in which the artistic gesture becomes the origin of a possible world, a conceptual opening. This shift—from form to thought, from matter to idea—marks a turning point.

Following this trajectory, Studio Azzurro emerges as a crucial link between sculpture and immersive installation, between material art and digital environments.

In their works, space is no longer merely traversed; it is digitally constructed, not only conceived but actively lived.

Their video-interactive installations make the viewer a participant, displacing the axis of sculpture from objectual presence to immersive experience.

This evolution paves the way for contemporary practices in which the artwork exists at the intersection of **idea, matter, and code**.

Studio Azzurro, with its sensitive rooms and interactive tables, is thus not an exception but a visionary bridge, one that carries sculpture into the narrative and technological dimension of the present.

From materials to methods: the next section examines how tools and techniques reshape sculptural practice and authorship in the digital studio.

1.2 Contemporary Art as Narrative: Sculptural Space and the Creation of Worlds

As outlined in section 1.1.4.4, the passage from Fontana's breaches to Marchese's thresholds of silence and Cavaliere's ecosystems of memory marked a decisive shift: sculpture became narrative space.

This section moves forward from that transformation to explore how, in the digital age, narrative expands into code, algorithms, and virtual environments.

Rather than a rupture, this shift represents a continuum of expansion. The conceptual openings of Lucio Fontana and the immersive, narrative environments of Studio Azzurro laid the groundwork for a sculptural language that moves seamlessly between tangible and virtual dimensions.

Artists working with 3D modeling, virtual reality (VR), and generative algorithms treat **digital space as a new sculptural material**. The mesh becomes a dynamic surface; the algorithm, a tool of emergence; the interface, a threshold between viewer and work. In this context, sculpture evolves into a performative and computational system, where form arises from the interplay between machine and intention, perception and interaction.

This contemporary shift also draws sculpture into dialogue with **storytelling**. Interactive installations, AR environments, and generative video works are no longer static objects to observe but narrative spaces to explore. The sculptural gesture becomes a narrative act—a way to construct meaning through experience and to invite the viewer into a story unfolding in space and time.

The artist becomes not merely a maker of forms but a designer of immersive, symbolic systems, where aesthetics intersect with memory, fiction, and emotion.

In this expanded field, the boundaries between sculpture, installation, and digital experience dissolve. What matters is not the singular object but the ecosystem it generates: a constellation of code, perception, material, and imagination. Sculpture thus extends beyond the studio or gallery and enters new domains: urban landscapes, virtual platforms, and augmented layers of reality. And through this expansion, it continues its ancient mission: **to give form to thought, body to vision, and structure to new worlds**.

1.2.1 The Digital Turn in Sculpture

Since the 1980s, contemporary sculptors have increasingly integrated digital code into their practice, enabling the artist's idea to manifest across both **physical and virtual realms.**

Where marble, bronze, and plaster once defined the ontology of sculpture, artists now work within immaterial datasets—meshes, point clouds, voxel fields, and procedural structures. These constitute a new materiality, one that is informational, fluid, and infinitely reconfigurable.

The initial transposition from physical to the digital often begins with digital modeling, where artists create original sculptural forms using specialized software, or with 3D scanning technologies such as structured light, laser triangulation, or photogrammetry. Digital modeling allows for the conception of complex geometries from scratch, offering a creative starting point that can be refined or combined with scanned data.

These systems capture surface topology with precision ranging from millimeter-level (consumer devices) to micrometer-level (professional scanners), generating dense polygonal meshes (typically 100K-10M+ polygons) or point clouds. Each scanning method offers different advantages depending on resolution, scale, and material properties, and must be carefully calibrated to ensure both geometric fidelity and manageable data volume.

Once digitized, the sculptural form becomes a manipulable dataset, encapsulated in file formats like OBJ, STL, PLY. These formats act as containers of geometry and texture, enabling interoperability across platforms and software environments.

The metaphor mixing "gipsoteca" (Italian) with technical terms needs clarification: The digital model becomes a kind of virtual gipsoteca (plaster cast gallery), an archive of sculptural possibilities preserved not in gypsum, but in vertices and polygons.

Mesh processing workflows—including retopology, smoothing, and decimation—optimize these models for computational efficiency while retaining critical surface detail.

At this stage, the digital sculpture can undergo transformations unimaginable in the physical studio: parametric deformations, Boolean operations, procedural generation, and other algorithmic interventions that radically expand the sculptor's formal vocabulary.

1.2.2 Hybrid Aesthetics and Virtual Possibilities

The integration of digital code also allows artists to transcend physical limitations, giving rise to hybrid practices where sculptures exist simultaneously as material objects and programmable data structures. Artists use software not just as a planning tool but as a **generative engine**, crafting geometries unachievable through traditional means.

These forms are then realized through advanced fabrication technologies—3D printing, CNC milling, robotic carving—or displayed within virtual environments and AR/VR platforms.

The result is a new aesthetic logic, where the artist's idea is no longer tethered to a single medium but manifests across multiple ontologies: physical, digital, interactive.

This hybridization also challenges conventional notions of authenticity, permanence, and spatial presence. A sculpture can exist as a file, a simulation, an immersive installation, or a printed object—each iteration equally valid, each context activating different layers of meaning.

As a result, sculpture today does not fix form in time but generates fluid systems of meaning that evolve with context, technology, and viewer interaction.

1.3 The Present Turn: Project-Based and Hybrid Art

Contemporary artistic practices are increasingly shaped by hybrid methodologies that blend traditional craftsmanship with digital technologies.

This fusion enhances the creative process, enabling artists to explore new forms of expression, interactivity, and audience engagement through thoughtful project development.

Artists today operate as designers, coders, and makers, traversing both physical and virtual environments to develop new aesthetic paradigms. This chapter explores the emergence of project-based approaches and the redefinition of artistic identity through hybrid practices.

In this context, design thinking and project-based methodologies have become essential, particularly in response to the spatial challenges posed by new technologies. Whether creating immersive environments, interactive installations, or virtual spaces, the contemporary artist must conceive form, function, and experience in advance—projecting creative gestures into dynamic, multidimensional contexts. The act of making is increasingly preceded by the act of conceiving, structuring, and simulating, as spatial design becomes a key element in shaping artistic meaning and technological interaction.

1.3.1 The Hybrid Artist

In the contemporary landscape, the figure of the artist evolves into that of a hybrid practitioner—blending manual skills with computational intelligence.

Sculptors often begin with traditional modeling in clay or wax and then transition into digital environments using software like Blender or ZBrush.

Here, they refine, simulate, and transform the form entirely, creating objects that exist simultaneously in physical and digital realms.

This shift marks the emergence of a design-oriented mindset, drawing from art, industrial design, architecture, engineering, and new media.

The methodology of Studio Azzurro offers a paradigmatic example: their collaborative, interdisciplinary approach united visual artists, programmers, scriptwriters, and musicians to generate immersive works that transcend disciplinary boundaries. In this model, the artist becomes not only a creator but a coordinator of complex systems and team processes.

1.3.2 Redefining Art Production

Hybrid methodologies challenge the traditional boundaries of artistic production. Physical materials such as wood, metal, resin, or fabric are now conceived as components of a broader workflow that begins with digital modeling and culminates in tangible form through tools like 3D printing, CNC milling, or robotic carving.

An artwork may be born as a parametric sketch, evolve through algorithmic manipulation, and materialize as a sculptural object—closing the loop between idea, code, and matter.

This approach emphasizes process over product, positioning the artist as an innovator who navigates between concept, digital code, and fabrication, often merging physical touch with virtual simulation.

1.4 Contemporary Practices: Between Code, Space, and Perception

To conclude the historical overview, we present a selection of significant works that integrate the theoretical perspectives discussed earlier.

These examples highlight how sculpture, space, and digital technologies converge, merging physical and virtual dimensions.

Contemporary artists operate at the intersection of traditional techniques and technological innovation, redefining space as a perceptual, relational, and computational environment.

Often their sculptures activate viewers as co-creators, transforming the medium into a dynamic field where narrative, presence, and virtuality converge.

1.4.1 Lucio Fontana: Spatial Environments and Environmental Works

Alongside his iconic *Concetti Spaziali,* Fontana developed a groundbreaking series of large-scale environmental installations—known as *Ambienti Spaziali*—which redefined the role of space, light, and gesture in the construction of meaning. Conceived between the late 1940s and the late 1960s, these works were not autonomous objects but immersive environments to be entered, experienced, and traversed.

Space became a sculptural medium, light a tangible material, and the viewer's movement an active component of the work's unfolding.

Through monochromatic rooms, suspended forms, neon lines, and disorienting spatial layouts, Fontana created an expanded field of perception in which the body was no longer separated from the artwork but became a generator of meaning. These *Ambientazioni* stand among the most radical and visionary components of Fontana's oeuvre, anticipating key elements of contemporary immersive art—from the dissolution of disciplinary boundaries to the creation of total environments where perception itself becomes the work.

1.4.1.1 Hangar Bicocca (2017): Reimagining Fontana's Spatial Environments in the Digital Present

The exhibition *Ambienti/Environments* at Pirelli Hangar Bicocca (Milan, 2017), curated by Marina Pugliese, Barbara Ferriani, and Vicente Todolí, presented a selection of Lucio Fontana's spatial environments.[18]

---

[18] As explained on Google Arts & Culture: "The exhibition 'Ambienti/Environments' brings together for the first time in the Navate space nine 'Spatial Environments' and two environmental interventions, created by Lucio Fontana between 1949 and 1968 for Italian and international galleries and museums. The exhibition presents a body of work that highlights the innovative and pioneering force of a great master of the twentieth century."

https://artsandculture.google.com/story/5QWRDROPeWEVLA

Several of Fontana's ephemeral environments have been reconstructed from drawings, photographs, and technical documentation—not as historical replicas but as spatial experiences.

This method is especially interesting for its focus on the viewer's perspective and spatial perception.

In this sense, the materials from the *Ambienti/Environments* exhibition at Hangar Bicocca provide a basis for digital reinterpretation using tools such as Blender, Unity, or Unreal Engine.

These reconstructions, as I propose in this conceptual extension (not implemented in the 2017 exhibition or by any official Fontana-related institution), translated into VR, AR, or metaverse platforms, allow for responsive environments where light, scale, and sound can change in real time through user interaction or generative algorithms.[19]

Rather than nostalgic replicas, they function as conceptual extensions of Fontana's idea of space as presence.

Today, this approach aligns with digital practices in 3D modeling and XR, transforming light, void, and movement into programmable parameters.

Such projects also offer educational and curatorial potential, bringing Fontana's vision into contemporary frameworks of perception, interaction, and immersive experience.

1.4.2 Nam June Paik: Integrating Technology in Video Sculpture

Nam June Paik (1932–2006) is widely recognized as the pioneer of video art and one of the first artists to integrate electronic technology into sculpture.

His works fuse the material presence of sculpture with the flow of information, transforming static forms into temporal, performative structures.

---

[19] They also open new curatorial and educational pathways, enabling immersive reconstructions for research and public engagement. Platforms like Spatial, VRChat, Kunstmatrix, and New Art City can host Fontana-inspired environments, alongside works by contemporary artists such as TeamLab, Olafur Eliasson, or Studio Azzurro—bridging historical experimentation and current digital practices.

`https://www.spatial.io`

`https://www.teamlab.art`

A key figure in the Fluxus movement, Paik emphasized performance, interactivity, and the body's role within media systems, merging art and life through sound, gesture, and transmission.

Landmark works such as *TV Buddha* (1974), *TV Garden* (1974), and *Electronic Superhighway* (1995) exemplify his vision of technology not merely as a tool but as both medium and message.

He reimagined the television not as a passive screen but as a sculptural element—an active agent in a new aesthetic experience, capable of generating presence, tension, and poetic resonance in real time.

1.4.2.1 *Electronic Superhighway (1995)*: Sculpture as Network, Light, and Signal

One of Nam June Paik most iconic pieces, *Electronic Superhighway: Continental U.S., Alaska, Hawaii* (1995), features a massive wall of neon-outlined states filled with 336 televisions broadcasting fragmented audiovisual content.

Here, the video monitor becomes a sculptural unit, and the network itself becomes the artwork: an early metaphor for digital connectivity and distributed perception.

In his practice, screens, wires, and feedback loops function as artistic media, rather than technical supports.

Paik was among the first to envision the artist as an **electronic shaman**, capable of shaping cultural consciousness through technology.

Paik's approach resonates strongly with today's hybrid art:

- He collapses the boundaries between object, screen, and system.
- His works create spatial fields of information.
- He anticipates the integration of networks, interactivity, and code into the sculptural domain.

Today, his legacy continues in works that integrate real-time data streams (social media, weather, biometrics, markets), transforming information flow into visual/sonic/spatial forms, and in generative media that evolve autonomously via algorithms or machine learning.

1.4.3 Studio Azzurro

As discussed in section 1.1.5, Studio Azzurro blends sensorial experience, narrative immersion, and technological experimentation, operating at the intersection of space, media, and relational aesthetics.

1.4.3.1 *KUNDE (2000)*: Memory, Movement, and Relational Space

KUNDE (Dortmund, 2000) constructs an interactive space of memory and testimony, built around the personal stories of migrants.

Voice recordings, projections, and sensor-based interactions allow visitors to activate narrative fragments by moving through the environment. The space is relational: walking, pausing, or touching triggers storytelling.

KUNDE exemplifies Studio Azzurro's methodology:

- Narration is distributed across space, rather than fixed in time.
- The viewer becomes co-author through gesture and attention.
- The artwork functions as a sensorial archive, constantly reactivated through presence.

This practice anticipates developments in XR installations, interactive museum design, and AI-driven narrative spaces—fusing sculpture, performance, and interface into a relational infrastructure.

1.4.4 Fabrizio Plessi

Fabrizio Plessi (b. 1940) is a pioneer of video installation in Europe, among the first Italian artists to explore the sculptural potential of electronic media.

His work fuses primordial elements—water, fire, stone, wood—with the artificial light of monitors, crafting a language where technology becomes organic and the screen becomes material. Active since the 1970s, his installations challenge the separation between nature and artifice, proposing a media-based poetics of energy, transformation, and memory.

Rather than using video to narrate or document, Plessi treats it as vibrating matter. His screens do not represent images; they radiate presence, acting as containers of flowing energy.

Thus, the monitor shifts from transmission device to sculptural unit, capable of evoking myth, ritual, and the sublime.

1.4.4.1 Roma (1987–2005): Fire, Architecture, and Electronic Memory

A paradigmatic example is *Roma*, first presented at Documenta 8 in Kassel (1987) Venice Biennale (1987) and reconfigured in subsequent versions up to 2005.

A large architectural structure—resembling a collapsed Roman temple in rusted steel and volcanic rock—houses monitors that display images of fire, flickering across the fragmented space.

Here, the fusion of material decay and digital vitality is at its most intense: the burning screens suggest a technological anima within the ruins of history. Fire is symbolic and regenerative, an electronic presence animating a memory of empire and collapse.

The piece articulates media-architecture: a structure that breathes, glows, and remembers. The ancient and the contemporary coexist in luminous ruins.

In its interplay of mass and void, *Roma* recalls the symbolic tension of works such as Henry Moore's *Atom Piece* (1964-65). In both cases form acts as a vessel for invisible forces—nuclear energy in Moore, digital fire in Plessi.

Within digital and post-digital aesthetics, *Roma* prefigures practices exploring the hybridity of cultural heritage and media environments—an immersive archaeology in which the past is not reconstructed but reanimated.

1.4.5 Rafael Lozano-Hemmer

Mexican contemporary artist Rafael Lozano-Hemmer is known for his large-scale interactive installations that merge art, science, and technology.

His work often explores public participation, sensory engagement, and collective memory, employing tools such as biometric sensors, projection mapping, and immersive soundscapes.

1.4.5.1 Voice Tunnel (2013): Light, Sound, and Participatory Space

One of his most emblematic works is *Voice Tunnel* (2013), created for the *Summer Streets* festival in New York City.

Created for New York City's Summer Streets, *Voice Tunnel* transformed the 426-meter Park Avenue Tunnel into an immersive audiovisual environment. The installation featured 288 theatrical lights controlled in real time by visitors' voices. Participants spoke into a microphone at the entrance; their recordings were translated into pulses of light whose brightness and rhythm were modulated by pitch and volume, producing a personalized luminous wave.

A layered soundscape played back previous recordings, creating an evolving echo of past voices. Each contribution became a temporary visual and acoustic trace woven into the environment—an artwork continually reshaped by its audience. *Voice Tunnel* exemplifies Lozano-Hemmer's vision of art as a relational and participatory space, where architecture, the body, and technology converge.

This work can be understood through the following lens:

- The tunnel breathes with light and sound, becoming a living architecture of sensation (architecture as a sensory space).
- Each voice is a fleeting trace, an echo that lingers, altering the rhythm of the space (active participation).
- Memory unfolds in layers: past presences intertwine with the now, shaping a continuous flow (layered memory).
- Technology is not a tool but a pulse—transforming time, space, and emotion into a shared, luminous narrative (technology as a creative amplifier).

In *Voice Tunnel,* every voice becomes light and shared memory.

1.4.6 Mario Klingemann: Machine Vision and Generative Aesthetics

German artist Mario Klingemann is an AI-driven generative art.

Often described as an **artist-programmer**, he works at the intersection of art, machine learning, and computational creativity. His practice uses neural networks (including GANs) and custom algorithms not simply as tools but as collaborators capable of aesthetic invention and unpredictable form-making.

Though rooted in data, Klingemann's aesthetic remains poetic and uncannily human. He treats visual culture as code and the neural network as a kind of subconscious capable of hallucinating alternate realities.

His process typically involves:

- Collecting large datasets (such as historical paintings or facial images)
- Training GANs to learn visual patterns
- Fine-tuning and curating the generative outputs
- Displaying the results in time-based, interactive, or generative formats

His work interrogates authorship, originality, and the role of intuition in creative processes.

By training systems to "dream," mutate, or remix visual data, Klingemann challenges traditional notions of artistic control, offering a new paradigm in which human and algorithmic agencies are deeply entangled.

1.4.6.1 Memories of Passersby I (2018): Machine Hallucination and Generative Portraiture

Memories of Passersby I is a generative installation in which a neural network continuously produces never-before-seen portraits of imaginary people on two adjacent screens (Figure 1-10).

Figure 1-10. Mario Klingemann, Memories of Passersby I, 2018.
Installation view at Espacio SOLO, Madrid.
*Photo by **Namile17**, licensed under **Creative Commons Attribution-ShareAlike 4.0 International (CC BY-SA 4.0)** via Wikimedia Commons.*
https://commons.wikimedia.org/wiki/File:Memories_of_Passersby_by_Mario_Klingemann_at_Espacio_SOLO.jpg

Running autonomously, the AI model is embedded in a vintage cabinet, suggesting a hybrid of technological device and classical furniture. Trained on thousands of portraits from the 18th to the 20th century, the system generates a hypnotic, uncanny flow of faces that never repeat—reframing portraiture through machine vision.

In *Memories of Passersby I*, Klingemann reconsiders key concepts in contemporary art:

- Artist as coder: Klingemann embodies the new figure of the artist who writes systems instead of carving matter.
- Aesthetics as process: Beauty is no longer static but emerges from dynamic computation.
- Intelligence as medium: GANs become co-authors, enabling forms that no single human could imagine alone.
- From Form to Flux: The artwork is not a finished object but a perpetual becoming.

His work exemplifies the shift toward **dematerialized creation**, where the object may not exist as a stable form but as a **generative process**.

1.4.6.2 Uncanny Mirror (2018): AI, Perception, and the Fragmented Self

An interactive "mirror" reconstructs the viewer's face via a neural network trained on thousands of images. As the visitor moves, the screen generates shifting, distorted portraits—familiar yet unsettling—evoking Freud's *unheimlich*. The piece probes identity, surveillance, and machine perception. The AI does not reproduce but interprets, projecting a self that is fragmented, generative, and open to transformation.

1.4.7 Refik Anadol: Sculpting the Latent Space

Refik Anadol is a pioneering media artist whose practice explores the intersection of data, machine intelligence, and immersive spatial environments. Trained in visual communication and computational design, he treats digital data not as representation but as a material for sculptural transformation.

His installations inhabit the boundary between real-time computation and perceptual space, creating algorithmic environments where data itself becomes form.

Anadol's approach is emblematic of a new paradigm in digital art:

- Use of institutional/public datasets to ground works in cultural memory
  - He converts **data into immersive visual environments**, not static representations, but fluid, multisensory experiences unfolding in time.
  - He shifts authorship from the singular sculptor to a **collaborative process with artificial intelligence**, in which the artist becomes a curator of emergence rather than a controller of form.
  - His artworks operate as **open systems**, continuously transforming, where no final version exists and the experience is always in motion.

In Anadol's practice, modeling[20] becomes cognitive navigation through a space of latent potential. Here selection replaces execution, and the artist acts as a meta-designer of emergence.

His environments are immersive, not as fixed spaces but as temporal flows—where data, code, and perception converge into a new form of digital materiality.

1.4.7.1 Unsupervised (MoMA, 2022)

For *Unsupervised,* Anadol trained a generative adversarial network (GAN) on 138,000 images from the MoMA collection.

The resulting AI system created an evolving digital sculpture that reimagined the museum's visual memory in real time.

Rendered in real time on a large-scale LED display in the museum's entrance, the piece continuously generates forms that have never existed, **hallucinations of what art might have looked like but never did**.

Unsupervised is not a retrospective of past works but a speculative fiction generated by the museum's own visual subconscious—an ever-changing memory of what art might be.

1.5 Possible Worlds: Between Matter, Code, and Creativity

Within this historical and contemporary framework, an idea rooted in my own creative research and production.

Alongside traditional techniques of modeling, painting, and sculpture, my work incorporates digital tools such as 3D sculpture, procedural modeling, 3D printing, and artificial intelligence, engaging in a continuous dialogue between physical matter and virtual imagination.

[20] In the context of generative art, Machine Learning (ML), and artists like Refik Anadol, modeling takes on a data-driven and statistical meaning, shifting from the act of defining a geometric shape to that of structuring possibilities within a vast, digital space of information.

I use these instruments as I would brushes or chisels—techniques and gestures through which to express ideas—so that code, algorithm, and virtual space become extensions of my hand (Figure 1-11).[21]

Figure 1-11.* *Gianpiero Moioli. Suspended Spaces, 2025.
A space between realities: sculptures shaped by hand and code, brought together in a virtual installation rendered in Blender

This hybrid approach allows me to explore new aesthetic and conceptual dimensions, where the artwork is no longer limited to the physical realm but emerges as a **fluid form** that **exists across multiple levels of reality: as ideas, images, data, and as new objects.**

These are works in progress but also works of projection.

They exist not as absence but as presence in the virtual, fully formed in vision, waiting to materialize.

They offer a glimpse into a future where nature, architecture, memory, and technology are no longer separate territories but parts of a single, interconnected horizon of imagination.

---

[21] These and other hybrid creations can be explored further at `www.gianpieromoioli.it`.

The possibility of working on objects and spaces that exist in my mind—but already have form, scale, material, and spatial relationships—opens up infinite worlds that would otherwise remain invisible.[22]

My work explores the boundaries between matter and imagination, visible and invisible.

It is a continuous dialogue between physical gestures and digital transformations.

Paintings are developed through a two-step process.

First, I begin with a direct, physical gesture, working with paper, cardboard, brushes, pencils, and colors. This manual phase is rooted in traditional, tactile practices.

Then, the work crosses into the digital realm: the image is scanned or photographed and further developed using artificial intelligence and digital painting tools.

This transformation allows the painting to evolve, expanding, reconfiguring, and generating new visual variations that blend human gestures with algorithmic logic.

Sculptures are developed through two main approaches.

In the first workflow, the work begins with manual modeling—shaped by hand using traditional materials—and then captured through 3D scanning, allowing it to enter the digital domain.

In the second method, the sculpture is conceived and created entirely within virtual space, using digital tools and software.

In both cases, the resulting digital models can either be translated back into the physical world through 3D printing—transforming virtual forms into tangible, material objects—or remain in the digital realm, where they take shape as immersive environments within platforms such as *Unity* or *Spatial*.

When produced physically, these prototypes can lead to the creation of final products in materials such as resin, bronze, aluminum, or ceramic—each chosen to express a particular formal quality or to convey a specific resonance of gesture and material memory.

Alternatively, when preserved in their native digital form, these models become accessible in virtual reality, experienced through headsets as navigable spaces.

They are no longer just objects to be viewed but environments to be entered, interactive and immersive artworks where spatiality is programmed and perception becomes an act of participation.

[22] In my practice, I explore these worlds through a hybrid approach, combining traditional, hands-on techniques with digital tools, allowing ideas to move seamlessly between the physical and virtual realms.

Finally, painting and sculpture converge in immersive installations, suspended spaces that tell stories, where art, narrative, and technology merge, transcending the boundaries of dimension, form, and language.

Through this ongoing dialogue between real and virtual, between human gesture and algorithm, I seek to build geometries of the invisible, emotional maps, traces of possible worlds.

1.5.1 States of Transformation and Landscapes and Forces

My artistic practice unfolds within a conceptual framework structured around two complementary axes: *States of Transformation* and *Landscapes and Forces.*

The first axis, *States of Transformation,* is primarily focused on the technical and technological development of the work, exploring how materials, gestures, and tools evolve across analog and digital environments.

The second, *Landscapes and Forces,* is more oriented toward creative exploration, addressing the symbolic, spatial, and emotional dimensions of the artwork.

Over time, these two axes have increasingly converged, giving rise to a form of sculpture that is not only materially and formally hybrid but also deeply connected to meaning, narrative, and storytelling.

1.5.1.1 States of Transformation

This section refers to the material and technological processes at the core of my practice, what I consider the *transformative states of matter and image.*

It encompasses the continuous movement between the physical and the digital, between fluid gestures and structured forms, between manual work and algorithmic systems.

Here, transformation is not only a technical phase but a conceptual one. Clay becomes a 3D scan; a drawing evolves into a digital painting; a virtual form returns as a printed object or remains suspended in an immaterial, interactive space.

These works do not inhabit a single medium but move across states: gestural, virtual, sculptural, encoded.

The transitions themselves are part of the artwork.

In this sense, *States of Transformation* also reflects the plural nature of my techniques: I integrate traditional materials such as plaster, clay, cardboard, and ink with 3D scanning and digital modeling (Blender 5.0), 3D printing, AI image synthesis (Stable Diffusion 3.5, Midjourney v7), and real-time environments (Unity 6, Spatial 2025 1.0).

Each step of the process generates a new state, a new material and conceptual presence, shaped by memory, code, and the physical act of making.

This dynamic process is exemplified by *Mechanical Idol* (2024) (Figure 1-12). On the left, a virtual model created and rendered in Blender reveals its conceptual construction, exploring parametric forms and iterative configurations. On the right, a sequence of digital variations produced in Stable Diffusion demonstrates how the same idea unfolds in virtual space, through AI-driven adjustments and generative reconfigurations. Together, these images embody the logic of transformation: one concept shifting across media, scale, and states of existence and oscillating between matter and code.

Figure 1-12. *Left:* ***Mechanical Idol, 2024****, mixed media, 3D model designed and rendered in Blender 4.4 (cm 229 (h) × 103 × 102). Right:* ***Mechanical Idol with Planets, 2024****, AI-generated variations produced with Stable Diffusion. These images illustrate a hybrid workflow in which the sculptural form evolves through virtual modeling and generative reinterpretation*

Each step of the process generates a new state, a new material and conceptual presence, shaped by memory, code, and the physical act of making.

1.5.1.2 Landscapes and Forces

If *States of Transformation* defines the processes, *Landscapes and Forces* articulates the content.

This section gathers five thematic trajectories that reflect the conceptual and aesthetic core of my recent work which I will explore in depth in Chapter 8: Cosmic and Artificial Worlds, Flames and Energy, Spaces of Memory, Metaphysical Architectures, and Flowing Horizons.

Each one explores a different aspect of the relationship between nature, architecture, and imagination, moving from elemental energies to artificial horizons.

These conceptual "landscapes" are not geographic but symbolic. They include fire and energy, rivers and forests, metaphysical cities, mediterranean light, and planetary architectures.

They are inhabited by forces—visible and invisible—that shape the environment and the experience of space.

These works are not representations of reality, but speculative constructions, mental and emotional maps of a world where memory, imagination, and digital transformation converge.

The following visual example illustrates this hybrid process, showing a physical-digital loop where a 3D-modeled sculpture rendered in Blender becomes the starting point for AI-driven transformations using Stable Diffusion.

The example in Figure 1-13, *Alien Forest* (2024), demonstrates this hybrid loop between material and digital states. On the left, the sculpture modeled in Blender and prepared for realization in metal and polymer materials embodies a tangible presence; on the right, its AI-generated reinterpretation reimagines the same form within a virtual landscape. Together, they reveal how a single idea can shift between physical matter and algorithmic vision, opening a continuum where sculpture evolves simultaneously as object and as speculative construction.

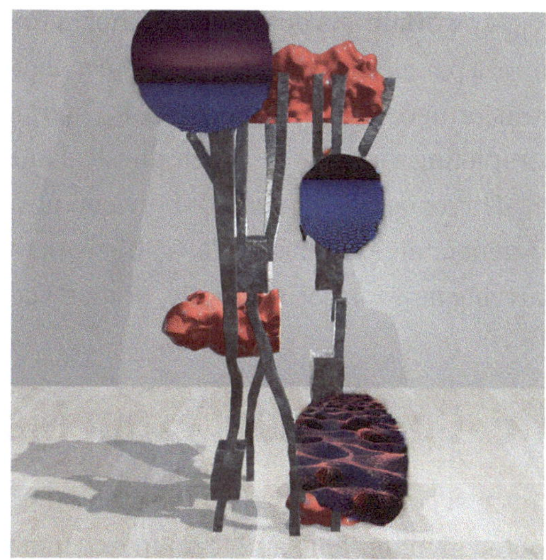

Figure 1-13. Gianpiero Moioli, Alien Forest, 2024.
On the left: mixed media sculpture, modeled in Blender and prepared for realization in metal and polymer materials (cm 238 (h) × 122 × 91).
On the right: AI-generated interpretation produced with Stable Diffusion, reimagining the work within a virtual landscape

Together, *States of Transformation* and *Landscapes and Forces* form the conceptual foundation of my hybrid artistic language. They are two intersecting paths: the first one oriented toward process and material mutation, the other toward symbolic environments and conceptual resonance.

1.5.2 Sculpting Across Dimensions

Each work emerges through a layered process that spans drawing, painting, sculpture, coding, and immersive installation, techniques and modes of making that are mapped visually in the structure of *Part I: States of Transformation.*

The image introducing this first part outlines the expressive techniques that form the basis of my approach: physical drawing and painting, 3D sculpture, digital modeling, algorithmic generation, and artificial intelligence.

While this section offers a personal and conceptual overview, each of these techniques will be examined in greater depth in Chapter 5, where I explore their material, technological, and poetic implications.

My workflow is not linear. Rather, it unfolds across multiple dimensions of space and time: a pencil drawing may become a digital image; a clay model may be 3D scanned, transformed, and reprinted; an AI-generated image may be painted over by hand, completing the cycle between physical and virtual.

This constant movement between physical modeling, digital sculpting, and AI-generated expansion allows the work to exist across multiple states, each stage carrying new formal, symbolic, or material qualities.

1.6 Conclusion: From Matter to Experience

This first chapter has traced the gradual transformation of sculpture from a discipline rooted in materiality and form to one that increasingly embraces space, perception, and technology as essential components of artistic language.

From the spatial ruptures of Fontana to the performative environments of Studio Azzurro and from Paik's electronic architectures to Plessi's elemental media, each of these practices has expanded the sculptural field toward narration, immersion, and interaction.

In doing so, they have laid the conceptual foundations for contemporary artists who work not only with stone, wood, or bronze but with code, light, data, and presence.

The artwork becomes a site of passage, a hybrid territory where gesture meets algorithm and where meaning is no longer fixed in matter but emerges through experience.

In this expanded field, the sculptural gesture is no longer bound solely to the manipulation of matter but extends into the orchestration of processes across physical and virtual domains. This conceptual shift sets the stage for the next chapter, which will explore in detail how contemporary modeling practices—both manual and digital—operate within hybrid workflows, merging traditional craftsmanship with computational precision to redefine the act of sculpting in the digital age.

CHAPTER 2

Modeling as Creative Gesture: Processes of Digital Creation

In this second chapter, we examine the transition from traditional sculptural techniques to digital modeling.

Digital tools, from 3D modeling software to AI-driven systems, enable the manipulation of form within virtual environments, merging the tactility of manual craftsmanship with the precision of algorithmic processes.

Within this **expanded artistic practice environment**, modeling becomes a hybrid act, at once technical, conceptual, and project-based.

Physical gestures, digital workflows, 3D scanning, and additive manufacturing converge into a seamless continuum.

The artist no longer shapes only matter but orchestrates a sequence of actions that is manual, virtual, and generative.

In contemporary digital paradigms, modeling encompasses all creative gestures within[1] virtual space.

The convergence of 3D modeling, scanning, artificial intelligence, and digital fabrication reshapes the boundaries between the physical and virtual realms.

As digital art moves beyond the constraints of physical form, it also reconnects with spatial and perceptual concerns rooted in the historical avant-gardes.

From Fontana's spatial cuts to Paik's electronic installations, sculpture expands to include video, light, code, and interactivity.

---

[1] As established in the preceding chapter, contemporary modeling paradigms are hybrid, incorporating not only manual and digital 3D creation but also algorithmic processes and the statistical structuring of data required by AI systems.

G. Moioli, *Art Between Matter and Code*, https://doi.org/10.1007/979-8-8688-2376-3_2

Contemporary platforms such as Blender, Unity, TouchDesigner, and Spatial extend this trajectory, projecting sculptural thinking into immersive and programmable environments where object and space merge into networks of data and experience.

In this context, digital modeling emerges as an autonomous creative gesture: a process that reshapes how form is conceived and redefines the relationship between art, technology, and perception, opening new aesthetic and conceptual pathways for contemporary practice.

2.1 The Transformation of the Artwork: From Concept to Physical Object to Expanded Idea

This section discusses how artworks evolve from ideas to tangible objects to conceptual entities in the digital age, emphasizing the shift from material-centric to idea-driven art.

In the digital context, modeling transcends its traditional role as the shaping of physical material and becomes the primary generative act of contemporary creation.

No longer limited to the sculptor's manipulation of clay, marble, or physical materials, modeling unfolds within a multidimensional space where data, code, and algorithms interact to give rise to both virtual and material forms (Figure 2-1).

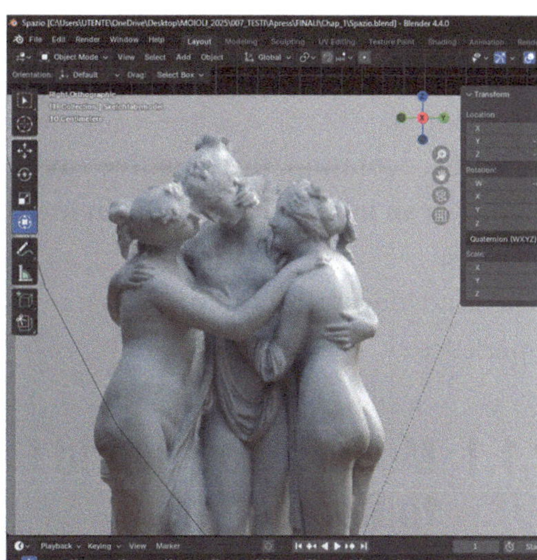

Figure 2-1. From classical sculpture to digital modeling.
Left: Antonio Canova, Three Graces (1813–1816, marble, h. 182 cm, Hermitage Museum, St. Petersburg). Public Domain
Right: Digital reinterpretation scanned and imported in Blender. (`https://skfb.ly/oCO8u`) by pickle, licensed under Creative Commons Attribution.
The juxtaposition underscores the shift from material sculpture to computational form

This shift transforms the artwork from a fixed object into a dynamic framework of possibilities, a fluid system where structure, process, and transformation coexist across multiple layers of interaction and media.

Contemporary digital art embraces this multiplicity, extending the notion of sculpture into immersive and performative systems.

From Studio Azzurro's pioneering experiences with "ambienti sensibili"—installations that responded to touch, movement, and presence emerged a new paradigm: the artwork as environment, the viewer as participant, the interface as form.

Today, this concept of the *sensitive environment* is no longer confined to physical space. Through extended reality platforms such as Blender, Unity, or Spatial and through real-time engines like TouchDesigner, the environment becomes **virtual, dynamic, and networked**.

The sensibility of the system—once driven by sensors and video feedback—is now amplified by **artificial intelligence**, which adds unpredictability, generative behavior, and semantic responsiveness.

AI enables the creation of spaces that not only react but imagine producing new images, generating textual responses, or mutating form based on interaction, language, or data input.

In this evolution, the sensitive environment becomes both metaversal and cognitive: an immersive space that learns, suggests, adapts, and evolves with its users.

It is no longer simply a space that responds, but one that collaborates, a co-author of experience.

2.1.1 Modeling as Hybrid Gesture: From Craft to Computation

At its core, modeling as a creative gesture preserves the intimate act of giving form to thought.

Yet this gesture today operates within hybrid environments. It may originate from a hand-drawn sketch or a physical maquette but rapidly extends into digital domains where virtual modeling tools, procedural logics, and AI-driven transformations intervene to expand and reinterpret the initial idea.

Virtual modeling allows for extensive experimentation, enabling designers to create numerous iterations and variations of the designed shape within computational and practical constraints.

Whether constructing volumetric forms through 3D modeling software such as Blender 3.x+, elaborating complex procedural geometries via node-based systems (Blender Geometry Nodes, Grasshopper), or developing visual compositions through AI-powered image synthesis platforms like Stable Diffusion 1.5/2.1 or DALL·E 2/3, modeling today constitutes a fluid interplay of data, processes, and algorithmic structures.

For instance, a hand-created clay or plaster model may be captured through 3D scanning, digitally refined, 3D printed, and subsequently transformed into an artwork of any material and scale.

Meanwhile, a simple pen-and-ink drawing can evolve into a complex multilayered image through iterative processes of virtual painting, neural image expansion, and manual re-intervention.

Similarly, the procedural generation of my *Mediterranean Landscape* or *Bio-mechanical Structure* works can emerge from algorithmic growth models, where I define parameters rather than forms.

In all these cases, creating becomes a hybrid process, merging physical gestures, virtual simulations, and AI-generated variability.

My *Mediterranean Landscape* (Figure 2-2) works are rooted in the cultural and environmental matrix of Italy: they evoke the geometry of Renaissance piazzas, the luminous clarity of the Mediterranean climate, and the metaphysical atmosphere of De Chirico's urban visions.

Yet they also open toward surrealist displacements and alien horizons, where familiar architectures are transformed under an unreal, incandescent light.

In these works, the Mediterranean is not represented as a literal place but as a symbolic and atmospheric space, a threshold where history and imagination, memory and invention, converge.

Figure 2-2. Gianpiero Moioli, Mediterranean Landscape (Hybrid Versions), 2025.
Left: Original hand-painted work with layered paper and cardboard collage.
Right: Two AI-generated reinterpretations created through inpainting, modifying selected areas of the original drawing while preserving its overall structure. Mixed media and AI-generated image.
The work explores the integration of manual gesture and algorithmic transformation within a Mediterranean imaginary

The example shown here exemplifies this hybrid logic.

On the right is the original hand-made composition, created through drawing and collage with superimposed papers and cardboard. To the right, the same work is reimagined through prompt-driven iterations in MidJourney, where algorithmic processes extend and transform the initial material gesture.[2]

This process of transformation is further extended through video, creating temporal dimensions of the work:

> Video: The sequence demonstrates the evolution of the concept from static image to temporal movement, generated using Midjourney V7 and subsequently edited and finalized in Blender 5.0.
>
> Music Licensing: The soundtrack for this video is utilized under a royalty-free license from Pixabay. The required attribution is: Music by FreeMusicForVideo from Pixabay.
>
> Link: https://vimeo.com/1144819891

What emerges is a dialogue between manual construction and computational expansion, where the physical artwork opens itself toward parallel worlds of representation.

A more detailed discussion of these techniques and their implications will follow in Chapter 5.

The contemporary artist no longer simply shapes inert matter but orchestrates interactive systems where sculpture, painting, sound, installation, performance, and generative computation converge into a unified field of dynamic creation.

Modeling expands into the creation of landscapes and universes, where matter and imagination converge in a generative totality.

It is no longer solely about form-making; it becomes an open-ended framework for experimentation, iteration, and continuous transformation across both material and immaterial domains.

---

[2] One of the prompts created by me and used for the AI reinterpretations reads: "Under the big orange sun, Mediterranean vegetation dances in the evening breeze.

"Sinuous lines evoke ancient roots, while vibrant colors blend harmoniously. Red and gold recall prosperity and vitality, evoking distant yet familiar landscapes. The horizon is a balance between nature and abstraction, between earth and dream."

Within this expanded field, artistic practice also extends into **raster and vector-based digital painting (Figure 2-3).**

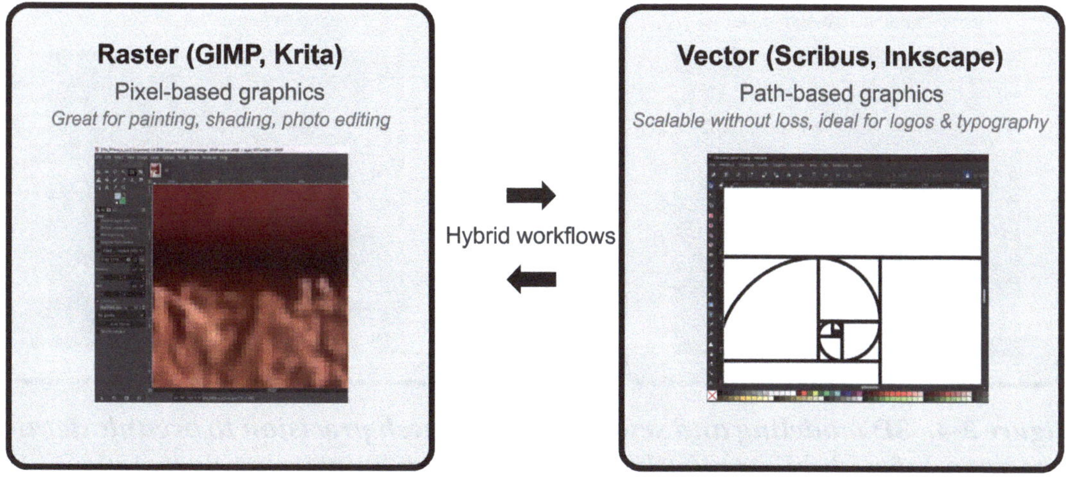

Figure 2-3. Raster vs. vector in digital painting and design.
Hybrid workflows integrate pixel-based and path-based graphics for versatile creative outcomes

Tools such as GIMP and Krita allow the creation of pixel-based, resolution-dependent images, ideal for painting, shading, and photo editing.

Conversely, Scribus and Inkscape operate with vector paths, offering resolution-independent graphics particularly suited to logos, typography, and scalable design.

Often, these two approaches are combined in hybrid workflows, where painterly textures and geometric structures intersect to form versatile visual languages.

Beyond two-dimensional practices, the field of digital art extends into **3D modeling and sculpting**, where software such as Blender, ZBrush, and Nomad Sculpt enable the creation of complex volumetric forms.

These environments allow artists to move from organic and fluid geometries to architectural and structural compositions, combining the immediacy of manual sculptural gestures with the precision of digital tools. In this sense, digital modeling does not represent a simple translation of traditional practices into virtual space but rather a hybrid methodology in which hand-driven intuition and algorithmic calculation coexist.

These software environments form the foundation of contemporary design workflows: they allow ideas to evolve from an initial sketch or digital maquette into articulated forms that can be visualized, iterated, and ultimately materialized (Figure 2-4).

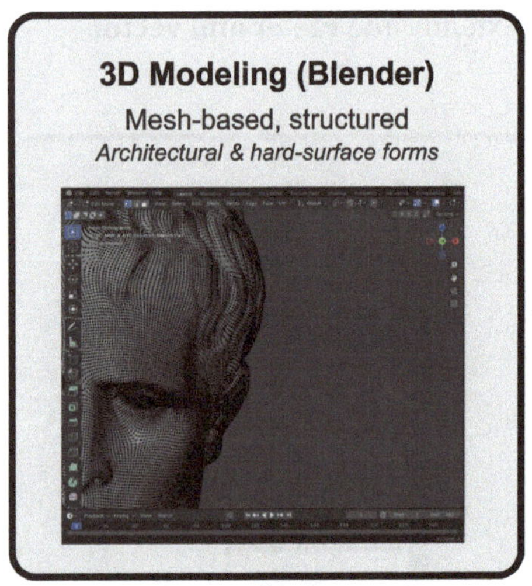

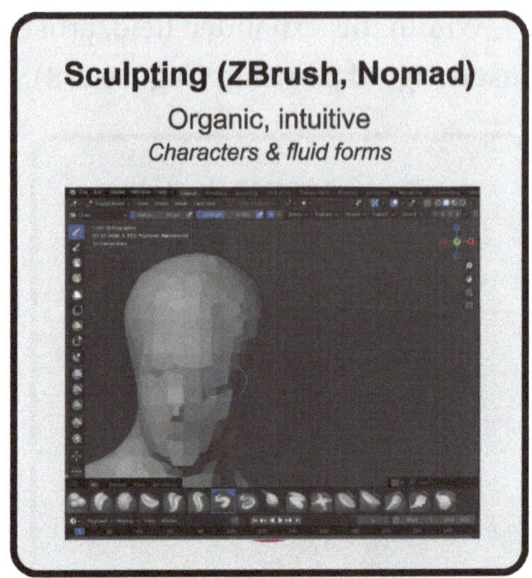

Figure 2-4. ***3D modeling and sculpting: from mesh precision to organic detail.*** *Integration of mesh-based modeling and organic sculpting: a hybrid workflow combining geometric precision with expressive freedom*

Building on this foundation, **procedural generation** and **AI-driven creativity** expand the workflow into algorithmic and generative domains, allowing for the creation of adaptive and complex forms beyond the scope of purely manual techniques (see Figure 2-5).

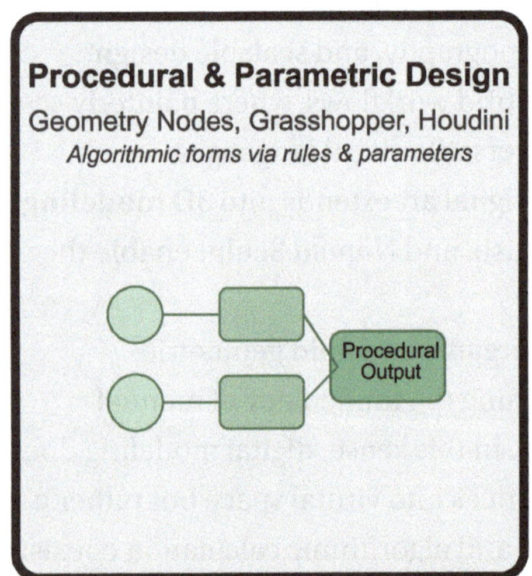

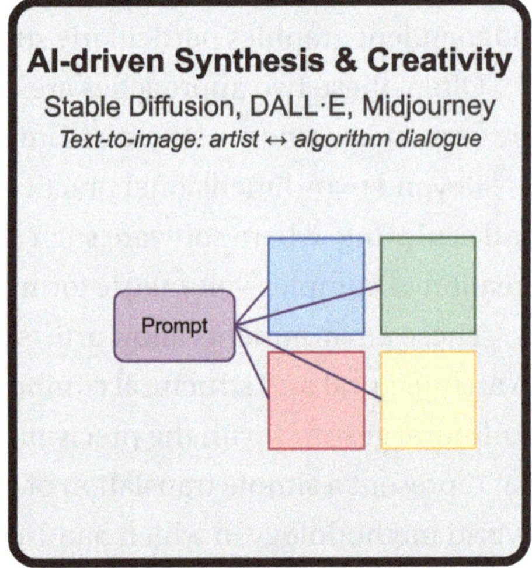

Figure 2-5. ***From procedural and parametric design to AI-driven synthesis.*** *Hybrid workflows merging rule-based generation with adaptive, algorithmic creativity*

Through platforms such as Blender's Geometry Nodes, Grasshopper for Rhino, or Houdini, forms are no longer modeled directly but generated algorithmically.

The artist operates by defining parameters, constraints, and relationships rather than shapes themselves, allowing geometry to emerge as the result of mathematical rules or computational processes.

Alongside procedural methods, the rise of AI-driven synthesis and computational creativity has expanded the field even further. Platforms such as Stable Diffusion, DALL·E, and Midjourney generate images from textual prompts, turning language itself into a modeling tool.

Here, creation unfolds as a dialogue between artist and algorithm: the human provides intuition, vision, and direction, while the machine introduces new associations, unexpected outcomes, and alternative interpretations. Rather than replacing artistic intention, these systems extend it, offering new spaces of experimentation where imagination is filtered through computation.

Expanding on **interactive installations, immersive environments, and extended realities** bring these responsive systems into fully spatialized, multisensory worlds, where audience participation becomes an integral part of the artistic experience (see Figure 2-6).

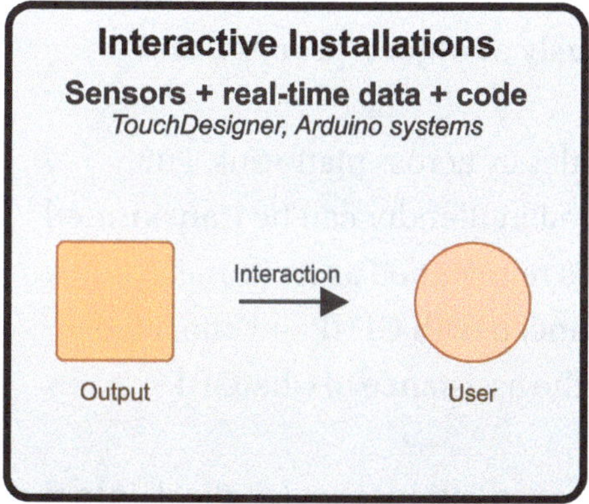

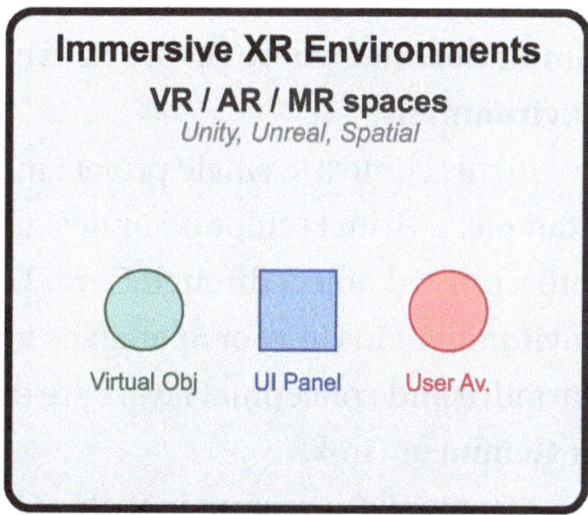

Figure 2-6. Interactive installations and immersive XR environments. *Hybrid workflows that merge responsive systems with multisensory spaces blending physical and virtual dimensions*

In **interactive installations**, the artwork is rooted in physical space: it becomes a responsive environment that can react to movement, sound, or temperature, transforming external stimuli into visual, acoustic, or spatial experiences. These works unfold in the material world, evolving into living systems co-authored by the artist and the participants who activate them through their presence and actions.

By contrast, **immersive environments and extended realities (XR)** expand this logic into the domain of virtuality. Using engines such as Unity, Unreal Engine, or Spatial, artists can design augmented, mixed, or fully virtual spaces that go beyond the physical gallery—ranging from realistic replicas of exhibition venues to fluid, multisensory worlds where perception is reshaped and the laws of space itself can be reimagined.

These environments are not merely simulated stages but experiential landscapes, where viewers become active participants in an expanded field of interaction.

In this way, immersion and interactivity converge, opening new horizons in which the boundaries between real and virtual, material and immaterial, dissolve into hybrid forms of artistic presence.

These modes are not isolated disciplines but interconnected modalities within a broader ecosystem of post-material creation.

The contemporary studio becomes a hybrid interface where gesture meets simulation and where the work exists simultaneously as object, process, and environment.

In this context, a single project might move seamlessly across platforms. For example, a virtual sculpture or designed object shaped in Blender can be transformed into a printed object through Cura. That same form is reimagined as an immersive environment in Unity or Spatial; its textures are enhanced with GIMP or Krita, while narrative and conceptual layers are developed with the assistance of ChatGPT or Gemini or Grok.

Meanwhile, a prompt in Stable Diffusion generates variations that feedback into the original model, forming a loop of image and idea.

Most of these tools are **open-source**, fostering experimentation, accessibility, and shared innovation. They are not merely technical utilities but conceptual prosthetic interfaces where tradition and invention converge.

Within this environment, creation unfolds as a continuum of gesture, simulation, and computation.

Here, shaping form also means shaping process: designing behaviors, encoding variation, orchestrating data flows.

The artist operates as both maker and meta-designer, navigating a landscape where objects, models, and algorithms coalesce into new aesthetic and conceptual terrains.

2.1.2 From Physical to Conceptual Artworks

Historically, sculpture relied on materials like terracotta, marble, and bronze to give tangible form to artistic vision.

Today, digital tools unlock unprecedented freedom, enabling infinite formal variations and a level of control previously unimaginable.

Since the advent of **3D modeling**, software artists can build virtual volumes from scratch, working with meshes, modifiers, and procedural techniques to define shape, proportion, and surface detail.

Digital environments allow for infinite iteration, real-time transformation, and the simulation of complex geometries before any material realization takes place.

Alongside modeling, **3D scanning** technologies enable the capture of existing physical objects, translating real-world forms into accurate digital models. These scans can be refined, reworked, or integrated into larger virtual compositions.

The next section explores these techniques, examining how tools like Blender, in combination with scanning hardware and photogrammetry software, support the creation and transformation of sculptural forms within the digital domain.

2.1.2.1 3D Modeling and Acquisition: From Virtual Creation to Physical Transformation

Contemporary digital sculpture unfolds along a dynamic spectrum that includes manual modeling, physical acquisition, digital post-processing, and even a return to material realization through techniques like 3D printing.

Rather than following a linear sequence, this process allows for circular and flexible movement between physical and virtual domains, enhancing the artist's ability to experiment, iterate, and transform sculptural ideas across different stages.

Before diving into specific techniques, let's look at the main tools and workflows available to the digital sculptor today.

2.1.2.1.1 Modeling from Scratch: Virtual Creation

The modeling process often begins entirely in the virtual domain, where an idea, a sketch, or a reference image serves as the seed for a digital form.

Using software such as Blender, ZBrush, or Maya, artists construct volumes and structures without physical constraints, working in an environment where scale, gravity, and material resistance are suspended (Figure 2-7).

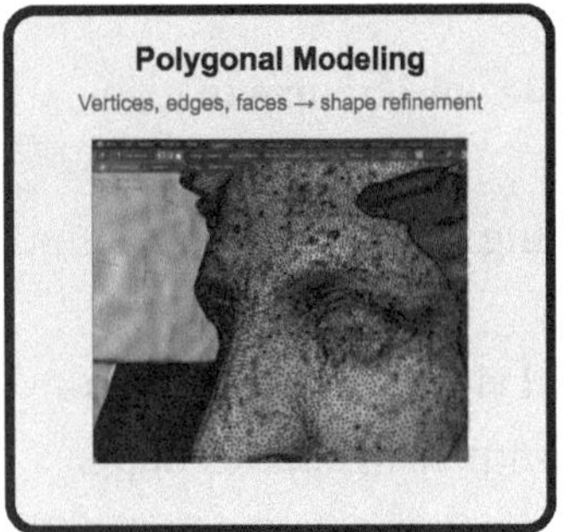

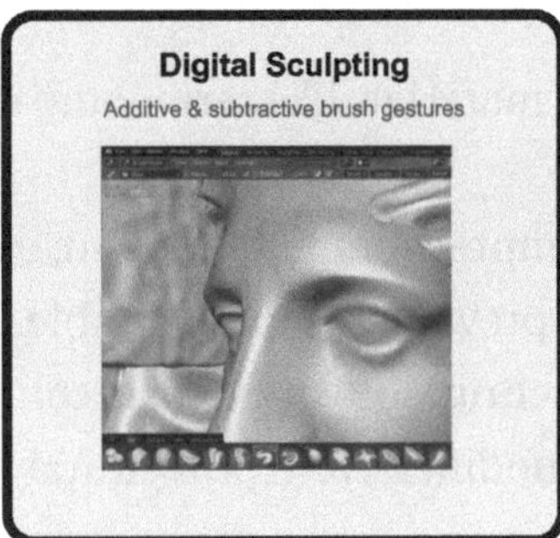

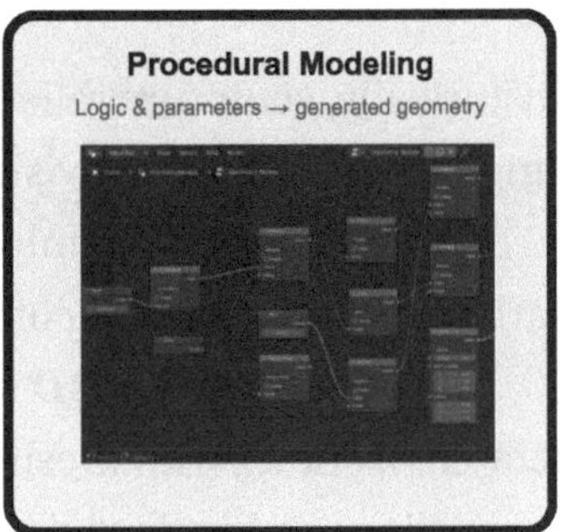

Figure 2-7. Three primary approaches to digital form-making.
Polygonal modeling for mesh refinement, digital sculpting for expressive surface shaping, and procedural modeling for logic-driven geometry generation

Several techniques are commonly employed:

- **Polygonal modeling**, which involves shaping a mesh by directly manipulating vertices, edges, and faces
- **Digital sculpting**, where artists use brush-based tools to simulate the additive and subtractive gestures of traditional clay modeling
- **Procedural modeling**, which allows the form to emerge from logic and parameters—often using node-based systems like **Blender's Geometry Nodes**

These approaches result in a digital 3D mesh, exported in formats such as OBJ, FBX, or STL, ready for rendering, animation, simulation, or other virtual or physical output.

This method is ideal when the form is entirely imagined or speculative—unconstrained by existing physical objects or traditional media.

2.1.2.1.1.1 Manual Modeling Techniques: From Structure to Gesture

Digital manual modeling refers to the direct, hands-on shaping of virtual forms, where the artist works on geometry much as they would with traditional materials—guiding every curve, edge, and surface.

In this context, the digital environment becomes an extension of the sculptor's hand, providing the precision of software tools while preserving the immediacy of manual gesture.

This section introduces the main techniques used in manual modeling within Blender and comparable 3D applications.

We will examine practical examples of these methods in section 2.5.1.

Object Mode: Composing with Volumes

Think of Object Mode as working with blocks of marble or clay before carving. Here you don't alter the internal shape of an object but move and arrange it as a whole.

- You place **primitive forms** (cubes, spheres, cylinders) as starting blocks.
- You adjust **size**, **rotation**, and **position**, like placing elements on a pedestal.
- You can apply **basic transformations and symmetry** (mirroring, duplication).

This stage is about **composition and structure**, not detail.

(In Blender, add objects with Shift+A, transform with G/R/S, organize in Collections, apply modifiers like Mirror or Array.)

Edit Mode: Constructing the Mesh

Edit Mode is where you actually shape the stone, cutting into its geometry. You work directly on the skeleton of the object, made of vertices, edges, and faces.

- You can **extrude surfaces** to extend them, like pulling clay outward.
- You can **insert loops and cuts** to refine contours.
- You ensure the **flow of edges** is clean, so the form bends and deforms correctly.

This stage transforms a block into a structured figure.

(In Blender, press Tab to enter Edit Mode; use Extrude (E), Insert Edge Loop (Ctrl+R), and Knife Tool (K).)

Sculpt Mode: Modeling by Gesture

Sculpt Mode brings you closest to the physical act of sculpting. Brushes simulate hands and tools working the material.

- The **Grab Brush** moves large sections, like pushing clay.
- **Clay Strips** build volume layer by layer.
- **Smooth** softens transitions.
- **Crease** carves fine lines and folds.

This is where expression emerges. Surfaces breathe, gestures come alive, and organic detail appears.

(In Blender, choose Sculpt Mode, and select brushes such as Grab, Smooth, Clay, Inflate.)

Retopology and Finishing

After expressive work, the digital sculpture may be "heavy"—like a clay maquette that needs a cast before display. Retopology rebuilds the surface into a lighter, cleaner structure, making it ready for animation, printing, or texturing.

- This ensures the form is **technically sound** while preserving artistic gestures.
- At this stage, you also prepare **UV maps and textures**, painting or projecting details onto the surface.

(In Blender, use the Shrinkwrap modifier, snapping tools, Subdivision Surface for preview, UV unwrap, and texture baking.)

2.1.2.1.2 3D Acquisition: Capturing Physical Form

When the goal is to bring an existing object—be it a handmade maquette, a historical statue, or a natural form—into the digital environment, 3D acquisition becomes the starting point.

3D scanning allows artists to digitize physical objects by translating them into point clouds or polygonal meshes.

This process enables faithful documentation, reinterpretation, and creative transformation of existing forms (Figure 2-8).

Figure 2-8. 3D model of the Bust of Napoleon Bonaparte in the Sketchfab interface.
Released by Virtual Museums of Małopolska under CC BY 4.0

In the image, we can see an example of a high-resolution 3D scan[3] of the *Bust of Napoleon Bonaparte*, digitized and released online by the Virtual Museums of Małopolska in Kraków, Poland,[4] as part of its open-access initiative.

[3] The 3D scan of the *Bust of Napoleon Bonaparte* is available on Sketchfab under a Creative Commons Attribution (CC BY) license: `https://sketchfab.com/3d-models/the-bust-of-napoleon-bonaparte-a177bf0e121641bea6cf1d58ad3efc5b`.

[4] The Virtual Museums of Małopolska is a regional digital platform curated by the Małopolska Institute of Culture and the Regional Digitalisation Lab in Kraków.

It provides open access to digitized cultural heritage from more than 41 museums in the Małopolska region, including the National Museum in Kraków.

You can explore the broader collection here: `https://muzea.malopolska.pl/`.

The 3D model is freely accessible on Sketchfab, where it can be explored online in multiple render modes and inspected down to the finest surface detail.

Released by the museum under a Creative Commons Attribution (CC-BY) license, it may be downloaded and reused for education, research, artistic reinterpretation, or integration into VR/AR environments, provided proper attribution is given.

This high-fidelity digital replica preserves both the overall proportions and the subtlest textures of the original sculpture, offering an unprecedented tool for study and creative re-appropriation.

Within the broader field of art and cultural heritage, the integration of 3D acquisition technologies has opened new pathways for preservation, reinterpretation, and creation.

From the digital documentation of classical sculptures to the development of new works rooted in material tradition, these tools serve both historical fidelity and contemporary experimentation.

In practice, their use spans a wide spectrum—from the digitization of classical sculptures such as those by Canova or Michelangelo, creating high-fidelity archives for study, education, and public dissemination, to the documentation for conservation and restoration, as in the *Scan the World* project,[5] where precise 3D records guide preservation strategies.

For example, Antonio Canova that embodies the fusion of technical mastery, philosophical reflection, and the neoclassical pursuit of the ideal, represents a conceptual reference point [1].

His extraordinary sensitivity to proportion, gesture, and finish provides a historical lens for rethinking how such values might be translated, reinterpreted, or even challenged through today's code-driven, algorithmic modeling practices.

For contemporary artists and sculptors, however, 3D scanning becomes a living tool: it enables the instant capture of clay or plaster models to generate digital doubles that can be freely scaled, deformed, combined, or reinterpreted without risking the original maquette.[6]

---

[5] The "Scan the World project" is an initiative that digitizes artworks and monuments through 3D scanning and makes them freely available online: `https://www.myminifactory.com/scantheworld/`.

[6] This vision was also championed by Leopoldo Cicognara (1767–1834), theorist and close friend of Canova. In his Storia della scultura dal suo risorgimento in Italia al secolo di Canova (1823), he celebrated Canova's work and framed sculpture as a civic and intellectual enterprise, anticipating the integration of aesthetic, nstitutional, and philosophical dimensions still relevant in today's technologically mediated art practices.

To enable these applications, artists, conservators, and institutions rely on three primary technologies.

The first is **photogrammetry**, which reconstructs a 3D model from a series of photographs taken from multiple angles, translating two-dimensional images into accurate three-dimensional geometry.

The second is **structured light scanning**, in which projected patterns of light and shadow are analyzed to capture surface geometry with high detail and accuracy.

The third is **LiDAR (Laser Scanning)**, which uses time-of-flight measurements to map physical volumes with exceptional precision, making it especially valuable for large-scale works or architectural contexts.

Once the raw data is acquired, specialized software—such as Meshroom, Kiri Engine, RealityCapture, or Artec Studio—processes the information to generate a high-resolution 3D mesh, often complete with texture maps that faithfully reproduce the surface appearance.

This workflow is essential when digitizing real-world forms for archiving, restoration, manipulation, or integration into new digital and immersive compositions.

2.1.2.1.3 Post-Processing and Integration

Whether created from scratch or captured via scanning, a model typically enters a **post-processing** phase before effective use in creative workflows.

In this stage, the raw mesh is **cleaned and optimized**: polygons reduced, surfaces smoothed, and topology corrected. Scanned models often require **noise removal, hole filling, and re-meshing**, with textures refined or re-projected. Only after this digital "polishing" does the model become a reliable base for further sculpting, procedural work, or fabrication.

This process includes:

- **Mesh cleaning**, which removes noise, fills holes, and eliminates artifacts
- **Retopology**, where the geometry is restructured for better performance, especially for animation or real-time rendering
- **UV mapping and texturing**, which allow surfaces to be painted, shaded, or mapped with real-world materials
- **Rigging** (if needed), to add bones and control points for animation or interactive manipulation

This step bridges the gap between raw digital form and its application in fields such as **VR/AR**, **video games**, **animation**, or **fabrication**.

2.1.2.1.4 Digital to Physical: Materializing the Virtual

In many cases, digital artworks are brought back into the material world through digital fabrication techniques, such as 3D printing, CNC milling, or casting.

These methods translate virtual models into tangible forms, allowing digital concepts to acquire physical presence while retaining their computational origins.

This final phase may involve:

- **3D printing**, using resin, filament (FDM), clay, or powder-based systems (SLS)
- **CNC milling**, for subtractive processes in wood, metal, or stone
- **Casting**, using printed prototypes to produce forms in bronze, ceramic, or other traditional materials

This closes the loop, transforming virtual creations into tangible sculptures that can inhabit physical space while retaining their digital origin, a topic that will be explored in detail in Chapter 6.

2.1.2.1.5 AI-Driven 3D Modeling: Emerging Practices and Current Limits

Artificial intelligence is beginning to enter the realm of 3D modeling, although its development is still at an earlier stage compared to other creative fields such as image generation or text synthesis.

Contemporary AI-driven tools for 3D creation continue to concentrate primarily on accelerating the early phases of the modeling process - ideation, rough geometry generation, and rapid prototyping - rather than delivering fully production-ready assets with optimised topology, clean UVs, rigging, and seamless integration into professional pipelines.

Significant progress in 2025 has nonetheless reduced the distance between "concept" and "final" through automated retopology, texture synthesis, and export optimisation modules that are now increasingly automated.

The principal approaches are:

Image-to-3D conversion, exemplified by Kaedim (v3), Spline AI (v2.5), and Luma AI Genie (v1.5), which transform single- or multi-view photographs, sketches, or reference images into textured, quad-dominant base meshes. These tools now routinely include automatic retopology, basic LOD generation, and preliminary UV unwrapping.

Text-to-3D generation, led by Meshy AI (v3.2), Tripo3D Rodin (v1.5), and Sloyd AI (v2.0). Building on the diffusion-model foundations established by earlier research prototypes such as OpenAI's Point-E (2022) and Google's DreamFusion (2022), these commercial systems produce textured, game-ready or print-ready models in seconds to minutes, with improved prompt fidelity, PBR material assignment, and direct export to Unity, Unreal Engine, or Blender.

NeRF- and Gaussian-Splatting-based reconstruction, represented by Luma AI's NeRF Suite v2.0, NVIDIA Omniverse Instant NeRF 2.0, and hybrid pipelines in 3D AI Studio.

These methods reconstruct photorealistic, navigable volumes from multi-angle photographic or video datasets.

Despite these advances, outputs from all three families still generally require manual or semi-automated intervention before they can be considered production-ready for high-end animation, AAA games, or physical fabrication.

The principal value of current AI tools therefore lies in dramatically accelerated concept exploration and mid-fidelity prototyping, enabling artists to iterate dozens of formal solutions in the time previously required for a single traditional maquette, while the final stages of professional asset creation remain a collaborative endeavour between human expertise and algorithmic assistance.

2.1.3 Expanded Art through Digital Iterations

Digital technologies make artworks expanded: iteratable, simulated in real time, and open to interaction.

Artists can develop multiple versions in software like Blender, testing formal, material, and spatial options before any physical outcome.

Interactive systems may respond to data, presence, or algorithms, transforming the work into an open, evolving system.

This shift redefines the artwork as a fluid conceptual entity situated in a continuum of process, interaction, and code.

Figure 2-9 summarizes the expanded conditions of digital practice: the artwork is no longer confined to material production but unfolds within infrastructures of software, data, and platforms. These conditions enable continuous iteration, simulation, and interaction, positioning the artwork as a fluid system in constant transformation.

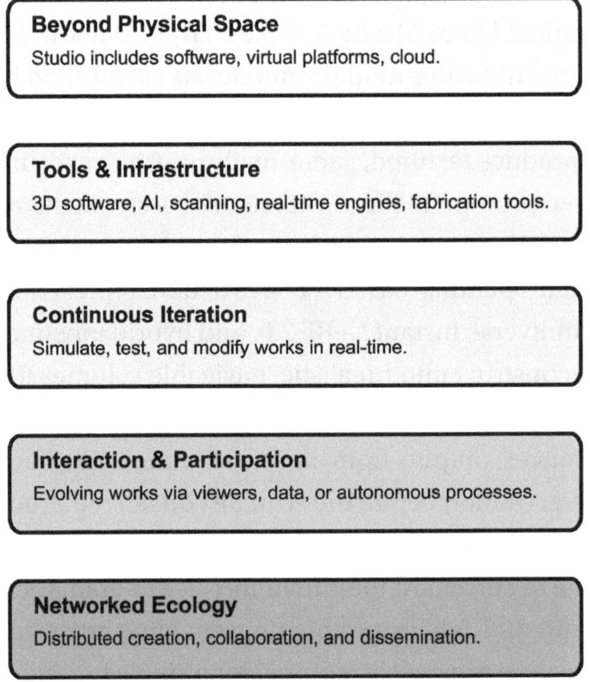

Figure 2-9. Framework of the expanded digital artwork.
From virtual infrastructures and tools to iterative processes, situating creation within a continuum of process, interaction, and code

The Expanded Studio can be understood through several key nodes that articulate its functioning and scope:

- **Beyond physical space:** The studio extends into software, virtual platforms, and the cloud, detaching practice from a single location.
- **Tools and infrastructure:** Core elements such as 3D software, AI, scanning, real-time engines, and fabrication technologies.
- **Continuous iteration:** Works can be simulated, tested, and refined in real time, making process an open cycle.

- **Interaction and participation:** Viewers, data, or autonomous systems contribute to evolving forms.
- **Networked ecology:** Creation, collaboration, and dissemination unfold within distributed and connected platforms.

This framework moves from the idea of an ecosystem to that of a practice.

In this sense the Expanded Studio blends traditional methods, sketches and maquettes, with computational ones.

Initial physical artifacts are digitized for iteration in the virtual space. The final files are used for virtual deployment or 3D printing, completing the cycle where the initial tactile gesture informs both the digital and physical output.

Section 2.2 explores how the expanded studio translates into practice, showing how virtual modeling can function as a kind of drawing—fluid, spatial, and continuously reconfigurable.

2.2 Real Sculpture and Virtual Modeling: Drawing in Digital Space, Fluid Matrices

This section contrasts physical sculpting with virtual modeling, emphasizing the flexibility of digital tools in shaping malleable, transformable forms.

As we noted before, from Antonio Canova's plaster and terracotta *bozzetti*[7]—tangible three-dimensional sketches—to Henry Moore's maquettes,[8] where ideas materialize as relations of mass and void, the sculptural sketch has long operated as a projective design process. **Virtual modeling is its contemporary equivalent: a drawn maquette in space that extends this exploratory logic into an open, potentially infinite digital continuum.**

Digital tools provide what we may call fluid matrices—virtual environments where form is never fixed but remains open to continuous transformation. Within these matrices, shapes can be stretched, warped, or reshaped without material

[7] Antonio Canova often created *bozzetti* in clay or terracotta as preparatory studies. These models were part of a systematic process, serving as tangible "thinking tools" to test proportions and gestures before moving to plaster and marble.

[8] Henry Moore used plaster maquettes as "three-dimensional sketches," small forms he could turn in his hands, view from every angle, and freely imagine at any scale. They embodied a process where ideas materialized in space as part of his design method.

resistance. Scale, texture, and structure may be altered in real time so that ideas evolve through iterative, nondestructive adjustments, more akin to drawing than carving.

In this context, virtual modeling becomes a form of drawing in three dimensions—a technical process that digital sculpture elevates into an artistic act. Software such as Blender, ZBrush, or Rhino enables the creation of forms unbound by gravity, scale, or material constraints, where speculative, impossible, or purely conceptual structures coexist with precise simulations of physical behavior.

This dual capacity, to invent and to simulate, makes digital modeling a hybrid space of intuition and computation, where the artist can shift seamlessly between abstraction and realism, speculation and materiality (Figure 2-10). **The concept of the fluid matrix captures this condition: an environment of perpetual becoming, in which the artwork is less an object than a process.**

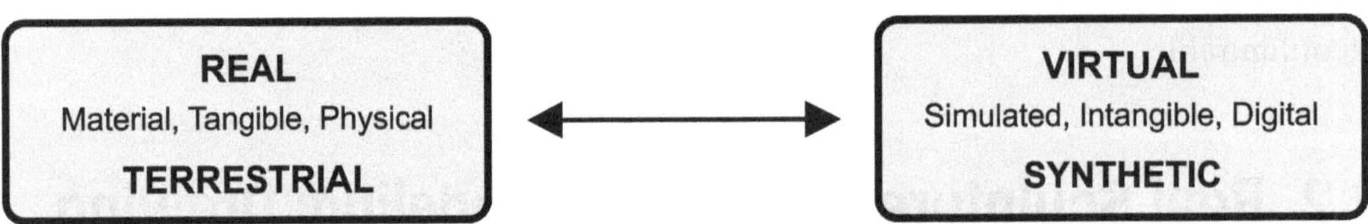

Figure 2-10. Real and virtual.
A fundamental polarity in contemporary artistic practice.

Such polarity mirrors a central tension in contemporary art: the interplay between the real and the virtual. Digital modeling operates precisely along this axis, enabling the artist to traverse domains once perceived as separate—material and immaterial, terrestrial and alien, or synthetic.

A simple sphere or even a flat plane can become a generative seed.

Through iterative modeling sessions—combining manual adjustments with algorithmic operations—it can evolve into **biomorphic forms** reminiscent of coral, vascular networks, or alien organisms.

My own practice often begins this way: extruding, applying modifiers, and progressively articulating shapes through a balance of direct sculpting and procedural logic.

In virtual space, the artist works directly with form as a spatial construct—defining contours, extruding volumes, and developing complex topologies with immediacy. Symmetry tools, mirror modifiers, and **nondestructive editing** allow intricate designs to emerge quickly, while the absence of physical inertia frees structures to float, interpenetrate, or defy terrestrial scale. The virtual model thus becomes a **fluid laboratory** for exploring formal possibilities unconstrained by fabrication.

In art today, the boundary between **real and virtual**—between dream and reality—is increasingly blurred, not only on screens or through headsets but within lived experience itself. A striking example is ***The Weather Project* (2003) by Olafur Eliasson**, presented at Tate Modern in London, where a constructed, simulated sun became an **immersive, almost tangible environment** for the viewers.[9]

2.3 Hybrid Modeling Workflows

Hybrid modeling workflows integrate manual craftsmanship with digital and computational processes, establishing a continuous exchange between the physical and virtual realms.

A clay or plaster model can be digitized via 3D scanning (structured light, photogrammetry, laser triangulation), producing meshes that preserve tactile nuances while enabling digital refinement. Conversely, virtual models can be re-materialized through 3D printing, CNC milling, or casting.

Figure 2-11 visualizes the cyclical flow of hybrid modeling, showing how manual, digital, computational, and AI-based processes interconnect and lead back into physical output.

[9] In this installation, a giant artificial sun—created using monochromatic lights, mirrors, and artificial mist—transformed the Turbine Hall into an immersive environment.

Although physically present in a real space, the audience experienced something dreamlike and almost virtual, where sensory perception was altered without the use of visible digital technologies.

This kind of work demonstrates how illusion and virtual experience can emerge within physical reality itself, making the boundary between what is real and what is perceived increasingly blurred.

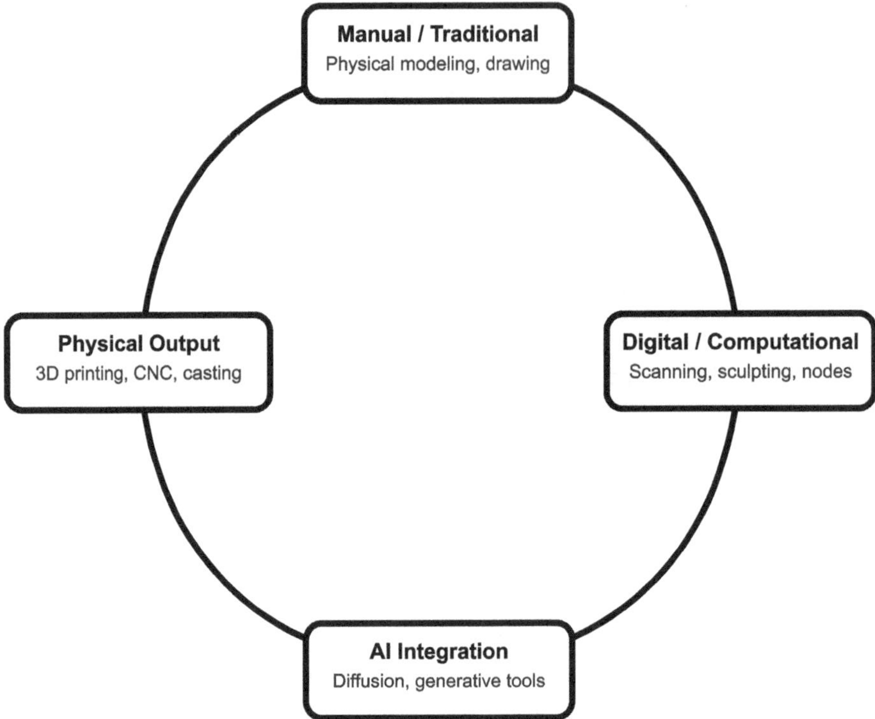

Figure 2-11. Hybrid workflow map.
A Cyclical model connecting manual, digital, computational, and AI-based practices with physical output, illustrating the continuity between traditional craftsmanship and contemporary parametric processes

This workflow can be broken down into four interrelated phases, each representing a node in the cycle:

- **Manual/Traditional**: Physical modeling, drawing, tactile gestures
- **Digital/Computational**: 3D scanning, digital sculpting, procedural modeling, parametric design
- **AI Integration**: Generative models, diffusion systems, algorithmic co-creation
- **Digital Fabrication**: 3D printing, CNC milling, casting, post-processing

In this continuum, hybrid workflows reveal that modeling is no longer confined to a technical stage of production but functions as a true mode of thinking: a dynamic process where ideas take form through cycles of materialization and abstraction.

The act of modeling thus becomes both reflective and projective, simultaneously testing possibilities and generating visions.

To make this shift explicit, the next section frames **modeling as a thought process**, introducing a design workflow that situates digital practices within broader cognitive and artistic strategies.

2.4 Modeling as Thought Process

Digital modeling is framed here as a cognitive and creative act: like philosophical inquiry, it lets artists test, visualize, and revise ideas in real time.

Modeling becomes a form of generative thinking in which form emerges from the interaction of intuition, algorithm, and material translation.

In this continuum, hybrid workflows reveal that modeling is not confined to a technical stage of production but functions as a true mode of thinking: a dynamic process where ideas take form through cycles of materialization and abstraction.

The act of modeling thus is both reflective and projective, simultaneously testing possibilities and generating visions.

Categories—painting, sculpture, digital image—become porous; each work can exist as file, object, projection, or immersive environment.

Modeling thus becomes a central engine of contemporary practice, inscribing imagination within data, code, and hybrid materialities.

This broadened conception lays the groundwork for the next inquiries into procedurality and artificial growth.

As we will explore further in Chapter 3 and Chapter 7, the sculptural gesture increasingly evolves toward autonomous generative systems where algorithms play an active role in shaping and evolving form.

2.4.1 Modeling as Cognitive Exploration

Digital modeling operates as **thought in motion**. Ideas are externalized through iterative manipulations of form, continuously refined by immediate visual feedback.

Like sketching, it enables rapid cycles of **hypothesis ➤ test ➤ revision**, keeping ideas in productive flux through simulation, deformation, and recomposition.

In this way, modeling is both **a space of imagination** and **a tool for conceptual clarity**, bridging **gesture and code, vision and execution**.

To understand how this reflective and technical process unfolds, we outline a design workflow common to contemporary art, design, and emerging technologies.

Figure 2-12 supports seven steps diveded into two phases: Conceptual and Technical Development.

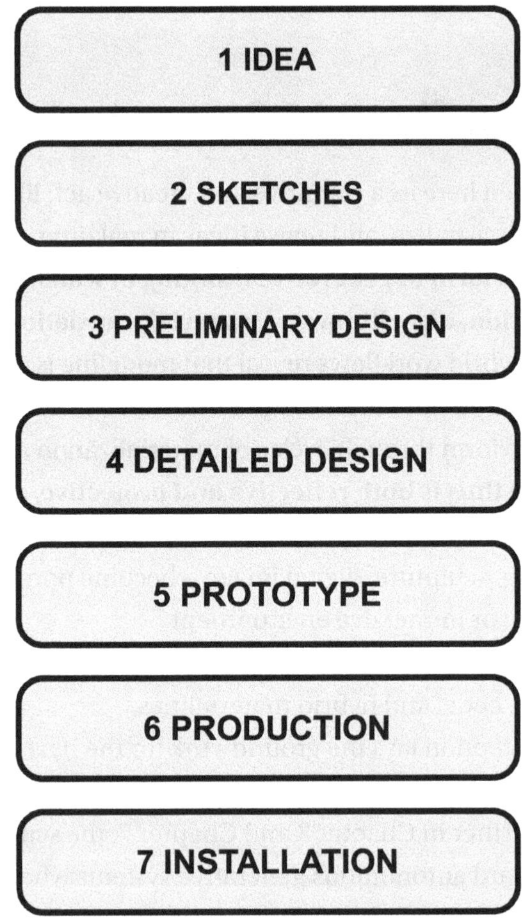

***Figure 2-12.** The creative design process: from idea to realization.*
Diagram illustrating the typical workflow in art, design, and new media projects

Beginning with an initial idea, the process unfolds through sketches, concept development, technical modeling, prototyping, and final production, culminating in the spatial installation of the work, whether in real or virtual form.

Each phase reflects a progressive articulation of form, material, and meaning, but also a continuous negotiation between intuition and technique.

In this sense, modeling serves as the connective tissue of the creative process: it translates vision into form, mediates between physical and virtual realms, and ensures that the artwork remains open to revision until its final spatial encounter with the viewer.

2.4.1.1 The Creative Design Process

In contemporary artistic practice, the creative process unfolds as a sequence of interconnected stages, each one influencing and reshaping the next.

Far from being a rigid, linear progression, this workflow is flexible and iterative, allowing the artist or designer to move back and forth between phases as ideas evolve. Figure 2-13 offers a synthesis of this process.

The artistic workflow can be understood as the articulation of two interconnected phases.

2.4.1.1.1 The Imaginative Phase

The process begins with an initial idea that unfolds through sketches, concept development, and preliminary models. In this stage, form is shaped as a projection of thought, where intuition, experimentation, and conceptual exploration gradually define the vision of the work.

Figure 2-13 illustrates the Imaginative Phase, where the process evolves from the initial idea through sketches and preliminary designs. This stage emphasizes intuition, exploration, and conceptual development.

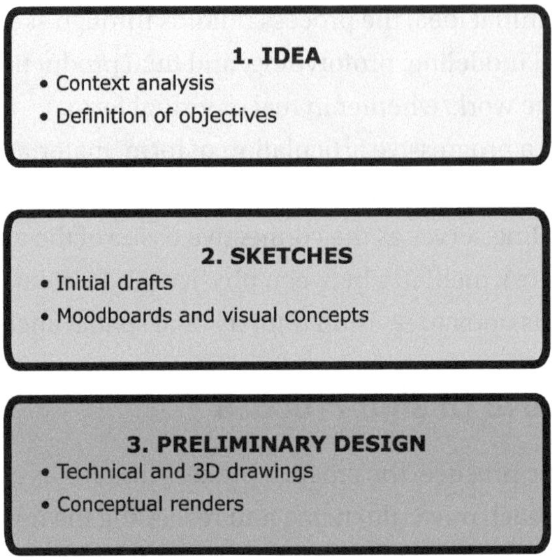

1. IDEA
- Context analysis
- Definition of objectives

2. SKETCHES
- Initial drafts
- Moodboards and visual concepts

3. PRELIMINARY DESIGN
- Technical and 3D drawings
- Conceptual renders

Figure 2-13. The Imaginative Phase of the design process.
From the initial idea to sketches and preliminary design, this phase focuses on intuition, exploration, and conceptual development

In this sequence, each step of the workflow is detailed, showing how the process progresses from conceptual exploration to material realization, culminating in the final installation.

1. **Idea**

   The project begins with an intuition, a spark that sets the direction.

   Here, the artist frames the context and defines objectives, identifying conceptual references and the scope of the work.

2. **Sketches**

   Quick drawings, mood boards, and visual concepts begin to give form to the idea. These early explorations help clarify intent, test possibilities, and communicate the emerging vision.

3. **Preliminary Design**

   The concept is translated into technical drawings, 3D models, and conceptual renders. These tools enable spatial testing, proportion adjustments, and material hypotheses before committing to production.

From detailed modeling to prototyping, fabrication, and final installation, the work enters a stage of progressive materialization.

2.4.1.1.2 The Productive Phase

Here, digital tools and traditional craftsmanship converge, translating concepts into tangible presence.

Each step refines the articulation of form, material, and meaning, while keeping the process open, iterative, and reversible. Modeling thus serves as the connective tissue between vision and realization, ensuring continuity across the two phases.

Figure 2-14 illustrates the Productive Phase, tracing the progression from detailed design to prototyping, production, and installation. This stage emphasizes technical precision, material translation, and the integration of digital and manual practices.

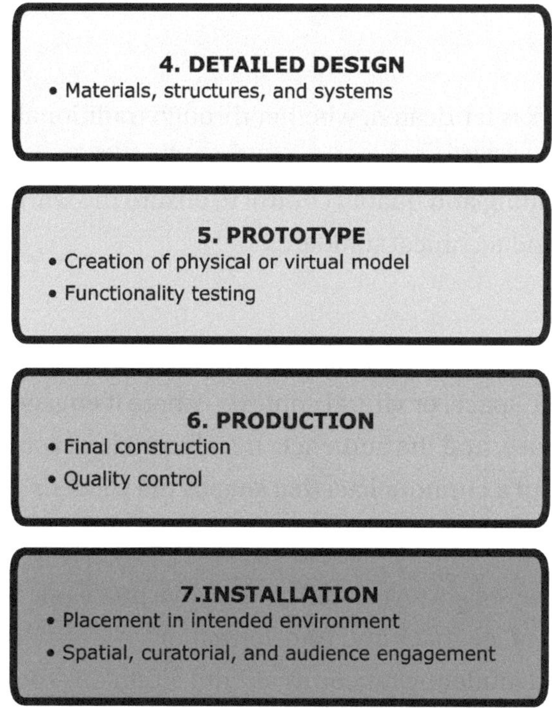

Figure 2-14. The Productive Phase of the design process.
From detailed design to prototyping, production, and installation, this phase focuses on material translation, technical precision, and the convergence of digital tools with traditional craftsmanship

Each step of the productive workflow can be further specified, highlighting how technical modeling, fabrication, and installation articulate the progressive materialization of the artwork.

4. **Detailed Design**

   At this stage, the focus shifts to feasibility. Materials, structural systems, and functional components are selected and integrated. From the smallest details to the overall assembly, technical precision ensures the coherence of the concept.

5. **Prototype**

   A transitional phase where the work is tested in physical or virtual form. Prototypes validate functionality, aesthetics, and spatial presence, informing final adjustments before full-scale realization.

6. **Production**

   The final work is fabricated, whether through traditional craftsmanship, CNC machining, or 3D printing. This phase includes finishing and quality control to ensure the work meets its conceptual and technical standards.

7. **Installation**

   The completed piece is placed in its intended environment—gallery, public space, or virtual context—where it engages with light, space, and the audience. Installation is not simply placement, but a curatorial act that shapes the viewer's experience.

Taken together, these stages reveal that the creative process is less a straight path than a dynamic system of feedback and transformation.

At every step, digital modeling functions as both a thinking tool and a material testbed, ensuring that each decision is informed, deliberate, and open to revision.

Across all stages, **modeling** acts as the **cognitive hinge**. It connects intuition with evaluation (renders, simulations), informs **material translation** (CNC/printing), and supports **multiple states** of the work (file/object/environment).

Many artists and designers work through hybrid workflows. For instance, *Marsyas* (2002–03) by Anish Kapoor and Cecil Balmond is a monumental example of digital form-finding and structural simulation realized physically in Tate Modern's Turbine Hall.[10]

Likewise, Studio Azzurro's "sensitive environments," such as *Tables (1995)*[11] or *Coro* (1995),[12] demonstrate the integration of manual gesture, video, sensors, and generative logic to produce immersive, interactive installation systems.

2.4.2 Creativity, Design Thinking, and Technology in Contemporary Art

In this sense, design for art, industrial design, and new technologies plays a crucial role.

These disciplines share many commonalities, and their design processes often overlap in structure and methodology.

Whether creating a sculpture, a functional object, or a digital experience, the workflow tends to follow similar phases of ideation, modeling, testing, and refinement.

This approach increasingly embraces a design-driven process, evolving from the initial hand-drawn sketch to a fully developed conceptual form.

As virtual space offers boundless possibilities, the design phase becomes a central act of creation, no longer a preliminary step, but the core of the artistic process itself.

In this expanded digital environment, the artist can iterate, transform, and refine the work beyond what would be possible in the physical world. Materials, scale, and even gravity become fluid parameters.

The act of modeling blends the artist's instinct with the logic of code. This allows sculptors to explore complex ideas (such as spatial relationshipsor fluid dynamics) in real-time, maintaining creative control instead of letting the algorithms decide on their own.

---

[10] The official Anish Kapoor website features a detailed page on *Marsyas*, offering insight into the artist's design process from initial concept to final installation: `https://anishkapoor.com/156/marsyas-3`

[11] The Studio Azzurro archive presents documentation of their interactive installations, revealing how concepts evolve through collaborative and technological processes. `https://www.studioazzurro.com/opere/tavoli-perche-queste-mani-mi-toccano/`

[12] Project pages in the Studio Azzurro archive show how works evolve from conceptual research to interactive environments, illustrating a design process that merges artistic vision with technological innovation. `https://www.studioazzurro.com/opere/coro/`

Modeling thus becomes a thought process that bridges creative vision with computational capabilities.

2.5 Practical Applications: Bridging Ideas, Materials, and Code with Historical and Contemporary Artists

At the end of each chapter, a practical section will provide ideas and techniques on how to translate the dialogue between historical references, conceptual approaches, materials, and digital tools into contemporary practice.

In this chapter, the focus will be primarily on **3D scanning and manual modeling**, understood as bridges between gesture and digital form. Reference software for this book is Blender 3.6+ (free download from blender.org), which requires minimum 4GB RAM, OpenGL 3.3 support, and works on Windows 10+, macOS 10.13+, or Linux distributions. It will be used to explore techniques of **digital modeling**, **virtual sculpture**, and **form generation** through a hands-on approach aligned with the chapter's core themes.

At the beginning of this section, a few simple examples of manual modeling will be presented, serving as accessible entry points before moving into more complex and hybrid workflows.

Then we will deepen the interplay of ideas, materials, and digital code, drawing inspiration from historical and contemporary figures who exemplify this expanded sculptural paradigm.

2.5.1 Introductory Manual Modeling Studies in Blender

These examples introduce the fundamentals of manual modeling in Blender, moving from broad, object-level manipulation to detailed mesh editing and expressive sculpting.

Each example follows a consistent structure—*Introduction, Technique, Conclusion*—to provide both conceptual context and actionable steps.

2.5.1.1 Base Form Manipulation in Object Mode

Object Mode is the foundation of manual modeling. Here, artists define overall scale, proportions, and placement before adding details. This stage is akin to blocking out a clay maquette, focusing on balance, mass, and composition (Figure 2-15).

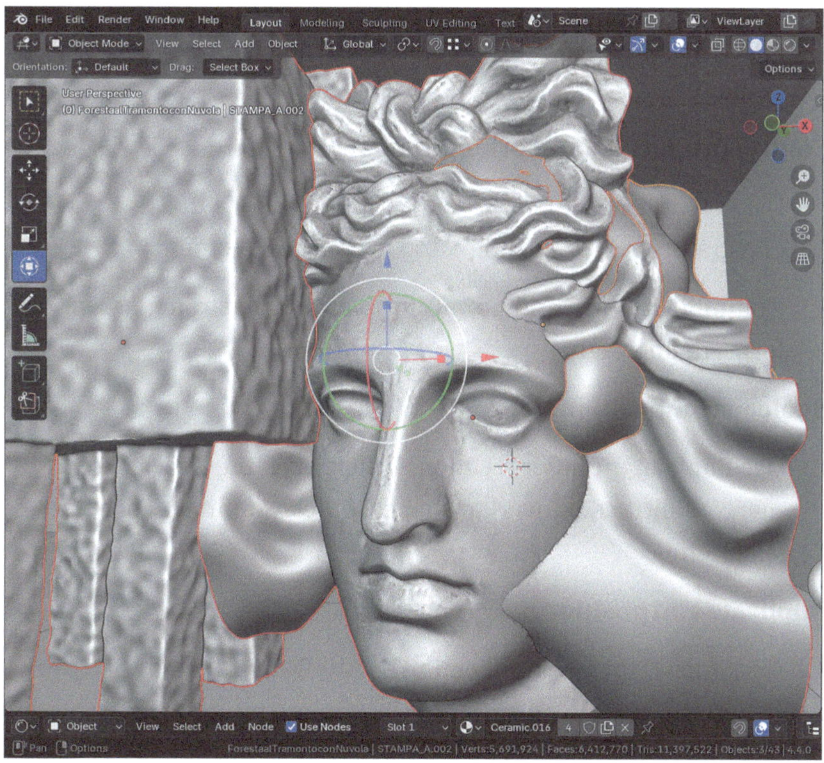

Figure 2-15.* *Piazza Metafisica, hybrid sculpture (Object Mode).
Piazza Metafisica belongs to my explorations in hybrid sculpture, where traditional methods meet digital processes. In Object Mode, the base form is defined through scale and proportion

2.5.1.1.1 Technique

1. **Establish primary volumes.**
   - Add primitive meshes (Shift+A → Mesh → Cube, UV Sphere, Cylinder, or custom shapes).
   - Think in terms of *architectural mass* and *negative space* before details.
2. **Control proportion and orientation.**
   - Use *G* (Grab/Move), *R* (Rotate), and *S* (Scale) with axis constraints (X, Y, Z) to align and proportion elements.
   - Combine uniform and nonuniform scaling to stretch or compress forms deliberately.
3. **Boolean composition.**
   - Use Boolean modifiers (Union, Difference, Intersect) to merge, subtract, or overlap shapes, quickly defining complex silhouettes.[13]
4. **Duplicate and position.**
   - Use Shift+D for free duplication or Alt+D for linked duplicates (where changes to one affect all), enabling modular construction.
5. **Arrange spatial composition.**
   - Consider camera perspectives and viewer movement in 3D space.
   - Use snapping (Shift+Tab) for precise alignment when building architectural or mechanical assemblies.

[13] Boolean operations require clean, manifold geometry to work properly. Non-manifold edges, duplicate vertices, or intersecting faces can cause Boolean failures. Always check mesh integrity before applying Boolean modifiers.

6. **Prepare for refinement.**
   - Apply transformations (Ctrl + A ➤ All Transforms) before entering Edit or Sculpt Mode to bake scale, rotation, and location values into the mesh data. This prevents unexpected behavior in modifiers, sculpting brushes, and export processes.
   - Keep topology simple if the object will be remeshed for sculpting, or more structured if it will undergo retopology later.

2.5.1.1.2 Conclusion

Object Mode establishes the sculptural "architecture"—a clean, intentional base that can be refined in Edit Mode, shaped in Sculpt Mode, or rebuilt through retopology. This foundation ensures later stages are faster, cleaner, and more expressive.

2.5.1.2 Precision Editing in Edit Mode

Edit Mode provides direct access to vertices, edges, and faces, enabling precise adjustments to form and topology. It bridges broad shapes from Object Mode with the detailed structures needed for sculpting or production (Figure 2-16).

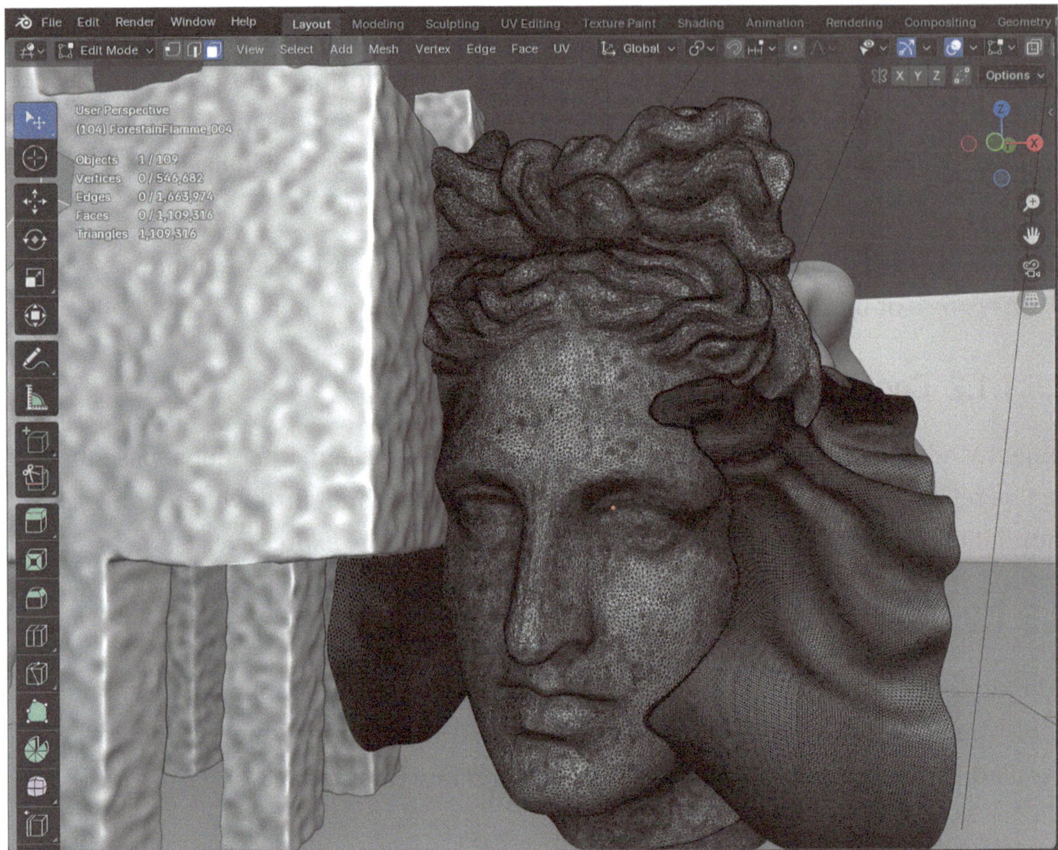

Figure 2-16. Piazza Metafisica*, hybrid sculpture (Edit Mode).*
Piazza Metafisica belongs to my explorations in hybrid sculpture, where traditional methods meet digital processes. In Edit Mode, geometry is refined or left fragmented

2.5.1.2.1 Technique

1. **Enter Edit Mode.**
    - Select the object and press Tab to switch from Object to Edit Mode.
    - Toggle between **Vertex**, **Edge**, and **Face** selection modes (1, 2, 3 keys).

2. **Shape manipulation.**
    - Use *G* (Move), *R* (Rotate), and *S* (Scale) to adjust selected components.
    - Apply proportional editing (*O*) for smooth, gradient-based deformations.
3. **Topology refinement.**
    - Insert *edge loops* (Ctrl+R) to add resolution where needed.
    - Use *Knife Tool* (K) for custom cuts and complex geometry control.
4. **Extrusion and insetting.**
    - Use *E* (Extrude) to extend geometry for limbs, walls, or protrusions.
    - Use *I* (Inset Faces) to create panels, frames, or thickness control.
5. **Merging and cleanup.**
    - Merge vertices (M) to remove unnecessary points.
    - Use 'Merge by Distance' (formerly 'Remove Doubles' in Blender 2.7x) to eliminate duplicate vertices and overlapping geometry.
6. **Preparing for smoothing or sculpting.**
    - Maintain quads instead of triangles for cleaner subdivision results.
    - Ensure consistent face orientation (Shift+N to recalculate normals).
    - Apply modifiers like *Subdivision Surface* to preview smoothness, but keep the base topology simple.

2.5.1.2.2 Conclusion

Edit Mode is where structure and precision meet artistic intent. A clean, well-organized mesh not only looks better but also behaves predictably when sculpted, animated, or printed. It bridges the raw massing of Object Mode with the expressive detailing of Sculpt Mode, ensuring a seamless creative workflow.

2.5.1.3 Organic Detailing in Sculpt Mode

Sculpt Mode transforms modeling into a tactile, gestural act, enabling artists to shape forms as if working with clay. It is ideal for creating organic surfaces and expressive details (Figure 2-17).

Figure 2-17.** **Piazza Metafisica, hybrid sculpture (Sculpt Mode).
Piazza Metafisica belongs to my explorations in hybrid sculpture, where traditional methods meet digital processes. In Sculpt Mode, surfaces are shaped with digital brushes

2.5.1.3.1 Technique

1. **Prepare the base mesh.**
   - Start from a clean, evenly subdivided model. Use Subdivision Surface modifier for smooth, quad-based topology, or Remesh for uniform triangle/quad distribution. Subdivision preserves original geometry flow; Remesh creates new topology with even density.
   - Apply *Scale* (Ctrl+A ➤ Scale) to avoid distortion in brush strokes.
2. **Enable Sculpt Mode.**
   - Select the object, and switch to *Sculpt Mode* from the Interaction Mode menu.
3. **Choose brushes for form-building.**
   - Grab Brush (G): Adjust large proportions and silhouette.
   - Clay Strips/Clay Thumb: Build up forms incrementally.
   - Inflate/Pinch: Accentuate or tighten edges and ridges.
4. **Surface texturing.**
   - Use texture masks with procedural patterns (Clouds, Noise) for organic surface irregularities.
   - Combine Draw and Smooth brushes to create convincing natural transitions.
5. **Dynamic topology and multi-res.**
   - Dynamic Topology (Dyntopo) in Blender 3.0+ automatically adds/removes mesh resolution during sculpting.[14]
   - Multires Modifier for working across multiple detail levels, ideal for workflows involving displacement maps.

[14] Dyntopo works only with triangle-based meshes and cannot be used with certain modifiers simultaneously.

6. **Final pass and cleanup.**
   - Smooth artifacts with the Smooth Brush or *Shift* shortcut.
   - Ensure consistent form flow to support later processes like baking, texturing, or 3D printing.

2.5.1.3.2 Conclusion

Sculpt Mode offers a direct, expressive link between the artist's hand and the digital surface. By combining broad gestures with fine detailing, it allows for a nuanced treatment of form that recalls the immediacy of physical sculpture while benefiting from the flexibility of a virtual workspace. Proper preparation and mesh management ensure that even the most complex surfaces remain controllable and production-ready.

2.5.1.4 Boolean Construction

Boolean operations perform set theory operations on 3D meshes - Union (combines volumes), Difference (subtracts one volume from another), and Intersection (keeps only overlapping areas). These operations require manifold (watertight) geometry to work reliably.

2.5.1.4.1 Technique

1. **Lay out primitives.**
   - Block the overall mass with primitives (Cube, Cylinder, Sphere) in Object Mode.
   - Apply transforms (Ctrl+A ➤ Scale/Rotation) to avoid Boolean artifacts.
2. **Nondestructive setup.**
   - Add a **Boolean** modifier to the main object. Choose **Union**, **Difference**, or **Intersect**.
   - Pick the cutter/operand object via the **Object** field (keep operands in a dedicated *Cutters* collection).

3. **Solver and order.**
    - Prefer **Solver: Exact** for reliability (switch to **Fast** only for speed on simple cases).
    - Keep Booleans **above** Bevel/Subdivision in the modifier stack for cleaner edges.
4. **Refine the cut.**
    - For chamfered cuts, add a **Bevel** modifier after the Boolean; use **Weight** or **Angle** to control which edges are beveled.
    - For thickness, add **Solidify** (before Bevel) and tweak *Offset/ Thickness.*
5. **Clean geometry (if applying).**
    - When ready to commit, **Apply** the Boolean(s).
    - Enter Edit Mode: remove stray edges, **Merge by Distance**, and **Recalculate Normals** (Shift+N).
    - If topology is messy, use **Voxel Remesh** (Object → Remesh) to reflow volumes for subsequent sculpting.
6. **Prepare for output.**
    - For rendering: enable **Auto Smooth** or **Weighted Normals** to fix shading.
    - For 3D printing: ensure watertight meshes using 3D-Print Toolbox ➤ Check All, close holes, and verify minimum wall thickness (typically 0.8-1.2mm for FDM, 0.3-0.4mm for resin printers, depending on material and printer specifications).

2.5.1.4.2 Conclusion

Boolean construction accelerates complex form-finding while remaining editable and reversible. Used with careful stack order and post-cleanup, it produces strong base meshes that can be beveled, subdivided, or remeshed—perfect stepping stones to Sculpt Mode, precise Edit-Mode refinement, or fabrication.

2.5.1.5 Retopology for Clean Geometry

Retopology rebuilds a mesh with optimized polygon flow, ensuring it is suitable for animation, texturing, and 3D printing.

2.5.1.5.1 Technique

1. **Prepare source and target.**
    - Keep the high-res mesh (sculpt/Boolean result) visible and non-selectable.
    - Create a new low-poly object (e.g., a Plane) as the retopo mesh; place it in a separate collection.
2. **Mirror and shrinkwrap.**
    - Add **Mirror** (if symmetrical).
    - Add **Shrinkwrap** (Target: high-res mesh). Start with **Nearest Surface Point** (or **Target Normal Project** for cleaner projection) and a tiny **Offset** (e.g., 0.001–0.003).
3. **Snapping setup.**
    - Enable **Snap to: Face** and tick **Align Rotation to Target** (if available).
    - Work in Edit Mode with snapping active so new vertices/edges conform to the source surface.
4. **Block primary loops.**
    - Use **Poly Build**, **Extrude**, and **Edge Slide (G,G)** to lay down clean quads along major features and silhouette lines.
    - Place supporting loops around curvature changes and potential deformation areas (hinges, joints, folds).
5. **Maintain topology quality.**
    - Favor **quads**; keep poles (5-valence) away from high-deformation areas.

- Even out spacing with **Relax/Smooth Vertices** and use **LoopTools ➤ Relax** (if enabled) to regularize density.
- Preview with a **Subdivision Surface** modifier (last in stack) to verify edge flow.

6. **Finalize and prepare for production.**
   - Apply **Mirror** and **Shrinkwrap** when satisfied; **Recalculate Normals** (Shift+N).
   - Mark seams for UVs; ensure consistent texel density if texturing.
   - For printing, ensure manifold geometry, add **Solidify** for thickness if needed, and run final checks (3D-Print Toolbox).

2.5.1.5.2 Conclusion

A disciplined retopology converts exploratory or procedurally complex forms into clean, controllable geometry. With correct edge flow, even density, and sound normals, the model deforms predictably, unwraps cleanly, and is ready for texturing, animation, or fabrication.

2.5.2 Pathways into Practice

These pathways are not meant to lead directly to finished works but to open small thresholds where gesture, matter, and code begin to converse. As Henry Moore often began from small natural fragments—a stone, a shell, a piece of bone found on the shore—these modest starting points suggest how practice can grow from the incidental toward the monumental. Through simple experiments—scanning a fragment, cutting a surface, reshaping a digital form—you can sense how ideas translate into practice and how practice itself becomes a field of discovery.

2.5.2.1 3D Scan and Digital Transformation

A simple sculpture or clay model, scanned with mobile photogrammetry apps such as Kiri Engine (iOS/Android) or alternatives like Polycam or RealityCapture mobile can serve as the raw material for digital exploration. Once imported into Blender (supporting formats: OBJ, PLY, STL, FBX), the scanned mesh may appear irregular, incomplete, or fragmented. Large meshes (>1M polygons) may require decimation before import on systems with limited RAM (Figure 2-18).

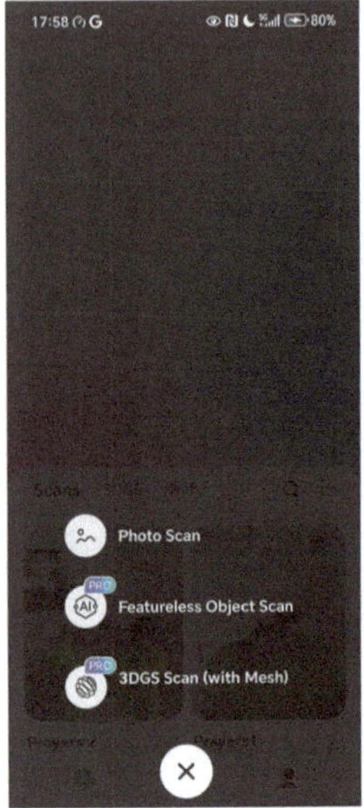

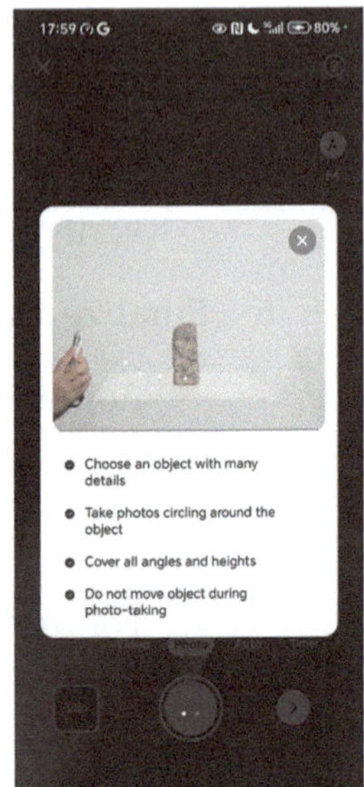

Figure 2-18. Photogrammetric scanning with Kiri Engine.
The app allows a bust or small object to be captured through a sequence of photographs, producing a 3D mesh that can then be cleaned, regularized, or transformed in Blender. This simple workflow demonstrates how everyday tools can bridge manual modeling and digital experimentation

Through modifiers like Remesh (with voxel size 0.01-0.05), Subdivision Surface (levels 1-3), and Displacement (using procedural textures or height maps), the bust can be progressively transformed. Each modifier requires specific parameter tuning to achieve desired results while maintaining mesh integrity. The mesh may first be **cleaned and regularized**, or deliberately left rough and incomplete, turning its imperfections into a generative resource.

As with Cragg's stratified sculptures, the digital process does not merely reproduce the original but subjects it to an evolution. Each procedural step crystallizes a new possible variation, extending the material gesture of modeling into a generative digital continuum

2.5.2.2 Fontana's Spatial Cuts and Environments in Virtual Space

Lucio Fontana's iconic cuts can be reinterpreted as manual interventions within virtual environments.

Starting from a simple digital plane, the *Knife Project* or *Boolean Difference* tools can simulate the decisive gesture of incision. However, successful digital simulation requires sufficient vertex density and strict geometric preparation (clean topology, manifold geometry) for the boolean operations to execute accurately: a technical precision that underscores the dialogue between artistic intent and computational constraints.

This connection between technique and realization is not exclusive to digital processes. Indeed, as Lucio Fontana himself explained in an interview with Carla Lonzi [1], the foundational material understanding remains paramount: "Technique, for us, was clay, marble, bronze, and you really had to know how to use them because you had to model, and in the modeling, you gave it all the life, you gave it all the form (...)"

In Blender, these cuts may be animated over time, visualizing the act of opening space as a performative sequence rather than a static mark.

Extending this into procedural sculpture or augmented Reality, the viewer can move around the cut, perceiving it as both surface and void, tangible and intangible.

Similar to Anish Kapoor's reflective sculptures such as 'Cloud Gate' (2004, Millennium Park, Chicago, Stainless steel), 'Tall Tree & The Eye' (2009, Guggenheim Museum Bilbao, Stainless steel and carbon steel), or his other mirror-polished stainless-steel works, as we will examine in the next chapter's discussion of procedural repetition and variation.

Fontana's digital cuts become algorithmic events, instances of opening space within a potentially infinite series of gestures, suspended between physical reference and virtual projection.

2.6 Conclusion

In contemporary practice, modeling is no longer a linear path from ideas to finished objects.

It is a **dynamic and cyclical process**, where physical gesture, computational logic, and material translation coexist in constant dialogue.

The ability to work iteratively — constantly modifying, undoing, duplicating, and comparing variants in seconds — transforms digital modeling from a mere technical skill into the very core of the design process. The artist now thinks by doing, and every gesture — every extrusion, subtraction, or undo — is an authentic act of design. Exploration and projection of ideas thus gain an unprecedented degree of liberty.

This chapter has explored modeling as both creative gesture and design system—a process where the artist defines not only forms but also the conditions under which forms can emerge, transform, and adapt.

Within this **expanded studio**, the artist becomes a mediator between realities—physical and virtual, tangible and simulated—able to shape not just objects but experiences and processes.

In this framework, the artwork is never a fixed endpoint; it is a momentary crystallization within a larger field of transformation, always capable of evolving into new iterations and contexts.

The next chapter will deepen this investigation by turning to procedurality and artificial growth.

It will examine how algorithmic systems can generate, evolve, and even autonomously transform sculptural forms, shifting the artist's role from sole maker to designer of generative conditions.

Reference

[1] See Lucio Fontana, interview by Carla Lonzi, in Autoritratto (Bari: De Donato, 1969).

CHAPTER 3

Procedurality and Artificial Growth: Algorithmic Logics in Art Practices

Building on the hybrid workflows explored in Chapter 2, where manual gesture and digital computation coexist, we now turn to a further shift: procedurality.

If hybrid modeling unites gesture and computation within a single creative space, procedurality pushes this union further, replacing the direct shaping of form with the design of rules, parameters, and behaviors through which form can emerge.

This chapter examines the evolution of contemporary sculptural practices in relation to new technologies, with particular attention to the transformations introduced by procedural modeling and algorithmic processes.

These developments are redefining aesthetic paradigms through dynamic, generative forms and innovative approaches to creative and design processes.

Today, the focus is shifting from direct manipulation to the design of generative systems, where the artist defines the logic rather than every detail of the form.

Within this context, emerging AI tools suggest a possible next stage—one in which algorithms may adapt and evolve—but this evolution will be explored in depth in Chapter 7.

Procedural modeling tools—such as Blender's Geometry Nodes—allow the construction of intricate structures through networks of interconnected nodes operating according to algorithmic rules.

G. Moioli, *Art Between Matter and Code*, https://doi.org/10.1007/979-8-8688-2376-3_3

These rules can generate grids, modular assemblies, iterative patterns, and organic morphologies, further enriched by procedural textures such as Noise, or Voronoi, enabling controlled variation and unpredictability within the creative process.

This procedural logic increasingly intersects with concepts of **artificial growth**, drawing on biological analogies such as cellular division, branching systems, and morphogenetic patterns—transformative processes where form evolves autonomously, echoing the dynamics of living organisms.

3.1 Digital Modeling and Procedural Modeling

From traditional manual modeling—where form is shaped directly by the artist's hand—to rule-based and algorithmic systems, three-dimensional practices are reshaping sculpture, video sculpture, and art with emerging technologies.

The focus is shifting from manual digital modeling of forms to dynamic and autonomous processes that emulate natural phenomena, challenge notions of authorship, and prioritize process-driven aesthetics and immateriality.

This transition can be mapped as a continuum of modeling paradigms, from manual to AI-driven systems.

Figure 3-1 maps four key stages: manual modeling, digital modeling, procedural modeling, and ai-mediated/data-driven practices.

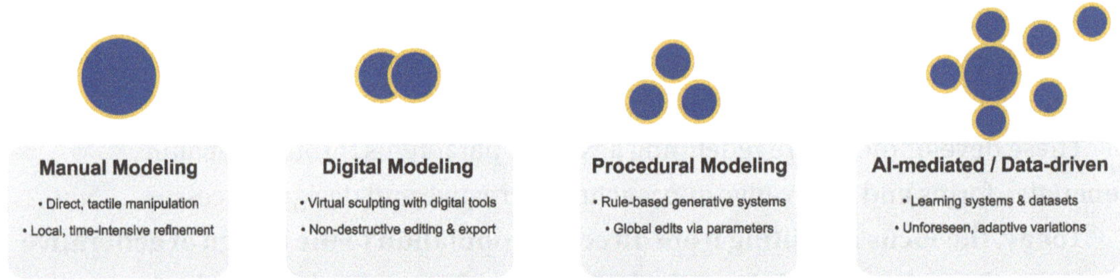

***Figure 3-1.** Evolution of modeling paradigms.*
From manual and digital modeling to procedural and AI-mediated systems, this diagram maps the shift from direct form manipulation to the orchestration of generative processes and data-driven creation

This shift redefines gesture, moving it beyond the artist's hand to include algorithmic, light, and data-based expressions.

Its lineage runs from Picasso's 1949 light drawings to today's procedural and AI-driven practices.

3.1.1 The Immaterial Gesture: From Picasso to Procedural Logic

The transformation of matter, gesture, and form in virtual space links past experiments to present-day digital practices.

In Chapter 1, we asked: *"What happens to matter, gesture, and form when they enter the virtual?"*

We have already begun to outline an answer through the Milanese line that runs from Canova to Fontana to Studio Azzurro, showing how material, space, and perception evolve in dialogue with technology.

Here, we extend this trajectory by tracing another path: from early experiments in capturing gesture—such as the luminous drawings of the late 1940s—to today's procedural logic.

An AI-generated reinterpretation of light-based gestures thus functions as a bridge between historical experimentation and contemporary digital practices.

Figure 3-2, produced in Midjourney through a custom prompt,[1] translates the ephemeral trace of light into a code-driven, digitally mediated form.

[1] The images were generated in Midjourney using the following prompt: "A long-exposure light painting in a dark space, inspired by Picasso's 1949 light drawings, glowing white trails forming abstract shapes in mid-air, photography-style, black background, cinematic lighting, high contrast."

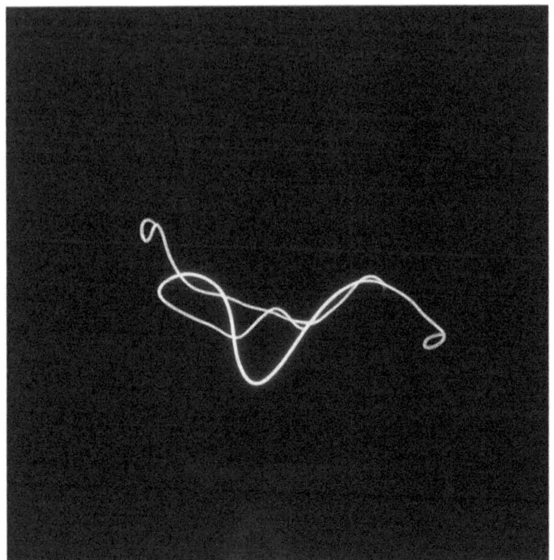
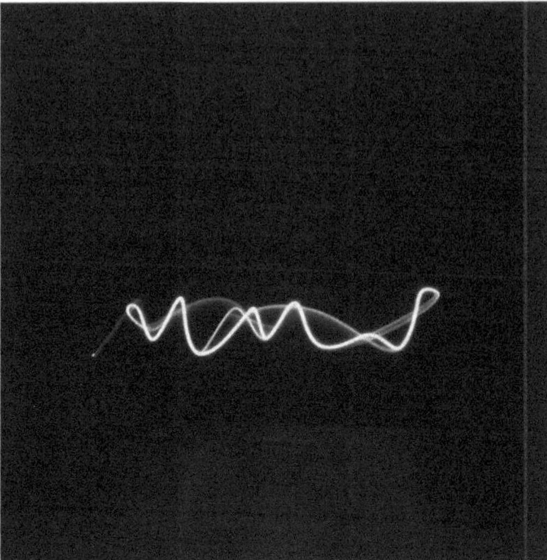

Figure 3-2. ***AI-generated reinterpretations of luminous gestures.*** *Produced in Midjourney with a custom prompt. These images translate the ephemeral trace of light into a code-driven, digitally mediated form, bridging historical experimentation and contemporary procedural practices*

This is an extension of Picasso's research serving as an example of how AI tools can replicate and reinterpret historical techniques, anticipating the generative processes explored in this chapter and leading, in the next, to a reflection on the question of authenticity in art.

In 1949, Pablo Picasso stepped into a darkened room holding a small electric light.

In collaboration with photographer Gjon Mili, he traced luminous lines in the air, drawing with light itself.[2]

These ephemeral gestures, captured through long-exposure photography, suspended motion in time and space.

Picasso's light drawings were not just experiments in photography, they marked a radical rethinking of the act of drawing itself.

The line, once bound to paper or canvas, was released into space and suspended in time. What remained was not a stable object, but a fleeting gesture captured by the camera's eye.

[2] For historical context on Picasso's 1949 light drawings, see "Behind the Picture: Picasso Draws with Light," *LIFE Magazine*, available at: `https://www.life.com/arts-entertainment/behind-the-picture-picasso-draws-with-light/?utm`

The luminous line, once performed in darkness, is here reimagined as an open-air gesture. Freed from its original setting, it expands into the horizon, transforming into a digital trace suspended between nature and code into an artificial environment.

In other words, a physical gesture—whether drawn by hand or recorded through motion capture—becomes the initial input for a procedural system that transforms it into a transient visual event, visible only for the duration of the simulation, echoing the impermanence of Picasso's light drawings (Figure 3-3).

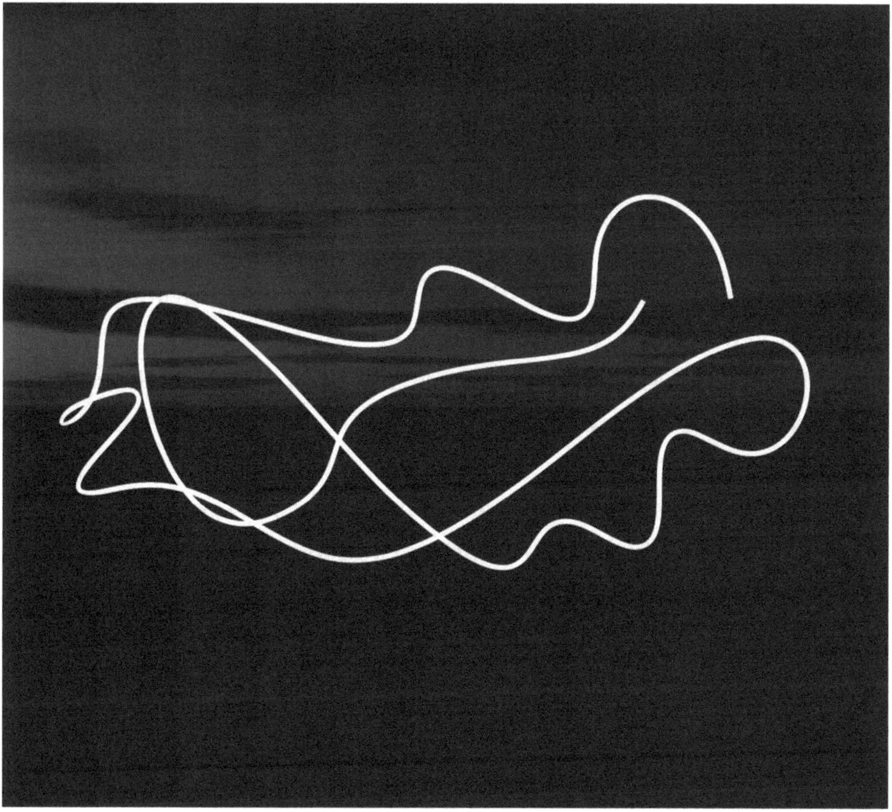

Figure 3-3. Luminous gesture in an open landscape.
A procedurally generated light-trace reimagined in an outdoor environment. Freed from its original darkness, the luminous line expands into the horizon, suspended between natural atmosphere and digital code

This principle can be extended into immersive environments using Blender's built-in VR features (via VR Scene Inspection add-on) combined with SteamVR/OpenXR.[3]

While Picasso relied on long-exposure photography to capture movement within a static image, Blender transforms these gestures into persistent 3D geometric data. In our example, they allow *spatial drawing* within virtual reality using motion-tracked controllers.

In Blender, these gestures are recorded as curves or meshes, which can then be processed through Geometry Nodes to add luminous effects, dynamic animations, and procedural transformations, providing one of the most direct ways to replicate the physicality of Picasso's light drawings within a virtual context.

In the practical examples section of this chapter, we will see how to create such a gesture using Blender's Geometry Nodes, while in Chapter 9 we will develop this approach into a full VR Gesture Drawing in the Metaverse.

Though analog, these experiments foreshadowed key elements of our current digital landscape: the immaterial gesture, the dissolution of form into movement, and the transformation of action into data.

Picasso's light drawings anticipated the aesthetic of procedurality: artworks that do not exist as fixed material entities but unfold through processes, systems, and time.

Just as Lucio Fontana's spatial cuts opened the canvas to gesture and void, his *Ambienti spaziali* and luminous neon works expanded this gesture into immersive environments, transforming space, light, and time into sculptural elements.

Both gestures projected the artwork beyond the static object, toward the immaterial, the spatial, the performative.

Today, digital artists, working with procedural modeling, artificial intelligence, and generative systems extend this lineage.

The gesture has not disappeared; it has multiplied.

It has become logic, a sequence, a flow, repeating, mutating, evolving.

---

[3] In 2026, Blender's VR capabilities—via the official VR Scene Inspection add-on (OpenXR-compatible with SteamVR) combined with add-ons like Freebird XR enable immersive scene navigation and spatial drawing using motion-tracked controllers. These tools record gestures as curves or annotations, which can be processed via Geometry Nodes for luminous effects, animations, and procedural transformations offering a direct digital extension of Picasso's light drawings.

This chapter explores how these procedural logics shape contemporary artistic practice. **From code-based modeling to artificial growth, from unpredictable algorithms to endlessly generative forms, we will examine how artists today create works that are not finished but becoming; not stable, but shifting; not defined by matter, but by transformation.**

3.1.2 From Digital Handcraft to Procedural Systems

A luminous gesture traced by hand in the air encapsulates the essence of manual creation: direct, embodied, and fleeting. Once transposed into the digital domain, such a gesture can be recorded, reconstructed, and transformed, marking the passage from tactile immediacy to algorithmic modulation.

In this trajectory, **Manual digital modeling** represents the first step: the artist manipulates vertices, edges, and surfaces point by point, echoing the hand's craft in physical sculpture. This "digital handcraft" retains the logic of localized intervention but acquires new possibilities through nondestructive workflows, sculpting tools, and the flexibility of scaling, exporting, or repurposing forms across different media.

Procedural modeling marks the next stage. Here, the artist no longer defines every detail directly but designs systems of rules that generate and transform form. Parameters, algorithms, and modular logic govern the structure: a single change can ripple across the entire model.

The paradigm shift is illustrated in Figure 3-4, which contrasts digital manual modeling with procedural modeling. This stage forms the conceptual foundation for the further expansions discussed later in this book.

Figure 3-4. Modeling paradigms.
Comparison between digital manual modeling—direct, point-by-point construction—and procedural modeling, which uses algorithmic rules and nondestructive tools for efficient, system-driven creation

In procedural workflows, changing a single parameter can propagate throughout the entire model, instantly reshaping its structure. Tools such as Blender's Geometry Nodes or Houdini's procedural operators enable complex modular or organic assemblies—grids, lattices, morphologies, or iterative patterns—to emerge from interconnected operations. This shifts authorship toward system design, where creativity lies in orchestrating generative behavior: deciding which parameters vary, which remain fixed, and how randomness or external data influence the outcome.

Procedural modeling thus expands sculpture into a field of continuous potential, where a model is not a fixed object but a living system—mutable, reconfigurable, and capable of generating infinite formal permutations.

3.1.3 Contrasting Procedural and AI-Mediated Modeling

This trajectory continues into AI-mediated and data-driven modeling, where learning algorithms process datasets, adapt to changing parameters, and generate forms beyond the scope of precoded rules—introducing adaptive variation, unpredictability, and new dimensions of authorship.

The progression from manual to digital modeling (Figure 3-4) lays the groundwork for the leap toward procedural and AI-mediated approaches (Figure 3-5), where form emerges from systems of rules, parameters, and adaptive processes rather than from point-by-point intervention.

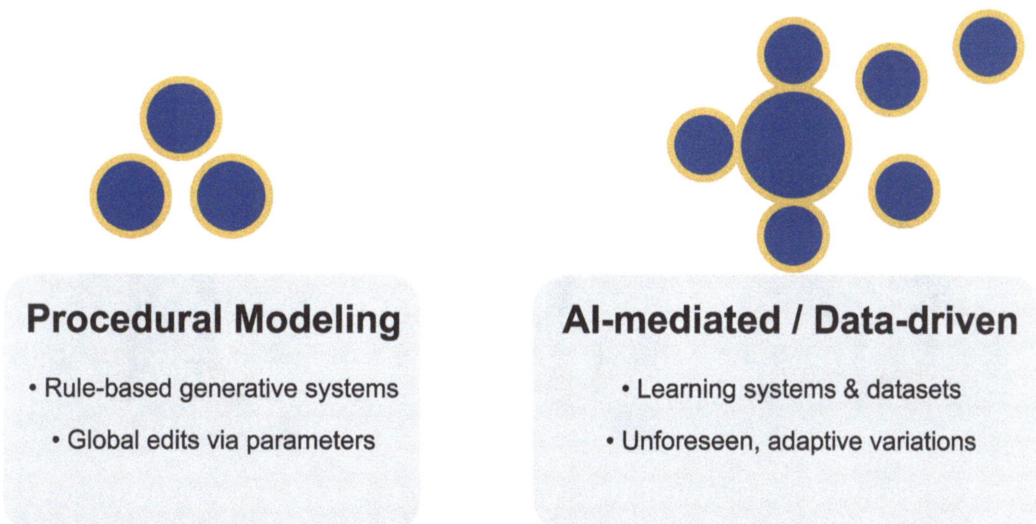

Figure 3-5. Modeling paradigms, part 2.
Comparison between procedural modeling—rule-based systems enabling global edits through parameters—and AI-mediated/data-driven modeling, where learning systems process datasets to produce unforeseen, adaptive variations. This diagram represents the culmination of the modeling paradigm shift outlined in this chapter

This opens the way to methods capable of generating intricate, evolving structures, an approach explored in the following section.

This conceptual shift is not only theoretical but also deeply embedded in my own artistic practice, as shown in the following sequence of works entitled *Synthetic Circulation* (Figure 3-6).

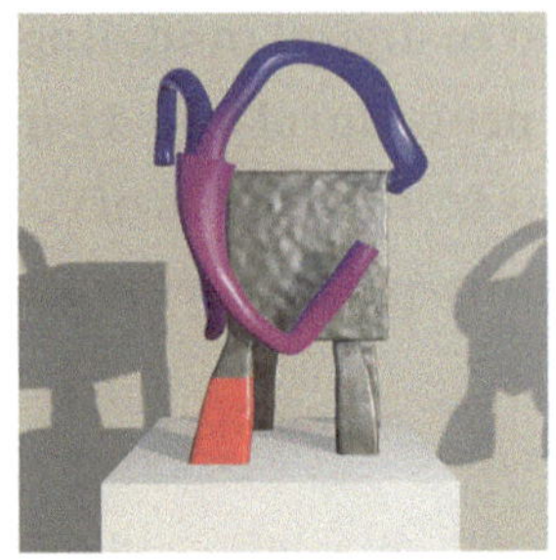

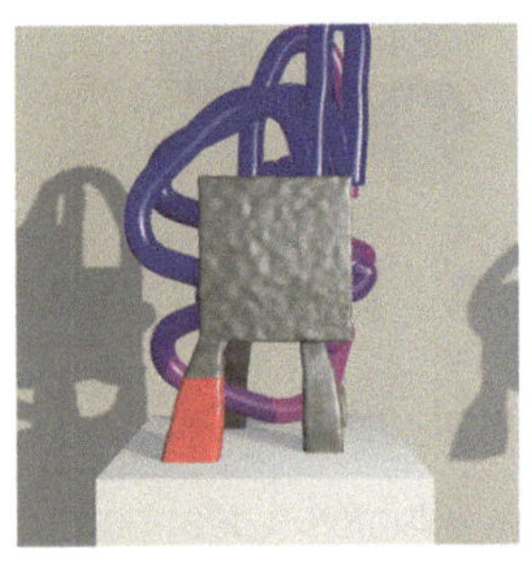
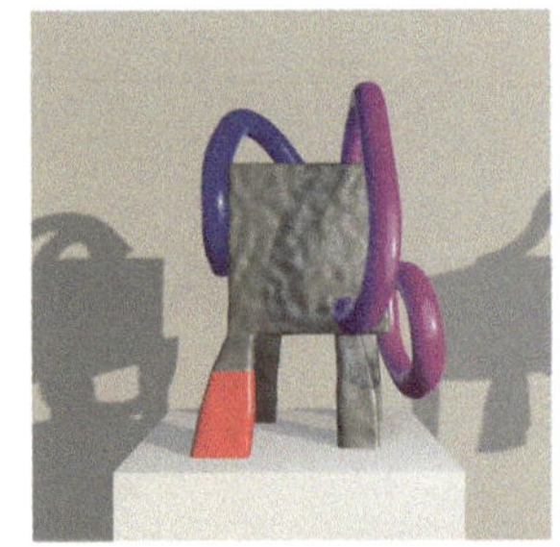

Figure 3-6. Synthetic Circulation.
Comparison across three modes of creation. The first row presents three digital sculptures, modeled directly in Blender, where form follows the hand's intention. The second row unfolds as procedural sculptures, generated by Geometry Nodes, where rules and parameters shape variation.
The third row emerges from artificial intelligence, where the gesture expands into unforeseen interpretations beyond control

Synthetic Circulation is conceived as an artificial, autonomous flow that exceeds its initial intention.

What begins as a modeled form in Blender is progressively reinterpreted through procedural logics and finally transformed by AI-driven variations.

The work explores circulation not as a fixed design but as an evolving process, where each stage introduces new layers of complexity and unpredictability.

In this way, the sculpture embodies a system in motion, at once controlled and generative, deliberate and emergent.

Here the metal structure reads as architecture—spine, scaffold, city—while the polymer wire, sometimes transparent and luminous, unfurls as circulation, a vital current threading the form with breath.

A quietly surreal organism of steel and light, it is an edifice that dreams of blood: geometry learning to pulse.

The works presented here share a common conceptual origin but diverge radically in their formative logics.

The **virtually modeled version**, created directly in Blender, reflects the logic of digital handcraft: point-by-point sculpting, incremental refinement of surfaces, and the direct translation of an idea into form. It mirrors the immediacy of manual making, while gaining the flexibility of undo/redo, scalability, and integration into multiple outputs such as rendering, animation, or 3D printing.

The **procedural version**, realized entirely through Geometry Nodes, shifts the process from direct manipulation to the design of systems. Each curve, intersection, and volume emerges from predefined parameters and generative rules. A single adjustment—such as changing noise amplitude or curve offset—reshapes the entire composition while preserving coherence. Here, authorship resides in orchestrating the rules and calibrating relationships that ensure structural consistency across infinite variations.

The **AI-mediated version**, by contrast, is produced by feeding the same conceptual brief into a trained model. The resulting geometry is not the execution of explicit rules but the interpretive response of a vast dataset. The system introduces unforeseen variations—color dynamics, textural nuances, and formal deviations—that exceed programmed intent. Authorship lies not in direct instruction but in curating and refining the machine's proposals.

Placed together, these three approaches reveal a continuum: from the immediacy of virtual craft to the generative logic of procedural systems to the adaptive interpretive agency of AI.

3.1.4 Enabling Complexity Through Code

Procedural methods make it possible to generate intricate, evolving forms that would be impractical—or impossible—to craft manually.

For instance, a network of nodes can generate a point grid, instance objects onto it, and modulate their properties—such as scale, rotation, or material—using procedural textures like Noise or Voronoi.

Such workflows can emulate natural phenomena such as growth, erosion, or fractal branching, or produce entirely abstract geometries unattainable through direct manipulation.

Beyond efficiency, procedural modeling embraces a process-driven aesthetic in which variability, unpredictability, and transformation are not side effects but central values.

This conceptual evolution sets the stage for section 3.2, which examines how these algorithmic processes are not just tools for generating form but catalysts for rethinking the very foundations of sculptural creation.

3.2 Procedural Sculpture and New Formative Logics

If procedural modeling transforms the act of creation into the orchestration of systems, procedural sculpture extends this principle in relation to space, into the physical or immersive realm.

Here, algorithmic rules become formative logics, processes that not only define form but also govern its growth, transformation, and interaction with space.

Whether realized through 3D printing, robotic fabrication, or real-time generative environments, these works embody an intrinsic dynamism, existing as open systems rather than fixed objects.

This part of the chapter examines how procedural methods redefine sculptural creation by introducing new formative logics rooted in algorithmic processes.

From a historical perspective, Nietzsche's distinction between the Apollonian and the Dionysian can be seen as an early anticipation of this shift, framing creation as a dynamic tension between order and chaos, structure and transformation.[4]

In his philosophy, the opposition between Apollonian and Dionysian originally described the contrast between sculpture and music, between form, clarity, and measured control on the one hand, and chaos, transformation, and ecstatic dissolution on the other.

This aesthetic polarity now finds new resonance in the field of digital creation, where it extends from traditional sculptural modeling to virtual modeling, procedural systems, and AI-driven processes.

Each step in this progression entails a gradual loss of control on the part of the artist but also a radical expansion of possibility, from shaping material by hand to programming behaviors to training systems that generate unexpected results.

The Apollonian ideal survives in the precise design of virtual forms, yet it is continually disrupted by the Dionysian unpredictability of algorithmic operations, procedural variation, and machine learning.

In this new terrain, the artist becomes a mediator between opposing forces, no longer sculpting matter alone, but orchestrating systems, navigating between order and emergence, between conceptual intention and generative autonomy.

Rather than cancelling each other out, these energies coexist in a productive tension that defines the hybrid nature of contemporary digital aesthetics.

3.2.1 Algorithmic Sculptures and Natural Processes

Procedural sculptures often draw from **the logic of natural processes—growth, erosion, crystallization, or fluid dynamics—not as metaphors but as active models for form generation.**

An artist might code the branching of trees, the accretion of coral, or the deposition of minerals, creating sculptures that evolve within a digital environment **as if obeying natural laws.**

[4] Friedrich Nietzsche, *Die Geburt der Tragödie aus dem Geiste der Musik* (The Birth of Tragedy), 1872. In this work, Nietzsche introduces the concepts of the Apollonian (order, clarity, measure) and the Dionysian (chaos, transformation, ecstasy) as complementary forces in art and culture.

This affinity with organic processes not only shapes their visual language but also bridges the computational and the biological, preparing the ground for the exploration of artificial growth in the next section.

3.2.2 Challenging Authorship and Embracing Complexity

The autonomy of procedural methods challenges traditional notions of authorship. The artist sets the initial conditions, but the algorithm determines the unfolding of form, producing structures that reflect system-driven complexity rather than direct manual intervention.

This shift reframes sculpture as a collaborative act, first between **human and human**, in the atelier or collective studio, where dialogue and shared making have long been central to artistic practice; then, in the post-digital era, between **human and machine**, where algorithms and AI systems become active partners in the creative process.

Anticipations of this expanded collaboration can already be found in the work of Studio Azzurro. Born as a collective, their practice affirmed from the outset that creation is never solitary but woven from many voices, many gestures, many gazes. In their *ambienti sensibili*, this human dialogue began to resonate with the presence of machines. Light, sound, and image became responsive, almost alive, listening to the body and answering its movements. What started as a collaboration among humans unfolded into a collaboration with technology itself—an alliance at once fragile and visionary. In this sense, Studio Azzurro foreshadowed today's procedural and AI-mediated practices, where authorship dissolves into a shared field of intention and emergence, between human and nonhuman, flesh and code.

3.3 Algorithms, Artificial Growth, and Unpredictable Forms: Simulating Organic Processes

Building on the interplay of predictability and surprise outlined in the previous section, this section highlights how algorithms mimic organic growth, leading to unpredictable outcomes that introduce a new aesthetic paradigm.

Yet, in procedural sculpture, this natural logic is mediated by the artist's control over parameters—allowing growth to be guided, accelerated, or transformed in ways that nature alone would not permit.

Algorithms can replicate natural phenomena, such as cellular growth or branching structures, to create sculptures that feel both organic and alien.

For example, using L-systems or cellular automata, artists generate forms that mimic biological processes, producing sculptures that evolve dynamically in digital space.

One of the most striking natural examples of this kind of organized complexity is found in the spiral structure of galaxies, whose geometry reflects the same proportional harmonies that appear in plants, shells, and other living systems (Figure 3-7).[5]

Figure 3-7. NGC 1232.
A spiral galaxy with a companion shaped like the Greek letter "theta," about 70 million light-years away in Eridanus.
By ESO/IDA/Danish 1.5 m/R.Gendler and A. Hornstrup.
http://www.eso.org/public/images/ngc1232b/,
File: Spiral Galaxy NGC 1232 (wallpaper).jpg - Wikimedia Commons CC BY 4.0,
https://commons.wikimedia.org/w/index.php?curid=25034867

[5] Like the spirals of shells or sunflower seeds, its structure follows proportional harmonies found in nature—patterns also explored in procedural sculpture.

A particularly compelling use of mathematical progression as a generative principle is found in the Fibonacci sequence, where each number is the sum of the two preceding ones.

This mathematical rhythm is deeply embedded in nature, shaping spirals, seed patterns, and branching forms that have inspired artists and architects for centuries (Figure 3-8).[6]

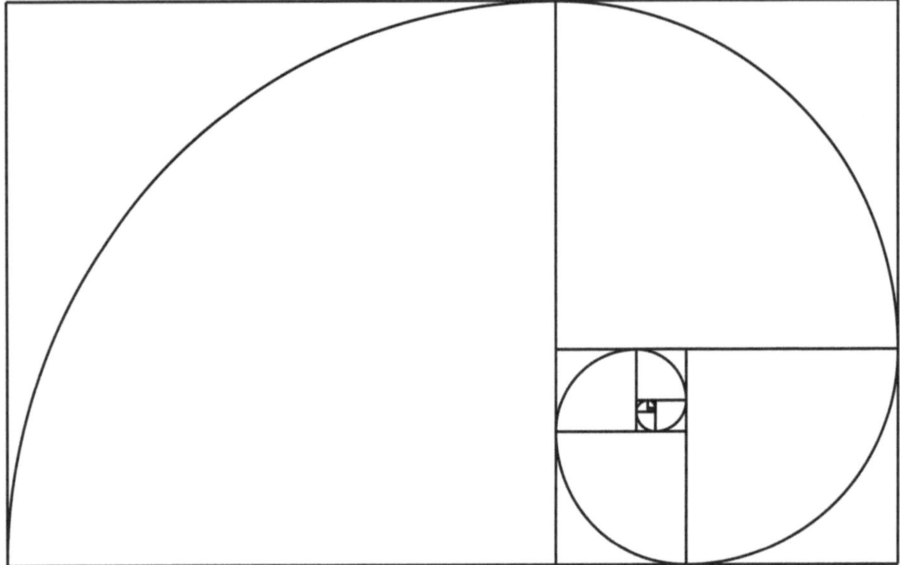

Figure 3-8. Golden spiral as a metaphor for the flow of life.
Echoing the organic rhythms of the body and the circulatory system.
Image by Icey at English Wikipedia, transferred from en.wikipedia to Commons, Public Domain,
File: Fibonacci spiral.svg - Wikimedia Commons
`https://commons.wikimedia.org/w/index.php?curid=37349753`

Found in **the phyllotaxis of plants, the spiral of shells, and the arrangement of sunflower seeds**, this mathematical progression expresses an inherent logic of expansion and proportion.

The same mathematical principle that shapes the perfect curve of the golden spiral also governs the arrangement of seeds in a sunflower.

[6] The Fibonacci sequence (1, 1, 2, 3, 5, 8, 13...) is closely related to the golden ratio and appears in many natural structures, from nautilus shells to sunflower seeds. A clear overview can be found at `mathworld.wolfram.com/FibonacciNumber.html`.

Both reveal nature's tendency to organize growth through proportion and rhythm, patterns that procedural sculpture can translate into dynamic, evolving forms.

By translating such principles into code, artists can design works that not only imitate natural patterns but also reinterpret them in unprecedented ways.

This approach recalls the practice of Italian Arte Povera artist Mario Merz, who famously employed the Fibonacci sequence in neon numbers spiraling across architectural façades, using mathematics as both a visual rhythm and a metaphor for organic growth.

The relationship between nature and mathematics has long fascinated scientists, philosophers, and artists. From the spiral of a nautilus shell to the branching of trees and the symmetry of crystals, natural forms often emerge from underlying mathematical principles or vice versa.

Geometry, proportion, and rhythm are not merely aesthetic qualities; they are the very structures through which life organizes itself.

Among these principles, the **Fibonacci sequence** stands out as a universal model of growth. Expressed as 1, 1, 2, 3, 5, 8, 13[7]..., each number is the sum of the previous two, producing a spiral whose proportions echo throughout biological and cosmic forms. Mario Merz's installations demonstrated how this mathematical law could be transposed into art. His illuminated sequences of numbers transformed buildings into metaphors for living organisms, merging architecture with a natural rhythm of expansion (Figure 3-9).

[7] The sequence given (1, 1, 2, 3, 5, 8, 13...) is the widely used practical form. The sequence's formal mathematical definition, however, begins with F(0) = 0, making the full sequence (0, 1, 1, 2, 3, 5, 8, 13...).

Figure 3-9. Mario Merz, The Philosopher's Egg, 1992.
Permanent neon tube installation representing the Fibonacci sequence, Zürich Main Station.
Fibonacci numbers at Zurich Main Station, Fibonacci numbers in popular culture, Wikipedia
By Gorodilova, Own work, CC0,
`https://commons.wikimedia.org/w/index.php?curid=24740888`

In the digital age, algorithms have become the tools through which these **natural patterns of organization**—spirals, branches, waves, and fractures—can be studied, replicated, and transformed.

Procedural systems translate the logic of growth into computational processes: the phyllotaxis of plants modeled through Fibonacci spirals, the ramification of roots or coral through recursive branching algorithms, and the irregularities of erosion through stochastic noise functions. Together, these patterns reveal how complexity in nature arises from simple rules, and how digital art can reinterpret them as evolving sculptural forms.

In Blender's Geometry Nodes, for example, a Fibonacci-based organic growth effect can be achieved by instancing mesh elements along a spiraling curve whose radius expands according to the golden ratio ($\varphi \approx 1.618$). Parameters can modulate rotation, scaling, and branching angles, while noise textures introduce natural irregularities. Combined with proper node setup for rotation and scaling, gradually revealing curve segments produces the illusion of a living form expanding in space—whether a plant shoot, a seashell, or an abstract organism (Figure 3-10).

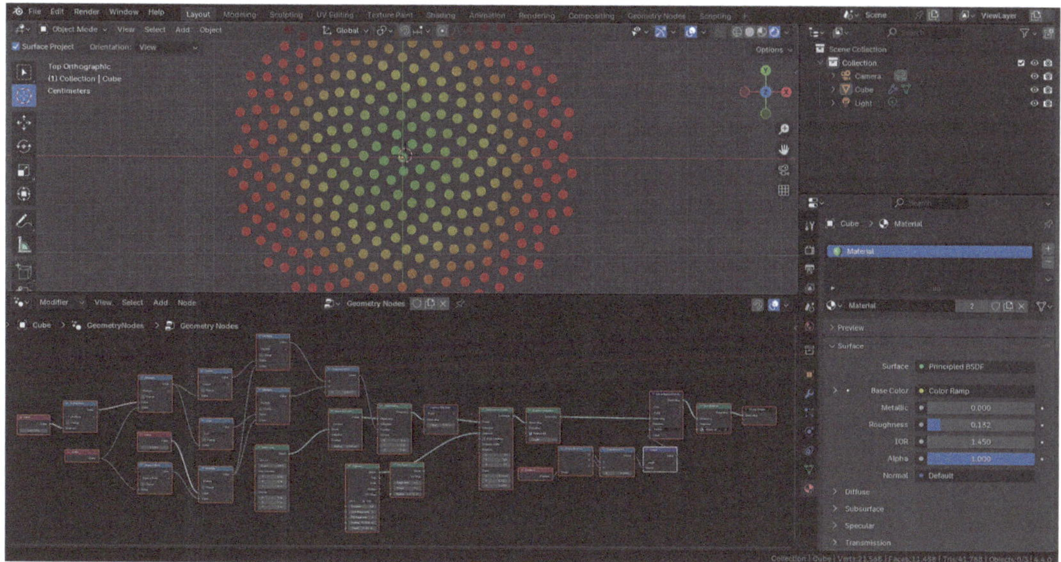

Figure 3-10. Procedural Fibonacci sequence.
Visualization created in Blender 4.4 through a custom Geometry Nodes setup, simulating organic growth patterns

These methods do more than imitate nature; they open a creative space where natural laws can be bent, exaggerated, or hybridized with artificial ones.

The result is a new aesthetic paradigm in which sculpture is no longer static but becomes a dynamic organism, evolving according to rules that balance order and unpredictability.

At the same time, each adjustment of parameters can trigger unforeseen variations, turning the algorithm into an active partner.

What begins as rule-driven design becomes a dialogue with code itself, laying the ground for collaborative creation.

3.3.1 Unpredictability and Collaborative Creation

The unpredictability of algorithmic outcomes introduces a new aesthetic where artists surrender partial control to the system. By setting parameters and allowing algorithms to generate unexpected forms, artists collaborate with code, embracing serendipity as a creative force.

This dynamic redefines the artistic process, positioning the algorithm as a co-creator in producing novel, organic-like sculptures.

Yet this openness to chance is not new. The unconscious, the accidental, and the unexpected have long accompanied art, whether in the Surrealist embrace of automatism or in the collective play of the *cadavre* exquis.[8]

Many 20th-century artists deliberately sought to integrate chance, unconscious processes, and material accident into their work.

In Surrealism, André Masson experimented with *dessin automatique*, letting the hand wander across the page without rational control so that unconscious impulses could emerge directly in line and form.[9]

A few decades later, Jackson Pollock radicalized this principle in his drip paintings. By moving around the canvas laid flat on the ground, he allowed paint to fall in unpredictable trajectories, where gravity, viscosity, and gesture combined into a dynamic equilibrium of control and accident.[10]

Arte Povera further embraced the poetics of chance, opening form to the transformative agency of raw materials themselves.[11]

What is different today is that this "other voice" no longer comes only from matter or gesture, or nature but from the machine itself.

Algorithms become companions in this search for surprise, bending rules and multiplying possibilities like a hidden nature made of numbers and code.

Thus, sculpture enters a surreal terrain where human intention and machinic suggestion entwine.

---

[8] *Cadavre exquis* (Exquisite Corpse) was a Surrealist collaborative drawing (or writing) game developed around 1925 by André Breton, Yves Tanguy, Jacques Prévert, and Marcel Duchamp, in which each contributor added imagery or text without viewing previous parts, producing uncanny, unexpected compositions.

https://www.museoreinasofia.es/en/collection/artwork/cadavre-exquis-exquisite-cadaver

[9] André Masson, *Automatic Drawing* (1924), in Dawn Ades (ed.), *Surrealist Art*, Thames & Hudson, London, 1974.

[10] Jackson Pollock, *My Painting* (1947), in *Possibilities I*, Winter 1947–48; see also Kirk Varnedoe and Pepe Karmel (eds.), *Jackson Pollock: New Approaches*, The Museum of Modern Art, New York, 1999.

[11] Germano Celant, *Arte Povera*, Mazzotta, Milan, 1969; see also Carolyn Christov-Bakargiev (ed.), *Arte Povera*, Phaidon, London, 1999.

Forms arise as if whispered by invisible forces: crystalline forests, spirals of liquid stone, architectures suspended between growth and collapse.

In this continuum, the artwork is no longer fixed but an apparition, alive in its continual becoming, unpredictable yet strangely inevitable, echoing both ancient impulses and future worlds.

In the same way that automatism or dripping once allowed chance to guide creation, today procedural and AI-based methods extend this principle into the digital domain.

A simple recursive rule in Blender's Geometry Nodes may proliferate into coral-like morphologies or galactic spirals, producing emergent organisms the artist could not have foreseen in detail, yet which carry the unmistakable imprint of collaboration between human intention and algorithmic growth.

3.4 Procedurality as a New Aesthetic

Procedurality does not simply describe a technique but defines a new artistic paradigm.

Here, the artwork is no longer confined to a single materialized form but exists as a continuum of possible states, each generated by the interplay of parameters, algorithms, and systemic logic.

This shift reorients sculpture away from the fetish of the unique object, toward a poetics of process, transformation, and variation.

3.4.1 Prioritizing Process Over Product

Procedural aesthetics give primacy to the act of generation rather than the final artifact.

While traditional sculpture measures itself against permanence and stability, procedural sculpture celebrates fluidity, transience, and evolution.

In this perspective, the "true" artwork lies not only in the output—be it a 3D print, an immersive installation, or a virtual simulation—but equally in the **algorithmic DNA** that drives its production.

The artist's gesture is displaced from direct manipulation of matter to the design of rules, parameters, and transformations.

This emphasis resonates with broader cultural shifts, where creativity is increasingly seen as an iterative dialogue between human intention and system dynamics.

3.4.2 Celebrating Complexity and Variation

If traditional aesthetics privileged harmony and proportion, procedural aesthetics elevate complexity, unpredictability, and multiplicity as sources of beauty.

The intricate morphologies produced by recursive rules, stochastic variations, or data-driven inputs reveal a fascination with the elegance of systemic behavior.

Viewers are invited not merely to admire a finished form but to sense the unfolding logic that animates it: the algorithm's silent choreography beneath the visible surface.

Each iteration of a procedural system becomes a unique manifestation of an underlying generative potential—a constellation of variations rather than a singular, definitive work. Beauty emerges from the very process of transformation, where every outcome carries traces of its origin but diverges into unforeseen paths.

This aesthetic contrasts sharply with the static traditions of sculpture, aligning instead with a vision of art as open, living, and infinite, a terrain where every variation is both complete in itself and incomplete without the series of possibilities it implies.

This redefinition of authorship and form inevitably leads to a broader question: what happens when the artwork exists not as matter but as code itself?

This question does not admit a single answer; rather, it unfolds across the following chapters, where the artwork as code will appear in turn as material, as process, as space, and as identity.

3.5 The Role of Immateriality

Procedural artworks frequently take the form of executable code, existing independently of any physical manifestation.

Rather than being bound to a single object, they can be stored, modified, and displayed virtually, or generated anew at every execution.

3.5.1 Artworks as Code and Data

In this way, the artwork is not only spatial but temporal. It unfolds in time, reconfiguring itself at each execution. Every run of the code becomes a new "performance" of the sculpture, where parameters, randomness, or data inputs produce variations that no longer fix the work into one definitive state. The sculpture becomes animated, a living presence that exists as duration as much as form (Figure 3-11).[12]

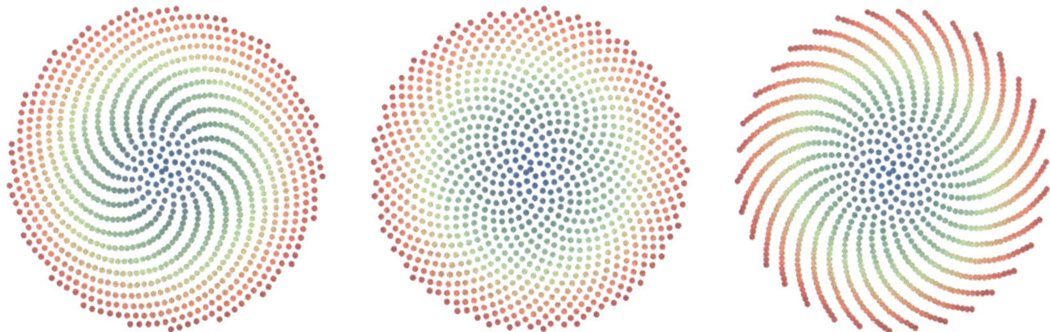

Figure 3-11. Vogel's spiral.
Algorithmically generated distribution of points based on golden angle, visualizing immaterial formImage by Wecoc, own work, CC0, `https://commons.wikimedia.org/w/index.php?curid=97505440`

This temporal dimension opens the door to narration and storytelling. Procedural works can be structured as evolving sequences, where forms shift like episodes in a story, responding to data streams, environmental inputs, or user interactions.

Instead of a static object to contemplate, the viewer witnesses a narrative unfolding in code, an artwork that tells itself through transformations.

In such contexts, art enters a hybrid field between object and event, between architecture and theatre.

Each variation is both a sculpture and a scene, both an artifact and a story. This narrative potential, intrinsic to procedural immateriality, recalls the ancient role of art as myth-making yet now transposed into a digital register, where algorithms replace words and transformations replace plots.

3.5.2 Infinite Reproducibility and New Artistic Paradigms

The immaterial nature of procedural art enables infinite reproducibility and adaptability, as code can be executed repeatedly to generate variations or shared across platforms.

[12] See: The Vogel Spiral Phenomenon, CodeProject

Category:Vogel's model, Wikimedia Commons

These aspects intersect with the certification and authenticity debates that will be explored in Chapter 4, especially regarding digital provenance.

The procedural system presented in Figure 3-12 was designed to generate different shapes from a single base form.

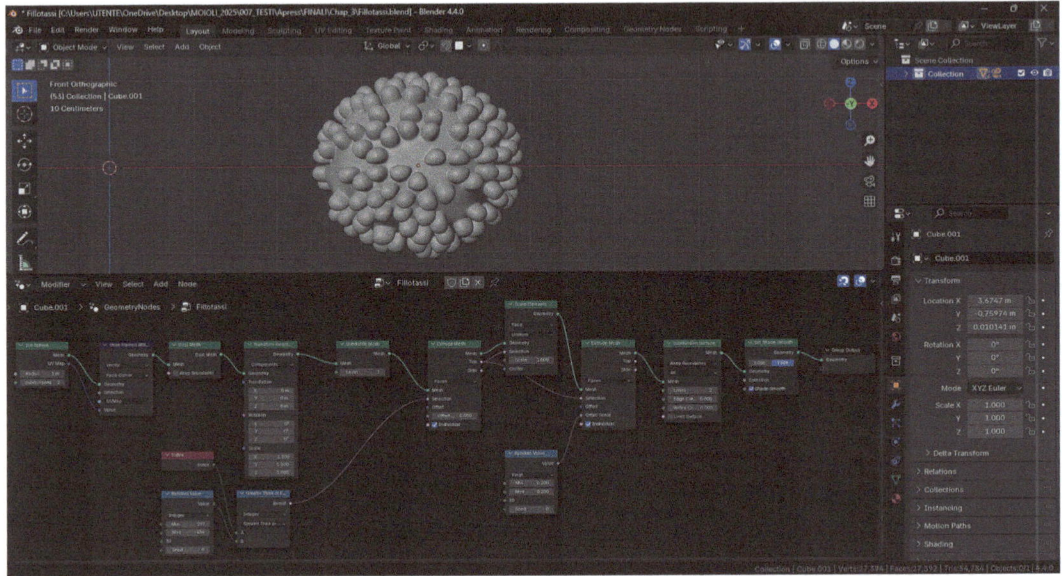

Figure 3-12.** **Procedural sculpture generated in Blender using a phyllotaxis-based Geometry Nodes setup.
This configuration allows infinite variations by simply adjusting parameters, illustrating how form can be continuously modified without altering the underlying generative code. Model, node configuration, and render © Gianpiero Moioli, 2025. Blender interface © Blender Foundation

The result is not an isolated exercise in geometry but a vocabulary of organic morphologies that also inhabit the structural components of my sculptures.

These forms, born within Blender through parametric rules, become both autonomous objects and fragments of larger architectures, cells, clusters, or circulations that can be recombined into more complex compositions.

In the following sequence, six variations of the same base object demonstrate the principle of infinite reproducibility in procedural art.

By modifying parameters such as scale, distribution, rotation, and extrusion depth, the sculpture updates dynamically (calculation time depends on mesh complexity), revealing a continuum of possible forms.

Each variation is not a copy in the traditional sense, but a unique instance generated from the same algorithmic **"genetic code."**

This phyllotaxis-based system, the arrangement of elements following geometric patterns observed in plant growth and implemented in Blender's Geometry Nodes, arranges elements according to mathematical principles such as the golden angle and Fibonacci sequence. Subtle parameter changes can radically transform morphology, shifting from dense, fruit-like clusters to spiky, radiating structures or compact architectural volumes. The process demonstrates how a single procedural setup can yield an infinite spectrum of formal outcomes, each carrying the imprint of its shared generative logic (Figure 3-13).

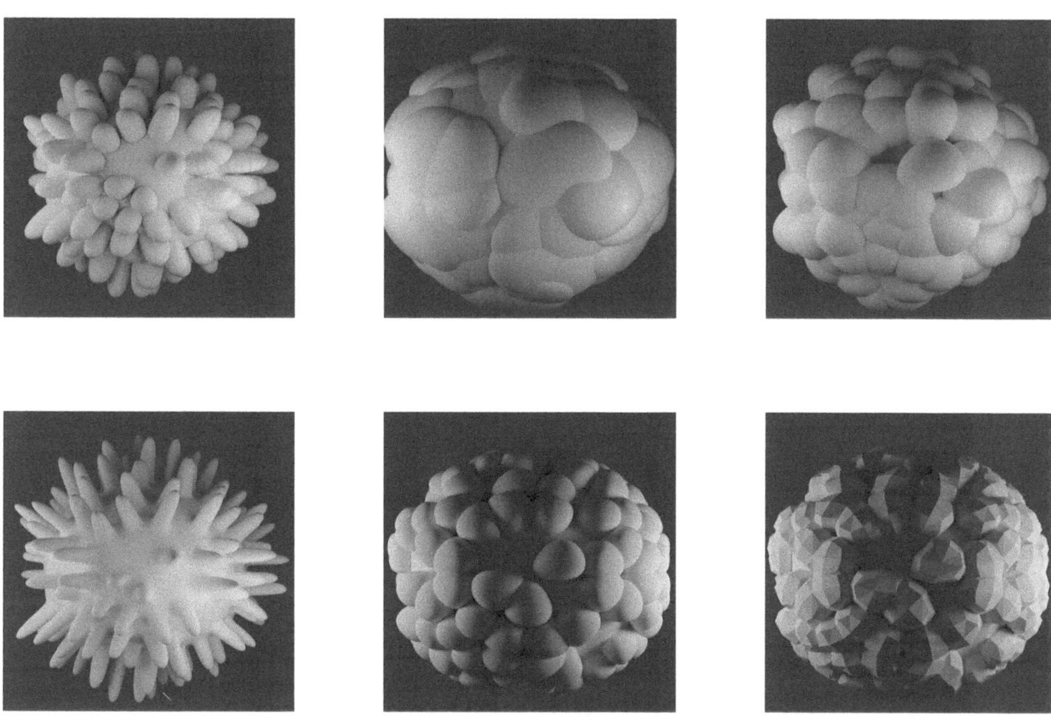

Figure 3-13. Six unique variations derived from the same phyllotaxis-based procedural system in Blender.
Sharing an identical algorithmic "genetic code," these forms emerge through subtle changes in scale, distribution, and rotation, revealing the transformative potential of generative sculpture. Like snapshots of an ongoing process, they suggest an endless evolution of shapes that could continue to unfold without limit.
Image and render by the author.

Algorithms become companions in this search for surprise, bending rules and multiplying possibilities like a hidden nature made of numbers and code. Sculpture enters a surreal terrain where human intention and machinic suggestion entwine: forms arise as if whispered by invisible forces—crystalline forests, spirals of liquid stone, architectures suspended between growth and collapse.

3.6 Examples of Procedural and Artificial Growth

This section presents simple practical examples of procedural and artificial growth workflows, demonstrating how artists can use algorithmic tools to create virtual artworks that emulate natural or synthetic processes.

Inspired by the expressive evolution from Picasso's fragmentations to Kapoor's reflective voids and Cragg's proliferating biomorphic structures these workflows balance Apollonian order (algorithmic rules and logic) with Dionysian flux (organic, unpredictable growth).

In this sense, procedural methods align with the book's broader narrative of merging tradition and technology, extending sculptural language into algorithmic and artificial terrains.

The workflows include, for example, the creation of complex procedural surfaces in Blender that can be integrated into contemporary sculptural practice and prepared for 3D printing using FDM/FFF methods.

These techniques allow for organic, mechanical, or hybrid effects, perfectly suited to artists exploring the intersection of technology and living form.

3.6.1 Introductory Procedural Studies in Blender: Modifiers and Geometry Nodes

As in the previous chapter we introduced the practical concepts of manual digital modeling, here we turn to procedural approaches.

These short examples illustrate how artists can generate complex, evolving forms in Blender without direct manual sculpting, relying instead on procedural logic, parametric control, and simulation. Each study begins with a simple base mesh and transforms it through modifiers, Geometry Nodes, texture-driven displacement, or dynamic simulation, allowing for easy experimentation, animation, and reproducibility across both static and interactive works.

3.6.1.1 Organic Surface with the Displace Modifier

Transforms a flat mesh into a complex relief by applying procedural displacement textures. Ideal for creating surfaces that evoke skin, geological terrain, or alien membranes.

3.6.1.1.1 Introduction

Natural surfaces—from alien membranes to eroded landscapes—often share a common quality: complex relief generated by repeating but irregular patterns. This example uses Blender's *Displace* modifier to create such textures procedurally, turning a flat plane into a richly detailed surface.

3.6.1.1.2 Technique

1) **Create the base mesh.**
    - Add a **Plane** (Shift+A ➤ Mesh ➤ Plane).
    - This will serve as the starting surface for the displacement effect.
2) **Increase geometry.**
    - Enter **Edit Mode** (Tab), right-click the plane and choose **Subdivide**.
    - Repeat the subdivision **four to five times** to ensure there is enough geometry for the displacement to work smoothly.
    - Return to **Object Mode** and add a **Subdivision Surface** modifier (Levels: 2–3) for a smooth, high-poly surface.
3) **Add displacement.**
    - Add a **Displace** modifier to the plane. Displacement requires high mesh density; the initial Subdivision Surface modifier helps manage this.
    - Click **New** in the modifier panel to create a new texture slot for the displacement map.

4) **Select texture type.**

   - Go to the **Texture tab** (Properties → Texture).
   - From the **Type** drop-down, choose a procedural texture such as **Musgrave**, **Clouds**, or **Voronoi** to generate the surface relief.

5) **Refine details.**

   - Add a second Subdivision Surface modifier (Levels: 2–3) at the bottom of the modifier stack (below the Displace modifier). This second instance will smooth the final, displaced surface for a high-poly result.
   - In the **Displace** modifier, adjust **Strength** to control the height of the displacement and **Midlevel** to shift the neutral plane (Figure 3-14).

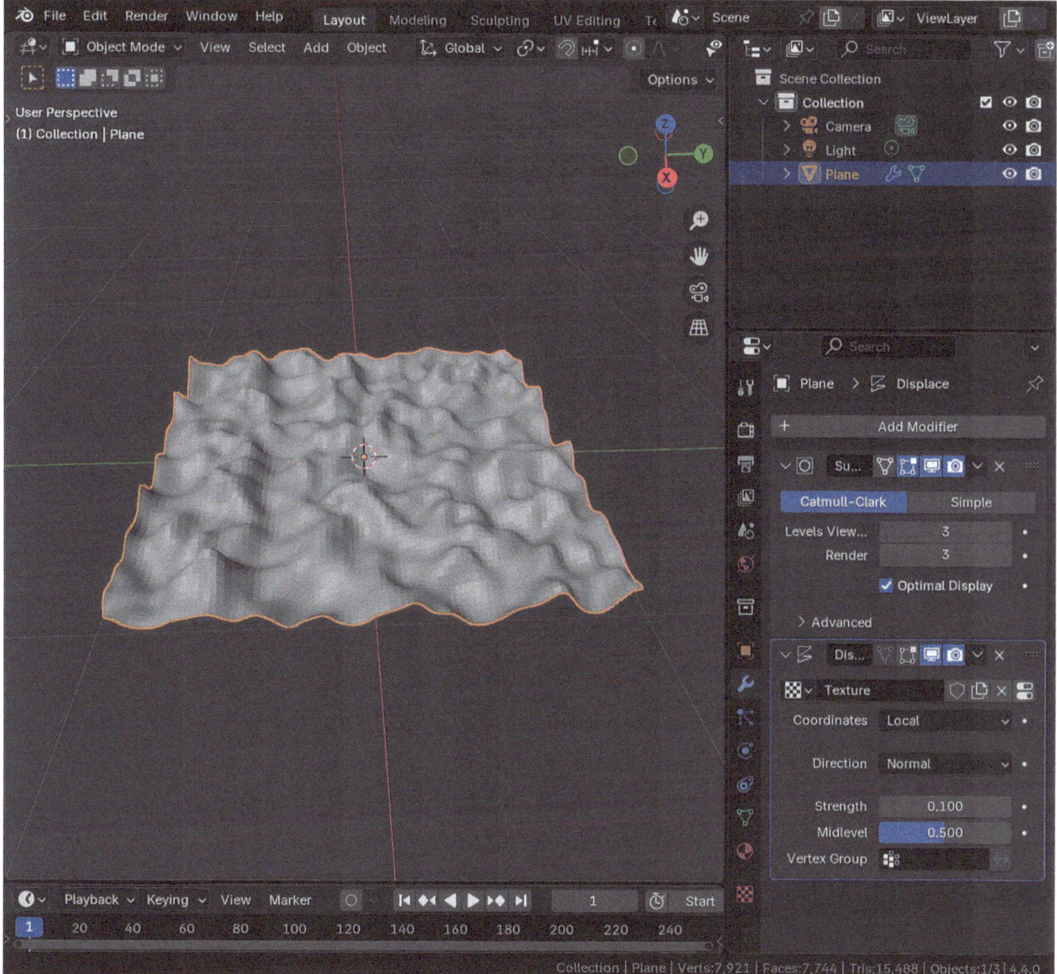

Figure 3-14. Blender interface showing the use of the Displace modifier with a procedural texture.

*By adjusting **Strength**, **Midlevel**, and texture parameters such as **Size** and **Detail**, the base plane is transformed into a dynamic surface with organic undulations and complex geometries*

- In the **Texture settings**, tweak **Size** and **Detail** to achieve the desired complexity—from soft, organic undulations to sharp, alien-like membranes.

3.6.1.1.3 Conclusion

The Blender 4.4 interface in Figure 3-14 shows the Displace modifier with procedural texture settings. Interface may vary in different Blender versions. By adjusting parameters, the plane evolves into an undulating surface. This is an approach that recalls the layered, transformative logic found in the sculptural processes of Tony Cragg and Anish Kapoor.

The result is a versatile organic surface that can be adapted to evoke skin, geological terrain, or alien environments. Its parametric nature allows rapid variations for use in sculptures, architectural elements, or as a base for further procedural growth.

3.6.1.2 Repeating Patterns with Geometry Nodes

Uses instancing to generate modular patterns across a surface or volume.[13] Scale, rotation, and density are varied procedurally, producing results from ordered grids to organic clusters.

3.6.1.2.1 Introduction

Many natural and artificial systems are built from repeating modules—cells, crystals, honeycombs, or mechanical panels. Geometry Nodes allows us to replicate a single element across a surface or space while varying scale, rotation, and position procedurally.

3.6.1.2.2 Technique

1) **Create the base surface.**
    - Add a **Grid** (Shift+A ➤ Mesh ➤ Grid) or any other mesh.
    - This mesh will act as the foundation on which the instances will be placed.
2) **Open Geometry Nodes.**
    - Add a **Geometry Nodes** modifier to the object.
    - Click New to create a new node group.

---

[13] The workflow requires Blender 4.2 LTS or newer (5.0+ strongly recommended in 2025).

High-density procedural patterns (e.g., millions of phyllotaxis instances) can still be extremely demanding on RAM and VRAM; 32–64 GB system RAM and a modern GPU with ≥12 GB VRAM are advised for smooth real-time editing.

3) **Distribute points.**

- Add a **Distribute Points on Faces** and an **Instance on Points** node.
- Connect **Group Input ➤ Distribute Points on Faces ➤ Instance on Points** as in Figure 3-15.

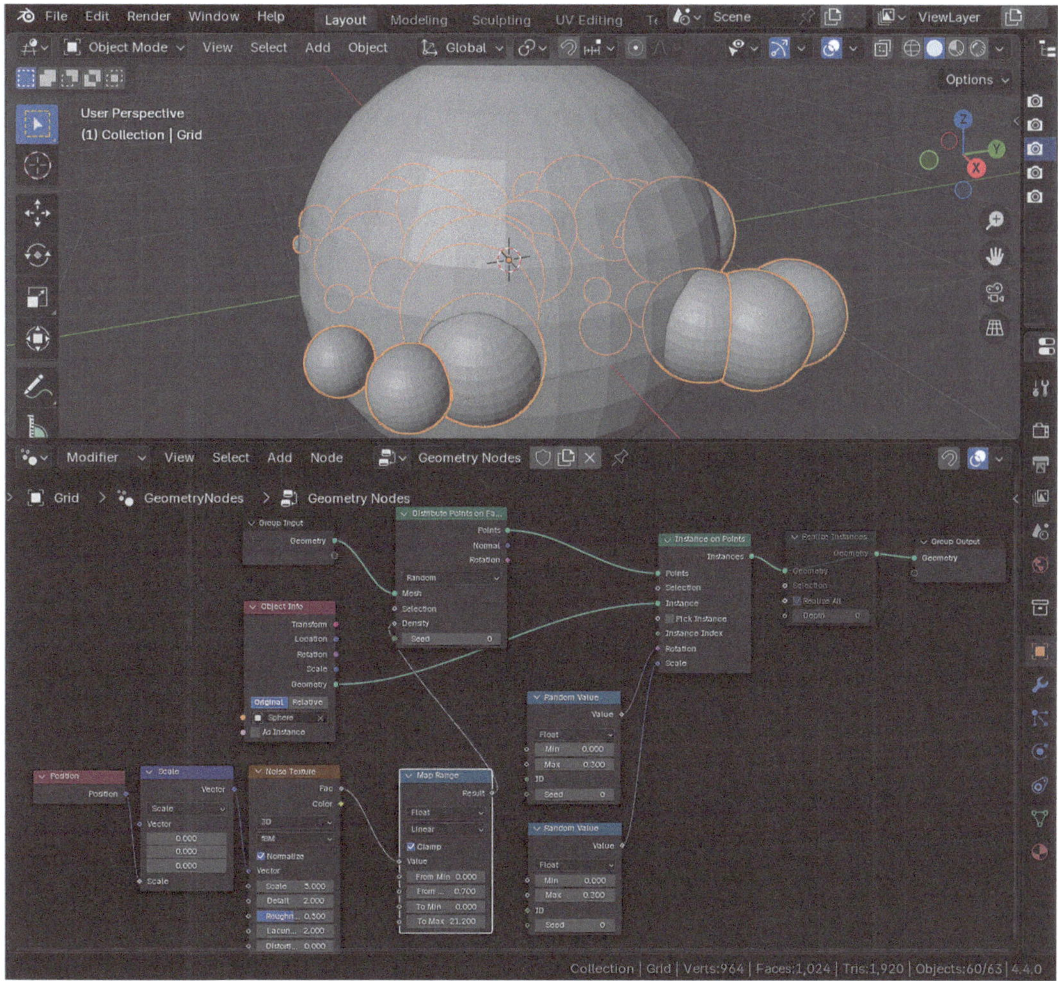

Figure 3-15. ***Blender Geometry Nodes setup generating modular spheres.*** *By adding Realize Instances before Group Output, the geometry becomes editable, allowing further refinement. This flexible workflow demonstrates how procedural networks can shift from ordered patterns to complex organic arrangements*

- This nodes control the points where instances will be generated.

4) **Load the module object.**

    - Add an **Object Info** node and set it to the object you want to repeat (e.g., a **Sphere**).
    - Connect its **Geometry** output to the **Instance** input of **Instance on Points**.

5) **Add variation in scale and rotation.**

    - For **scale**, add a **Random Value** node and set its Type to Vector (crucial for 3D scale) or Float. Connect its Value output to **Instance on Points ➤ Scale**.
        - Example values: Set Min to (**1.2, 1.2, 1.2**) and Max to (**3.0, 3.0, 3.0**) for uniform randomized scaling.
    - For **rotation**, add another **Random Value** node (set Type to Vector or Float) and connect its Value output to **Instance on Points ➤ Rotation** if desired.

6) **Control patterns with noise.**

    - This process allows for procedural control of density using a texture, introducing organic irregularities.
    - Add a **Position** node.
    - Add a **Vector Math** node and set its operation to **Scale**.
    - Connect Position node to Scale input of Vector Math; then connect the **Vector** output of Scale to the Vector input of a **Noise Texture** node.
    - Add a **Map Range** node. Connect the **Factor** output of the Noise Texture into the Value input of the Map Range node.
    - Example Map Range values: Set From Min = 0, From Max = 1, and To Min = 0, To Max = 2 (or a desired max density value).
    - Connect the **Result** output of Map Range to **Distribute Points on Faces ➤ Density**.

7) **Finalize.**

- If you need editable geometry, add **Realize Instances** before **Group Output** (Figure 3-15).

3.6.1.2.3 Conclusion

This setup produces adaptable pattern fields ranging from precise grids to chaotic organic arrangements. By replacing the module object, the same network can shift from mechanical panels to biological textures, making it a powerful tool for hybrid aesthetics.

This flexible workflow demonstrates how procedural networks can shift from ordered patterns to complex organic arrangements, echoing sculptural processes of growth, modularity, and variation.

3.6.1.3 Hollow and Lattice Structures

Converts solid forms into lightweight frameworks using Wireframe or Remesh modifiers. The open structures recall bone, coral, or architectural trusses.

3.6.1.3.1 Introduction

Lightweight frameworks are common in both biology (bone structures, corals) and technology (trusses, meshes). Blender's *Wireframe* and *Remesh* modifiers allow for quick conversion of solid objects into open, structural lattices.

3.6.1.3.2 Technique

3.6.1.3.2.1 Wireframe Method

1. **Create the base mesh.**
   - Model a starting shape or import an existing mesh.
2. **Add the Wireframe modifier.**
   - In the Modifiers panel, add Wireframe.
   - Enable **Even Thickness** to maintain consistent edge width.

3. **Adjust parameters.**
    - Modify **Thickness** to control the strut width.
    - Use **Offset** to position the lattice relative to the original surface.

3.6.1.3.2.2 Remesh Method

1. **Add the Remesh modifier.**
    - In the Modifiers panel, add Remesh and set **Mode** to Sharp.
2. **Set the resolution.**
    - Adjust **Octree Depth** to control the mesh resolution.
3. **Optional irregularity.**
    - Add a Decimate modifier to break uniformity and introduce organic variation (Figure 3-16).

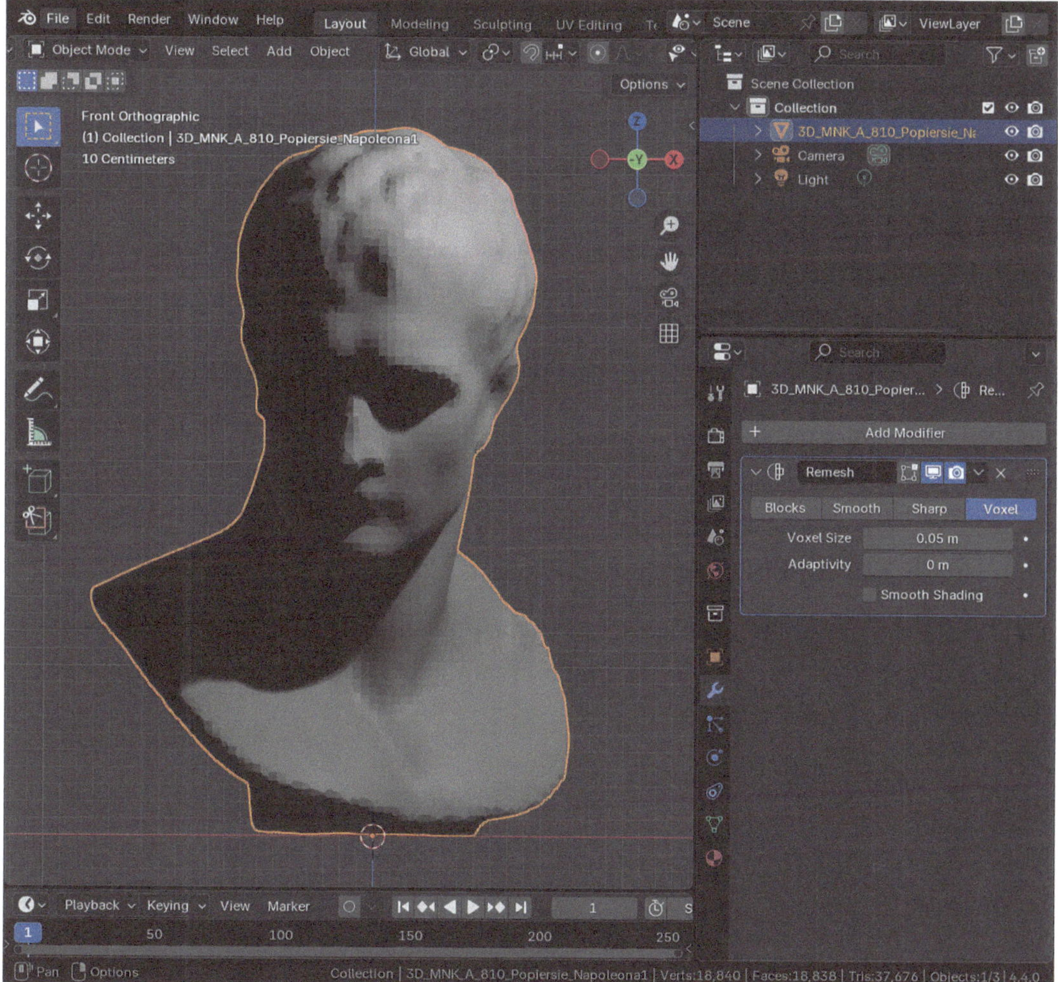

Figure 3-16.** **Application of the Remesh modifier in Blender on a scanned bust.
By adjusting the Voxel Size, the mesh resolution changes, producing denser or more porous lattice structures

The application of the Remesh modifier in Blender on a scanned sculpture, (in this case the 3D model of the Bust of Napoleon Bonaparte released by Virtual Museums of Małopolska downloaded from Sketchfab) converts the surface into a voxel lattice.

The Remesh modifier is not a manual sculpting tool, but rather an algorithmic transformation based on fixed rules.

Here, the Remesh modifier in Voxel mode is used with a resolution of 0.05 meters to modify the geometry.

This digital process echoes traditional sculptural methods of roughing-out or schematization, where solid mass is reduced to structural essence.

3.6.1.3.3 Conclusion

Both methods produce lightweight, visually permeable structures that can be scaled up for installation work or printed in smaller formats as experimental sculptures. They are especially effective for evoking biomechanical or architectural hybrids.

3.6.1.4 Techno-Mechanical Surfaces via Image Displacement

This effect embosses mechanical or abstract detail onto a surface using grayscale height maps.[14] The effect merges digital aesthetics with sculptural form.

3.6.1.4.1 Introduction

Height maps derived from technical or scientific imagery can be used to emboss mechanical detail directly into a 3D surface, creating forms that appear engineered yet organically integrated.

3.6.1.4.2 Technique

1. **Create the base mesh.**
    - Add a Plane or any other base mesh (Shift+A → Mesh → Plane, for example).
2. **Increase geometry.**
    - Enter Edit Mode (Tab), right-click the plane, and choose Subdivide.
    - Repeat the subdivision four to five times to ensure there is enough geometry for the displacement to work smoothly.
    - Return to Object Mode and add a Subdivision Surface modifier (Levels: 2–3) for a smooth, high-poly surface.

[14] Mechanical circuit-board pattern (CC0) suitable as a height map; this is ideal for embossing structured detail onto 3D surfaces via displacement.

3. **Apply displacement.**
   - Add a Displace modifier.
   - Click New to create a texture slot, then load a grayscale image (e.g., circuit diagram, topographic map, or astronomical data).
4. **Adjust relief.**
   - In the Displace modifier, set **Strength** and **Midlevel** to control the height and depth of the displacement.
5. **Increase resolution.**
   - Add another Subdivision Surface modifier to increase mesh density for cleaner, more precise results (Figure 3-17).

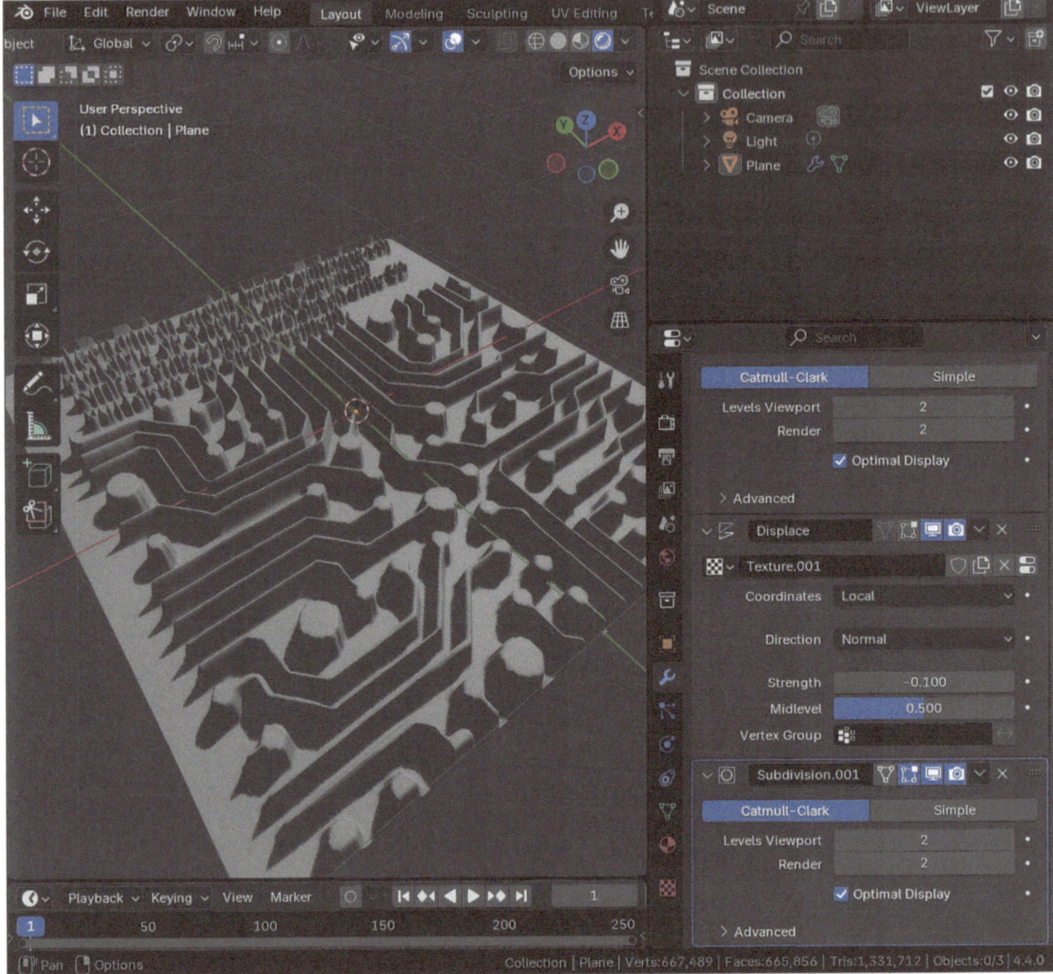

Figure 3-17. Blender interface showing the use of the Subdivision Surface modifier with Displace.
Increasing mesh density allows grayscale height maps to generate precise techno-mechanical patterns across the surface

3.6.1.4.3 Conclusion

This method creates surfaces that merge digital aesthetics with sculptural form. By altering the image input, the same mesh can take on radically different mechanical or abstract identities, making it ideal for hybrid works at the intersection of technology and art—a digital counterpart to both traditional bas-relief carving and the embossed textures of industrial surfaces.

3.6.1.5 Fluid Simulation in Blender's Geometry Nodes

This effect simulates continuous, flowing deformation within a procedural system. Animated ripples and distortions evoke organic movement or molten material.

3.6.1.5.1 Introduction

This workflow demonstrates how Blender's Geometry Nodes can be used to create fluid-like forms that simulate continuous organic growth. Inspired by the dynamic energy of *Breath of Fire* (Chapter 8.1), the process merges Dionysian fluidity with Apollonian structure through procedural logic.

3.6.1.5.2 Technique

1. **Base mesh.**
    - Create a low-poly object such as an Icosphere to serve as the foundation.
2. **Geometry Nodes deformation.**
    - Add a Geometry Nodes modifier.
    - Build a noise-based displacement system to distort the mesh, giving the impression of liquid movement.
3. **Animate the deformation.**
    - Use a Scene Time node to drive parameters such as noise offset or scale, creating continuous ripples and surface evolution (Figure 3-18).

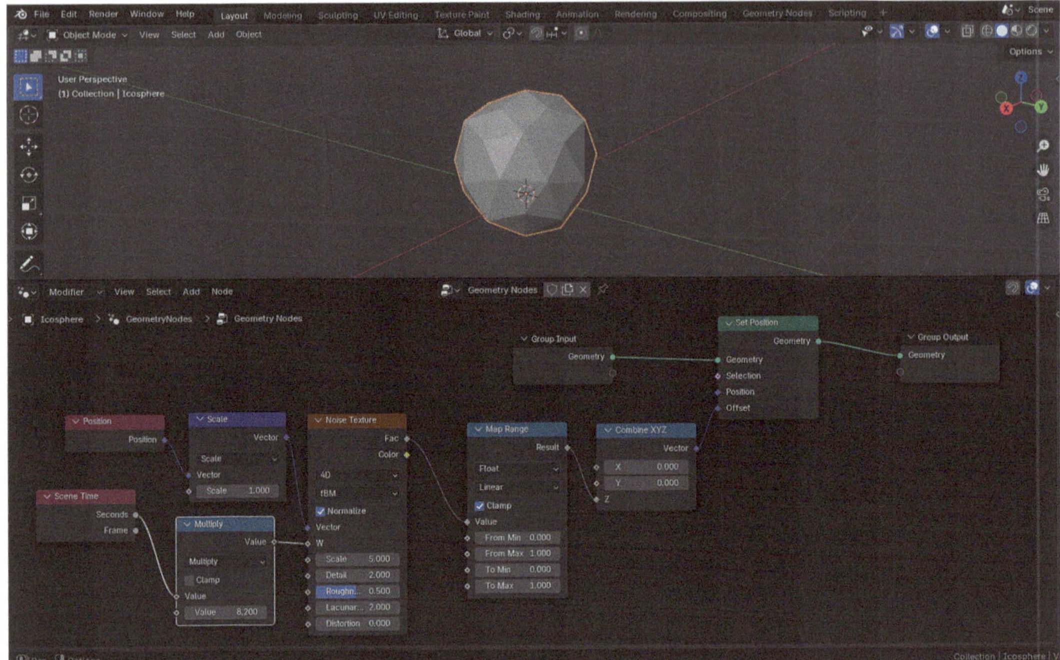

Figure 3-18. Blender Geometry Nodes setup driving a fluid-like transformation of a polyhedral form.
The system simulates continuous flow and deformation, positioning the object between digital sculpture and dynamic performance, and evoking processes of material metamorphosis

4. **Export.**

    - Export as GLB (GL Transmission Format) for integration into virtual exhibition platforms (see Chapter 9.6.1.2).

      GLB is generally the recommended standard as it is web-optimized and bundles the geometry, materials, and potential animations into a single file.

      However, it is essential to verify the specific format requirements of the target virtual platform (which may sometimes prefer FBX, OBJ, or specific low-resolution formats).

    - Alternatively, apply all modifiers and export as a static mesh for physical fabrication (see Chapter 6).

3.6.1.5.3 Conclusion

The resulting form exists between sculpture and performance, reacting to both internal procedural logic and potential user interaction. Like a digital echo of traditional casting or fluid modeling, it suggests forms in constant transformation. As part of a metaverse installation, it can respond to viewer input, extending the concept of growth into a participatory digital environment.

3.6.2 Picasso's Procedural Gesture

Picking up from the earlier discussion on Picasso's gestural line, this example shows how his intuitive drawing logic can be transposed into the digital domain.

Here, a Bézier curve, drawn freely by hand, is transformed through Geometry Nodes into a three-dimensional object.

Using the Trim Curve function, the line itself can be animated, unfolding progressively as if it were being traced in real time—a direct digital echo of the artist's hand.

The most elementary graphic gesture—a line traced in space—thus becomes a volumetric form with thickness and substance.

It demonstrates how a simple mark can evolve into digital sculpture. From the artist's immediate stroke emerges a fluid structure, modifiable and capable of generating infinite variations.

Figure 3-19 illustrates how digital tools can translate the immediacy of a hand-drawn gesture into volumetric form, revealing the continuum between intuitive drawing and computational modeling.

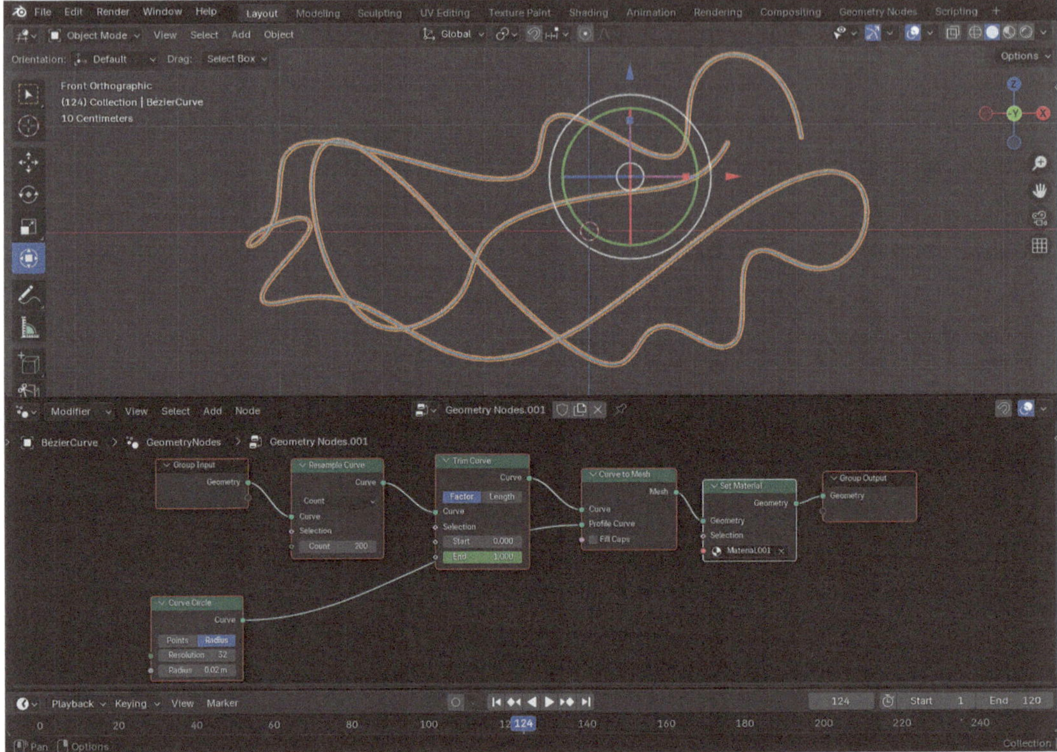

Figure 3-19. Procedural interpretation of a luminous gesture.
Re-creation of a light-drawing-inspired gesture using Blender's Geometry Nodes. A Bézier curve, manipulated through node-based operations, is converted into a 3D mesh with adjustable thickness and material, translating Picasso's 1949 luminous line into a procedural and modifiable digital Figure

In this way, gesture and algorithm converge within a single continuum, where intuition meets procedural logic. What was once a fleeting trace on paper now unfolds into a dynamic system: a sculptural entity that can be stretched, duplicated, animated, or even materialized through digital fabrication. The hand's immediacy persists, but it is amplified by computational processes, revealing a new paradigm where drawing is no longer just representation, but the seed of generative form.

3.6.3 Contemporary Hybrid Artworks with Digital Code

In contemporary sculpture, the integration of digital processes is more pervasive than it might appear at first glance. Even when not explicitly stated—or only mentioned in passing—artists incorporate procedural modeling, algorithmic transformations, and other computational tools in the conception and production of their works.

These technologies may be used to prototype forms, generate complex geometries impossible to model manually, or simulate material behaviors before fabrication.

This hybridity often remains invisible in the finished piece. The final sculpture may appear purely handcrafted, yet beneath its surface lies a digital lineage of parameters, simulations, and procedural logic.

Some artists deliberately conceal the technical processes behind their work to focus the viewer's attention on its aesthetic or conceptual impact, while others openly celebrate the algorithmic origins of their forms.

This spectrum—from discreet digital assistance to fully generative workflows—is well documented across several platforms and research initiatives, which collectively showcase how generative art brings algorithmic thinking to the forefront of contemporary creative practice.[15]

In what follows, I will examine two case studies—Tony Cragg and Anish Kapoor—whose works illustrate distinct ways in which procedural logic informs contemporary sculpture.

3.6.3.1 Tony Cragg: Material, Scale, and Procedural Design

Tony Cragg (b. 1949) has developed a sculptural practice that, in his recent works, is in some way rooted in the monumental tradition of artists such as Henry Moore and distinctly shaped by contemporary digital and procedural methodologies.

His large-scale works often appear as fluid, stratified forms or biomorphic towers that emphasize materiality and volume.

[15] See: `https://aiartists.org/` for a mapping of contemporary AI and generative art practices; see `https://archive.aec.at/` for an extensive collection of media and generative artworks presented at the Ars Electronica Festival and Prix; and see `https://artbase.rhizome.org/` for the preservation and contextualization of born-digital and algorithmic works.

Though to the untrained eye the role of software and algorithmic processes is rarely visible in the final outcome, procedural techniques are integral to the design and realization of these sculptures, enabling complex structural balances and large-scale production.

Cragg's work thus embodies a dialogue between organic form, industrial process, and procedural logic, situating him as a bridge between modern sculptural traditions and computational design.

3.6.3.1.1 Stak: From Procedural Growth to Sculptural Form

Tony Cragg's monumental sculptures, from the 1990s onward, achieve fluid and natural-looking results through their layered surfaces and organic torsions, using an almost scientific and cumulative method of procedural modeling and stratification. His bronze work *Stack*, for example, is composed of stratified, undulating volumes that seem to grow upward in rhythmic layers, simultaneously recalling geological formations and fluid motion.

In digital terms, such a sculpture could begin from something as simple as a rectangular block, gradually subdivided and transformed through operations that deform and articulate the surface. Modifiers like subdivision surfaces, which smooth geometry, or displacement driven by layered textures, could generate undulating rhythms, cavities, and protrusions reminiscent of Cragg's sculptural language (Figure 3-20).

Figure 3-20. Tony Cragg, Stack (2011)*, collocata a Shoe Lane, Londra. By Matt Brown, CC BY 2.0,* `https://commons.wikimedia.org/w/index.php?curid=142793781`

What is crucial, however, is not the technical details but the underlying principle: the sculpture is the result of a process of evolution.

Each digital operation corresponds to a step in the transformation, and the final work we see is like a snapshot—a crystallized moment—within a potentially endless series of variations. In this way, Cragg's sculptures resonate with the logic of procedural generation: the visible object is not only a finished form but also a trace of the continuous flux from which it emerged.

As highlighted in IGNANT's essay "Sculptor Tony Cragg Creates Bold Works That 'Embody A Frozen Moment Of Movement'" (2019),[16] his practice embodies precisely this paradox: forms that appear fixed, yet pulsate with the memory of motion.

[16] *"Sculptor Tony Cragg Creates Bold Works That 'Embody A Frozen Moment Of Movement,'"* IGNANT, August 26, 2019. The article highlights Cragg's abstract, fluid sculptures as embodying "a frozen moment of movement," emphasizing his view of sculpture as a dynamic and imaginative discipline.

Sculptor Tony Cragg Creates Bold Works That "Embody A Frozen Moment Of Movement," IGNANT

Cragg himself has emphasized sculpture as a discipline of infinite possibilities, where the task of the artist is to find "where it becomes more meaningful."

His stratified towers and torsional volumes can therefore be seen as materializations of energy, as if matter itself were arrested in a dynamic blur, embodying a frozen moment of movement.

Figure 3-21, taken in Blender, demonstrates how procedural modifiers reproduce this principle in digital space. The Displace modifier, controlled by strength values and animated over the timeline, generates evolving surfaces that simulate geological layering and organic torsion.

By adjusting the parameters of the Displace modifier, the very form of the sculpture is continuously reshaped. While the analogy remains conceptual, just as Cragg's physical sculptures seem to solidify a living flux, the digital model makes processes of growth and mutation visible as an editable, ongoing transformation.br /It is not documented whether Tony Cragg employs procedural modeling in his practice, yet the generative logic underlying his sculptures—where form emerges through accumulative, stratified, and torsional operations—shows an intriguing methodological affinity with procedural workflows. Both approaches rely on iterative transformations and on the idea that form is not imposed but discovered through a dynamic process. In this sense, digital procedural modeling can serve as an analytical parallel that makes explicit the kind of continuous metamorphosis that Cragg achieves materially.

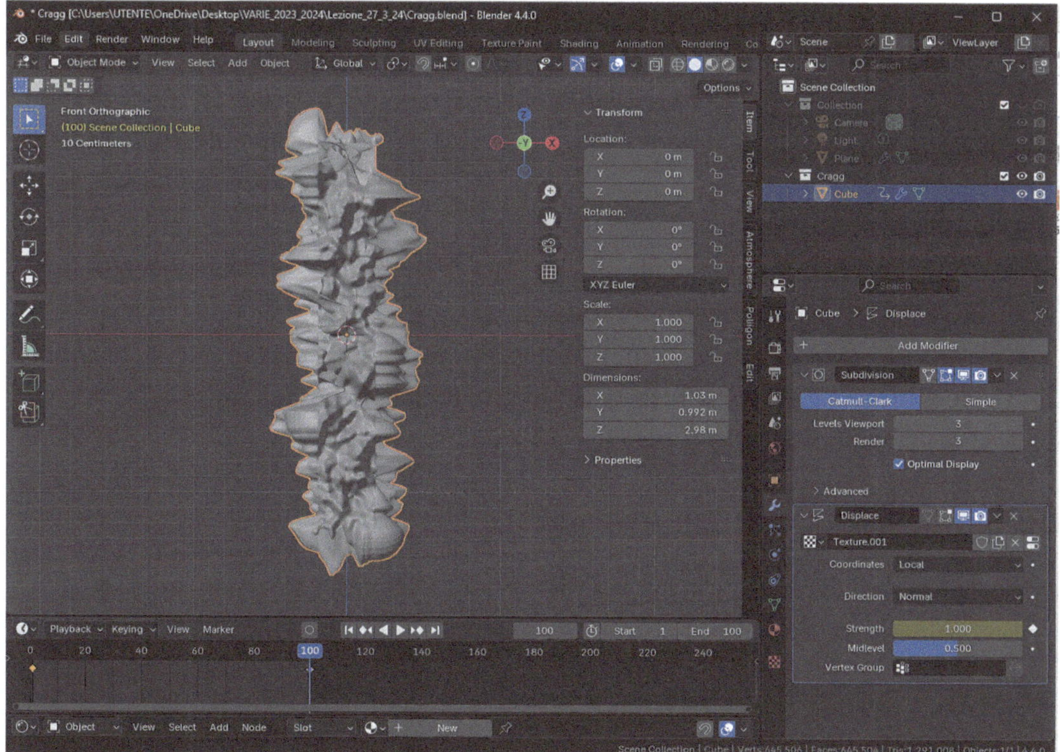

Figure 3-21. The Displace modifier.
This algoritm here, adjusted through strength values and animated along the timeline, generates stratified surfaces that simulate geological layering and organic torsion. This digital workflow illustrates how Cragg's sculptural language—forms embodying a "frozen moment of movement"—can be understood as the crystallization of an evolutionary process

By modifying the parameters of the Displace modifier, the very form of the sculpture is continuously transformed.

Just as Cragg's physical sculptures seem to solidify a living flux, the digital model visualizes growth and mutation as an editable, ongoing process.

3.6.3.2 Anish Kapoor: Procedural Thinking and Conceptual Space

Anish Kapoor (b. 1954) has consistently employed digital tools and procedural approaches to develop sculptures that merge material innovation with conceptual investigation. Works such as *Cloud Gate* (2004–2006), with its seamless stainless steel skin reflecting and distorting the surrounding cityscape, exemplify this integration of material and idea.

Yet Kapoor's procedural thinking can be traced back much earlier: in *Circle to Square Drawing* (1973),[17] he already explored systematic transformation as a generative principle.

Later, in the monumental installation *Marsyas* (2002),[18] designed for Tate Modern's Turbine Hall, he relied on advanced software-based simulations and procedural form-finding to realize a vast, stretched membrane that redefined spatial perception.

Kapoor's practice, therefore, demonstrates how procedural design underpins not only the technical realization of his works but also their conceptual power, where material, reflection, and space converge into immersive experiences.

3.6.3.2.1 Anish Kapoor: Tall Tree and The Eye

Anish Kapoor's *Tall Tree and the Eye* is a monumental vertical column composed of mirrored spheres, reflecting and distorting the surrounding environment (Figure 3-22).[19]

[17] *Anish Kapoor - Circle to Square Drawing (1973)*, `https://anishkapoor.com/331/diagram`.

Early computer-based experiment where Kapoor defined circle and square as endpoints, leaving the intermediate transformation to be generated algorithmically (`https://anishkapoor.com/331/diagram`).

[18] *Anish Kapoor - Marsyas (2002)*, Anish Kapoor Official Website, diagram description: the work is formed between three very large steel rings, stretched between them like a flayed skin (`https://anishkapoor.com/156/marsyas-3`).

[19] *Tall Tree & The Eye* by Anish Kapoor (2009) is a monumental sculpture composed of 73 reflective stainless steel and carbon spheres, designed to interact dynamically with its surroundings (`https://www.guggenheim-bilbao.eus/en/the-collection/works/tall-tree-and-the-eye`).

It is installed at the rear of the Guggenheim Museum Bilbao, in a small water basin overlooking the Nervión River, positioned to reflect the museum's architecture, La Salve Bridge, and the surrounding urban environment (bigcitiesbrightlights.wordpress.com).

Figure 3-22. *Anish Kapoor,* ***Tall Tree and The Eye*** *(2009), Guggenheim Museum Bilbao.*
Stainless steel and carbon steel, 1297 × 442 × 440 cm.
Image by Zarateman, own work, CC0,
https://commons.wikimedia.org/wiki/File%3ABilbao_-_Museo_Guggenheim_-_Tall_Tree_and_the_Eye_%28Anish_Kapoor%29_4.JPG?utm

Its apparent simplicity hides a complex interplay of repetition, variation, and balance, making it a perfect case study for procedural reproduction in 3D.

To digitally recreate Anish Kapoor's *Tall Tree and the Eye*, three main approaches can be used, each with its own balance of realism and control.

The first is physical simulation with Rigid Body dynamics, where forces and collisions naturally arrange the spheres into a vertical column, which is very organic though time-consuming and parameter-sensitive.

The second is a fully procedural method with Geometry Nodes, which distributes spheres inside a cylindrical volume with precise density and variation controls (Figure 3-23).

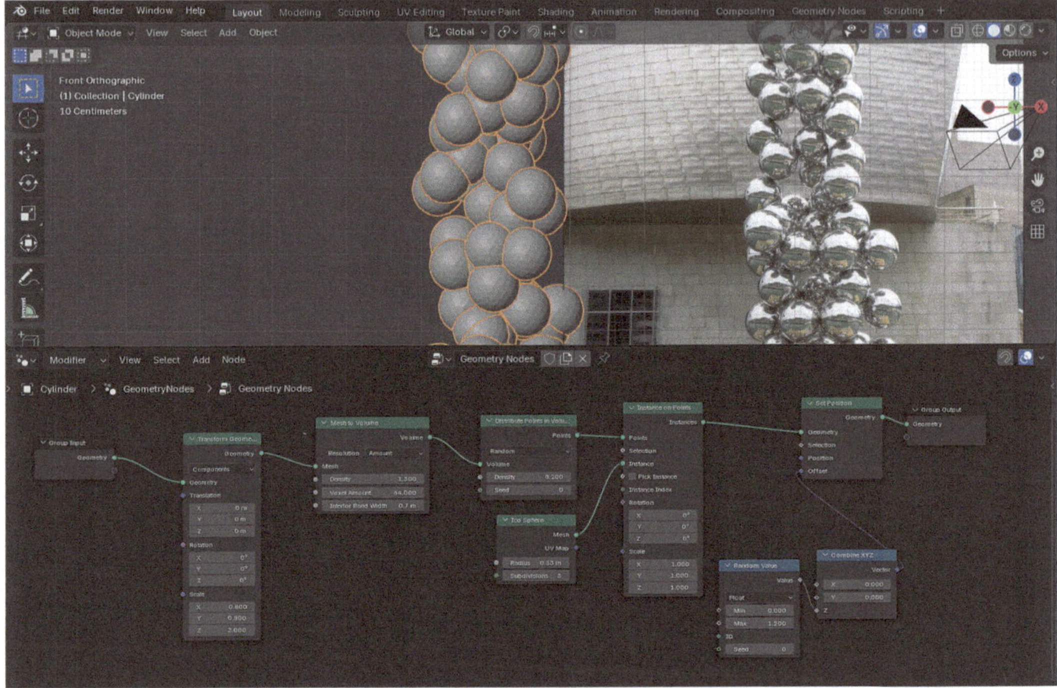

Figure 3-23. Using Geometry Nodes.
Spheres are distributed within a cylindrical volume and varied through scale and positional offsets. This setup illustrates Kapoor's Tall Tree and the Eye as a generative system, where repetition and variation create a volumetric column of mirrored forms

Finally, a hybrid method blends procedural generation with a simulation zone, allowing the spheres to "relax" into place, achieving a natural yet efficient result.

In particular, Geometry Nodes provide a direct parallel to Kapoor's artistic logic: by defining rules of distribution, scale variation, and positional constraints, the system generates complex structures of reflection and balance without manually modeling each sphere.

Much like Cragg's stratified towers embody a crystallized process of growth, Kapoor's mirrored spheres can be understood as algorithmic instances within a generative field, where the visible sculpture is both a singular object and a trace of procedural repetition.

3.7 Conclusion

Across the works examined in this chapter, procedurality emerges as both method and language, shifting the artist's role from manual maker to creator of worlds, as all great artists have, in fact, been.

Rather than producing a single, fixed object, the artist defines rules and parameters that generate potentially infinite variations.

In this way, artworks become dynamic states, adaptable across contexts, materials, and media.

Procedural modeling bridges natural and artificial logics, translating growth patterns, physical forces, and cultural motifs into new formal vocabularies. It enables precision and unpredictability, balancing Apollonian control with Dionysian emergence.

In contemporary practice, it connects disciplines: supporting fabrication with adaptable geometries, extending into virtual and metaverse spaces, and integrating with AI to produce hybrid forms.

Ultimately, procedurality invites the artist to shape not only the object, but the very conditions under which it can continuously evolve.

The next chapter will explore how such generative potential challenges traditional ideas of uniqueness, authenticity, and authorship, from Walter Benjamin's notion of the *aura* to contemporary blockchain-based certification.

CHAPTER 4

Uniqueness, Identity, and Digital Certification: From Aura to Blockchain

> ***"In the age of its technical reproducibility, what withers in the work of art is its aura.***
>
> *This process is symptomatic; its significance extends far beyond the realm of art.*
>
> *It signals the perception of the masses in modern times. What fades in the era of technical reproducibility is the authority of the artwork."*
>
> *Walter Benjamin*

This chapter examines the evolution of the artwork's identity from Walter Benjamin's concept of *aura* to contemporary practices involving metadata, blockchain, and networked ecosystems.

We begin with a historical and cultural foundation in Walter Benjamin's seminal essay "The Work of Art in the Age of Mechanical Reproduction" (1936), where the idea of *aura*—the singular presence of an artwork in time and space—was first problematized in the context of mass reproducibility.

Historical cases such as the Musée Rodin, which continues to produce authorized posthumous casts from the artist's original molds, reveal how questions of authenticity and legitimacy have long extended beyond the artist's lifetime.

These practices demonstrate that the aura of an artwork can be preserved or reconstructed through legal, institutional, and documentary frameworks.

G. Moioli, *Art Between Matter and Code*, https://doi.org/10.1007/979-8-8688-2376-3_4

Alongside these historical precedents, we will analyze the role of open-source and Creative Commons licensing systems that offer artists new ways to balance openness and authorship in the digital environment.

Such frameworks highlight how authorship today is not only protected by copyright but also negotiated through licenses that can encourage circulation, sharing, and derivative creation while maintaining artistic identity.

In the second part, attention shifts to nonfungible tokens (NFTs) and the new forms of collecting they enable. We will consider emblematic cases such as Sotheby's auctions of large-scale digital collections—like the sale of 500 drawings tokenized as unique editions—which illustrate how the art market is experimenting with new paradigms of ownership and scarcity.

Through this trajectory—from Benjamin's reflections on aura to blockchain-enabled certification—the chapter interrogates how art, law, and technology converge to redefine what it means for an artwork to be unique, authentic, and owned in the digital age.

4.1 Aura and the Question of Uniqueness

This section explores the concept of an artwork's aura[1]—its unique presence in time and space—and how digital reproduction challenges traditional notions of uniqueness and authenticity.

[1] For Walter Benjamin, aura is what makes a work of art unique and unrepeatable. It arises from the work's authentic presence in time and space, from the history and tradition that accompany it, and from the sense of distance and reverence that surrounds it, preserving its halo of mystery and authority.

Long before the digital era, both art and sculpture had already confronted this issue. Through molds, casts, and bronze foundries, the same work could be reproduced multiple times. Were all these casts equally authentic? How many impressions of a print or bronzes from a mold could still claim the status of "original"?[2]

These questions, central to the history of sculpture, resurface today in the age of digital reproduction.

Benjamin's seminal essay "The Work of Art in the Age of Mechanical Reproduction" provides a cultural foundation, arguing that mechanical reproducibility erodes an artwork's aura.[3]

According to Benjamin, aura is tied to authenticity and the "here and now" of the original work: a singular presence that is diminished when identical copies circulate.

In this section, we first examine Benjamin's ideas on the loss of aura in the age of mass reproduction, while also considering how the problem of reproducibility was already evident in traditional sculpture.

We will then move forward to ask how digital technologies might undermine and reconfigure aura through tools such as metadata, blockchain, and new certification systems.

---

[2] Throughout the history of editioned art, legal and ethical standards have emerged to define "original" multiples, balancing artistic intent with market value. For prints such as etchings and lithographs, the industry convention typically limits the original edition to 150–200 impressions, plus a small number of Artist's Proofs (A.P., often 10–15% of the edition), though this varies by technique and artist. `https://tinyurl.com/3wmedvnw`

For bronze sculpture, legal precedents are particularly stringent. In France, the Musée Rodin is restricted by law to a maximum of 12 casts per work (8 numbered editions + 4 A.P.), ensuring the integrity of posthumous reproductions. `https://www.musee-rodin.fr/en/museum/institution/original-bronze-casts`

For photography, gallery editions are generally limited to 25 or fewer prints to preserve scarcity and value, often with 5–10 A.P. reserved for the artist. `https://www.artsy.net/article/artsy-specialist-buying-limited-editions`

These standards reflect evolving debates on authenticity, with further details and citations provided in the full bibliography (see Ellis, The Print Collector's Handbook, 2015; Musée Rodin Charter, 2023).

[3] Walter Benjamin, "The Work of Art in the Age of Its Technological Reproducibility," first published in French as *L'œuvre d'art à l'époque de sa reproductibilité technique*, in Zeitschrift für Sozialforschung, Paris, 1936. Canonical German version in *Schriften*, edited by Theodor W. Adorno and Gershom Scholem, Frankfurt am Main, Suhrkamp Verlag, 1955. The specific translation used in this chapter is "The Work of Art in the Age of Its Technological Reproducibility," translated by Edmund Jephcott (Harvard 2003), which corresponds to the Third German Version of the essay (1939).

4.1.1 Benjamin and the Loss of Aura

Benjamin famously argued that mechanical reproduction devalues a work's aura, the unique presence of an artwork in its original time and place.

In his view, the ability to create identical copies, through photography, film, printing, etc., strips the artwork of its "mystical halo" and authority.

The aura, as Benjamin defined it, is tied to authenticity and tradition—the "unique interweaving of time and space" that gives an artwork its singular authenticity in the here and now.[4]

Mechanical reproduction undermines this uniqueness. When any number of identical prints or photos can exist, the distance and reverence for the original diminish.

In short, "even the most perfect reproduction of a work of art is lacking in one element: its presence in time and space." And with each reproduction the original's aura and historical depth falter.

The conceptual diagram in Figure 4-1 visually represents Benjamin's notion of the aura: the authentic presence of an original artwork, expressed in the Latin phrase *hic et nunc*.

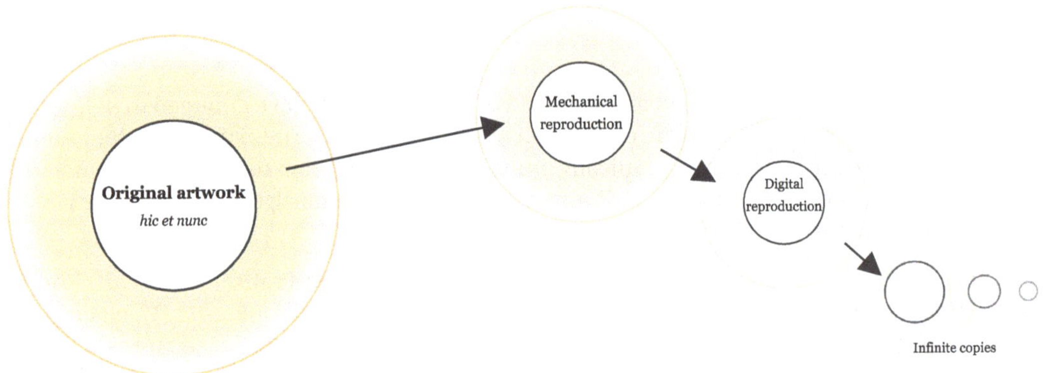

Figure 4-1. The Loss of the Aura.
This diagram illustrates the progressive shift from manual modeling, where form emerges through direct, tactile gestures, to digital modeling with virtual tools, to procedural modeling based on algorithmic rules, and finally to AI-mediated or data-driven approaches. While the graphic reduces the process to four stages, each stage encapsulates a transformation in authorship and reproducibility: from unique, unrepeatable gestures to systems capable of generating infinite adaptive variations

[4] Benjamin's phrase "unique interweaving of space and time" deliberately recalls the inseparable fabric of spacetime in Einstein's relativity. The aura, for Benjamin, is the last enclave of an absolute, nonrelativized "here and now" in a world that has become fully measurable and reproducible.

The luminous "aura" surrounding the work gradually fades as it transitions from mechanical to digital reproduction and finally to infinite copies, illustrating the progressive loss of uniqueness and authority that Benjamin described.

In the digital era, Benjamin's concern is amplified.

The result is a crisis of reproducibility: the concept of a singular, authentic original piece is deeply challenged by the ease of duplication in digital media.

Just as photography shattered the aura of unique paintings, the Internet's unlimited copying capabilities seemingly render aura obsolete in the realm of digital art.

4.1.2 New Forms of Aura Through Digital Tools

In the contemporary digital context, authenticity and originality are being redefined not by physical uniqueness but by digital certification.

For instance, artists and technologists are using metadata and blockchain to create a verifiable record of a digital artwork's origin and ownership. By embedding unique metadata in a file or minting an NFT on the blockchain to represent the work,[5] they can create digital scarcity,[6] a quality of uniqueness that is attached to the work's digital certificate rather than its physical form.

NFTs create a verifiable chain of ownership for a token that references an artwork. However, they do not automatically authenticate that the person who minted the token was the legitimate creator—this requires external verification through artist signatures, platform vetting, or community recognition.

Even though the underlying digital image or video can still be copied freely, the NFT token is unique and owned by a single entity, introducing an aura of exclusivity around an otherwise reproducible piece. In this way, digital tools shift the source of aura from the **object's physical presence** to its **secure identity**.

The artwork's value and authenticity are anchored in verifiable data—who created it, when, how, and who owns it all recorded immutably.

[5] It is crucial to distinguish between: (a) metadata embedded within a file itself (easily altered, not scarce), (b) cryptographic hashes of files (prove a specific version existed at a time, but don't prevent copying), and (c) NFT tokens on blockchain (scarce, tradeable, but merely point to files that may or may not remain accessible).

[6] Digital scarcity refers to the creation of uniqueness in the digital realm, where files can normally be copied infinitely. Through blockchain and NFTs, a digital asset can be marked as "original" and limited in number, mimicking the scarcity of physical objects.

This marks a reconfiguration of Benjamin's concept: aura in the digital age is no longer a purely material phenomenon but a combination of cryptographic proof, metadata context, and the collective agreement that a given certified instance of the work is special.

In sum, while the traditional aura "withers" in the age of technical reproducibility, a *new aura* can emerge through digital certification and the perceived integrity it grants to digital art.

In traditional sculpture, the problem of authenticity was already clearly present. Works could be reproduced through casting. For example, a mold made from an original model could generate multiple bronzes or plaster copies, just as an engraving plate could yield countless impressions.

But which of these should be considered authentic? Only the first exemplar? All those produced under the artist's supervision? Or only a defined limited series?

The very notion of originality has long been entangled with the distinction between the unique piece, the numbered edition, and the open reproduction.

This dilemma resurfaces in the digital sphere in amplified form.

Just as bronze casting raised doubts about the originality of each exemplar, digital printing and file duplication pose the same question with even greater intensity. Here the difference is that digital copies are not just multiple; they are indistinguishable and theoretically infinite.

Reproducibility and authenticity—from traditional techniques to digital paradigms—have always been intertwined.

Direct techniques such as carving stone, modeling clay, or welding steel preserve the authentic gesture of the artist, leaving behind an unrepeatable trace.

Indirect techniques, by contrast, rely on molds or matrices: casting in plaster, terracotta, or bronze allows multiple identical copies.

However, the difference is not always clear-cut.

In today's digital context, the question resurfaces with even greater force. A digital file, unlike a plaster cast, can be copied endlessly without degradation.

If in traditional sculpture the matrix raised doubts about originality, in the digital sphere infinite perfect duplication radically challenges the very notion of authenticity.

Figure 4-2 illustrates this tension, showing how direct/manual techniques embody uniqueness, while indirect/reproducible techniques anticipate the broader cultural debate on reproducibility and originality in modern and digital art.

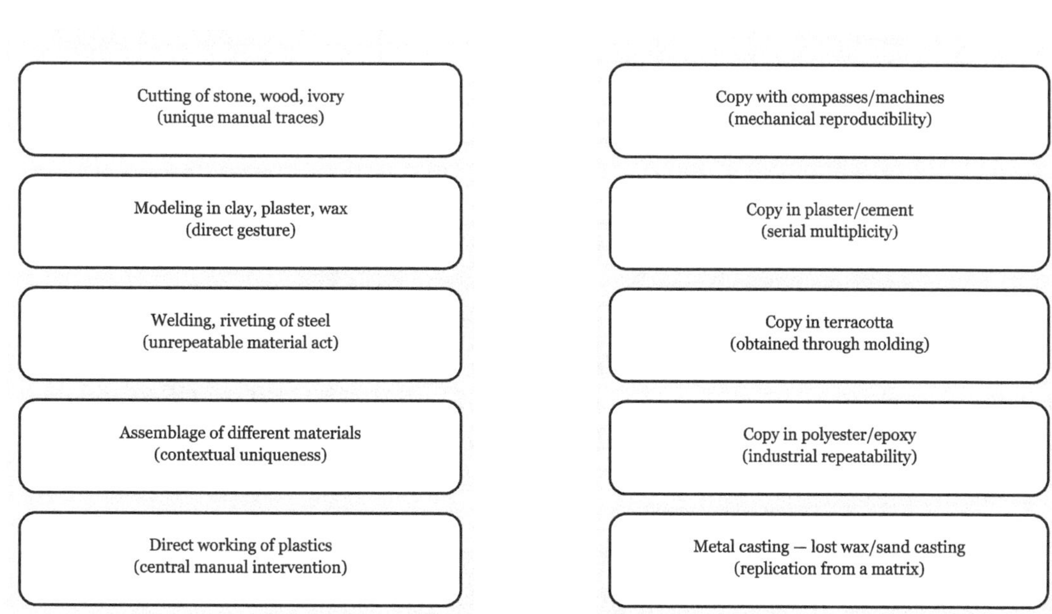

Figure 4-2. Direct vs. indirect techniques.
This diagram illustrates the distinction between traditional direct and indirect sculptural techniques

A further complication arises with 3D printing, which blurs the boundary between traditional casting and digital duplication.

Like bronze casting or engraving, 3D printing can generate multiple physical instances from a single matrix; yet, because its source is a digital file, it not only allows identical replications but also the effortless creation of many different variations.[7]

In this way, the boundary between authenticity and reproducibility becomes even more blurred, as each copy may be both unique and derivative at the same time.

Figure 4-3 expands this trajectory, tracing the three major levels of reproducibility: traditional, mechanical, and digital.

[7] 3D printing complicates the question of authenticity also by combining artisanal customization with industrial scalability. It blurs the line between unique craftsmanship and mass production, while inheriting the digital logic of infinite reproducibility, a phenomenon already explored in digital craftsmanship studies (Rautray 2021). https://www.cambridge.org/core/services/aop-cambridge-core/content/view/41420A80655DFD1FB74F4EE638BDD080/S2732527X2100033Xa.pdf/additive-manufacturing-enabling-digital-artisans.pdf

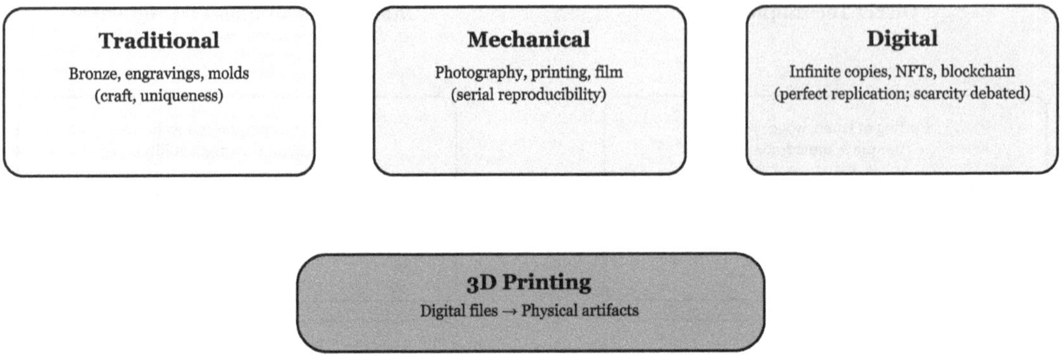

Traditional
Bronze, engravings, molds
(craft, uniqueness)

Mechanical
Photography, printing, film
(serial reproducibility)

Digital
Infinite copies, NFTs, blockchain
(perfect replication; scarcity debated)

3D Printing
Digital files → Physical artifacts

Figure 4-3. Levels of Reproducibility.
The diagram distinguishes three levels of reproducibility: traditional techniques, rooted in craftsmanship; mechanical techniques, linked to industrial processes; and digital techniques, grounded in algorithmic computation

Each stage intensifies the problem of authenticity, culminating in the paradox of infinite digital copies and the emergence of blockchain as a potential solution which seeks to restore uniqueness through certification rather than material presence.

It is precisely in this space of tension that questions of authorship and identity come to the fore.

Who is the author when a work can be endlessly copied, remixed, or generated by algorithms? From traditional sculpture to digital files, authenticity has never been a matter of the object alone, but also of its attribution, metadata, and cultural framing.

The next section will therefore turn to issues of **identity, authorship, and post-authorship**, exploring how digital works carry both material and immaterial layers, how open licensing and Creative Commons reshape rights of use, and how generative art and AI complicate the very notion of the author.

4.1.3 From the Aura of the Hand to the Aura of the Project

Imagine an artist who begins with hand-applied pigment forms and later moves to large, engineered works.

In the first phase, the aura lives in the trace of the hand: the grain of the powder, uneven saturation, tiny imperfections left by touch.

When the practice becomes more project-based, the aura doesn't disappear; it shifts.

It lives in an authored protocol: a distinctive geometry, a specific material recipe, fabrication tolerances, and—above all—the site-specific calibration of the work: light, acoustics, visitor flow.

In short, aura moves from the trace to the conditions that make the work singular.

As a concrete instance of the "hand-trace aura," Anish Kapoor's early pigment pieces saturate the gallery space in color; the powder's grain and uneven density make the artist's touch visibly legible (Figure 4-4).

Figure 4-4. Anish Kapoor, interior view at MUAC—Museo Universitario Arte Contemporáneo, Mexico City, 25 May 2016.
Photograph taken during the exhibition opening.
Photo: Gobierno CDMX, CC0, via Wikimedia Commons

At this point the very notion of aura migrates. It is no longer the trace of the artist's hand on matter, but the certified bond between digital authorship and its situated realization.

What becomes unique is not an unreproducible object, but a verifiable relationship between a master file and its instantiation in place.

The cryptographic hash functions as the contemporary equivalent of the sculptor's mold.

Parametric seeds act as the artist's signature inscribed in the space of possibilities, governing every permissible variation.

Calibration logs and material certificates document the precise dialogue between code, light, color, sound and architecture.

A distributed ledger ties every physical or experiential instance back to its immutable source.

Thus, originality no longer inheres in the singular artefact, but in the authenticated encounter of file and context—matter and code activated together, "here and now."

4.2 Identity, Authorship, and Post-Authorship

If reproducibility destabilizes the uniqueness of the artwork, it also unsettles the very foundation of authorship.

This section examines how artworks can exist as both tangible objects and code, how new licensing models allow hybrid forms of rights, and how generative art pushes us toward a concept of post-authorship.

Authorship in the digital realm becomes fluid; it is tied not just to a single creator but to networks of contributors, code, and audiences.

We explore the dual nature of digital works as physical and digital entities, the emergence of hybrid rights regimes like open licenses combined with exclusive tokens, and generative art's implications for the very notion of author and artwork.

4.2.1 The Dual Nature of Digital Works and Metadata

Many contemporary artworks now exist simultaneously in physical and digital forms, raising questions about where the true "art" resides.

For example, an artist might create a sculpture as a 3D-printed object in resin or PLA and also distribute the digital 3D model file online.

The physical piece and its digital twin are both authentic manifestations of the work.

The value and meaning of such a work are distributed across both realms—the gallery display and the file circulating on the Internet.

This challenges the traditional notion of a singular original. Instead, the artwork is a hybrid entity experienced in multiple contexts: physical space, virtual space, on-screen, in VR, etc.

In this context, metadata becomes crucial to preserving identity and authorship.

Digital files can carry embedded information such as the creator's name, creation date, or edit history.

This metadata functions as a kind of digital fingerprint for the artwork.

The metadata travels with the file and helps authenticate it, answering questions like: Who made this? When? Has it been altered?

For a digital sculpture file, metadata might record the artist, the software used, and any modifications made, establishing a chain of provenance much like a signature on a painting. In fact, metadata often serves as the digital signature of the artist in lieu of a physical mark.

It ensures that even if the work is copied, there's a traceable thread back to the source.

As a result, the identity of a digital artwork is increasingly defined by its documented history and data, rather than by an unrepeatable physical presence.

The artwork becomes as much about the process and record—the story encoded in its data—as about the final image or object we see.

4.2.2 Metadata in 3D Files: Between Internal Notes and Certified Records

Unlike photography or graphic design, where metadata standards such as EXIF or IPTC are widely adopted, 3D environments lack a universal system for embedding authorial or copyright information.

In software like Blender, the user can add custom properties at the level of a scene, object, or mesh.

These properties can record details such as author, title, or date, and they remain inside the.blend file.

However, they are not automatically exported to other formats (such as .fbx or .obj), nor are they recognized as standardized metadata by external platforms.

This means that while such properties are useful as conceptual demonstrations—showing how a digital file can carry traces of authorship—they do not function as official certification. The data remains internal, editable, and potentially invisible once the file circulates across different environments.

For this reason, in digital art the role of metadata operates on two levels:

1. **Internal and informal**: Annotations or custom properties embedded directly in the file (for example, within Blender or EXIF data in images). These provide a trace of authorship or process but remain fragile, since they can be altered or lost.

2. **External and certified**: Systems such as blockchain records, Creative Commons licenses, or museum databases, which ensure persistence, recognition, and legal validity. These forms of metadata serve as durable guarantees of authorship and authenticity across platforms and time.

In short, while a sculptor can inscribe their name on the base of a marble statue, in 3D files authorship is not naturally "carved" into the data.

It requires intentional embedding and external systems of certification to preserve authorship and authenticity in the long term.

Similarly, the authenticity of physical artworks cannot be guaranteed by a signature alone; it depends on consistent documentation, verified provenance, and expert assessment.

4.2.2.1 Certifying 3D Files

While Blender does not offer built-in certification tools, artists can secure authorship and authenticity of their 3D files using external systems.

These pathways illustrate how authorship can be anchored across different levels of visibility and authority, providing artists with flexible strategies according to their needs and contexts.

Figure 4-5 summarizes the main approaches available to certify 3D files, ranging from basic cryptographic proofs to institutional and blockchain-based systems.

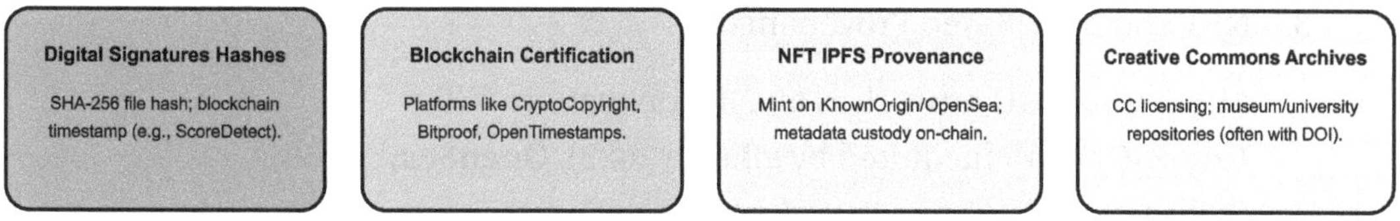

Digital Signatures Hashes
SHA-256 file hash; blockchain timestamp (e.g., ScoreDetect).

Blockchain Certification
Platforms like CryptoCopyright, Bitproof, OpenTimestamps.

NFT IPFS Provenance
Mint on KnownOrigin/OpenSea; metadata custody on-chain.

Creative Commons Archives
CC licensing; museum/university repositories (often with DOI).

Figure 4-5. Main Approaches to Certifying and Proving Provenance of 3D Files. *Diagram showing the main approaches for certifying 3D files, from cryptographic hashes to blockchain platforms, NFTs, and institutional archives*

These methods ensure authorship is traceable, legally recognized, and digitally persistent, far surpassing the capabilities of internal file metadata alone.

The following are practical solutions for artists to establish and verify authorship of their 3D files.

These methods leverage cryptographic techniques, blockchain anchoring, and open standards to provide tamper-proof proof-of-existence and ownership, ensuring long-term protection in an era of easy replication.

1. Digital Signatures and Hashes

   Compute a cryptographic hash (e.g., SHA-256) for your .blend file, which uniquely identifies it and changes if the file is altered.

   Services like **ScoreDetect**[8] simplify timestamping by anchoring the hash to the Ethereum blockchain, providing verifiable proof of the file's existence at a specific time.

2. Blockchain Certification Platforms

   Platforms like **CryptoCopyright**[9] and **Bitproof**[10] allow artists to upload a file, generate its hash, and register it immutably on a blockchain, issuing a certificate of proof for authorship verification. Alternatively, **OpenTimestamps**,[11] a free open-source tool, timestamps files on Bitcoin's blockchain, enabling independent verification.

[8] *ScoreDetect* is an online platform that generates a verification certificate for your digital content by recording its checksum on a public blockchain. This creates an immutable timestamp, offering credible proof of authenticity and ownership—even if the original file remains private. `https://www.scoredetect.com/`

[9] See: `https://crypto-copyright.com/`

[10] See: `https://www.bitproof.com/`

[11] See: `https://opentimestamps.org/`

3. NFT and IPFS-Based Provenance

   Minting your 3D artwork as an NFT on platforms like **KnownOrigin**[12] (acquired by eBay in 2022), **OpenSea,**[13] or **Foundation**[14] registers it on the blockchain, storing metadata such as author, title, and file hash immutably.[15]

   The file can be stored on IPFS (a distributed storage network), and the blockchain records the IPFS Content Identifier (CID) linking to that file. However, artists should understand that:

   (a) IPFS files are publicly accessible to anyone with the CID,
   (b) files must be 'pinned' by at least one node to remain available, and (c) pinning services may charge ongoing fees.
   This process, however, involves gas fees and platform commissions.

4. Creative Commons and Institutional Archives

   Noncryptographic options include publishing 3D files under Creative Commons licenses to ensure legal recognition of authorship and reuse conditions.

   Alternatively, depositing files in institutional repositories, such as university databases or museum collections, provides curatorial validation and permanence.

   These archives often issue DOI identifiers, making works citable in academic and professional contexts.

For basic proof of existence, free services like OpenTimestamps suffice.

[12] See: `https://knownorigin.io/`

[13] See: `https://opensea.io/`

[14] See: `https://foundation.app/`

[15] The NFT platform landscape has undergone significant consolidation since 2021. Artists should research platform stability, user reviews, and terms of service before committing to any marketplace.

For legally recognized certification, paid platforms like CryptoCopyright or ScoreDetect offer robust solutions.[16]

To enter the digital collectibles market, NFT marketplaces provide visibility but involve costs like gas fees and commissions.

These distinctions are summarized in Figure 4-6, which maps the progression from basic proofs of existence to legal certification and market-oriented frameworks.

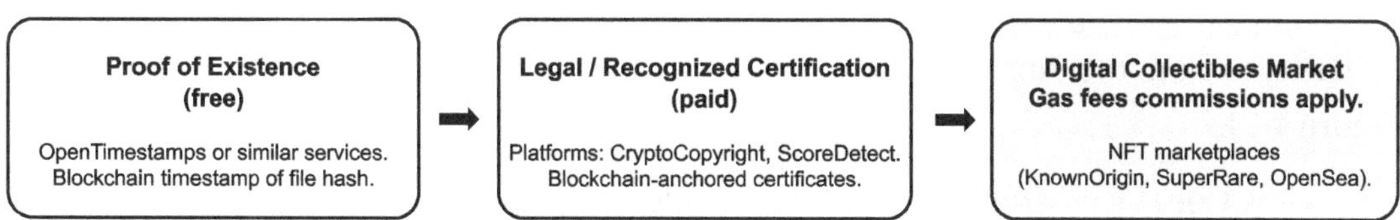

Figure 4-6. Three levels of 3D file certification.
From basic proofs of existence to legally recognized certification and the digital collectibles market

Taken together, these certification models define the technical and legal foundations of authorship in the digital realm.

Yet authorship is not only about proving existence or ownership, but it also concerns the ways works can be shared, remixed, or collaboratively expanded.

This leads directly to the question of licensing and hybrid rights, explored in the next section.

4.2.3 Licensing and Hybrid Rights

The rise of digital art has also led to innovative ways of managing copyright and usage rights, resulting in hybrid models of authorship and ownership.

Traditional copyright is often seen as too restrictive for the collaborative, share-friendly environment of the Internet.

[16] Practical Workflow for Certification

- Export your file (.blend, .obj, or .gltf).
- Hash your file (e.g. via SHA-256).
- Choose a platform: ScoreDetect, crypto-copyright, OpenTimestamps, KnownOrigin.
- Register the hash on blockchain receive proof/certificate.
- Keep the certificate alongside the file as verifiable proof of authorship.

In response, many artists have embraced open licensing systems like Creative Commons (CC) and open-source models, which allow controlled sharing, remixing, and even collaborative development of works.

Since 2002, Creative Commons has provided standardized licenses that let creators predefine how others can use their work.

These licenses span a continuum between full openness and more restrictive forms of protection, offering a balance between circulation and control.

Ordered from the most open to the most restrictive, the main licenses are as follows (Figure 4-7):

- **CC0:** The creator waives all rights, releasing the work into the public domain for maximum reuse.
- **CC BY:** Others can reuse and modify the work, as long as they credit the original author.
- **CC BY-SA:** Derivative works must be licensed under the same terms (share-alike), in addition to requiring attribution.
- **CC BY-ND:** Others can reuse the work and distribute it, but they **cannot modify it** (No Derivatives), requiring attribution.
- **CC BY-NC:** The work can be shared or remixed for noncommercial purposes only, with attribution.
- **CC BY-NC-SA:** This is a combination requiring **non-commercial** use and **share-alike** licensing for derivative works, with attribution.
- **CC BY-NC-ND:** The most restrictive license. The work can be shared for **noncommercial** use only and **cannot be modified** (No Derivatives), with attribution.

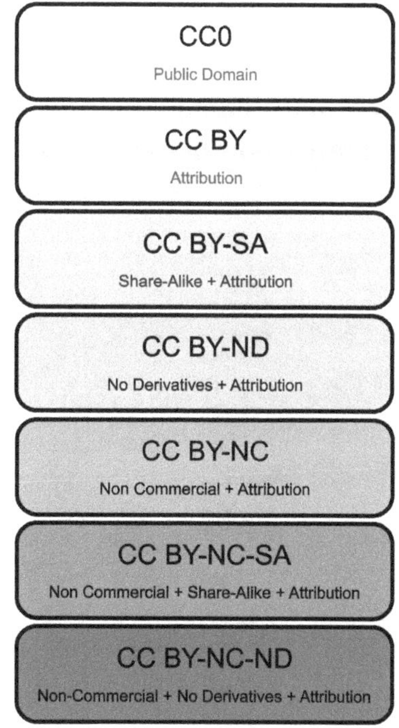

Figure 4-7. Creative Commons Licences.
Creative Commons licenses range from maximum openness (CC0) to more restrictive conditions (CC BY, CC BY-SA, CC BY-ND, CC BY-NC, CC BY-NC-SA, CC BY-NC-ND), allowing artists to balance reuse, recognition, and control

By deploying these licenses, digital artists can encourage the circulation and transformation of their art while still retaining authorship credit. For example, an artist might publish an image under CC BY, allowing it to spread widely (building reputation and cultural impact) yet still be acknowledged as the creator wherever it travels.

Importantly, open licensing doesn't mean giving up all economic benefits.

Many artists are combining open distribution with exclusive monetization in what we can call hybrid rights strategies.

An artist can now release a work freely online—even allowing remixing under noncommercial or fully open licenses—while simultaneously selling limited physical editions or NFTs of the same piece to collectors.

In this way, openness drives cultural reach and community building, while controlled scarcity generates revenue.

Beeple (Mike Winkelmann) offers the clearest illustration of this dual strategy.

For more than a decade he published every single daily artwork from his Everydays series (2007–present) under a CC0 (Public Domain Dedication) license, making the 5,000+ high-resolution images and animations permanently free for anyone to download, use, or remix without restriction-free (Figure 4-8).

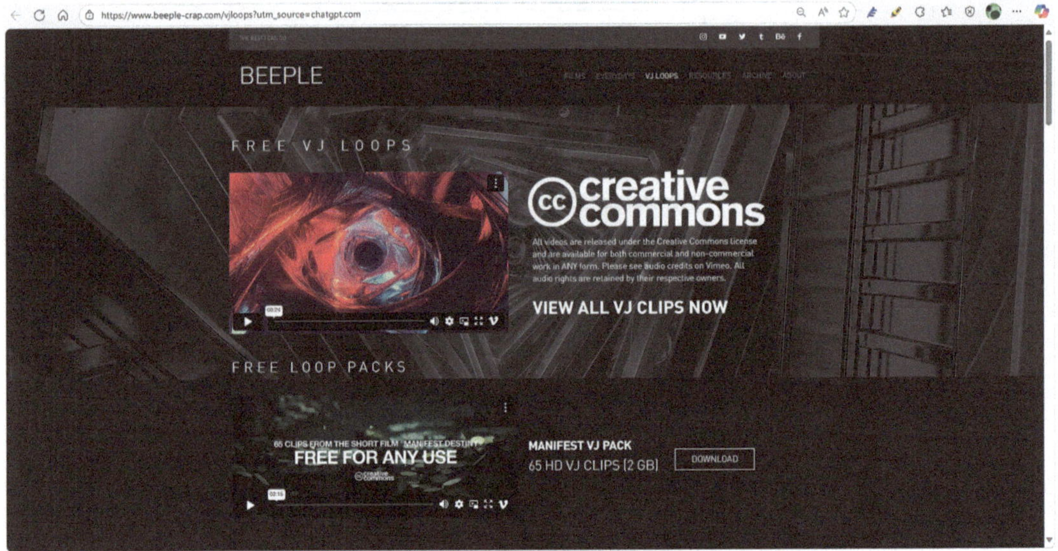

Figure 4-8. Beeple's Website.
Screenshot from Beeple's official website, where hundreds of animated loops can be freely downloaded under Creative Commons licenses, alongside open-source Cinema 4D project files released for educational and creative use

This radical generosity built him an enormous global following long before NFTs existed.

When the NFT market emerged, Beeple was able to monetize that reputation at unprecedented scale. The same images that anyone can still download for free were assembled into the collage *Everydays: The First 5000 Days*, sold at Christie's in March 2021 for $69.3 million as a single authenticated token.

The Beeple case therefore demonstrates that open licensing and blockchain-enforced exclusivity are not contradictory. They are complementary layers.

Openness creates cultural aura and audience; the NFT re-introduces verifiable uniqueness and provenance, allowing the artist to capture economic value without ever withdrawing the work from the commons.[17]

Such examples point to a future where authorship is "negotiated" across different channels. The artist remains the author, but the way a work is experienced and owned can vary. Some rights are given to the public, some are reserved for collectors.

These hybrid models mean an artwork's identity and value are co-defined by legal frameworks, like CC licenses, community engagement, and market mechanisms.

Authorship becomes less a static ownership of a work and more a dynamic management of rights, choosing when to invite the public in and when to assert exclusivity.

In essence, today's digital artists often wear two hats, as open sharers and as rights holders, crafting a balance that maintains their artistic identity while leveraging the power of networks and markets.

4.2.3.1 Blender and the Open-Source Paradigm

A paradigmatic case in the field of digital art is represented by Blender,[18] the open-source 3D modeling and animation platform distributed under the GNU General Public License (GPL).[19] Unlike proprietary software, which limits use, modification, and redistribution, Blender's licensing model guarantees artists full freedom to access the code, customize it, and share their modifications with the community.

---

[17] Beeple (Mike Winkelmann) has released 12 VJ loop project files—such as Box_Beat, WRMMM, and Cleanroom—along with five additional .c4d files for short films, all available for commercial or noncommercial use without attribution (though he welcomes notifications of derivative projects). Shared in an **"open access"** spirit, these resources can be downloaded from his official website at `https://www.beeple-crap.com/resources`.

[18] Blender was originally developed as proprietary software by the Dutch company Not a Number (NaN) in 1998. Following NaN's bankruptcy in early 2002, Ton Roosendaal launched the "Free Blender" crowdfunding campaign, which successfully raised €100,000. In October 2002, Blender was officially released as open-source software under the GNU General Public License (GPL).

[19] The GPL is a free software license created by the Free Software Foundation (FSF). It guarantees users the freedom to run, study, share, and modify software, while requiring that derivative works be released under the same license ("copyleft"), thus ensuring openness across all future versions.

See: *Free Software Foundation*, "GNU General Public License," `https://www.gnu.org/licenses/gpl-3.0.html`

This model demonstrates how licensing can function not as a restriction but as a catalyst of creativity. Artists are not only users of a tool but participants in a collective ecosystem where improvements, add-ons, and workflows are constantly generated and redistributed.

In this regard, my own artistic and academic practice offers a telling example.

For more than 15 years, Blender has been central to both my teaching and my sculptural production.

In the mid-2000s, together with Stefania Albertini, we worked under the name *Albertini and Moioli* producing joint projects.

Some of those works are still viewable on YouTube.[20] We explored the possibilities of virtual sculpture, focusing on the creation of immersive and interactive environments within free platforms such as OpenSimulator (OpenSim).

From the beginning, we have embraced open-source tools—not only Blender but also GIMP, Krita, Inkscape, Scribus, and many others—because their licenses guarantee the most essential freedom: the freedom to shape our own instruments.

This openness has allowed us to work without imposed limits, to adapt tools to artistic needs, and to share knowledge in a spirit of collaboration and exchange.

Over time, Blender became the foundation of both our real and virtual works.

After the collaboration with Stefania Albertini concluded, I carried this approach forward into my individual practice.

It now functions as a bridge between traditional sculpture and immersive digital practices.

Beyond individual use, my engagement with Blender also extended to teaching and training, where open-source tools provided not only technical resources but also a shared cultural and pedagogical framework.

This commitment was also acknowledged through my role as a Blender Foundation Certified Trainer (BFCT), as shown in the official certificate in Figure 4-9.[21]

---

[20] You can find some more videos on my YouTube channel at `https://www.youtube.com/@GiugiogiaAuer`.

[21] Note: The author, Gianpiero Moioli, was a Blender Foundation Certified Trainer (BFCT) during the period 2008–2011 (when the original program was officially discontinued). For training, the Blender Foundation provides free resources like the official Manual, tutorials, and Blender Studio courses, while encouraging community contributions via the bf-education group—no formal certifications are offered anymore.

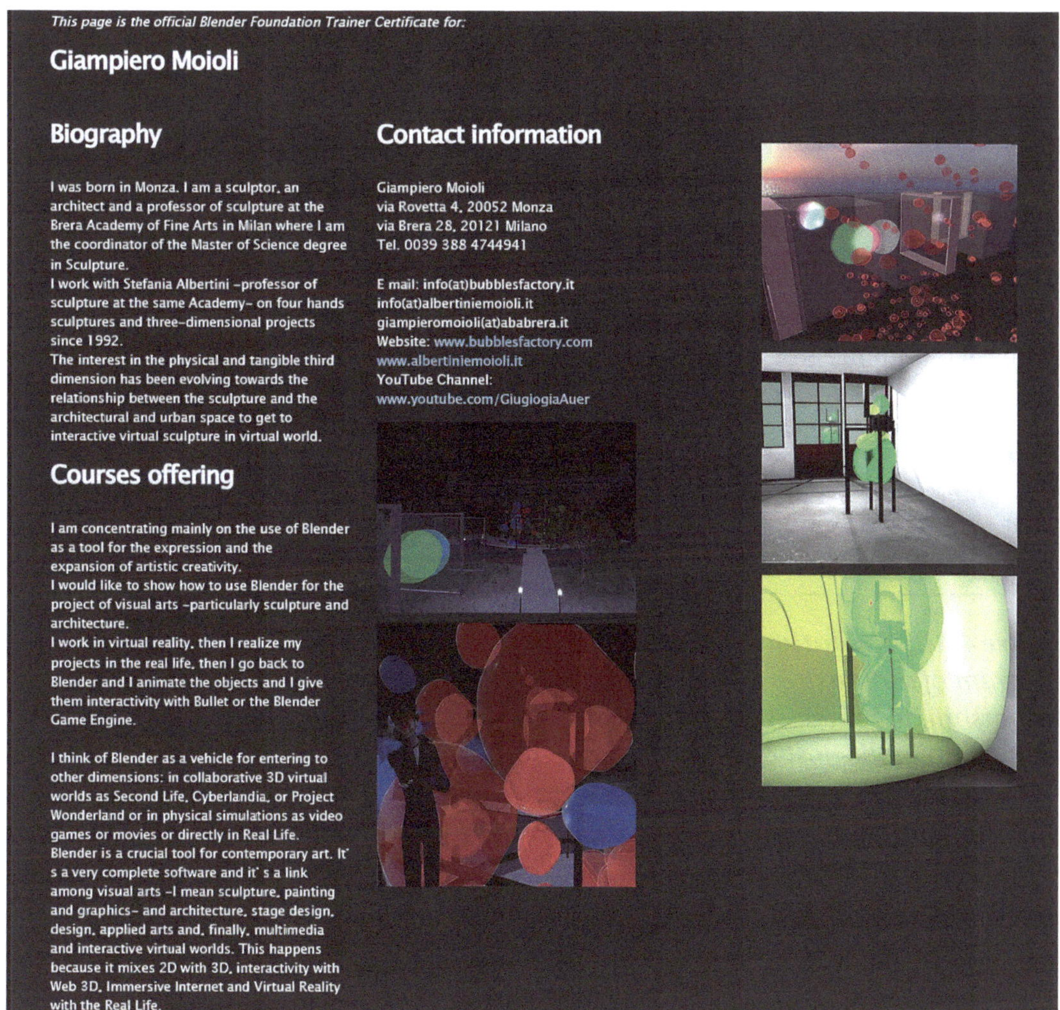

This page is the official Blender Foundation Trainer Certificate for:

Giampiero Moioli

Biography

I was born in Monza. I am a sculptor, an architect and a professor of sculpture at the Brera Academy of Fine Arts in Milan where I am the coordinator of the Master of Science degree in Sculpture.
I work with Stefania Albertini -professor of sculpture at the same Academy- on four hands sculptures and three-dimensional projects since 1992.
The interest in the physical and tangible third dimension has been evolving towards the relationship between the sculpture and the architectural and urban space to get to interactive virtual sculpture in virtual world.

Courses offering

I am concentrating mainly on the use of Blender as a tool for the expression and the expansion of artistic creativity.
I would like to show how to use Blender for the project of visual arts -particularly sculpture and architecture.
I work in virtual reality, then I realize my projects in the real life, then I go back to Blender and I animate the objects and I give them interactivity with Bullet or the Blender Game Engine.

I think of Blender as a vehicle for entering to other dimensions: in collaborative 3D virtual worlds as Second Life, Cyberlandia, or Project Wonderland or in physical simulations as video games or movies or directly in Real Life.
Blender is a crucial tool for contemporary art. It' s a very complete software and it' s a link among visual arts -I mean sculpture, painting and graphics- and architecture, stage design, design, applied arts and, finally, multimedia and interactive virtual worlds. This happens because it mixes 2D with 3D, interactivity with Web 3D, Immersive Internet and Virtual Reality with the Real Life.

Contact information

Giampiero Moioli
via Rovetta 4, 20052 Monza
via Brera 28, 20121 Milano
Tel. 0039 388 4744941

E mail: info(at)bubblesfactory.it
info(at)albertiniemoioli.it
giampieromoioli(at)ababrera.it
Website: www.bubblesfactory.com
www.albertiniemoioli.it
YouTube Channel:
www.youtube.com/GiugiogiaAuer

Figure 4-9. BFCT Certificate.
My official Blender Foundation Certified Trainer (BFCT) certificate, including biography, teaching profile, and examples of projects developed with Blender (2008)

The implications go beyond software: they resonate with broader transformations in contemporary art, where authorship is increasingly distributed across networks of contributors, remix practices, and generative systems.

From here, the discussion naturally moves toward the notion of **post-authorship**, which will be addressed in the following section.

4.2.4 Generative Practices and Post-Authorship

Building on the open-source ethos exemplified by Blender, generative practices extend the notion of shared authorship from tools to artworks themselves.

New creative practices like generative art and algorithmic creation are pushing the concept of authorship into uncharted territory.

In generative art, the artist doesn't produce a single finished piece directly; instead, it creates a **system, set of rules, or algorithm** that can generate artworks, often with some degree of randomness or autonomy (Figure 4-10).

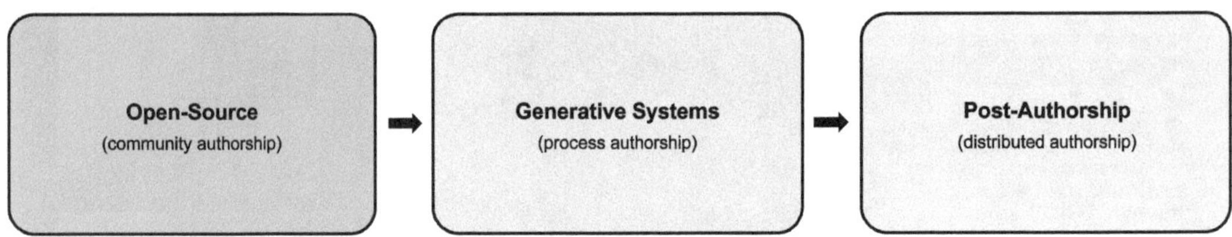

Figure 4-10. Evolution of Authorship in Generative Art.
Diagram of authorship in generative art: from open-source and community authorship, to process-based authorship in generative systems, to distributed authorship in the post-authorship scenario

In this post-authorship scenario, who "owns" the work or the creative output?

The question of rights becomes complex. If an algorithm creates a thousand images based on an artist's code, is each image individually authored by the artist, or by the algorithm, or jointly?

Some generative artists have addressed this by using open licenses, effectively saying anyone can use these outputs, as the concept of a singular authorship is less relevant.

Others use **smart contracts on blockchain** to embed rules for usage and royalties directly into the generative system.

For instance, a smart contract might ensure that whenever a generative piece is resold, a percentage automatically goes back to the original artist, acknowledging their indirect authorship role.

This kind of automated rights management means the code itself helps govern authorship and compensation, reducing the need for external enforcement.

Generative art highlights a shift from owning a static art object to engaging with a dynamic art system.

The artist's role becomes more like a composer or a designer of a process, rather than a crafter of a single artifact.

The identity of each artwork in a generative series may be less important than the identity of the underlying system and concept.

We start to see the artwork as an "open field of potentialities" a range of possible outputs and variations rather than one fixed image or object.

This blurs the boundaries between creation and reproduction. If an artwork can endlessly produce new forms, the line between an original and a copy loses meaning.

A striking prefiguration of these dynamics can be found in Maurizio Cattelan's *Comedian* (2019), the banana duct-taped to a wall and sold at Art Basel Miami.

The work itself was ephemeral and reproducible, yet its market value resided entirely in the accompanying certificate of authenticity rather than in the perishable fruit.

Indeed, the banana does not even need to be reproduced; it is produced by nature itself, underscoring that the "artwork" resides not in the object, but in the artist's act of selection and in the contractual and conceptual system that legitimizes it.[22]

In this sense, Comedian did not anticipate NFTs[23] as it highlighted the same logic on which they are based: the object is infinitely replaceable, but authorship and value are anchored in a contract that defines ownership.[24]

In *Comedian*, the buyer does not purchase the banana itself but a certificate of authenticity issued by the Perrotin gallery.

This document includes precise instructions on how to install and maintain the work, from the type of duct tape to the replacement of the fruit.

The gesture places Cattelan within a lineage that runs from Duchamp to Sol LeWitt. The work lies in a conceptual and contractual act, while its material component is merely a temporary expression.

What changes in the digital era is not the logic but the medium that sustains it.

Digital artists now encode authorship and ownership through algorithms and smart contracts.

---

[22] This shift from object to decision recalls Marcel Duchamp's *ready-mades*, where the artist's act of selection replaced manual creation as the source of artistic meaning.

[23] *Comedian by Cattelan is not a case of "pre-NFT thinking," since NFTs already existed, with CryptoPunks in 2017 and SuperRare in 2018, to name two examples.*

[24] The work was also acquired by Justin Sun, founder of Tron and already active in the crypto world, thus confirming the direct connection between Cattelan's conceptual performance and the dynamics of digital collecting.

The same mechanism of validation migrates from the gallery to the blockchain, from the physical signature to cryptographic verification.

Within this framework, authorship becomes shared and iterative.

The artist is no longer the sole originator of form but a facilitator who defines the rules of a system and sets creativity in motion.

Questions of authorship evolve into questions of governance. Who controls the parameters, who may modify them, and who benefits from the process?

Creative Commons licenses offer models for sharing, while blockchain protocols trace provenance and distribute ownership or revenue.

The result is a networked conception of creation, where artist, audience, and machine contribute together to the work's ongoing life.

Ultimately, artificial intelligence pushes this paradigm to its limit. Is the author the artist, the algorithm, or the collective memory embedded in data?

This unresolved question marks the current frontier of creativity in the digital age.

4.3 Blockchain and NFTs: New Paradigms of Authenticity

Before analyzing their artistic implications, it is useful to explain what we mean by blockchain, fungible tokens, and NFTs through simple images.

A **blockchain** can be imagined as a great collective notebook, shared and copied across thousands of computers at once.

Each time someone adds a page, that page is permanently sealed and attached to the previous ones so that the story cannot be erased or rewritten. Unlike a private archive, this notebook is public, transparent, and practically impossible to falsify, an incorruptible memory.[25]

A **fungible token** works like money.

[25] A blockchain is a decentralized, distributed ledger technology that records transactions across a network of computers in a secure, transparent, and tamper-resistant way. Each transaction is grouped into a block, which is cryptographically linked to the previous one, forming an immutable chain. Once validated through consensus mechanisms (such as Proof of Work or Proof of Stake), data cannot be altered without changing all subsequent blocks, making falsification practically impossible. This structure makes blockchain particularly suitable for guaranteeing provenance, authenticity, and traceability in contexts such as digital art, supply chains, and financial transactions.

One euro coin is worth the same as another euro coin, and we can exchange them without distinction. The same applies to cryptocurrencies such as Bitcoin. Each unit is interchangeable with another. Its value lies precisely in being identical and substitutable.[26]

An **NFT**, instead, is more like an autograph on a book or a unique collector's card. The content—a novel, an image, a digital file—can be copied infinitely, but the autograph or the card remains unique, tied to a specific owner.

An NFT is essentially this digital autograph: a certificate on the blockchain that says, "This file belongs to you," even though millions can look at or duplicate the image.

Its function is not to prevent copying but to establish originality and ownership.[27]

With these concepts clarified, we can better understand how blockchain and NFTs have introduced a radical shift in art: a reversal of the logic of infinite reproducibility.

If Walter Benjamin spoke of the loss of the aura in the age of mechanical reproduction, NFTs attempt to reintroduce aura into the digital domain, creating uniqueness where everything seemed destined to be endlessly multiplied.

It is worth noting that the concepts of uniqueness and originality vary across different art forms.

In literature, a novel has one author, yet countless identical copies circulate freely without diminishing its authorship.

In music, the score or recording may be endlessly reproduced, but its originality still lies in the composer or performer.

Contemporary art, through blockchain and NFTs, seems to be moving closer to these models: the value no longer resides in the material singularity of the object, but in the recognition of authorship and the framework that defines it.

[26] A fungible token is a digital asset whose units are interchangeable and identical in value. Like money or cryptocurrencies such as Bitcoin and Ether, one token can always be exchanged for another of the same type without loss or difference. Their value lies precisely in their substitutability.

[27] An NFT is a unique, indivisible digital asset recorded on a blockchain. Unlike fungible tokens, each NFT has a distinct identity and metadata that certify its originality and ownership. NFTs are widely used in digital art, collectibles, and virtual assets, functioning as certificates of authenticity and provenance rather than preventing duplication of the underlying file.

4.3.1 Blockchain as Certification and the NFT Paradox

Blockchain is essentially a public, immutable ledger, a database spread across many computers that securely records transactions and information.

In the art world, this technology is being used to guarantee authenticity and provenance of digital works.

When an artist 'mints' a work as an NFT on a blockchain, they create an immutable record (the token) that contains metadata about the work and a reference to where the digital file is stored. Critically, the NFT and the artwork file are separate: the token is permanently recorded on blockchain, but the artwork file's longevity depends on how and where it is hosted.

Thanks to the transparency and tamper-resistant nature of the blockchain, that record cannot be easily changed or forged, giving the work a lasting mark of authenticity.

For example, platforms like Verisart[28] allow artists to officially certify physical or digital artworks on the blockchain, creating a verifiable provenance record accessible to anyone.[29]

This kind of certification is not limited to art: luxury brands have formed the Aura Blockchain Consortium[30] to similarly track product authenticity from creation to sale.

In the realm of digital art, blockchain tackles the medium's core paradox: how can a file that can be copied infinitely ever be considered "unique"? By enforcing verifiable digital scarcity through NFTs and smart contracts, blockchain re-creates—artificially—the conditions of traditional art markets. Yet the very need for scarcity remains deeply contested. Many digital artists argue that the true spirit of Internet culture lies in open distribution, attribution, and collective access rather than artificial exclusivity and private ownership. This tension—between the digital commons and the logic of property—is one of the most significant cultural debates sparked by the rise of blockchain-based art.

---

[28] Founded in 2015, *Verisart* is a platform that certifies artworks on the blockchain. It generates a digital certificate of authenticity linked to the work, recording authorship, provenance, and ownership in a tamper-proof way. This allows artists and collectors to verify the history and authenticity of both physical and digital pieces.

[29] As of 2025, Verisart offers both free (limited) and paid subscription certificates, primarily utilizing the Bitcoin blockchain for timestamping. Artists should consider whether these paid certification services, which often include enhanced platform features, metadata management, and smart contract tools, offer advantages over free, basic blockchain timestamping services for their specific use case.

[30] The Aura Blockchain Consortium is a nonprofit platform founded in 2021 by LVMH, Prada, and Cartier. It uses blockchain to provide each luxury product with a secure digital identity, ensuring traceability, authenticity, and transparency throughout its lifecycle

NFTs are the answer that has gained the most traction.

An NFT is not the artwork file itself but rather a token that refers to the artwork and asserts ownership of it.

Think of the NFT as a title deed or certificate for the artwork.

The **NFT paradox** is that the token is unique, but the underlying work—an image, video, etc.—might be freely copyable by anyone.

When someone buys an NFT artwork, what they truly buy is the exclusive blockchain-backed proof of ownership of that work. They do not automatically gain copyright or control over all copies of the image.

As one legal commentary puts it, "When someone purchases an NFT, they buy the digital certificate of authenticity, but they do not own the copyright or the right to reproduce it."[31]

The NFT transfers the **aura of originality**, via the token, without stopping the digital file from being duplicated.

This is a paradox because it flips our intuitive understanding. The image that can be seen and saved by anyone is not what's scarce; the invisible token is what's scarce.

Yet this has proven to be a workable model, collectors value the NFT as the sign of true ownership.

In effect, blockchain confers a new kind of aura on digital art: the aura of the authenticated token.

An artwork's presence in the blockchain ledger becomes analogous to Benjamin's idea of presence in time and space.

The art still exists everywhere as a copy, but only one manifestation is cryptographically marked as **"the original"** in the eyes of the market and community. This re-uniquifying of digital art means that even in an age of perfect copies, we have reintroduced a concept of "the one." It just lives on a blockchain rather than in a single physical object.

[31] "When someone purchases an NFT, they buy the digital certificate of authenticity, but they do not own the copyright or the right to reproduce it." —from the article "What You Need to Know About NFT Agreements," published June 8, 2022. `https://contiguglia.com/blog/what-you-need-to-know-about-nft-agreements/`

4.3.2 Provenance, Markets, and Disintermediation

Beyond establishing uniqueness, blockchain also revolutionizes provenance tracking and the structure of art markets.

When an NFT is transferred directly between wallets on the blockchain (peer-to-peer), that transaction is permanently recorded in the public ledger. However, many NFT trades occur on centralized exchanges where ownership may be managed in private databases. Additionally, reading blockchain provenance requires technical knowledge interpreting raw transaction data on a block explorer like Etherscan is not intuitive for most art collectors.[32]

This level of transparency is unprecedented in the art world. Traditionally, provenance could be murky, documents could be lost or forged, and experts were needed to verify chains of ownership.

With NFTs, the ledger itself provides an instant provenance trail: anyone can see the list of owners back to the creator, simply by inspecting the token's history.

This helps combat forgery and theft; a buyer can verify if the NFT truly originated from the legitimate artist and see if an artwork is authentic in seconds.

Blockchain technology also reduces the need for intermediaries in transactions, a process known as *disintermediation*.

In a blockchain-based art ecosystem, artists and buyers can transact directly.

Smart contracts can include royalty terms, but enforcement depends on the marketplace respecting these terms.

Recent market competition has led some platforms to make creator royalties optional, highlighting that smart contract royalties are not automatically or universally enforced. The effectiveness of automated royalties remains dependent on the infrastructure through which NFTs are traded.[33]

This questions the traditional roles of galleries, auction houses, or notaries.

If a piece of art carries its own digital proof of authenticity, one might not need a gallery's reputation or a third-party appraiser to establish trust.

---

[32] To view an NFT's complete provenance: (1) find the token's contract address and ID, (2) view on Etherscan.io or similar blockchain explorer, and (3) interpret the transaction history noting that transfers to exchange wallets may represent sales that are then handled off-chain.

[33] *Smart contracts* are self-executing programs on the blockchain. They automatically carry out agreed rules—such as transferring ownership or paying royalties—without the need for intermediaries.

As a report on this trend noted, "Creators and audiences can engage in direct, secure, and certified transactions without the need for galleries, auction houses, or notaries, since everything is recorded on a distributed public ledger."[34]

In other words, the blockchain itself acts as the trusted ledger, replacing functions previously served by art dealers and institutions.

Of course, major auction houses have not stood idle; they have embraced NFTs to maintain relevance.

Sotheby's and Christie's have held high-profile NFT auctions, demonstrating that even the intermediaries can adapt by facilitating NFT sales.

For example, Christie's record-breaking auction of an NFT collage in March 2021 signaled that the traditional art world was willing to validate blockchain-certified art at the highest level.

Sotheby's, similarly, launched its own digital platform and sold collections of hundreds of NFT artworks in innovative formats.

Sotheby's entered the NFT market in April 2021 with Pak's The Fungible (USD 16.8 million) and, six months later, launched Sotheby's Metaverse with the curated sale Natively Digital 1.2 (USD 18.7 million). These record-breaking auctions established the house as a leading institutional force in digital art. After 2022, however, Sotheby's quietly discontinued its dedicated Metaverse platform and now includes NFTs only occasionally within its broader contemporary-art sales.

These events had a profound cultural impact, marking the moment when digital art entered the prestigious art market on its own terms.

Together, they demonstrated that verifiable digital authenticity could sustain markets and prices once reserved for physical masterpieces.

---

[34] "NFTs are often compared to digital certificates of ownership. The certificate, in the form of data recorded on a blockchain, signifies ownership of an associated digital item not contained in the data itself...." — U.S. Congressional Research Service, *Non-Fungible Tokens and Intellectual Property: A Report to Congress*, March 12, 2024. `https://www.myartbroker.com/art-and-tech/articles/blockchain-tech-authentication-in-art`

4.3.3 Environmental Considerations for Artists

While blockchain brings opportunities, it also introduces new challenges and risks. Environmental concerns arose due to the high energy consumption of early blockchain protocols, though later improvements—such as Ethereum's 2022 transition to proof-of-stake—have helped to mitigate this impact.

Artists engaging with blockchain must weigh its environmental implications against its benefits, particularly as sustainability becomes a core ethical concern in cultural production. The energy demands of PoW systems have drawn widespread criticism, but PoS alternatives and mitigation strategies offer pathways forward.

Figure 4-11 provides a comparative overview of annual energy consumption for major blockchains commonly used in NFT minting and provenance, highlighting the dramatic variance between proof-of-work and proof-of-stake models (data aggregated from 2025 estimates, normalized to TWh/year).[35]

Blockchain	Estimated Annual Consumption	Environmental Impact
Ethereum (PoS)	≈ 0.01 TWh	Green
Tezos	≈ 0.0006 TWh	Green
Algorand	≈ 0.0002 TWh	Green (carbon-negative)
Polygon (Layer 2)	≈ 0.0003 TWh	Green
Solana	≈ 0.001–0.002 TWh	Green/Yellow
Flow	≈ 0.001 TWh	Green
Bitcoin (PoW)	150–200 TWh	Red

Figure 4-11. Estimated Annual Energy Consumption of Selected Blockchains (2025).
The figure compares the estimated annual electricity consumption of the blockchains most commonly used for NFT minting and digital provenance

Green indicates negligible or carbon-negative consumption; yellow marks very low but still measurable impact; red signals extremely energy-intensive networks.

[35] Data for 2025 aggregated from Cambridge Centre for Alternative Finance, Ethereum Energy Consumption Index, TRF Carbon Ratings Institute, and the official sustainability reports of the respective foundations.

For artists, the practical guidance is straightforward. When environmental impact matters, prioritize energy-efficient PoS blockchains such as Ethereum (post-Merge), Tezos, Algorand, Polygon, or Flow. Leading platforms including SuperRare, Foundation, Zora, and Manifold now default to these low-carbon chains, while tools like ScoreDetect and OpenTimestamps offer near-zero-impact timestamping on Ethereum Layer 2 or Bitcoin calendars.

The debate nevertheless persists. Even the most efficient networks consume energy for transactions that are often speculative and may not produce lasting cultural value, prompting legitimate questions about whether blockchain is necessary for every form of digital art.

In response, several platforms have introduced robust carbon-offset programs—Tezos funds on-chain climate initiatives, Algorand has been carbon-negative since 2021 through verified offsets, and others support reforestation or renewable-energy certificates—allowing artists to neutralize their emissions entirely.

Market volatility remains another critical challenge; the 2021 hype cycle demonstrated both meteoric rises and precipitous collapses in NFT prices.

Nonetheless, the deeper paradigm shift is undeniable and enduring. In a direct reversal of Benjamin's diagnosis, we are moving from infinite multiplicativity to re-uniquization. Blockchain has made possible the creation of digital singularities—assets that carry verifiable authenticity, scarcity, and provenance in ways that echo the aura of the physical original, thereby profoundly redefining what it means to collect, own, and transmit art in the digital age.

4.3.4 Reproducible Certification Protocol

It is one thing to recognize the theoretical possibility of a renewed digital aura; it is quite another to implement it with rigor and transparency in actual creative practice. The present work therefore adopts a fully reproducible cryptographic certification protocol that turns the abstract promises of blockchain provenance into a concrete, verifiable reality. Every step—from the initial AI generation to the final production-ready mesh—is bound by an unbroken chain of SHA-256 hashes, with optional anchoring to the Bitcoin blockchain through OpenTimestamps.

Full technical details and open-source code are provided in Appendix A (for Ethical, Legal, and Provenance Implications of the Certification Protocol, see Appendix G in Chapter 5).

4.3.5 Case Studies and Cultural Impact

The interaction of NFTs with the art world has been exemplified by several key case studies, which also highlight the broader cultural impact of this technology.

The arrival of NFTs in the institutional art world is best measured by two watershed moments that occurred within weeks of each other in 2021.

The first—already emblematic of the new economic model described earlier—was Christie's sale on March 11, 2021, of Beeple's *Everydays: The First 5000 Days* for $69.3 million (Figure 4-12). At the time this was the third-highest price ever achieved by a living artist (after Jeff Koons and David Hockney).[36]

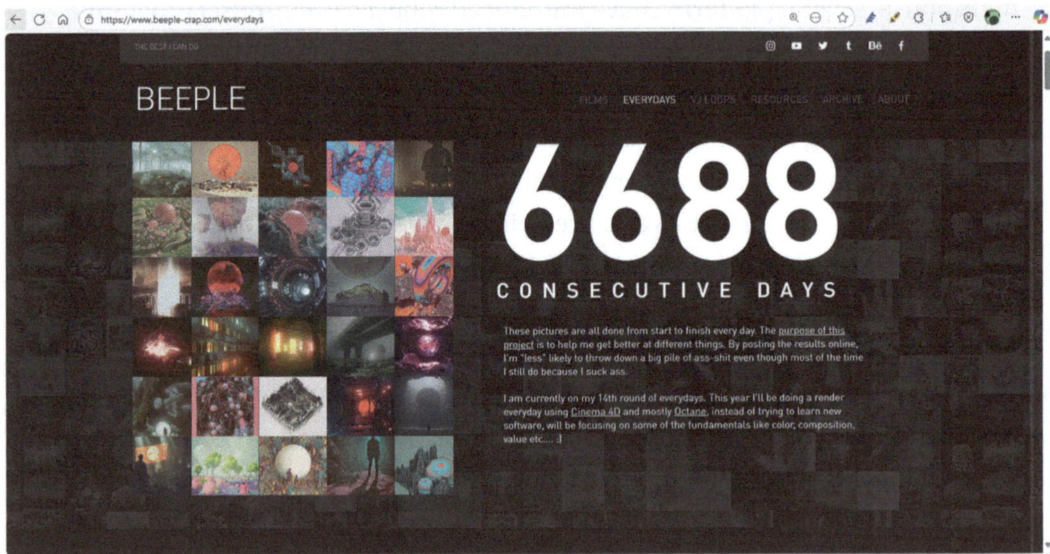

Figure 4-12. Beeple's Website.
Screenshot from Beeple's official website (beeple-crap.com), showing the Everydays project with 6,688 consecutive daily works. This long-term practice, begun in 2007, has later culminating in the famous Everydays: The First 5000 Days NFT auction

[36] The auction's resonance was amplified and complicated by several crucial factors. (1) The buyer, MetaKovan (Vignesh Sundaresan), was later revealed as a crypto entrepreneur who owned tokens from his Metapurse project (B.20), which included fractional ownership of Beeple works, raising conflict-of-interest concerns as B.20's value surged 6,000% post-sale. (2) The sale accepted cryptocurrency (Ether), marking Christie's first major crypto transaction. (3) It sparked debates on whether this represented genuine art market validation or crypto bubble speculation.

Sotheby's soon followed, curating innovative digital-native auctions, such as the sale of hundreds of tokenized drawings presented as unique editions.

Their first NFT sale, in collaboration with the artist Pak, fetched more than $16 million, demonstrating both the scalability of NFT formats and the willingness of traditional institutions to embrace blockchain.

These auctions showed that the prestige economy of art was shifting, owning a notable NFT could carry as much cultural capital as owning a renowned painting, since ownership is public and value is transparent.

Beyond these high-end sales, NFTs empowered a wider range of creators.

Artists who previously struggled to monetize digital works found new revenue streams by minting NFTs, while communities emerged around collections like CryptoPunks or Bored Ape Yacht Club, blending art, pop culture, and identity.

This democratization of collecting, coupled with speculative enthusiasm, blurred boundaries between art, finance, and social networks.

Importantly, these cases forced new debates about authenticity and ownership in culture. When an NFT of a tweet, meme, or viral image can be sold, it challenges conventional ideas of what creative expressions can be "owned."

The cultural impact of NFTs thus extends beyond art institutions. It reshapes intellectual property debates, expands who can be a collector, and merges art with the ethos of tech culture.

4.4 Authenticity Across Time

Authenticity in art is a question that has continuously evolved.

This section situates today's changes in a broader perspective by recalling historical precedents, considering how the notion of authorship might evolve in the future, and examining how authenticity frameworks are also applied beyond the art world.

We will look at examples where authenticity and originality were legally or institutionally managed—showing that aura can be preserved or even constructed—before imagining future scenarios in the age of AI and networks.

4.4.1 Historical Precedents

Long before the advent of digital reproduction, artists and institutions confronted the challenge of preserving an artwork's authenticity and aura through time.

A particularly illuminating case is that of Auguste Rodin.

When he died in 1917, Rodin bequeathed to the Musée Rodin his entire estate, including thousands of models, molds, and plasters, as well as the legal rights to his work.

By decree of the French state, the museum was granted exclusive authority to supervise the production of posthumous bronzes.

According to French law,[37] each authorized edition is limited to 12 casts, ensuring that new bronzes remain "originals" within the framework of authenticity.[38]

This legal and institutional system was designed both to preserve the integrity of Rodin's oeuvre and to disseminate his art through controlled reproduction: a practice that continues today under the museum's supervision.

The case of *The Thinker* (*Le Penseur*) exemplifies this complexity.

First conceived in 1880 as part of The Gates of Hell, the work was realized in a small model around 1880–81, and by 1902–1904 it had taken monumental form.

The first large bronze cast, produced by the Alexis Rudier Foundry, was exhibited in Paris in 1904 (Figure 4-13).

[37] Decree no. 93-163 of 2 February 1993, art. 2.5, codified in Article R. 122-3 of the Intellectual Property Code, limits authorized posthumous bronze editions of Rodin's sculptures to twelve casts in total: eight numbered editions offered for sale and four artist's proofs reserved for public collections.

[38] On Rodin's posthumous bronzes, see Musée Rodin, *Original bronze casts*, Musée Rodin official website, accessed August 22, 2025; https://www.musee-rodin.fr/en/museum/institution/original-bronze-casts; Alexander Nemerov, interview in Stanford News, "What Makes a Rodin a Rodin? Stanford Scholar Explains the Famed Sculptor's Process," July 2020, https://news.stanford.edu/stories/2020/07/makes-rodin-rodin-stanford-scholar-explains-famed-sculptors-process; NPR/CapRadio, "Rodin's Bronzes: Original, Copy or Both?," June 2020, https://www.capradio.org/news/npr/story?storyid=900006469.

Figure 4-13. Auguste Rodin, The Thinker.
The Thinker by Auguste Rodin, located in the garden of the Musée Rodin, Paris. Posthumous bronze cast (produced after 1917, the year of Rodin's death. Made under the legal authorization granted to the museum.By AndrewHorne (talk), Public Domain, Wikimedia Commons

This cast, personally supervised by Rodin, is currently located at the Musée Rodin in Paris and is identifiable by the foundry mark "Alexis Rudier Fondeur Paris" stamped on the back of the figure, along with Rodin's signature "A. Rodin" and a patina typical of Rudier's early 20th-century work (dark brown with greenish highlights, applied under Rodin's direct oversight).[39]

After Rodin's death, authorized casts continued to be produced by selected foundries and under the Musée Rodin's supervision.

Over the 20th century and beyond, dozens of casts have been realized, each with its own casting record. Determining the exact year of a given example—such as those at the Musée Rodin or the Metropolitan Museum of Art—depends on identifying its specific record.[40]

Although made decades after Rodin's death, these casts are still considered authentic artworks because they derive from the original molds and are legally sanctioned.

Here authenticity is less an inherent quality than a legal and institutional construct.[41]

The aura of Rodin's work has thus been extended through documentation, rights, and controlled production, not solely through the artist's direct hand.

This precedent highlights the flexibility of the notion of "original."

In Rodin's case, the medium of bronze already implied multiples, and authenticity was determined by the authority of the French state, which in 1916 accepted Rodin's bequest and later established legal limits on posthumous casts.

---

[39] Worldwide, there are *approximately* 28 monumental bronze casts of Rodin's *The Thinker*—life-size or larger—produced either during the artist's lifetime or posthumously under the legal authority of the Musée Rodin. In addition to these large-scale versions, numerous smaller bronzes and plasters were made from Rodin's original models over the decades.

Because each casting has its own documented history, the total number of authenticated versions varies across catalogs, but specialists consistently recognize *The Thinker* as one of the most widely disseminated sculptures in modern art, despite its production remaining strictly regulated under French law (maximum 12 posthumous casts per model).

[40] For a detailed chronology: 1880 conceived as part of The Gates of Hell; 1880-1881 first small plaster model; 1902-1904 enlargement to monumental scale; 1904 first monumental bronze cast by Alexis Rudier Foundry, exhibited in Paris; 1917 upon Rodin's death, the Musée Rodin was granted legal rights to authorize posthumous casts; 1917-present numerous authorized casts produced by foundries including Rudier, Godard, and Coubertin, under museum supervision.

[41] The authenticity of posthumous casts remains debated within the art world. While legally sanctioned casts are considered "original" under French law, the art market makes significant price distinctions between lifetime casts (cast during Rodin's lifetime, typically valued three to five times higher) and posthumous casts. Critics argue that posthumous casting lacks the artist's direct supervision and quality control. This debate parallels contemporary questions about posthumous prints from photographer's negatives or posthumous editions of design objects.

The same logic applies to printmakers and photographers, who traditionally produced limited editions.

Each impression is regarded as original if it has been authorized, numbered, and documented by the artist.

What determines authenticity is the artist's intention, the declared edition size, and the supporting documentation—such as certificates of authenticity, edition registers, and provenance records—that attest to the work's legitimacy.

Figure 4-14 illustrates this logic with a hand-retouched intaglio print.

Figure 4-14. Albertini & Moioli, Cell Culture, 2004.
Intaglio print, edition of four, each copy hand-retouched

In this case, the work exists in four copies, but the manual intervention on each impression enhances its individuality, blurring the line between unique piece and limited edition.

Other historical strategies to preserve aura include restoration practices and provenance documentation.

Museums and archives established trust by maintaining detailed ownership and exhibition records.

A painting accompanied by such provenance carried an enhanced aura, not just because of the object itself but because of its narrative continuity, its passage through history, collectors, and exhibitions.

This mirrors the role of metadata and blockchain records today. Provenance then was built through manual scholarship, whereas now technology can automate and secure it.

In summary, authenticity has never resided in the object alone.

It has always depended on a support system of rights, expert verification, and contextual narratives.

Practices such as authorized posthumous casts or certified limited editions anticipated today's digital authenticity tools.

They demonstrate that aura can be preserved—or even constructed—through authoritative control and certification, whether it comes in the form of a museum's stamp or a smart contract on Ethereum.

4.4.2 Future Authorship

Digital art blurs the line between physical and immaterial, challenging conventional ideas of an artwork's identity and the role of the author.

This section examines how artworks can exist as both tangible objects and code, how new licensing models allow hybrid forms of rights, and how generative practices push us toward a concept of post-authorship.

Authorship in the digital realm becomes fluid: it is tied not just to a single creator but to networks of contributors, code, and audiences.

In the previous sections we examined the transformations of authorship, authenticity, and rights in the digital era: from Creative Commons and open-source models to blockchain certification and generative practices.

In this final section, we shift the focus toward their convergence in practice: how these ideas come together in networked artworks and what their implications are for artists, institutions, and audiences today.

Figure 4-15 provides a visual map of this progression, from the traditional figure of the individual author to distributed and hybrid forms of authorship, and finally to the post-authorship paradigm shaped by AI and networks.

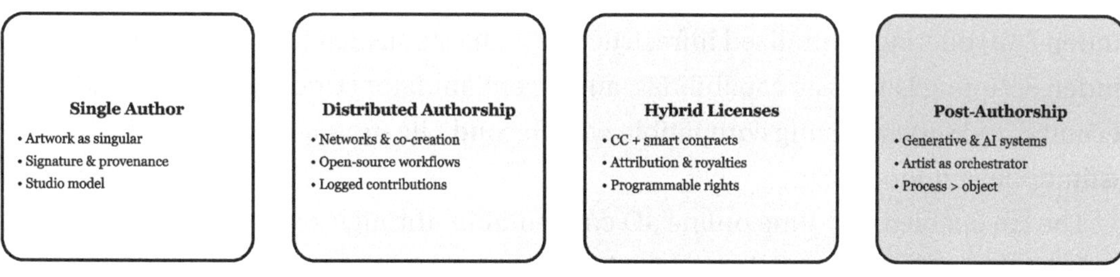

***Figure 4-15.** Identity, authorship, and post-authorship.*
From single authorship to distributed, hybrid, and generative models

4.4.2.1 Distributed Authorship and Open-Source Art

Looking to the future, authorship is likely to become increasingly distributed.

Works are no longer conceived as the product of a solitary artist but as the outcome of convergent processes involving many contributors.

This can take the form of community-driven projects, collaborative art in virtual worlds, or AI systems trained on vast datasets of human creativity.

Authorship, in this sense, becomes shared and fluid, with multiple agencies—human, machinic, and communal—shaping the final work.

The logic of open-source art exemplifies this: just as software evolves through countless edits and contributions. Artworks may be continually edited and remixed by communities. Blockchains could even log and certify each contribution, turning provenance into a multi-authored chain rather than a single point of origin.

4.4.2.2 Case Study: Brera Academy Virtual Lab (2008–2012)

A pioneering example of such distributed creativity was the Brera Academy Virtual Lab, launched in 2008 on the virtual platforms Second Life and OpenSim by Stefania Albertini and Gianpiero Moioli, professors at the Brera Academy of Fine Arts in Milan, together with Bruno Aliprandi, the Academy's technical director.[42]

The project utilized two distinct virtual world platforms: Second Life (proprietary, Linden Lab) offering centralized infrastructure with established user base and Linden Scripting Language capabilities, and OpenSimulator (Open Source) providing decentralized server hosting compatible with Second Life protocols but ensuring institutional autonomy.[43]

The lab enabled real-time online 3D collaboration through shared exhibitions, conferences, and workshops that merged the physical and the virtual, **allowing participants to co-create and shape works together in a shared digital space.**

A landmark event was Immersive Wor(l)ds (Milan, June 2012), staged simultaneously in the historic Salone Napoleonico of the Academy and on its virtual island in Second Life (Figure 4-16).

[42] Documented in the volume *Brera Academy Virtual Lab. Un viaggio dai mondi virtuali alla realtà aumentata nel segno dell'open source* (FrancoAngeli, 2010), edited by Gianpiero Moioli and Mario Gerosa, with a preface by Philippe Starck, the project is presented as an open and collective experiment in creativity.

See: `https://www.francoangeli.it/Libro/9788856825060/Brera-Academy-Virtual-Lab.-Un-viaggio-dai-mondi-virtuali-alla-realt%C3%A0-aumentata-nel-segno-dell'Open-source?id=18468`

[43] Technical context circa 2008-2012 included avatar-based real-time 3D interaction, in-world building tools using primitive shapes and sculpted prims, and interactive scripting capabilities, but faced significant limitations including graphics quality constraints, simultaneous user capacity of approximately 40–50 avatars per region, and bandwidth requirements limiting accessibility.

Figure 4-16. Immersive Wor(l)ds, streaming from the Salone Napoleonico of the Brera Academy of Fine Arts (Milan).
With simultaneous participation on the Academy's virtual island in Second Life, June 2012. The event exemplified the convergence of physical and digital presence, where avatars and audiences interacted in a shared performative space

Writers and visual artists created works inspired by literature, which were presented in parallel physical and virtual spaces, enabling avatars and in-person audiences to interact.

The project *Brera Academy Virtual Lab* thus became a performative experiment in distributed presence and hybrid authorship, as documented in the eponymous essay mentioned in note 43 (Figure 4-17).

Figure 4-17. Brera Academy Virtual Lab.
A Journey from Virtual Worlds to Augmented Reality in the Sign of Open Source (FrancoAngeli, 2010). The volume reflects on the implications of virtual worlds for art, design, and architecture, highlighting how the project was grounded in open-source principles and the freedom of licenses

The book emphasized how the initiative was rooted in open-source principles and in the freedom of licenses, framing the Virtual Lab not only as a pioneering artistic experiment but also as a critical reflection on collaborative creation in the digital age.

4.4.2.3 Hybrid Licenses and Smart Contracts

Future authorship may also be shaped by new licensing models.

Traditional copyright, often too rigid for collaborative environments, could be complemented by blockchain-based smart contracts[44] that automate recognition and compensation. Imagine a license that states: "Anyone can add to this artwork,

[44] Smart contracts are self-executing programs on a blockchain that automatically enforce agreements once predefined conditions are met. Introduced with Ethereum (2015), they are widely used in NFTs to automate royalties and rights management.

but all derivatives must credit prior contributors and share revenue with them." Such mechanisms combine the ethos of Creative Commons with the enforceability of blockchain, ensuring that co-creators are acknowledged and rewarded. Early examples can already be seen in NFT projects where token ownership grants the right to create derivative works, or where resale royalties automatically return to the original artist. This creates an evolving, community-owned framework of authorship.

However, while smart contracts can successfully automate revenue splitting (distributing NFT sale proceeds to multiple wallet addresses according to predefined percentages) and implement programmable royalty standards like ERC-2981, they face critical limitations that prevent them from functioning as comprehensive licensing systems. A more accurate description is that smart contracts can automate financial distribution within cooperating platforms according to predefined rules, while attribution, derivative detection, license compliance, and off-chain enforcement remain dependent on traditional copyright law, social norms, and community governance. They function best as complementary tools for streamlining transactions within communities that already share normative commitments to fair compensation, rather than as replacements for legal and social enforcement mechanisms.[45]

[45] However, it is crucial to recognize what smart contracts *cannot* do, thereby defining the true limits of code-enforced digital rights. Their limitations center on the inability of the code to interact meaningfully with the external, human world:

- They cannot verify off-chain compliance, as blockchain records wallet addresses, not human identities, and attribution occurs in social/cultural contexts code cannot monitor.
- They cannot detect derivative works, lacking any on-chain mechanism to identify visual similarity or conceptual borrowing.
- They cannot enforce cross-platform rules, as contract rules apply only within their specific blockchain and cooperating platforms, unable to prevent copying or commercial use elsewhere.
- They cannot verify share-alike provisions, making Creative Commons–style restrictions technically unenforceable through code alone.

Existing implementations reveal this reality: while platforms like Mirror.xyz enable functional revenue splitting for transactions within their ecosystem, royalty standards are often not universally honored by marketplaces (following the 2022–2023 enforcement crisis). Furthermore, derivative tracking remains non-functional, requiring manual declaration rather than technical verification.

4.4.2.4 Post-Authorship and AI

Generative practices and artificial intelligence further complicate the picture.

In generative art, the artist does not design a single final piece but creates a system or algorithm that generates endless variations.

Authorship is distributed between the human who writes the code, the machine that executes it, and sometimes the audience that interacts with it.

In this "post-authorship" scenario, the focus shifts from producing a static object to orchestrating processes and frameworks.

Questions of authorship become questions of governance: who controls the system, who can intervene, and who benefits from its outputs?

For instance, projects such as Refik Anadol's data-driven installations or the generative NFT platform Art Blocks exemplify this shift through distinct technical mechanisms.[46]

The artist designs the system's possibility space but cannot predetermine specific outcomes, shifting creative agency from executing a singular vision to orchestrating generative processes where human intentionality, computational logic, and (in some cases) collector participation converge to produce each unique instance.[47]

In this way, the "death of the author," to borrow Roland Barthes' phrase,[48] is not an end but a transformation. Creativity persists, but as a networked ecosystem sustained collectively by artists, machines, and communities.

---

[46] Refik Anadol's works (such as *Unsupervised*, 2022, displayed at MoMA) employ machine learning algorithms trained on institutional archives to generate ever-evolving data sculptures, where the artist designs the training parameters and aesthetic filters but the neural network produces forms emergent from dataset patterns.

[47] Art Blocks (launched 2020) operates through a different mechanism: artists upload generative code (typically JavaScript using p5.js library) stored on-chain. When collectors mint an NFT, the blockchain transaction hash serves as a pseudorandom seed input to the algorithm. This creates deterministic yet unpredictable outcomes (the same hash always produces identical output), but the hash itself is unknowable before minting. Notable examples include Tyler Hobbs' *Fidenza* (999 editions, 2021) and Snowfro's *Chromie Squiggle* (open edition, 2020), where each collector receives a unique artwork generated at the moment of purchase. The authorship distribution differs between models: Anadol's installations reflect ongoing machine interpretation of data, while Art Blocks creates fixed outputs co-determined by the artist's algorithm, blockchain randomness, and collector's minting action.

[48] Roland Barthes, "The Death of the Author," first published in Aspen, no. 5-6 (1967, published 1968); reprinted in Image-Music-Text, ed. and trans. Stephen Heath (New York: Hill and Wang, 1977).

4.4.3 Beyond Art

The concepts of authenticity, provenance, and aura that we've discussed are not confined to the art world.

In fact, digital certification systems are increasingly applied in other sectors—from luxury goods to everyday products—effectively extending the idea of an aura of authenticity to them. One prominent example is the luxury fashion industry. Companies are using blockchain to assure customers of the authenticity of high-end products like handbags, watches, or jewelry. The Aura Blockchain Consortium, founded by major luxury brands, creates a shared ledger where each product gets a "digital passport" recording its origin, materials, and ownership history.

A customer buying a designer purse can scan a code and see the entire lineage of that item, confirming it's not a knock-off.

In a sense, the luxury item gains a digital aura: an added layer of value coming from trust and transparency.

Beyond luxury, supply chains for food, wine, and other commodities are also adopting blockchain for authenticity and ethics.

For example, some vineyards now tag wine bottles with NFTs or blockchain codes to guarantee that a bottle of vintage wine is genuine and to provide provenance from grape to table.

Similarly, diamonds can be tracked on blockchain to ensure they are conflict-free, each stone carrying a record from mine to jeweler.

Interestingly, this broad adoption circles back to Benjamin's notion of aura in a new way.

For consumer products, an aura was traditionally conferred by brand prestige or craftsmanship.

Now, aura is being reconfigured as trust and transparency provided by technology. A luxury handbag might be one of thousands, not unique in a material sense, but if it has a secure digital identity that verifies it and perhaps even shows a personalized history, it gains an aura of uniqueness in the eyes of buyers.

The "mystique" is in the data attached to the item.

This demonstrates how aura the sense of specialness is being deliberately engineered through digital means outside of art.

Another area to mention is collectibles and media.

Sports leagues are selling video highlight clips as NFTs, giving a collectible aura to something that is otherwise just a video clip anyone can watch.

Fans buy the NFT because it's an official edition, numbered and signed by the blockchain, so to speak.

We also see experiments in literature and music such as authors releasing chapters as NFTs, musicians dropping limited digital albums with NFT liner notes.

All these create scarcity around digital content that normally would be infinitely replicable.

In summary, the innovations that were perhaps first tested in digital art, using blockchain to create authenticity and uniqueness, are now permeating various domains.

We are witnessing the rise of a "network of authenticity" that spans art, fashion, food, and more, where each object or piece of content can have a record making it special.

This broad application suggests that our entire culture is grappling with an overload of copies and information, and we're using technology to carve out pockets of authenticity and rarity.

The aura, once thought lost in mass production, is making a comeback in distributed form: a halo of data that travels with an item to vouch for it.

Thus, the boundaries of what is considered an "artwork" or a special artifact might expand, as anything with a certified story can claim a kind of aura in the digital age.

4.5 Toward a Networked Artwork and Practical Applications

In this final section, we bring together the concepts discussed so far under the notion of the networked artwork: art that takes shape, circulates, and is experienced within technological and social networks.

We examine how authorship becomes distributed across these ecosystems, outline practical applications of blockchain and digital platforms in creative fields, and reflect on how such changes are reshaping the aura of art for the future.

Essentially, this section bridges theory and practice: after exploring aura. Authenticity, and authorship in the digital age, we now turn to how artists and institutions actually implement these ideas.

4.5.1 Distributed Authorship and New Ecosystems

In a networked environment, the creation and meaning of art emerge as distributed processes.

Artworks are no longer the product of a single studio in isolation but take shape through interactions across online platforms, social media communities, and collaborations between artists and audiences.

Digital artists might share works in progress on forums or Discord, iterating publicly with feedback.

New ecosystems have arisen to support this model. Decentralized platforms allow several artists to contribute to a shared project, while collective NFT galleries distribute ownership among many investors.

In some generative art collections, collectors influence the final state of the work at purchase.

As Duchamp argued in *The Creative Act* (1957), the creative process is not carried out by the artist alone. The spectator completes the work by interpreting and giving it meaning.

This act of completion creates what Duchamp called the **"art coefficient"**: the differential between the artist's intention and the unintentional realization.

In this sense, artist and spectator act together as co-authors of the artwork, bringing it fully into existence.[49]

It is crucial to note that Duchamp's framework emphasized *hermeneutic participation* (meaning-making),[50] where spectators add value through reception, whereas contemporary distributed authorship (as in Art Blocks) involves collectors in the *technical generation process* itself.

---

[49] Marcel Duchamp, *The Creative Act,* lecture given at the Convention of the American Federation of Arts, Houston, April 1957, transcription at `https://www.ubu.com/papers/duchamp_creative.html`

[50] Duchamp's essay specifically states: "All in all, the creative act is not performed by the artist alone; the spectator brings the work in contact with the external world by deciphering and interpreting its inner qualifications and thus adds his contribution to the creative act." The distinction matters: Duchamp described hermeneutic participation (meaning-making, an epistemological level), while blockchain-based generative art enables ontological participation (work-making, a material/technical level). Both represent distributed authorship but operate at different levels.

This intuition resonates uncannily with the *Five-Way Portrait of Marcel Duchamp* (1917), a photographic experiment made at the Broadway Photo Shop in New York (Figure 4-18).

***Figure 4-18. Five-Way Portrait of Marcel Duchamp**, Portrait multiple de Marcel Duchamp), Broadway Photo Shop, New York City, 21 June 1917. By Anonymous National Portrait Gallery, Public Domain*

In this image, created through sequential exposures or a mirror arrangement, Duchamp multiplies his own likeness into five overlapping views, as if mocking the very idea of a singular, stable author.[51]

With his characteristic irony, Duchamp seems to anticipate the notion of distributed authorship: the author as a fractured, evolving figure whose identity is less fixed than it is dispersed across multiple presences.

In this way, the portrait becomes a playful prophecy of today's networked creativity, where authorship itself is fluid and collective.

[51] The image, a conceptual gesture disguised as a commercial studio portrait novelty, was achieved using a sequential portrait technique (likely multiple exposures on a single plate or mirror arrangement), creating five distinct profile and frontal views of Duchamp arranged in an overlapping composition.

This logic extends into virtual worlds and the metaverse. Platforms like *Second Life* or *Decentraland* host immersive environments where artworks change through visitor engagement and where multiple creators contribute to the same digital space.

For a detailed comparative analysis of the technical architectures, scripting systems, economies, and generative capabilities of these platforms, see Appendix B.

The result is a living gallery, never identical twice, shaped by an ongoing network of contributions.

In this sense, the artwork's "aura" or significance is no longer tied to a single origin story but distributed across many nodes in the network.

This shift invites us to value process over product, continuity over singularity.

It also challenges institutions to experiment with new attribution and economic models such as smart contracts that automatically split revenues among contributors.

Increasingly, the ecosystem itself becomes the "author," providing the fertile ground from which creative content continually grows.

4.5.2 Practical Applications Across Media and Platforms

Many of the concepts discussed so far are already being implemented in practice across diverse media and technological platforms.

The infrastructure of the digital art landscape is characterized by constant flux, and the platforms discussed here represent a snapshot as of the publication date.

Platform viability changes rapidly, often leading to the restructuring or outright discontinuation of services. Historical examples such as the closure of KnownOrigin's minting and on-chain marketplace (acquired by eBay) or the shifts in operations for early platforms like Nifty Gateway and Foundation illustrate this inherent instability.

This creates a paradox central to the field. While the blockchain offers immutable records of existence and ownership, the commercial platforms that host, display, and manage the associated artwork files (metadata and images) are impermanent, introducing significant risk to long-term content sustainability.

To better situate these dynamics, Figure 4-19 maps some of the most relevant platforms and tools through which concepts of authenticity and networked authorship are currently operationalized.

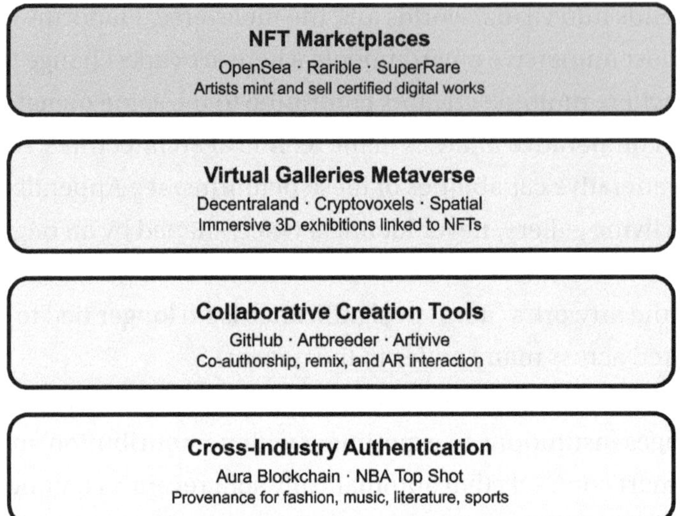

Figure 4-19. Practical applications across media and platforms. *These platforms show how authenticity and authorship are redefined across digital and physical media*

For an introductory critical caveat paragraph, see Appendix C.

From NFT marketplaces to collaborative platforms and cross-industry authentication systems, these examples show how the practices discussed so far are being concretely implemented across different media and technological domains.

The following examples illustrate how authenticity and networked authorship take form today:

- **NFT Marketplaces for Digital Art**

  Platforms such as OpenSea, Rarible, and SuperRare enable artists to mint NFTs for their digital artworks and sell them directly to collectors. These marketplaces handle blockchain interactions and provide storefronts.

  Artists upload files (images, 3D models, music, etc.) with embedded metadata (title, description, creator info), which are then linked to tokens on blockchains like Ethereum.

  Collectors purchase these tokens, which certify authenticity and ownership. This system bypasses traditional gatekeepers, allowing creators to monetize digital works that were previously difficult to sell.

- **Virtual Galleries and Metaverse Platforms**

  Virtual worlds such as Somnium Space, Cryptovoxels, or Spatial function as networked exhibition spaces.

  For an introductory critical caveat paragraph, see Appendix D.

  Artists and museums use these to stage immersive galleries where visitors, represented by avatars, experience art in 3D environments.

  Artworks can be linked to NFTs, allowing users to view blockchain certificates or even purchase pieces directly. These platforms also support collaborative events, such as opening receptions in VR, where artists and audiences interact in real time.

  > Exhibitions no longer unfold solely on the walls of physical galleries, but also within shared digital environments.
  >
  > In Decentraland, for instance, exhibitions are positioned within a vast online map of virtual parcels (Figure 4-20). The "location" of an exhibition is not a building but a node in a global network, persistently accessible to anyone with an Internet connection.

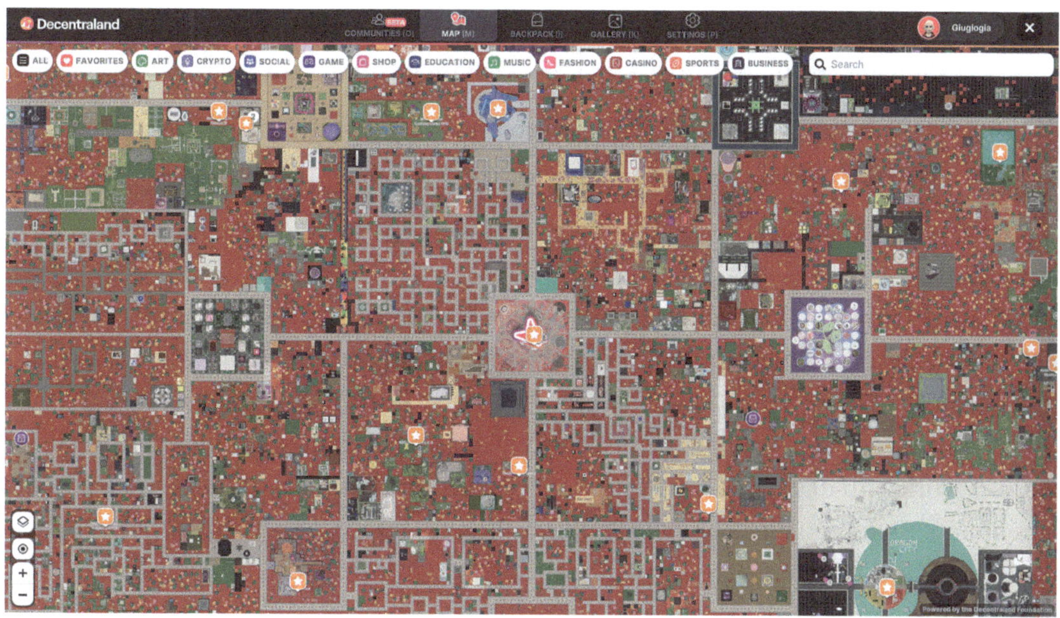

Figure 4-20. The world of Decentraland.
Screenshot of the Decentraland map, a virtual world where users can navigate immersive spaces, visit galleries, and interact with blockchain-linked exhibitions (©Decentraland, fair use for academic discussion)

- **Collaborative Creation Tools**

  A range of platforms encourage co-authorship. GitHub, originally designed for code, is used by digital artists to co-create works by sharing software, 3D assets, or procedural scripts.

  Artbreeder, an AI-based tool, allows users to collectively generate and remix images, where each image may have multiple "parents." Augmented reality apps like Artivive invite viewers to add digital layers or commentary to physical works, turning spectators into contributors.

  These collaborative tools highlight how creation can be iterative and distributed, with version control and licenses ensuring credit.

  For a detailed multiplatform analysis, see Appendix E.

- **Cross-Industry Authentication Systems**

  As we have just seen, the logic of authentication has expanded far beyond art.

  Blockchain turns verification into a universal grammar of value, allowing any object, image, or idea to claim its digital aura.

  The mechanisms once used to preserve artistic uniqueness are now scripting authenticity across the entire landscape of production.

In practice, adopting these technologies requires artists and institutions to develop new technical skills.

Museums now employ digital strategy teams to explore blockchain for collections and AR for exhibitions, while artists increasingly manage crypto wallets and metadata standards.

This convergence of art and technology is also a convergence of professions. Creators work with developers, galleries hire blockchain experts, and audiences become participants. Together, these practical applications are building the infrastructure for a new cultural era, where physical and digital, individual and collective, intersect in the making and experience of art.

4.5.3 The Reconfiguration of the Aura

Walter Benjamin described aura as the unique presence of an artwork in time and space.

In the digital age, this notion has not disappeared but undergone a profound reconfiguration.

This transformation shifts aura from the **mystical and distant**, which was based on reverence and ritual, to the **transparent and data-driven**, founded instead on trust in protocols and verifiable records.

Where Benjamin emphasized reverence and unapproachability, today aura often emerges from trust in protocols, consensus, and verifiable records. What once relied on tradition and ritual now requires transparency and certification.

Aura, however, is not only technical; it is also collectively produced.

A meme or a digital artwork gains aura through cultural recognition, circulation, and community engagement.

Projects like Nouns, for example, adopt a CC0 licensing model that actively encourages remix and reuse of the artwork, detaching the visual identity from exclusive control (Figure 4-21).[52]

Figure 4-21. Example of Noun.
Noun1 and Noun1562, part of the open-source, CC0-licensed Nouns project, where images are freely reusable and remixed while ownership and provenance are certified on-chain

[52] The Nouns project is an example of CC0 generative art, where each token is released with no copyright restrictions, allowing unlimited reuse and remix. See OpenSea: `https://opensea.io/blog/articles/nouns`

This open-source approach allows the visual brand to become ubiquitous, exponentially increasing the project's cultural presence and community ownership.

This demonstrates a crucial paradox: high valuation and cultural significance (aura) can be generated by broad circulation and open licensing, rather than by exclusivity or scarcity.

Once authenticated on-chain, this cultural aura merges with digital certification, creating significance beyond the image itself.

In digital culture, this creative agency expands. Aura is generated not just by artist and audience but by machines, networks, and markets that mediate and redistribute artistic presence.

A striking example is provided by generative platforms such as Art Blocks, where the artwork does not exist until the moment of purchase.

The buyer's minting action generates a unique variation from the artist's algorithm so that authorship is distributed between code, collector, and blockchain transaction.[53]

Aura is also increasingly distributed. Because a digital artwork can exist simultaneously across countless screens, its aura no longer depends on a singular physical location.

It emerges instead from the network: from recognition, consensus, and the shared belief in its significance.

An NFT does not owe its aura to aesthetic qualities alone but to its historical role and to the community's acknowledgment of its uniqueness.

In this sense, the aura of contemporary art is a fusion of old and new: a unique story of creation amplified by technology, reinforced by community, and preserved by consensus.

---

[53] On Art Blocks, each NFT is minted directly from an algorithm.

The collector's action determines the unique outcome. This process relies on the transaction hash serving as the seed input for the algorithm, ensuring deterministic but unpredictable outputs. Authorship is distributed across three stages: (1) The Artist (uploads the generative code), (2) The Collector (initiates the transaction and provides the unknowable hash seed), and (3) The Blockchain (executes the contract and stores the record). This reliance on a final, unknowable input clarifies the philosophical shift from fully deterministic (pre-designed) systems to systems co-determined by code and chance. Famous projects include *Chromie Squiggles* by Snowfro and *Fidenza* by Tyler Hobbs, where every mint yields a distinct generative artwork. (See for example *Chromie Squiggle*:

`https://opensea.io/item/ethereum/0x059edd72cd353df5106d2b9cc5ab83a52287ac3a/1455`

It is no longer the silent aura of a relic but the dynamic aura of a networked beacon, illuminating what it means for art to be authentic in a digitized and distributed cultural landscape.

4.6 Conclusions

Part I has shown that contemporary sculpture cannot be reduced to a simple opposition between tradition and innovation.

From Canova to Fontana, from the Lombard masters to digital and AI-driven practices, each step reveals a continuous dialogue between matter and immateriality, gesture, and code.

At the same time, the creative act itself is being reshaped by new tools. Modeling, simulation, and procedural design transform the sculptural process into a dynamic system capable of generating, evolving, and adapting forms.

The artist's gesture extends into algorithms, and the project becomes an evolving dialogue between intuition and computation.

The notion of *aura*, once bound to the unrepeatable presence of the artwork, now persists within digital networks as trust, recognition, and shared narrative.

What was once a silent, mystical quality becomes distributed and interactive yet still sustains a sense of singularity.

Crucially, the digital aura differs from Benjamin's concept. While the traditional mechanism relied on material presence and ritual, the digital relies on technical protocols, consensus, and verifiability.

This transformation raises critical questions for ongoing scholarship regarding authenticity, platform dependency, and the phenomenological immediacy of digital works.

This transformation—from *aura to network*, from *object to system*, from *gesture to code*—defines the threshold on which the next part of the book begins: the concrete techniques and creative processes through which **matter and code are now sculpted together.**

4.7 Appendix A: Reproducible Digital Certification Procedure

To ensure the authenticity, integrity, and full traceability of every asset throughout the entire generative pipeline—from the initial AI-generated output to the final production-ready 3D mesh—a rigorous cryptographic certification protocol based on hashing and timestamping is implemented.

The complete application of this protocol (including optional registration on a Distributed Ledger Technology such as a blockchain) is detailed in this appendix.

4.7.1 Cryptographic Hashing Method (Digital Fingerprint)

Every critical output (high-resolution image, prompt/parameter file,.obj or .stl mesh, etc.) must be processed with a cryptographic hash function.

- **Algorithm:** SHA-256 (Secure Hash Algorithm 256 bit), current industry standard.
- **Purpose:** Produces a unique, fixed-length alphanumeric identifier. Even a single-bit change in the file results in a completely different hash.

4.7.2 Timestamping and Chain Linking

The generated hash is immediately bound to a precise timestamp (date and exact time) and linked to the hash of the previous version (or the original source file).

- **Purpose:** Establishes an immutable chain of provenance and the exact chronological order of transformations.

4.7.3 Certified Digital Manifest (CDM) Format

The Certified Digital Manifest (CDM) is the formal output of this protocol, serving as the immutable Certificate of Provenance for the digital asset. Certification data for each new file (A) derived from a previous file (B) are stored in a standardized, machine- and human-readable format (JSON recommended). **The CDM contains all critical metadata fields necessary for cryptographic verification and legal compliance.**

Field	Description
id_version	Unique identifier of the current version (e.g., Mesh_V2)
file_name	Name of the certified file
sha256_hash	SHA-256 hash of the current file (A)
timestamp	Creation/certification date and time (ISO 8601 format)
previous_hash	SHA-256 hash of the source file (B)
transformation_tool	Software/tool used for the transformation (e.g., Midjourney v6, Blender 4.2 + RetopoFlow)
notes	Optional free-form notes (e.g., "Optimized for 3D printing manifold mesh")

4.7.4 Reference Implementation (Python)

The following production-ready Python snippet calculates the SHA-256 hash of any file (images, meshes, parameter files) and generates a complete, verifiable certification record:

```
import hashlib
import json
import datetime

def sha256_hash(filepath: str) -> str:
    """Compute SHA-256 hash of a file (streaming for large
    files)."""
    hasher = hashlib.sha256()
    with open(filepath, "rb") as f:
        while chunk := f.read(65536):  # 64 KB chunks
            hasher.update(chunk)
    return hasher.hexdigest()

# --- Example Usage ---
current_file = "Mesh_Final_V2.stl"
current_hash = sha256_hash(current_file)
```

```
# Hash of the previous step (e.g., AI-generated source image or
earlier mesh version)
previous_hash = "a7c2d8e4f1a9b3c5d7e0f9a8b1c3d5e7f0a9b8c7d6e5f4a3
b2c1d0e9f8a7b6c5"

certification_record = {
    "id_version": "Mesh_V2_Cert",
    "file_name": current_file,
    "sha256_hash": current_hash,
    "timestamp": datetime.datetime.utcnow().replace(microsecond=0).
    isoformat() + "Z",
    "previous_hash": previous_hash,
    "transformation_tool": "Blender 4.2 + RetopoFlow addon",
    "notes": "Manifold mesh optimization for 3D printing,
    watertight, 2 million triangles"
}

# Canonical JSON serialization (critical for reproducible hashing
of the record itself)
def canonical_json(obj):
    return json.dumps(obj, ensure_ascii=False, sort_keys=True,
    indent=None, separators=(',', ':'))

record_bytes = canonical_json(certification_record).encode("utf-8")
certification_record["record_self_hash"] = hashlib.sha256(record_
bytes).hexdigest()

# Save certification record
with open("certification_Mesh_V2.json", "w",
encoding="utf-8") as f:
    json.dump(certification_record, f, ensure_ascii=False,
    indent=4)

print(f"SHA-256 of {current_file}:\n{current_hash}\n")
print("Certification record (certification_Mesh_V2.json) created
and self-hashed.")
```

4.7.5 Recommended Enhancements for Maximum Trust

- Replace or complement local timestamps with RFC 3161-qualified timestamps or OpenTimestamps (Bitcoin-anchored, free).
- Store the final certification manifest and assets on permanent decentralized storage (IPFS/Arweave) for public verifiability.
- Optionally inscribe the root hash on a public blockchain (Polygon, Ethereum, Tezos, Bitcoin Ordinals, etc.) or register via Verisart/Artory-style certificate of authenticity.

This protocol provides mathematically provable authenticity and a complete, auditable transformation history equivalent to or exceeding standards used by leading generative artists and digital art certification platforms.

4.8 Appendix B: Comparative Analysis of Metaverse Platforms for Generative Art (2025 Update)

The integration of generative artworks into immersive environments requires a technical understanding of the underlying platform architectures.

This analysis compares **Second Life** (a mature, centralized virtual world) and **Decentraland** (a blockchain-native, decentralized platform), focusing on the technical and economic specifications relevant for creative implementation as of late 2025.

4.8.1 Technical and Economic Specifications

Characteristic	Second Life (Linden Lab)	Decentraland (DAO/Ethereum)
Infrastructure	**Centralized.** Proprietary servers (sims) managed by Linden Lab. Offers guaranteed persistence for paid land.	**Decentralized.** Open-source platform (SDK) running on the Ethereum blockchain (for land/asset ownership) and peer-to-peer servers.

(*continued*)

Characteristic	Second Life (Linden Lab)	Decentraland (DAO/Ethereum)
Building System	**In-World Modeling.** Relies on *Prims* and imported mesh assets.	**Off-World Modeling.** Requires external development using the SDK (JavaScript/TypeScript). Assets are uploaded and referenced in code.
Scripting	**Linden Scripting Language (LSL)** or **SLua** (new Lua-based beta, Dec 2025: **~50% faster execution**, modern features for procedural loops). Highly effective for real-time physics/behavior.	**SDK (JavaScript/TypeScript).** Based on webGL engines (Babylon.js) for scene logic, animations, and interactions.
Economy	**Linden Dollar (L$).** Consolidated, stable currency (approx. L$260/USD, 2025). Focus on continuous royalties for content creators (L$ market ~$60M USD/year).	**Crypto/NFT-Based.** Uses **MANA Token** (~$0.18 USD, Dec 2025; volatile but DAO-governed) and **LAND** (tokenized property as NFT). Treasury ~23.7M MANA (Jun 2025 transfer).
Current Status (2025)	**Mature and Stable, with Innovation.** Dedicated user base (peak concurrency ~50,000). Key updates: **SLua scripting beta** (Dec 2025) and mobile app enhancements (Q4 2025). Focus on community-driven creation and economy.	**Rapidly Evolving and DAO-Driven.** ~300,000 monthly active users (up 15% YoY). Key updates: **Regenesis Labs launch** (Oct 2025) for agile execution; roadmap includes Mobile/VR clients (Q4 2025) and high-quality games.
Permanence	Dependent on centralized management and continuous land fee payments to Linden Lab. Guarantees "always-on" for scripted installations.	**Theoretical permanence tied to Ethereum** (LAND NFTs immutable), but content persistence depends on user-hosted nodes (risk of desync if low activity; ~80% parcels inactive, 2025 data).

4.8.2 Critical Distinctions and Generative Behavior

The choice between platforms dictates the optimal type of generative art and user engagement.

4.8.2.1 Critical Distinctions

Feature	Second Life	Decentraland
Control & Rights	High control for content creators; stable royalties. Ideal for consistent, long-term installations.	Property (LAND, NFT) is decentralized. Ideal for speculative art where value is tied to blockchain transactions.
Generativity Focus	Optimized for **Behavioral Generativity** (systems based on real-time physics, continuous LSL/SLua event response).	Optimized for **Transactional Generativity** (art that changes based on blockchain data, NFT ownership, or MANA staking).
Project Fit (Example: *Symphony of the Labyrinth*)	SL's behavioral generativity is ideal for real-time "dialogue" (e.g., LSL/SLua responding to visitor proximity with procedural vine growth).	DL's transactional focus is ideal for NFT-minted variants (e.g., MANA-staked evolutions tied to DAO votes), enabling blockchain-driven forks of the Open Source process.

4.8.3 Artwork Behavior Specification

Artwork interactions must distinguish the immediate user-model loop from genuine model adaptation, leveraging 2025 tools:

- **Trigger Events:** User actions (proximity, *touch, pointer events*) activate procedural changes in the artwork's geometry, color, or texture.
- **External Data Feeds:** Artworks autonomously generate variations based on external data (e.g., real-world weather, financial feeds).

- **Input-Driven Narrative (LLM Integration):** Visitors input text to an LLM (e.g., **Grok API** or **Llama 3** via SLua/JS integration, 2025), which returns data used to structurally or texturally modify the visual art in real-time. This achieves the dynamic blend of generative text and visual output required by the project.

4.9 Appendix C: Infrastructure Context and Platform Viability (Critical Caveat) 2025 Update

The rapid evolution of digital infrastructure demands that any mapping of contemporary creative platforms be viewed with critical caution.

The following analysis serves as an essential caveat to the operational diagrams presented in the book, emphasizing the fragility of even the most established systems as of December 2025.

4.9.1 The Impermanence of Digital Infrastructure

It is critical to understand any architectural diagram, such as that presented in Figure 4-19, as merely a **snapshot of the digital art infrastructure landscape as of late 2025**.

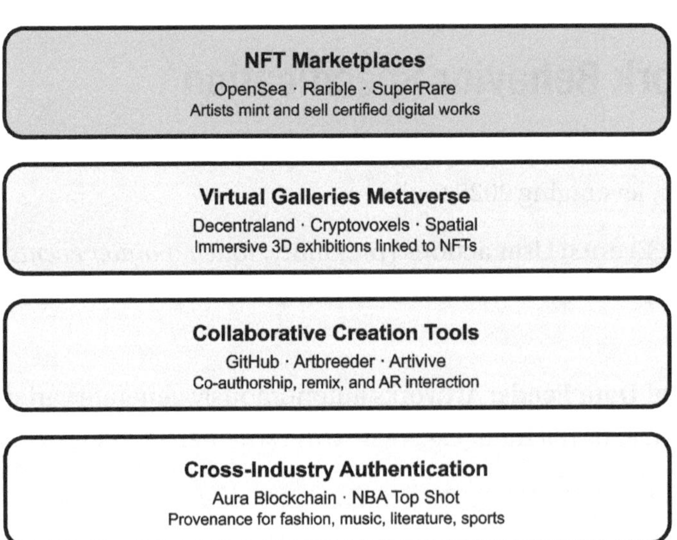

The viability and structure of platforms and services within the Web3 and generative art space change at an accelerated pace—often driven by market shifts, acquisitions, regulatory pressures, and technological pivots.

The history of this field is defined by examples of services that have been restructured, discontinued, or whose functionality has been abruptly altered, demonstrating the fundamental risks associated with centralization and dependency on third-party servers.

4.9.2 Historical Precedents of Platform Restructuring and Discontinuance

The market volatility in 2024–2025 underscores the fragility of commercial platforms relative to the permanent record of the blockchain:

Platform Category	Example Platform	Status/Impact on Artists (2025 Update)
Marketplace Evolution	**KnownOrigin** (Acquired by eBay 2022)	**Ceased operations in early 2025.** Artists who relied on its curated environment were forced to migrate to secondary markets (OpenSea), disrupting workflows and visibility.
	Foundation	Undergoing strategic shifts (mid-2025) towards enhanced community curation and hybrid AI-Web3 integrations to sustain engagement against market consolidation.
Centralized Gateways	**Nifty Gateway**	**Pivoted dramatically (April 2024)** from pure marketplace to "Nifty Gateway Studio," a creative production arm. Implements **IPFS-pinned metadata** (Phase 2 completed April 2025) but de-emphasized core marketplace mechanics.
Early Web3 Services	**Bitproof**	**Long superseded.** Its decentralized notary functions have been absorbed into more robust tools (like Ethereum's native attestation protocols), forcing legacy users to manually migrate proof data.

(*continued*)

Platform Category	Example Platform	Status/Impact on Artists (2025 Update)
Generative Tools Volatility	**Async Art**	**Shuttered its core platform in Q1 2025** after funding contraction, forcing programmable art migrations to self-hosted IPFS setups.
	Art Blocks Factory	Saw **deprecations** in favor of more sustainable DAO-governed models, requiring system maintenance by the community.

4.9.3 The Blockchain Paradox and Sustainability Risk

This dynamic context highlights a paradox at the heart of digital art: the contrast between immutable records and impermanent commercial platforms.

While blockchain technologies offer an immutable, decentralized record of authenticity and ownership, the actual commercial platform (the website interface, the display API, or the execution environment) remains a centralized entity subject to standard business vulnerabilities, maintenance costs, and strategic pivots.

The **sustainability risk is therefore high and multifaceted**. The artwork's authenticity may be recorded permanently on-chain, but the accessibility, interface, and interpretive context provided by the platform are inherently fragile—exacerbated in 2025 by rising Ethereum gas fees, regulatory scrutiny on NFT royalties (e.g., EU's MiCA updates), and the shift toward AI-hybrid models that demand constant backend upgrades.

For artists engaging in networked and generative creation, this means that the longevity of the work requires prioritizing **technical resilience**: self-hosting on **IPFS** or **Arweave** for metadata; open-source code under **MIT/GPL licenses** for scripts; and **hybrid models** that decouple frontend experiences from proprietary servers.

Only through such measures can the integrity and accessibility of works endure beyond the lifecycle of any single commercial service, ensuring that generative art remains a living, evolvable ecosystem rather than a relic of transient platforms. In an ecosystem characterized by the short lifecycles of commercial platforms, genuine permanence stems from decentralized protocols, open-source licensing, and self-sovereign storage solutions, thereby transforming generative art from a transient product into a durable cultural heritage.

4.10 Appendix D: Virtual Exhibition Platforms: Operational Status and Critical Analysis (2025)

Virtual worlds like **Somnium Space**, **Voxels** (formerly Cryptovoxels), and **Spatial** serve as networked exhibition spaces, enabling artists to host immersive galleries and interactive installations.

As of December 2025, these platforms remain operational but vary significantly in scale and underlying infrastructure.

This appendix outlines their operational status, user metrics, and critical challenges, highlighting the metaverse's potential for art while underscoring issues of sustainability and equity.

4.10.1 Comparative Analysis of Virtual Exhibition Platforms (2025)

Feature	Somnium Space	Voxels (formerly Cryptovoxels)	Spatial
Operational Model	VR-native, Persistent World	Browser-based, Voxel World	Cross-Platform (Web, Mobile, VR)
Blockchain Base	Ethereum (NFT Land)	Ethereum/Polygon (NFT Land, Low Fees)	Centralized (Web/Cloud) with NFT integration
Active Users (Dec 2025)	~15,000 monthly (VR-focused; up 12% YoY)	~5,000 monthly (Stable niche community)	500,000+ monthly (Web/Mobile; up 25% YoY)
Sustainability Model	**Strong:** $CUBE Token upgrades, community governance, persistent worlds.	**Niche but Steady:** Reliant on Ethereum fees and low maintenance costs.	**Robust:** Backed by enterprise focus (brands), subscriptions, and hybrid accessibility.
Technical Infrastructure	VR1 Headset Integration (Quest 3); Serverless (AWS); **File Storage: IPFS**	Voxel-based WebGL; Persistent worlds via Polygon; **File Storage: Arweave**	Unity SDK; WebGL + WebXR Hybrid; Cloud-hosted (AWS/GCP); **File Storage: Centralized CDN with IPFS backups**

(continued)

Feature	Somnium Space	Voxels (formerly Cryptovoxels)	Spatial
Accessibility Focus	VR-focused (headset required for full features); Screen-reader support partial.	Browser-based (no download); Keyboard navigation; Barriers: High Ethereum gas fees for new users.	**Leading in Inclusivity:** Web/Mobile entry; Voice commands; AI-generated alt-text. Barriers: Complex Unity SDK for advanced builds.
Economic Model	$CUBE token; Land sales ($100–$10,000/parcel); Revenue: 70% from NFTs.	Parcel sales (floor 0.0199 ETH); Marketplace fees (2.5%). Low trading volume (stable for niche artists).	Freemium ($10–$50/mo); NFT integration (MetaMask); Revenue: 60% subscriptions, 40% events.

4.10.2 Critical Infrastructure Questions

The democratization of exhibition through these platforms highlights key challenges for long-term integration with generative art:

1. **File Storage and Persistence:**

    - **Decentralized Resilience:** Somnium Space uses **IPFS** and Voxels uses **Arweave** for asset storage, ensuring better decentralized permanence.

    - **Centralization Risk:** Spatial's reliance on a Centralized CDN risks **data loss** if proprietary servers fail, requiring artists to actively manage their IPFS backups. All face the risk of "link rot" for embedded media.

2. **Operational Sustainability:**

    - **Longevity:** Somnium's consistent tokenomics and updates support longevity; Spatial's enterprise focus ensures robust funding. Voxels' low activity, conversely, risks market stagnation.

3. **Accessibility Barriers and Equity:**
   - **Hardware Costs:** VR hardware costs ($300–$3,000) exclude low-income users, hindering true global access.
   - **Blockchain Fees:** High Ethereum fees (0.01–0.1 ETH) deter emerging artists from minting their first works. Spatial's web-first entry and Somnium's free trials mitigate these barriers, but the global digital divide remains a persistent challenge for equitable participation.

These platforms democratize exhibition but require hybrid approaches (e.g., self-hosting web backups) for true resilience, a necessary condition for any generative work designed for long-term evolution (see Appendix E).

4.11 Appendix E: Multiplatform Analysis of Collaborative Creation Tools (2025 Update)

The following platforms exemplify how contemporary digital creation shifts from singular authorship to complex co-authorship, necessitating technical understanding of version control, licensing, and content persistence. This update reflects developments as of December 2025, including enhanced AI integrations and AR accessibility tools.

4.11.1 GitHub (Version Control for Generative Scripts)

Feature	Description for Digital Artists	Legal/Technical Implications (2025 Update)
Technical Function	**Version Control (Git):** Allows artists to track every change (commits) to code or assets. Essential for **procedural art** where generative scripts (e.g., Python, JavaScript) are the final artwork.	**Authorship:** Git logs establish clear, timestamped contribution history, resolving ambiguity in code-based co-authorship. **AI Integration: GitHub Copilot** (integrated with LLM APIs like Grok Code Fast 1, GA Oct 2025) directly assists in code generation, enabling agentic workflows for procedural loops.

(continued)

Feature	Description for Digital Artists	Legal/Technical Implications (2025 Update)
Use for Co-Creation	Multiple artists can simultaneously contribute to the same generative script, 3D asset library, or shader code (*forking* the project), merging changes iteratively.	**Licensing:** Artists typically use **Open Source Licenses (MIT, GPL)** to define reuse terms. **Persistence:** Content is highly persistent, relying on a vast distributed network of repositories.

4.11.2 Artbreeder (AI-Based Image Remixing)

Feature	Description for Digital Artists	Legal/Technical Implications (2025 Update)
Technical Function	Utilizes **Diffusion Models** to blend ("breed") multiple source images ("parents") into a new output, allowing exploration of the public **latent space**.	**Licensing: CC0 is mandatory for all outputs** (reaffirmed Oct 2025), simplifying distribution but complicating the claim of sole ownership. Users retain personal rights for non-commercial use.
Collaborative Image Generation	Users contribute to a continuously evolving lineage of images. Each output has a long, traceable parent history.	**Ownership Ambiguity:** Authorship is complex due to multiple human and algorithmic inputs. **Persistence Risk:** Content persistence is **server-dependent**, although **JSON export** of lineage metadata mitigates some loss risk.

4.11.3 Augmented Reality (AR) Platforms (e.g., Artivive, Blippar)

Feature	Description for Digital Artists	Legal/Technical Implications (2025 Update)
Technical Mechanism	**Marker- or GPS-Based Triggers:** Physical artworks are linked to digital overlays (animations, 3D models). **Blippar's no-code Blippbuilder** (with AR glasses compatibility ongoing into 2025) lowers entry barrier.	**Authorship:** AR apps act as hosts. **Persistence Risk:** High dependence on the platform's API and server maintenance (e.g., Blippar's AR glasses integration increases reliance on app lifecycle).
Viewer Contribution	Platforms allow viewers to add digital layers or commentary (e.g., **Artivive open calls** for "transient co-contributors" on themes like bias visualization).	**Legal Ambiguity:** User-added content may introduce licensing conflicts. **Compliance: GDPR compliance** is required for user-added content; persistence is tied to app maintenance (Artivive grants royalty-free licenses for promotional use).

4.11.4 Conclusion: Legal Ambiguity and Server Dependency

The shift toward co-authorship highlights two critical issues:

- **Legal Ambiguity:** While platforms like GitHub offer clear contribution records, AI remixing and AR contributions introduce ambiguity regarding derivative work rights and licensing when multiple human and algorithmic inputs are involved.
- **Content Persistence:** Except for self-hosted solutions or platforms like GitHub, the longevity and accessibility of the collaborative work are highly vulnerable to platform governance and the maintenance of proprietary servers and APIs. For long-term integrity, artists must prioritize self-hosting or hybrid models (e.g., utilizing **IPFS** for decentralized persistence of AR assets) to ensure the collaborative work endures beyond platform lifecycles.

PART II

From Real to Virtual

The first part of this book traced a historical and conceptual path from neoclassical ideals to digital reproducibility, showing how sculpture has continually negotiated the relationship between tradition and innovation, aura and reproducibility, uniqueness and openness.

This provided a framework for understanding how artistic identity and authorship have been redefined in successive technological contexts.

Part II now shifts the focus from theory to practice.

Here we enter the expanded studio of contemporary artists, where manual gestures, digital tools, and algorithmic processes intersect.

Sculpting is no longer confined to marble, bronze, or clay; it extends into 3D modeling environments, photogrammetry scans, AI-generated forms, and additive manufacturing. Rather than replacing traditional media, these processes hybridize them, producing new forms of materiality that oscillate between physical and virtual.

The studio itself has become distributed, spanning the workbench, the screen, and the network.

It is within this expanded space that new possibilities for art and sculpture emerge: where matter and code are sculpted together and where the gestures of the past meet the algorithms of the present.

CHAPTER 5

States of Transformation: Painting, Sculpture, and Digital Expansion

Art today unfolds in states of transformation, where matter and image, manual gestures and digital processes, continuously merge and reshape one another.

This chapter examines how creative techniques in the digital era generate hybrid artworks that span physical, virtual, and immersive dimensions.

It considers manual and virtual painting, AI-driven expansions, sculpture combined with 3D scanning, and prototype-oriented 3D printing, showing how these practices redefine artistic creation.

By integrating tools such as Blender, Stable Diffusion, and 3D printers, artists collaborate with digital systems to craft works that blend tangible materials with immaterial aesthetics, opening new territories of possibility.

The precise software versions and hardware specifications required for methodological reproducibility are fully detailed in section 5.1.

Starting from my own artistic practice—where traditional sculptural methods are reinterpreted through digital experimentation—I will outline workflows that combine modeling, scanning, and AI-driven synthesis.

My work sometimes also incorporates fragments of Greek, Roman, Renaissance, and Neoclassical art and architecture, reassembling them into speculative landscapes where historical memory is transformed into new iconographic readings.

The use of cultural heritage fragments, even though the original works are in the public domain, requires strict attention to digital provenance.

Scans and 3D models generated by institutions (museums, archives) are often subject to restrictive licenses on the digital file itself, which must be verified.

G. Moioli, *Art Between Matter and Code*, https://doi.org/10.1007/979-8-8688-2376-3_5

The author commits to meticulously verifying the license of every digital source and utilizing only those with permissive licenses (such as Public Domain, CC0, and certain other Creative Commons licenses) in the correct manner.[1]

It is essential to always ensure full attribution, discussing the curatorial implications and respect for the original object's historical memory.

This chapter could also be understood as *Sculpting the Invisible*. In Blender and other 3D modeling software, it is possible to create sculptures that do not yet exist physically but already possess concrete attributes: dimensions, materials, spatial presence.

Soon, artificial intelligence will open the same horizon, shaping forms that emerge from data as if they were dreams given volume.

Placed within Part II, the chapter complements the broader exploration of virtual modeling and AI-driven creation, distinguishing itself from the historical perspective of Chapter 1, the introduction of digital modeling in Chapter 2, and the focus on procedure in Chapter 3.

5.1 Hybrid Techniques

Hybrid methods are not just techniques but thresholds.

They mark a liminal zone where manual and digital practices intersect, creating spaces of exchange between drawing, modeling, 3D processes, procedural systems, and artificial intelligence.

Within this framework, traditional gestures—such as painting, drawing, or sculpting with clay and plaster—are reinterpreted and expanded through digital tools, while algorithmic structures and AI systems introduce forms of unpredictability that extend beyond the artist's direct control.

Hybrid techniques thus generate artworks that inhabit both the material and the virtual realm, unfolding between tactile presence and immaterial code (Figure 5-1).

[1] Where institutions apply more restrictive licenses (e.g., CC-BY-NC, CC-BY-ND, rights reserved, or specific contractual terms), I will either refrain from using the digital surrogate or will limit its use strictly to the permitted conditions, always citing the exact source and license.

Figure 5-1. Gianpiero Moioli. Alien Landscape at Dawn, 2025.
Digitally modified acrylic painting on paper and cardboard with pen drawing, cm. 150 (h) x 200.
Multiple hybrid forms are suspended between matter and code. Here, the materials and the hand's gesture meet the logic of algorithms, shaping a threshold where memory, imagination, and future worlds intertwine

They are not merely about combining different media but about establishing a condition in which **memory and innovation** coexist, where **matter and algorithm** co-construct aesthetic forms.

Drawing on contemporary practices my work seeks to establish a dialogue with the structured proportions of Canova and the spatial experimentation of Fontana, reinterpreting these legacies through 3D manual and virtual modeling and procedural algorithms.[2]

This trajectory can also be traced in other fields: Picasso and Duchamp redefined artistic languages by transforming gestures and contexts, while Philippe Starck demonstrated how design can become a metaphorical machine, a projection of future imaginaries where dematerialization and invisibility reshape everyday life.

In this perspective, the digital can be understood as an extension of the studio, where code acts almost like clay and virtual growth acquires a sculptural presence.

So, at this point, it is crucial to establish the technological framework that underpins this practice. To ensure the transparency and reproducibility of the workflows detailed later in this chapter, the following tables define the specific software environments, AI checkpoints, and hardware configurations utilized.

The necessary technical foundation relies first on the hardware infrastructure that supports both intensive AI inference and the subsequent large-scale physical fabrication.

Figure 5-2 details this configuration.

Component	Model / Detail	Role in the Workflow
GPU (for AI/Rendering)	NVIDIA GeForce RTX 4070 Ti	VRAM: 12 GB – used for AI inference and real-time rendering
System RAM	32 GB	—
Operating System (OS)	Windows	—
3D Printer (FDM)	Anycubic Kobra 2 Max	Used for prototyping and large-scale production of final artworks
3D Printer (Alternative)	Elegoo Neptune 4 Max	Used for comparison, testing, and dimensional variations

Figure 5-2. Hardware configuration and fabrication.
Details the physical computing environment (GPU, RAM, and OS) and the specific 3D printer models used for the physical realization of the digital work

In parallel with the physical components, the digital environment and generative models are key.

Figure 5-3 provides the specific versions and checkpoints utilized to ensure that the mesh transformation, texturing, and image synthesis processes are fully transparent and reproducible.

---

[2] My approach combines manual techniques with digital processes. Beyond the overview of my works available on my website at `www.gianpieromoioli.it`. This article explores how I integrate virtual modeling and artificial intelligence into my sculptural practice: `https://mp.weixin.qq.com/s/ow3zOTqtMzaDoqLVwX_73Q`.

Tool	Version / Checkpoint	Notes on Usage
3D Modelling	Blender 4.4 (LTS)	Used for scanning processing, mesh retopology, and preparation of models for 3D printing.
Image/Texture Synthesis (Interface)	ComfyUI	Node-based workflow environment. Python 3.11.9, PyTorch 2.4.1.
Image/Texture Synthesis (Checkpoint)	Stable Diffusion 1.5	Primary model for texture synthesis and generation of attached illustrative images.
Image/Texture Synthesis (Service)	Midjourney (latest production version)	Used for supplementary high-quality image and texture generation.

Figure 5-3. Software Environment and AI Models Used in the Generative Pipeline (2025–2026 Versions).
Specifies the versions of the 3D modeling and AI synthesis tools (Blender, ComfyUI, Midjourney), including the Stable Diffusion checkpoint (v1.5) essential for texture generation

With this complete technical overview established, the methodology is fully defined. A brief technical clarification is necessary:

- Local tools (e.g., Stable Diffusion via Automatic1111, ComfyUI, or InvokeAI) require a powerful GPU (≥12 GB VRAM, ideally RTX 4080/4090 or higher) and 32–64 GB RAM for efficient high-resolution work.
- Cloud-based platforms (Midjourney V7, Kling 2.5, Runway, Luma, etc.) run entirely on remote servers; any recent laptop or smartphone with Internet access is sufficient, as the heavy computation is handled by the provider.

This hardware distinction is crucial because it determines practical accessibility. Local tools (Stable Diffusion) are free but require a powerful GPU, while cloud tools (Midjourney, Kling 2.5, Runway, etc.) need a browser and a paid subscription.

Such a synthesis suggests possible pathways for artists interested in combining historical sensibilities with contemporary technological processes, generating forms that oscillate between immaterial and physical realms.

In this chapter, I will examine in detail **contemporary hybrid artistic techniques**, in which painting and sculpture merge with digital tools and algorithms, redefining the boundaries between the real and the virtual.

At the core lies my artistic research. Through concrete examples and current workflows, I will reflect on the relationship between the materiality of the artwork, the algorithmic nature of new tools, the identity of the artist, and the imagination enhanced by new media.

To clarify this expanded notion of hybridity, two complementary diagrams are introduced at the beginning of this chapter.

Figure 5-4 positions New Technologies as the starting node from which two trajectories emerge.

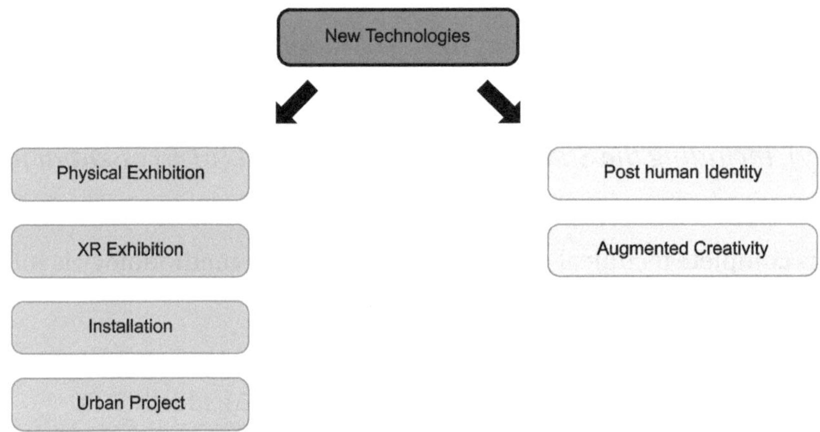

Figure 5-4. Hybrid workflow: conceptual overview.
Diagram showing the outcomes of hybrid artistic processes.
This diagram complements the next one by focusing on outcomes and conceptual directions rather than technical workflows

On the left, it presents contexts of display:

- **Physical Exhibition**: The traditional setting of museums and galleries, where works produced with hybrid methods enter into dialogue with established institutions
- **XR Exhibition**: Immersive environments combining VR, AR, and MR, in which the viewer actively navigates and interacts with the work
- **Installation**: Site-specific approaches blending physical and digital elements—screens, projections, sensors—into enveloping environments
- **Urban Project**: Extensions of hybrid practices into the public sphere, embedded in architectural and urban contexts where community and technology intersect

On the right, the diagram highlights conceptual trajectories:

- **Post-Human Identity**: The reconfiguration of subjectivity in the encounter between biological existence and technological augmentation
- **Augmented Imagination**: The expansion of cognitive and aesthetic possibilities through algorithmic systems, which act as catalysts for unforeseen forms, speculative narratives, and symbolic landscapes

Together, these dimensions demonstrate that hybrid practices operate simultaneously as modes of production, systems of exhibition, and fields of thought that reshape both artistic identity and cultural imagination.

Figure 5-5 complements this view by focusing on the operational flow of hybrid creation: manual painting and sculpting lead to 2D and 3D scanning, digital painting, AI image generation, and prototyping through 3D printing, before branching toward exhibition formats and technological extensions shown in the first diagram.

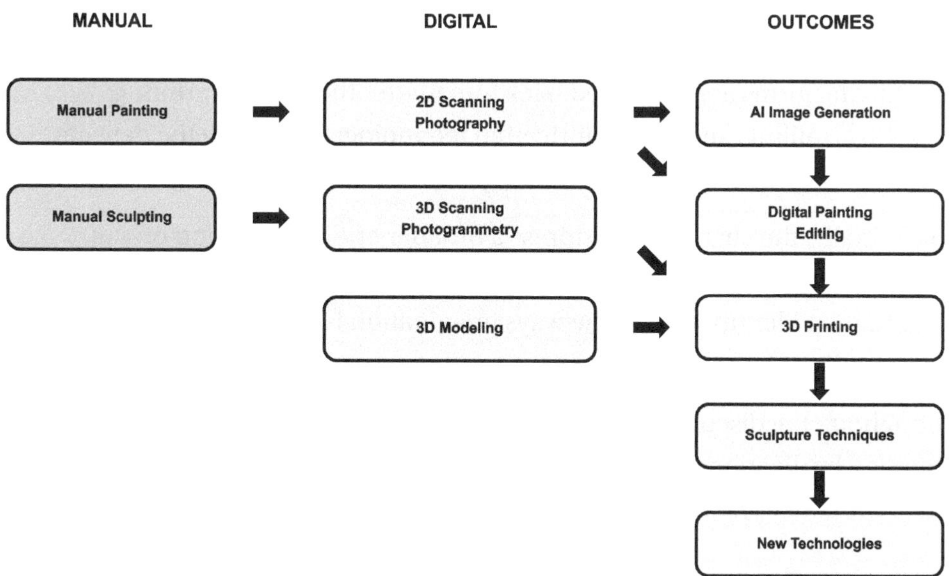

Figure 5-5. Hybrid workflow: technical process.
Diagram illustrating the technical workflow from manual painting and sculpting to digital scanning, digital painting, AI-based processes, and prototyping through 3D printing.
The scheme emphasizes the integration of traditional and digital techniques as part of a continuum that extends sculpture and painting into hybrid practices

It defines hybrid techniques in methodological terms, as a continuum between physical and digital processes.

Taken together, these diagrams demonstrate that hybrid methods should not be understood as isolated tools, but as interconnected thresholds where artistic creation evolves across material, digital, and conceptual dimensions.

In the following sections, I will explore how hybrid artistic techniques unfold across different domains of practice.

- Painting will be considered first, showing how the manual gesture extends into digital environments and generative AI, where the traditional act of brush and pigment is reconfigured as code and algorithmic transformation.
- Sculpture will then be examined in its passage from manual modeling to virtual 3D environments, scanning, and virtual reality, establishing a continuous dialogue between material presence and virtual projection.
- From there, the focus will turn to prototyping processes, in which digital forms are translated back into matter through 3D printing, CNC milling, and other fabrication technologies, probing the delicate relationship between virtual design and tangible materiality.
- Finally, the chapter will address a broader critical reflection on the intersection of matter and code, focusing on the notion of post-human identity and on the ways imagination is augmented by algorithmic systems.

Throughout, the discussion will be grounded in practical examples and case studies, accompanied by diagrams and images that clarify the operational workflows and illuminate the conceptual stakes of this expanded field of practice.

5.1.1 Generative Tools: Artificial Intelligence as a Creative Partner

This section focuses on contemporary generative instruments and how they are reshaping not only painting and sculpture but also the very modalities of artistic production.

From neural networks[3] to procedural systems driven by code,[4] artists today engage with new algorithmic agents: collaborators capable of generating unprecedented visual configurations by operating through rule-based structures or reference datasets.

In recent years, user-friendly platforms such as Stable Diffusion, Midjourney,[5] and RunwayML have made powerful AI models for generating images and videos accessible to creatives without programming skills.

Meanwhile, the open-source community has developed a spectrum of powerful interfaces, from the accessible and widely used Stable Diffusion WebUI Automatic1111 to the fully customizable, node-based ComfyUI (Python 3.11.9, PyTorch 2.4.1).

Running the Stable Diffusion 1.5 checkpoint on an NVIDIA GeForce RTX 4070 Ti (12 GB VRAM), these tools generate a standard 512×512 image in approximately 2.5–4 seconds and support advanced techniques such as inpainting and outpainting.

Generative AI can thus be considered a new artistic medium, endowed with its own language and potential.

Two main approaches to its use in the visual arts can be distinguished: the generation ex novo and the transformation and hybridization of existing images

5.1.1.1 Generation Ex Novo

In this approach, the artist provides only a textual description (prompt), and the model generates an entirely original image that did not previously exist.

Systems such as DALL·E, Midjourney, and Stable Diffusion operate in this way, sometimes supplemented by image-based workflows.

---

[3] Neural networks are computational models inspired by the brain, composed of layers of interconnected artificial neurons capable of recognizing and reproducing complex patterns. Deep architectures enable generative AI systems to synthesize images, texts, and forms from learned representations.

[4] Procedural systems are rule-based generative processes, where forms emerge from algorithms and parameters rather than direct modeling.

Neural networks learn from data to generate new patterns, while procedural systems produce forms through rules and parameters explicitly defined by the artist.

[5] Midjourney is among the most widely used generative AI platforms, transforming text, images, and videos into new visual outputs. It now extends beyond still imagery to workflows for videos, characters, and story-driven sequences; see the official update page at `https://updates.midjourney.com/`.

The artist here acts as a *director* or curator of possibilities: refining prompts, selecting outputs, and iterating until the desired result is achieved.

For example, with Stable Diffusion one might generate a painting in the style of Turner depicting a futuristic sunset city, producing a spectrum of variations rather than a single result.

Such outputs highlight how the "prompt" does not prescribe a fixed image but activates a field of potentialities, where the artist intervenes as a curator of emergence.

Similarly, the model can be directed to reinterpret a subject in the style of Picasso.

Similarly, the model can be instructed to reinterpret a subject "in the style of Picasso" or "in the manner of Caravaggio." What emerges is not a genuine historical collaboration but a simulated dialogue across time, in which the algorithm recombines fragments of the collective visual archive. These cases underscore both the power and the limits of generative AI: its capacity to situate images in new contexts and open speculative trajectories, yet its fundamentally derivative nature, built on the assimilation of vast corpora of pre-existing visual material.

Although works by long-deceased artists are safely in the public domain, prompting an AI with the styles of living artists or with copyrighted material can produce unauthorized derivative works. Artists therefore bear both curatorial and legal responsibility to ensure outputs are sufficiently transformative (fair use) or properly licensed.

5.1.1.2 Transformation and Hybridization of Existing Images

The second approach is the transformation and hybridization of existing images.

The second approach begins with visual inputs provided by the artist—photographs, scans, drawings, or pre-existing artworks—and modifies or extends them according to a specific intention. This includes style transfer, variation generation, inpainting (filling missing or masked zones), and outpainting (extending borders). Here the AI functions less as an independent creator and more as a sophisticated creative filter or collaborator.

A particularly emblematic and widely discussed example is the 2022 OpenAI demonstration in which DALL·E 2 was used to outpaint Vincent van Gogh's *The Starry Night* (1889). Starting from the original canvas, the model generated coherent continuations of the swirling sky, the cypress tree, and the village, effectively "uncropping" the painting and producing new hybrid territories that blend the historical masterpiece with AI-generated content. This experiment—conducted by the OpenAI team and released in September 2022—remains the canonical illustration of outpainting capabilities and of the broader paradigm of transformation and hybridization.

Other common practices within this category include:

- Fine-tuning models on personal datasets via DreamBooth (Stable Diffusion) or Custom Models (Midjourney) to teach the AI a specific face, object, or personal style
- Using ControlNet, IP-Adapter, or img2img workflows to force structural or stylistic continuity with source material
- Iteratively completing damaged artworks or extending unfinished sketches

In all these cases, the creative value resides not in automatic production but in the conceptual framework and human curation of the process.

It is precisely within this tension between automation and artistic authorship that the present series of post-human portraits takes shape.[6]

5.1.2 Portraits: Post-Human Visages

This hybrid procedure lies at the core of my series of post-human portraits.

Each work begins with a real face—photographed or 3D-scanned—and then deliberately contaminated by abstract fields, metaphysical landscapes, or symbolic objects that attempt to exteriorize the subject's inner world.

The AI is tasked with generating variations of the face (deformed, fragmented, multiplied) or with inventing dreamlike backgrounds; I subsequently intervene to weld these elements together, ensuring that the result is not mere illustration but the construction of a new visual mythology of the person.

[6] DreamBooth is a method introduced in 2022 for personalizing text-to-image models such as Stable Diffusion using just a few images of a subject. It fine-tunes the pretrained model to recognize that subject (or style) as a unique identifier, enabling the creation of new images that are consistent with the visual characteristics of the input data. `https://machinelearningmastery.com/training-stable-diffusion-with-dreambooth/`

Figure 5-6 illustrates the actual technical and artistic pipeline employed in this series.

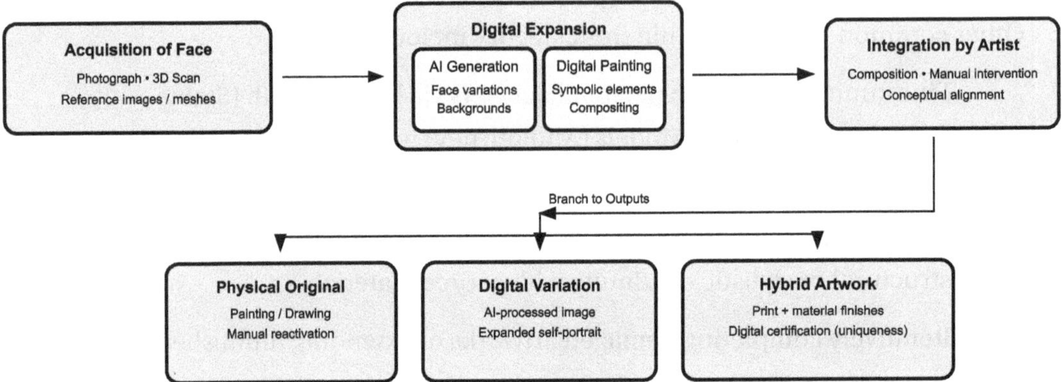

Figure 5-6. Workflow of post-human portraits.
From face acquisition to digital expansion and artistic integration, the process deliberately branches into three possible outcomes—physical, digital, or hybrid artworks—reflecting the ontological multiplicity of the post-human subject

The process begins with the acquisition of a real face—either through high-resolution photography or through 3D photogrammetry (producing both reference images and polygonal meshes).

These data are then fed into a digital expansion phase: using Stable Diffusion 1.5 (via ComfyUI) and a combination of img2img, inpainting, and ControlNet/OpenPose workflows, the AI generates multiple face variations (deformations, fragmentations, colour inversions) and symbolic/metaphysical backgrounds.

At the same time, manual digital painting (GIMP/Procreate/Photoshop) introduces deliberate chromatic fields and compositional elements that the algorithm alone cannot produce.

The artist then performs the decisive integration: compositional alignment, conceptual refinement, and manual re-intervention (both digital and, when required, physical).

From this single expanded core the workflow deliberately branches into three parallel outcomes—physical original (reactivated by hand on the initial support), digital variation (high-resolution file, often further iterated), and certified hybrid artwork (limited-edition print on archival medium + material finishing + NFT or certificate of authenticity).

This tripartite structure is not accidental: it materializes the post-human condition itself, in which a single identity simultaneously inhabits the realms of matter, code, and certified uniqueness.

I term this process **hybrid painting**.

The choice of final medium is never neutral. It determines the ontological status of the piece and the layers of meaning it carries.

In a series of digital and hybrid self-portraits, AI functions as a space of convergence between the real and the virtual.

Geometric fields, chromatic contrasts, or symbolic elements merge with facial features, generating compositions that are simultaneously intimate and otherworldly (Figure 5-7).

Figure 5-7. Gianpiero Moioli, Self-portrait, 2025.
AI expansion, print on paper, 50 × 50 cm each.
Post-human self-portraits in which my scanned face is transformed through digital processes and combined with metaphysical landscapes and symbolic elements

Identity here does not fragment into art-historical references but unfolds through the interplay of real physiognomy and virtual imagination.

Each portrait becomes a layered construction: at once a trace of the body, a digital transformation, and a speculative vision of the self.

My portraits—whether paintings or sculptural compositions—evoke faces, gestures, hands, or gazes but always through deformed, partial, or hybrid forms. Sometimes a face emerges from a smooth block or a realistic hand protrudes from a geometric structure, which are signs of presence, traces of stories, fragments of memory.

The portrait becomes an interrogation of the body and the self in an age of technique and transformation.

The portrayed faces are never realistic in the traditional sense; rather, they appear hybrid, suspended between the human and the abstract.

AI here functions as an instrument of creative estrangement. It decomposes and recomposes features, suggesting visions that the artist alone might not have conceived but that resonate when aligned with the underlying concept.

In this way, AI acts as an **amplifier of imagination**, enabling the exploration of alternative or fantastical versions of real subjects.

Through this iterative experimentation, the portrait becomes not a fixed likeness but an evolving field of identity, suspended between matter and code.

5.1.3 The Artist as Curator of Generative Systems

The adoption of AI tools in art has sparked both ethical and aesthetic debates.

Some fear the risk of visual homogenization, while others highlight their democratic potential. The analogy with photography is often evoked: a medium initially contested, yet ultimately one that liberated painting from mimetic duties and paved the way for the avant-gardes.

AI may similarly free the artist from certain technical constraints, acting as a catalyst for new aesthetics.

As early as the 1960s, pioneers such as Harold Cohen[7] created algorithms capable of drawing autonomously; those early forms of artificial creativity were based on explicit rules defined by the programmer.

Today, with neural networks, we witness emergent behaviors. The model produces outputs not programmed image by image but arising from statistical learning.

[7] Harold Cohen (1928–2016) was a British artist and pioneer in computer art.

In the early 1970s he developed AARON, one of the first programs capable of generating autonomous drawings. Unlike today's neural networks, AARON was based on rule-based procedures explicitly coded by Cohen, anticipating later explorations of artificial creativity.

This shift redefines the artist's role toward the curation and orchestration of complex systems. **The artist becomes, at least in part, the designer of a process rather than a direct executor.**

As curator of generative systems, the artist selects training sets or pre-trained models, defines constraints and directives, and then refines the results.

The parallel with parametric design is clear. Instead of drawing every single element, one establishes rules and parameters, and the software calculates variations.

In art, this approach leads to works that evolve and generate infinite outcomes, sometimes even in real time, when AI is integrated into installations.

The artwork thus becomes a process rather than a static object, echoing performance and conceptual art, but implemented through algorithms (Figure 5-8).

Figure 5-8. Coop Himmelb(l)au, Dalian International Conference Center (2008–2012).
A landmark of parametric architecture, where forms arise from algorithmic rules rather than manual drafting, echoing the generative approach in art, where the work is conceived as a process rather than a fixed object.
By 準建築人手札網站 Forgemind ArchiMedia `https://www.flickr.com/photos/eager/14302092083`

Equally important is reflection on the imaginary.

AI draws upon vast collections of existing images and therefore represents, in a certain sense, the collective visual imagination.[8]

Using it means to confront stereotypes and archetypes embedded in datasets.

Yet precisely because these systems produce unexpected results, they can help the artist to see differently, discovering forms that previously existed only as remote possibilities.

Collaboration with the machine, if critical and conscious, can thus enrich creation. Generative AI has become a companion in artistic experimentation; it does not replace the artist's vision but amplifies and sometimes challenges it, compelling creators to define their role and intentions with greater clarity.

5.2 Beyond the Canvas: Painting Between Manual Gesture and Algorithm

Painting, traditionally understood as the artist's gesture inscribed on a bounded surface, is now entering a renewed phase of expansion through digital tools and generative AI.

The hand and pigment remain central, but the image is no longer confined to material surfaces. It can extend virtually without limits, reinterpreted and transformed through digital painting, algorithmic processes, and new technologies.

This trajectory echoes earlier ruptures in art history, anticipating today's hybrid practices where painting, sculpture, and digital media intertwine in continuous transformation.

Painting thus becomes a hybrid act, where tactile matter—acrylic, watercolor, ink—coexists with immaterial data, layers, and procedural variations.

[8] The collective visual imaginary of diffusion models is shaped primarily by their training data.

Stable Diffusion, for instance, relies heavily on LAION-5B—an uncorrected scrape of more than five billion Internet images—thereby inheriting societal biases (gender, racial, and cultural stereotypes) and frequent copyrighted material.

Artists must therefore actively counter these inheritances through rigorous output auditing (similarity searches, lineage tracing tools), deliberate use of diverse and curated reference datasets, and systematic negative prompting. Only conscious, critical engagement prevents the unconscious reproduction of the dataset's ideological and legal contaminants.

Digital platforms reproduce the textures of traditional media while allowing endless iterations, while AI-driven systems generate new image fragments consistent with the original style or subject, extending the painterly field into previously unattainable dimensions.

Through these processes, the canvas becomes both surface and interface: a threshold where memory and gesture encounter the logic of the algorithm.

5.2.1 Manual Painting as a Foundation

Manual painting, rooted in physical media like oils or acrylics, provides a tactile foundation for hybrid artworks. Its expressive qualities can now be expanded through AI, which reimagines and extends the painterly gesture into new dimensions.

Artists often begin with physical sketches or canvases, capturing expressive gestures or conceptual ideas.

This grounding in material gesture preserves the emotive quality of manual work while opening avenues for digital enhancement.

By layering paper, cardboard, and pigment, I create a surface that is already hybrid before entering the digital domain.

In *Labyrinth with Planets*, 2023, (Figure 5-9) acrylic and collage construct a stratified surface that anticipates its own digital transformation: matter becomes a threshold, waiting to be reconfigured by code.

Figure 5-9.** **Gianpiero Moioli, Labyrinth with planets, 2023.
Acrylic on paper and cardboard collage, 70(h) × 100 cm.
This work is the starting point of the hybrid painting process, where painting and manual layering become the foundation for subsequent digital reimaginations

Once translated into data, these works expose the tension between physical matter and algorithmic process, where gesture and calculation co-construct the image.

This conversion from gesture to calculation necessitates a meticulously documented digital transformation pipeline, detailing every stage from raw acquisition format to final archival output to ensure the reproducibility and traceability of the work's core metadata, scale, and authorship.

The transition from physical matter to algorithmic data follows a strict, fully documented pipeline designed to ensure methodological reproducibility and integrity:

1. **Acquisition:** Initial physical artworks and reference photographs are captured and stored as lossless PNG files.

2. **3D Modeling:** Physical geometry is imported into GIMP 3.0.8 as PNG, or Blender 4.4 (LTS) as OBJ or STL meshes. Scene units are set to metric (m or cm) and the standard Blender Z-up coordinate system is maintained for vertical alignment.

3. **AI Expansion:** Digital assets are processed in Midjourney or ComfyUI (Stable Diffusion 1.5 checkpoint). All outputs are saved as high-resolution PNGs with full embedded generation metadata (prompt, seed, sampler, CFG, workflow JSON).

4. **Final Output:** Composite artworks are exported as archival PNG (for physical printing) or GLTF/GLB (for virtual display and certification).

Authenticity and Provenance: No NFT or on-chain token is minted. However, final manifests are optionally anchored to the Bitcoin blockchain exclusively for tamper-proof timestamping via OpenTimestamps (a free, noncommercial standard that does not create tradeable assets). This specific implementation relies on the reproducible cryptographic provenance protocol detailed in Section 4.3.4 (Reproducible Certification Protocol).

After this example from my own practice, it is useful to recall a modern precedent that resonates with these ideas.

Paul Klee's *Destroyed Labyrinth* (1939), as shown in Figure 5-10, portrays the fragmented remains of a maze, often interpreted as a metaphorical scene reflecting the chaos of its historical moment.

Figure 5-10. Paul Klee, Destroyed Labyrinth, 1939.
Oil and watercolor on paper mounted on burlap.
Klee's interleaving of oil and watercolor generates depth across the surface, offering an early model of hybrid materiality within modern painting.
Public Domain: `https://commons.wikimedia.org/w/index.php?curid=118146370`

Klee's manual layering of oil and watercolor creates a rich texture and fine detail, giving the work a tactile, organic feel.

The hybrid technique, combining oil paint with watercolor washes, was innovative for its time and added depth to the surface.

Klee's use of multiple mediums in one piece exemplifies a hybrid approach to painting, albeit on a two-dimensional surface.

This demonstrates how manual experimentation with materials and techniques can already generate a sense of hybridity, where the surface itself becomes a site of transformation and layered meaning.

Building on this premise, the next step is to explore how digital environments expand the painterly field even further.

5.2.2 Virtual Painting in Digital Environments

Although often considered very recent, digital painting has a longer history.

As early as the 1980s and 1990s, pioneering artists experimented with computer-based tools that translated brushstrokes into pixels, anticipating today's immersive workflows.[9]

A more contemporary reference is David Hockney's iPad drawings, such as *The Yosemite Suite*,[10] which show how manual expression—once bound to paper or canvas—can find continuity in the digital interface.

Just as layers of paper and pigments in traditional collage create depth, Hockney's digital brushstrokes preserve the presence of the hand while extending it into luminous, immaterial space.

In both cases, whether through acrylic and cardboard or pixels and screens, the surface becomes a hybrid threshold: at once material and virtual, tactile and immaterial.

Painting is not eclipsed by digital media; it becomes a point of departure for new expansions, where gesture and imagination are prolonged into unforeseen dimensions.

What has changed is the accessibility and sophistication of the tools.

Today, software such as GIMP, Krita, Photoshop, Adobe Fresco, Procreate, or Sketchbook can reproduce all the effects of traditional media while expanding them with new possibilities of layering, iteration, and transformation.

Digital brushes emulate the textures of manual work but also enable processes that exceed the physical medium.

In my digital painting *Large Green Machine with Spherical Mechanisms*, for example, I used digital painting to layer chromatic effects with textures recalling pencil, felt pen, or watercolor.

Such works demonstrate how material gesture is redefined. The digital does not replace the manual but regenerates and prolongs it.

Beyond the creative act itself, digital tools also allow for technical control and enhancements once unthinkable in traditional media.

---

[9] Early experiments in digital painting date back to the 1980s and 1990s. Notable examples include David Hockney's pioneering use of computer-based drawing in the late 1980s and later on iPads, as well as Andy Warhol's experiments with the Amiga computer (1985), where he produced digital reinterpretations of his iconic images. These early works translated the painterly gesture into pixels, foreshadowing the immersive and hybrid workflows available to artists today.

[10] You can explore David Hockney's full range of digital works, including his groundbreaking *Yosemite Suite*, on his official website at `https://www.hockney.com/works/digital`.

For instance, as in Figure 5-11, it is possible to generate multiple variations from a single matrix or original work, introducing processes of recomposition and expansion that were never available to traditional painting.

Figure 5-11. Gianpiero Moioli, Large green machines with spherical mechanisms, 2023.
Digital paintings. Cm 100 x 100.
Two digital paintings created with GIMP and Adobe Fresco

Different platforms highlight distinct potentials.

The digital painting tools utilized in this practice fall into two main categories: desktop applications (optimized for power and compositing) and mobile/tablet applications (optimized for immediate, gestural input).

Desktop applications such as **Photoshop** (the professional standard for layering, color management, and compositing) and its open-source counterparts **GIMP** and **Krita** are primarily optimized for high-resolution processing and complex, multilayered workflows executed via mouse or pen display. Krita, specifically developed for digital art, emphasizes advanced brush engines and customizable textures that simulate oils, inks, and watercolors with remarkable sensitivity, creating a continuity with manual practice.

Conversely, mobile and tablet applications such as **Adobe Fresco**, **Autodesk Sketchbook**, and **Procreate** are designed with the immediacy of drawing in mind.

They privilege gesture, tactile feedback, and real-time responsiveness on touchscreens, offering brushes that reproduce the spontaneity of pencil, pastel, or watercolor.

Fresco, for instance, integrates “live brushes” that mimic the diffusion of water or the thickness of oil paint, while Procreate (a cornerstone of tablet-based creation) and Sketchbook excel in speed and intuitive sketching, bridging the gap between notebook and digital tablet.

These platforms bring the digital environment closer to the embodied experience of drawing and painting, allowing fluid transitions between study, draft, and finished work.

Another key feature of digital painting is its **flexibility of format**. Unlike traditional painting, a work has no fixed size. It may begin on a small tablet screen and later be adapted for large-scale printing or projection.

The final material scale of the work is deliberately decoupled from the resolution of its original digital creation. This is achieved through:

- Vector formats (SVG, PDF), inherently resolution-independent.
- Raster images enhanced by AI upscaling tools. Controlled tests with Topaz Gigapixel AI v8.4.4 (4× enlargement) yield SSIM > 0.95, confirming suitability for monumental prints. Equivalent open-source results are obtained with Real-ESRGAN or SwinIR.

The artist can therefore prioritize gesture, composition, and color during creation and decide the physical dimensions only at the exhibition stage. The same logic now applies to moving images. AI super-resolution and frame-interpolation tools (e.g., RIFE, Topaz Video AI) transform modest sequences into fluid, high-definition projections suitable for large-scale immersive installations.

In the end, what emerges is a porous boundary between manual and virtual creation, where each dimension continually expands and redefines the other.

5.3 Hybridizations and Expansions with Artificial Intelligence

We have explored the intersections of real and digital painting, where manual gestures and virtual tools converge. Now we take a further step.

If digital painting extends the canvas into a space of infinite layers and modifications, Artificial intelligence introduces another dimension: the capacity of the image to generate itself through algorithmic processes.

AI-powered tools such as Stable Diffusion, Midjourney, and DALL·E transform painting into a space of co-authorship, where the artist's input—manual, digital, or textual—meets the algorithm's ability to produce unforeseen textures, forms, and atmospheres.

In my own practice, this idea takes shape in the series hybridizations and expansions. **Hybridizations** fuse heterogeneous sources—paintings, drawings, digital sketches, photographs—into new compositions where fragments intertwine and unexpected continuities emerge.

Expansions, instead, begin from a fragment or bounded work and push its limits outward, unfolding the image into new environments.

Conceptually, these operations parallel the **AI techniques of inpainting and outpainting**, where images are either completed from within or extended beyond their original frame.

They do not produce static pictures but fields of evolving possibilities, where boundaries between styles, media, and temporalities dissolve.

Painting becomes an expanded space, open to continuous reconfiguration.

In Figure 5-12 I present a virtual gallery created in Blender, in which works from the *Expansions* series are installed as looping video projections within fully navigable 3D spaces.

Figure 5-12. Gianpiero Moioli, Expansions, 2023–2025.
Virtual gallery created in Blender, displaying a series of manually painted works subsequently modified and expanded through artificial intelligence, and installed as video projections within Blender's virtual spaces

Here, manual paintings are reinterpreted and extended by AI, showing how traditional gestures, once bound to the canvas, can unfold into new spatial and aesthetic dimensions. In virtual space installations, these expanded fields migrate into immersive digital environments, where outpainting techniques allow painted forms to envelop viewers in 360-degree or VR experiences, dissolving physical boundaries and inviting ongoing, interactive reconfiguration of the artwork within boundless simulated architectures.

5.3.1 Hybridizations and Expansions with Artificial Intelligence

In my practice, *Hybridizations* emerge when two or more of my distinct real works are merged through digital painting and AI into a single composition or into a sequence of images.

I use this method to construct visual narratives, where painted forms become protagonists in unfolding stories.

The procedure does not simply overlay elements but creates a new continuity in which fragments intertwine, generating unforeseen visual logics and symbolic connections.

Expansions, by contrast, begin with a single manual painting whose boundaries are digitally pushed outward. The content generated in the expanded areas is then guided and hybridized by the visual syntax and chromatic fields extracted from other reference drawings, introducing a controlled formal contamination into the single final work.

AI becomes a means to amplify rhythm, add depth, and open trajectories beyond the canvas, transforming the original work into a field of evolving variations.

The resulting images do not remain fixed but continue to branch, unfold, and reconfigure themselves into alternative possibilities.

These processes also extend beyond static images, giving rise to video works in which hybridized and expanded paintings evolve through time as moving sequences.

Painting shifts from a static object to an open system of perpetual reinvention.

In this way, the work opens itself to new levels of interactivity and imagination.

***Hybridizations* invite the viewer to follow a thread of visual storytelling, while *Expansions* immerse the gaze in proliferating spaces that stretch beyond the initial frame.**

Two videos from this series can be viewed here:

- Hybrid Xenoscape: Looping metamorphosis (exemplifying Hybridizations)

  `https://vimeo.com/1141859810`

- Horizon Labyrinth: Iterative horizontal proliferation (exemplifying Expansions)

  `https://vimeo.com/1141886537`

The other steps of this trajectory will be addressed later: **Variations** in Chapter 7 and **Continous Spaces** in Chapter 10, which represent the dynamic developments of hybridizations and expansions.

5.3.1.1 Hybridizations

Hybridizations become interactive fields, expanding beyond their origins and resonating across dimensions of form, memory, and imagination.

Their creation unfolds in four stages:

1. **Initial gesture on canvas.** The process begins with a traditional work—an acrylic painting, drawing, or sketch—whose textures, marks, and expressive intention provide the authorial imprint (Figure 5-13).

Figure 5-13. Gianpiero Moioli, Cosmic Labirinths, Hybridization. 2023. *Three hand-made drawings serving as initial sources for Hybridizations, where manual gestures provide the foundation for subsequent digital transformations*

2. **Digital processing and AI blending.** The physical work is digitized, via scanner or photography, and then processed through generative AI.

   By combining it with another image, the algorithm creates hybrid compositions, weaving together fragments of style, form, and color into novel visual constellations that neither of the originals could anticipate.

3. **Material return.** The resulting hybrid image can be printed on paper or canvas and once again reworked manually. This stage reconnects algorithmic synthesis with human gesture, producing layered works where analog and digital signs coexist.

4. **Multiplicity of outcomes.** Hybridizations often yield parallel outputs: the unique physical original, the digital hybrid generated by AI, and a mixed form: the printed and manually retouched version.

   Each outcome embodies a different degree of transformation and meaning, situating the work within a continuum rather than a fixed state (Figure 5-14).

Figure 5-14.* *Gianpiero Moioli, Cosmic Labirinths, Hybridizations. 2023. *From three hand-painted works to a sequence of hybridizations, where manual gestures merge with digital processes to generate new visual continuities*

5.3.1.2 Expansions

Expansions reveal the painting as a process in growth, capable of projecting itself outward and multiplying its trajectories:

1. **Outward unfolding.** Using AI outpainting techniques,[11] the system analyzes the colors, textures, and rhythms of the original canvas, generating new sections that prolong its visual continuity. The painting thus becomes an "organism in growth," in which forms extend beyond the initial frame.

2. **Depth and rhythm.** Expansion is not merely spatial but also compositional. AI introduces variations in rhythm, adds layers of depth, and opens trajectories that the manual work alone could not anticipate.

3. **Reintegration and re-painting.** As with hybridizations, the expanded image can be re-materialized through high-quality prints. On these, the artist intervenes again with brushes, pens, or pigments, reactivating the work through manual gesture.

4. **Dynamic potential.** Expansions demonstrate how AI is not only a generator of alternatives but a catalyst that prolongs the lifespan of an artwork, allowing it to transform, branch, and reappear in multiple forms.

   What begins as a finite painting evolves into a field of variations, each one open to further reinterpretation (Figure 5-15).

[11] Outpainting, often perceived as intuitive, actually involves a complex negotiation between image and algorithm; see: `https://news.artnet.com/art-world/dall-e-outpainting-2171195#:~:text=Outpainting%20might%20seem%20intuitive%2C%20but,do%20touch%20ups%20by%20erasing`.

Figure 5-15. Gianpiero Moioli, Expansions, 2023–2025.
Above: "Dragon's Heart." Below: "Gravitational Field." Series of expansions where manual paintings are extended through AI, unfolding into new symbolic and spatial dimensions

In both hybridizations and expansions, painting unfolds across multiple layers of reality.

5.3.1.3 Authorship, Authenticity, and the Expanded Artwork

This practice raises crucial questions of authorship and authenticity.

The artist remains the author of all stages yet partially shares aesthetic authorship with the generative algorithm, which introduces unforeseen forms.

However, it is the **act of selection** that ultimately defines the work: the moment when intention and judgment turn potential into form.

Each AI output is critically evaluated, and only those results that align with the artist's vision are refined and integrated into the process.

In this sense, the creative gesture persists even within algorithmic systems. The decisive act is not the generation itself, but the **choice that transforms possibility into meaning**.

My experience suggests the emergence of a new concept: the **expanded artwork**, not as a single object but as an ecosystem of related images, connected by a shared visual DNA and a traceable lineage of transformations.

5.3.1.4 Toward Video and Multimedia Expansions

From images that multiply and transform, a natural step is their extension into time and sound, where painting expands into moving sequences and multimedia environments (Figure 5-16).

Figure 5-16. Gianpiero Moioli, Alien Gravitational Field, 2024.
Four frames from a video sequence generated with AI, expanding a manual painting into a time-based narrative dimension

This methodology also extends into the time-based dimension of video.

With tools such as Stable Diffusion or Midjourney, it is possible to create animated sequences. The artist defines a starting point and an end point, while the AI generates the intermediate passages.

5.3.1.4.1 Mini-Tutorial: Creating Short Video Sequences Using Midjourney V7 and Blender 5.0

Contemporary AI tools enable artists to craft concise animated sequences from two static images—whether original artist-created works digitized via scanning or modified through platforms like Midjourney—by leveraging text-to-video generation for intermediate frames and nonlinear editing for assembly.

This workflow produces clips of variable lengths and dimensions, suitable for immersive art, exhibitions, or digital publications.

The following is a step-by-step guide using Midjourney V7's image-to-video capabilities and Blender 5.0's Video Sequence Editor (VSE), emphasizing seamless morphing between start and end points.

1. Prepare keyframes in Midjourney.

   Upload or generate two images representing the sequence's start and end.

2. Generate video clips from keyframes and prompt.

   Add a start, an end clip, and a prompt. Activate Auto Sound or Auto Speech. Choose Duration and Quality Mode. Click Create.

   Create multiple sequences that you can then edit together.

3. Final Assembly in Blender 5.0 (Video Sequence Editor).

   Open Blender ➤ Switch to Video Editing workspace.

   - Add ➤ Movie ➤ Import all the clips to the sequencer.
   - Export: Output Properties ➤ FFmpeg Video (H.264) ➤ Render Animation (Ctrl+F12).

This method yields a coherent, emotionally resonant video narrative, where AI handles interpolation and Blender ensures professional polish.

For artists, it democratizes animation, turning digitized sketches into immersive experiences without specialized software.

When these short AI-generated clips are combined (cross-faded and layered with sound), they become powerful visual stories of strong emotional resonance.

Today, platforms such as Kling 2.5 and Runway Gen-3 go further by integrating autogenerated music, ambient sound, voice synthesis, and narrative scripts, giving rise to fully AI-driven storytellers capable of weaving coherent visual-auditory experiences in a single click.

A preliminary example of this workflow can be seen in the short morphing video that directly inspired my installation Labyrinth with Vector Physical Field, presented in Chapter 10.

You can find the video at `https://vimeo.com/1142208704`.

The sequence was generated using Midjourney V7 from selected renders of the 3D model originally created in Blender. These AI-generated clips were subsequently refined, synchronized, and combined into the final montage using Blender 5.0's Video Sequence Editor (Figure 5-17).

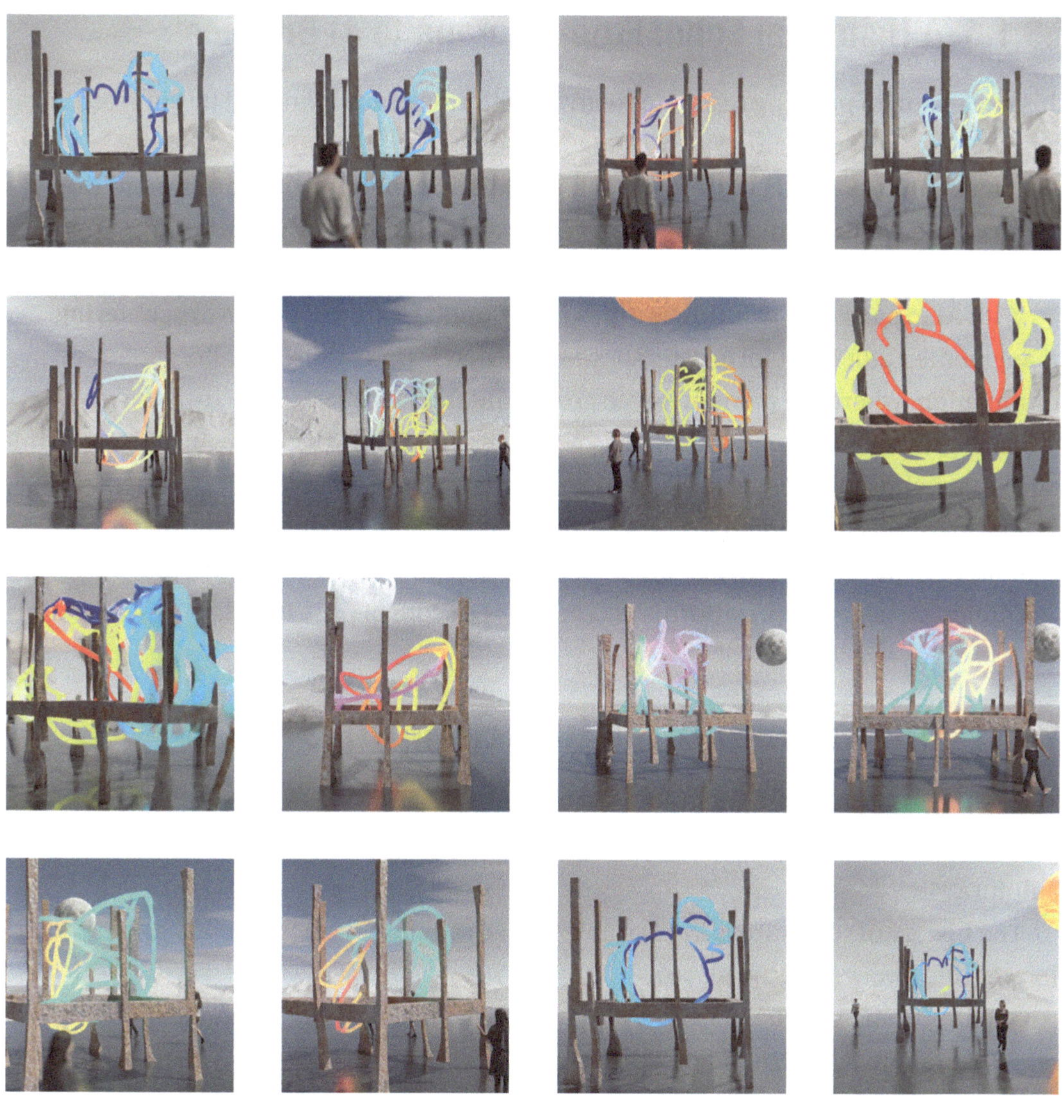

Figure 5-17. Gianpiero Moioli, Labyrinth with Vector Physical Field, 2025. *Selection of frames from the AI-generated video, based on a 3D model in Blender, later refined through Blender's Video Editor. The work explores the dialogue between physical structures and algorithmic light trajectories in a virtual environment*

Taken together, these outputs constitute a continuum of transformations, each digitally certified through the reproducible cryptographic provenance protocol described in section 4.3.4, thereby ensuring full authenticity and traceable versioning without reliance on central authorities.

5.3.1.5 A Historical Echo: From Fontana to AI Brushes

This expansion of painting resonates with ambitions already glimpsed by 20th-century artists.

Lucio Fontana, in his manifestos of Spatialism, called for the abolition of the illusory space of the canvas in favor of real space,[12] incorporating temporal and technological dimensions into art.[13]

With AI expansions, painting escapes the bounded frame of the canvas, entering an augmented albeit virtual artistic space—one that is potentially infinite, generated by computation, where the painted image grows and transforms.

Conceptually, AI can be regarded as an extension of the artist's brush, an algorithmic brush that paints following rules derived from vast archives of images.

The artist sets the parameters or text prompts, and the model generates; it is an indirect gesture, yet still a gesture, much like a composer writing notes that an interpreter, the algorithm, performs according to a score of possibilities.

5.4 From Manual to Virtual Sculpture

Moving from the domain of two-dimensional images to the volumetric realm, we encounter similar phenomena of hybridization and transformation in contemporary sculpture.

The history of sculpture is inseparable from the materials that embody artistic ideas: clay, marble, bronze, wood, plaster.

Each substance has been more than a medium. It has carried symbolic meanings of weight, durability, ritual, and transformation.

To model in clay, to carve stone, and to cast bronze meant to work with resistance, to submit imagination to matter's demands, and at the same time to project permanence into form.

---

[12] See *Concetto spaziale (Spatial Concept)*, Museo Reina Sofía. https://www.museoreinasofia.es/en/collection/artwork/concetto-spaziale-spatial-concept-1#:~:text=Lucio%20Fontana%20,concept%20of%20Spatialism%2C%20published

[13] See "Spatial Concept 'Waiting' by Lucio Fontana," *Singulart Blog*, April 2, 2024. https://www.singulart.com/blog/en/2024/04/02/spatial-concept-waiting-by-lucio-fontana/?srsltid=AfmBOoq1vKA4tP9BZKhOy1NXNVEUnT7oqy1Fea1lu9zIRbbeCZE1pzCd#:~:text=Lucio%20Fontana%27s%20Spatial%20Concept%2C%20Waiting%3A,dimensionality

Yet in the 20th century, with the *Manifesto of Spatialism* (1947), Lucio Fontana called for a radical rethinking: to move beyond the "illusory space" of the canvas or the traditional block of marble and to embrace real space and real time as new dimensions of art.

In this vision, sculpture was no longer confined to the closed object but opened toward the immaterial—light, energy, void—anticipating the conditions of the digital.

Today, the passage from manual sculpture to virtual sculpture continues this trajectory.

The digital matrix extends material gestures into new domains, gravity-free, infinitely scalable, and reversible.

What endures is the gesture. Whether chiseling marble or sculpting in VR, the artist shapes presence through absence, giving form to thought across different material and immaterial substrates.

5.4.1 Manual Sculpture as a Starting Point

Manual sculpture, using materials such as clay, wood, plaster, or metal, allows artists to give tangible form to ideas in a direct, physical way.

- Modeling clay by hand captures expressive detail and the immediacy of gesture
- Carving stone or wood emphasizes resistance, durability, and permanence
- Metalworking introduces constructive processes—welding, assembling, bending—that transform industrial materials into artistic form

These physical objects, born of tactile sensibility and manual labor, embody the dialogue between imagination and resistance.

A clay figurative model preserves the impression of the artist's hands; a bronze casting transforms a malleable sketch into a monument of endurance.

Each material carries its own ontology of form, and together they represent the foundation upon which contemporary translation into the digital can occur.

For example, the sculpture in Figure 5-18 combines steel structures with translucent resin highlighting the tension between weight and transparency. During daylight, the dark rigidity of the bars anchors the organic red volumes, while at night colored light turns the resin into a glowing presence.

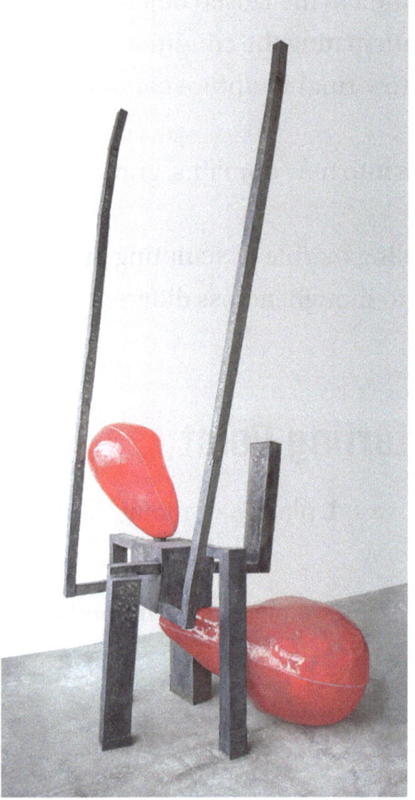

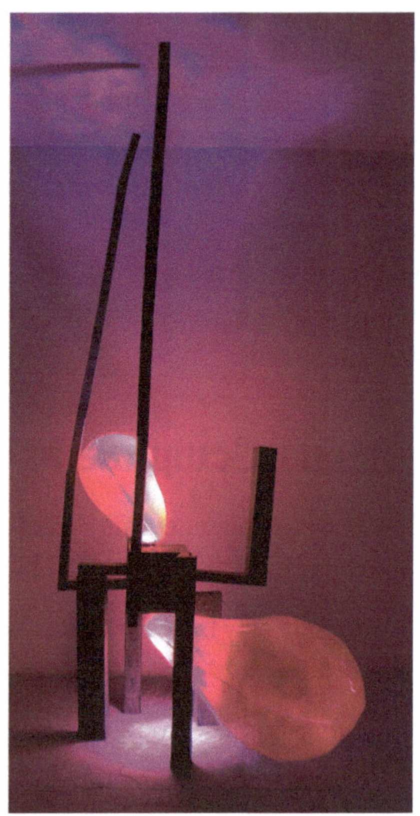

Figure 5-18. Albertini & Moioli, Bubbles Making Machine, 2007.
Iron, methacrylate, and LED. 350 (h) × 150 × 168 cm.
Iron and methacrylate structure with LED light, evoking a fantastical bubble-making device that turns a simple game into a poetic, visionary machine

Such examples show how manual sculpture remains a vital starting point. Each material—whether clay, wood, or resin—introduces its own logic of form, resistance, and expressivity. These physical objects, born of manual labor and tactile sensibility, can serve as foundations for digital translation.

Once scanned or reinterpreted in virtual space, they preserve the traces of material making while opening new horizons of transformation and exploration.

This represents one of the possible pathways by which manual sculpture enters into dialogue with digital processes.

5.4.2 Virtual Sculpture

In traditional sculpture, the process is additive, modeling clay or assembling materials, or subtractive, carving stone or wood, always leaving traces of physical gesture in matter.

In digital sculpture, too, processes remain additive or subtractive. Artists build up forms by extruding, inflating, or depositing virtual clay with digital brushes, or they carve away volume through Boolean operations, dynamesh subtraction, or surface erosion. These immaterial gestures faithfully mirror traditional sculptural logic while granting absolute precision, infinite undo, and impossible scales.

Here, physical matter is replaced by a purely mathematical representation—a polygonal mesh, subdivision surface, or implicit function—manipulated in real time through software interfaces.

Early digital modeling relied on mouse and keyboard, building geometric primitives point by point. Over time, tools became increasingly tactile and intuitive:

- 3D scanning (structured-light, laser triangulation, and photogrammetry) captures existing physical models or bodies with submillimeter precision, preserving the gestural traces of traditional making while opening them to digital metamorphosis. Full technical protocols—including device models, camera/lens specifications, capture counts, point-cloud density, alignment methods, and post-processing pipelines—are documented in Chapter 6.
- Blender and ZBrush introduced digital clay and sculpting brushes that behave like their physical counterparts.
- VR sculpting environments such as Gravity Sketch and Adobe Medium allow artists to work at real scale with tracked hand controllers, circling and shaping the virtual object as if standing inside the studio.

In my own practice, I have employed all three approaches—manual polygonal modeling in Blender, high-fidelity 3D scanning, and procedural generation—often combining them within a single workflow.

The digital domain offers expanded possibilities. Forms can be suspended without gravity, variations can be endlessly tested and undone, and motifs can be replicated and scaled with precision, allowing flexibility and openness to transformation that surpass traditional material constraints.

Once slow, point-by-point operations can now be generated, transformed, and scaled with unprecedented freedom.

Virtual sculpture extends the artist's gesture beyond matter, allowing the creation of works that oscillate between presence and absence, permanence and fluidity, embodying the very essence of Spatialism in the digital age.

The virtual sculptures illustrated in Figure 5-19 emerge precisely from this convergence. Real-world elements, captured through high-resolution 3D scanning, are incorporated into the compositions, preserving the tactile memory and accidental traces of their material origin.

Figure 5-19. Gianpiero Moioli, Virtual sculptures modeled in Blender. *Combining manually sculpted objects with algorithmically generated forms. The works explore the encounter between hand-driven gesture and procedural logic, material and digital presence*

Alongside them, manually sculpted components—shaped in Blender's Sculpt and Edit modes—retain the expressive imprint of the hand-guided gesture translated into virtual space.

Finally, algorithmically generated structures, driven by procedural and parametric logic, expand the sculptural vocabulary beyond the limits of individual gesture.

The resulting works stage a continuous dialogue between hand and algorithm, material memory and digital invention.

5.4.3 Algorithmic Growth: Toward Procedural Sculpture

One of the most disruptive aspects of contemporary sculpture is the introduction of procedural and parametric methods.

Tools such as Blender's Geometry Nodes or Houdini allow the artist to define networks of algorithmic rules that generate geometry from parameters rather than from direct manual modeling (Figure 5-20).

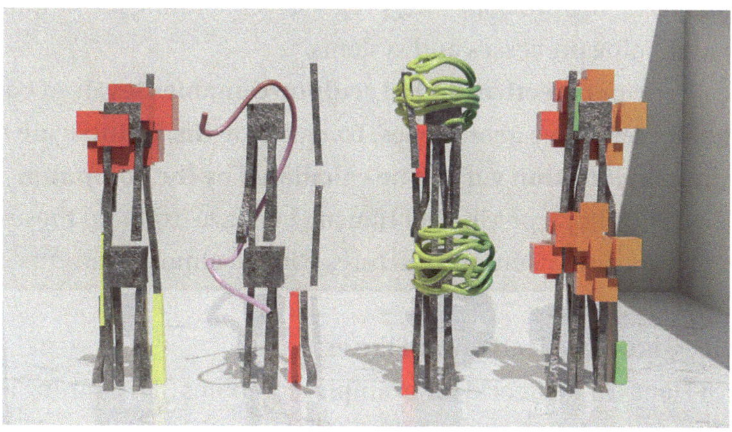

Figure 5-20. Gianpiero Moioli, Virtual procedural sculptures in Blender. *Manually modeled grey structures are combined with procedurally generated organic colored forms*

In this paradigm, the sculptor no longer shapes a single object but designs a system capable of producing potentially infinite objects.

A set of nodes might generate branching patterns, or modular grids that expand and transform according to density, curvature, or scale. Adjusting parameters reshapes the entire structure in real time, establishing a dynamic relationship between form and process.

This approach simulates processes of artificial growth and morphogenesis, shifting the focus from the finished object to the rules of its becoming.

As discussed in Chapter 3, this redefines the artistic gesture itself.

A practical example comes from my own practice, where I employ modifiers and node systems in Blender to generate procedural textures and surface patterns.

These often echo natural fractals or classical geometric motifs, creating a bridge between historical ornament and algorithmic generation.

5.4.4 Sculpting Processes: From Hands to Code to AI

The spectrum of techniques available to sculpture today is vast.

As outlined in Figure 3-1 in Chapter 3, the continuum of sculptural processes can be mapped through their interconnections.

This trajectory unfolds across four stages: manual real modeling, manual digital modeling, procedural generation, and AI or data-driven practices.

Each stage builds on the previous one, progressively shifting the emphasis from shaping matter to shaping processes and systems.

From an aesthetic perspective, digital sculpture enables levels of complexity once unimaginable: recursive geometries, fractal growths, or intricate interlacings that challenge human intuition yet can be calculated by the computer.

Artists such as Julius Popp or Michael Hansmeyer have explored these directions, producing columns and architectural structures with an almost "baroque" density of detail.

Other practices, however, lean toward the essential.

Belgian artist Hans Op de Beeck, for example, combines 3D scanning and digital modeling to create monochromatic sculptural worlds, rarefied and meditative.

In his recent exhibition *Nocturnal Journey* (2025), he presented 39 life-size sculptures derived from digital captures of everyday objects and human figures, reproduced manually in grey resin with a uniform dusty finish.[14]

His method—digital scanning in the design phase, followed by manual refinement of the resin sculptures—unites the precision of reality with poetic reinterpretation.

Op de Beeck's authorship emerges in the overall composition, while his works balance digital precision with the tactile presence restored through resin finishing.

As Guendalina Perelli observes, "(...) the scanner reproduces reality, but the artist reinterprets, organizes, and rewrites it sculpturally; (...) the result is not a cold copy, but a poetic echo, filled with temporality and emotion."[15]

This poetic echo emerges precisely from the meeting between digital replication and human interpretation.

Though "born from pixels," the sculpture ultimately speaks through the silence of matter, engaging the viewer in a tangible and contemplative experience.

Op de Beeck's example demonstrates that new technologies do not necessarily lead to shiny, high-tech aesthetics; on the contrary, they can renew timeless sculptural themes—vanitas, dream, memory—through contemporary means.

5.5 Hybrid Practices Between Real and Virtual Sculpture

Just as painting has expanded into the digital dimension, sculpture too undergoes a profound transformation.

A new kind of sculpture is born in the void of virtual space, where forms grow like organisms shaped by code, algorithms, and the artist's hand.

On the screen, every curve and tension is sculpted immaterially.

Increasingly, these forms are modeled and experienced in virtual reality, where the artist can walk around the work, sculpt at real scale, and test spatial relationships in immersive environments.

---

[14] *Nocturnal Journey* by Hans Op de Beeck at the KMSKA in Antwerp (March 22 - August 17, 2025), Exhibition: https://kmska.be/en/kmska-presents-hans-op-de-beeck-nocturnal-journey

[15] Guendalina Perelli, *Art and Design: Digital and Handcrafted Sculpture,* TheSignSpeaking, June 11, 2025. https://www.thesignspeaking.com/enart-and-design-digital-and-handcrafted-sculpture/#:~:text=One%20of%20the%20most%20original,remains%20unmistakably%20a%20visual%20storyteller

Yet the work does not remain suspended in data: through 3D printing it acquires matter, layer by layer, like a sedimentation of time.

The initial PLA print—fragile, imperfect, biodegradable—is then translated into durable bronze or ceramic via lost-PLA casting or slip-casting techniques (full print parameters, mold-making steps, shrinkage compensation, and observed dimensional tolerances are documented in Appendix F).

This back-and-forth movement expands the very idea of sculpture.

The digital file becomes the authenticated original matrix. Its integrity is cryptographically verified and its provenance tracked on a blockchain ledger (technical details of hashing, signing, and NFT metadata standards are provided in Appendix G).

Each physical manifestation—whether in PLA, bronze, or ceramic—is accompanied by a certificate attesting to its derivation, while digital versions themselves may circulate as NFTs.

In this way, sculpture lives as a passage between worlds: an idea translated into code and returned to matter.

The following sections will explore how this hybrid condition unfolds—through 3D scanning and material translation, as well as through digital fragments that preserve memory in new, unexpected forms.

5.5.1 From the Real to the Virtual and Back Again: 3D Scanning and Printing

3D scanning digitizes manual sculptures into virtual models, enabling further manipulation in modeling software and acting as **a two-way bridge between the physical world and the digital domain.**

In my sculptural workflow I adopt two approaches:

- In the first, the work is physically modeled by hand—or a classical artwork is scanned—and then captured through 3D scanning to be transferred into virtual space.
- In the second, the sculpture is conceived and created directly in the digital realm using software.

The resulting model can be retopologized, cleaned, modified, combined with other elements, and eventually brought back into the physical world through 3D printing, transforming immaterial forms into tangible objects. It can also be experienced in immersive virtual environments, becoming a sculptural space of exploration.

These technologies greatly facilitate the design process, not only for sculpture but also for video sculpture, installations, and hybrid works where digital experimentation converges with traditional materials and new technologies.

3D printing relies on different methods: **fused deposition modeling (FDM)**, which deposits layers of melted plastic; **laser sintering (SLS/DMLS)**, which fuses metallic or polymer powders; and **stereolithography (SLA)**, which uses light to solidify resin into finely detailed forms. **Each of these technologies (FDM, SLA, SLS) offers a distinct balance of speed, precision, and material compatibility, critically determining the choice of the final object's characteristics.**

The comparative analysis of these methods, including their specific operational parameters, materials, and impact on the final sculptural outcome, **will be explored in detail in the following chapter.**

All share the ability to generate complex forms directly from a file, layer by layer.

In art, they are used for both prototypes and finished works.

In my practice, I often print PLA models as preliminary prototypes, which then serve as molds for casting in bronze or ceramics.

In this way, the qualities of classical materials—tactility, color, durability—combine with the formal freedom of digital design, creating a temporal short-circuit between tradition and future.

Scanning, in turn, is not only a tool for creation but also for knowledge and preservation. Projects like *Scan the World* are digitizing thousands of renowned sculptures and sharing the models online, making them available for anyone to print or remix.

Institutions such as the SMK - National Gallery of Denmark are also releasing digitized collections in open access, expanding the global circulation of cultural heritage (Figure 5-21).[16]

[16] SMK - National Gallery of Denmark, 3D digitized collections on Sketchfab: `https://sketchfab.com/smkmuseum`

Figure 5-21. Apollo Belvedere, 3D scan.
3D model released under CC0 license by SMK - National Gallery of Denmark, available on Sketchfab

Platforms like Sketchfab[17] further amplify this process by making many 3D models freely available under various licenses, thereby encouraging reuse by artists, educators, and enthusiasts worldwide.[18]

This marks a radical change: volumetric data of works once accessible only in person now circulate globally.

Imagine a Corinthian capital or an ancient fragment scanned and then reinserted, via 3D printing, into a contemporary installation: the boundaries between original and copy, quotation and innovation, blur, opening new layers of meaning.

[17] Sketchfab is an online platform for publishing and sharing 3D models, including open access collections from major museums and institutions. `https://sketchfab.com/`

[18] License Audit Note: While Sketchfab hosts significant open-access content, practitioners must verify the specific Creative Commons (CC) license assigned to each model before reuse, as not all licenses permit commercial use or the creation of derivatives. The detailed analysis of CC license types (CC0, CC BY, CC BY-NC, CC BY-ND) and their implications for generative practice is fully outlined in section 4.2.3.

In this sense, 3D printing for sculpture is what photography was for painting: enabling reproducibility and manipulation, while simultaneously pushing creativity into uncharted territories.

It frees sculpture from many technical constraints, while raising new ontological questions: is a printed sculpture less "authentic" than one carved by hand, or simply different?

From an operational perspective, scanning and printing workflows often require technical expertise and collaboration.

High-definition digitization may involve laser or structured-light scanners, followed by extensive mesh cleaning; software such as Blender streamlines these operations; 3D printers or foundry artisans complete the translation into traditional matter.

This recalls the production model of the Renaissance workshop, now updated as the digital workshop.

Another key value is scalability. The same file can be printed small for study, or enlarged to monumental scale.

Variations in form or dimension can be achieved simply by adjusting the file.

This leads to new aesthetics. Some works deliberately expose printing striations or low-resolution polygons, integrating them as a visual language; others, conversely, erase all traces of digital process, restoring an aura of classical timelessness.

5.5.2 Lost Codes: Fragments of Memory in Digital Clay

A series of my works rooted in these concepts is titled *Lost Codes,* which evokes the silent persistence of memory within ruins.

Here, fragments of classical forms—broken, recomposed, reimagined—become new signs, suspended between past and future. They are not conceived as inert relics but as living codes, calling us to reread what history has left in fragments.

At the core of *Lost Codes* lies the dialectic between memory and erasure, between what humanity has preserved and what risks dissolving into oblivion.

The sculptures are not neutral abstractions; they carry with them hidden histories, much like archaeological remnants unearthed from unknown civilizations—echoes of lost knowledge that demand interpretation.

For example, in *Metaphysical square with Apollo, 2025, mixed media, cm.53(h) x 65 x 43* (Figure 5-22), I drew inspiration from Giorgio De Chirico's *Piazze d'Italia,* in particular *The Song of Love* (1914).

That painting, with its enigmatic juxtaposition of classical fragments and metaphysical urban space, became the initial spark for my design.

In the work, I integrated a 3D scan of a real object—Apollo's head—into the virtual scene.

I downloaded the scan of a plaster model made by Danis from Sketchfab, released under a CC BY 4.0 license,[19] and modified it for my composition.

Methodological Note on Derivatives:

The original mesh was subjected to significant modifications to integrate it into the work *Metaphysical Square with Apollo.*

The process involved both destructive and generative steps:

1. **Destructive shaping:** The mesh was **cropped and selectively cut** to create a fragment.
2. **Architectural integration:** This fragment was then **integrated into the overarching architectural or metaphysical structure** of the scene.
3. **Digital refinement:** Finally, the resultant form was subjected to further digital processing, including **retopology**, **re-shading**, and the **integration of procedural damage via Blender Geometry Nodes** to fit the narrative.

In accordance with the CC BY 4.0 license, this modified derivative is attributed to the original creator (Danis), and the resulting file is also made available under CC BY 4.0.

To programmatically ensure license compliance, the required attribution text and the original asset URI are permanently embedded in the metadata section of the Certified Digital Manifest (CDM) established in Appendix A.

By merging a scanned cultural fragment with newly modeled geometry, the virtual model itself became a collage of temporal layers, where past and future coexist in deliberate tension, like a metaphysical stage suspended between eras.

The *Lost Codes* series embraces the weight of matter and the logic of structure, unlike purely imaginative modeling, where forms may ignore gravity or material constraints (Figure 5-22).

[19] Model "Apollo (Head)" (`https://skfb.ly/oPAI8`) by Danis is licensed under Creative Commons Attribution 4.0 (CC BY 4.0) (`http://creativecommons.org/licenses/by/4.0/`). Required Attribution Text: "Apollo (Head) by Danis, licensed under CC BY 4.0, modified by the author."

Figure 5-22. Gianpiero Moioli, Metaphysical Square with Apollo*, 2025, mixed media, cm.53(h) x 65 x 43.*
A 3D scan of the Apollo Belvedere merges with digital forms in a alien world and a suspended time

Every digital stroke is conceived with gravity, stability, and durability in mind so that the works can truly stand in space.

This produces an atmosphere of suspension, where the fragments do not belong entirely to the past nor fully to the future but remain poised in a timeless interval.

In many of these projects, classical and neoclassical sculptures, acquired through 3D scanning, provide the raw material.

Once celebrated as emblems of reason, harmony, and spiritual aspiration, they are digitally fragmented, recomposed, and reinterpreted.

Through this process, ancient symbols are not merely quoted; they are given new life.

Their aura is displaced, yet never extinguished, it mutates, opening the door to new readings.

This dynamic is embodied in works such as *The Dragon in the Labyrinth, 2025, mixed media, cm. 88(h) x 58 x 55,* where metallic fragments and vibrant digital forms converge, suggesting the ruins of an alien world reimagined as a metaphysical stage between past and future (Figure 5-23).

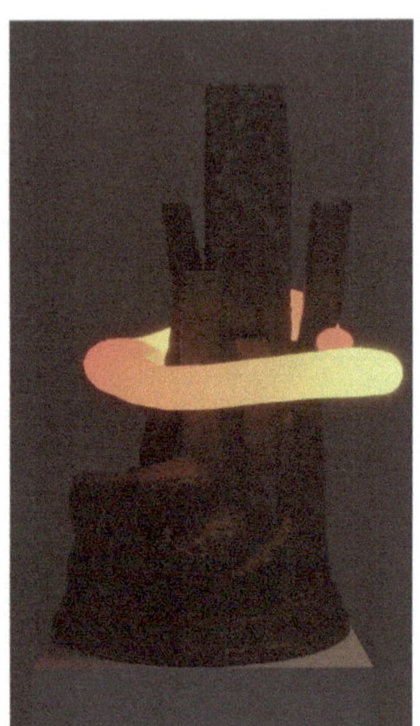

***Figure 5-23. Gianpiero Moioli, The Dragon in the Labyrinth, 2025**, mixed media, cm. 88(h) x 58 x 55.*
A luminous serpentine form coils around metallic ruins, evoking memory and suspended time

Thus, the *Lost Codes* works appear as if they were ruins from an alien world: remnants of an unknown civilization, at once familiar and estranged.

Their forms evoke a metaphysical stillness but also the uncanny silence of extraterrestrial landscapes scattered with enigmatic monuments.

Lost Codes are not nostalgic ruins but living seeds of possibility.

They transform memory into invention, archaeology into speculation, opening thresholds where antiquity resonates with visions of alien futures.

5.6 Beyond Sculpture and Painting

This last section examines 2D and 3D modeling and scanning as creative processes that translate physical forms into digital models, enabling new artistic possibilities.

Together with 3D printing, these processes frame the relationship between real and virtual art, showing how physical and digital dimensions can coexist and inform one another.

To better understand these dynamics, Figure 5-24—similar to those presented at the beginning of the chapter (Figures 5-4 and 5-5)—maps the technical processes and operational flows between real and virtual, two-dimensional and three-dimensional.

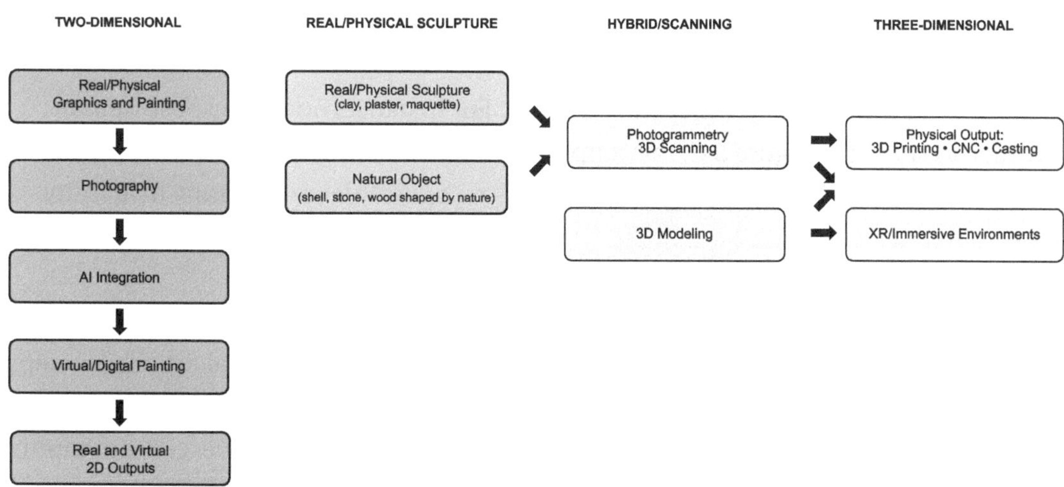

Figure 5-24. Hybrid workflow: from two-dimensional to three-dimensional practices.
Diagram mapping the continuum from manual graphics, painting, and sculpture through hybrid processes such as 3D scanning, toward digital modeling, XR environments, and physical fabrication

I refer here also to Figure 2-12 in Chapter 2 to connect this new diagram to the broader design framework.

This diagram illustrates the continuum from manual graphics, painting, and sculpture through hybrid processes such as 3D scanning, toward digital modeling, XR environments, and physical fabrication.

It reveals how contemporary workflows are not linear but relational. Each phase can feed back into the others, creating cycles of transformation in which manual, digital, and algorithmic practices converge and expand the boundaries of artistic creation.

At the core of this continuum is the reciprocal relationship between matter and code.

Matter represents the physical support, charged with permanence, tactility, and uniqueness. Code, by contrast, embodies the immaterial domain—the algorithm, the digital file, the bit—marked by reproducibility, mutability, and speed of dissemination.

In today's hybrid works, these two dimensions no longer remain separate.

Such works embody a double ontology. They are at once ideas and objects, processes and products.

5.6.1 Multiple Dimensions

All these dynamics also reflect on other aspects. For instance, one of my post-human portraits, as shown in Figure 5-7, may appear as a canvas print, a video file, or an NFT, and in each case the same conceptual imprint is recognizable: a continuity of identity across different states.

This fluidity compels us to reconsider the notion of the original.

In classical art, the original was tied to matter: the one canvas painted by the artist, the unique bronze casting, or a limited and numbered edition. In digital art, the concept of originality becomes elusive, since a file can be copied perfectly.

It is no coincidence that systems like blockchain and NFTs have emerged, attempting to guarantee digital uniqueness through cryptographic certificates.

In my works, every element is provided with certification, as if to affirm that originality resides in the authentic link between the different states rather than in the medium itself.

This principle is operationalized through the **Certified Digital Manifest (CDM)**, established in Appendix A, which serves as the auditable record for the entire transformation chain.

The detailed template, examples, and procedures for secure signing and archival storage (PGP, DOI/Zenodo) are fully detailed in Appendix C.

We are thus confronted with an expanded concept of authenticity, where the creative trace matters more than the aura of a single object.

This transformation recalls what happened with the invention of printmaking and photography, but here it is amplified: not only is the artwork reproducible, it is also pluripresent in different formats.

The relationship with tradition, in this context, becomes dialectical.

On the one hand, technology literally allows tradition to be incorporated into the work—through the scanning of classical fragments or the AI stylization of historical pictorial genres—ensuring continuity of memory.

On the other, it challenges traditional values: manual skill partly gives way to the ability to conceive and direct; permanence yields to potential evolutivity, as in generative works that change over time or in successive versions of a software-based artwork.

After all, the Brera Academy itself was founded precisely to combine artistic and artisanal practice with conceptual and theoretical dimensions.

From its Enlightenment origins, the institution did not aim solely at manual mastery but sought to train **artists, designers, and experts in new technologies** capable of integrating technical expertise, critical reflection, and openness toward the sciences.

5.6.2 Post-Human Identities

One particularly significant theme that has emerged in this chapter is that of identity.

In classical figurative art, identity was often represented in stable terms, the portrait fixed the features of a person in a moment.

In my post-human portraits, identity is captured in its becoming, in its multiplicity.

Faces and bodies are fragmented, hybridized with foreign elements, as if to suggest that in the technological age, human subjectivity itself becomes a pliable material.

The use of AI to generate faces that do not exist—or to merge multiple identities into a composite face—reflects the idea of **the post-human**, in which the individual is no longer confined to the boundaries of its own flesh but extended and transformed through the digital. This raises urgent questions: can AI capture something of a person's essence, or does it only produce an empty simulacrum?

What is the role of the artist in ensuring that these images carry depth and meaning, rather than becoming mere aesthetic manipulations? To prevent the latter, the artist's intervention is critical.

From the cases examined, it becomes clear that the key lies in poetic intention that provides the necessary human intentionality to the algorithmic output.

Another dimension to consider is the role of the viewer.

In these hybrid and transformative works, the viewer is often called to an active or interpretative role.

Consider a digital sculpture experienced in virtual reality. Here, the viewer explores a simulated space in 360°, instead of physically moving around it. The screen—or headset—becomes itself an exhibition medium.

Already in the 1980s and 1990s, artists such as Studio Azzurro spoke of works existing on two dimensions of reality, concealing technology to highlight poetic and participatory experiences.

Today, technology is even more pervasive, yet paradoxically invisible. The artist, therefore, inherits the responsibility to bridge this gap.

The contemporary viewer must therefore educate their gaze: to discern when they are encountering matter, when code, and to appreciate the intertwining of the two.

In conclusion, matter, code, identity, and imagination today form a unified connective tissue for the most innovative contemporary art.

My own practice—constantly oscillating between real and virtual—offers an emblematic example of how an artist can "construct geometries of the invisible: emotional maps, traces of possible worlds" within this hybrid fabric.[20]

Matter is no longer only visible and tangible, but also invisible and algorithmic; code is not mere calculation but becomes poetic matter, a new clay to be modeled; identity is no longer fixed, but a story in becoming; imagination knows no clear boundaries between dreamed and realized, because machines help us visualize the nonexistent with startling realism.

5.7 Conclusion

The works presented in this chapter—painterly expansions, AI hybridizations, digital and post-human sculptures—bear witness to states of transformation in which every medium contaminates the other: painting becomes a virtual environment, sculpture turns into data and then back into body, the artist becomes a programmer, and the program almost a co-author.

What emerges is a fascinating and still largely unexplored territory, where each technical innovation not only unlocks new expressive possibilities but also raises new critical questions.

The horizon that takes shape is that of a *transmedial* and *transmaterial* art, where the real and the virtual no longer oppose each other but converge into a single augmented reality of imagination.

Like a palimpsest, where history leaves its traces and fragments while the present overwrites them with digital languages, today's art layers together different times and media.

It is up to the artist—and to the viewer—to discover within this palimpsest the resonances, the threads of meaning, and the visions of the future.

[20] See: https://gianpieromoioli.it/blog/

In this horizon, states of transformation are no longer transitory moments but the permanent condition of art in the 21st century: an art in perpetual metamorphosis, a mirror of a world in which **change itself has become the only constant**.

The exploration of this condition consequently demands a methodological focus that extends from guaranteeing **authenticity and provenance** (ensured by the certification of the digital matrix) to its precise and reproducible **translation into matter**.

This very translation, through 3D printing and physical fabrication processes, will be the subject of our analysis in the next chapter.

5.8 Appendix F: Detailed Fabrication and Casting Protocols

This appendix provides the comprehensive, reproducible technical specifications and quality control metrics necessary to replicate the physical conversion of the certified digital assets (Appendix A) into durable physical artworks (bronze or ceramic).

5.8.1 3D Printing (PLA): Master Model Generation

This phase establishes the initial physical positive (master model) used for subsequent silicone molding.

Parameter	Detailed Value	Reproducibility Note
Device Used	Prusa i3 MK3S+ or equivalent (FDM)	Standard Fused Deposition Modeling printer.
Filament	PLA (White or Gray), 1.75 mm	Chosen for ease of post-processing.
Layer Height	**0.12 mm**	Optimal balance between speed and surface detail.
Infill Density	**15% (Gyroid Type)**	Ensures rigidity with minimal weight for handling.
Support Removal	Manual post-print, finished with light sanding/filler to eliminate layer lines.	

5.8.2 Silicone Molding and Casting Preparation

The PLA master model is used to create a flexible mold for producing a sacrificial wax copy.

Phase	Method/Material	Technical Detail
PLA Preparation	Fine sanding (up to P400 grit)	Essential to remove FDM layer lines and achieve a smooth finish.
Silicone Mold	Platinum Cure Silicone (e.g., Smooth-On Mold Star 30)	Two- or multi-part mold designed for easy release.
Casting Wax	Microcrystalline Casting Wax	Low-pressure injection to ensure fidelity of detail.
Gating System	Manual addition of **sprues and vents** to the wax copy.	Critical artisanal step to prevent air pockets and miscasts.

5.8.3 Lost-Wax Casting (Bronze Investment Casting)

The casting protocol adapts the digital model for permanent metallic realization.

Parameter	Detailed Value	Rationale/Impact
Metal	Silicon Bronze (e.g., C87500)	Offers good flow properties and surface finish.
Digital Shrinkage Compensation	**+2.0%** (Applied to the.stl file pre-print)	Compensates for the average shrinkage of bronze during cooling; crucial for dimensional accuracy.
Investment Material	Ceramic Shell (e.g., Ultravest or equivalent)	Supports high temperatures and fine detail capture.
Casting Temperature	Varies (typically $1050^\circ C - 1100^\circ C$)	Rigorously controlled to prevent *short pours* and porosity.

5.8.3.1 Observed Failure Modes (Examples)

1. **Surface Porosity:** Caused by insufficient venting of gases in the investment or incorrect casting temperatures. Solution: Welding and grinding repair.
2. **Extreme Shrinkage (Warping):** Due to uneven wall thickness in the original digital model. Solution: Revision of the initial digital model.

5.8.4 Quality Control and Dimensional Verification

Final verification between the digital file and the finished bronze object.

Measured Metric	Result (Example on 300 mm Model)	Purpose
Measured Actual Shrinkage	$\approx 1.95\%$ (after digital compensation)	Validates the effectiveness of the preventative digital scaling.
Maximum Deviation (Post-Finish)	**<0.5 mm**	Ensures the final physical work is faithful to its digital origin.
Final Mesh Triangle Count	2.5 million – 5 million	Confirms that digital complexity is substantially maintained in the physical form.

These protocols ensure that the physical work is not a mere reproduction, but a faithful and certified continuation of the original creative gesture, closing the loop between bits and matter in a single chain of verifiable authenticity.

5.9 Appendix G: Ethical, Legal, and Provenance Implications of the Certification Protocol

While **Appendix A** details the cryptographic methodology for establishing file integrity, this appendix addresses the consequential frameworks.

It operationalizes the concept of "expanded authenticity" by exploring the legal and ethical implications of using verifiable blockchain provenance in artistic practice, clarifying authorship, ownership, and the role of the certified digital matrix.

5.9.1 Technical Definition of "Authenticated and Certified"

Before examining the legal landscape, it is essential to translate the philosophical claims of digital uniqueness into precise technical definitions grounded in the data structure of the **Certified Digital Manifest (CDM)**.

- **Authentication (Integrity):** Achieved via the **SHA-256 Hashing Algorithm** (Appendix A). The unique hash serves as the verifiable digital fingerprint of the file.
- **Certification (Timestamping):** Achieved by linking the SHA-256 hash to an immutable time source (e.g., **OpenTimestamps** anchored to the Bitcoin blockchain, as outlined in Appendix A). This proves the file existed unchanged from that time onward.
- **Chain of Custody/Signing:** The previous_hash field in the certification record (Appendix A) creates a verifiable, unbroken chain of transformations, effectively signing the entire workflow from initial input to final output.

5.9.2 Implications for Intellectual Property (IP) and Rights

The certification protocol clarifies ownership and creation rights, crucial in a generative pipeline:

1. **Creation Date:** The timestamp provides incontestable proof of when the digital file was finalized, which can be critical in disputes over prior art or simultaneous creation.
2. **IP Rights (Original Matrix):** Certifying the initial file establishes it as the **original matrix** (the source data). Any subsequent physical or digital version is derived from this certified source, strengthening the author's claim over all resulting works.
3. **Copyright Protection:** While hashing does not *create* copyright (which is automatic upon creation), it provides **strong technical evidence** supporting the copyright claim against potential infringement, as the certified file's integrity and creation date are provable.

5.9.3 Provenance and Resale Rights

The protocol enhances provenance far beyond traditional methods:

- **Immutable Provenance:** The chain of custody (hash links) provides an auditable history of the asset, demonstrating every step (AI transformation, human refinement, 3D modeling) taken by the artist.
- **Secondary Market:** For future sales, the buyer can verify the integrity of the digital matrix (or the final physical manifest) against the publicly recorded hash. This eliminates doubt regarding authenticity and forgery, significantly enhancing the asset's value.
- **Resale Rights (Ethical Consideration):** Although no NFT is minted to enforce automatic royalties, the artist may specify in the *Certification Record Notes* (Appendix A) or in a separate contract (Bill of Sale) a commitment to honor future **Droit de Suite/Resale Rights**. The certified record acts as a binding document for this ethical commitment, even without automated smart contracts.

5.9.4 Technical Conflicts: NFT Marketplaces

The choice to use a noncommercial standard (OpenTimestamps) necessitates specific considerations when interacting with marketplaces (even if only for documentation):

- **Metadata Standards (ERC-721/1155):** Standard NFT marketplaces rely on the Ethereum/Polygon infrastructure and metadata schemas (e.g., ERC-721). Since this project avoids minting, the certified manifest replaces standard NFT metadata.
- **Mapping:** The key fields in the Appendix A Certification Record (sha256_hash, timestamp, transformation_tool) effectively serve the same function as NFT metadata, providing the necessary verifiable data points, but anchored to Bitcoin/OTS rather than the marketplace's proprietary contract.
- **Code Example:** The Python code in Appendix A already provides the necessary function (sha256_hash) to compute the file hash, which is the foundational technical step required by this process.

5.9.5 Public Implementation: Certificate of Derivation

While the Certified Digital Manifest (CDM, defined in Appendix A) establishes the cryptographic integrity and provenance chain, the **Certificate of Derivation** serves as the publicly accessible, human-readable document delivered alongside the final artwork (physical or digital).

This certificate translates the technical data of the CDM into a legal and transparent statement of the work's origin, thereby operationalizing the concept that originality lies in the authentic link between states.

5.9.5.1 Template of the Certificate of Derivation

The certificate extracts, summarizes, and signs the most critical fields from the underlying CDM records:

Field	Description	Source Data	Relevance to Authenticity
Title of Work	Official title of the final artwork (e.g., *Metaphysical Square with Apollo*)	Metadata	Unique Identification
Author / Artist	Principal creator	Metadata	Intellectual Property Assertion
Final File SHA-256 Hash	Cryptographic fingerprint of the final certified file (.obj, .stl, or final rendering)	sha256_hash of the final record	**Verifiable Integrity**
Creation Date (Initial)	Date and time of the earliest certified event in the chain	timestamp of the initial record	Proof of Prior Art
Provenance Chain Root	Hash of the original source file (link to the first CDM record)	Aggregated previous_hash	Transformation History Trace
Upstream License Check	Details on the license and attribution of incorporated third-party materials (e.g., CC BY 4.0)	notes	**Legal Compliance Assurance**
Signature Method	Method used to cryptographically secure the certificate	External Data	Proof of Authorship and Non-Tampering

5.9.5.2 Example Certificate: Metaphysical Square with Apollo

This example illustrates the practical application of the CDM data for the artwork discussed in Chapter 5:

Field	Example Value
Title of Work	Metaphysical Square with Apollo (Edition: Bronze 1/5)
Author / Artist	Gianpiero Moioli
Final File SHA-256 Hash	7f1a3b8c2d5e0f9a456...a4f1a9b3c5
Creation Date (Initial)	2025-10-27T14:30:00Z
Provenance Chain Root	Root Hash: 6b2c1d0e9f8a7b6c... (Full log available via Appendix A protocol)
Upstream License Check	Source material "Apollo (Head)" licensed under CC BY 4.0 by Danis. Attribution text embedded in CDM metadata.
Signature Method	PGP Signature (Key ID: 0x1234ABCD)

5.9.5.3 Secure Signing and Archival Storage

To ensure the Certificate of Derivation is trustless and permanent, two mandatory security steps are implemented:

- **Secure Signing (PGP):** The final Certificate of Derivation (and the underlying CDM record) must be digitally signed by the author using a cryptographic key pair (**PGP/GPG** recommended). This step provides mathematical proof that the document originated from the artist and has not been altered since its issuance.
- **Institutional Archival (DOI/Zenodo):** To ensure long-term persistence and academic citability, the full Certified Digital Manifest (JSON file) and the final technical asset are deposited in an institutional repository (such as **Zenodo**).

  This service provides a **Digital Object Identifier (DOI)**, creating an immutable reference that links the physical or final digital artwork to a permanent, independently verified record of its transformation chain.

In conclusion, the certification protocol—via SHA-256 hashing, OpenTimestamps on Bitcoin, and verifiable chain-of-custody—operationalizes expanded authenticity by linking digital origins to physical outcomes through the Certified Digital Manifest and the human-readable Certificate of Derivation. It delivers strong, verifiable evidence of authorship, provenance, and transformation history, aligns with growing legal acceptance of blockchain timestamps in IP disputes, and affirms that originality today lies in the traceable continuity across all states of the work—fostering ethical transparency and a sustainable bridge between tradition and technological evolution.

CHAPTER 6

From Virtuality to Matter: 3D Printing and Material Translation

The passage from virtual to material represents one of the most radical shifts in contemporary artistic practice.

Digital creations, once confined to the screen, can now be transformed into tangible objects through advanced 3D printing and innovative fabrication techniques.

This chapter explores that transition: the evolving dialogue between immaterial design and physical matter, as well as the ways artists today bridge conceptual imagination with material form in unprecedented ways.

Contemporary artists embrace this duality, materializing their visions while adopting new strategies—such as digital certificates or NFTs—to preserve the authenticity and value of each piece.

At the same time, 3D printing blurs traditional boundaries. Like bronze casting or engraving, it allows multiple physical instances to emerge from a single matrix. Yet because its origin lies in the digital file, it also carries the logic of infinite reproducibility.

While the digital file exhibits perfect reproducibility (each copy is bit-identical), physical 3D prints inherit variations from machine state, material batch properties, and environmental conditions, meaning no two prints are truly identical within typical tolerances (±0.1-0.2mm for FDM). More significantly, the economic logic differs bronze casting becomes more efficient at scale (amortizing mold costs across many casts), while 3D printing maintains linear time and material costs per unit, making "infinite" reproduction theoretically possible but practically constrained. This positions 3D printing in unique territory: reproducible in principle (like casting), variable in practice (like hand-making), and economically linear (unlike both).

G. Moioli, *Art Between Matter and Code*, https://doi.org/10.1007/979-8-8688-2376-3_6

In this sense, the technology disrupts the neat opposition between direct and indirect methods, positioning itself as a hybrid practice that both materializes and multiplies the digital.

Finally, 3D printing reconfigures the distinction between craftsmanship and industry.

On one side, it supports artisanal experimentation. Small, customized, and even improvised works can be created directly in the studio. On the other hand, the very same file can be scaled for industrial manufacturing, replicated across multiple machines worldwide.

This dual nature makes 3D printing unique: at once intimate and global, singular and serial, artisanal and industrial.

It is precisely this tension—between uniqueness and reproducibility, tradition and innovation—that defines the new terrain where virtual ideas meet material presence.

6.1 From Virtual Model to Material Object

This section examines the journey from a digital 3D model to a physical object.

It explores how artists conceive and design virtual sculptures and then bring them to life through 3D printing.

For me, the enduring dream of every artist is to materialize an idea: to transform an immaterial vision into a tangible presence.

In my own practice, I begin with immediate and malleable substances such as clay and plaster, which allow gestures to be captured almost as quickly as they are imagined.

These traditional materials embody a form of immediacy; the hand shapes them while the mind envisions.

Once the concept is established, more advanced methods can consolidate and refine the work.

Here 3D printing becomes invaluable. It extends the logic of sketching in paper, clay, or plaster into a new technological domain, where ideas can be preserved, tested, and realized in durable form.

In this sense, 3D printing occupies ambiguous territory within traditional sculpture taxonomies.

It is clearly an indirect method requiring the intermediary digital file rather than direct manipulation of final material, yet it disrupts the temporal and economic structures of traditional indirect methods. Where bronze casting involves a long processes through foundries and mold-makers, 3D printing can progress from file to finished form in days, collapsing the distance between conception and realization.

Moreover, the digital file exists as information rather than material object, enabling instantaneous global transmission and perfect duplication more difficult for physical molds. This dual nature, indirect in structure, immediate in execution, positions 3D printing as a hybrid practice that both materializes individual instances and multiplies the underlying design without material degradation.

The focus here is the practical workflow of moving from bits to atoms: modeling, slicing, printing, and post-processing, all while preserving the creative vision.

The workflow is not a straight line but a living cycle whose seven stages constantly feed back into one another:

1. Digital modeling (CAD/3D software)
2. Mesh preparation (repair, wall-thickness verification, orientation)
3. Slicing (layer height, supports, infill)
4. Printing
5. Support removal and inspection
6. Post-processing (sanding, filling, priming, finishing)
7. Evaluation against the original creative intention

Each stage feeds back into the others. A failed print forces changes in the model, post-processing reveals details that demand new digital gestures, and the material's behavior under the nozzle suggests revised parameters.

The practical workflow is therefore never linear; it is an iterative cycle in which every error becomes a source of refinement.

Yet these stages also form a true continuum. The spontaneity of the first digital gesture survives intact through every translation. The slicer interprets it in the technical language of layers and supports; the printer deposits it, drop by drop, into physical reality; post-processing finally restores the tactile warmth and visual subtlety the artist imagined from the outset.

In this sense, 3D printing is far more than a technical tool: it is an extension of creativity itself—a living bridge between thought, code, and matter.

6.1.1 Designing Virtual Models for Fabrication

Digital sculpting and modeling software serve as the starting point for works destined to become physical or to exist as fully immersive experiences in VR.

In my practice, I approach virtual modeling with a clear idea that evolves through successive design phases, as discussed in section 2.4 in Chapter 2.

I work iteratively in the digital stage before any printing begins.

Tools such as Blender's 3D Print Toolbox add-on help me verify geometric printability—identifying nonmanifold geometry, intersecting faces, and minimum wall thickness (I typically set 2-3mm for PLA structures), and checking for overhangs exceeding printable angles (~45° without supports for FDM).

For actual structural integrity analysis, I rely on physical prototyping and empirical testing, with balance assessment performed by manual center-of-mass calculation in Blender.

For large works, I often design modular parts to be printed separately and later assembled.

The modular design and assembly approach requires technical elaboration on tolerance management and registration systems. Parts are designed with a minimum tolerance gap (typically 0.2–0.4mm depending on the printer) and utilize simple registration keys or interlocking mechanisms (pins and holes or tongue-and-groove joints) to ensure alignment and structural rigidity during the final bonding phase.

It is important to note that, unlike mechanical engineering, the requirements in art are centered on visual and structural integrity rather than precision functionality; this allows for a greater degree of flexibility in tolerance management, as minor imperfections are often mitigated during the post-processing and finishing stages.

This process highlights the hybrid nature of digital design: at once creative and engineering-oriented.

The sculpture *Little Metaphysical Piazza with a Cloud* exemplifies this principle. Its modular architecture suggests stability, while the cloud element shows how digital logic can integrate organic, lightweight forms.

In the renders shown in Figure 6-1, the work is still virtual yet already conceived in physical terms. Every aspect—proportions, dimensions, and materials—has been defined as if it were real.

Figure 6-1. Gianpiero Moioli, Little Metaphysical Piazza with a Cloud, 2025, *mixed media, cm. 52 (h) x 46 x 37.*
The work illustrates the transition from virtual modeling to fabrication. The architectonical structure evokes stability, while the cloud element shows how digital design integrates organic and light forms

At this stage, the digital sculpture is no longer just an image or a sketch, but a structure fully prepared for translation into matter.

The virtual design phase is more than preparation. It is already the first act of materialization.

The transition to slicing marks a threshold where imagination must adapt to the language of gravity, supports, and fabrication.

Figure 6-2 highlights the software interface and the adjustments required to ensure that the digital form remains consistent with both the aesthetic vision and the technical constraints of fabrication.

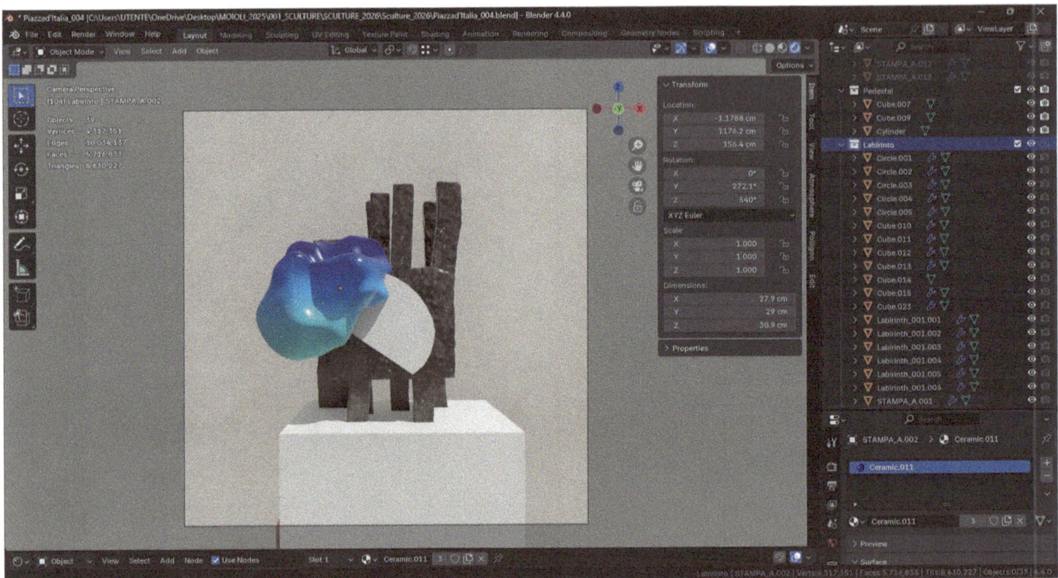

Figure 6-2. Little Metaphysical Piazza with a Cloud (2025).
The sculpture depicted during the virtual modeling stage in Blender. The software environment allows the artist to refine proportions, check structural feasibility, and prepare the digital model for subsequent 3D printing

In this sense, modeling is not only the prelude to printing but already the first act of materialization, where imagination is gradually aligned with the language of machines.

6.1.2 Materializing Digital Designs with Advanced Printing

Once the digital model is fabrication-ready, the next step is slicing.

Software such as Ultimaker Cura or Anycubic Slicer Next converts the 3D model into G-code, translating geometry into layers.

In this stage, artists set parameters like layer height, infill density, and supports, while many aspects are optimized automatically by the program.

For example, when *Little Metaphysical Piazza with a Cloud* is loaded into Anycubic Slicer Next, each cross-section is previewed.

The software rotates the piece for optimal orientation and adds supports for the overhanging cloud.

This preparation bridges the poetic design and the realities of the printer's capabilities (Figure 6-3).

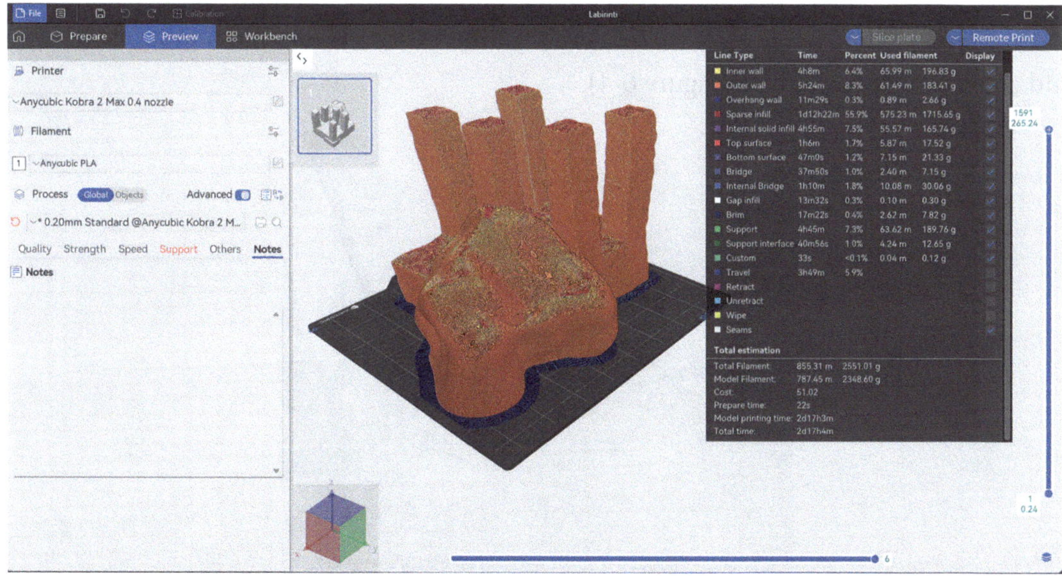

***Figure 6-3.** The 3D model of Little Metaphysical Piazza with a Cloud.* *The sculpture is ready for printing in a slicing program (Anycubic Slicer Next). The software generates layer-by-layer toolpaths from the virtual design, here showing a preview of the object and its supports before printing*

The printer then extrudes material along the defined tool paths, building the object layer by layer, like a sedimentary accumulation of ideas turned into matter.

In my case, an Anycubic FDM printer with PLA bioplastic was used for the first version of *Little Metaphysical Piazza with a Cloud.*

Yet the initial print is rarely the final step.

A PLA prototype may later serve as a master for bronze or ceramic casting or be reprinted in specialized resins.

In this way, each material translation transforms both physical properties (texture, durability, weight, patina) and aesthetic experience while maintaining geometric and compositional continuity from the digital source.

Whether this constitutes "preserving a conceptual core" depends on one's theoretical position. Idealist approaches treat the digital model as embodying an immaterial concept that material instantiations express, while materialist approaches (following theorists like Tim Ingold) argue that each material translation generates distinct meanings through its specific affordances, sensory qualities, and cultural associations suggesting that a work exists as a constellation of related but nonidentical material versions rather than multiple instances of a singular concept. In my practice, I embrace both perspectives. The digital model functions as a generative source enabling controlled variation, while each material realization offers distinct phenomenological and conceptual possibilities (Figure 6-4).

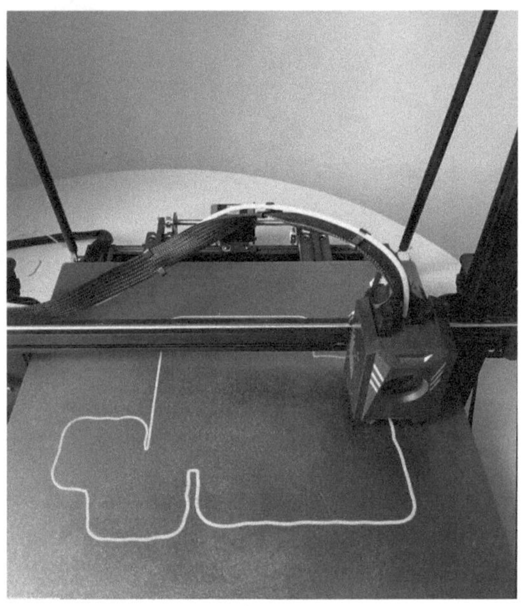

Figure 6-4. First layer of the 3D printing process.
The nozzle deposits the initial contour in PLA bioplastic, marking the very beginning of the sculpture's emergence from digital code into matter

The PLA version of my sculptures serves as a steppingstone: relatively fragile compared to engineering plastics, compostable under industrial conditions (though persistent in typical environmental exposures), bearing the imperfections of the printing process, receiving form through slow deposition, layer by layer, like a sedimentation of time.[1]

[1] PLA requires industrial composting facilities (58°C+) to biodegrade within three to six months. In ambient conditions, degradation is minimal. Artists should not dispose of PLA prints as "biodegradable" waste without access to proper composting infrastructure. This accuracy is essential for ecological credibility of arguments about material sustainability.

Each phase—from virtual model to plastic print to a metal or ceramic cast—is a material translation that adds new texture and longevity without losing the conceptual core.

The raw print also requires finishing: removing supports, sanding, priming, and sometimes painting.

Often prints are produced in sections that must be assembled by hand.

At this stage, digital precision meets artisanal skill, and the artist interprets the work anew in matter.

By the end of this journey, the once-virtual idea stands as a tangible artifact—a materialized digital design—ready to engage viewers in the physical world (Figure 6-5).

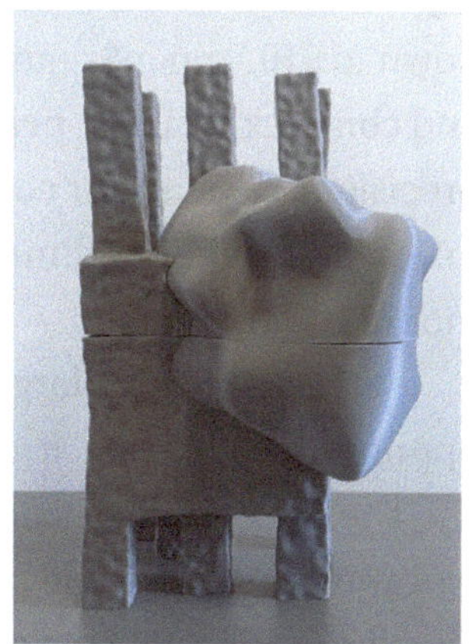

Figure 6-5. Little Metaphysical Piazza with a Cloud (2025), *mixed media, 52 × 46 × 37 cm.*
The sculpture printed in two separate sections and subsequently assembled. The PLA version is shown here before post-processing and surface finishing

Here the artist's role is crucial: technical precision merges with aesthetic judgment.

Digital skills for design are combined with manual and artisanal expertise in the finishing process. The digital work is not simply reproduced but reinterpreted in matter, each layer embodying both algorithmic logic and human intention.

Thus, the passage from virtual model to physical sculpture is not a neutral transfer but a creative act where algorithmic logic and human intention converge in a tangible presence.

6.2 Techniques, Materials, Processes

Today, in the mid-2020s, 3D printing has fully evolved from a niche prototyping tool into a sophisticated platform for creation, enabling artists to materialize complex forms with unprecedented precision and speed.

This shift, accelerated by advancements in multi-material printing, AI-driven optimization, and sustainable bio-inks, has expanded its role beyond rapid iteration to the production of end-use artworks, including hybrid sculptures that blend digital design with organic textures.[2]

Artists today can rely on high-precision systems—such as **ultra-fine resin printers**, capable of XY resolutions between 22 and 35 microns (μm) and layer heights down to $10 \mu m$—and multi-material jetting to produce works of exceptional detail and complexity. **High-precision FDM systems** also contribute significantly, offering precision adequate for complex assembly with layer heights routinely reaching $50 \mu m$ or less, and high-dimensional accuracy (down to $\pm 0.1 \text{mm}$) crucial for modular work.

At the same time, large-format extrusion and powder-bed processes expand opportunities of scale, material diversity, and structural performance.

These technologies not only surpass the limits of traditional methods but also open pathways to sustainable practices, employing recycled or biodegradable composites and enabling applications at architectural scale.

Cutting-edge approaches such as multi-material printing and robotic fabrication allow intricate structures once deemed impossible, with designs that mimic organic growth or respond dynamically to their environment.

[2] Key 2025 innovations include generative AI for lightweight structures (Raise3D, 2025), carbon-negative materials like chitin composites (Meshy AI, 2025), and seamless prototyping-to-production pipelines (Materialise, 2025). These capabilities, now standard in tools like Blender 5.0 and Prusa MK4 printers, democratize high-fidelity fabrication for artists, reducing costs and environmental impact while supporting serial editions and custom installations.

Pioneering figures like Neri Oxman have demonstrated some of the numerous possibilities offered today in digital fabrication. Her team, for example, used a multi-material 3D printer to design an intricate mask for musician Björk, integrating multiple textures into a single piece to reflect the complexity of human anatomy.[3]

Such innovations are dramatically expanding the artist's toolkit, blending technology and creativity in ways that redefine what a sculpture or installation can be.

Equally transformative is the explosion of material choices now available for 3D printing, which profoundly influence both the appearance and the structure of an artwork.

Material has always functioned as artistic language from Michelangelo's marble to Serra's steel, material choice shapes meaning as much as form.

What 3D printing changes is the ease of medium experimentation. The same digital model can be rapidly tested in multiple materials, making comparison an explicit part of the creative process rather than a commitment made early in conception.

This separation of form-conception from physical realization enables artists to explore how identical geometries speak differently in PLA, resin, metal, or ceramic, treating material choice as a variable to be systematically explored rather than a predetermined constraint.

Plastics and resins remain staples for their fine detail and versatility; metals allow the creation of durable pieces with metallic luster; ceramic and clay bring earthy textures and a handcrafted quality; concrete enables architectural-scale forms with rugged presence.

Each medium imbues the work with distinct aesthetics and physical properties. A resin print might appear delicate and translucent, while a metal print conveys strength and permanence.

Beyond these familiar media, artists are experimenting with novel and hybrid materials.

---

[3] For a detailed case study of multi-material 3D printing in wearable sculpture, see Neri Oxman's "Rottlace: A Series of 3D-Printed Masks for Björk," *Architect Magazine*.
`https://www.architectmagazine.com/technology/neri-oxman-designs-rottlace-a-series-of-3d-printed-masks-for-bjork_o`

For example, Neri Oxman's research has explored **biomaterials.**[4] Her Aguahoja I pavilion, for instance, was fabricated using a biocomposite derived from chitosan (from shrimp shells), cellulose (from plant matter), and pectin (from fruit).[5] This process utilized **multiple digital fabrication methods, including robotic 3D printing**, to create an organic structure that naturally biodegrades and enriches its environment instead of polluting it (Figure 6-6).[6]

Figure 6-6. Neri Oxman, Subterrain (2008).
Part of the Material Ecology series, exploring natural growth, erosion, and biodegradation as design principles. By ercument gorgul, Flickr, CC BY 2.5

[4] See also "3D Printed Art: Neri Oxman Uses FDM Technology for Latest Installation," Stratasys Direct. `https://www.stratasys.com/en/stratasysdirect/resources/case-studies/neri-oxman-3d-prints-art/`

[5] The core innovation of the Aguahoja project lies in its biocomposite material composition (chitosan, cellulose, pectin) and its robotic fabrication method, primarily through water-based 3D printing that integrates computational design with self-assembling hydrogels.

This process draws on multiple techniques, including robotic extrusion and environmental self-assembly, to produce works that fully biodegrade. The material data for the Aguahoja pavilion (5,740 fallen leaves, 6,500 apple skins, and 3,135 shrimp shells) is taken from the project's official description by Neri Oxman and the Mediated Matter Group. `https://oxman.com/projects/aguahoja`

[6] For a visual behind-the-scenes of Neri Oxman's design and fabrication process, see *Rottlace by Neri Oxman / Mediated Matter - Getting Ugly* on YouTube. `https://www.youtube.com/watch?v=14flotuAzfY&t=1s`

This kind of radical material experimentation opens new aesthetic possibilities: imparting organic textures, translucencies, or even living qualities to art, while also embedding deeper conceptual meanings.

An artwork can now be designed to **evolve or decay** as part of its lifecycle, aligning with environmental principles.[7]

By embedding such natural dynamics into design, Oxman demonstrates a present in which objects are conceived not as static artifacts but as living systems open to transformation.

She calls this approach "material ecology," intentionally designing with processes like growth and biodegradation in mind to create sustainable, adaptive works.[8]

In short, from advanced printing technologies to an eclectic range of materials, artists in 2025 have an expanding toolkit that allows them to tailor both the look and the structural behavior of their artworks to an unprecedented degree, marrying form with function in imaginative new ways.

At the same time, it is useful to distinguish between the comprehensive technical classification of additive manufacturing processes, as defined by ISO/ASTM standards,[9] and the subset of techniques most relevant to artistic practice.

While ISO/ASTM identifies seven main process families of 3D printing, ranging from industrial-scale processes to highly experimental methods,[10] this chapter focuses on the four most relevant to artistic practice: Material Extrusion (FDM/FFF) for its accessibility and versatility; Vat Photopolymerization (SLA/DLP) for high-resolution detail; Powder Bed Fusion (SLS/SLM) for its structural strength and durability; and Material Jetting

[7] See "Material Ecology: Nature // Humanity," SFMOMA — an insightful exploration of how Neri Oxman integrates natural systems and 3D printing in her work. `https://www.sfmoma.org/read/material-ecology-nature-humanity-neri-oxman/`

[8] See: `https://lifestylesmagazine.com/nox25/#1`

[9] The international technical standards that officially define and classify additive manufacturing (AM) processes. See ISO/ASTM 52900: "Additive manufacturing - General principles - Terminology" (2015, updated 2021).

[10] The ISO/ASTM standard identifies seven AM process categories: (1) Binder Jetting, (2) Directed Energy Deposition, (3) Material Extrusion (includes FDM/FFF), (4) Material Jetting (includes PolyJet/MultiJet), (5) Powder Bed Fusion (includes SLS, SLM, DMLS, EBM), (6) Sheet Lamination, (7) Vat Photopolymerization (includes SLA, DLP, CLIP).

Each category encompasses multiple technologies, ranging from industrial-scale processes for aerospace and biomedical engineering to experimental methods with limited diffusion.

(multi-material systems) for its unique aesthetic and chromatic capabilities. Large-format applications are addressed separately as they represent scaling of these core technologies rather than distinct processes.

This streamlined framework reflects the processes that have had the greatest impact on contemporary artistic production, without losing sight of the broader technological landscape.

In the following sections, each of these key techniques will be examined in detail.

6.2.1 Advanced 3D Printing Techniques

Contemporary artists employ diverse 3D printing technologies, each offering distinct advantages: **FDM** excels in material variety, large format capability, and mechanical strength; **SLA/DLP** provides superior surface finish and fine detail for small to medium parts; **SLS/SLM** enables complex geometries without support structures and metal material options; and **Material Jetting** allows multi-material and full-color capabilities (Figure 6-7).

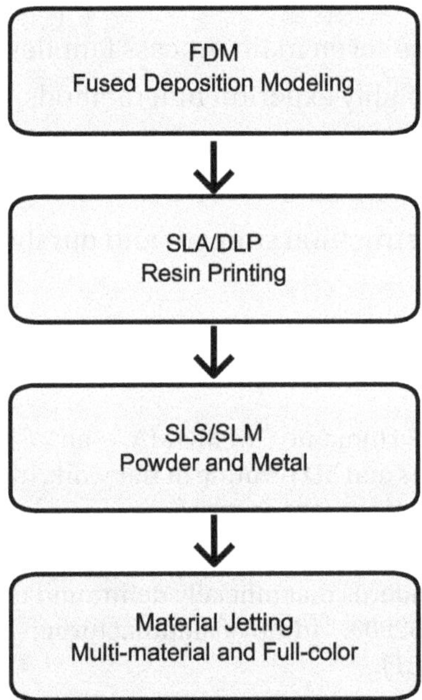

Figure 6-7. Advanced 3D printing techniques.
From FDM as the most accessible method to SLA/DLP for high-precision resin prints, SLS/SLM for powder and metal fabrication, and Material Jetting for multi-material and full-color capabilities

Technology selection depends on the specific requirements of each artwork resolution needs, material properties, scale, production quantity, and post-processing tolerance rather than hierarchical advancement.

For **Fused Deposition Modeling (FDM)**, or **Fused Filament Fabrication (FFF)**, the most widespread and accessible method works by heating and extruding a thin filament of thermoplastic such as PLA or ABS through a nozzle, depositing the material layer by layer until the object is complete. This is a principle often compared to a hot glue gun guided by digital instructions.[11]

When a design includes overhanging elements, the printer generates temporary support structures, later removed or dissolved.

Valued for its affordability and versatility, FDM nevertheless produces visible layer lines.

For some artists these marks become a new aesthetic language, openly revealing the object's digital origins, while others smooth the surface through post-processing such as sanding, priming, or painting to align the final piece with their intended vision.

Recent research has shown that PLA filaments enhanced with agricultural by-products, such as carrot pomace and ground walnut shells (at 1–5% concentrations), can be optimized for FDM printing while maintaining mechanical viability for artistic applications.[12]

While these bio-additives increased flexural strength by up to 44.9% (compared to pure PLA), they simultaneously reduced breaking stress by ~15% (and extensibility by ~9.5% at lower concentrations), demonstrating a clear trade-off between stiffness and ductility.

Crucially, the fillers also enhanced biodegradability, with weight loss rising to 7.6% after 120 days in acidic soil (pH 5.5)—up to 6.35% faster than pure PLA—further expanding the sustainable material palette available to artists, though higher additions may increase brittleness and extrusion inconsistencies.

---

[11] See: https://www.researchgate.net/publication/385997251_A_Survey_of_Fused_Deposition_Modeling_FDM_Technology_in_3D_Printing

[12] "Mechanical properties and biodegradability of samples obtained by 3D printing using FDM technology from PLA filament with by-products," Nature Scientific Reports, February 18, 2025. https://www.nature.com/articles/s41598-025-89984-0

By contrast, **Stereolithography (SLA)**[13] and **Digital Light Processing (DLP)**[14] adopt a radically different principle.

Instead of extruding melted plastic, these vat-photopolymerization methods use light to cure liquid resin layer by layer: a laser in the case of SLA or a projected image in the case of DLP. Working at far higher resolution than FDM, they produce exceptionally smooth surfaces where layer lines are often invisible to the naked eye.

For artists, this means the ability to capture the subtlest of details—expressive gestures, fine textures, or translucent effects—that FDM would blur.

Printers such as the Formlabs Form 4 or the Anycubic Photon Mono M5s Pro make it possible to produce small figurative or organic pieces with a finish close to glass, ideal for evoking immateriality, fragility, or ethereal presence.[15]

In this way, SLA and DLP bring the material properties of the print into closer alignment with the nuances of the digital model, ensuring that even the finest elements of a virtual vision survive the passage into physical matter.

Selective Laser Sintering (SLS)[16] and **Direct Metal Laser Sintering (DMLS)**[17] extend digital sculpture into the realm of strength and permanence.

Using lasers to fuse powder materials—whether plastics such as nylon or metals such as steel and bronze—these systems can produce durable objects with complex geometries. Unlike FDM or resin printing, they require no added support structures, since the surrounding powder stabilizes the form during fabrication. A digital sculpture printed in metal through DMLS acquires the solidity and reflective finish of traditional casting while allowing for far more intricate designs.

---

[13] See: https://formlabs.com/blog/ultimate-guide-to-stereolithography-sla-3d-printing/?srsltid=AfmBOopW1xqMiNeLU9lxRKA4q3SpiC1aovID5Ebfo_k84b4u5hdkrUJA&utm

[14] See: https://www.stratasys.com/en/resources/blog/digital-light-processing-dlp-3d-printing-explained

[15] The Form 4 offers an XY resolution of 50 microns and layer heights down to 25 microns, while the Photon Mono M5s Pro achieves 16.8 × 24.8 µm XY resolution and 10-micron layers, enabling exceptional detail in compact build volumes (200 × 125 × 210 mm for Form 4; 223.78 × 126.38 × 200 mm for M5s Pro).

[16] See: https://formlabs.com/uk/blog/what-is-selective-laser-sintering/?srsltid=AfmBOorZBoITRZH7th7qgIfb2aexaEE9h29r-wRUsSx67mPtJH4C1nXt&wtime=%7Bseek_to_second_number%7D&

[17] See: https://www.protolabs.com/en-gb/resources/insight/direct-metal-laser-sintering/

Artists turn to these processes for medium-scale sculptures or jewelry-like works where strength, detail, and luster are essential, and where iteration is faster than in conventional foundry practice.

Another frontier opens with **multi-material and color 3D printing**, where the printer itself becomes a tool for mixing textures, transparencies, and hues directly during fabrication. Unlike single-material processes, these systems can deposit or solidify different materials within the same build, enabling effects once achievable only through manual painting or assembly.

In **Material Jetting (MJP)** technologies such as **Stratasys PolyJet**, dozens of nozzles spray droplets of different photopolymer resins, which are immediately cured by UV light.[18]

This makes it possible to combine different materials into a single print—rigid and flexible zones, transparent and opaque elements, or even smooth gradients of color and mechanical properties—achieving color fidelity, texture variety, and ultra-fine detail in one workflow.

Full-Color Binder Jetting (CJP)[19] follows a different principle. Starting from a powder bed of plastic, gypsum, or sand, a print head selectively deposits liquid binder and colored inks layer by layer. Once consolidated with resin or infiltration, the result is akin to a 2D inkjet print expanded into three dimensions, producing models with intricate motifs or photographic shades embedded in the material itself.

The goal is to integrate material and color variation during printing rather than adding it afterward.

Alongside these, **Powder Bed Fusion technologies** extend polymer printing (SLS) into high-strength materials: Selective Laser Melting (SLM) and Electron Beam Melting (EBM) produce durable metallic parts for structurally demanding artworks, while Multi Jet Fusion (MJF) offers fast polymer fabrication for end-use prototypes.

These processes are crucial for artists seeking robust, functional sculptures.

By contrast, the **Material Jetting family**—including PolyJet (Stratasys) and MultiJet Printing (MJP, 3D Systems)—transforms the printer into a volumetric palette. Textures,

[18] See: "PolyJet Technology for 3D Printing," Stratasys guide to technologies and materials. `https://www.stratasys.com/en/guide-to-3d-printing/technologies-and-materials/polyjet-technology/`

[19] See "How to Design Parts for Binder Jetting 3D Printing," Hubs Knowledge Base. `https://www.hubs.com/knowledge-base/how-design-parts-binder-jetting-3d-printing/`

colors, and material gradients are deposited drop by drop, enabling intricate, multi-material compositions conceived as three-dimensional paintings.

6.2.2 Beyond the Studio: Large-Format Granulate Fabrication

Large-format fabrication represents the next step in this trajectory.

If multi-material and color printing transform the 3D printer into a painter's tool, large-format approaches turn it into an architectural instrument.

They extend additive manufacturing from the scale of small objects to that of monumental sculpture and outdoor installations, as well as experimental architectural components.

This is the realm of Large-Format Fused Granulate Fabrication (FGF), where extrusion machines no longer rely on fine filament spools but instead process raw granulates such as plastic pellets. An example is the Ginger Additive G1,[20] a pellet-based 3D printer with a build volume of one cubic meter, designed for large-scale fabrication in recycled or technical plastics.

Through the direct use of plastic granules, this approach reduces costs and supports circular design principles, making it particularly relevant for sustainable production in the arts.

Another branch of large-format 3D printing focuses on clay and concrete extrusion systems, which push additive manufacturing into the realm of architecture and construction.

WASP's Crane system can print the primary structural shells of habitable dwellings using a biocomposite material based on locally sourced soil and clay mixed with natural fibers and binders.

Projects such as TECLA (2021) demonstrate this capacity, though conventional construction methods are still required for building systems (electrical, plumbing), openings (doors, windows), and finishes.[21]

[20] See `https://www.gingeradditive.com/`.

[21] WASP's earth-based printing material is a precise biocomposite typically comprising local soil/clay (70–80%), water (15–20%), rice husk or straw fibers (5–10% for mechanical reinforcement and crack reduction), and a small percentage of hydraulic binder (such as lime, 1–5%) to control rheology and setting time. Specific ratios are calibrated on-site based on local soil composition for optimal extrudability and structural integrity.

Similar approaches are being tested with concrete, enabling experimental pavilions and structural components.

In this sense, large-format 3D printing is more than a tool. It is a strategy for rethinking material cycles and for designing works that embody both scale and sustainability.

Each advanced technique can be seen as a different "brush" or chisel in the artist's toolkit.

What unites them all is that technology is never an end, but always a means to serve the artwork's vision, ensuring that the final physical piece conveys the essence of the digital concept with maximum force.

6.2.3 Material Choices for Aesthetic and Structural Impact

Just as important as the printing method is the choice of material, which profoundly influences an artwork's look, feel, and longevity.

Figure 6-8 summarizes the principal categories of materials—plastics, resins, metals, ceramics and concrete, and experimental composites—highlighting how each shapes both aesthetics and structural behavior.

Plastics
PLA, ABS, PETG
versatile, accessible

Resins
SLA/DLP
ultra-fine detail, smooth finish

Metals
SLS/SLM/DMLS
strength, durability

Ceramic Concrete
Earthy texture, architectural scale

Experimental / Hybrid
Bio-based, composites,
biodegradable

***Figure 6-8.* Diagram of material categories used in 3D printing for artistic practice.**
Each group offers distinct aesthetic and structural qualities: plastics (versatile and accessible), resins (ultra-fine detail and smooth finish), metals (strength and durability), ceramic/concrete (earthy texture and architectural scale), and experimental or hybrid composites (bio-based, biodegradable, or innovative blends)

In 3D printing, artists are no longer confined to plain plastics.

Today they can draw on a broad spectrum of substances, each with its own aesthetic qualities and structural behavior. Choosing a material is not merely a technical step but part of the creative dialogue, shaping how a sculpture appears, feels, and endures.

Plastics remain the most common entry point.

PLA, ABS, and PETG are staples of FDM printing, with PLA especially favored in artistic contexts.

Derived from corn, it is easy to use, available in countless colors, and affordable.

Its intrinsic fragility can even become a conceptual asset. In works like *Alien Landscape with Clouds,* (Figure 6-9) PLA's ephemerality underscores themes of impermanence.

At the same time, the material can be painted or polished to elevate a raw print into a finished artwork, as shown in Figure 6-9, where surface treatments and color variations enhance the expressive quality of the form.

***Figure 6-9. Gianpiero Moioli, Alien Lansdcape with Clous, 2025**, PLA, cm.41(h) x 33 x 39 cm.*
The work exemplifies the use of PLA printing refined with surface finishing

A 3D printing model can also be enriched with fillers—such as marble for a stone-like density, wood for organic warmth, metal powders for a reflective sheen, or carbon fibers for a matte, high-tech finish with increased structural strength—each imparting distinct textures and symbolic resonances.

In its carbon-fiber composite version, PLA becomes a medium of contrasts: light yet resistant, synthetic yet capable of evoking the tactile aura of traditional materials.

Raw, stratified surfaces coexist with polished and spray-painted areas, as exemplified in *Alien Landscape with Sunset* in Figure 6-10.

Figure 6-10. Gianpiero Moioli, Alien Landscape with Sunset, 2025*, mixed media, cm. 55 (h) x 58 x 35.*
This version of the work exemplifies the use of carbon-fiber PLA, with some areas left raw and others refined through post-processing such as smoothing and spray painting

Here, material duality itself becomes metaphor: between impermanence and endurance, between the digital trace and its transformation into tangible presence.

For artists seeking intrinsic smoothness and finer details from the outset, **Resin** brings an entirely different character.

Photopolymer resins used in SLA and DLP technologies produce prints of striking smoothness and detail.

A translucent resin can generate ethereal, glowing effects when backlit, while opaque resin creates a porcelain-like finish that recalls small figurines or delicate craft objects.

Resin is more brittle than plastic, so it suits works not meant to endure mechanical stress, but its ability to reproduce fine reliefs and intricate geometries with minimal post-processing makes it invaluable for artists who want their digital subtleties to survive intact in physical form.

Metal pushes digital sculpture into the territory of tradition.

Printing in steel, bronze, or titanium through SLS, DMLS, or binder jetting produces pieces with the weight, strength, and patina of classical metalwork.

A geometric shape imagined on screen can take on a reflective sheen in stainless steel, inviting comparisons with modernist sculpture.

Complex lattice structures or filigree meshes that would be impossible to cast conventionally can be realized directly from a digital file.

Durable and weather-resistant, metal 3D-printed parts—especially in stainless steel 316L, bronze, titanium Ti6Al4V, or aluminum AlSi10Mg—open the door to permanent outdoor installations and monumental works, combining the gravitas of classical metal sculpture with unprecedented formal freedom.

Current commercial build envelopes for high-quality metal powder-bed systems (DMLS/SLM) typically reach around 400–600 mm per side on industrial machines, while binder-jetting metal systems are limited to approximately 400 mm in the longest dimension.

These constraints necessitate modular design and assembly techniques for truly large-scale works, bridging the gap between digital conception and monumental physical realization.

Ceramic and **concrete** carry art back to the earth.

Printing in clay allows for firing into true ceramic, giving works a handcrafted aura, complete with slight surface variations that contrast with their digital origins.

Concrete, by contrast, lends itself to large, monolithic forms: sculptures at the scale of building fragments, heavy and brutalist in presence.

Systems like WASP's large-format printers make it possible to realize such massive pieces, turning virtual designs into architectural experiments.

Clay speaks of craft and intimacy, while concrete embodies solidity and permanence, yet both arise from the pliability of digital modeling.

Finally, **experimental materials** push 3D printing into new poetic territory. Artists explore wood composites that smell like carved timber when sanded, flexible filaments that mimic rubber, or recycled plastics that bring ecological awareness into the work.

Others employ biodegradable filaments infused with coffee, hemp, or other organic matter, making the material itself part of the artwork's metaphor.

A piece about nature's fragility, for example, might be printed in a compostable bioplastic, destined to dissolve over time.

Material choice, then, is never neutral. It mediates between concept and form, between the digital idea and its tangible manifestation.

Figure 6-11 visualizes the interplay between 3D printing techniques and material categories, mapping how different processes (FDM, SLA/DLP, SLS/SLM, Material Jetting) align with major material categories (plastics, resins, metals, ceramic/concrete, experimental hybrids).

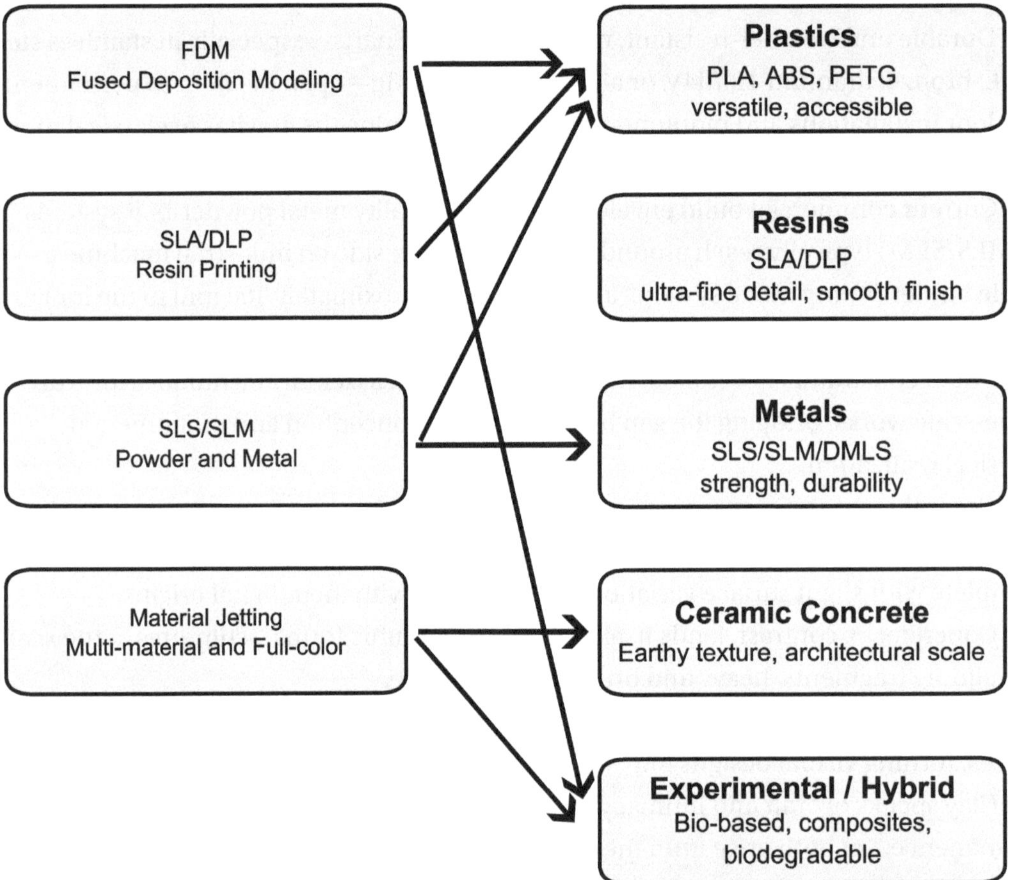

Figure 6-11. Diagram showing the relationship between major 3D printing techniques.
It represents the printing techniques (FDM, SLA/DLP, SLS/SLM, Multi-material printing) in relation to the material categories (plastics, resins, metals, ceramic/concrete, experimental hybrids)

Each combination shapes not only feasibility but also aesthetic expression.

Beyond technical compatibility, these connections highlight how the artist's decision on process and medium actively mediates between digital concept and physical presence, transforming technical constraints into aesthetic opportunities.

6.3 WASP: Ceramic 3D Printing and Sustainable Architecture

Inspired by the potter wasp, which builds its nest patiently from local mud, the World's Advanced Saving Project (WASP) has developed a philosophy that unites technology, sustainability, and biomimicry.

Just as the wasp uses what it finds around itself to create shelter, WASP emphasizes locally sourced materials to construct habitats directly on-site.[22]

This natural metaphor is not a simple anecdote but a true design principle.

It reflects a vision of digital fabrication rooted in ecological awareness, where 3D printing becomes not only a tool of production but also a means to reestablish a dialogue between art, architecture, and the earth itself.

For this reason, I have chosen to dedicate an entire paragraph to WASP, whose projects demonstrate how technological innovation can converge with environmental ethics and artistic imagination.

WASP's research extends from ceramic 3D printers designed for artistic practice to robotic arms capable of shaping complex forms and up to the Crane WASP system, a large-scale construction platform for eco-sustainable housing, which we have already mentioned.

Each development stems from the same guiding metaphor: technology that, like the potter wasp, builds by using the soil around it as raw material.

6.3.1 Ceramic 3D Printers and Robotic Arms in Art

At the artistic scale, this philosophy takes form through WASP's ceramic 3D printers.

[22] See: https://www.3dwasp.com/en/

Instead of depositing mud, they extrude clay and porcelain, layer by layer, transforming digital models into tangible forms.

Once dried and kiln-fired—following protocols carefully adapted to their variable wall thicknesses and intricate geometries—these works become true vitrified ceramics, even though their fabrication and material behavior diverge profoundly from traditional wheel-throwing or hand-building.

The printed pieces retain unmistakable traces of their digital origin in surface stratification and algorithmic patterning, creating hybrid objects that exist simultaneously within the millennia-old tradition of fired clay and the contemporary realm of robotic fabrication and computational design.

For artists, this means that clay is no longer confined to the hand or the wheel. Complex lattices, extreme overhangs, and filigrees once impossible to achieve manually can now be realized with robotic precision, expanding the expressive vocabulary of ceramics far beyond the limits of physical gesture.

This potential is tangibly realized in projects such as TECLA (Figure 6-12), where WASP's 3D printing technology transforms local **raw earth** into high-performance architectural envelopes—proving that robotic precision can bypass the limits of manual crafting, even when working with unfired, sustainable materials.

***Figure 6-12. Crane WASP robotic arm** for the semi-automated construction of sustainable housing.*
The TECLA project was developed by WASP in collaboration with Mario Cucinella Architects. Photo by: Alfredo Milano (Drone views: Italdron), via Wikimedia Commons. License: CC BY 2.5

The introduction of six- or seven-axis robotic arms—exemplified by WASP's CEREBRO system—dramatically extends the possibilities of large-format clay printing.

With working envelopes typically ranging from 1.5 to 3 meters, these robots break free from the constraint of strictly horizontal layering and can follow nonplanar, curved, or even vertical toolpaths.

Yet the material's rheology and gravity still impose limits. Freshly deposited clay or earth must be viscous enough to hold its shape, restricting extreme overhangs and requiring careful control of deposition speed, layer height, and curing time.

The robot can print onto existing armatures or curved molds, dynamically tilting the nozzle to improve interlayer adhesion or to achieve specific surface orientations.

This flexibility, however, demands sophisticated robotic CAM programming (usually Grasshopper + KUKA|prc, Robots (ABB), or WASP's own CEREBRO software) to guarantee collision-free paths and consistent material flow.

In practice, the robot becomes both printer and sculptor, translating digital intent into a continuous, gravity-aware gesture at architectural scale.

This expanded choreography is vividly captured in the work of RobotLab (Figure 6-13), where a KUKA industrial arm performs complex calligraphy.

Figure 6-13. Example of a KUKA industrial robotic arm used for highprecision tasks.
In this installation by RobotLab, the robot performs complex calligraphy, retranslating the Martin Luther Bible into a traditional Schwabacher font. This demonstrates the machine's ability to translate digital code into fluid, organic gestures.
Photo by: Marc Wathieu, via Wikimedia Commons. License: CC BY 2.0

Here, code and gesture converge. Algorithms dictate motion, yet the result carries the immediacy of a sculptural act.

Artists who adopt this technology do not merely reproduce traditional pottery forms on a larger scale; they leverage this robotic limb to translate digital code into fluid, organic gestures that were previously exclusive to the human hand. In these works, this technological mediation allows clay to reclaim its identity as raw earth, yet it is rearticulated through algorithms and machines that act as extended hands, bridging the gap between ancestral material and digital future.

6.3.2 Crane WASP and Eco-Sustainable Architecture

On a larger scale, the **Crane WASP** system translates the logic of the "vespa vasaia" into monumental sculpture and architecture.

Here, the raw material is not only clay but the very soil of the site: mixtures of earth, straw, fibers, and water, extruded into walls that rise stratum after stratum like a monumental pot.

This approach prioritizes locally sourced materials: no imported concrete, no industrial bricks, but the land itself, returned to inhabitable form.

Structures such as **Gaia** (2018) and **TECLA** (2021), demonstrate that entire dwellings can be printed using local earth (Figure 6-14).

Figure 6-14. ***TECLA****: Eco-sustainable 3D printed house made of local raw earth. The project was engineered and printed by WASP in collaboration with Mario Cucinella Architects and a network of specialist partners including School of Sustainability (SOS), Mapei, and Milan Ingegneria. Photo by: Alfredo Milano (Drone views: Italdron), via Wikimedia Commons. License: CC BY 2.5*

Their walls, thick and layered, combine thermal efficiency with a sculptural rhythm. The striations of extrusion become both structure and ornament, a new kind of digital masonry.

In TECLA, two dome-shaped volumes were printed simultaneously by synchronized Crane WASP arms, forming a futuristic yet ancestral dwelling.

The surface, ribbed with the traces of extrusion, resembles a geological formation rather than a conventional house. It is an architecture that appears grown from the ground, as if it had always been there.

From an artistic perspective, such projects blur the boundary between sculpture and habitat. **A Crane WASP house is not only shelter but also land art: inhabitable sculpture shaped by algorithms yet composed of the most archaic of materials: earth.**

The process is reversible too. These walls, if left to erosion, would dissolve back into the soil, completing a cycle of impermanence.

Thus, Crane WASP redefines architecture as a form of sustainable sculpture.

It is site-specific by nature, because each building is literally made from its site.

In this convergence of tradition and digital precision lies a profound message: technology can serve not to dominate nature but to collaborate with it, as the potter wasp teaches, transforming mud into home.

6.4 Dialogue Between Digital and Material: Iteration, Feedback, and Authenticity

In this section, we explore the dynamic interplay between digital designs and physical materials.

Creating art with 3D printing is rarely a one-way trip from computer to object; instead, there is a continuous dialogue.

Materials influence design decisions, and the results of physical fabrication often feed back into the digital process for refinement.

We also address how artists are managing issues of authenticity and editioning in an era when digital files enable infinite reproducibility.

By embracing techniques such as iterative prototyping and adopting certification methods, artists ensure that the story of the artwork spans both virtual and physical realms in a cohesive and meaningful way.

6.4.1 Material as an Extension of Digital Design

Materials are never neutral in the making of an artwork.

They shape not only the physical appearance of a piece but also its meaning, atmosphere, and longevity.

In the context of 3D printing, this choice becomes even more complex. Every material carries specific properties—density, transparency, texture, or durabilitythat directly affect how a digital design is perceived once translated into matter.

When a digital model becomes physical, the chosen material effectively becomes an extension of the design itself, adding its own voice to the artwork's expression.

Artists treat material selection as part of the creative concept, not as an afterthought.

To illustrate these variations, Figure 6-15 maps the main categories of additive manufacturing processes and the materials they employ, the same techniques discussed in section 6.2.

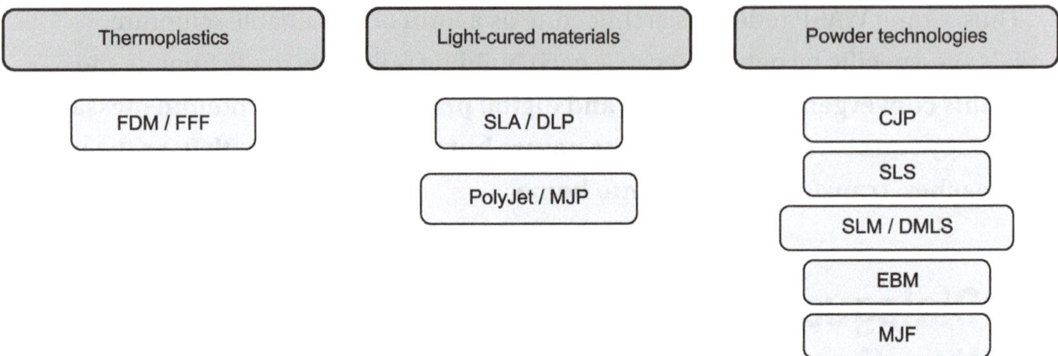

Figure 6-15. 3D Printing: Matter and Method.
Schematic overview of the main additive manufacturing techniques and their associated material families

Each pathway offers distinct expressive possibilities for artists, shaping both technical feasibility and aesthetic meaning.

In this sense, my sculpture *Dragon in the Forest* provides a concrete illustration of how material choice extends and transforms a digital design (Figure 6-16).

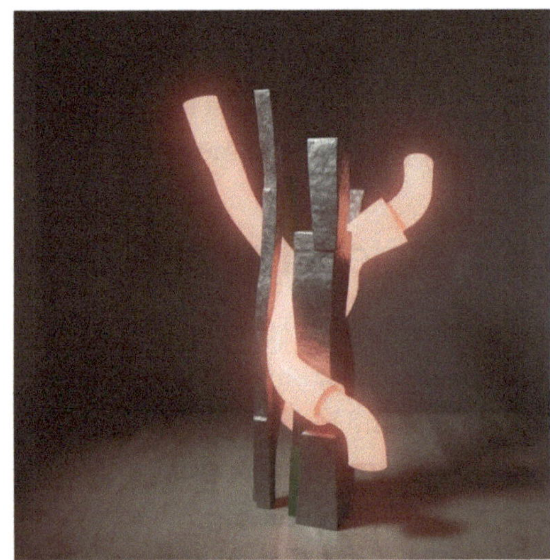

Figure 6-16. Gianpiero Moioli, Dragon in the Forest, 2025, mixed media, cm.150 x 72 x 71.
Front and back views.
Material Variations of a Digital Sculpture. Metallic trunks form an artificial forest, within which a dragon shifts from translucent to transparent lighted plastic

The same underlying model takes on radically different qualities depending on whether its elements are realized in traslucent or in semi-transparent plastic.

Through these variations, the case demonstrates how 3D printing does not end with form-making but extends into the realm of materials, where each choice transforms the expressive and conceptual voice of the work.

Artists often experiment by printing test pieces in different materials or colors to see how each impacts the look and feel.

3D printing is particularly suited to this process, commonly referred to as prototyping.

In my own practice, I typically produce three to eight test prints per work, exploring variations of form, color, material simulation, and structural stability. For a small-scale sculpture/maquette (approximately 150 to 200mm in largest dimension), each PLA test print requires 8 to 15 hours printing time plus 2 to 4 hours post-processing (support removal, preliminary sanding, test assembly) and consumes approximately $5 to 15 in material.

Approximately 50% of test prints reveal issues requiring digital model revision; common problems include inadequate wall thickness in thin sections, unsupported overhangs causing sagging, poor joint registration between multi-part assemblies, or aesthetic issues with surface texture and layer visibility.

For a small-scale sculpture this iterative investment of approximately 45 to 80 total hours and $30 to $120 per completed sculpture is essential to achieving the final vision, as many structural and aesthetic issues only become apparent in physical form.

With medium-sized printers I can also realize quite large works, constructed from multiple parts.

I created the sculpture *Dragon in the Forest* in Blender and printed it using an Anycubic Kobra 2 Max, dividing the digital model into several components to fit the printer's build volume (Figure 6-17).

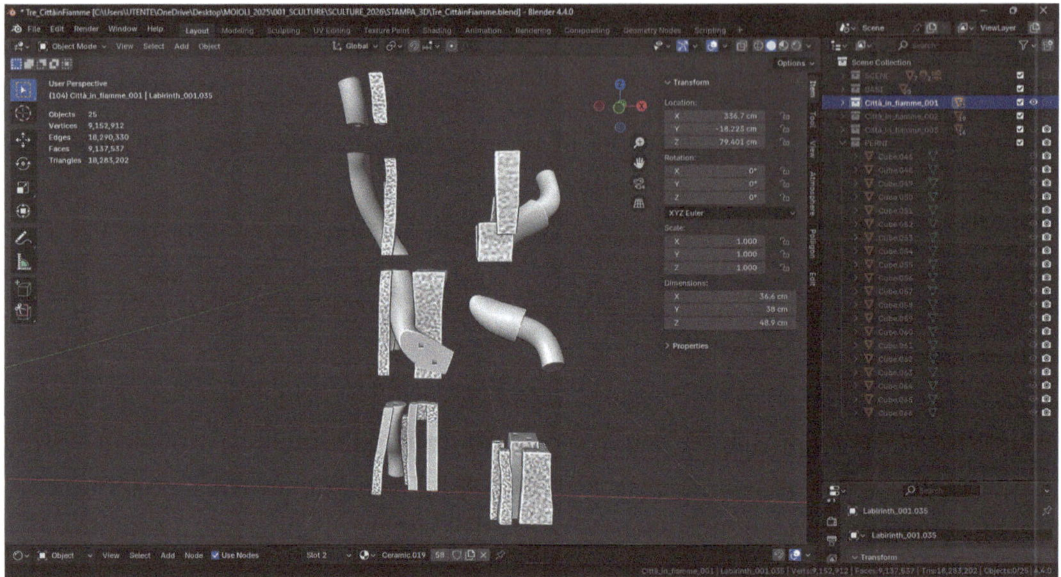

Figure 6-17. Preparation of the sculpture Dragon in the Forest in Blender. *The digital model is divided into printable components to match the build volume of an Anycubic Kobra 2 Max. Each part is later assembled with 3D-printed pins and adhesive, before undergoing post-production finishing*

The sculpture, standing 150 centimeters tall, was then assembled by joining the parts with 10 mm square profile 3D-printed PLA pins in clearance-fit holes and two-part epoxy, followed by body filler and sanding. Pin connections were designed with 0.5 mm tolerance to ensure ease of assembly and prevent rotation while maintaining structural strength across the height.

This case illustrates how digital conception and material execution are inseparable: each phase, from modeling to assembly, influences the next.

Similarly, material choice itself can radically transform the character of a work.

A geometric pavilion prototype, for instance, will take on very different qualities depending on the chosen material.

In gray concrete, it can highlight mass and solidity, evoking industrial or brutalist architecture, recalling the large-scale earthen and concrete experiments we have just seen with WASP.

In white ABS or PLA, it may emphasize sharp edges and lines while also playing with light and shadow. In clay it can evoke a more handcrafted or timeless character.

By aligning material properties with the digital model's intent, the artist creates a harmony between what the piece looks like and what it is.

6.4.2 Material as Medium

My *Metaphysical Piazzas* series (2025) provides a telling example (Figure 6-18).

These works depict sculptural and architectural structures in a surreal manner.

Through 3D printing and the simulation of various materials with surface finishes, the digital theme of frozen time and mental space is carried into the material itself.

The sculptures do not simply represent relics from a metaphysical city; they embody them.

I printed the series in PLA to maximize experimentation with surfaces, colors, and material simulations.

The *Metaphysical Piazzas* series, shown in Figure 6-18, does not merely allude to ruins of an imagined city; it conjures them into being.

Figure 6-18. Gianpiero Moioli, Metaphysical Piazzas, 2025.
Four views of the digital sculptures from the series Metaphysical Piazzas, where architectural fragments and abstract elements combine with virtual clouds and chromatic volumes

Each printed column, arch, or tower rises like a fragment suspended between memory and invention, a relic from a civilization that never existed yet feels strangely familiar.

By layering digital precision with material patina, the sculptures crystallize time itself, freezing moments of thought into permanent architectures.

At the same time, the series operates at the threshold between architecture and sculpture, between digital imagination and material artifact: as if silent Renaissance and Metaphysical piazzas had been reconstructed through 21st-century algorithms and given body by 3D printing.

What emerges is not paradox but a palimpsest: a city both ancient and futuristic, both virtual and concrete.

In this way, the *Metaphysical Piazza* series invites viewers to inhabit a landscape of suspended time, where the dialogue between past and future, matter and code, becomes physically present.

This exploration of architecture and space finds a natural counterpart in another work, *Still Life with Fruit Basket,* where the focus shifts toward painting and the tradition of representation (Figure 6-19).

Figure 6-19. Gianpiero Moioli, Still Life with Fruit Basket, 2025*, mixed media, cm.53 (h) x 51 x 39.*
A digital reinterpretation of the still life genre, freely inspired by Michelangelo Merisi da Caravaggio and Antonio Canova's marble Fruit Basket

Here, the vocabulary of digital sculpture intersects with the pictorial genre of the still life, translating its play of forms and colors into three dimensions.[23]

The fruit basket itself derives from a marble sculpture of Antonio Canova, which I have freely reinterpreted and recontextualized within a contemporary digital workflow that transforms a neoclassical artifact into part of a hybrid composition.[24]

With PolyJet™ 3D printing, the process becomes a way of "painting in three dimensions." Color, texture, and transparency are integrated directly into the build, allowing the work to acquire the vivid tonalities of a Renaissance canvas while inhabiting the sculptural realm.

In this fusion, past, present, and future converge.

In essence, the choice of colors, surfaces, and materials enables the physical artwork to reflect the virtual concept on a sensory level, reinforcing what was imagined in software through tangible qualities such as texture, weight, and transparency.

Crucially, materials also carry symbolic weight. Printing in biodegradable plastic or fragile composites can deliberately comment on ephemerality. The piece will not last, echoing decay or transition.

Conversely, producing a digital design in bronze connects it to history and permanence. Artists exploit this contrast. One may print an algorithmic form in bronze to affirm its classic status, while another may print a classical bust in neon-green bioplastic to subvert expectations.

The dialogue between digital and material is where meaning is forged, an alchemical step where code meets clay, and something new and resonant emerges.

This alchemy between code and matter resonates with a longer artistic lineage.

Caravaggio's *Basket of Fruit* (c. 1596) transformed an everyday subject into a meditation on abundance and decay, freezing ephemerality on canvas.

Centuries later, Canova's marble *Fruit Basket* translated the still life into neoclassical sculpture, fixing fragility in stone (Figure 6-20).

---

[23] See: `https://en.wikipedia.org/wiki/Still_life`

[24] Antonio Canova, Fruit Basket, c. 1783, Museo Correr, Venice. A rare still life in marble within Canova's oeuvre, today part of the Correr Canova collection.

***Figure 6-20. Michelangelo Merisi da Caravaggio, Canestra di frutta (Fruitbasket), (1595–96)**, oil on canvas, 31 × 47 cm.*
Caravaggio's Basket of Fruit freezes organic decay on canvas, mirroring how modern digital fabrication allows artists to choose between ephemeral or permanent media to manifest virtual intent. By Caravaggio - Own work, user: Lafit86, Public Domain, `https://commons.wikimedia.org/w/index.php?curid=10478675`

My own *Still Life with Fruit Basket* reinterprets this dialogue in digital terms, where 3D modeling and printing merge painting, sculpture, and code into a hybrid form.

Another decisive factor in the passage from virtual to material is scale. It is not merely a technical parameter but a conceptual choice that shapes how a work is experienced.

At small scale, the object functions as a study or maquette, documenting the passage from digital to material while pointing toward potential expansion at monumental size.

At larger scales, perhaps through systems like Crane WASP, the work becomes immersive architecture. Scale is never neutral; it is an aesthetic and symbolic decision that suggests possibilities beyond the exhibited object.

Artists today can choose among multiple 3D printing paths: from full-color polymers, to binder-jet systems, to metal PBF processes. These workflows, converging with rendering and AR/VR previews, blur the boundary between virtual models and physical artworks.

To safeguard authorship in a world of copyable files, many artists now adopt digital certifications or NFT editions.

In short, contemporary sculpture is conceived in code, materialized through diverse print technologies, and authenticated by cryptographic proof.

Beyond this, the passage from virtual to physical is rarely linear. It advances through iterative cycles of prototyping and refinement, where questions of authenticity also emerge.

6.4.3 Iterative Feedback: Prototyping and Authenticity in the Digital Age

The passage from digital model to physical sculpture is rarely linear.

Artists work through iterative feedback loops. A first print may reveal weaknesses or unexpected effects, prompting adjustments in the digital file and new prototypes.

Light, scale, and material responses guide refinements so that the artwork emerges from a dialogue where matter "speaks back."

In this sense, 3D printing echoes printmaking: a single matrix generates multiple outcomes, but here variations produce cohesive yet distinct series such as *Metaphysical Piazza*.

This reproducibility naturally raises the issue of authenticity, already discussed in Chapter 4. Here it is enough to note that artists often limit editions and pair each physical piece with a digital certificate or blockchain record, ensuring uniqueness within an iterative process.

Some artists have begun experimenting with digital authentication methods including blockchain-based certificates (NFTs) or centralized digital registries, though traditional documentation (signed/numbered editions, certificates of authenticity, gallery provenance records) remains the predominant authentication method in the 3D-printed art market as of 2025.

Blockchain approaches face practical challenges: linking digital tokens to physical objects requires additional mechanisms (embedded NFC chips, QR codes) vulnerable to separation or damage; platform dependency creates long-term preservation concerns; and legal recognition remains inconsistent across jurisdictions.

For artists adopting these methods, the authentication system itself often becomes part of the conceptual framework, addressing questions of digital reproducibility and material uniqueness directly.

In short, iterative prototyping turns digital sculpture into a living process, constantly evolving between code and matter, while thoughtful certification preserves its integrity across versions.

6.5 Contemporary Case Studies: Digital Fabrication in Art

In this final section, we turn to a selection of recent artworks that embody the key themes of this chapter.

These case studies show how contemporary artists employ digital fabrication not merely as a technical tool but as a medium of invention: reimagining classical genres, engaging with metaphysical ideas, and constructing entirely new landscapes.

At the same time, the chosen examples highlight the diversity of approaches that coexist today, from monumental sculpture to architectural speculation, from bio-fabrication to conceptual installations.

They demonstrate how virtual design and material execution intertwine, enriching the dialogue between tradition and technology.

Taken together, these works confirm that digital fabrication has become a creative language in its own right, enabling hybrid practices that weave together historical references, digital imagination, and physical craft.

6.5.1 Bruce Beasley: Sculptural CAD into Monumental Form

The first example is that of Bruce Beasley, an American sculptor (b. 1939) who has been an early and influential adopter of digital modeling as part of a sculptural workflow.

Since the 2000s he has relied on CAD to conceive complex interlocking forms, using 3D printing at prototype scale to iterate proportion and structure before translating the results into monumental works in bronze or aluminum (Figure 6-21).[25]

[25] See: `https://makezine.com/article/craft/fine-art/maker-profile-bruce-beasley`

***Figure 6-21.* *Bruce Beasley, Spokesman II (1994)*, *bronze. Bad Homburg, Germany. A public-art example of Beasley's large-scale metal work. By Karsten11, own work, Public Domain,* `https://commons.wikimedia.org/w/index.php?curid=6869674`

The Rondo series, developed over the past decade and beyond, exemplifies this dialogue between virtual design and enduring materials.

What begins as a malleable digital model is honed through small printed maquettes and ultimately realized at monumental scale, where the intricate interplay of light, shadow, and negative space within the interlocking toroidal forms activates the sculpture in continuously changing ways throughout the day.

In Beasley's practice, 3D printing is not merely a means of reproduction but **a design instrument**—an intermediate stage that allows for precise refinement of geometry and balance—bridging thought, code, and matter in service of sculptural presence.

The sculpture in Figure 6-21 by Bruce Beasley, composed of interlocking geometric volumes, embodies dynamic balance and monumentality.

Today, a similar work could be easily modeled in Blender and 3D printed in various materials, including direct metal fabrication through SLM or DMLS.

6.5.2 Anish Kapoor: Forms Between Voids, Reflective Surfaces, and Digital Experimentation

Anish Kapoor (India/England, b. 1954) is renowned for his monumental, often site-specific sculptures that explore matter, voids, reflective space, and perception.

Kapoor has long adopted digital tools such as CAD and 3D modeling to conceive complex forms, curved surfaces, and biomorphic volumes, as well as to verify the structural and visual feasibility of his large-scale works.

Throughout his career, he has consistently integrated technological innovation into both the design and fabrication of his sculptures, making digital processes a permanent component of his artistic method rather than an occasional support.

A first significant example is the cement-printing experiment that Kapoor developed in collaboration with Factum Arte.[26] It is a series of works emerged from experiments with 3D concrete printers, where different cement mixtures were exploited to generate forms through digital-mechanical processes.

Even in well-known pieces such as Cloud Gate, Kapoor employed digital modeling to define the surfaces, curvatures, and internal structure. Producing the perfectly curved steel plates required a detailed CAD process, prototyping, and digital verification (Figure 6-22).

[26] Further details can also be found in this article:

`https://www.factum-arte.com/pag/49/greyman-cries-shaman-dies-billowing-smoke-beauty-evoked`

Figure 6-22. Anish Kapoor, Cloud Gate (2006)*, stainless steel sculpture, Millennium Park, Chicago.*
The work exemplifies the use of advanced digital modeling and engineering to achieve seamless reflective surfaces and complex curvature.
Photograph by Marco Verch, Creative Commons 2.0.
https://foto.wuestenigel.com/cloud-gate-sculpture-in-chicago/

In his practice, digital experimentation is an integral part of the creative and constructive process. The digital dimension makes it possible to explore formal possibilities, test variations, and conceive complex geometries that would otherwise be difficult to achieve with traditional methods.

Today, similar methodologies make it possible to produce smaller 3D-printed models, even with experimental materials, or metal, to study light, reflections, and spatial interactions before scaling up to monumental formats.

6.5.2.1 Factum Arte: Chance, Unpredictability, and the Organicity of the Artwork

Digital experimentation characterizes Kapoor's collaboration with Factum Arte, where experiments in 3D cement printing in the late 2000s produced works such as *Greyman Cries, Shaman Dies, Billowing Smoke,* and *Beauty Evoked* (2009).

In these projects, digital instructions encounter the unpredictable behavior of material: the extrusion of cement, subject to gravity, viscosity, humidity, and vibration, generated organic and irregular forms that blurred the boundary between human authorship, algorithmic logic, and material agency.

Here, the digital file functions not as a rigid script but as a triggering device, opening a field of possibilities in which matter itself chooses its path.

Surfaces bend, collapse, and stratify in ways that recall geological or biological processes, with fissures and folds emerging from the interplay between control and chance.

In this sense, 3D printing becomes a laboratory of contingency, where Kapoor uses digital technology for embracing unpredictability, yielding an aesthetic of the quasi-living.

We can see the effects of this experimentation in the publication *Unconformity & Entropy* (Factum Arte, Madrid 2010), a catalog that documents Kapoor's cement-printing experiments through images of prototypes, renderings, cement mixtures, and emergent surfaces, illustrating the dialogue between digital processes and material behavior in his creative practice.[27]

Figure 6-23 offers a visual example of the concrete 3D printing technology employed in this type of experimentation.

[27] You can find the PDF here: `https://www.factum-arte.com/resources/files/fa/publications_PDF/Kapoor_Unconformity_Entropy.pdf`

Figure 6-23. TU/e Built Environment's Rohaco 3D Concrete Printer being extensively used for Concrete Printing Research.
This gantry system exemplifies the specialized machinery required to translate digital complexity into large-scale concrete forms, bridging the gap between industrial research and monumental artistic practice. By Misanthropic One - https://www.flickr.com/photos/22902505@N05/26587585494/, CC BY 2.0

What emerges is a field in which sculpture, architecture, nature, and technology intertwine, with chance acting as a generative force rather than a disturbance.

A similar historical example is the medieval helical column at Avallon, which was carved to resemble a twisted rope, where architectural regularity merged with an organic sense of growth and torsion, intertwining nature and mathematics in a single form.[28]

In Romanesque and Gothic architecture, such motifs often embodied the union of structure and ornament, translating vegetal rhythms into stone and giving the impression that architecture itself could grow like a living organism (Figure 6-24).

[28] The Church of Saint-Lazare in Avallon, Burgundy (12th century), preserves one of the rare Romanesque portals with a helical "rope" column, an ornamental motif where geometry and vegetal symbolism are intricately intertwined. Several images of the west portal of Collégiale Saint-Lazare, Avallon, can be found here: https://commons.wikimedia.org/wiki/Category%3AWest_portals_of_Coll%C3%A9giale_Saint-Lazare_d%27Avallon

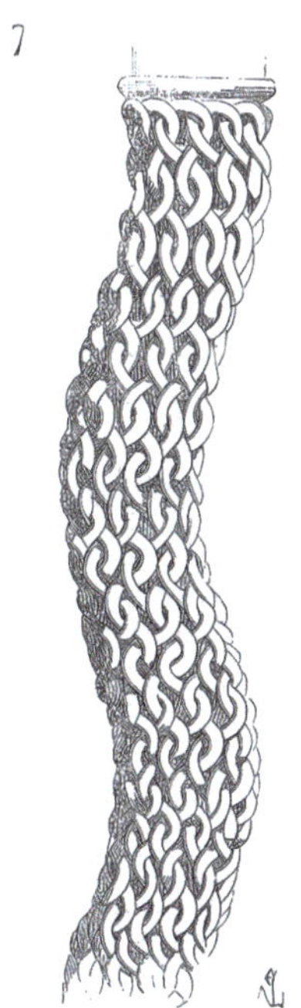

Figure 6-24. Helical column from the portal of Saint-Lazare, Avallon.
A rare Romanesque motif where architectural geometry intertwines with vegetal rhythms, evoking the union of structure and nature.
Drawing: Public Domain,
Photograph by NateBergin, own work, CC BY 4.0

These forms remind us that the dialogue between geometry and nature, order and organic vitality, has long been inscribed in the very fabric of architecture.

By contrast, the 3D-printed cement fragments realized by Kapoor in collaboration with Factum Arte evoke the same principle in a radically different way: instead of a smooth and controlled surface, the material unfolds as a chaotic weave of filaments.

In this new context, torsion becomes emergent and unpredictable through additive manufacturing. Filaments bend, collapse, and intertwine, generating organic contingencies.

6.5.2.2 Cloud Gate: Digital Design, Prototyping, and 3D Printing Between Art and Architecture

With Cloud Gate, the other pole of Kapoor's research emerges as digital precision as the foundation of an architectural sculpture.

The geometry was defined through NURBS/CAD modeling, tested with rapid prototyping and 3D-printed models to assess reflections, curvatures, and structural stress points, and then translated into engineering practice: calendared stainless steel panels, millimetric tolerances, welding, and mirror polishing.[29]

Here, 3D printing is not the end point but a decisive design stage. It enabled rapid iterations, optical-spatial verification, and coordination between designers, engineers, and workshops. The result is an artwork in which art and architecture converge: a continuous skin that deforms the surrounding landscape through reflection, supported by a digitally optimized structural core.

Cloud Gate demonstrates how digital NURBS modeling, finite element analysis, and precision CNC fabrication can transform an immaterial vision into a large-scale public sculpture.

While the final work was constructed through traditional welding of 168 steel plates, the complex geometry required digital modeling throughout the design process to calculate curvatures, reflections, and structural loads.

6.5.3 Antony Gormley: The Body in Digital Translation

Antony Gormley (UK, b. 1950) is internationally recognized for his sculptural investigations of the human body—often cast from his own figure—and for his reflections on the relation between the individual and space.

One example of this approach is *Another Place* (2005): 100 life-size cast-iron figures installed along a roughly 3 km stretch of Crosby Beach near Liverpool, facing the horizon and rhythmically revealed and submerged by the tides (Figure 6-25).

[29] The article "Effects of Digital Technology on Anish Kapoor's Works" (Rethinking The Future) is illustrated with numerous images, most notably those related to the design and construction of *Cloud Gate:* `https://www.re-thinkingthefuture.com/know-your-architects/a2494-effects-of-digital-technology-on-anish-kapoors-works/`

Figure 6-25. Another Place (2005), installation by Antony Gormley on Crosby Beach, UK.
One of 100 cast-iron figures facing the horizon.
Photo by Chris Howells. Edited version of Another Place3.jpg., CC BY 2.5,
`https://commons.wikimedia.org/w/index.php?curid=968318`

The work invites reflection on isolation and collectivity, permanence and transience, as the human form is set against the vastness of the sea and the cyclical movement of water.

While *Another Place* grounds the body within elemental nature, Gormley has also explored how computational systems, and digital tools can generate new sculptural environments.

This trajectory finds an ambitious expression in *Quantum Cloud* (1999), a 30-meter-tall lattice of tetrahedral steel units installed beside the Millennium Dome (now The O2) in London.

This work reflects a synthesis of sculpture, architecture, and mathematics, producing a structure that is at once monumental and immaterial.

We will return to *Quantum Cloud* in Chapter 7 as a pivotal example of how code, form, and matter intersect to create a metaphysical presence at architectural scale.

Since the early 2010s, Gormley's practice has increasingly relied on high-resolution 3D scanning of his own body and the algorithmic manipulation of point-cloud and voxel data, allowing him to fragment, pixelate, or radically abstract the human figure into entirely new sculptural languages.

The artist himself has repeatedly described the decisive break with the old plaster-mold process—which required hours of immobile posing and restricted posture—in favor of digital scanning that captures precarious, unstable positions in seconds.[30]

In the 2014 BBC documentary *Antony Gormley: What Do Artists Do All Day?*, he is shown working with a digital body scan and manipulating its geometry on screen. This footage provides rare insight into how the scanned body is translated into schematic or modular structures that later inform the production of new works.[31]

In these works, the scanned body becomes a matrix that can be expanded, fractured, or reorganized into polyhedral or block-like formations, establishing a dialogue between anatomy, architecture, and computational structure.

In this evolving workflow, the body is first translated into digital data; that data is then reshaped through modelling processes that abstract, compress, or re-grid the human form; and the resulting digital model ultimately guides fabrication in materials such as cast iron, steel, or aluminum. Rather than abandoning the logic of casting, Gormley extends it into the computational realm, preserving the intimate, indexical connection between his own body and the sculptural object while opening it to new forms of geometric and spatial experimentation.[32]

6.5.3.1 Expansion Field: Gormley's Digital Translation of the Human Body

A striking example of this approach is Expansion Field (2014), a large-scale installation in the exhibition hall at the Zentrum Paul Klee, composed of 60 geometric body-forms distributed across a vast exhibition space.[33]

---

[30] See the text *"Bodybuilding"* (Rebecca Comay, in *Expansion Field*, 2014), available on the artist's official website: `https://www.antonygormley.com/resources/texts/bodybuilding`

[31] Antony Gormley: What Do Artists Do All Day?, BBC Four, first broadcast 2014.

[32] Body Politic: An Interview with Antony Gormley, Polly Bates (2024): `https://www.artistsrespondingto.co.uk/post/body-politic-an-interview-with-antony-gormley`

[33] An article detailing Expansion Field can be found on the Zentrum Paul Klee website: `https://archive.zpk.org/en/exhibitions/review/2014/antony-gormley-802.html`

Each element derives from scans of Gormley's body, digitally processed and transformed into block-like volumes that appear at once corporeal and architectural.

The repetition and variation of these forms create a field of presences, where the human figure is abstracted into a sequence of inhabitable geometries.

Here the use of digital scanning and computer-assisted fabrication is essential. It enables the translation of bodily experience into modular units that articulate space much like an architectural grid.

While grounded in the physical reality of the artist's body, *Expansion Field* demonstrates how digital processes allow Gormley to reinvent the body as structure, extending sculpture into the language of architecture and spatial design.

6.5.4 Neri Oxman

As already discussed in section 6.2, Neri Oxman (b. 1976), architect, designer, and former associate professor at the MIT Media Lab, where she founded and directed the Mediated Matter group, has become a leading figure in exploring how biology, design, and digital fabrication can converge into a new paradigm of creation.

Her concept of *material ecology* proposes that design should be understood as a symbiosis between natural processes and technological systems, where growth, biodegradation, and environmental adaptation become integral to form-making.

Among her best-known projects is the *Silk Pavilion* (2013), in which 6,500 silkworms were guided to weave their cocoons over a digitally fabricated scaffold, demonstrating a design method that collaborates with biological organisms.

Other works expand on this principle at architectural scale, experimenting with multi-material 3D printing that incorporates structural, optical, and environmental functions directly into the printed form.

In Oxman's vision, additive manufacturing becomes not only a tool of production but a medium for embedding biological logics into design, opening the way toward architectures that are grown, adaptive, and ecologically responsive.

Oxman's practice redefines what architecture and sculpture can be: no longer static artifacts, but dynamic systems conceived in dialogue with life itself.

By merging advanced 3D printing with biomaterials, her work points toward a future in which material and environment coalesce, offering an ecological alternative to the permanence of industrial production.

6.5.4.1 Silk Pavilion: Nature, Technology, and Mediated Growth

The Silk Pavilion (2013), conceived with the Mediated Matter group at MIT, combined robotic fabrication and biological processes.

A primary structure of computer-numerically-controlled (CNC) deposited silk served as the base, onto which a secondary layer was created by introducing approximately 6,500 silkworms (Bombyx mori).

As the larvae moved across the scaffold seeking pupation sites, they deposited silk filaments whose density and orientation were influenced by the geometry of the underlying framework. The resulting structure exhibited gradient opacity and fibrous texture arising from the interaction between designed scaffold and biological behavior, though the exact pattern and density of silkworm-deposited silk remained indeterminate.

The result is a hybrid environment where human design, digital simulation, and natural agency converge.

The geometry reflects computational modeling, but its final texture and density are co-authored by living organisms.

In this sense, the Silk Pavilion is less a static object than a process; it is a collaboration between species that anticipates future forms of sustainable and adaptive architecture.

Through this work, Oxman extends the logic of digital design into the realm of the biological, demonstrating how growth, ecology, and computation can be woven together to produce structures that blur the line between the natural and the artificial.

6.5.5 Michael Hansmeyer: Algorithmic Ornament and Generative Complexity

Michael Hansmeyer (Germany/Switzerland, b. 1973) is an architect and computational designer whose work investigates how algorithmic processes can generate forms of extraordinary intricacy.

Rather than acting as a traditional "maker," he positions himself as a designer of rules and procedures, allowing code to elaborate structures that far exceed manual imagination.

The logic behind his practice stems from the concept of the subdivision surface, borrowed from computational design and 3D graphics.

Starting from a basic geometric form—such as a prism or a cylinder standing in for a column—Hansmeyer applies iterative subdivision algorithms that divide each face into smaller polygons.

With every cycle, geometry becomes more detailed and complex.

Unlike the smooth Catmull-Clark subdivision familiar from 3D software, his process introduces additional rules. Edges are sharpened, symmetries enforced, deviations inserted.

Ornament is thus not applied decoratively but arises as an emergent property of the algorithm itself.

In a sense, this recalls how ornament historically merged with structure in sacred architecture—for example, the twisted and sculpted columns of medieval church portals, such as the helical "rope" column at aforementioned Saint-Lazare in Avallon and the masterful figural sculpture found at Saint-Lazare in Autun—where geometry and ornament were inseparable.

The *Subdivided Columns* (2010) exemplify this approach.[34] From a classical reference, Hansmeyer generates columns with hundreds of thousands of facets, oscillating between the vegetal and the baroque, forms that seem hand-carved yet are entirely computational. Because the resulting digital models are too intricate to sculpt manually, he turned to advanced fabrication technologies.

Early prototypes were realized by stacking laser-cut sheets of cardboard, each slice representing a section of the model. This echoes, in another register, Tony Cragg's stratified sculptures of the 1990s, where layers of polystyrene were manually stacked to generate organic complexity.

Hansmeyer, however, translates algorithmic data into physical layers, repurposing stratification through digital means.

Later works employed large-scale 3D printing in sand and concrete, such as the **Digital Grotesque** (2013, with Benjamin Dillenburger), a project that expands this logic to architectural scale.

The installation, measuring 16 m^2 in floor area and 3.5 meters in height, comprises over 1.2 billion facets generated through custom subdivision algorithms.

[34] *Subdivided Columns* project by Michael Hansmeyer: layering method, algorithms, and fabrication details. Available at: michael-hansmeyer.com/subdivided-columns: `https://michael-hansmeyer.com/subdivided-columns`

It was fabricated using binder jetting technology (selective binding of sandstone powder) in 11 individual sections[35] measuring up to approximately 100×100×100 cm, the maximum build volume of the **D-Shape** printer used.

Sections were post-processed with resin infiltration for structural strength and precisely assembled on-site.

In sum, Hansmeyer's columns and architectural environments demonstrate how iterative algorithms can dissolve the boundary between structure and ornament.

Geometry here is no longer imposed by the artist's hand but emerges directly from code, revealing a new paradigm where digital logic itself becomes material form.

6.5.5.1 *Digital Grotesque*: Immersive Algorithmic Architecture

If the Subdivided Columns exemplify the generative potential of iterative algorithms applied to classical forms, Digital Grotesque (2013, with Benjamin Dillenburger) expands this logic of "chaos and order,"[36] to an architectural scale.

Conceived as a full-scale room printed in sand by a large-format 3D printer, the project demonstrates how computational processes can create spaces of unprecedented ornamental density.

The result is an immersive environment where every surface is saturated with detail, evoking associations that range from gothic cathedrals to coral reefs, from baroque ornament to organic growth.

Fabricated directly from the digital model without any manual intervention, Digital Grotesque challenges conventional distinctions between design and construction, structure and decoration.

Here, ornament is not applied but grown through code, while 3D printing serves as the only viable means of realizing the form's extreme complexity.

By entering the space, viewers find themselves enveloped in a world where geometry has become almost biological, revealing the potential of algorithmic architecture to dissolve boundaries between the natural and the artificial, the virtual and the material.

---

[35] Michael Hansmeyer and Benjamin Dillenburger, *Digital Grotesque: An Architecture of Complexity*, AD Architectural Design, Vol. 84, Issue 6, 2014, pp. 64–71. The data is also confirmed in the official project documentation (Digital Grotesque, project website) and reflects the operational constraints of the D-Shape printer used for fabrication.

[36] Later works employed large-scale 3D printing in sand and concrete, as in *Digital Grotesque* (2013). For material specifications, see `https://michael-hansmeyer.com/digital-grotesque-I#`.

6.5.6 Amy Karle: Bioart and the Body as Sculpture

Amy Karle (USA, b. 1980) works at the intersection of art, biology, and emerging technologies, **exploring how new fabrication methods can reimagine the human body and its materiality.**

She is internationally recognized for her projects in **bioart**, where 3D printing becomes a bridge between anatomy, data, and living systems.[37]

While many artists employ 3D printing to extend formal or architectural languages, Karle uses it to probe the body itself, transforming code and matter into a site of biocultural reflection. Her practice raises urgent questions about mortality, identity, and technological augmentation, expanding the very definition of sculpture into the realms of biotechnology and philosophy.

Alongside her biological experiments, Karle also employs multi-material 3D printing to produce wearable pieces and anatomical forms that combine transparency, flexibility, and structural strength, echoing the complexity of human tissues.

Among her projects, *Regenerative Reliquary* (2016) stands out as a paradigmatic case of this convergence and will be examined in detail below.

6.5.6.1 Regenerative Reliquary

Regenerative Reliquary is the clearest embodiment of Karle's approach, presenting a work that functions simultaneously as a technical prototype and a philosophical proposition (Figure 6-26).

[37] See the official site: `https://www.amykarle.com/`

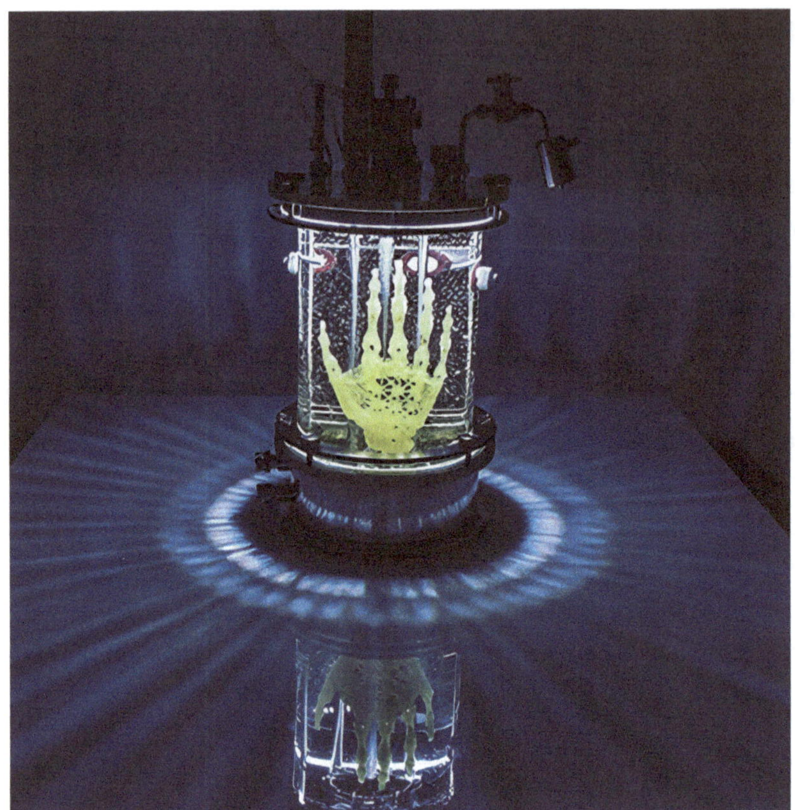

Figure 6-26. Amy Karle, Regenerative Reliquary (2016).
3D-printed PEGDA hydrogel scaffold of a human hand, seeded with human mesenchymal stem cells and placed in a bioreactor.
Photograph by Amy Karle, CC BY 4.0. `https://it.wikipedia.org/wiki/Amy_Karle`

The project begins with medical imaging data (CT scans) of a human hand, which Karle converts into a parametric CAD model designed to replicate the porous micro-architecture of trabecular bone.

The resulting file is 3D-printed as a delicate lattice scaffold in PEGDA (poly(ethylene glycol) diacrylate) hydrogel, a biodegradable material specifically engineered to promote cell adhesion and proliferation.

Once fabricated, the scaffold is placed in a bioreactor and seeded with human Mesenchymal Stem Cells (hMSCs).[38]

Over time, the intention is for the cells to differentiate into osteoblasts and mineralize the matrix; as the polymer degrades, it would theoretically leave behind only living bone tissue.

Although no functional bone tissue was grown to completion during the exhibition periods—from its premiere at Ars Electronica (Linz, 2016) to the YouFab Global Creative Awards (Tokyo, 2017–2018)—the work remains a powerful conceptual demonstration of the bioprinting workflow and the future possibility of cultivating bespoke tissues.

Conceptually, the work inverts the traditional religious reliquary.

While a historical reliquary preserves the dead remains of a saint, this container hosts the potential for future life.

What begins as a product of code and printing evolves through biological processes, transforming both its appearance and meaning.

The boundary between inert object and organic tissue dissolves; the sculpture's duration is no longer static but metabolic, asking a radical question: can sculpture cross the threshold into life itself?

6.6 Conclusions

This chapter has traced how 3D printing transforms digital imagination into tangible matter, not only through technical processes but by reshaping the very categories of artistic creation. We have seen how the dialogue between code and material dissolves traditional oppositions, between unique and multiple, artisanal and industrial, direct and indirect.

Through diverse case studies, it becomes clear that 3D printing is no longer a tool but a cultural medium: it allows artists to reimagine classical genres, invent new landscapes, and integrate ecological and hybrid materials into their practice.

[38] Amy Karle, Regenerative Reliquary: An exploration of the future of the human body and self-directed evolution, Official Project Documentation, 2016–2017, `https://www.amykarle.com/project/regenerative-reliquary/`; as detailed in bio-art and tissue engineering sources, including Ars Electronica Festival archives (2016) and YouFab Global Creative Awards proceedings (2017), confirming the use of PEGDA hydrogel as the biodegradable scaffold and hMSCs as the cell line for incubation.

It is at once a continuation of sculpture's long tradition and a radical rupture that expands it into new conceptual territories.

By embracing both the experimental intimacy of the studio and the global reproducibility of digital files, artists use 3D printing to interrogate authorship, materiality, and the future of artistic production itself.

In this duality lies its power: 3D printing embodies the paradox of being simultaneously a technique of materialization and a system of multiplication that preserves the aura of the unique object.

If 3D printing has shown how code can be materialized, the next chapter will explore how artificial intelligence now enables code itself to imagine, and, in certain cases, to dream for us.

CHAPTER 7

Artificial Intelligence as a Creative Tool: Collaboration Between Artist and Machine

In Chapter 3, we observed how procedural systems shifted the artist's role from direct manipulation to the design of generative rules.

AI-based generative systems, trained on large datasets, can produce outputs that exhibit patterns and combinations not explicitly programmed, introducing variation beyond deterministic procedural rules.

However, it is necessary to distinguish between **training**, the phase where learning from data occurs, and **inference**, the phase where generation occurs.

For example, models such as Stable Diffusion operate through latent diffusion processes during inference, rather than adapting or learning in real-time during use.

As covered in Chapter 5, where hybrid practices combined manual and digital processes, AI extends these dynamics, opening an even broader field of collaboration and unpredictability.

The artist's role has never been limited to artisanal mastery and technical skill; visionary ideas and conceptual strategies have always been central.

With AI, this role is amplified and transformed. The capacity to imagine worlds now coexists with actively shaping training data, steering probabilistic systems, and curating machine outputs in a genuine human–nonhuman collaboration.

This chapter examines how AI reshapes authorship, introduces unpredictability, and opens aesthetic territories inaccessible through traditional or procedural means.

G. Moioli, *Art Between Matter and Code*, https://doi.org/10.1007/979-8-8688-2376-3_7

Through text-to-image models such as Stable Diffusion, Midjourney, and DALL·E, artists generate 2D visual content that can serve as source material for hybrid works.

When integrated with 3D modeling software, fabrication technologies, and immersive platforms, these AI-generated images become components of works spanning physical, digital, and immersive dimensions.

This integration follows a pipeline of steps: **image generation** (AI output), **3D texturing/modeling** (digital processing), and **fabrication or VR deployment** (physical or immersive realization).

A practical section outlines workflows and examples—including my own experiments—showing how AI can be seamlessly integrated into creative processes.

In this way, Chapter 7 concludes Part II, which traced the transition from manual and material practices to virtual modeling, procedural systems, and AI-driven creation.

Together, these chapters reveal how the studio expands into a space where human imagination and algorithmic processes co-evolve, generating new forms, landscapes, and possible worlds.

7.1 Collaboration Between Artist and Machine

This section examines how AI can act as a collaborative partner, expanding the artist's vision with machine-generated outputs that introduce new creative possibilities.

The emergence of artificial intelligence marks a decisive turning point in the use of digital tools. AI systems no longer simply execute instructions or manipulate data but learn from experience and generate autonomous forms.

In other words, the artist can now collaborate with a system capable of learning and creating almost independently, surpassing the previous paradigms of manual and procedural modeling.

This evolution reflects a continuously transforming creative trajectory: from painting and manual modeling, where form emerged entirely from the **human gesture** to **digital tools** that expanded technical and formal possibilities but still remained subordinate to the artist's direct control.

Procedural systems then introduced a logic of rules and generative parameters, shifting the role of the artist from direct maker to designer of processes.

Finally, as illustrated in Figure 7-1, **AI-mediated modeling** marks a further step: a data-driven paradigm in which the machine learns patterns, adapts to contexts, and proposes autonomous forms, turning creation into a dynamic dialogue between human intention and algorithmic interpretation.

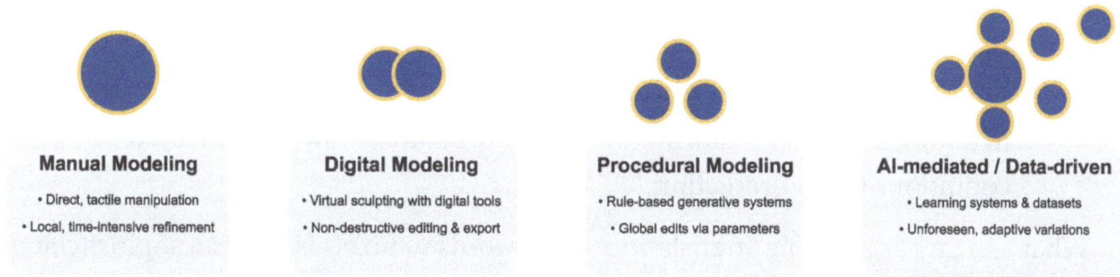

***Figure 7-1.** Evolution of modeling paradigms.*
From manual modeling to digital, from procedural approaches to data-driven AI-mediated modeling

7.1.1 The Prompt

The prompt is the central interface of AI-based image creation. It is the point where language becomes image. It is a textual instruction that is transformed into visual output through a complex probabilistic process.

In contemporary text-to-image systems, the prompt is first encoded into a high-dimensional embedding by a contrastive vision-language model, most commonly CLIP.[1]

This embedding lives in a joint text-image latent space where textual descriptions are aligned with visual features learned during pre-training.

[1] For the CLIP model and text-image embedding space, see:

Radford, A., Kim, J. W., Hallacy, C., Ramesh, A., Goh, G., Agarwal, S., ... & Sutskever, I. (2021). Learning transferable visual models from natural language supervision. Proceedings of the 38th International Conference on Machine Learning (ICML), PMLR 139, 8748–8763.

The resulting vector then conditions the generative model:

- In diffusion models (Stable Diffusion, DALL·E 3, Midjourney, Flux, etc.), it guides the iterative denoising process, usually performed in a compressed latent space.[2,3]
- In earlier GAN-based systems (DALL·E 1, VQGAN+CLIP), it steered latent-space sampling.
- In autoregressive transformer models (Parti, Muse, Imagen Video), it conditions token prediction.

What appears as a simple "translation" from words to pixels is in fact a sophisticated conditional sampling from the vast probability distribution internalized by the model during training.

Far from being a deterministic compilation—as happens, for example, when a short Python script in Blender reliably produces the same 3D scene every time it is executed (Figure 7-2)—the AI prompt triggers a probabilistic exploration of learned correlations.

[2] For the foundational architecture of Denoising Diffusion Probabilistic Models, see:

Ho, J., Jain, A., & Abbeel, P. (2020). Denoising diffusion probabilistic models. Advances in Neural Information Processing Systems 33 (NeurIPS 2020), 6840–6851.

[3] Rombach, R., Blattmann, A., Lorenz, D., Esser, P., & Ommer, B. (2022). High-resolution image synthesis with latent diffusion models. CVPR 2022, 10684–10695.

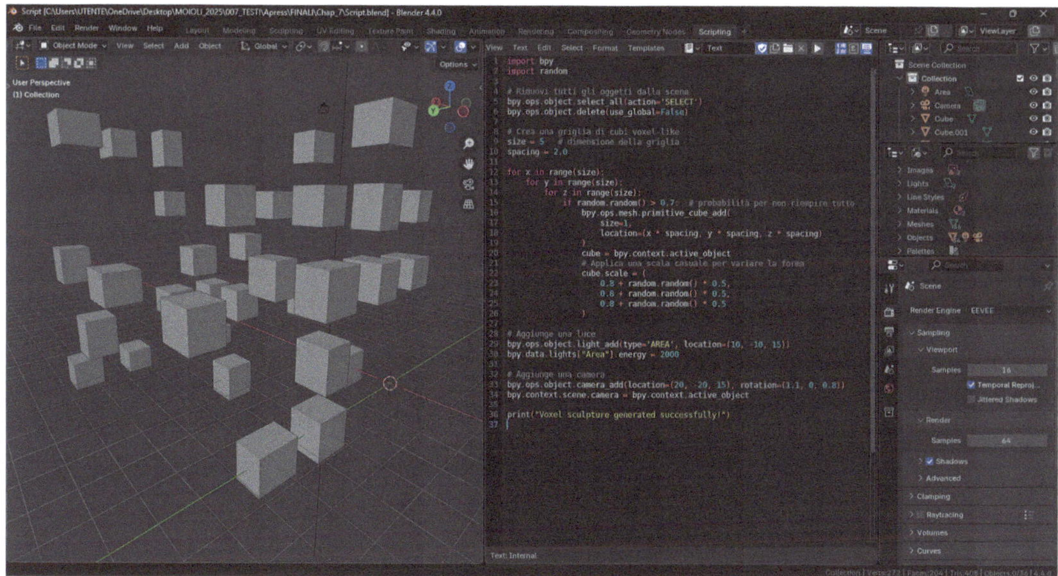

Figure 7-2. Python scripting in Blender.
A few lines of code deterministically generate a precise arrangement of voxel-like cubes. This traditional "text-to-form" paradigm (perfect fidelity, full reproducibility) serves as a revealing counterpoint to the probabilistic, non-deterministic nature of AI image generation from prompts

The same textual input can yield countless plausible variations, none of which is strictly prescribed by the prompt itself.

Yet the analogy with programming is not entirely misleading.

Both practices belong to a broader "text-to-form" tradition. In traditional computer graphics, symbolic instructions are executed with perfect fidelity; in generative AI, they are interpreted stochastically within the space of everything the model has seen.

The difference lies in the degree of control and predictability—and it is precisely this margin of unpredictability that transforms prompting from mere technical command into a genuinely creative act.

In the context of AI art, the prompt is therefore never just a list of keywords.

It is a micro-narrative that encodes intentions, atmospheres, and aesthetic directions while deliberately leaving room for the model's own contribution.

A well-crafted prompt functions almost like a film treatment or a short poetic fragment. It balances precision and ambiguity, materials and moods, structure and openness.

It can be broken down into several recurring layers: almost like the shots of a storyboard or the stanzas of a poem.

Crucially, while the prompt allows for creative variation, artists can exert technical control over the resulting randomness.[4]

Take, for instance, the description of a monumental abstract sculpture made of rusted steel frames and brightly colored tubular forms in red, orange, and yellow, set against a clear sky. This prompt conveys essential elements: material, form, color palette, context, and atmosphere.[5]

This single sentence contains at least six operative layers:

1. **Material and Physicality**. The sentence first defines the materials, such as rusted steel and concrete, anchoring the output in a tangible physicality.

   It is important to note, however, that the model does not "understand" the physical properties of rust or concrete; it reproduces the visual textures and patterns statistically associated with these material labels in its training data.

2. **Form and Structure**. Second, it specifies the form, voxel-like cubes, indicating a geometric structure that gives the model a recognizable compositional framework.

3. **Chromatic Palette**. Third, it establishes a chromatic palette of warm reds, oranges, yellows, and greens, ensuring that the generated image will resonate with a precise atmosphere.

4. **Context and Environment**. Fourth, it situates the object within the context, embedding the sculpture into a plausible environment rather than isolating it in abstraction.

---

[4] Parameters like the *seed* value ensure reproducibility, allowing the regeneration of the exact same image, while selecting specific *deterministic samplers* (like Euler or DPM++ 2S A) allows the user to balance the trade-offs between creative variation and dependable outcome generation.

[5] The example analyzed here refers to a structured prompt describing "A monumental abstract sculpture made of rusted steel frames and brightly colored tubular forms in red, orange, and yellow, set in a contemporary modern architecture under a clear sky. The structure consists of voxel-like cubes and geometric volumes, combining industrial and organic qualities. Photorealistic, cinematic composition with volumetric lighting and high contrast. As the viewer approaches, the sculpture emits a soft glowing light that intensifies, creating an immersive and dynamic atmosphere."

5. **Stylistic and Atmospheric Codes**. Fifth, the prompt invokes precise rendering conventions—photorealistic, cinematic, volumetric god rays, golden-hour lighting, hyper-detailed 8k—not merely as technical parameters, but as carriers of experiential intensity.

   These keywords function like filters in the darkroom or lens choices on a film set: they do not add content but radically inflect the emotional temperature and perceptual credibility of the resulting image.

6. **Cues of temporality and latent interactivity**. Finally, the prompt may slip in a subtle narrative tense—"as the viewer approaches, the glow intensifies," "light pulsing softly," "a figure just turning its head"—suggesting duration, proximity, or response. These are poetic fictions inscribed within an irrevocably static frame.

   Current text-to-image models cannot produce actual movement or interaction; they can only simulate its visual after-image through motion blur, parallax cues, radiating light shafts, or vectors of implied kinesis.

   The generated picture does not react, yet it masterfully performs the memory of a reaction—a frozen promise of interactivity that has become one of the most haunting signatures of contemporary AI imagery.

In sum, a good prompt functions almost like a micro-script. It balances precision and openness, describing materials, forms, colors, contexts, stylistic codes, and even dynamic cues, while leaving space for the algorithm to generate its own unforeseen variations.

7.1.2 Cosmic Labyrinth

To make this more concrete, let us now turn to a practical example that demonstrates how such principles can be applied in the creation of one of my works.

Figure 7-3 presents *Cosmic Labyrinth* created in Blender through 3D modeling.

Figure 7-3. Gianpiero Moioli, Cosmic Labirinth, Mediterranean Landscape. 2023, *272 h × 249 × 223 cm.*
Created in Blender with sub-object modeling, modifiers, and Geometry Nodes, with the integration of a 3D scan of the Baroque portal of Acireale (CC0 1.0 Universal)

The sculpture was conceived as a virtual object with real-world dimensions (272 h × 249 × 223 centimeters), designed from the outset to be directly translatable into physical form through 3D printing.

The **main gray metal structure**—the rigid, labyrinthine framework that holds the entire piece together—was built through classic polygon modeling in Blender. Starting from a simple primitive cube, I worked primarily in Edit Mode at the subobject level (vertices, edges, and faces) using proportional editing, extrusions along normals, and loop cuts to articulate the complex network of interlocking Corten-steel beams.

To break the excessive rigidity of the raw geometry and give the metal beams a weathered, slightly tortured appearance, I applied a first Subdivision Surface modifier (Catmull-Clark, levels 2–3) followed by a Displace modifier driven by a high-resolution Clouds texture (strength ~0.001–0.05) to introduce subtle organic undulations and micro-imperfections.

A second Subdivision Surface modifier was then stacked on top to smooth the displaced surface without losing the newly acquired turbulence, producing a final skin that feels simultaneously industrial and eroded by time—a controlled chaos that would have been almost impossible to sculpt manually vertex by vertex.

The second key component is the **ornate Baroque portal from the Duomo of Acireale**, which was introduced as a high-resolution 3D scan (approximately 1.0 million polygons).

The scan was cleaned, re-topologized where necessary, and then strategically deformed to produce a deliberate clash between 17th-century opulence and brutalist minimalism.

The orange tubes form a single, perfectly continuous mesh. The Curve to Mesh node (with "Fill Caps" enabled) automatically connects each consecutive beveled circle with a smooth cylindrical surface, so the entire system—no matter how long or tortuous—remains one seamless, watertight piece of geometry.

No gaps, no separate objects, just one living orange artery that can be deformed, lengthened, or twisted in a single gesture.

Figure 7-4.** **Gianpiero Moioli, Cosmic Labirinth, Mediterranean Landscape. 2023.
Architectural skeleton in rusted metal with integrated fragment of the Baroque portal of Acireale. The juxtaposition of the abstract framework and the historical element creates a dialogue between structural modernity and Mediterranean memory

These three distinct production logics—traditional subobject polygon modeling, digital appropriation of cultural-heritage 3D scans, and fully procedural generation via Geometry Nodes—coexist within the same file and are continuously negotiated during the creative process.

Their friction and reconciliation are precisely what gives Cosmic Labyrinth its hybrid character: a single work that is at once hand-crafted, archaeologically sourced, and algorithmically alive.

7.1.2.1 Modeling in Blender: Manual Control and Geometry Nodes

This modular construction echoes architectural logics, where each element can be adjusted independently but contributes to the coherence of the whole.

The digital base architecture was first manually modeled to establish a precise and tangible sense of structure.

On this foundation, a second layer was introduced. To reconnect the work to the themes of the Piazze d'Italia and Paesaggi Mediterranei, I incorporated a 3D scan of the Baroque portal of Acireale, freely reinterpreted and integrated into the sculpture.

The original model, created through photogrammetry with a smartphone and downloaded from MyMiniFactory under the CC0 1.0 Universal license,[6] required standard technical cleanup before integration. This was necessary because high-density scan meshes often contain flaws and excess geometry.

The cleanup of the mesh typically involved four key steps:

1. **Hole Filling**, implementing automatic hole filling to ensure the model was topologically closed and watertight (essential for 3D printing).
2. **Decimation** from a high-density initial mesh (likely several million polygons) down to the optimized count of approximately **1 million polygons** for performance efficiency.
3. **Remeshing** for a more uniform polygon distribution (even topology).
4. **UV unwrapping** to correctly map and apply the existing textures onto the simplified mesh.

This portal, located in Acireale at the foot of Mount Etna, represents a lava-stone entrance associated with the local Baroque tradition, a material expression deeply rooted in the architectural culture of the region.

Its re-elaboration within the sculpture introduces a historical and urban resonance into an otherwise abstract composition, linking the digital structure to layers of memory, place, and cultural identity.

In this way, heritage itself becomes a catalyst for visionary creativity, bridging past and future.

The historical reference does not remain static but becomes the starting point for new digital processes.

[6] While CC0 allows unrestricted use including commercial applications, ethical practice suggests acknowledging sources and considering whether AI transformation of heritage artifacts raises questions about cultural context and reinterpretation. For readers: always verify license terms before using scanned heritage objects, as some jurisdictions maintain rights over heritage sites regardless of photographic copyright. The model analyzed here is available for verification: `https://www.myminifactory.com/object/3d-print-baroque-portal-in-acireale-188515`

After the integration of the Baroque portal, the workflow shifts with the tubular forms from manual modeling to a procedural logic through Blender's Geometry Nodes, employed to generate fluid, continuous trajectories.

These "pipes" intertwine with the rigid digital frame and, with the historical architectural element, creating a dialogue between geometric stability and organic movement.

Geometry Nodes enable the artist to define rules, relationships, and parameters that automatically generate and transform complex structures. Instead of constructing each element individually, the artwork emerges from a network of instructions that determine how forms are distributed, scaled, or connected.

In this sense, *Cosmic Labyrinth* demonstrates how Blender can serve not only as a tool for static modeling but also as a platform where procedural and generative methods expand the creative process—as Figure 7-5 clearly shows by simply varying a single parameter and anticipating later integrations with AI-based transformations.[7]

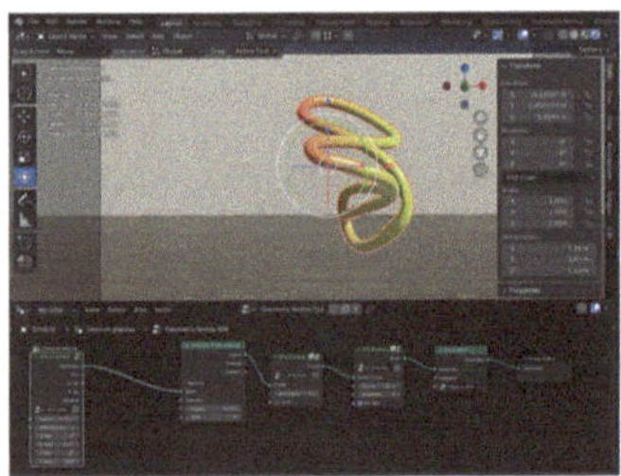
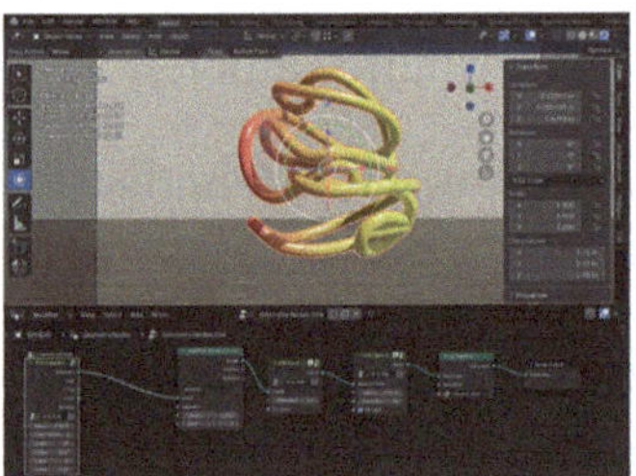
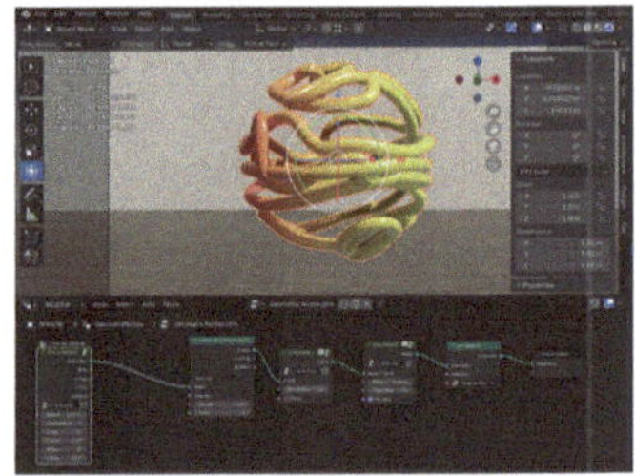

Figure 7-5. Procedural variations of the tubular structure in Cosmic Labyrinth.
By modifying only the density parameter within Blender's Geometry Nodes, the form evolves from sparse configurations to dense, intertwined networks, exemplifying the generative potential of a single procedural system

This exemplifies one of the key strengths of Geometry Nodes: the ability to generate complex variations from a single procedural definition. The artist sets a framework of conditions—density, scale, curvature—and the system computes all possible configurations.

[7] In the screenshot of the Geometry Nodes editor (Figure 7-5), changing the Density value of the Distribute Points on Faces node from 0.7 to 2.3 to 4 is enough to radically transform the orange tubular system. At low density the tubes become sparse and sinuous, almost calligraphic; at higher values they proliferate into dense, vascular clusters.

This instantaneous, nondestructive reconfiguration exemplifies the shift from traditional modeling to real-time parametric authorship—a logic that prefigures the stochastic variation typical of AI-driven workflows.

Such flexibility not only accelerates the creative workflow but also resonates conceptually with themes of growth, transformation, and multiplicity, aligning with the hybrid dialogue between organic movement and structural clarity that defines *Cosmic Labyrinth.*

Building on this procedural foundation, the work was further expanded through the integration of **AI-generated variations**.

Here, the **Baroque portal of Acireale**, previously integrated as a scanned architectural fragment, becomes the catalyst for a new phase of experimentation. The historical element is no longer merely quoted but offered to the AI as a generative seed, prompting the model to hallucinate alternative architectural futures from its ornamented curves.

Using the finalized Blender models of Cosmic Labyrinth as structural seeds, I generated an entire family of images through a repeatable Midjourney (V6.1) workflow:

1. Original Blender render exported as PNG with resolution 1152 x 2048, transparent background, clean lighting.
2. Uploaded to Midjourney and processed via img2img/remix with a fixed denoising strength of 0.65 (preserving roughly 35 % of the original structure while allowing 65 % speculative mutation).
3. Prompt engineering: The core prompt was the one documented in note 5.
4. Multiple generations: six to eight grids of four variants each, using the default V6.1 sampler; seeds left free to maximize diversity; then the most promising results were upscaled and further varied.
5. Manual curation of 7–10 final candidates.
6. Light post-processing in GIMP: Gentle S-curve in Curves for contrast and warmth; selective orange saturation boost (+15 on the orange channel only); occasional layer-mask compositing of two variants to recover the best arch deformation; final non-destructive upscale via Lanczos 3 and subtle unsharp mask.

Figures 7-6 and 7-7 illustrate some of the results of this process.

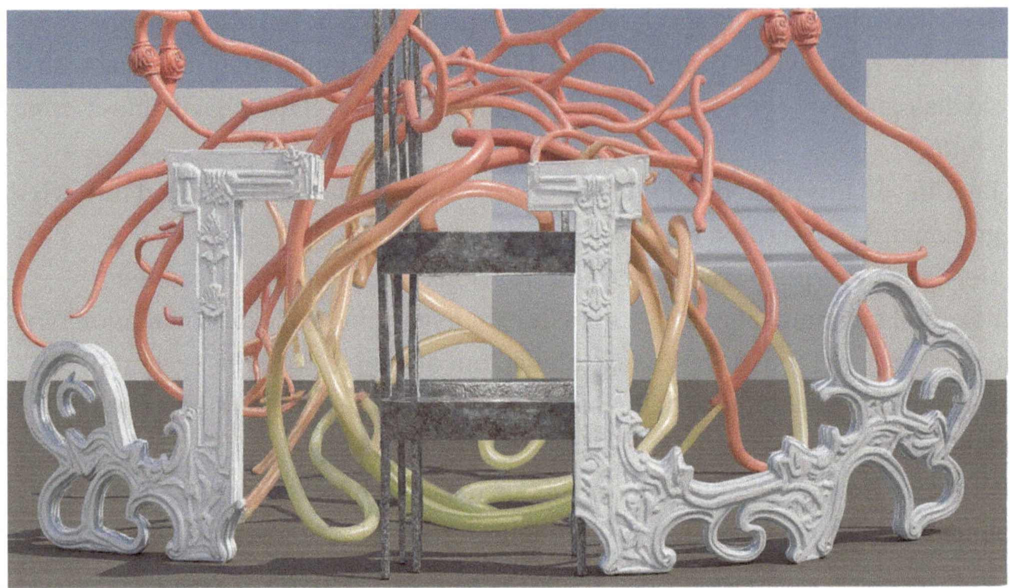

Figure 7-6. Cosmic Labyrinth reworked with AI.
The Baroque portal of Acireale is reshaped into new architectural thresholds, intertwining with the sculptural structure and tubular forms

Figure 7-7. Cosmic Labirinth. AI-generated variation.
The historical portal expands into a sequence of imagined colonnades, transforming the original trace into a fragment of invented and alien architectures

In Figure 7-6, the Baroque portal is reshaped into new architectural thresholds, intertwining with the sculptural framework and the tubular forms.

In Figure 7-7, an AI-generated variation extends this transformation. The historical portal evolves into a sequence of imagined colonnades, merging echoes of classical architecture with futuristic invention.

The same principle of metamorphosis was also applied to the tubular structures, whose curvature, thickness, and chromatic gradients were modified through AI-based image transformation, producing dynamic variations that evoke organic growth or energy flows.

Out of the many possible results generated through this iterative process, these two examples were selected to illustrate the initial phase of experimentation. They reveal how the algorithm can reinterpret both architectural and sculptural elements, translating them into new visual harmonies that oscillate between structure and fluidity.

This generative idea, however, does not remain confined to the digital image.

It can be further refined and reinterpreted by the artist—evolving from an AI-generated vision into a tangible three-dimensional work.

The same configuration can thus be materialized as a sculpture, expanded into a scenographic environment, or reimagined as an urban installation, bridging the virtual and the physical through processes of digital fabrication or architectural translation.

In this sense, *Cosmic Labirinth* exemplifies how procedural and AI-based methods can converge. Algorithmic geometry defines the structure, while artificial intelligence expands its symbolic and visionary dimensions.

7.1.2.2 AI Expansions: From Object to Space

This work reveals a dual trajectory, almost as if it possessed two distinct lives.

The first is that of a three-dimensional object, conceived and modeled in Blender with precise control of structure and materiality.

The second life unfolds through its transformation into image, scenery, and landscape, when the original renderings are reinterpreted by AI systems such as Stable Diffusion and, more recently, Midjourney.

In this way, the object ceases to be merely a static form and becomes a narrative space—one that, as we shall see in the following chapters, is capable of genuine interactivity in two radically different registers.

In Chapter 9, interactivity remains fully virtual. The spectator navigates, manipulates parameters, and receives real-time visual and auditory feedback inside a simulated environment.

In Chapter 10, instead, interactivity migrates into the physical world. The work reacts to the actual presence and movement of bodies through sensors, producing computational light, sound, and responses in real space.

Thus, the same generative seed that began as a fixed sculpture in Blender and then proliferated into AI-reimagined images finally blossoms into two distinct forms of lived experience—one immaterial and screen-based, the other fully embodied and situated in the gallery or landscape (Figure 7-8).

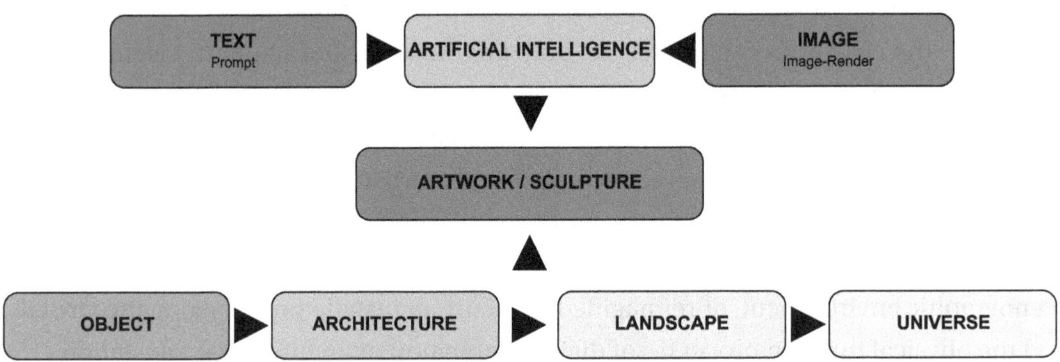

Figure 7-8. Conceptual scheme of AI-based expansion.
The creative process evolves progressively, moving from object to architecture and urban space, to landscape, and finally toward an entire universe.
This trajectory illustrates how AI enables artworks to transcend their initial form and generate ever-expanding narrative and spatial dimensions

This scheme already hints at the broader trajectory of expansion, achieved primarily through **compositional scaling** and **prompt manipulation** in the AI image generation process. This trajectory can be broken down into four conceptual stages:

- **Stage 1: Local Modification:** The sculpture begins to modify and to influence the space immediately around it. (This is achieved through minimal scale changes and low denoising in img2img, preserving the original background.)
- **Stage 2: Architectural/Urban Integration.** It transforms into an urban space or architectural presence. (This is achieved by prompting specific architectural styles and adjusting perspective to place the object within a recognizable human scale).

- **Stage 3: Extended Landscape.** It unfolds into an extended landscape. (This is achieved by widening the compositional frame and prompting natural or vast environmental elements).
- **Stage 4: Cosmic Universe.** Finally, it expands into a cosmic universe. (Achieved by extreme scale manipulation and prompting speculative or cosmic environments).

All of this originates from the initial 3D modeling and is further amplified and reimagined through AI, demonstrating how a single object can evolve into an entire world.

Together with 3D modeling and image generation, the prompt is the central operator. Far from being a simple descriptive prelude, it is the active vector of scalar and narrative transformation, the textual device that continuously repositions the same seed form across ever-larger orders of reality.

Far from a static command, it enters continuous dialogue with the image: words describe, stretch, reinterpret, and each new variation is born as much from language as from geometry.

The process is potentially infinite. The work escapes the boundaries of its original file and proliferates into imaginary cities, alien planets, nebulae, and entire universes: no longer an object among others, but the generative matrix of whole worlds.

7.1.2.2.1 The Sculpture Extends Beyond the Object

The first stage of our expansion begins with the transformation of the 3D renderings produced in Blender.

Sculpture, like architecture, has always existed in relation to space, but here what was initially conceived as a static configuration becomes the subject of metamorphosis. Volumes are stretched or compressed, and surfaces acquire transparency or reflective depth.

Artificial intelligence acts as a catalyst for these transformations, reinterpreting the sculptural renderings through prompt-based processes in Stable Diffusion and Midjourney.

Although both rely on diffusion models, Stable Diffusion offers surgical control and iterative precision (open weights, ControlNet, LoRAs, local execution), while Midjourney v6.1 delivers instant aesthetic polish and unexpected conceptual leaps—tools that, far from competing, have become complementary stages of the same workflow.

Text prompt: *A monumental abstract sculpture of steel and glowing tubular forms, fused with alien spaces and architectural elements.*

Prompt Development Context (method used for all four stages)

This final prompt is the result of an **iterative and structured refinement process.**

It was designed not merely as a description but as a technical command encoding the artwork's **hybridity** and **conceptual scale.**

Every prompt is built in four rational layers:

1. Core subject & scale
2. Primary materials and production logics
3. Hybridizing/expansive agent (the lever that triggers the scalar jump)
4. Rendering and atmospheric directive

This structure guarantees both conceptual coherence and maximum leverage on the model (Figure 7-9).

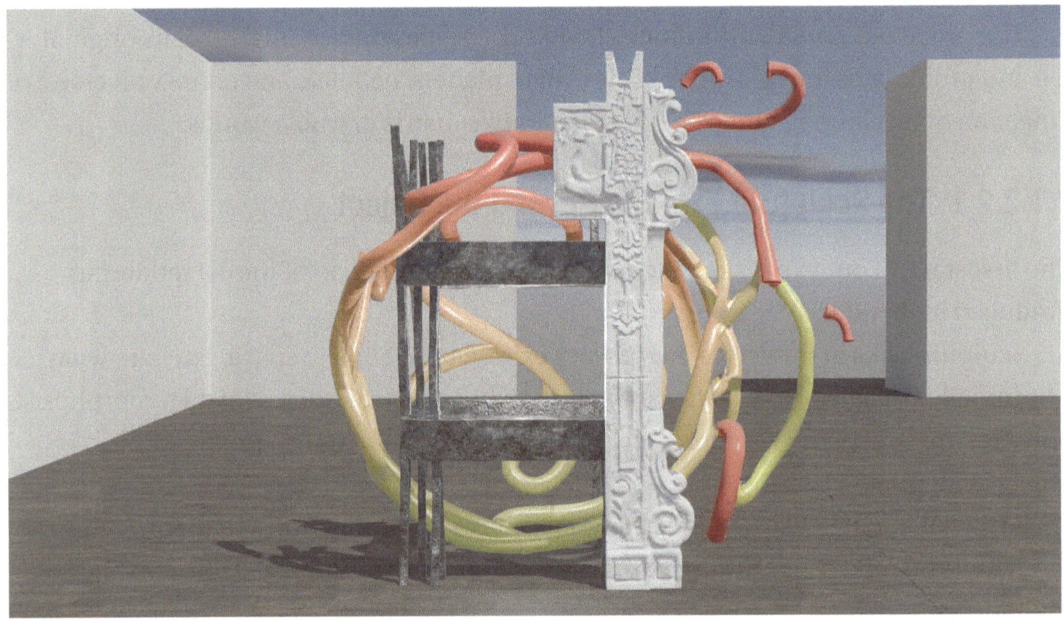

Figure 7-9. Phase 1 – From Object to Space.
3D rendering of Cosmic Labyrinth. The sculpture, modeled in Blender, begins to change, hinting at a scenographic dimension that extends beyond the object itself

This first evolution starts with the modification of the object and space, laying the groundwork for the subsequent stage where the sculpture begins to generate urban space and architecture.

7.1.2.2.2 Thresholds of the Imaginary Urban Space and Architecture

The second stage moves from object to urban space, architecture, and scenography (Figure 7-10).

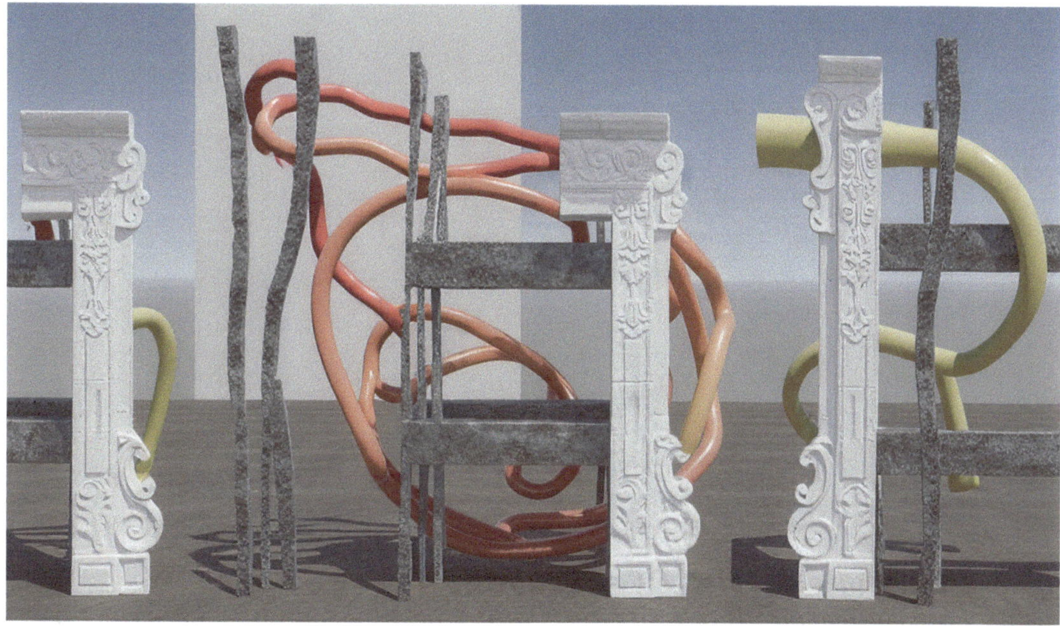

Figure 7-10. Phase 2 – Thresholds of the Imaginary Urban Space and Architecture.
The sculpture expands into an architectural presence: portals and tubular forms dissolve into pathways and plazas, generating a hybrid space between monument and urban environment

The sculpture ceases to be a mere presence within its surroundings; it transforms into an environment in itself.

By modulating the prompts, the object evolves into a container of space, producing spaces, architectures, and atmospheres that viewers can imagine inhabiting.

Text Prompt: *Abstract monumental sculpture as a metaphysical square in rusted steel and stone. Warm Mediterranean light, surreal atmosphere. The structure dissolves into pathways and plazas, merging monuments and environment.*

The work becomes a threshold: at once sculpture, architecture, and urban space, an open frame for collective imagination.

7.1.2.2.3 Cities and Landscapes of Memory and Light

From architecture the work evolves into the landscape (Figure 7-11).

Figure 7-11. Phase 3 - Toward Landscape.
Cosmic Labyrinth expands into city and landscape, intertwining with planetary and organic forms. The sculpture ceases to be an isolated object and becomes a generator of horizons, atmospheres, and terrains

The sculpture first becomes an urban frame, an imaginary city made of thresholds and voids.

From there it extends further: luminous horizons evoke Mediterranean light.

Text prompt: *Monumental labyrinthine sculpture expanding into city and landscape, rusted steel and stone. Variations: neon night, surreal arches, metaphysical piazza with Mediterranean light.*

The sculpture unfolds into city and landscape alike, its form echoing the layered processes of the stratifications of nature and culture. It no longer exists as an isolated object but as a generator of horizons, atmospheres, and terrains.

7.1.2.2.4 Cosmic Horizons

In the fourth stage, the sculpture expands beyond earthly space (Figure 7-12). It dissolves into a cosmic scenography, where planets, moons, and luminous nebulas orbit its structure. No longer bound to the ground, it becomes an architecture of the universe, a generator of infinite horizons.

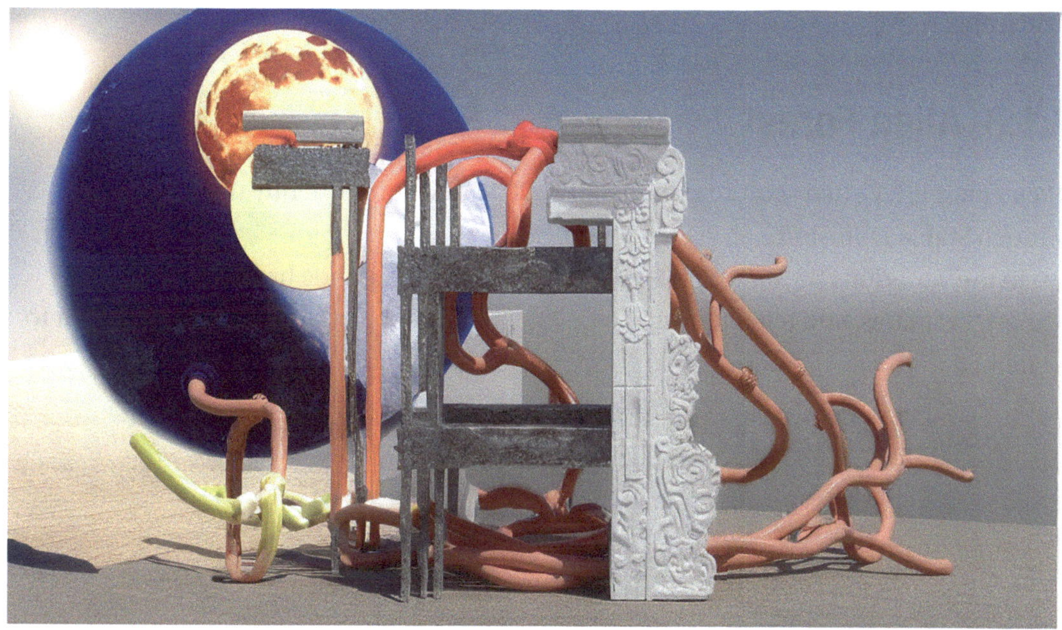

Figure 7-12. Phase 4 – Cosmic Horizons.
Cosmic Labyrinth expands beyond terrestrial space, entwining with planetary and lunar presences. The sculpture dissolves into a cosmic scenography, becoming an architecture of the universe and a generator of infinite horizons

Text prompt: *Abstract monumental sculpture as cosmic architecture, surrounded by planets and moons, glowing nebulas, vast galactic horizon, cinematic light. Beautiful space with sun and planets and sunlight shining through the trees, serene, peaceful, high detail.*

The sculpture becomes universe: a constellation of forms and lights, projecting the work into a boundless dimension where art, space, and cosmos converge. This cosmic convergence finds a new terrestrial—yet equally visionary—echo in.

Alien Forest. This work concerns a different sculpture already introduced in Figure 1-13 of Chapter 1.

This work demonstrates how the same principles of expansion can be applied across distinct forms and contexts, confirming that **the dialogue between image, 3D modeling, and AI** does not remain tied to a single object but opens an entire horizon of possibilities.

In the next section, these ideas will be translated into **a new environment**, intertwining organic forms and speculative architectures to generate an unprecedented landscape.

7.1.3 Alien Forest

Alien Forest is a virtual sculpture modeled in 2024 and subsequently transformed through Stable Diffusion.

In the variations presented in Figure 7-13, the work expands by incorporating planets, branches, and alien landscapes, evolving from object to space, from content to container.

Figure 7-13. Gianpiero Moioli Alien Forest (2024).
AI variations. The digital sculpture expands into surreal and cosmic landscapes, showing the open-ended potential of AI-based transformation

These images suggest how the sculpture can transcend its digital condition and generate new extensions through screens, projections, and immersive environments, opening an inexhaustible creative potential.

With the introduction of AI, this trajectory of art as gesture and manual practice encounters a turning point: the machine does not merely assist but actively participates in the creative process, producing scenarios that exceed the logics of traditional drawing and modeling.

In this perspective, AI emerges as a genuine creative partner, capable of amplifying imagination and transforming artistic practice into a continuous dialogue with the algorithm.

This principle of computational extension is further realized through video, creating temporal dimensions that unfold from the static image:

> Video I: The first video sequence was generated using Stable Diffusion 1.5, with subsequent editing and temporal sequencing managed in Blender 4.2.
>
> Music by AudioCoffee: `https://www.audiocoffee.net/` from Pixabay `https://pixabay.com`
>
> Link: `https://vimeo.com/1025475802`
>
> Video II: The second video, demonstrating advanced aesthetic coherence, was generated entirely within Midjourney V7 (including the AI-generated soundscape) and edited/post-produced using Blender 5.0
>
> Link: `https://vimeo.com/1144800932`

In summary, the case studies of *Cosmic Labirinth* and *Alien Forest* collectively establish a **new hybrid methodology** in digital art.

This practice is defined by the convergence of precise, manually controlled 3D modeling (which provides structural stability and defined form) and AI-driven transformation (which enables rapid, imaginative expansion and unexpected aesthetic exploration).

The **prompt** acts as the central interface, translating conceptual intent into visual possibility. Through this continuous dialogue between the structured work of the artist and the stochastic process of the algorithm, the digital object transcends its physical boundaries, transforming from a static piece of content into an **unfolding generative space** that establishes the foundation for further immersive and interactive experimentation.

7.2 New Creative Possibilities and Conceptual Challenges

In this section, we explore how AI introduces radically new creative possibilities while simultaneously challenging traditional notions of authorship, aesthetics, and artistic intention.

On the one hand, AI opens unexplored imaginative horizons; on the other, it raises conceptual questions about originality and the artist's role in relation to a creative machine.

7.2.1 AI as a Creative Partner

Working with AI involves interacting with a statistical system that generates outputs probabilistically rather than executing deterministic commands.

The model samples from learned distributions patterns extracted from training data producing variations that can appear surprising or suggestive to human observers.

This "surprise" isn't intentionality or agency in the model; rather, it reflects the vast multidimensional space of possibilities encoded in its parameters, portions of which may be unexpected to the user.

Understanding AI as a probability engine rather than a creative entity helps artists leverage its capabilities effectively. **They're exploring a learned latent space of visual patterns**, not conversing with an artificial mind.

The "dialogue" is between artist and statistical process, mediated by prompts that weight different regions of this probability space.

A prompt, a drawing, an image, or a sculpture can become the starting point for new visual outputs that broaden the artist's horizon, offering directions never previously considered.

The experience is comparable to reading a novel by Emilio Salgari or Jules Verne.

Just as the reader was transported into exotic or submarine worlds never seen before, the artist, through AI, gains access to otherwise inaccessible visual universes: landscapes and forms that extend the boundaries of their own imagination.

However, this comparison requires scrutiny.

While Verne and Salgari created original imaginative visions, AI systems generate outputs by recombining and interpolating patterns from training data they cannot produce anything truly outside the distribution of what they've seen.

The sense of accessing "otherwise inaccessible visual universes" comes not from AI generating the genuinely novel but from its capacity to produce unexpected combinations and variations at a scale and speed impossible for individual humans.

The artist's role therefore is critical. They curate, guide, and interpret these statistically generated possibilities, recognizing which combinations carry aesthetic or conceptual value. This is closer to a curator sifting through a vast archive than an explorer discovering genuinely uncharted territory though the curatorial act itself remains deeply creative.

Unlike reading a novel, however, this is not a solitary journey. The encounter with AI takes the form of a creative dialogue, in which the machine responds, diverts, and surprises.

This collaboration blends human intent with machine interpretation, generating a dynamic interplay that expands the artist's creative scope.

In my project *Symphony of the Labyrinth: the Tale of the Clock and the Tree*, I used ChatGPT and DALL-E to create a narrative, as I will explain later.

Yet my starting point was always artistic inspiration—painting in this case—before allowing the algorithm to suggest new narrative and visual pathways.

7.2.1.1 Case Study: Symphony of the Labyrinth

> *"... in a labyrinthine city, built of interwoven streets and shifting squares there were the Clockwork Master, a mechanical idol of gears and engineering, and the Nature Shaman, an organic idol of plants and animals.*
>
> *Though opposites, they embodied complementary aspects of the same reality.*
>
> *When a mysterious plant began to grow among the city's gears, the two collaborated to weave it into the maze square, blending mechanics and nature.*
>
> *The city was transformed into a harmonious environment where duality became unity, and the coexistence of technology and nature was celebrated as a source of creativity and wonder..."*

From a series of drawings, I developed a tale. The project began in 2023 with five hand-painted drawings: simple, almost archetypal images of labyrinths, idols, holographic symbols, mechanical cities, and dual realities, with the support of ChatGPT and DALL·E.

These paintings became the seed for a three-stage process:

- **Manual genesis**: I created drawings with simple colors and materials, concentrating on elementary ideas such as labyrinths, forests, idols, cities, and plazas.
- **AI expansion**: I turned to AI to expand these initial visions. Artificial intelligence helped me push beyond the limits of my own style, opening horizons that might otherwise have remained inaccessible. For an artist, one of the greatest risks is becoming confined within personal habits or repeating familiar patterns. AI became a way to break free from this cycle, offering new perspectives and unexpected variations.
- **Hybrid synthesis**: I brought manual and digital versions together. I selected from among the virtual adaptations generated by AI, refining them further with digital painting. In this way, the process became a dialogue between hand and algorithm, tradition and innovation, where each stage enriched the next.

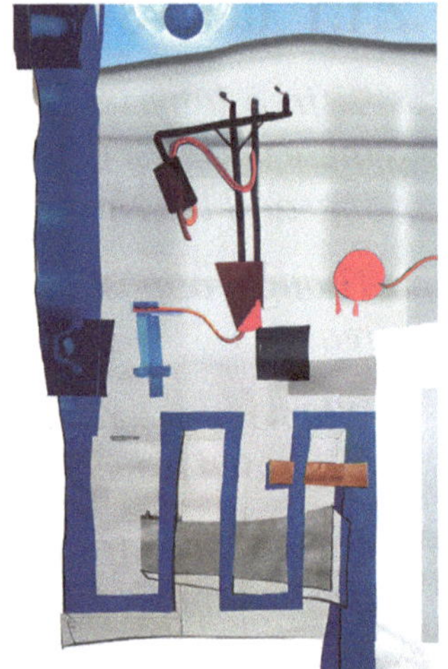

Figure 7-14. Gianpiero Moioli, Mechanical Idol with Gears, Primitive Holographic Idol, Labyrinth with Holograms.
Digitally modified acrylic paintings on paper and cardboard with pen drawing, cm 150 (h) × 100

The narrative that emerged from this synthesis unifies the central elements of the drawings. **Mechanical Idol with Gears** (Figure 7-14) became the Clockwork Master, embodying the mechanical essence of the city.

Primitive Holographic Idol (Figure 7-14) was reimagined as the Nature Shaman, a symbol of organic and ancestral life.

Labyrinth with Holograms (Figure 7-14) provided the scenography of their encounter: a plaza animated by holographic symbols of duality and interconnection.

Mechanical Labyrinth City (Figure 7-15) turned into a shifting plaza of giant gears, endlessly reconfiguring its pathways.

Finally, **Dual Reality with Holograms** (Figure 7-15) expressed the coexistence of parallel realities, reflected in the interaction between the Clockwork Master and the Nature Shaman.

Figure 7-15. Gianpiero Moioli, Mechanical Labyrinth City and Dual Reality with Holograms.
Digitally modified acrylic paintings on paper and cardboard with pen drawing, cm 100 (h) × 150

From this dialogue emerged a concise allegorical tale.

In a labyrinthine city of shifting squares and interlocking gears lived two guardian idols: the Clockwork Master (pure mechanism) and the Nature Shaman (pure organism).

When a mysterious vine began to grow inside the city's machinery, the two rivals chose collaboration instead of conflict, weaving living branches through steel cogwheels until the entire metropolis became a single hybrid organism. A place where technology and nature were no longer opposites but the two voices of the same symphony.

This synthesis of visual art and storytelling thus forms not only the conclusion of one experiment but also the opening toward a broader reflection: the new ecology of visual creation, where images, texts, and AI interact in a continuous cycle.

In this sense, *Symphony of the Labyrinth* is less a finished work than a first movement of an **open-source process**: not "open source" in a strictly legal or software sense, such as CC0 licensing or Blender's GNU license but as a conceptual condition of openness. **This work is designed to be replayed, re-orchestrated, and extended indefinitely by human and nonhuman players alike, embodying the principles of a networked artwork** where the project's integrity resides in its potential for continuous transformation and application.

7.2.2 The New Ecology of Visual Creation

After outlining the evolution of modeling paradigms, it is useful to focus on the new ecology of visual creation inaugurated by artificial intelligence.

Today, the relationship is no longer linear—from the artist to the tool—but takes the form of a dynamic network where text and image intertwine and where humans and AI influence each other reciprocally.

More precisely, the relationship is iterative but asymmetrical.

The artist influences AI outputs through prompt engineering and parameter adjustment, while AI outputs influence the artist's subsequent decisions and directions introducing unpredictability and a recursive influence.

However, standard text-to-image interfaces do not adapt or learn from individual user sessions and the model remains static.

The "reciprocal influence" is actually the artist's internal creative process responding to generated results, not mutual learning between two agents.

For most artists using web-based tools (Midjourney, DALL·E), the interaction is user ➤ model ➤ output ➤ user evaluation ➤ refined prompt. The model never learns from the individual user or permanently adapts to their aesthetic; it simply responds to each new prompt.[8]

Figure 7-16 illustrates the interaction flows that define contemporary creative practice with AI.

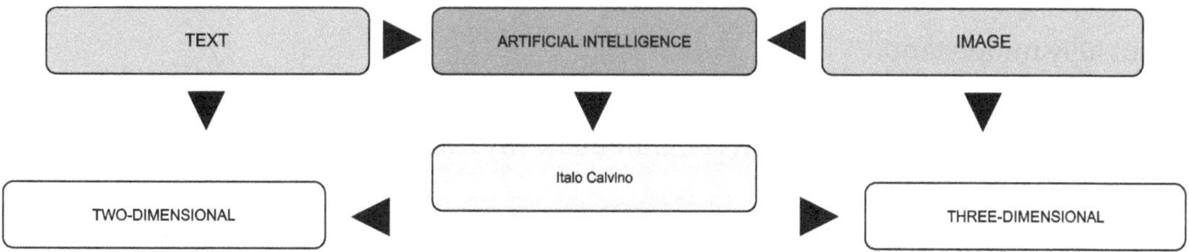

Figure 7-16. Relationships between text, image, human, and AI.
The diagram illustrates the interactive flows that define contemporary creative practice with AI

Texts and Images guide the generation of new images, while AI reworks data and produces unforeseen visions. The artist, in turn, interprets, selects, and reintroduces the results into the process, creating a continuous cycle of collaboration.

In my own practice, I always start from an image, which is then expand through prompts and models.

This new ecology of visual creation, as in Figure 7-16, shows how the process is no longer linear but circular and interactive. Texts, images, artist, and AI interweave in a continuous flow, in which each result becomes the starting point for further transformations.

If AI introduces the unexpected, it is the role of the artist to interpret and guide this dialogue, selecting and refining the outcomes.

This dynamic finds a profound echo in literary reflection.

As Italo Calvino suggested in his reflections on visibility and multiplicity, **imagination has always been a network of images, stories, and symbols capable of expanding beyond the individual mind.**

---

[8] The only current exception is fine-tuning (DreamBooth, LoRA, custom checkpoints), which truly teaches the model an artist's style.

It requires high-end GPUs (≥ 16 GB VRAM), technical expertise, curated datasets, and hours-to-days of training: barriers that keep it out of reach for most artists using mainstream web tools.

Calvino, in his 1985 Harvard lecture "Visibility" (from Six Memos for the Next Millennium),[9] described imagination as an inherently interconnected process: images beget images, stories branch into multiplicity, symbols resonate across collective memory.

Caution is needed, however, when mapping this humanistic vision onto computational systems. Calvino's "cinema of the mind" referred to the mysterious, embodied capacity for internal visualization and creative synthesis—processes we still do not fully understand.

AI image generation, by contrast, operates through learned statistical correlations in high-dimensional vector spaces. It is mathematically tractable yet conceptually alien to human cognition.

The similarity lies in the networked, associative nature of both; the difference lies in substrate (neurons versus silicon), mechanism (biological synthesis versus gradient descent), and intentionality (meaning making versus pattern matching).

Borges, too, envisioned infinite libraries and labyrinths of narratives, each path opening onto new worlds.[10]

In this sense, AI does not replace creativity but amplifies a process that has always been relational and open-ended, extending it into a new, algorithmic dimension.

As in the examples of expansions and hybridizations, as covered in Chapter 5, the goal is to obtain increasingly creative and diverse works.

Through this iterative dialogue, from an apparent chaos emerges an abstract yet harmonious composition that reflects my original intention.

This **tension between chaos and order** finds its clearest expression in the following case study.

7.2.2.1 Case Study: Gravitational Field

Gravitational Field is not a single work, but an open series generated from one hand-drawn matrix (Figure 7-17).

[9] Italo Calvino, "Visibility," in Six Memos for the Next Millennium. Cambridge, MA: Harvard University Press, 1988.

[10] Jorge Luis Borges, "The Library of Babel," in Ficciones (1944; English trans. Grove Press, 1962).

Figure 7-17. Gianpiero Moioli, Gravitational Field (2023).
Original manually painted composition (left) and seven AI-generated variations. The work explores the dialogue between geometry and chromatic tensions, where field and labyrinth merge into a dynamic map of attraction and repulsion

It emerges through a dynamic interplay of geometric forms and chromatic tensions, which seem to attract and repel each other.

Using Midjourney V6's advanced Inpainting workflow, I repeatedly masked and regenerated selected areas of this base composition with the prompt "gravitational field" and a high Guidance Scale (28). This forced strong conceptual adherence while allowing the model's latent-space interpolations to introduce unforeseen chromatic and formal configurations.

Rigid lines evoke a labyrinth, yet within this grid unexpected trajectories unfold. Field and Labyrinth merge into a spatial and mental map, where direction and disorientation coexist, embodying a creative process that oscillates between deliberate control and algorithmic emergence.

The result is a genuine human-AI collaboration. Midjourney contributed statistically rich, often surprising visual proposals, while each variant was rigorously evaluated, refined, or discarded through new masks and adjusted prompts until it aligned with my aesthetic and conceptual framework.

Because every piece shares the same originating matrix yet diverges through iterative AI intervention, the series remains radically open**: a living, expandable archive of possibilities that can be reconfigured into wall installations, projections, or time-based video sequences without ever reaching a definitive closure.**

7.2.3 Expanding Creative Horizons

AI enables artists to explore visual territories that would be difficult or time-consuming to reach through traditional means alone. It helps creatives generating unexpected combinations and extending the range of imaginable forms unfolding alien, fantastical, and imagined worlds.

From a single prompt, paintings, sculptures, and architectures can blossom into immersive landscapes where viewers do not simply look but enter.

In this way, the work transcends representation to become an experience, anticipating Part IV's exploration of virtual creation.

The previous examples—*Cosmic Labyrinth* and *Alien Forest* in 3D and *Gravitational Fiel*d in 2D—form the basis for synthetic alien landscapes.

Through AI, these works evolve into visions of unknown worlds, rich in astonishing details: unfamiliar geological formations, iridescent skies of other planets, and atmospheres that exceed the limits of human experience, while maintaining the language and style of the artist, transforming them into visionary landscapes where matter and imagination intertwine.

For the artist, such images offer raw visual material to be developed and reimagined.

From these scenarios, immersive environments can emerge—whether virtual or physical. **What begins as a static work can be transformed into a navigable virtual world or an interactive installation, where viewers step inside and become participants.**

In this way, the traditional genre of sculpture, scenography, and architecture expands into an immersive experience, and the artist ventures into creative territories once inaccessible.

AI thus extends the horizon of imagination, enabling hybrid works that unite painting, virtual reality, and experimental storytelling.

This is the idea behind my *Spazi Continui* (*Flow*, or *Continuous Spaces*), interactive and noninteractive video installations.

7.2.3.1 Continuous Spaces: From Static Image to Flowing Vision

The notion of a **continuous space** begins with an intuition (Figure 7-18). It is a space that is never still, always in motion, endlessly transforming like a three-dimensional procedural texture generated in real time through noise functions (Perlin, Voronoi, or wavelet turbulence) combined with animated distortion and displacement nodes.

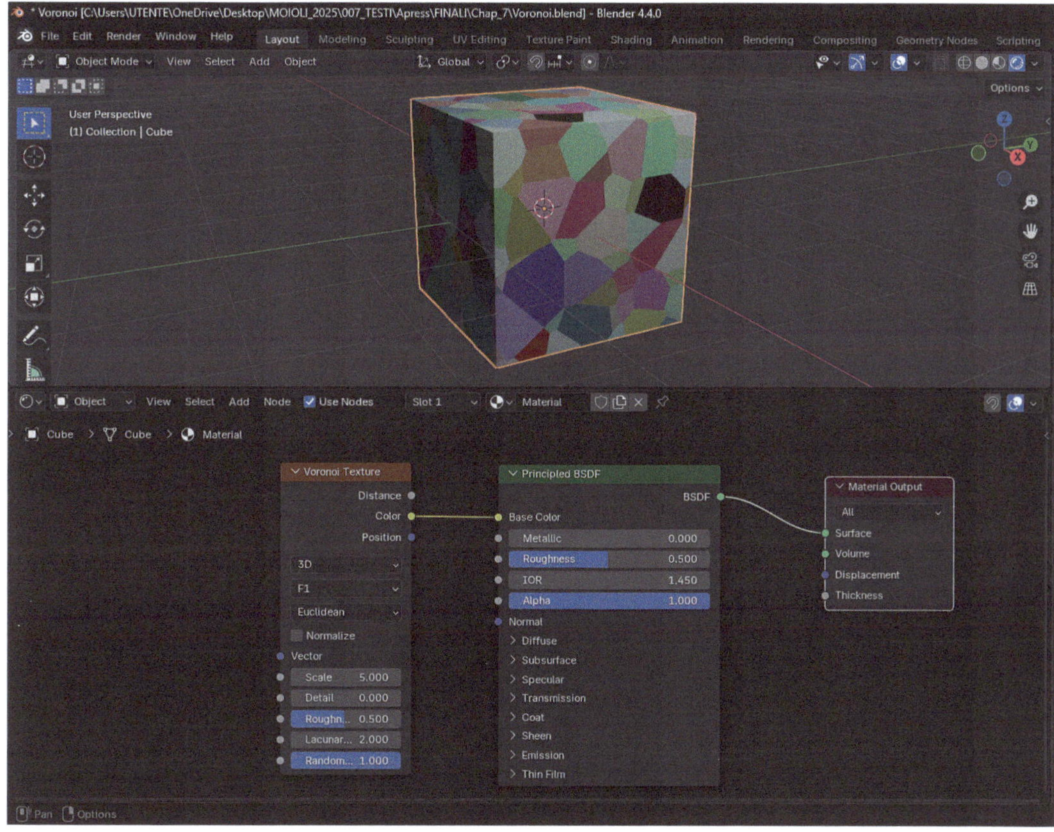

Figure 7-18.** **Procedural texture in Blender.
A three-dimensional pattern generated through nodes. Like continuous spaces, it never repeats itself but unfolds through variations and fluctuations, evoking a world in perpetual transformation

Thanks to this computational approach—typically implemented in Blender's Geometry Nodes or Shader Nodes (see Figure 7-18)—the pattern never truly repeats: each point in space is evaluated independently as a function of its coordinates and time, producing infinite, non-tiling variations that evoke a world in perpetual becoming.

The crucial difference, however, lies in origin. My continuous spaces are not the product of an autonomous algorithm but of human creativity. Hand-drawn compositions that, once fed into the AI, becomes the seed for infinite transformations.

From this perspective, *Continuous Space* is not merely a technical experiment but a new poetics of space and time.

The models of the work (or the core idea) manifest as a series of evolving videos, generated through Midjourney Kling 1.6's Image-to-Video process (a video generation model integrated within the Midjourney workflow). Two hand-drawn keyframes, combined with a targeted prompt, expand into seamless, evolving sequences where the visual field refuses to remain static.

Yet I deliberately constrained this boundless evolution, anchoring it to the trace of my own manual gesture—a technique fully illustrated in Chapter 10.

From these sequences, a theoretically infinite series of images can be generated, both through digital painting and once again through artificial intelligence.

Specifically, keyframes are extracted from the video flow and reworked—via virtual brushes or Image-to-Image models like Stable Diffusion—to introduce focused texture, detail, and stylistic variation, yielding printable virtual artworks, like the one in Figure 7-19, that can be precisely adapted to the scale and proportions of any exhibition space.

Figure 7-19. Gianpiero Moioli, Alien Birds, 2025*, Digitally modified acrylic painting on paper and cardboard with pen drawing, cm 50 (h) × 200. Still from the video of a continuous space. The hand-drawn composition, reworked through AI, unfolds into an endless flow of colors and forms, exemplifying the concept of continuous spaces*

Alternatively, these sequences can evolve into dynamic videos, as in *Alien Birds – Continuous Space* (2025), available at `https://vimeo.com/1144276173`, where crystalline avian forms dissolve and reform in cosmic migration, demonstrating the iterative fusion of hand-drawn origins and algorithmic metamorphosis. This is a preliminary manifestation of the project's unrealized potential, awaiting physical instantiation in future iterations.

The concept resonates with a rich lineage of artistic exploration, echoing the kinetic energy of Umberto Boccioni's *Unique Forms of Continuity in Space* (1913), where the sculpted figure seems to surge forward, its form sculpted not just by matter but by the invisible currents of motion (Figure 7-20).

Figure 7-20. Umberto Boccioni, Unique Forms of Continuity in Space, 1913. *Bronze, Museum of Modern Art, New York. Public Domain via Wikimedia Commons.*
Photo by Wmpearl, own work, Public Domain, `https://commons.wikimedia.org/w/index.php?curid=6909304`

This futurist masterpiece captures movement as a tangible force, molding bronze into a fluid embodiment of speed and dynamism.

In a similar spirit, my work *Gravitational Field*, as in Figure 7-17, or *Alien Birds*, as in Figure 7-19, reinterprets motion as a field of tensions rather than a single trajectory.

Here, geometry and color are pulled into orbits of attraction and repulsion, generating visual currents that recall both physical gravity and psychological disorientation.

Similarly, Lucio Fontana's Spatial Concepts (starting in the 1940s) pierced the canvas to reveal an infinite void, transforming a two-dimensional surface into a gateway to three-dimensional space.

These historical precedents made art a bridge between the tangible and the boundless.

In the digital age, these ideas find new life as fluid continuums of vision, evolving into a realm where the boundaries of medium and time dissolve.

This dissolution occurs as static images are transformed into navigable virtual environments, real-time video installations, and interactive flows, leveraging algorithmic computation to integrate painting, sculpture, and time-based media into a single hybrid work.

Imagine a digital canvas animated by AI, where forms shift and flow in real time, echoing Boccioni's dynamism while opening Fontana's voids into living space.

Here, painting becomes a dialogue between artist and algorithm, expanding into time as a fourth dimension.

The work no longer ends with its creation but evolves continuously, reshaping itself through the viewer's gaze and the pulse of the environment, becoming a living sculpture of movement and transformation (Figure 7-21).

Figure 7-21. Gianpiero Moioli, Alien Birds (2024).
Frames from the video Alien Birds in the Continuous Space *series. Starting from two drawings, AI generates a sequence of transformations where one image flows into another, creating a continuum of color, motion, and metamorphosis*

Continuous Space becomes both image and flow, both surface and time. It is a bridge between past artistic utopias and the emergent languages of algorithmic creativity.

From this perspective, the discussion naturally turns to the broader implications of working with AI.

7.2.4 Conceptual Challenges of AI Art

AI challenges traditional notions of authorship and originality, since machine-generated outputs inevitably raise questions of creative ownership.

Rather than treating AI as a substitute, artists can integrate it as part of their process, using, for instance, Stable Diffusion to generate textures or spatial atmospheres that, once reworked by hand, expand into environments.

In this way, authorship is not erased but redistributed across a dialogue between human and machine.

To explore these conceptual tensions, Figure 7-22 presents some sculpture from my series *Metaphysical Piazza* (Figure 7-22). Already introduced in the previous chapter, this project is revisited here to highlight how 3D modeling and AI generative systems reinterpret the atmospheres of sculpture and architecture.

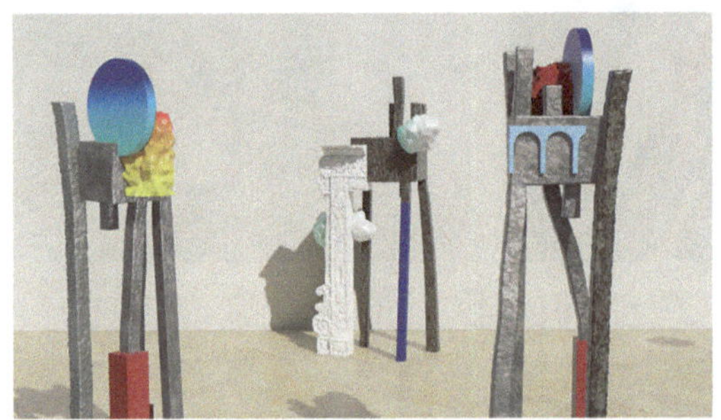
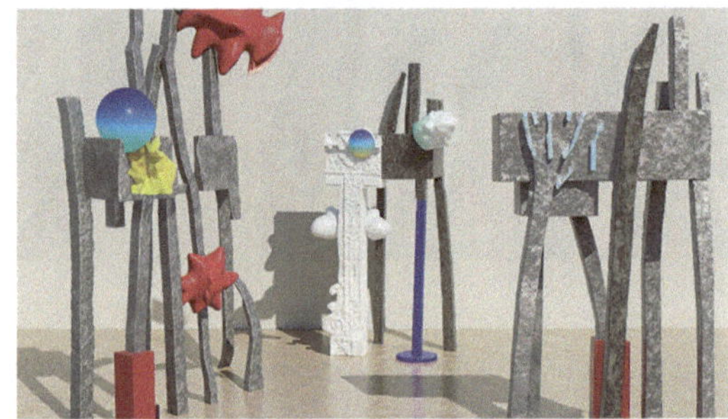

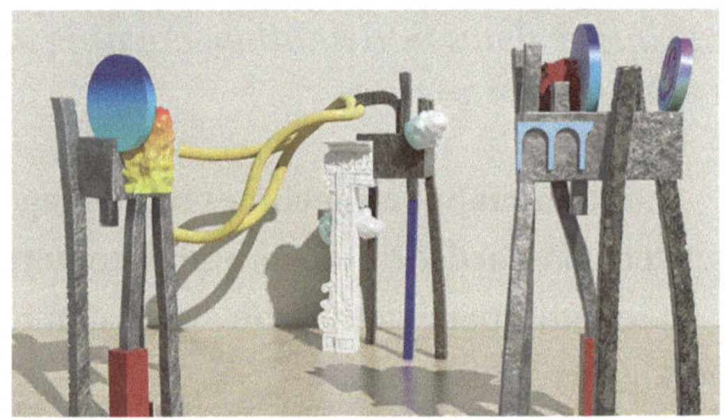

Figure 7-22. Metaphysical Piazza, sequence of 3D and AI-generated variations. *Hybrid compositions combining digital modeling and AI re-elaborations, reinterpreting metaphysical atmospheres through architectural fragments, chromatic contrasts, and elongated forms*

The resulting images are not replicas but hybrid visions of deserted piazzas with elongated shadows, unexpected chromatic shifts, and surreal distortions.

They embody the unresolved balance between homage and reinvention, between historical memory and algorithmic autonomy. This reinvention is made possible precisely by the manual seed—the initial drawing—which anchors the algorithm to deliberate human intention, preventing it from lapsing into pure randomness.

Placed in dialogue with this, Figure 7-23 shows James Turrell's environmental installation, where light alone, through calibrated modulations, transforms architecture into a threshold of perception. Here, space itself becomes magical and metaphysical, suspended between material presence and immaterial glow.

Figure 7-23. James Turrell, Sculpting the Immaterial.
View through the atrium of the Diözesanmuseum in Freising to the light space created by the artist. Di Flocci Nivis, Opera propria, CC BY 4.0, `https://commons.wikimedia.org/w/index.php?curid=167324718`

This juxtaposition underscores a crucial point. Just as Turrell achieves a metaphysical atmosphere through pure light, AI-driven re-imaginations of metaphysical piazzas expand painted or sculptural fragments into immersive environments.

In both cases, the work transcends representation to become an experiential space—whether luminous or algorithmic—that redefines our sense of presence within image and architecture. This algorithmic expansion, however, remains firmly rooted in the artist's initial manual seed: the project that serves as the deliberate anchor, guiding the AI away from randomness and toward a coherent, intentional metaphysical vision.

7.3 Generative Algorithms Overview

This section explores generative algorithms [11] as one of the true engines of AI-driven art, where creation becomes less a fixed object and more a living process.

These algorithms, guided by rules or trained on vast datasets, do not stop at producing a single outcome; instead, they give rise to entire constellations of variations—each formally coherent yet never identical.

The artwork no longer belongs to the logic of permanence but to that of becoming. It unfolds as a sequence of shifting possibilities, each version echoing the others while opening unexpected directions.

In this sense, generative algorithms transform art into a dynamic field, where repetition is never mere duplication but the seed of evolution, rhythm, and discovery.

7.3.1 Principles of Generative Art

The term *generative algorithms* encompasses two fundamentally distinct approaches that produce forms evolving with varying degrees of predictability.

[11] Generative algorithms are computational procedures designed to create outputs—such as images, sounds, or forms—based on rules, mathematical functions, or trained data. In the arts, they are used to generate variations, explore infinite possibilities, and simulate processes of growth and transformation.

For a general introduction, see `https://en.wikipedia.org/wiki/Generative_art`.

1. **Machine Learning (ML) Generation:** Systems like **Stable Diffusion**, **Midjourney**, or models hosted on platforms like **RunwayML** operate by sampling from learned probability distributions.

   They do not follow explicit rules but encode implicit statistical patterns from massive training datasets (neural networks like transformers and U-Nets). The output is based on learned statistical associations, and the same prompt typically produces different outcomes due to stochastic sampling, unless the *seed* is fixed. This results in forms that evolve **unpredictably**.

2. **Rule-Based/Procedural Generation:** Systems utilizing **L-systems**, **cellular automata**, **particle systems**, or procedural noise functions (Perlin, Voronoi) operate deterministically from explicit, human-defined rules.

   Given the same initial parameters or seed, they produce identical outputs. Unpredictability here arises only from intentionally introduced randomness or the complexity of rule interactions (emergent behavior).

3. **Hybrid Systems (The Convergence):** It is important to note the rise of **Hybrid Systems**, which combine both generative approaches.

   These systems, for instance, utilize procedural logic (like depth maps or edge detection) to constrain the statistical outputs of an ML model (as seen with **ControlNet in Stable Diffusion**). These hybrids attempt to merge the **controllability** of rule-based systems with the **generative surprise** of ML systems.

The result is often a family of related objects—multiple versions of the same theme—each with subtly different variations, while still rooted in the same algorithmic premises.

This spectrum of possibilities complements the artist's vision, enabling the exploration of an entire space of forms rather than a single, static result.

These characteristics sharply distinguish generative art from the traditional procedural approaches discussed in Chapter 3.

Whereas classical procedurality generally follows deterministic rules fixed by the artist—yielding highly controllable and repeatable outcomes—machine learning algorithms introduce stochastic variability that is inherent to their probabilistic core.

Although procedural systems can also incorporate randomness (e.g., seeded noise), ML's variability is bounded only by the model's training distribution and therefore not truly "autonomous." Yet it enables complex, emergent visual proposals that significantly expand the expressive potential of the work.

Take Yayoi Kusama's Pumpkin, one of her celebrated works realized in bronze and covered with her characteristic dotted patterns (Figure 7-24). Its repetitive, infinite motifs prefigure the multiplicity of generative outputs, where a single seed blooms into endless, yet thematically coherent, variations.

Figure 7-24. Yayoi Kusama, Pumpkin. Bronze sculpture.
The dotted pumpkin, one of Kusama's most iconic motifs, exemplifies the idea of infinite variation and serial form, placing organic shape and obsessive pattern into dialogue, a theme resonant with generative processes in contemporary AI art. By Zlatko, own work, CC0, `https://commons.wikimedia.org/w/index.php?curid=154016797`

It is an iconic piece that bridges sculpture, installation, and environment, transforming a natural form into the obsessive imagination of the artist.

In dialogue with the discourse on infinite variation and the creation of families of forms, Kusama embodies the human and obsessive dimension of repetitive generation, while AI represents its algorithmic counterpart.

Reducing her practice to mere pattern production would flatten its profound intentionality. Kusama's dots are never neutral. Born from hallucinations of proliferation and obliteration, they function simultaneously as psychic exorcism, self-dissolution into the infinite, and critical commentary on consumer society and mass reproduction.

In the *Infinity Mirror Rooms*, repetition becomes a device for altering perception and engulfing the viewer in boundless space.

By contrast, AI generates similar multiplicities through learned statistical associations, without lived experience or conceptual intent.

Yet the parallel remains illuminating: both practices construct infinite yet structured worlds through repetition—one driven by the psyche and cultural critique, the other by latent-space probabilities—revealing two distinct vectors of the same contemporary obsession with boundless variation.

A practical example of these principles can be observed in my paintings *Gravitational Field* (see Figure 7-17).

This work emerged from an image and a prompt designed to simulate the physical forces of a gravitational field acting upon virtual particles.

It is essential to clarify that this "gravitational field" is a conceptual and aesthetic descriptor used in the prompt to guide AI generation toward specific visual qualities: attraction and repulsion, orbital paths, radiating force lines, and dynamic tension between forms.[12]

Such results can be expanded into interactive multimedia experiences, artistic installations, digital scenographies, live performances, and immersive VR environments where the viewer navigates inside the flux itself.

For future hybrid developments that integrate true physics-based force fields with AI-generated aesthetics, see Appendix H.

[12] A technical clarification: no actual physics simulation was performed to generate *Gravitational Field*; the "field" exists purely as a visual metaphor and aesthetic evocation within the AI-generated imagery, not as a computational simulation of force dynamics. This distinction is vital for maintaining technical rigor, as the output relies on the model's learned visual association of the term *gravitational field*, not scientific processing.

A generative image, for instance, may become the basis for a projection mapping sequence; particle simulations can be synchronized with sound in a live performance; or a dynamic field like *Gravitational Field* can be transformed into a VR installation.

As illustrated in Figure 7-25, the interface of TouchDesigner allows visual nodes to be connected into a network that transforms inputs—such as images, videos, or data—into trajectories, geometries, and dynamic flows.

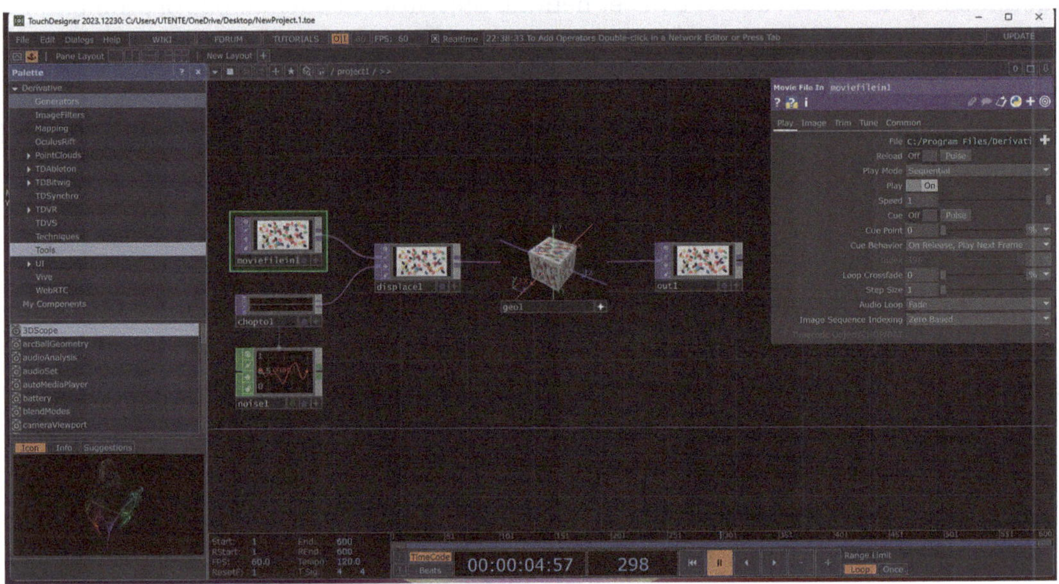

Figure 7-25. TouchDesigner interface.
Example of a visual programming environment where images and data are processed through interconnected nodes. In this case, a video input is displaced and mapped onto a 3D cube, illustrating how generative rules can be defined and modified in real time, producing evolving visual patterns

For a detailed technical introduction, including the functional distinction between its core data families (TOPS, CHOPs, SOPs, and DATs) and implementation guidance, see Appendix I.

Through this process, generative outputs do not remain static but become performative environments. Images turn into projections, movements into spatial choreographies, and data into immersive audiovisual landscapes.

Each execution of the generative script produces unique variations of this visual gravitational field.

The artist, partly assuming the role of observer, can allow the computational process to execute continuously based on the established algorithmic or statistical premises, or intervene to adjust parameters and achieve different effects. This **observational role** involves two distinct workflows: **real-time intervention** (adjusting parameters—such as *Guidance Scale* or *Noise Seed*—during generation for immediate effect,[13] particularly within live environments like TouchDesigner) or **post-hoc curation** (reviewing and selecting from a batch of statistically sampled outputs to guide subsequent iterations).

Gravitational Field thus demonstrates how, by embracing the principles of generative art, the artist creates forms in continuous evolution, drawing on phenomena of controlled chaos.

The element of unpredictability inherent in the generative system becomes part of the final aesthetic, enriching it with complexity and depth.

This approach fully embodies the spirit of generative art. It arises from the interplay of predefined rules and algorithmic spontaneity.

From this tension emerges a repertoire of forms that extends the artist's imagination in ways impossible to achieve through manual techniques or deterministic procedural generation alone.

7.3.2 Integrating Generative Outputs into Artworks

Artists can integrate generative outputs into their creative workflow by combining them seamlessly with manual or digital processes.

For example, a generative algorithm in Stable Diffusion can produce a dynamic texture for a 3D model designed in Blender.

This AI-generated texture (Phase 1) is then integrated into the 3D workflow through specific technical steps such as UV unwrapping the Blender model, applying the texture as a PBR material, and ensuring the final geometry is correctly remeshed and decimated (Phase 2). The model may then be rendered as a virtual sculpture or materialized through 3D printing (Phase 3), which requires final conversion to a watertight mesh and export to a manufacturing file format (e.g., STL or OBJ).

[13] In environments like TouchDesigner, this is achieved by connecting generative nodes (e.g., Stable Diffusion integration via custom operators) to live controls, enabling instantaneous changes to guidance scale, seed values, and ControlNet conditioning strength while previewing the evolving output.

In this way, the visual information created by AI becomes material again: a process of transference between the digital and the analog, the immaterial and the tactile.

A concrete example of this integration is Sougwen Chung's *Drawing Operations Unit (D.O.U.G.).*[14]

In this long-term series, the artist collaborates with robotic arms programmed to draw alongside her.

Sometimes the robots replicate her gestures in real time; in others, they rely on neural networks trained on her previous works.

The resulting drawings are neither purely algorithmic nor entirely manual, but hybrids born of a dynamic negotiation between human intention and machine interpretation.

Here, AI outputs—gestural traces, patterns, visual textures—are directly inscribed on physical supports, transforming immaterial computation into tangible mark-making.

The final works fuse analog and digital dimensions. The robotic line carries the memory of the artist's hand while extending it into unforeseen variations.

Drawing Operations exemplifies how a generative process, though immaterial in origin, can be integrated into concrete works through careful artistic mediation.

In doing so, it reveals AI not as a replacement for the human gesture, but as a collaborator that amplifies it—a bridge between code and matter, between calculation and creation.

7.4 AI and Unpredictability

This section explores how the unpredictability of artificial intelligence can become a source of creative innovation.

Far from being a limitation, the unexpected behavior of AI systems often acts as a catalyst for invention.

In this sense, AI introduces a form of *guided chance,* opening aesthetic opportunities of serendipity that would not otherwise emerge.

[14] See `https://sougwen.com/`.

7.4.1 Harnessing Unpredictability

Random variations generated by platforms such as DALL·E or Midjourney often lead artists toward paths they might never have imagined.

AI becomes a mythopoetic agent, capable of evoking archetypal images and symbols that the artist can interpret as new visual mythologies.

Its spontaneous combinations tap into a latent reservoir of forms and meanings, generating narratives that are unplanned yet strangely resonant.

To harness unpredictability is precisely this: to recognize in AI's accidents a hidden potential, and to learn how to ride it steering its direction while letting its force expand one's expressive vocabulary.

7.4.2 Curating Unpredictable Results

Once the images are generated, the artist must transform abundance into coherence.

Dozens of variations may appear, especially when working with systems like Stable Diffusion, but only a few carry the right energy or compositional strength.

Through a process of selection, refinement, and recombination—adjusting tones, merging fragments, removing artifacts—the artist turns chance into form.

This curation ensures that the algorithm's unpredictability enriches rather than overwhelms the work, filtering randomness through a critical eye.

A concrete example is my *Portraits* series, previously introduced in Chapter 5 and expanded here (see Figure 7-26).

***Figure 7-26.** **AGianpiero Moioli, AI-Based Self-Portraits, 2024**.*
Digital prints, variable dimensions.
A series of experimental self-portraits generated with manual painting and AI, where facial physiognomies are hybridized with architectural and landscape elements. The resulting images explore the fluidity of identity through surreal and unplaceable forms

In these AI-based self-portraits, I explored identity through deformation and hybridity: faces fused with architecture, bodies dissolving into landscape, fluid physiognomies without a fixed place.

Not all images entered the final sequence.

Unpredictability becomes a controlled ingredient of artistic practice—not a threat to authorship but a tool for reimagining it.

7.4.3 The Genealogy of Chance in Art

This method echoes a long tradition in art history, where accident and unpredictability have often served as creative tools.

From Leonardo's advice to find figures within stains or clouds to Arcimboldo's composite portraits, artists have long drawn inspiration from the accidental.

In the 19th century, Victor Hugo developed visions from ink blots and spontaneous, while William Blake channeled visionary spontaneity through his direct, expressive marks in illuminated printing.

With Dada, Hans Arp composed collages "according to the laws of chance," letting cut-out shapes fall randomly onto paper.

Later, Max Ernst explored frottage and grattage—rubbing or scraping to reveal textures beneath—deliberately introducing the unexpected into creation.

In the 20th century, Jackson Pollock radicalized this principle through dripping, letting gravity dictate the movement of paint, while John Cage extended it into music through the *I-Ching*.

In each case, composition was shaped not only by control but by accident elevated to a principle of form: traces that the artist then interpreted and transformed into coherent vision.

Seen in this continuum, AI's unpredictability is not a rupture but a new chapter in the long genealogy of chance as a generative force in art.

The difference lies only in the medium: today, unpredictability is algorithmic, born from neural networks, yet it still requires the artist's eye to transform randomness into meaning.

7.5 Practical Applications: Creating AI-Augmented Artworks

In this final section, I provide examples of practical workflows through which artists can integrate procedural logic and AI into their creative processes.

These examples are inspired by contemporary practices, including my own work.

My artworks, augmented by AI, function as a bridge between the traditional and the virtual. The aim is to demonstrate in practice how collaboration with the machine can enrich artistic production.

7.5.1 AI-Generated Visuals

As we have seen, one of the most widespread and immediate developments of artificial intelligence in art is the generation of digital images from textual or visual prompts.

These outputs are not simply finished illustrations but intermediate materials: raw matter that the artist can select, refine, and expand.

A single prompt can give rise to a sequence of variations: landscapes, figures, architectural structures, or abstract patterns.

These do not appear as definitive solutions but as open possibilities.

This happens because a prompt is not a command but a textual instruction interpreted by an AI model trained on vast datasets of images and descriptions.

The model translates the text into visual forms, producing multiple outcomes that remain coherent yet never identical.

The artist can then intervene by:

- **Training custom models** on their own archive, imprinting a personal style into the outputs
- **Providing reference images**, which function as *sources of inspiration* to guide the algorithm toward specific atmospheres, textures, or compositional logics

In this way, the dialogue between **text, model, and image** expands the creative process into a multidimensional field where **chance and intention intertwine**.

7.5.1.1 Functions of AI Outputs

From this dialogue emerge results that serve a dual purpose.

On the one hand, they are **experimental**, enabling the artist to explore visual universes that go beyond the limits of their imagination or manual techniques.

On the other, they are **operative**, forming the first step toward more complex digital works—virtual paintings, immersive scenographies, VR installations—where AI images become textures, environments, or compositional elements within a 3D workflow.

In this sense, AI acts as a generative engine of possibilities, while the artist's role is to transform these raw visions into works with formal and conceptual coherence.

7.5.1.2 Developments with Midjourney

Among the many available platforms, Midjourney exemplifies this evolution.[15]

Initially conceived as a tool for generating highly detailed still images from prompts, it has progressively evolved into a space for expanded creativity.

Its generative logic now extends beyond images to narrative and storytelling, enabling sequences that resemble storyboards or visual scripts (Figure 7-27).

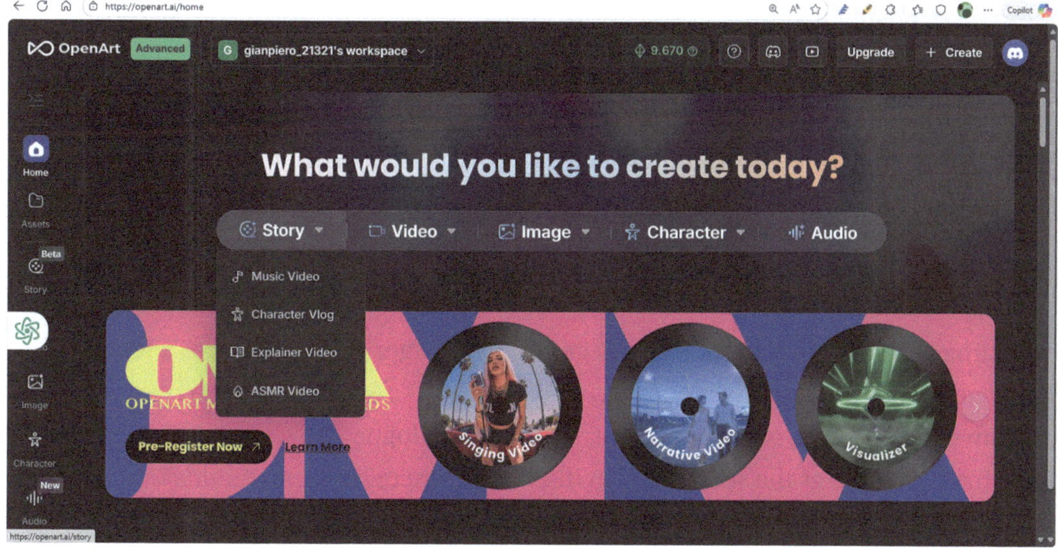

***Figure 7-27.** Screenshot of the Midjourney OpenArt interface (2025). The platform exemplifies the new creative ecosystems of AI, where storytelling, images, videos and sound converge into algorithmically mediated environments*

In practice, this multidimensional logic unfolds through five main domains:

- **Stories**: From *music videos* to *character vlogs* and *explainer formats,* narrative sequences emerge as visual scripts enriched by AI's generative logic

[15] Midjourney is a generative artificial intelligence platform. It is widely used by artists, designers, and researchers to explore visual languages and imaginative scenarios. Available at: `https://openart.ai/home`

- **Videos**: Including *lip-sync animations, text-to-video,* or *image-to-video,* expanding still imagery into cinematic time-based forms
- **Images**: Not only *creation* but also *editing* and *conversational refinement,* enabling continuous visual evolution from a single source
- **Characters**: Design of avatars or visual figures, both as *standalone portraits* and as elements inhabiting broader environments or narratives
- **Audio**: Generation of voices, soundscapes, and experimental compositions that connect the visual field with immersive atmospheres

Through such tools, AI no longer merely generates isolated images but opens the way to a broader creativity that ranges from painting to storytelling, from sculpture to immersive scenography, positioning itself as a partner in a continuously expanding artistic practice.

7.5.1.3 Animating AI Outputs for Immersive Art

Animating an immersive space from AI-generated images or videos is less a technical challenge than an imaginative journey.

With Midjourney, a static image born from the dialogue between text, image, and algorithm can serve as the seed of a moving vision, where stillness unfolds into flow.

The process begins with the generation of a single image.

From there, the interface allows words, images, or a constellation of both to evolve into sequences of motion.

Each variation becomes a possible path. Some may be discarded, others refined, while the most compelling can be further shaped and recomposed in Blender.

An abstract pattern might slowly mutate like a living organism, or a group of images may evolve into a continuous metamorphosis, as in *Alien Birds* (2024) and the other *Continuous Spaces* explored in Chapter 10.

As Figure 7-28 shows, Midjourney's interface is deceptively simple, yet it opens onto infinite scenographies once its outputs are animated, where the static becomes dynamic and vision expands into immersive experience.

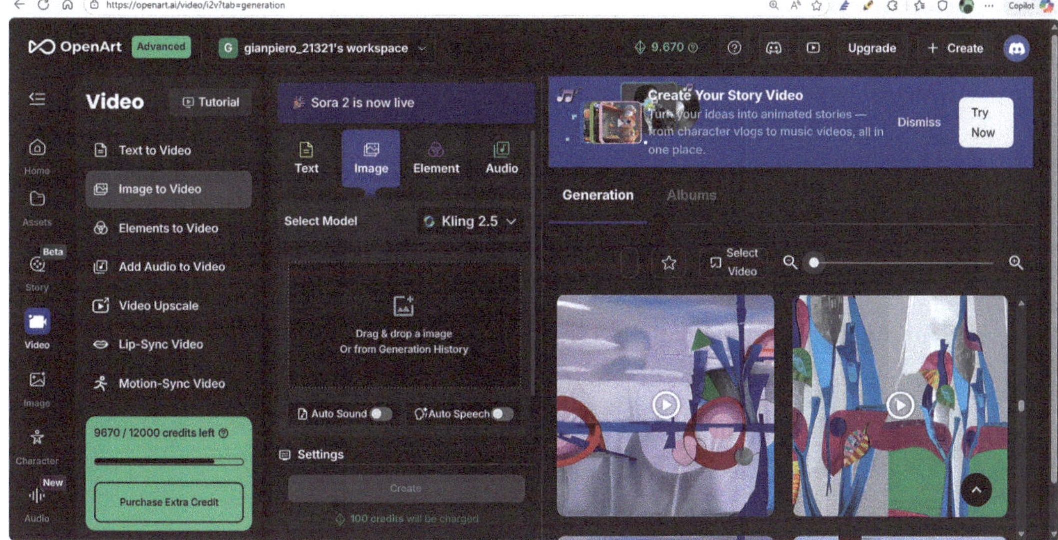

Figure 7-28. ***Midjourney's video interface.***
Through a simple and intuitive layout, text, images, and prompts can be transformed into animated sequences, where static forms evolve into dynamic scenographies and immersive environments

In the simplest case, once the AI-generated animation has been created, we can import it into Blender and apply it as a moving texture on the surface of a 3D model, whether a simple cube, a sphere, or a more organic form.

From here, the scene can be exported into a VR environment, through platforms like Unity, or Unreal Engine, and experienced with headsets such as modern VR headsets.

At this point, however, it is important to clarify how AI can control or influence textures inside VR, since there are different levels of integration:

1. **Pre-rendered AI animations (immersive but static)**

   In the simplest approach, the animation generated with AI is imported into Blender or Unity as a video texture.

   In VR, this becomes part of the environment, creating the effect of a living painting or a moving surface. The texture is AI-driven, but it does not change once inside VR.

2. **Procedural textures influenced by AI (dynamic)**

   A second approach connects AI to procedural systems, for instance, TouchDesigner or Unity shaders.

Here the AI continuously generates or modifies textures, which are projected in real time onto 3D objects. This produces environments that never repeat themselves, reacting to variables such as time, sound, or user movement. The result is a hybrid between AI-driven image generation and the logics of procedural animation.

3. **Interactive AI-driven textures (adaptive and responsive)**

   The most advanced level directly links the VR system to an AI model, via APIs for models such as Stable Diffusion or Runway. In this case, textures and materials are regenerated while the user interacts: looking at an object, touching a controller, or performing an action could trigger the AI to produce new variations.
   The environment thus becomes personalized and evolving, an endless dialogue between user and algorithm.

4. **Fully adaptive closed-loop systems (continuous feedback)**

   In this emerging level, the VR system uses real-time user data (e.g., gaze tracking or biometrics) to feed back into the AI model, creating a loop where textures evolve based on ongoing interaction. For example, environmental changes or haptic responses trigger new AI generations, ensuring a truly symbiotic experience.

In all four cases, the work is no longer a static object but an immersive artwork that evolves over time, reflecting the logic of continuous creative transformation.

While levels 1 and 2 are routine in contemporary installations, levels 3 and 4 remain at the cutting edge, with generation latencies of 0.5–3 seconds depending on model and hardware—a threshold that continues to shrink rapidly.

These levels of implementation, ranging from passive pre-rendered content (Level 1) to fully adaptive closed-loop systems (Level 4), form the core of the hybrid AI-VR roadmap outlined in Appendix L.

Compared with the hybrid painting processes discussed in Chapter 5, here the focus shifts toward a fully digital and dynamic experience, where **AI not only generates images but becomes an active engine of spatial and temporal change.**

7.5.2 AI-Augmented Sculptures

In digital painting, the outputs of artificial intelligence appear as images to be selected and transformed, while in sculpture AI takes on an even more incisive role. It becomes a generator of surfaces, textures, and formal details that are grafted onto three-dimensional matter.

It is not simply a matter of "translating" the image into volume but of experimenting with a hybridization in which the generative logic of AI merges with the practice of modeling and fabrication.

It should be noted, however, that while AI applications for 2D are now well established and widely disseminated, those for 3D are still in an emerging phase: less immediate, often experimental, yet extremely promising for the future development of digital sculpture.[16]

The contribution of AI for 3D modeling can manifest on two different levels.

On the **virtual** level, algorithms generate patterns, textures, or digital materials that overlay 3D models, transforming neutral geometries into complex and unexpected forms.

Here, the virtual surface becomes an active layer of invention rather than a simple covering.

On the **physical** level, these AI-generated surfaces can be transferred into fabrication processes.

A texture created by AI, for example, can be exported as a displacement map and applied to a 3D mesh, which is then 3D printed to reproduce its reliefs in tangible form.

Similarly, AI-generated patterns can guide CNC milling paths, engraving details directly into stone or wood. Even in traditional sculpture, the AI output may serve as a digital stencil or reference, informing manual carving or casting.

My recent sculptures, such as *Cosmic Labyrinth* or *Burning Archaic City*, presented earlier in this chapter, demonstrate how this hybridization can give rise to creations that no longer belong to a single aesthetic regime. The ancient and the futuristic, the real and the virtual, the manual gesture and algorithmic calculation intertwine within a single plastic body.

[16] Platforms like Kaedim3D, Tripo AI, Point-E (OpenAI), and GET3D (NVIDIA) generate meshes or objects from images and text, while Luma AI and Runway Gen-2 experiment with video-to-3D. These outputs usually need refinement in software like Blender or ZBrush, but they signal the rise of a new ecosystem for AI-augmented sculpture.

AI-augmented sculpture thus becomes a territory of experimentation, where art explores not only new forms but also new modes of existence, suspended between the physical and the digital dimension.

7.5.2.1 Virtual Sculpture with AI Textures

In the digital sphere, sculpture can take on a fully immaterial form, existing as an object of vision and interaction without ever being materialized.

This process often begins with the creation of a base model in Blender: a form that may echo the language of classical statuary, reference the clarity of architectural geometry, or embrace the fluidity of organic structures.

The model serves as a neutral canvas, awaiting transformation.

The next step introduces the contribution of artificial intelligence. Using tools such as Stable Diffusion or Midjourney, the artist generates textures guided by textual prompts, for example, "metallic organic arabesque pattern."

From countless algorithmic outputs, one or more high-resolution images are selected, carrying with them an element of unpredictability that enriches the creative process.

Back in Blender, these AI-generated textures become part of the sculpture's material presence.

By applying them as materials and experimenting with bump or displacement mapping, providing the surface with depth and relief, acquiring tactile qualities even in its virtual state.

A flat image is thus transformed into a complex skin, where the precision of geometry intertwines with the fluidity of generative patterns.

Finally, the virtual sculpture is placed in a digital exhibition space, whether on immersive platforms like Spatial, within high-fidelity XR hubs, or inside dedicated VR galleries.

Here, the work exists as a fully immaterial artifact: accessible from anywhere in the world, navigable as part of immersive environments, and open to new forms of interaction.

Moreover, through procedural algorithms or AI-driven animation, a virtual sculpture can remain perpetually alive and in motion: its surface animated by evolving textures or generative patterns that transform over time.

7.5.2.2 Physical Sculpture with AI Details: The Thrilling Alchemy of Code and Matter

If in the virtual realm AI can clothe neutral geometries with unexpected surfaces, in the physical dimension its contribution becomes even more striking. The algorithm's invention is translated into matter, leaving a tangible mark on the sculptural object.

The process usually begins with the creation of a digital base model, conceived in Blender, ZBrush, or captured through 3D scanning. This foundational geometry provides the essential ground upon which **AI interventions can unfold, transforming the possible into the realized.**

Through platforms such as Stable Diffusion, Midjourney, or **emerging image-to-3D tools** (see Appendix M), the artist generates a repertoire of surface motifs, patterns, or details: ornamental arabesques, eroded stone veins, metallic weaves, or organic skins.

These visual outputs are then selected and adapted, functioning not as decorative overlays but as creative elements that reshape the language of the sculpture.

Once reintegrated into the model, the AI-generated details are applied via displacement maps, mesh editing, or hybrid workflows.

The enhanced geometry can then be materialized through 3D printing, CNC milling, or traditional casting processes.

This materialization requires a critical technical step: ensuring the final mesh is "watertight" and optimized (decimated) for the chosen fabrication method before being exported as an STL or OBJ file.

At this stage, the immaterial invention of the algorithm crosses the threshold into the physical world, inscribing itself into stone, resin, metal, or ceramic.

When exhibited, the result is no longer just a digital simulation but a hybrid object, where AI's generative unpredictability coexists with the tactility of material processes.

Viewers can touch, move around, and inhabit a form that is both algorithmic and human, both digital and artisanal.

In this sense, **AI-augmented physical sculpture** becomes a laboratory of encounter between tradition and innovation, virtual imagination and tangible matter.

It suggests that the future of sculpture may not lie in choosing between physical and digital but in weaving them together, so that each dimension enriches the other.

7.5.3 Between Virtual and Physical: The Expanded Field of AI Sculpture

The virtual and physical dimensions of AI-augmented sculpture are not two separate territories but points along a single continuum of creative transformation.

In the virtual space, algorithms operate as instruments of vision, expanding the boundaries of imagination and allowing artists to sculpt with light, texture, and code.

In the physical realm, these same algorithms imprint their presence onto tangible materials, embedding digital invention into form and substance.

Across both domains, what emerges is a bold, new sculptural paradigm, where creation unfolds through cycles of translation: from data to image, from image to model, from model to object and vice versa.

This continuous exchange dissolves the traditional divisions between concept and realization, immaterial and material, digital and handmade.

In this expanded field, the artist becomes both designer and mediator, guiding the dialogue between algorithmic processes and human intent.

The result is a hybrid practice that extends the lineage of sculpture into the age of artificial intelligence: an art that no longer represents form but generates it, in collaboration with code.

This transition from algorithm to matter anticipates the next section, where these principles are reflected on a monumental scale.

Antony Gormley's Quantum Cloud (1999), rising beside the Thames as a vast lattice of steel and void, embodies the same logic of emergence: **a structure born from computational simulation, where the human figure materializes within a field of algorithmic forces.**

7.5.4 From Algorithm to Sculpture: Gormley's Quantum Cloud

Antony Gormley's *Quantum Cloud* (1999) was commissioned for the Thames waterfront beside the Millennium Dome in London.

At 30 meters high, it remains his tallest sculpture to date, surpassing even the Angel of the North.

The work is composed of thousands of tetrahedral units made from 1.5-meter long steel sections, assembled into a vast lattice that both contains and obscures the outline of a human body (Figure 7-29).[17]

Figure 7-29. Antony Gormley, Quantum Cloud, 1999.
Steel and air, 30 m height. Commissioned for the Millennium Dome, London. The sculpture consists of thousands of steel tetrahedrons forming a cloud-like lattice from which the human figure subtly emerges.
Photograph by Andy Roberts from East London, England, Flickr, CC BY 2.0, https://commons.wikimedia.org/w/index.php?curid=448926

What distinguishes *Quantum Cloud* is its computational genesis. The steel members were arranged according to a computer simulation based on a random walk algorithm.

[17] See: https://en.wikipedia.org/wiki/Quantum_Cloud

Starting from points on the surface of an enlarged digital model of Gormley's own body, the algorithm generated a chaotic yet coherent cloud, from which the faint silhouette of the figure emerges at the center.

Its monumental scale places the work in direct dialogue with the urban landscape of the *Millennium Dome*, while its method reflects a synthesis of sculpture, architecture, and mathematics.

It is a work of computational art ante litteram, where artist's body, digital code, and material structure converge to create a metaphysical presence: a figure simultaneously dispersed and crystallized within an architectural cloud of steel.

Seen from today's perspective, Quantum Cloud anticipates the logic of AI-augmented sculpture: a process where algorithms generate structural complexity, and the artist acts as both initiator and interpreter of a system that evolves autonomously.

In this sense, Gormley's work can be viewed as a precursor to contemporary practices where computation becomes not merely a tool, but an active agent in shaping form, space, and meaning.

7.6 Critical Methodologies and Philosophical Constraints: The Open Work and the Code Canvas

The preceding sections established the practical power and innovative application of generative systems.

However, a rigorous analysis of AI-augmented artistic practice must address the critical methodological and ethical challenges that define this emerging field.

This final section outlines the essential standards for technical verifiability, ethical practice, honest assessment of limitations, and the philosophical question of authorship.

7.6.1 The Code as the Inseparable Canvas

For generative art, the philosophical shift is profound: unlike traditional media, the code is inseparable from the canvas.

This premise is the foundation for all methodological and ethical discussions that follow.

The concept is deeply linked to Umberto Eco's philosophy of the "**Opera Aperta**" (The Open Work).[18]

In this context, the generative code is the contemporary equivalent of Eco's "open score" (partitura aperta).

It is not the finished work, but the system of rules that allows infinite potential variations to emerge.

This means that the artwork is defined by its systematic possibility rather than a single fixed realization.

Despite the frequent metaphor of "co-creation," the AI is never a co-author: authorship, responsibility, and intentionality remain unequivocally human. This is a distinction that is not only technical and legal, but profoundly ethical.

The artist becomes the executive mediator, executing the code's score through parameters and prompts (as detailed in Appendix M).

The requirement for verifiability, the scrutiny of the algorithm's statistical limitations, and the shifting locus of intentionality are all direct consequences of this fundamental inversion.

7.6.2 Methodological Rigor: Sourcing and Versioning

For generative art to be treated as a serious subject of technical and academic discourse, the principle of verifiability is paramount.

Since the artwork is the system (the "Open Work"), transparency of the system is non-negotiable.

Project Toolchain Statement

The methodological rigor applied throughout this book relies on a hybrid toolchain of open-source and proprietary software, designed for maximum verifiability and interoperability.

---

[18] The concept of *Opera aperta* was introduced by Umberto Eco in his foundational 1962 essay, *Opera aperta: forma e indeterminazione nelle poetiche contemporanee* (Milan, 1962).

Translated as "The Open Work," by Anna Cancogni (Cambridge, MA: Harvard University Press, 1989).

The theory emphasizes the role of the reader/spectator as a co-author who actively participates in defining the work's meaning.

The workflows utilized in this study were executed on a robust computational environment featuring the NVIDIA GeForce RTX 4070 Ti GPU. The specific software configuration included: Blender 4.4 (LTS) for 3D mesh modeling, Stable Diffusion 1.5 as the primary model for texture synthesis, and Midjourney V6 as the latest high-quality service for supplemental image generation. All code and versioning requirements are managed via GitHub, as documented in Appendix E. Currently, as of early 2026, this toolchain has transitioned to more advanced standards—including NVIDIA RTX 5090 (32 GB VRAM), Blender 5.1, and Midjourney V7—to support the real-time inference and high-fidelity simulations detailed in the subsequent.

Essential Verifiability Requirements

The declaration of the tool chain necessitates the adherence to three fundamental standards of documentation:

- **Version Control:** All execution environments, algorithms, and libraries used must be meticulously cited.

  Merely stating a name is insufficient; the specific version number (e.g., Stable Diffusion 1.5, Blender 4.4) must be logged and cited, with logs managed through collaborative tools (as detailed in Appendix E).

- **Replicability of Workflow:** Technical claims about the hybrid process must be accompanied by the precise parameters used, including the seed value (for predictability) and metrics like Guidance Scale and Steps (as partially illustrated in Figure 7-25).

- **Tool Agnosticism:** While platforms like Midjourney or Runway are accessible, the documentation must focus on the underlying model architecture they employ, treating the platform interface as merely the execution wrapper.

7.6.3 Ethics and Inclusivity in Generative Practice

The artist working with AI bears an ethical responsibility to ensure both the process and the output are accessible and ethically sound.

- **Output Accessibility:** Generative artwork, being highly visual, often excludes the visually impaired.

Artists must integrate accessibility into the final product. This includes creating AI-generated alternative text (alt-text) that describes the emergent qualities of the image and providing non-visual data streams (e.g., sound or haptic feedback) synchronized with the visual output.

- **Inclusive Tool Design:** The proliferation of complex, code-heavy generative tools must be balanced by the design of intuitive, inclusive interfaces (like TouchDesigner's node-based environment, as explored in Appendix I) that lower the barrier to entry for artists without extensive programming backgrounds.
- **Dataset Ethics:** The reliance of large models on vast training datasets raises ethical concerns regarding copyright and consent.

  The generative artist must remain engaged in the ongoing debate about the provenance of the training data and advocate for transparent, ethically sourced models.

7.6.4 Fundamental Limitations of Current AI Models

An optimistic view of AI capabilities must be tempered by an honest assessment of what current latent diffusion models fundamentally *cannot* do, thereby defining the true boundary of the human artist's role.

- **Lack of Causal Reasoning:** AI operates through statistical correlation and pattern recognition, not causal reasoning.

  It cannot understand *why* a gravitational field works, only what a gravitational field *looks like.*

  This leads to visual artifacts, illogical spatial relationships, and an inability to correctly render complex interactions beyond its trained distribution.
- **The Artifact Problem:** Outputs frequently contain statistical artifacts (e.g., distorted hands, floating geometry, incoherent perspective), which require the human artist's curatorial eye and post-processing intervention (editing and *in-painting*) to correct.

The human role is often defined by fixing the machine's statistical errors.

- **Pattern Recognition vs. Intention:** The system is an advanced pattern-matching engine.

  The *intention* to create a narrative, a critique, or a specific conceptual framework always remains outside the algorithm's capability, residing exclusively with the human practitioner.

7.6.5 The Locus of Intentionality: Authorship and Control

The philosophical shift from singular creation to co-creation human-AI collaboration necessitates a formal reconsideration of where artistic intentionality—and therefore authorship—resides.

- **Prompt as Intentionality:** The prompt moves beyond mere description to become the artist's primary statement of intent, setting the conceptual and aesthetic boundaries for the machine's exploration.

  The prompt, rather than the final pixel, is the initial act of authorship.

- **Curation as Control:** Since the AI's output is stochastic, the artist's role shifts heavily toward curation. The selection, refinement, and subsequent re-seeding of a specific output from a batch of statistically sampled images constitutes the most critical act of control and final approval.

- **Copyright Implications:** The ambiguous nature of co-creation challenges established copyright law.

  Assigning authorship requires determining whether the final work meets the threshold of human creative originality beyond the simple execution of a command. This tension mandates that artists document their manual interventions (editing, *in-painting*, procedural synthesis) to assert their claim to the final output.

The critical and philosophical questions raised in section 7.6 remain open and urgent; they define the ethical horizon of the practices explored throughout this book and of the art yet to come.

7.7 Conclusion

Antony Gormley's Quantum Cloud remains the perfect epilogue to this trajectory. It's a sculpture born from a random-walk algorithm applied to the artist's own body scan—personal data transmuted into collective spatial presence, resonating equally with mathematics, sculpture, and architecture. The path traced in this chapter reveals how generative algorithms—from the first procedural experiments to today's AI-driven systems—have liberated art from mere representation. Artists now engage processes of emergence, unpredictability, and transformation.

Works are no longer static objects but living systems. Through external inputs (environmental sensors, real-time audience tracking), they respond to the world and invite the viewer into dynamic, ever-shifting fields of experience. This responsiveness is not intelligence, but the deliberate choreography of algorithmic behavior by the human creator.

Generative art thus reveals its double nature: rigorously rational, rooted in rule-based structures, yet profoundly poetic—capable of evoking metaphysical atmospheres and new ecologies of vision.

It is in the fertile tension between algorithmic determinacy and artistic intentionality that a genuinely new space of creativity opens. The next chapter will push this horizon further, asking not only how artificial intelligence generates forms, but how it begins to imagine worlds—and what this means for authorship, creativity, and the future of visual art.

7.8 Appendix H: From Aesthetic Evocation to Computational Simulation: Future Perspectives

The distinction between the aesthetic evocation offered by current generative AI and the computational rigor of physical simulation defines the next frontier of human-machine collaboration.

Until now, AI has functioned as a dazzling mirror of the imagination, translating the metaphor of a "gravitational field" into a purely statistical hallucination.

The future challenge is no longer what the algorithm can draw but how it can behave and what it can calculate within a physically coherent virtual world.

By integrating Force Fields and Geometry Nodes (Blender 5.0+, Houdini 20) with latent-space sampling, the artist moves from selecting images to orchestrating genuine dialogues between **statistical randomness** (AI) and **deterministic causality** (Physics).

The result: works that are simultaneously dreamed by AI and calculated by physics—hybrid entities that breathe, collapse, and reform under the viewer's gaze.

7.8.1 The Three-Phase Hybrid Workflow (2026–2027)

This workflow outlines the necessary steps to synthesize the aesthetic richness of latent-space models with the physical coherence of computational simulation, transforming visual metaphor into kinetic reality.

Phase	Focus/Role	Key Tools & Concepts	Output
Phase 1	**AI Sketch (Conceptual Seed)**	Midjourney V7/Flux.1/Lumina-T2X. Defining aesthetic targets (chromatic palette, mood, compositional tension) through iterative prompting.	High-resolution "target feeling" image (pure aesthetic output; no physics).
Phase 2	**Physics Engine (Behavioral Core)**	**Blender 5.0+** (Geometry Nodes + Simulation Nodes) or **Houdini 20**. Driving particle systems, soft bodies, or cloth with real forces (Gravity, Vortex, Turbulence, Wind).	Physically accurate **4K animation** (weight, momentum, collision, destruction).
Phase 3	**Stylistic Synthesis (Recursive Feedback)**	**Image-to-Video/Frame-to-Frame** models (e.g., Kling 2.5 Pro, Runway Gen-4, or local Stable Video Diffusion). Using **ControlNet** (depth/normal maps) to guide the AI.	Final hybrid video: The AI's aesthetic applied on top of the physically correct motion.

7.8.2 Expansions: Toward Living, Reactive, Phygital Works

The hybrid workflow serves as a foundation for advanced artistic explorations, aiming to integrate the generated forms into the viewer's real-time experience.

Expansion	Goal & Technical Implementation	Future Impact
Real-Time Generative Environments (2026)	Porting the entire pipeline into **Unreal Engine 6** or **Unity** (using Barracuda + Sentis). The viewer's position (tracked via webcam/LiDAR) becomes a dynamic force node in the live simulation.	The artwork literally **breathes with the audience**, establishing a true recursive influence beyond the prompt window.
Audio-Reactive & Haptic Topographies	Live sound (music or voice) drives turbulence intensity and vortex strength in the simulation. Combine the visual output with **haptic floors** (butt-shaker plates) or **mid-air ultrasound haptics** (Ultraleap).	The viewer doesn't just see the invisible forces; they **feel them**, creating a visceral, multisensory experience.
Phygital Materialization 2.0	Moving beyond static prints. Using **robotic sand 3D printing** or **CNC foam cutting** to create physical "time-slices" of the simulation at different moments. The original animation is then projected back onto them via structured-light projection mapping.	The sculpture physically contains its own **past and future**, manifesting motion and time in a tangible object.

7.8.3 Closed-Loop Bio-Feedback (2026–2027): The Ultimate Human-Machine Symbiosis

This concept represents the pinnacle of immersive co-creation. The simulation is seeded with real-time biometric data (heart rate variability, skin conductance, electrodermal activity) from the viewer, captured via wearable (e.g., Empatica E4, developed in Boston/Milan) or facial tracking (MediaPipe in Unity).

The user's emotional state becomes a literal gravitational force inside the artwork. The more agitated the biometrics, the more the field distorts with amplified turbulence or repulsive particles.

The piece transforms into a mirror of inner chaos, materializing invisible human emotions as visible, calculated storms, **closing the loop between body, code, and perception in a deeply personal, therapeutic resonance.**

Early prototypes, like BARN's 2025 biofeedback installations, demonstrate its potential for collective mindfulness in public spaces.

7.8.4 Conclusion

In the end, the future of digital sculpture does not lie in replacing the artist's hand with the machine but in extending it, infinitely.

From the first hesitant pixel to the living, reactive, phygital artifact, every tool we have examined (from Blender's Geometry Nodes to Kling's latent-space video, from lost-PLA bronze to bio-reactive clay) serves a single purpose: to let **matter and code speak the same language.**

What began as a quest for precision and multiplicity has revealed itself as a new pact between intention and emergence, between control and surrender. The artwork is no longer an object fixed in time, but a process in perpetual becoming, open, iterative, and alive.

This is the true revolution. Not that machines create, but that they allow us to create more humanly than ever, by giving form to what we feel but cannot yet draw, calculate, or touch.

The hand remains. The algorithm has simply become its newest, boundless finger.

7.9 Appendix I: Technical Introduction to TouchDesigner (TD)

7.9.1 Overview (2025 Update)

TouchDesigner (Derivative, Toronto) remains the leading node-based **real-time visual programming environment** and the de facto standard for interactive installations, projection mapping, live visuals, and hybrid digital-physical artworks.

It functions as the **central nervous system** of contemporary hybrid practice, allowing AI outputs, physics calculations, and human intention to converge and execute in real time.

7.9.2 Core Data Families (2025)

TouchDesigner's framework is built upon five interconnected data families. Understanding these families is fundamental to building any complex generative network.

Family	Full Name	Data Type	Primary Artistic Use (2025)
TOP	Texture Operator	2D images, video, render buffers (GPU)	Real-time feedback loops, shader effects, multi-projector mapping, zero-latency sharing (NDI, Spout).
CHOP	Channel Operator	Time-series numeric data (data channels)	Audio reactivity, sensor fusion (LiDAR, biometric), DMX/OSC control, parameter smoothing.
SOP	Surface Operator	3D geometry (points, vertices, polys)	Procedural modeling, high-volume instancing (up to 10M instances), particle systems, signed-distance fields (SDFs).
COMP	Component	Containers & UI	Building reusable modules, designing user interfaces, managing VR/AR scenes, and structuring networked installations.
DAT	Data Operator	Tables, text, scripts	Python scripting (3.11), JSON/API handling, external ML model inference, network communication (OSC/MQTT/WebSocket).

7.9.3 Technical Dominance in Hybrid Workflows

TouchDesigner's speed and flexibility stem from its optimized GPU-native architecture and deep integration with modern computational standards.

- **Acceleration & Optimization:** Native GLSL TOP shaders, **CUDA-accelerated CHOPs**, and advanced rendering techniques like OptiX ray-tracing (available since version 2024.39900).
- **High-Volume Instancing:** Built-in Instancing allows the system to manage and render up to **10 million instances** of geometry at 60 fps (on high-end GPUs like the RTX 4090).
- **ML Integration: Python 3.11** and **TorchScript integration** allow artists to run small ML models (e.g., ControlNet depth or CLIP interrogators) directly inside TD for real-time creative steering.

- **Interoperability:** Direct **USD** import/export facilitates seamless round-trip workflows with Blender. **NDI 5** and **Spout/Syphon** ensure zero-latency video sharing across networks.
- **Sensor Bridge:** Native support for **OSC, MQTT, and WebSocket** makes it the perfect bridge for connecting biometric, environmental, and tracking sensors.

7.9.4 Role in the Continuous Spaces/Hybrid Workflow

Workflow Layer	Function in TD	Connection to Appendix H
Real-Time Generative Engine	Receives depth maps or normal passes from Blender simulations (Phase 2, Appendix H – B1) and drives millions of particles using CHOP-driven force fields.	Translates calculated physics into live, visual output.
AI ↔ Physics Bridge	Uses Python DATs to call local Stable Diffusion (via ComfyUI API) or remote Kling 2.5 frames, then **re-injects them as live textures** onto the real-time geometry.	Enables **Phase 3: Stylistic Synthesis** by merging statistical texture with procedural movement.
Audience Interaction Layer	Webcams, LiDAR, or biometric sensors are routed through MediaPipe and CHOPs to dynamically alter simulation parameters (e.g., viewer heartbeat modifies gravitational constants).	Drives the **Real-Time Generative Environments** and **Bio-Feedback** expansions.
Projection Mapping & Phygital Output	Maps the continuous, live animation onto complex 3D-printed time-slice sculptures with centimeter- level accuracy.	Essential for realizing **Phygital Materialization 2.0**.

7.9.5 Minimum Recommended Hardware (2025)

Component	Minimum for Development	Recommended for Complex/Live Projects
GPU	NVIDIA RTX 3060 12 GB	RTX 4080/4090 or A4000/A6000 (Workstation)
VRAM	10 GB	**24 GB+** (Critical for multiple high-res TOPS)
RAM	32 GB	64–128 GB (Crucial for Python/ML processes)
CPU	8-core (High Clock Speed)	16+ cores (Multi-threading for CHOPs/DATs)

7.9.6 Quick-Start Resources (2025)

- **Official Learning Hub:** `https://learn.derivative.ca`
- **Community Bible:** `https://derivative.ca/community-books` (excellent for conceptual understanding)
- **Video Tutorials:** Nvoid's "TouchDesigner for Artists" YouTube series (2024–2025 updates)
- **ML Integration Reference:** GitHub repository "TD-ML-Toolkit" (focus on LoRA and ControlNet integration inside TD, 2025)

7.10 Appendix L: AI-Driven Workflow for Virtual Reality (VR) and Extended Reality (XR)

This appendix outlines **a four-phase technical roadmap for integrating generative art into real-time interactive environments (VR/XR)**, ranging from high-efficiency static textures to computationally intensive, fully adaptive closed-loop systems.

This demonstrates the project's capacity to transition from theoretical model to embodied experience in immersive spaces.

7.10.1 The Four-Phase AI-VR Integration Model (2025 Roadmap)

The four phases represent increasing levels of **computational cost** and **user interactivity**. All levels are currently achievable using the listed software versions by late 2025.

Phase	Interactivity Level	Computational Cost	Key Technical Focus
1	Static (Passive Loop)	**Zero Real-Time Cost** (Pre-rendered)	Efficiency and Optimization
2	Dynamic (Non-Interactive)	Moderate (GPU-Bound Procedural)	Real-Time Noise and Feedback
3	Interactive (Responsive Trigger)	High (On-Demand AI Inference)	Low-Latency Network Streaming & Sensing
4	Fully Adaptive (Closed-Loop)	Very High (Continuous ML Inference)	Real-Time Depth Sensing and Material Swapping

7.10.2 Workflow Implementation Details

Phase	Technical Implementation (Inputs & Process)	Software & Hardware Environment	Outcome and State
Phase 1: Pre-rendered AI Animations (Static in VR)	**Input:** Generate 5–10 second seamless loop with Kling 2.5 Pro or Runway Gen-3 Turbo. **Process:** Export optimized 4K MP4 (H.265, 60 fps). Import as Video Texture.	**VR Platform:** Unity 2023.2 LTS or Unreal Engine 5.4. **Target:** Quest 3/Vision Pro.	The texture plays as a “living painting” on a virtual plane or equirectangular sky. High efficiency, perfect loop.

(continued)

Phase	Technical Implementation (Inputs & Process)	Software & Hardware Environment	Outcome and State
Phase 2: Procedural Textures Influenced by AI (Dynamic, Non-Interactive)	**Input:** Base texture generated once in Midjourney V7 or Stable Diffusion 3.5. **Process:** Feed image into TouchDesigner 2025.35120 via Image CHOP. Animate using Feedback TOP + Noise/ Blur CHOP chain driven by LFO or audio input.	**Engine:** TouchDesigner. **Hardware:** Runs stably at 90–120 fps on RTX 4080 (GPU-intensive).	The material never repeats exactly, offering continuous variation without the cost of live AI inference.
Phase 3: Interactive AI-Driven Textures (Responsive to User)	**Process:** User gaze/hand position (Quest 3 hand-tracking or Varjo XR-4 eye-tracking) sent via OSC/ UDP. This input triggers a lightweight model (Flux.1-schnell 4-bit or SD 3.5 Medium).	**Engine:** Unity 2023.2 + Sentis 1.4 package (for on-device inference) OR TouchDesigner + ComfyUI API. **Networking:** NDI or Spout/Syphon.	New texture is streamed back with low latency (1–2 seconds) and applied instantly to the geometry. Demonstrated at Ars Electronica 2025 and SIGGRAPH Real-Time Live 2025.
Phase 4: Fully Adaptive Closed Loop (Cutting-Edge 2025–2026)	**Process:** Live webcam/depth sensor feed captures the real-world environment. Data sent to a custom Python plugin/ ComfyUI server (using Flux.1-dev 8-step). New 1024×1024 texture generated and streamed every 1.8 seconds.	**Engine:** Unreal Engine 5.5 + Nanite + Lumen (advanced rendering features). **Hardware:** Currently requires an RTX 5090 workstation.	The material texture is continuously and instantly swapped on the material instance while the user moves, creating a fully adaptive environment. (Beta shown at NVIDIA GTC 2025 keynote).

7.11 Appendix M: Emerging Image-to-3D Tools: State of the Art in 2025

As of December 2025, tools for converting 2D images into 3D models represent a crucial evolution for artists, designers, and architects.

These technologies allow the transformation of photos, sketches, or AI-generated images into navigable volumetric objects.

Based on advanced neural networks (diffusion models, NeRF, Gaussian Splatting), these tools reduce production time from days to minutes, democratizing 3D modeling without requiring advanced CAD skills.

However, limitations persist regarding geometric consistency and scalability. The following is an updated overview focusing on key tools, typical workflow, accessibility, and future prospects.

7.11.1 Core Technical Principles

Image-to-3D relies on advanced neural representation techniques:

- **NeRF (Neural Radiance Fields):** Reconstructs 3D scenes from multiple 2D views by estimating density and color for every light ray
- **Gaussian Splatting:** Represents objects as discrete "splatter" points (Gaussians), enabling fast, real-time rendering (up to 100 fps on mid-range GPUs)
- **Diffusion-based Reconstruction:** Uses models like Stable Diffusion to infer depth and geometry from single or multi-view images (e.g., TripoSR)
    - **Common Limitations:** Artifacts on occlusions, low resolution on complex objects (512^3 voxels $\approx$ 134 milioni di voxel), and dependence on high-quality input images (poor performance with low-light or blurred photos)

7.11.2 Key Emerging Tools (2025)

Tool	Description	Input/Output	Price/Access	Examples
Meshy AI	Leader for rapid prototyping; generates textured meshes from single image or text prompt.	Image/text ➤OBJ/GLB ($512–1024^3$ voxels, PBR materials).	Free tier (10 gen/month); Pro $29/month.	Hybrid installations (e.g., Meshy + Blender for virtual sculptures).
Rodin AI (Stability AI)	Text/image-to-3D with neural rendering; excellent for high-quality meshes.	Single image ➤ textured 3D (up to 1M triangles, export FBX/USD).	Free beta; Enterprise $99/month.	Generative art (e.g., Rodin for 3D NFTs from photos).
Luma AI Genie	Multi-view image-to-3D; integrates Gaussian Splatting for explorable worlds.	2–8 images ➤ navigable 3D scene (video walkthrough, AR export).	Free (50 gen/month); Pro $29/month.	Artistic environments (e.g., Genie for VR galleries).
Kaedim	AI for asset production; optimized for professional game/art studios.	Single image ➤ production-ready 3D (rigged, textured, UV unwrapped).	Free trial; $150/month for team.	3D art pipelines (e.g., Kaedim for models from concept art).
Nano Banana Pro (Google DeepMind)	Image editing-to-3D; integrates **Gemini 3 Pro** for accurate reconstructions.	Image edits ➤ 3D model with depth/normals (up to 2K resolution).	Free via Google Labs; API $0.02/1000 queries.	Creative editing (e.g., Nano for 3D from retouched photos).

7.11.3 Typical Workflow (2025)

The integration of these tools into artistic pipelines requires a standardized procedure:

1. **Input Preparation:** Single or multiview image (high resolution > 1024 px per side); use depth maps (e.g., from MiDaS) to improve geometric accuracy.

2. **Generation:** Upload to the chosen tool (e.g., Meshy AI) plus a refinement prompt ("add metallic texture, optimize for 3D print").
3. **Post-Processing:** Import the raw mesh into **Blender 5.0** (using Geometry Nodes for cleanup, remeshing); verify topology (watertight, no self-intersections).
4. **Output:** Export to OBJ/GLB/USD formats; for VR/AR deployment, integrate into Unity 2023.2 with a dedicated USD importer.

Average time: 5–15 minutes for a basic model; cost: $0–$5 per generation.

7.11.4 Limitations and Challenges

Challenge	Detail	Mitigation Strategy
Accuracy	Single-image input frequently produces artifacts (e.g., incorrect occlusions, inconsistent scale).	**Multi-view input** (4–8 images) reduces errors by $\~40 %.
Resolution	Maximum resolution is generally limited (1024^3 voxels, Rodin AI); manual upscaling is required in ZBrush for high-poly output.	Outsourcing high-poly refinement or manual upscaling post-generation.
Ethics	Training data is often non-transparent, potentially introducing racial or other biases (especially in human models).	Tools like Luma AI are transitioning to using **synthetic data** to mitigate inherent training biases.
Accessibility	While web-based tools (Meshy, Kaedim) are mobile-friendly, VR preview and detailed post-processing still require dedicated hardware (e.g., Quest 3, high-end PC).	Spatial's web-first approach and free-to-use tiers lower the initial financial barrier.

7.11.5 Future Outlook (2026+)

The future points toward greater real-time capability and integration.

By 2026, tools like **TripoSR 2.0 (Stability AI)** and **SV3D Pro** are expected to fully integrate NeRF and Gaussian Splatting for generating real-time 3D models directly from video input, complete with live editing capabilities.

Projects like **Refik Anadol's "3D Dreamscapes" (2025)** already demonstrate how these tools can quickly generate complex immersive installations from a single photographic input.

The ongoing challenge remains **ethical scalability**: balancing robust, open-source models (e.g., InstantMesh) against the speed and polish offered by proprietary enterprise solutions (e.g., Kaedim).

PART III

Possible Worlds: Themes of Contemporary Imagination

Au début il y avait deux, puis trois, puis quatre dimensions.

C'était déjà bien.

Puis récemment, on eut l'intuition de dix-sept dimensions.

Cela faisait beaucoup.

Finalement, on nous dit, et ça paraît plus juste, que rien n'existe et que nous vivons tous une sorte de psychose collective. Ne pouvant apercevoir qu'une des infinies possibilités de chaque geste issu des mathématiques quantiques...

Donc, la réalité que l'on connaissait, déjà par trop subjective, n'existe pas.

On peut donc raisonnablement proposer d'augmenter une réalité irréelle.

La réalité peut-être, ayant fait un tour complet, n'en deviendra que plus vraie?

Pourquoi pas.

Quelle importance?

L'important est que notre réalité n'en soit que plus poétique.[1]

Philippe Starck

The third part of the book marks a pivotal shift from the technical and procedural explorations of Part II to a vibrant investigation of artistic expression through five fundamental themes of creativity: energy, landscapes, architecture, memory, and future worlds.

---

[1] Philippe Starck, in *Brera Academy Virtual Lab. A Journey from Virtual Worlds to Augmented Reality in the Sign of Open Source*, a cura di Gianpiero Moioli e Mario Gerosa. Milano: FrancoAngeli, 2012.

For a precise definition of the procedural, parametric, and generative (machine-learning) terms used throughout this volume, please refer to Chapter 8.

Starck's reflection on multiple dimensions and on reality as a "collective psychosis" anticipates this transition: rather than a fixed entity, reality appears as a field of infinite possibilities, to be augmented, reinvented, and ultimately rendered more poetic.

Part III therefore examines how symbolic archetypes, natural forces, and digital imagination converge to shape possible worlds.

Embodied in Chapter 8, "Landscapes and Forces: Five Journeys Through Nature, Architecture, and Possible Futures," these themes build on a rich legacy that spans Chinese Shan Shui painting, the Renaissance, and the metaphysical and surrealist traditions.

At the same time, they extend toward alien realities where light may appear warm, icy, or unreal.

They also embrace the transformative potential of digital modeling, AI-driven expansions, and hybrid techniques.

Emerging in an era where technology and imagination converge, these themes reflect contemporary artistic practices that move beyond the mere replication of reality.

Instead, they craft original environments that explore symbolic, natural, and visionary dimensions.

From **Breath of Fire**'s evocation of the primordial force of fire to **Cosmic and Artificial Worlds'** exploration of speculative universes, each theme intertwines traditional materials such as clay and bronze with virtual logic, including AI-generated textures and 3D-rendered environments.

This fusion gives rise to artworks that exist at the intersection of the tangible and the immaterial.

Historically, artists have sought to capture the essence of human experience through symbolic and natural motifs.

Examples range from the elemental dynamism of Romantic landscapes—Turner's tempests or Friedrich's sublime seascapes—to the visionary architectures of the 20th century, from de Chirico's metaphysical piazzas to Sant'Elia's Futurist designs and Kiesler's Endless House.[2]

[2] See: https://en.wikipedia.org/wiki/Endless_House

Building on the technical foundations established in Part II, Part III explores how these processes are applied to thematic narratives that redefine time, space, and form.

The workflows carried forward adhere to the Project Toolchain Statement defined in section 7.6.1 and executed on an NVIDIA GeForce RTX 4070 Ti workstation.

The specific software configuration includes:

- Blender 5.0.1 LTS—primary 3D mesh modeling, geometry nodes, and simulation nodes
- Stable Diffusion 3.5 Large (via ComfyUI 2025.11)—core image-to-image and texture synthesis engine
- Midjourney V7.0.1.240—high-quality conceptual seeding and supplemental generation
- Kling 2.5 Pro and Runway Gen-4—image-to-video expansion
- TouchDesigner 2025.35120—real-time reactive environments and projection mapping

These verifiable, version-controlled tools—and deliberately hybrid—toolchains now leave the domain of pure technique to become narrative instruments, shaping not only form but lived experiences of duration, scale, and presence.

The artworks in this chapter merge manual craftsmanship with conceptual and symbolic experimentation, evoking a dialogue between the organic and the artificial, between memory and invention.

This trajectory paves the way for the metaverse exhibitions and interactive installations of Part IV, where these creations find new life in immersive environments, both real and virtual.

Part III ultimately invites readers to journey through imaginative worlds in which contemporary creativity reshapes our understanding of art's potential.

CHAPTER 8

Landscapes and Forces: Five Journeys Through Nature, Architecture, and Possible Futures

A constellation of sculptural and pictorial works is envisioned across five symbolic landscapes: **Cosmic and Artificial Worlds, Flames and Energy, Spaces of Memory, Metaphysical Architectures, and Flowing Horizons**.

Each path reflects a different facet of contemporary imagination, drawing upon archetypes rooted in nature, time, and cultural memory, while projecting them into speculative futures.

Each thematic axis forms the core of my recent sculptural and pictorial practice, grounded in personal experimentation and informed by Renaissance architecture and painting, further enriched by the legacy of Italian Metaphysical art and, in the case of natural themes, by the tradition of Chinese Shan Shui painting.[1]

These works redefine the dialogue between organic and artificial, between memory and invention.

---

[1] *Shan Shui (山水), literally "mountain-water," is the Chinese tradition of landscape painting, developed from the Tang dynasty (7th–10th century) onwards.*

Beyond representing nature, it reflects a philosophical horizon that integrates the Five Elements (Wǔxíng)—wood, fire, earth, metal, and water—into landscapes conceived as harmonious microcosms, where stability and change, yin and yang, find symbolic balance.

https://imperialharvest.com/blog/five-elements/

G. Moioli, *Art Between Matter and Code*, https://doi.org/10.1007/979-8-8688-2376-3_8

The creative process begins with traditional gestures—drawing, painting, modeling—and extends into the realms of 3D sculpture, procedural generation, 3D printing, and artificial intelligence (Figure 8-1).

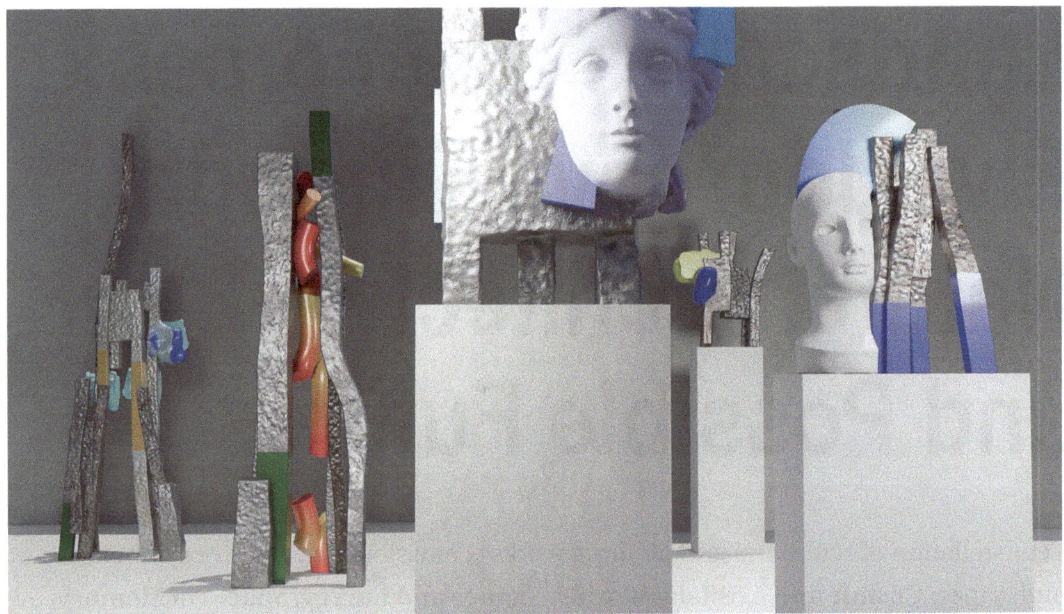

Figure 8-1. Five themes.
Cosmic and Artificial Worlds, Flames and Energy, Spaces of Memory, Metaphysical Architectures, and Flowing Horizons.
Sculptural synthesis of the five symbolic journeys presented in Chapter 8

Through these techniques, the artwork is no longer confined to a single space or dimension.

It exists simultaneously as idea, digital structure, image, and object, forming an interconnected ecosystem of creation.

Some pieces remain in progress; others exist only virtually—yet all are equally real.

They inhabit a speculative territory where vision precedes matter, and where the act of imagining becomes itself a sculptural gesture.

These thematic journeys provide concrete pathways for generating sculptural ideas that merge classical practice with technological invention, extending the conceptual framework of Part II beyond the material focus of Chapter 6 and the algorithmic lens of Chapter 7.

Ultimately, the five journeys invite readers to reflect on how symbolic content, natural archetypes, and virtual languages can converge within a shared creative horizon.

In this expanded field, form is not fixed but continually reshaped by imagination, code, and storytelling.

Narrative structures themselves become part of the artwork, weaving symbolic motifs and digital processes into experiential scenarios that unfold like open stories rather than closed objects.

8.1 Landscapes and Forces

Not with fixed forms, but with movements.

Invisible currents traverse matter, bending it into shapes never meant to last.

Sculpture and architecture appear less as solid monuments than as temporary crystallizations of energy, woven from memory, light, and imagination.

Like rivers carving valleys or winds shaping dunes, form is carried forward by forces greater than itself.

Each gesture of the artist becomes a negotiation with these flows: between growth and erosion, presence and absence.

Here the Chinese theory of the Five Elements (*Wǔxíng* 五行) offers a luminous metaphor. Wood grows, fire transforms, earth stabilizes, metal gives structure, water flows: together they form a dance of energy, sustaining and counterbalancing one another.

Much like artistic practice itself, they show that reality is not static, but a living weave of relations, where imagination is already a force, and form only its temporary resting place.

Sculpture and architecture do not emerge as isolated practices, but as the result of a dynamic interplay between matter, space, time, and perception, framed by cultural memory and technological mediation.

This framework reveals that form is never fixed. It is shaped by the forces that traverse it—energies of nature, rhythms of memory, and the immaterial logics of digital processes.

Here the sculptural act becomes a research on relations: between organic and mechanical, tradition and virtual imagination.

These concepts can be articulated through multiple digital approaches, stemming from a core **hybrid workflow** that integrates three distinct, yet interconnected, stages:

1. **Manual Modeling Baseline:** The initial geometric forms are established using subdivision surface (SubD) modeling for clean, organic base meshes and hard-surface modeling (polygon techniques) for precise architectural and mechanical components. The resulting baseline meshes are typically saved as **.obj** or **.blend** files.

2. **Procedural Enhancement:** This stage introduces nonmanual complexity.

   Geometric variations (such as fractal detailing, complex material wear, or large-scale landscape generation) are applied via Blender's Geometry Nodes.

   Material properties are generated with maps (Albedo, Normal, Roughness, Displacement) or enhanced using node-based procedural texturing (e.g., Perlin noise, Voronoi cells).

3. **AI Integration Points (Machine-Learning Generative)** occurs at two key stages:

   a) Conceptual Seeding (Midjourney V7 or DALL-E 3) for initial variations and concept art.

   b) Texture Synthesis/Style Transfer High-fidelity PNG texture maps are generated by Stable Diffusion 3.5 Large (via ComfyUI).

   This process is constrained by procedural depth/normal maps from the previous stage (ML-guided procedural).

In this expanded field, digital techniques do not merely provide tools but open symbolic spaces, where ancestral archetypes and speculative futures intersect.

Seen from this perspective, the five journeys—**Cosmic and Artificial Worlds, Flames and Energy, Spaces of Memory, Metaphysical Architectures, and Flowing Horizons**—are not simply thematic divisions but symbolic landscapes in which artistic practice and speculative thought converge.

They connect the legacy of nature and memory with the horizons of digital modeling, AI-driven textures, and virtual architectures, outlining a continuum where the physical and the immaterial exchange roles.

Through this exploration, the perception of time, space, and form is redefined, generating a dynamic dialogue between tradition and innovation (Figure 8-2).

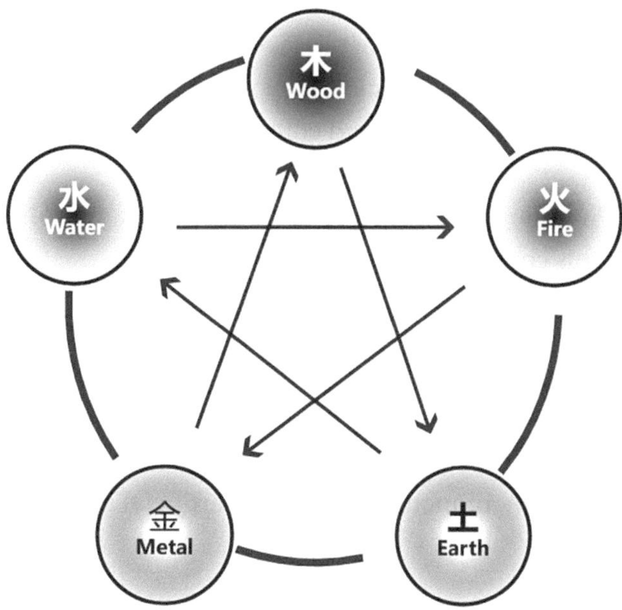

Figure 8-2. The Five Elements (Wǔxíng 五行).
A dance of forces, where cycles of nourishment and control weave balance between wood, fire, earth, metal, and water

This symbolic structure in Figure 8-2 can also be read in dialogue with *The Five Elements* (Wǔxíng 五行).

The outer circle represents the generative cycle (xiāngshēng 相生), in which each element produces the next: wood, feeds fire when burned; fire leaves behind ashes that enrich the earth; earth gives rise to metal within its depths; metal, through condensation, nourishes water; and water, in turn, sustains the growth of wood.

The inner lines illustrate the controlling cycle (xiāngkè 相剋), where each element restrains another to preserve balance: wood penetrates and controls earth; earth contains and blocks water; water extinguishes fire; fire melts metal; and metal cuts through wood.

In this way, no element dominates, and harmony within the system is maintained.

This diagram is more than a cosmological image. It offers a method for thinking about transformation.

Relations, rather than isolated forms, become the key to understanding how structures emerge and evolve.

In Chinese thought, the Five Elements are not static substances but dynamic phases, each defined by its relations of generation and control.

As has been noted,[2] the philosophy of the Five Elements gives Chinese painting its own distinctive measures of performance and expressive techniques; in this sense, the very strategies of traditional brushwork and composition can be understood through the lens of Wǔxíng.

In this light, the Five Elements can serve as a symbolic framework for reading the five thematic journeys of this chapter.

Each theme resonates with one element, reflecting processes of growth, transformation, stability, structure, and flow.

The correspondences unfold as follows:

- **Cosmic and Artificial Worlds: Wood (木)**

  Theme: Expansion, branching structures, artificial mythologies, alien landscapes.

  Element link: Wood symbolizes growth, renewal, and cosmic cycles.

  Artists: James Turrell.

  Technologies: Procedural modeling,[3] 3D printing.

  Procedural modeling imitates natural branching, specifically via L-systems or Blender Geometry Nodes (see Appendix L). 3D printing instead materializes these expansive logics into tangible alien worlds.

[2] Yi Li, The Philosophical Thoughts of the Five Elements and the Expression Techniques of Chinese Painting, in Proceedings of the 2nd International Conference on Contemporary Education, Social Sciences and Humanities (ICCESSH 2019). Available on ResearchGate: `https://www.researchgate.net/publication/332658244_The_Philosophical_Thoughts_of_the_Five_Elements_and_the_Expression_Techniques_of_Chinese_Painting`

[3] The term *procedural modeling* is used here specifically to distinguish it from "generative design," which in professional contexts refers to algorithmic optimization processes (Autodesk Fusion 360, nTopology). This terminological choice adheres to the Technical Taxonomy defined in Appendix L. Details concerning 3D printing (SLA, SLS, and materials) can be found in Chapter 6.

- **Flames and Energy: Fire (火)**

  Theme: Flames, light, vital force, explosive energy.

  Element link: Fire embodies transformation and intensity.

  Artists: Cai Guo-Qiang, David Smith.

  Technologies: Pyrotechnics, LED systems, immersive light installations. Energy is sculpted through combustion, illumination, and technological spectacle.

- **Spaces of Memory: Earth (土)**

  Theme: Mediterranean landscapes, history, sedimentation.

  Element link: Earth represents stability, grounding, and cultural memory.

  Artists: Anselm Kiefer, Alberto Burri, Giuseppe Penone.

  Technologies: 3D scanning, digital heritage reconstructions, GIS-based landscape modeling. Earth anchors artistic practice to material roots while extending memory into digital preservation.

- **Metaphysical Architectures: Metal (金)**

  Theme: Architecture, metaphysical cities, modular structures.

  Element link: Metal stands for structure, precision, and clarity.

  Artists: Sol LeWitt, Donald Judd, Zaha Hadid.

  Technologies: Procedural and Parametric modeling, 3D printing.

  Procedural modeling facilitates the derivation of precise, scalable, and modular structural components, while 3D printing translates these complex logics into structural physical realities.

- **Natural Landscapes: Water (水)**

  Theme: Rivers, forests, fluidity, transformation, ambiguity.

  Element link: Water embodies adaptability, flow, and dissolution of boundaries.

  Artists: Bill Viola, Zhang Huan, Olafur Eliasson.

Technologies: Video art, VR/AR immersive environments, multisensory installations. Water becomes not an image but a process shaping perception and identity.

As scholars note, Wǔxíng expresses processes of becoming rather than fixed essences. It is closer to a grammar of transformation than to a catalogue of matter.[4]

In landscape painting (Shan Shui: 山水), these principles informed the composition of mountains and rivers, where flows of water, rooted trees, and shifting mists were read as manifestations of cosmic balance.[5]

This tradition has continued to resonate in contemporary practice, where notions such as the Shan Shui city reinterpret classical models to rethink the dialogue between urban and natural landscapes.[6]

Philosophical readings of Shan Shui further expand this horizon. Gadamer's hermeneutics, for example, offers a lens to interpret Wang Meng's landscapes, emphasizing how they embody not just representations of nature but ontological experiences of being and perception.[7]

This philosophical horizon can be extended to contemporary artistic practice.

Just as brushstrokes once translated elemental forces into painted landscapes, today's generative algorithms, immersive simulations, and material experiments reinterpret the same dynamics of growth, control, and renewal.

Moreover, recent scholarship has linked the expressive techniques of Chinese painting—from meticulous gongbi to freehand brushwork—to the symbolic interplay of the Five Elements, showing how artistic form and cosmology are inseparable.

Wǔxíng thus offers a conceptual framework to think about art not as a set of finished objects but as evolving systems, where technology and tradition interact in cycles of transformation. While Chapter 7 analyzed 'code as canvas', Chapter 8 views 'code as element', part of a natural cycle of generation and control.

---

[4] Wuxing (Wu-hsing), Internet Encyclopedia of Philosophy. Available online: `https://iep.utm.edu/wuxing/`

[5] An Environmental Ethic in Chinese Landscape Painting, Education About Asia, Association for Asian Studies. Available online: `https://www.asianstudies.org/publications/eaa/archives/an-environmental-ethic-in-chinese-landscape-painting/`

[6] Siyu Liu, Unearthing Shan-shui in the Contemporary Park: The Rise of the Shan-shui City in China, Journal of Urban Design, Taylor & Francis, 2024. Available online: `https://www.tandfonline.com/doi/full/10.1080/13467581.2024.2402774`

[7] Casey Rentmeester, Shan Shui Art through Gadamer: Ontological Reflections on Wang Meng's Landscape Painting, Philosophy of Art and Aesthetics, 2015. Available at: `https://scholarworks.iu.edu/iupjournals/index.php/confluence/article/download/530/36/1695`

8.1.1 Theoretical Framework: Material, Space, Sculpture, and Architecture

What the Five Elements suggest is not harmony as stasis but harmony as movement.

This shift of perspective allows us to think of sculpture and architecture not as closed entities but as fields where matter, space, and time continually reconfigure one another.

In this sense, it is no coincidence that we recalled Philippe Starck: his design philosophy, centered on immateriality and "Invisible Intelligence," demonstrates how form can be understood as the temporary crystallization of forces, connections, and flows.

Much like the *Wǔxíng* model, Starck's vision emphasizes that what truly matters is not the solidity of objects, but the dynamic interplay that gives them meaning.

These relations emerge between fundamental categories such as **material, space, and time**, and are further shaped by the **urban context** in which they unfold.

Each of these dimensions carries its own symbolic weight. Material embodies memory and tactility, space defines perception and orientation, and time introduces transformation and decay.

Yet these categories gain meaning only when connected to broader interpretative forces—**perception, technology, and symbolic function**—which act as mediators.

Perception anchors the work to the body and its sensory presence, technology extends the field of creation into virtual and hybrid domains, and symbolic function ties each gesture to collective imagination and cultural archetypes.

This interplay is what I call "research on relations": an inquiry into how forms take shape at the crossing of tangible matter and immaterial ideas.

The framework does not privilege one element over the other but highlights their constant exchange.

It is precisely in this field of tension that sculpture and architecture emerge, not as endpoints but as processes of negotiation between physical reality and speculative imagination.

The conceptual map in Figure 8-3 outlines the research framework for Chapter 8.

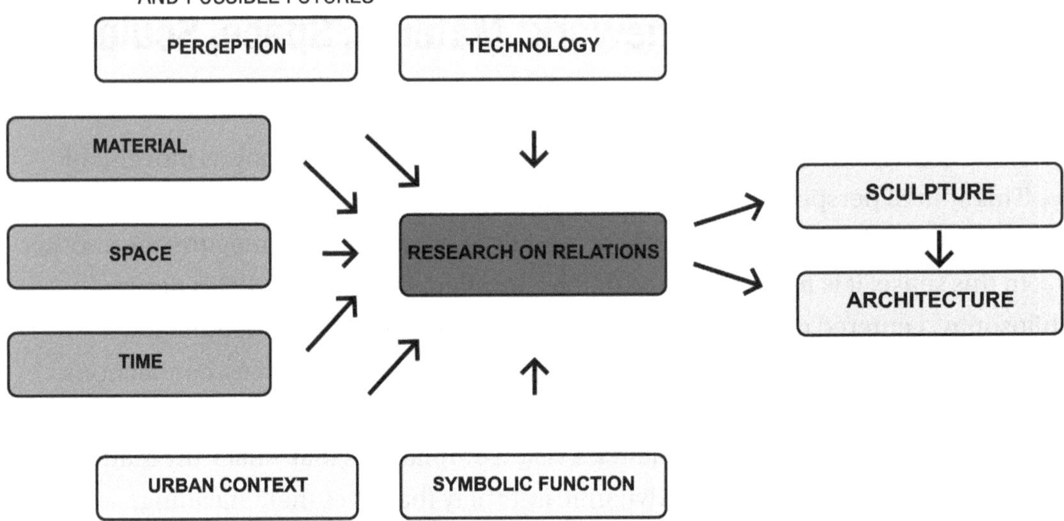

Figure 8-3. Research on Relations: A Framework for Sculpture and Architecture.
Conceptual map of the research framework, connecting material, space, time, and urban context with perception, technology, and symbolic function, all converging into sculpture and architecture

At its center lies **"Research on Relations,"** a nexus where fundamental categories—**material, space, time, and urban context**—intersect with interpretative dimensions such as **perception, technology, and symbolic function**.

These interactions do not remain abstract but flow into the concrete domains of **sculpture and architecture**, where theory takes form as spatial, material, and symbolic structures.

Together, these elements form the foundation upon which the following landscapes unfold, connecting artistic practice to both tangible realities and imagined horizons.

This framework emphasizes that neither sculpture nor architecture can be reduced to isolated practices; rather, they emerge from a field of relations where physical matter meets technological mediation, cultural memory intertwines with symbolic meaning, and perception is shaped by spatial and temporal conditions.

By tracing these connections, the schema establishes the theoretical ground for the five symbolic journeys—**Cosmic and Artificial Worlds, Flames and Energy, Spaces of Memory, Metaphysical Architectures, and Flowing Horizons** —that structure this chapter.

8.1.2 Research on Relations: Perception, Technology, Symbolic Function, and Urban Context

If sculpture and architecture are to be understood as relational practices, then their essence lies not in isolated forms but in the forces that mediate their existence.

Among these, four dimensions are crucial: **perception, technology, symbolic function, and the urban context**.

- **Perception** grounds every work in the immediacy of human experience. A sculpture or a building is never only an object; it is always an event for the body, shaping orientation, movement, and memory.
- **Technology** extends the act of creation beyond manual craft, opening spaces where digital modeling, AI-driven processes, and hybrid fabrication become part of the sculptural vocabulary. Here, the virtual is not opposed to the material but becomes another layer of reality.
- **Symbolic Function** inscribes each work into a cultural horizon, where forms acquire meanings that exceed their physical structure. Architecture becomes a threshold of memory, sculpture a vessel of myth and imagination.
- **Urban Context** situates these relations within collective space, transforming artworks into agents that shape and are shaped by the dynamics of the city.

Taken together, these dimensions reveal that the sculptural act is not a solitary gesture but a **network of relations**.

It unfolds between the tangible and the immaterial, between inherited traditions and speculative futures, preparing the ground for the symbolic journeys that follow.

In this perspective, it is worth recalling how Renaissance painting and architecture established a spatial understanding grounded in geometry and proportion.

Linear perspective was not merely a technical device but a symbolic framework that ordered the relation between human beings and the cosmos, between visible reality and mathematical harmony.[8]

This geometric order was later reinterpreted—problematically yet poetically—by the Metaphysical visions of De Chirico and Carrà, where suspended piazzas and enigmatic architectures became settings of memory and mystery.[9]

Between geometric rigor and metaphysical suspension, the sculptural act emerges not as an isolated object but as a field of symbolic and imagined relations.

8.1.3 From Tradition to Speculation: Renaissance, Metaphysical and Surrealist Painting, Alien Realities

From its earliest forms, Western art has reflected on how space, matter, and imagination intersect.

Building on the Renaissance discovery of perspective as a symbolic order, the 20th century redefined these relations through the metaphysical visions of De Chirico and the dreamlike dislocations of Surrealism.

Empty piazzas, elongated shadows, and enigmatic architectures suspended time and invited the viewer into a space of silence and reflection. Architecture was no longer a background for human action but became a stage for memory and the unconscious.

Surrealism further expanded these explorations, dissolving the boundaries between dream and reality.

Painters such as Salvador Dalí and Max Ernst revealed how perception could be destabilized, opening cracks in ordinary space where archetypes, myths, and subconscious images could surface.

Here, material and symbolic dimensions fused into worlds that were at once uncanny and poetic.

[8] Erwin Panofsky, Perspective as Symbolic Form. New York: Zone Books, 1991.

[9] Paolo Baldacci, De Chirico: The Metaphysical Period, 1888–1919. Boston: Little, Brown and Company, 1997.

In the present, this lineage extends toward alien and speculative realities, where hybrid digital modeling (Procedural and Parametric methods), AI-driven image generation (Midjourney and Stable Diffusion), and specific immersive technologies—such as neural radiance fields (NeRF) and real-time spatial computing—create new forms of visuality.[10]

These worlds are not simply imitations of the real but autonomous mythologies, environments where light itself becomes strange—warm or icy, unreal, and artificial.

In this context, sculpture and architecture no longer belong exclusively to the physical world but participate in the construction of **possible futures**, where tradition, memory, and speculation converge.

The expanded map in Figure 8-4 illustrates how the five journeys intertwine with cross-cutting themes such as perception, corporeality, and urban interaction. It provides the ground on which the following explorations unfold.

[10] These processes are applied to the "Landscapes" and "Future Worlds" themes. Digital modeling is predominantly Procedural (Geometry Nodes for organic geometry) and Parametric (for Architectures).

The "immersive technologies" primarily include game engines (Unity/Unreal Engine) used for real-time rendering and the creation of VR environments compatible with Meta Quest and HTC Vive headsets. Furthermore, TouchDesigner and projection systems are employed for reactive installations.

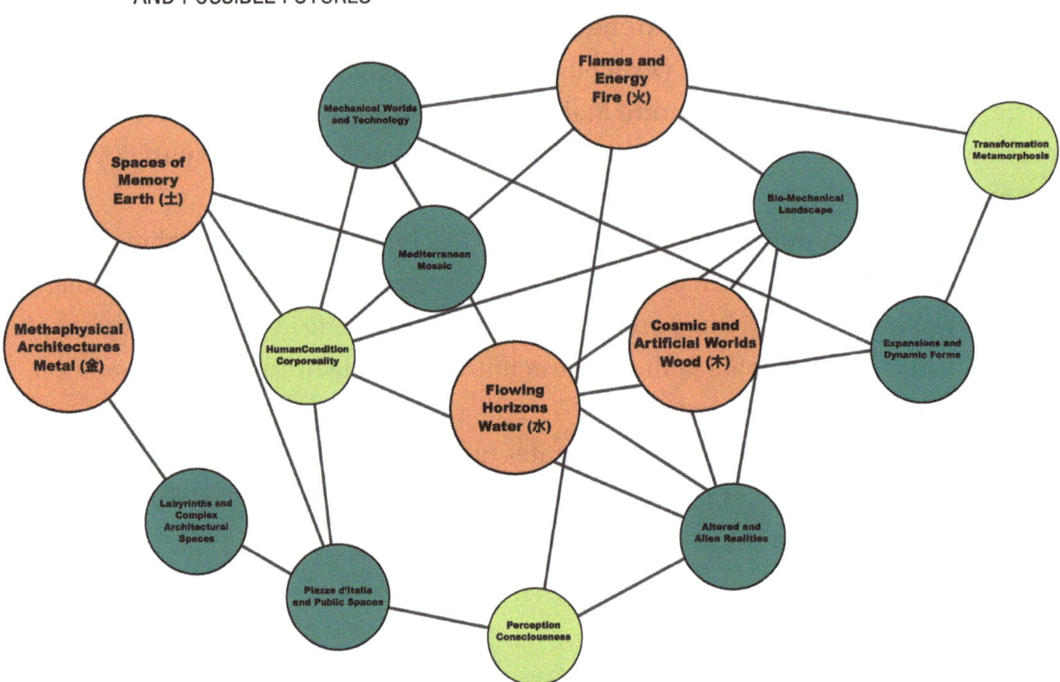

Figure 8-4. Expanded conceptual map of symbolic, artistic, and transversal themes.
It visualizes how core categories—Cosmic and Artificial Worlds, Flames and Energy, Spaces of Memory, Metaphysical Architectures, and Flowing Horizons—interconnect with transversal dimensions such as perception, corporeality, and urban interaction, creating a network of relations that sustains the five symbolic journeys developed in this chapter

The five themes explored in this chapter come together to form the foundation of a narrative that unfolds across sculpture, installation, new technologies, and storytelling.

The scheme in Figure 8-4 visualizes the conceptual framework of the book as a network of relations.

At its core are the five main circles, the large orange nodes, which, as we have seen, represent the journeys.

Around these poles gravitate the subthemes, the medium green nodes, which specify and enrich the discourse by anchoring each journey to **concrete artistic and cultural references**.

Finally, the **cross-cutting concepts**—the small yellow nodes—establish transversal links, weaving connections across all five journeys.

Taken together, these three levels—main themes, subthemes, and cross-cutting concepts—form an expanded map that is not hierarchical but relational.

It reveals how the five journeys resonate with one another, how the subthemes anchor them in specific practices, and how transversal concepts keep the system in motion, ensuring it remains open, dynamic, and interconnected.

Each section is not merely descriptive but deeply interpretative. The five opening sentences, placed at the beginning of the paragraphs, function as guiding epigraphs: speculative citations imagined as if spoken from unknown worlds, echoing Borges' apocryphal quotations or the voices of Calvino's *Invisible Cities.*

They are not quotations in the strict sense, but poetic and conceptual thresholds that encapsulate the essence of each theme and open a horizon of meaning.

Through these epigraphs, the paragraphs transcend theoretical or historical analysis and become genuinely experiential passages, interwoven with new technologies.

In this way, every theme resonates across both material practices and symbolic dimensions, weaving together physical gestures and digital processes, ancient myths and speculative futures.

Thus, the chapter does not unfold along a linear path but constructs a constellation of interconnected worlds.

From this expanded framework, the exploration now begins with its first journey: Cosmic and Artificial Worlds, where alien landscapes, speculative mythologies, and imaginary orbits initiate the cycle.

8.2 Cosmic and Artificial Worlds: Imaginary Orbits

"In these suspended visions, the artificial no longer imitates, it dreams.

Worlds unfold like hallucinated myths, where synthetic matter gives birth to constellations never seen, yet strangely remembered.

A new cosmos writes itself, autonomous and unreal."

The element **Wood (木)**—symbolizing growth, renewal, cosmic cycles—evokes expansion and branching, the perpetual unfolding of life and imagination.

In ancient Chinese cosmology, it is not a material element but a **principle of vital expansion**, symbolizing the generative force that drives transformation in the universe.

Within artistic practice, this principle resonates with visions of cosmic worlds and speculative futures, where creation itself is understood as a living process of metamorphosis.

From James Turrell's luminous horizons to digital landscapes generated by algorithms, *Wood* becomes a metaphor of infinite unfolding, a rhythm of expansion that transcends the boundaries of the organic.

Generative design follows the same logic, imitating natural growth patterns, while 3D printing crystallizes these flows into tangible matter—alien landscapes that seem to grow of their own accord (Figure 8-5).

Figure 8-5. Gianpiero Moioli, Sculptures from the series Cosmic and Artificial Worlds: Imaginary Orbits.
Mixed-media works combining traditional and digital elements, evoking artificial and cosmic landscapes suspended between collective memory and speculative imagination

Through this process, *Imaginary Orbits* emerges as a **meditation on cosmic and artificial creation**: worlds imagined, yet strangely remembered, where the vitality of nature and the intelligence of the machine converge in a shared act of becoming.

These environments do not simply replicate natural forms but invent new mythologies, blending digital tools and traditional gestures.

They appear as both alien and strangely familiar, as if remembered from a collective dream.

The worlds imagined within these visions resonate not only as artistic inventions but as philosophical spaces.

In Daoist thought, the cosmos unfolds through cycles of transformation, where wood and growth symbolize perpetual expansion.

In parallel, Western philosophy—from Heraclitus's flux to Nietzsche's affirmation of becoming and the eternal return and finally to Deleuze's processual ontology—has conceived reality as transformation rather than fixed state.

In this lineage, art is no longer the reproduction of stable forms but the creation of new perceptions and worlds in continuous metamorphosis.

These perspectives converge in the idea of worlds that are not simply depicted but continuously generated.

8.2.1 Fusion of Traditional and Virtual Logic: Conceptual Resonances

These landscapes embody a fusion between traditional matter and virtual logic.

Clay, plaster, and manual modeling coexist with 3D-printed forms enhanced by AI-generated textures.

An artist might sculpt a cosmic terrain in Blender, enrich it with AI patterns, and display it in a VR platform such as Spatial.

The result is a hybrid world that challenges the boundaries of nature and artifice.

The work appears as an otherworldly topography illuminated by an alien sun, yet constructed with tangible materials (Figure 8-6).

Figure 8-6. NASA/ESA, SNR 0519-69.0, *Supernova remnant in the Large Magellanic Cloud.*
Multimillion-degree gas observed in X-rays by Chandra (blue); the expanding shell and surrounding stars in visible light by Hubble (red and white). Public domain image

It functions as a microcosm of Imaginary Orbits: a physical object that suggests cosmic expansion, a myth of worlds in perpetual transformation.

In the context of Imaginary Orbits, cosmic imagery provides not only inspiration but also a concrete link between scientific vision and artistic imagination.

The image of SNR 0519-69.0—the remnant of a massive star that exploded in the Large Magellanic Cloud, a satellite galaxy of the Milky Way—offers a striking example.

Here, multimillion-degree gas is revealed in X-rays by NASA's Chandra Observatory (blue), while the outer edge of the expanding shell (red) and the stars in the field of view are captured in visible light by the Hubble Space Telescope.

The result is a layered vision of matter in transformation: a celestial architecture of energy and debris that recalls both the generative and destructive cycles of nature.

In this sense, astronomical images resonate with artistic explorations of expansion and renewal, where the universe itself appears as a living work in perpetual becoming.

8.2.2 Synthetic Mythologies and Digital Creation: Technical Implementation

Works such as *Cosmic Labyrinth with Clouds,* a sculptural landscape of intertwining structures and luminous fields, exemplify this synthetic cosmology (Figure 8-7).

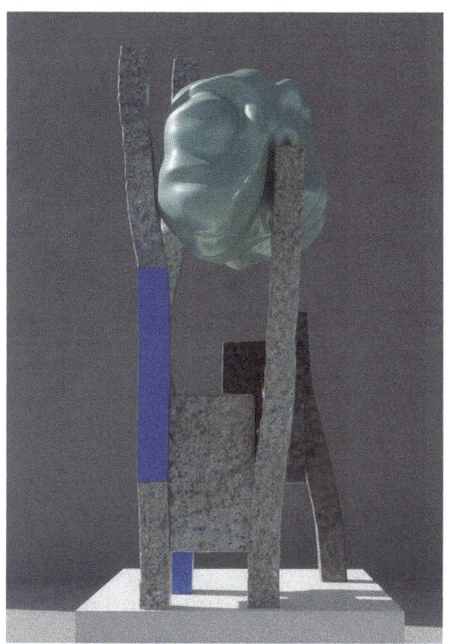

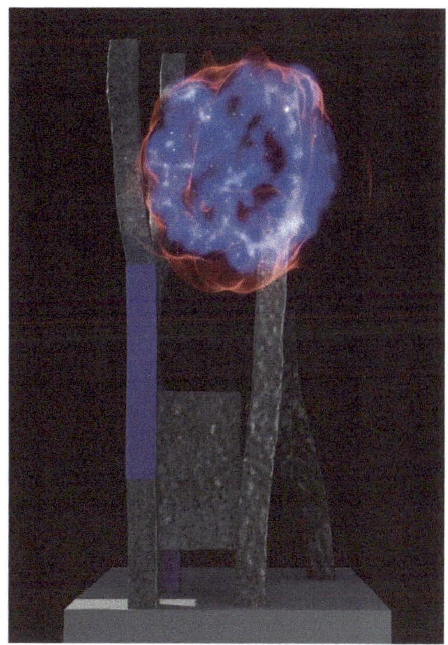

Figure 8-7. Gianpiero Moioli, Cosmic Labyrinth with Clouds*, 2025, mixed media, cm. 105 (h) x 51 x 41.*
The diptych of Cosmic Labyrinth with Clouds highlights the transition from tangible sculpture to digital transformation, where a physical form evolves into a supernova-like vision, bridging material reality and cosmic imagination

These works are configured as speculative environments that transcend conventional perception.

Their unique visual language is achieved through a rigorous hybrid workflow that systematically fuses detailed digital sculpting with cutting-edge artificial intelligence (AI) image generation.

The foundation of these ultraterrestrial landscapes begins in Blender 4.4. Here, the initial structures and forms are built using a duality of methods: manual modeling and procedural modeling. The final geometries were rendered using the Eevee engine, specifically set with 128 samples for noise reduction, an HDRI lighting setup, and exported at 2048x2048 resolution in PNG.

The finished 3D renderings were exported and then used in **Midjourney V6** via the **/blend** command (designed for combining multiple images) to generate the final images, directly combining them with the visual data from SNR 0519-69.0—the brilliant, ethereal remnant of a massive star that dramatically exploded within the Large Magellanic Cloud.

This specific combination was the core step to imbue the work with an atmosphere that is truly alien and vast.

Finally, individual frames were transformed into moving sequences through the Midjourney AI video platform, extending the work into temporal and immersive dimensions.

As captured in the phrase: "*Worlds unfold like hallucinated myths, where synthetic matter gives birth to constellations never seen, yet strangely remembered.*"

This work clearly demonstrates the technique I employ: a process that draws inspiration from the philosophical and artistic themes explored in this chapter and then expands through the use of new technologies.

Traditional sculptural gestures are reimagined through algorithmic variations, producing landscapes that are neither entirely natural nor artificial.

The result is not simply the reproduction of existing motifs but the invention of new mythologies, synthetic worlds that resonate with the memory of dreams and the logic of machines.

Through this process, the work unfolds as a living mythology—a constellation of worlds suspended between matter and vision—pointing beyond technique toward the philosophical dimension of becoming.

8.2.3 Synthetic Mythologies: Philosophical Resonances

Artists such as James Turrell, in works like *Split Decision*, create perceptual thresholds where light itself becomes a medium of transformation (Figure 8-8).

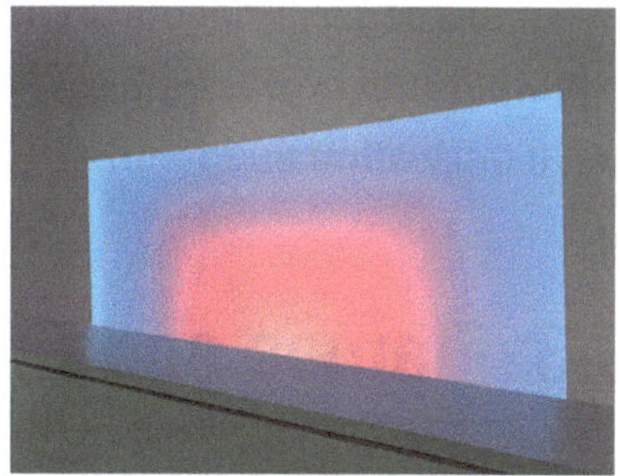

***Figure 8-8. James Turrell, Split Decision, 2018**, Kunsthalle Mannheim.*
Installation view of the light environment, where luminous fields create perceptual thresholds.
Photo by Immanuel Giel, CC0, via Wikimedia Commons

Turrell's environments remind us that perception is not passive reception but an active construction.

Similarly, Olafur Eliasson and Cao Fei expand these resonances into immersive and virtual spaces, where the visitor becomes co-creator of the environment.

Technological practices reinforce these philosophical perspectives. VR platforms such as Spatial and Unity, AI generative systems, and parametric design embody the notion of becoming through procedural logics. Forms are no longer fixed but emerge from rules and algorithms.

Just as Borges imagined infinite labyrinths and Calvino described cities suspended between reality and dream, these tools enable the creation of fluid ontologies in which every world remains provisional and open-ended.

James Turrell's Split Decision[11] exemplifies this approach.

In this walk-through environment, light becomes architectural matter.

[11] Several photographs of the installation Split Decision can be found on Wikimedia Commons: `https://commons.wikimedia.org/wiki/Category%3ASplit_Decision_%28James_Turrell%29`

The visitor crosses a corridor that leads to a luminous threshold. Color is not simply projected but inhabited, producing an immersive condition that transforms the perception of space.

The installation functions as an architectural space of light, where chromatic fields create immaterial zones and perceptual thresholds.

The title itself suggests a choice or divided passage. The spectator must cross a perceptual boundary between two suspended fields of color that appear without material support.

In this sense, Imaginary Orbits can be read as a speculative cosmology: an exploration of how art, philosophy, and technology converge to generate landscapes that are at once alien and familiar, material and immaterial, symbolic and procedural.

8.3 Flames and Energy: Breath of Fire

> *"Machines were no longer mere tools. They had become part of the life cycle, expanding and evolving like living organisms, blurring the boundaries between what was natural and what was not."*

Fire (火)—energy, transformation, combustion—represents the second stage of this journey.

It embodies flames, vital force, and the perpetual cycle of destruction and renewal, following the initial movement of cosmic expansion.

8.3.1 Fire as Material and Metaphor: Conceptual Resonances

More than a physical element, fire has always been a metaphor of change. From the myth of Prometheus[12] to the visions of modern technology, it is both origin and threat, a force that shapes matter while exceeding human control (Figure 8-9).

[12] See: `https://en.wikipedia.org/wiki/Prometheus`

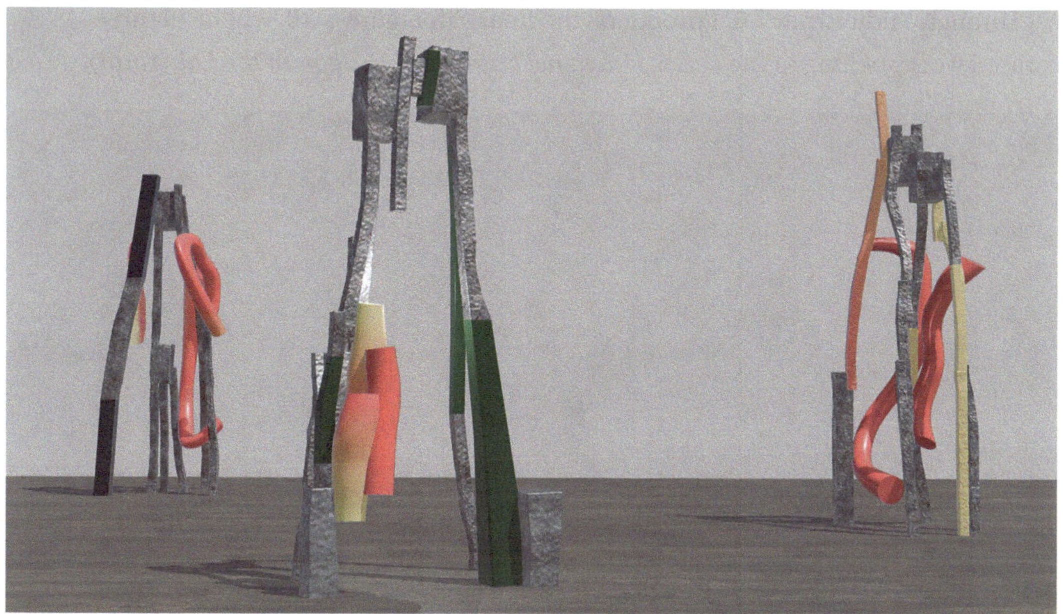

***Figure 8-9.** **Gianpiero Moioli, Sculptures from the series Fire, Energy and Transformation, 2025**, mixed media.*
Vertical structures combined with flowing, flame-like forms evoke energy, combustion and renewal, symbolizing the second stage of the journey through the elements

The sculptures shown in Figure 8-9, titled *Edifici in fiamme* (*Burning Buildings*), form part of a larger installation conceived as a city in flames.

Rising vertical structures are intersected by flowing, incandescent shapes, suggesting both architectural fragments and tongues of fire.

Together, they evoke an urban landscape consumed by combustion, where destruction and transformation are inseparably bound.

8.3.2 From Physics Simulation to AI-Driven Fire: Technical Implementation

I began the work in Blender 4.4, modeling the structures in 3D.

Using geometry nodes, I created the yellow and red tubes. While the architectural framework of the piece was modeled manually, the tubes—sinuously wrapping around the structure—were generated procedurally.

Building on this base, I then worked with AI.

Through Midjourney V6, I produced the image in Figure 8-10, where all three featured works belong to the series *Drago nel Labirinto* (*Dragon in the Labyrinth*).

Figure 8-10. Gianpiero Moioli, Dragon in the Labyrinth, 2025.
AI-generated image based on the 3D installation modeled in 3D and reinterpreted through digital and AI processes into fiery luminous forms

Starting from the 3D model of a related installation, *Edifici in fiamme* (Burning Buildings), the final aesthetic was refined using Midjourney V6. The image was generated using the Chat to Edit function by inserting the finished 3D rendering and the following prompt:

> "Transform the red and orange tubes into glowing light sources, as if illuminated by fire. Darken the surrounding environment so that the luminous tubes cast a radiant, fiery glow, enhancing contrast between light and shadow. Emphasize the atmosphere of burning energy within a dim architectural space."

This process of using the 3D rendering as a visual foundation and combining it with a highly descriptive prompt allows the AI to translate structural geometry into an expressive, atmospheric image, fulfilling the symbolic intent of the work.

In contemporary practice, this symbolism extends into technology. Artificial intelligence can ignite unexpected images like sudden sparks, generating visionary forms from textual prompts.

Just as fire transforms matter into energy, AI transmutes data and words into entire visual universes.

Likewise, immersive light installations translate the brilliance of fire into radiant environments, where light itself becomes sculptural energy, enveloping the spectator in fields of color and intensity.

Likewise, as exemplified by the approach of artists such as James Turrell and Olafur Eliasson, immersive light installations translate the interplay of elements (such as light, water, and mist) into radiant, sensorial environments.

In these spaces, light itself becomes sculptural energy, enveloping the spectator in fields of color and intensity and creating perceptual thresholds.

Fire has always carried a dual meaning. It consumes and destroys but also purifies and renews. In sculpture, it is both a literal process—melting, casting, transforming matter—and a symbolic force.

From ancient mythologies to modern narratives, fire stands as the threshold between chaos and creation.

In Chinese cosmology, fire (火 huǒ) occupies a central position within the Wu Xing cycle of elements.

It is the phase of growth and expansion, associated with summer, the color red, and the vital energies that rise upward.

Fire is movement.

For this reason, the natural extension of my three-dimensional works is animation. The transformation of static forms into dynamic ones.

I achieve this through two complementary approaches: 3D software and artificial intelligence.

In Blender, the animation process follows advanced production logic.

The animation of the camera and nonprocedural objects utilizes standard keyframe animation applied to transform properties (location, rotation, scale) to define paths.

For complex, interdependent motions, constraints, and driver-based animation are also employed.

The animation sequences are typically rendered at 24 frames per second (fps). Due to the high geometric complexity, rendering is handled by the Eevee engine, primarily leveraging GPU processing.

The output is exported as a video codec (e.g., H.264) using FFMpeg.[13]

AI offers a parallel method.

With systems like Midjourney, it is possible to generate animations by uploading individual frames and defining prompts that interpolate one image into the next.

More advanced models, such as ControlNet, extend this practice further.

For static transformations with structural preservation—such as turning structural elements into glowing tubes or shifting the atmosphere of a scene—I employ techniques based on structural conditioning (e.g., ControlNet using a depth map or Canny edge detection of the Blender render, or InstructPix2Pix for text-based editing).

This preserves the identity and structural integrity of the forms while applying sophisticated transformations directly from text instructions.

Thanks to their ability to perform precise local edits, maintain spatial coherence, and respond to context, these AI models are particularly suited to translational art practices: workflows that move fluidly between 3D modeling, rendering, and AI-mediated reinterpretation, where fire, as a metaphor of energy and transformation, becomes both process and image.

8.3.3 Synthetic Mythologies and Philosophical Closure

The same tension animates Cai Guo-Qiang's celebrated Explosion Events, where gunpowder is ignited on paper or across entire landscapes.[14]

His work treats fire as cosmology: sudden bursts of energy that inscribe themselves on earth and sky, echoing both the violence of creation and the poetry of transformation.

These explosions do not simply illustrate fire; they perform it, staging energy as spectacle and myth.

---

[13] The most significant temporal changes are achieved through Geometry Nodes. This allows parameters to be modified procedurally, producing flowing transformations over time.

Temporal changes are structured by connecting the Scene Time node to input parameters like Phase or Scale on various field/value nodes. For instance, by connecting the Scene Time node to a Wave Texture's Phase input and then using that texture to drive the displacement of a mesh via a Set Position node, we create an animated ripple effect that evolves procedurally.

[14] For an explanation of Cai Guo-Qiang's use of gunpowder to "draw" on surfaces—laying down explosive powder, igniting it, and capturing the resultant burns and residues—see *Gunpowder Drawings* at the Guggenheim. `https://www.guggenheim.org/teaching-materials/cai-guo-qiang-i-want-to-believe/gunpowder-drawings`

In his hands, fire becomes drawing, architecture, and cosmology—an elemental script that inscribes human imagination into the fabric of the universe.

Figure 8-11 shows a work by Cai Guo-Qiang in which gunpowder is used not to destroy, but to leave a lasting mark on a dress.

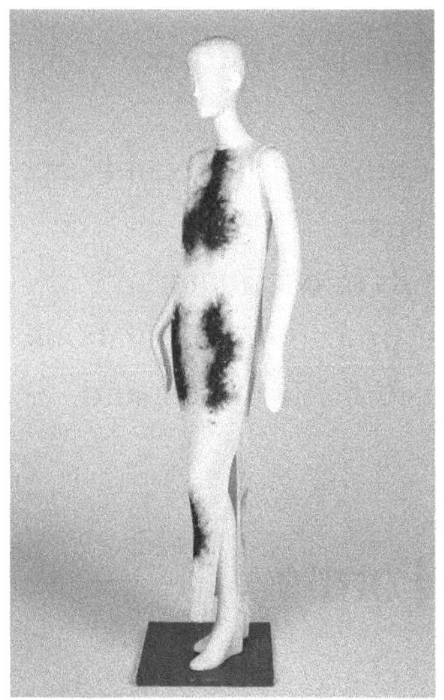
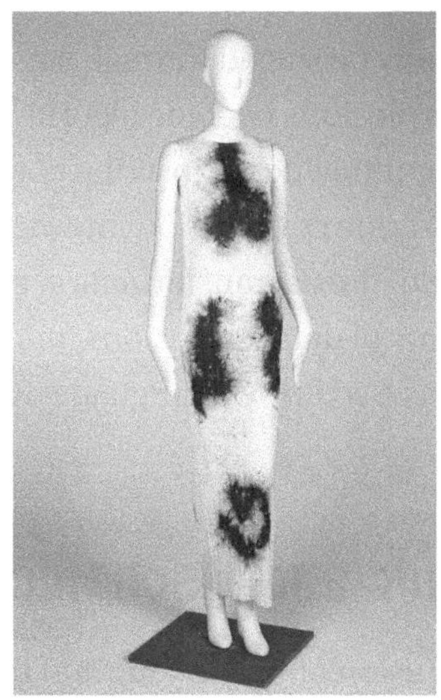
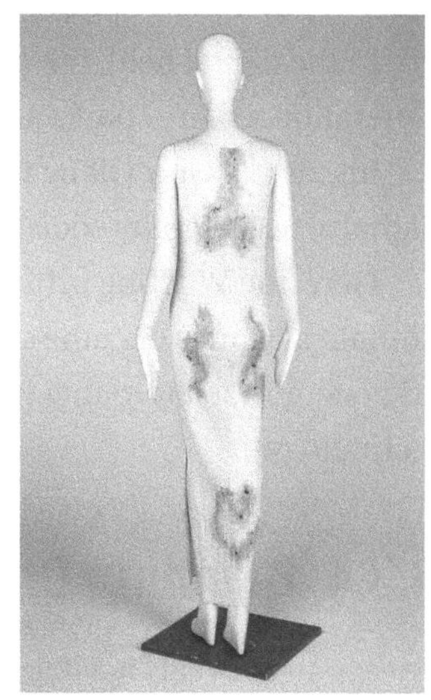

Figure 8-11. Cai Guo-Qiang, Gunpowder Dress for Issey Miyake, ca. 1998. *Pleated cotton, gunpowder. RISD Museum, Providence. Fotograph by: RISD Museum, licenza CC0.* *https://risdmuseum.org/art-design/collection/gunpowder-dress-20194, CC0*

In this way, combustion becomes both a creative and symbolic process, uniting fashion, sculpture, and performance in a single artistic gesture.

Cai Guo-Qiang placed gunpowder on white garments crafted in the shape of dragons, symbolizing life, and ignited it to imprint unique designs onto the fabric through the explosive process.

Issey Miyake later drew inspiration from these charred patterns, reproducing them as prints on fabric for his innovative Pleats Please line.[15]

In this work, fire (huǒ, 火) appears as a transformative principle; it consumes matter while simultaneously renewing and transfiguring it.

[15] Collaboration between Issey Miyake and Cai Guo-Qiang, where gunpowder explosions burned dragon motifs onto garments. https://www.metmuseum.org/art/collection/search/692445

Within the Wu Xing cycle, fire represents expansion and vitality, an energy that rises upward. Cai Guo-Qiang's dress bears the imprint of ignited gunpowder turning the violence of the explosion into an aesthetic trace.

Here, flame becomes both visual language and metaphor for an energy that fuses destruction and creation.

In the digital field, fire can now be staged through simulations and AI-driven generation, where sparks and explosions become algorithmic.

Just as Cai Guo-Qiang uses gunpowder to inscribe energy onto fabric and landscape, digital artists employ code to inscribe combustion into virtual space.

Here, the Wu Xing principle of fire as transformation expands into immaterial domains. Flames become streams of data, explosions unfold as procedural simulations, and energy itself is reimagined as a sculptural language that fuses myth, matter, and technology.

8.3.4 Blending Organic and Mechanical Forms

Energy also reveals itself in the fusion of the organic and the mechanical. In *Burning Buildings*, sculptures emerge as hybrid organisms where machinery grows like living tissue, and organic matter acquires technological rhythms.

In *Mechanical Forest*, in Figure 8-12, structures evoke a vital pulsation. Machines no longer appear as tools but as entities expanding and evolving like life forms.

Figure 8-12. Gianpiero Moioli, Mechanical Forest, 2025.
Digitally modified acrylic painting on paper and cardboard with pen drawing, cm. 100 x 150.
The work envisions a hybrid space where mechanical and organic logics intertwine, anticipating sculptural forms animated by energy and transformation

This blending has profound cultural resonances. Mary Shelley's *Frankenstein* framed the modern myth of technology as a spark that animates matter: a Promethean fire that both creates and threatens.

This is the case with *Royal Bird*, the sculpture of David Smith, where industrial metal becomes a vehicle for lyricism.

The work illustrated in Figure 8-13 may be read as a vision of an industrial and mechanical world: an environment where metallic structures and energetic flows mirror the pulse of technology itself.

Figure 8-13. David Smith, Royal Bird, 1947–48.
Welded steel. National Gallery of Art, Washington, D.C.
The work illustrated here can be read as a vision of an industrial and mechanical world—an environment in which metallic structures and energetic flows mirror the pulse of technology itself.
By Anthony Caro - Own work, Public Domain, `https://commons.wikimedia.org/w/index.php?curid=48393157`

A similar tension animates my work *Foresta meccanica* (Mechanical Forest, Figure 8-12), where metallic structures intersect with organic-like flows.

Foresta meccanica reflects a contemporary horizon in which the organic and the technological are inseparable, coexisting as parts of the same energetic field.

At the same time, it signals a further step: not only toward the digital and computational logics of informatics but also toward the generative and adaptive processes of artificial intelligence.

In fact, we are living through yet another transformation.

After the Industrial Revolution, the Digital Revolution, and the advent of the Internet, the rise of artificial intelligence marks a new and profound shift in our historical horizon.

Philip K. Dick, in *Do Androids Dream of Electric Sheep?* (1968),[16] shifted the focus from animation to consciousness, imagining artificial beings whose memories and emotions blur the very definition of the human.

Ridley Scott's *Blade Runner* (1982),[17] based on Dick's novel, visualized this ambiguity in iconic form: replicants whose inner flame is indistinguishable from human desire, set against dystopian architectures that pulse like mechanical organisms.

My works continue this dialogue in sculptural terms.

Structures recall mechanical origins, while organic shapes twist and grow like living matter.

Procedural simulations animate them with the fluidity of fire, making them appear monumental yet unstable, fixed yet alive with invisible forces.

The dialogue between organic and mechanical, natural and artificial, exposes their interdependence: energy as the connective tissue between matter, code, and imagination.

This fusion extends into moving images created with Blender and AI platforms such as Midjourney.

Physics engines and procedural nodes generate sequences where fire acts as both substance and symbol. These animations become laboratories in which digital organisms evolve frame by frame, the machine unfolding as a living script across time.

Here fire is more than metaphor: both medium and method, shaping artistic experience across physical and virtual dimensions.

Cai Guo-Qiang's explosions inscribe energy directly onto matter, while immersive light environments reinterpret fire as pure luminosity, capturing its brilliance in controlled fields.

In the digital domain, flames and sparks appear as algorithmic events: energy endlessly recomposed between code and image.

Fire thus embodies a continuum. From the violence of combustion to the immaterial glow of simulation, it becomes a sculptural principle uniting matter, light, and data within a single field of transformation.

---

[16] Philip K. Dick, *Do Androids Dream of Electric Sheep?* (1968)—see Wikipedia for summary and themes: `https://en.wikipedia.org/wiki/Do_Androids_Dream_of_Electric_Sheep%3F`

[17] Ridley Scott, *Blade Runner* (1982). See Wikipedia for details: `https://en.wikipedia.org/wiki/Blade_Runner`

Through these tools, sculpture enters the temporal dimension. It breathes, mutates, and dissolves, extending the Promethean spark into the immaterial space of data and simulation.

8.4 Spaces of Memory: Mediterranean Landscapes

> *"In the heart of Mediterranean light and stone, the boundary between body and place dissolves: here architecture breathes memory, and the void opens not to absence, but to the enduring whisper of the earth."*

Earth (土)—memory, roots, landscapes—is the element of grounding and permanence.

In the Wu Xing cycle, Earth is the center, the still point that nourishes and stabilizes every transformation.

8.4.1 Abstraction and Figuration: *Conceptual Foundations*

It is the slow accumulation of matter, the sedimentation of memory, the quiet resilience that lets life regenerate after fire and flood.

Earth is not inert substance; it is the symbolic matrix that gathers, protects, and transmits the continuity of existence.

Figure 8-14 presents works that embody this theme of Spaces of Memory.

Figure 8-14. Gianpiero Moioli, Paesaggi mediterranei (Mediterranean Landscapes), 2025.
Mixed media, variable dimensions. A series of works in which Mediterranean memory is evoked through the interplay of material structures and translucent forms, balancing figuration and abstraction

These spaces breathe Mediterranean light: ruins, olive trees, fragments of cities bathed in the gold of late summer, awakening the joy of cherished recollection. Yet in their silence lingers the shadow of nostalgia—every trace of beauty is also marked by loss.

8.4.2 Digital Transformation of Mediterranean Forms: Technical Implementation

The Mediterranean is not described here but reimagined through abstract structures and luminous, translucent volumes that recall ruins, trees, and suspended cities. Works such as Paesaggio mediterraneo (Mediterranean Landscape) and Città al tramonto (City at Sunset) balance fragile figurative echoes with bold abstract expansions, turning Earth into both matter and atmosphere, permanence, and dissolution.

This vision is further expanded through digital transformation.

Starting from a 3D rendering of the installation (produced in Blender with Eevee engine for contrasted effects), the image was reinterpreted in Midjourney using image-to-image prompting techniques, allowing the luminous elements to emerge as the sole sources of light within a darkened environment.[18]

The result is an atmosphere of late-summer twilight: a Mediterranean landscape detached from geography, suspended in abstraction, where color and light themselves become vessels of memory (Figure 8-15).

[18] Technical note on the AI workflow (for transparency and reproducibility):

(1) The reinterpretation in Midjourney was primarily achieved through image prompting with direct upload of the Blender render as a reference image, combined with iteratively refined descriptive prompts.

In some cases, the *Image to Prompt* command was used on the original render to generate base prompts, subsequently edited manually.

(2) The darkened environment was controlled via prompt engineering: positive keywords included "dark ambient atmosphere, dramatic chiaroscuro lighting, single internal light sources from glowing structures, no external sunlight, deep shadows, moody twilight"; negative prompts excluded "bright daylight, harsh sun, ambient fill light, overexposed." Only minor contrast adjustments were made in GIMP and Krita.

(3) Multiple attempts were required (20–50 generations per variant, starting with 4x grids), with selection based on structural coherence, internal luminosity, and nostalgic mood.

Success rate ~15–20 % for ideal outputs in initial batches; final images derived from upscales and remixes (Midjourney V6/V7, 2025).

(4) The 3D-to-AI translation inevitably sacrifices absolute geometric precision, rigid spatial arrangements, and exact color fidelity, introducing slight distortions and unpredictable color variations.

This loss is deliberate, as it enhances abstraction and the suspended quality of memory.

Figure 8-15. Gianpiero Moioli, Notturno mediterraneo (Mediterranean Nocturne), 2025.
AI-generated image from a 3D render in Blender 4.4, modified with Midjourney. The sculptures are reimagined as glowing presences in a nocturnal Mediterranean setting, where abstract forms radiate memory and atmosphere

This hybrid synthesis allows the work to move beyond the constraints of simulation, crystallizing the digital artifact into a specific visual poetics.

8.4.3 Earth as the Horizon of Memory: Philosophical Resonances

In Western thought, Earth has often been associated with memory and history.

From Aristotle's conception of the four elements as the fundamental principles of nature, Earth has been understood as the basis of stability and permanence, the substance that grounds all transformation.

Centuries later, Heidegger deepened this intuition in his reflection on "dwelling" (Bauen Wohnen Denken), describing Earth as the ground that shelters human existence and offers a place where being can take root.

In this sense, Earth is not merely inert matter but the horizon in which time leaves its imprint, where history, memory, and culture sediment into visible and invisible traces.

Mediterranean landscapes embody this double perspective.

They are both places of sedimented history—ruins, olive trees, stones, and stratified architectures—and spaces of light and rhythm, where matter is transfigured into atmosphere.

Artists like Alberto Burri and Anselm Kiefer have transformed earth into a field of memory, where cracks, burns, and accumulations reveal both trauma and resilience but become pictorial matter as in Sefiroth.[19]

In this work, reminiscent of the format of ancient altarpieces, Kiefer layers heavy materials such as lead to evoke sedimented landscapes of memory and transform Earth into a metaphysical field where history solidifies into matter (Figure 8-16).

[19] Detailed description and provenance of Sephiroth available at Kunsthalle Mannheim's official collection page: `https://www.kuma.art/en/node/12632`

Figure 8-16. Anselm Kiefer, Sephiroth, 2000.
Oil, emulsion, acrylic, shellac, lead on canvas and wood, 950 × 510 × 50 cm.
Kunsthalle Mannheim, Hector-Bau, Atrium.
Monumental vertical composition whose layered, scarred surface turns matter into a palimpsest of memory.
By Immanuel Giel, own work, CC0, https://commons.wikimedia.org/w/index.php?curid=168743830

Today, these logics extend into the digital domain. 3D scanning and digital heritage technologies preserve sites and artifacts, transforming earth into data, and thus into a new form of continuity between past and future.

In this sense, Earth becomes both a tangible material and a digital archive: a bridge where memory is transmitted not only through physical permanence but also through simulation and re-creation.

8.4.4 Light as Material Memory

This idea resonates with Heidegger's notion of dwelling, where Earth is understood as shelter and rooting.

It is reinterpreted in the work of Mario Merz,[20] whose *Igloos* merge primordial materials such as stone, clay, and branches, with contemporary symbols like neon writing.

These archetypal forms evoke the themes of roots, protection, and collective memory, embodying a continuity between ancient gestures and present experience (Figure 8-17).

[20] Mario Merz, a leading figure of Arte Povera, was previously discussed in Chapter 3 for his use of the Fibonacci sequence as a metaphor for organic growth.

In his series of igloos, Merz explored another archetype: the shelter. Built with primordial materials (stone, clay, branches) and, sometimes, contemporary signs (neon writing), the igloo embodies both protection and collective memory, resonating with Heidegger's idea of dwelling.

Figure 8-17. Mario Merz, Igloo di pietra, 1982.
Environmental sculpture at the Kröller-Müller Museum Sculpture Park (The Netherlands). The igloo, an archetypal form recurring throughout Merz's work, merges primordial materials with contemporary symbols, evoking roots, shelter, and collective memory.
Photo by Gerardus, own work, Public Domain, via Wikimedia Commons.
`https://commons.wikimedia.org/w/index.php?curid=4145439`

In dialogue with these artistic lineages, digital practices generate new "shelters of memory." Physical models can be scanned for preservation or reimagined in Blender as hybrid forms, inspiring new ideas and projects.

Thus, the Mediterranean landscape appears as a timeless field, suspended between matter and simulation, permanence and transformation.

My own works, such as *Natura Morta con Canestro di Frutta* (Still Life with Fruit Basket), continue this exploration (Figure 8-18).

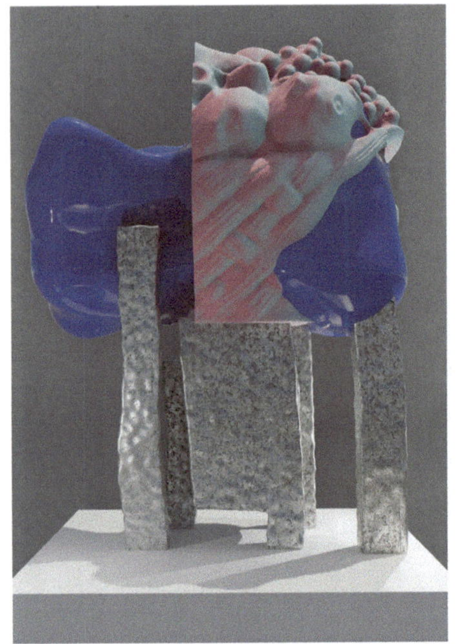

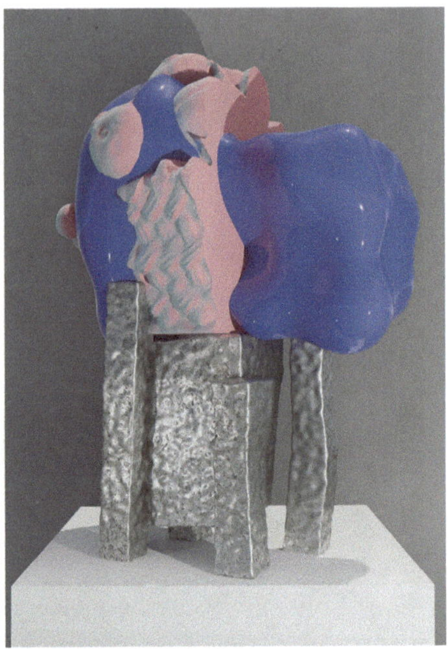

***Figure 8-18. Gianpiero Moioli, Still Life with Fruit Basket, 2025**, mixed media, cm.53 (h) x 51 x 39.*
In this work, the tradition of the still life is reinterpreted through luminous materials and digital processes. The fruit basket, a classical motif of permanence and fragility, becomes an atmospheric field where light itself is sculpted, evoking both joy and nostalgia within a Mediterranean horizon

In these pieces, light is treated as a material, captured through translucent metal and resin structures or reimagined in digital renderings with glowing effects.

This dreamlike quality arises from the way light is treated as a material presence, where physical matter glows and breathes in translucent structures and digital renderings alike.

By evoking the tradition of the "natura morta" (still life), these works connect with a long artistic lineage.

Historically, still life arranged fruit, vessels, or everyday objects as meditations on permanence, fragility, and the passage of time.[21]

[21] See: For background on the history and significance of still life (natura morta) in art, see the detailed article on Wikipedia: `https://en.wikipedia.org/wiki/Still_life#`.

Today, such compositions are reinterpreted in moments of uncertainty as sources of comfort and reflection.[22]

Once associated mainly with the domestic sphere, still life has gradually expanded into a symbolic language, able to address not only intimate reflections but also collective experiences and cultural memory.

Giorgio Morandi, for example, transformed bottles and everyday objects into meditations on memory, light, presence, and absence, demonstrating how still life could transcend the quotidian and become a vehicle for existential reflection.

In my Mediterranean reinterpretations, the still life becomes luminous and atmospheric: no longer a static table setting but a landscape of memory, where objects and light themselves become traces of joy, nostalgia, and transformation.

8.5 Metaphysical Architectures: Geometries of the Void

"Cities and squares were no longer inert settings, but living stages where memory, silence, and vision intertwined; spaces where architecture became thought, and presence opened to the imaginary."

Metal (金), in the Chinese Wu Xing system, represents structure, clarity, and contraction.

It is the element that defines form, sharpens contours, and brings order out of indeterminate matter.

Within Daoist cosmology, Metal embodies the principle of limitation that makes transformation possible; it draws borders, articulates rhythms, and allows emptiness to acquire shape.

Western philosophy has equally reflected on this relationship between form and void. Nietzsche imagined form as a counterpoint to Dionysian chaos, the Apollonian measure that opens space for thought and vision.

The dialogue between the formal definition of sculpture and the metaphysical suspension evoked in De Chirico's works forms the core of my series *Piazze d'Italia* (*Italian Squares*) (Figure 8-19) or *Metaphysical Spaces* (Figure 8-20).

[22] https://creativecommons.org/2021/02/11/still-life-art-that-brings-comfort-in-uncertain-times/

Figure 8-19. Gianpiero Moioli, Piazze d'Italia (Metaphysical Spaces), 2025, *mixed media, variable dimensions.*
A series of sculptural assemblages that reinterpret metaphysical squares through abstract fragments, architectural echoes, and luminous elements

Figure 8-20. Gianpiero Moioli, Piazze d'Italia (Metaphysical Spaces), 2025, *mixed media, variable dimensions.*
A threshold between material memory and digital imagination. Here, the Apollonian clarity of defined contours meets the Dionysian energy of raw matter and the enigmatic suspension of the void, transforming the city into a mental and visionary space

In these sculptures, the metaphysical legacy is reinterpreted through digital processes and architectural modeling, turning piazzas and essential geometries into spaces suspended between historical memory and contemporary imagination.

This Apollonian clarity can also be understood as a "lucidity of the dream": a capacity to give precise contours to Dionysian intensity.

In art, this emerges in certain surrealist and metaphysical works, where dreamlike visions are rendered with rigorous outlines and crystalline geometries, making the unconscious visible with almost architectural definition.

Christian Norberg-Schulz further developed these ideas in his notion of ***genius loci***, the "spirit of place."

For him, architecture gives form to existential space by making visible the character of a site—its atmosphere, orientation, and memory.

In this sense, form is not an abstract geometry but a way of dwelling that reveals the identity of a place and anchors human presence within it.

Titled "Geometries of the Void," this section explores imagined cities and timeless piazzas inspired by Italian metaphysical painting, reflecting emptiness, solitude, and the mental dimension of architecture.

This is what I have sought to convey through my *Metaphysical Architectures.*[23]

8.5.1 Piazzas as Thresholds

In this horizon, Mario Merz's igloos embody a different but complementary vision of metaphysical architecture.

Built from fragile fragments of marble precariously held together, they reveal the threshold quality of space: neither finished monument nor pure ruin but a place of passage where memory, fragility, and protection coexist.

The metaphysical piazza functions as a threshold between presence and absence, past and future.

Like Merz's igloos, it is never entirely stable: **a suspended space that gathers fragments, organizes silence, and opens a horizon for imagination.**

Merz began creating igloos in the late 1960s and continued throughout the following decades, experimenting with materials that combined fragility and resistance.

The versions built with marble slabs and clamps, such as the one now at the Kunsthalle Mannheim, in Figure 8-21, belongs the later phase between the 1980s and 1990s.

[23] AI-generated reinterpretations of these installations were created using Midjourney. Example prompt: "Transform the installation into a nocturnal Mediterranean piazza. The sculptures glow from within in shades of blue, turquoise, and pink, while the environment fades into darkness, illuminated only by the luminous forms—dreamlike and metaphysical atmosphere."

Figure 8-21. Mario Merz, Sculpture in Kunsthalle Mannheim, Germany. *An igloo constructed with fragments of marble slabs provisionally held together by clamps. Unlike the previous stone igloos, this work emphasizes fragility and incompleteness: the material of classical monuments becomes a precarious memory, continuously recomposed and never fixed.*
By Immanuel Giel - Own work, CC0, `https://commons.wikimedia.org/w/index.php?curid=164569135`

Here, the precarious assemblage of classical stone fragments evokes both ruin and reconstruction, a memory constantly recomposed rather than permanently fixed. In a similar vein, Fabrizio Plessi's liquid visions of Roma—the work previously mentioned in the first chapter—dissolve ancient monuments into flowing water and light, turning eternal stone into fragile, ever-shifting reflections; both artists render the classical as provisional and alive.[24]

[24] See: `https://www.artsy.net/artwork/fabrizio-plessi-roma-1`

8.5.2 Metaphysical and Digital Aesthetics

From Merz's material thresholds we move to a different but complementary lineage, one where rules and concepts themselves become the building blocks of form.

It is in this context that the work of Sol LeWitt proves decisive.

His practice resonates deeply with the principle of Metal as a system of limitation, order, and generative constraint (Figure 8-22).

Figure 8-22. Sol LeWitt, Wall Drawing 831, *Museo Guggenheim Bilbao, installation view.*
A monumental wall installation where geometric bands of vivid color expand across architectural surfaces. The work exemplifies LeWitt's conceptual approach, transforming simple rules into immersive environments that redefine space through rhythm, clarity, and abstraction.
Photo by Zarateman, own work, CC0, `https://commons.wikimedia.org/w/index.php?curid=40241089`

In LeWitt's art, the notion of structure is not imposed but unfolds from within **rule-based systems**. Walls become visual fields governed by instructions, with boundaries drawn by logic rather than by hand.

LeWitt's wall drawings and modular sculptures operate in this register. A set of rules determines which lines, colors, or modules appear, and within that constraint the work comes into being.

The boundaries are not restrictive but generative; the grid is not a cage but a field of possibility.

His works are procedural, architectural, and fundamentally design-based, emerging not from spontaneous gestures but from conceived systems.

In comparing LeWitt to Merz's igloos, we encounter two complementary gestures. Merz gathers fragments and breathes memory into thresholds, while LeWitt fashions entire fields of invisible rules, limiting to liberate vision.

In my own *Metaphysical Architectures*, these thresholds are reinterpreted through sculptural assemblages that merge classical echoes with digital processes, transforming the void into a geometry of memory and vision.

8.5.3 From Digital Geometry to Physical Matter: Technical Implementation

Works such as *Metamorfosi*, in Figure 8-23, explore this dialogue.

Figure 8-23. Gianpiero Moioli, Metamorphosis, 2025*, mixed media, cm. 662 (h) × 40 × 32.*
A sculptural assemblage where a fractured classical head is reimagined through metallic textures and translucent digital volumes.
The work embodies a state of transition, balancing memory and transformation, permanence and the immaterial

Classical forms are not merely cited but fractured, recomposed, and intertwined with luminous digital volumes, embodying a suspension between permanence and transformation.

Using digital modeling in Blender, I create suspended architectural forms that can be translated into 3D prints

The leap from digital imagination to physical sculpture is never automatic; it demands a disciplined, love-filled conversation between the virtual model and the real-world behavior of matter.

This workflow is not just a technical sequence; it is a ritual of translation in which the digital file learns to breathe, weigh, and age in the physical world, while never betraying the original poetic intention.[25]

These works express the idea that sculpture and architecture are a field of thought and imagination: an image of space and time.

In this way, the sculptures unfold between physical and digital dimensions, aligned with the chapter's exploration of invisible thresholds.

8.6 Flowing Horizons: Mountains, Rivers, and Forests

"In these forests where roots entwine with circuits and rivers carry both memory and code, the question is no longer who tames whom—only how far the current will carry us together."

[25] Everything begins in Blender 5.0. From the very first rough block-out, I export the STL file for preparation. Slicing is performed in Ultimaker Cura 5.8, targeting an Anycubic Kobra 3 Max (400 × 400 × 520 mm build volume). Because many of my metaphysical architectures exceed these dimensions, I split the model into two clean halves during the design phase, with integrated rectangular pins and sockets for perfect registration. Printing parameters are always the same family: 0.20 mm layer height, 15–20 % gyroid infill, tree supports only where strictly needed, and PLA+ filament (neutral or pre-colored). Once printed supports are removed by hand, the two halves are joined with two-component structural epoxy (Loctite HY 4070 or equivalent) under light clamping for 24 hours, followed by progressive sanding (180 ➤ 400 grit) and occasional spot-filling with epoxy putty. Final finish is applied by brush and spray in several thin layers: acrylic primer, polyurethane enamel (satin or metallic), and, when desired, subtle patina effects. When the PLA prototype is validated, I often create a silicone mold (platinum-cure, usually Smooth-On Rebound 25 or Dragon Skin 30) so the same form can be reborn in resin, bronze (lost-PLA casting), or other materials— thus completing the circle from digital dream to multiple material incarnations.

Water (水)—fluidity, transformation, flow—is the softest yet most powerful element, dissolving boundaries and carving paths through resistance (Figure 8-24).

Figure 8-24. Gianpiero Moioli, Mountains, Rivers, and Forests, installation, 2025.
This work reinterprets archetypal elements of the landscape—vertical forms as mountains and forests, fluid chromatic volumes as rivers and transformations—suggesting a symbolic topography where erosion and regeneration coexist

Water flows into immersive installations and AI-driven simulations, where fluid dynamics and real-time rendering generate rivers of light and sound.

As a principle, it embodies transformation itself. Dissolving solid forms into experience, it becomes the medium through which perception is reshaped and worlds are continuously remade.

This section explores landscapes, inspired also by Chinese Shan Shui painting, reinterpreted through a hybrid lens where nature and artifice merge.

Mountains, rivers, and forests are not neutral settings but archetypal structures, embodying permanence and transformation.

Sculpture here acts as a symbolic topography: a terrain where duration, erosion, and regeneration unfold.

8.6.1 Natural Dialogues

Landscapes are symbolic matrices shaping perception.

Mountains evoke solidity, rivers embody flow, and forests recall organic rhythm.

In these sculptures, vertical structures intersect with fluid, colored insertions.

In Daoist thought, water (水, shuǐ) is the most yielding of elements yet the most powerful, capable of carving valleys and eroding mountains.

Laozi wrote in the Daodejing: *"Nothing in the world is as soft and yielding as water. Yet for dissolving the hard and inflexible, nothing can surpass it."*[26]

In this sense, water here is not only a metaphor of flow but a spiritual principle of transformation, impermanence, and resilience.

Western philosophy, too, has seen the landscape as a mirror of inner states.

From Heraclitus' river, which reminds us that no one can ever step into the same waters twice, the flow of water has long symbolized change as the essence of existence.

The sculptural landscape inherits this duality and embodies the endurance of rock and the ceaseless passage of water, fusing them in a single form.

Through procedural modeling and AI recomposition, landscape ceases to imitate nature and instead generates new horizons of perception.

Just as in traditional Chinese Shan Shui painting, where mountains and waters are more than topography—acting as metaphors of harmony, balance, and spiritual energy—here the sculptural landscape is conceived as a symbolic field.

In digital rivers, sculpted through code, water is no longer fluid matter but a field of data, an artificial current that still evokes memory and flow.

Immersive technologies such as VR and AR extend this metaphor, producing navigable spaces where the viewer does not merely observe the landscape but drifts inside it, as if inhabiting a dream.

[26] Laozi, Dao De Jing, ch. 78: "Nothing in the world is as soft and yielding as water. Yet for dissolving the hard and inflexible, nothing can surpass it." Translation by Stephen Mitchell, 1988.

This movement from **natural archetypes** to **synthetic horizons** echoes the narratives of Calvino's *Invisible Cities,* where landscapes are symbolic constructions, thresholds between reality and imagination.

Similarly, algorithmic forests and artificial rivers are not simply simulations but new mythologies: places where nature is rewritten by code, and perception itself becomes the terrain of artistic invention.

In this dialogue between nature and artifice, Giuseppe Penone's works remind us that sculpture can itself become landscape.

Figure 8-25. Giuseppe Penone, Tra scorza e scorza (Entre écorce et écorce), 2003.

Bronze and oak, installation at the Parterre d'Eau of the Château de Versailles, part of the exhibition Penone Versailles. Set against the classical sculpture of Nymph and Zephyr, the work establishes a dialogue between nature and culture: "What interests me is when man's work begins to become nature." *(Giuseppe Penone).*

Photo by Jean-Pierre Dalbéra, CC BY 2.0 `https://commons.wikimedia.org/w/index.php?curid=37214903`

In *Tra scorza e scorza* (2003), installed at the Parterre d'Eau in Versailles, a carved wooden trunk rises among classical figures, evoking the transformation of human gesture into nature.[27]

As Penone states, "*What interests me is when man's work begins to become nature.*"

8.6.2 Fluid Landscapes and Synthetic Natures

If Calvino imagined cities as mirrors of desire and memory, here sculpture opens landscapes where matter itself seems to flow (Figure 8-25). This fluid interpretation of the environment resonates with Penone's vision, where the sculptural act does not merely depict nature but seeks to merge with its organic processes, turning the artificial back into the living.

In my work, this dialogue shifts toward a synthetic horizon where the organic is rewritten through the industrial and the digital. Metallic fragments rise like artificial cliffs, while translucent and luminous volumes recall water in perpetual motion.

It is within this context that *Alien Landscape with Sunset*, in Figure 8-26, appears, where fluidity is no longer only a quality of landscape but a principle of metamorphosis that reshapes the horizon itself.

[27] The motif of metamorphosis recalls Gian Lorenzo Bernini's Apollo and Daphne (1622–25, Galleria Borghese, Rome), where the body of the nymph is transfigured into tree bark and leaves, embodying the fusion of human and vegetal forms: `https://en.wikipedia.org/wiki/Apollo_and_Daphne_%28Bernini%29`

***Figure 8-26. Gianpiero Moioli, Alien Landscape with Sunset, 2025,** mixed media, cm. 55 (h) x 58 x 35.*
In this work, fluidity is no longer just a quality of landscape but a principle of metamorphosis that shapes space itself

Mythological echoes emerge in the shifting forms. The artificial sunset evokes ancient tales of transformation, where identities and elements dissolve into one another, embodying the ambiguity and transformative power of water.

Through its sculptural form, the work does not depict water directly but alludes to it symbolically, translating its flowing and transformative nature into a landscape of matter and light.

By contrast, Olafur Eliasson's immersive installations—mist, waterfalls, rainbows, or the blinding glare of artificial suns—no longer represent natural elements but evoke them as total sensorial experiences.

Light, temperature, humidity, and color dissolve bodily boundaries, turning the visitor into an integral part of a living, liquid landscape of perception.

In both cases, water is not merely an iconographic subject but an active principle shaping perception, identity, and the relationship with the environment.

Eliasson's work thus exemplifies a broader shift in contemporary art: from the representation of nature to its re-embodiment through immersive and participatory practices.

Here, water becomes not only a theme but a medium, dissolving the distance between artwork and spectator (Figure 8-27).

Figure 8-27. Olafur Eliasson, immersive installation.
From the exhibition "Olafur Eliasson. In Real Life/Bizitza errealean", co-organized by Tate Modern and the Guggenheim Bilbao, 2020–2021.
The work turns the exhibition space into a total chromatic environment, where fog and colored light envelop the visitor.
The body loses its visual bearings and plunges into a liquid landscape, conceived as a sensorial and spiritual experience.
Photo by Makeip, own work, CC0, Wikimedia Commons. `https://commons.wikimedia.org/w/index.php?curid=103497305`

This trajectory reflects the deeper transformation of artistic languages in the digital age, where elements are experienced as processes, environments, and relations rather than static forms.

In this sense, the aquatic principle resonates both with Daoist thought—where water embodies adaptability and transformation—and with Western aesthetics that explore fluidity as a metaphor for identity and becoming.

8.7 Conclusions

Chapter 8 has unfolded through five symbolic journeys—**Cosmic and Artificial Worlds, Flames and Energy, Spaces of Memory, Metaphysical Architectures, and Flowing Horizons**—each reflecting a different dimension of artistic imagination.

Taken together, they form a constellation where natural archetypes, cultural memory, and speculative invention converge.

The dialogue between organic and artificial and between tradition and technology is not resolved but continuously renegotiated, producing works that inhabit both matter and code, both image and story.

In this sense, the Five Journeys may also be read in resonance with the cosmology of the Five Elements (Wǔxíng 五行), where growth, transformation, and renewal arise from cycles of generation and control.

The artworks are not isolated artifacts but dynamic nodes in a process of becoming, shaped as much by imagination and narrative as by material or algorithmic form.

As a sculptor, I also work within this horizon. Through new technologies of animation, VR interactivity, and AI, form itself can be conceived as movement, flowing in time and space like a fluid entity rather than a fixed object.

By tracing these paths, the chapter points to a new horizon: a field where sculpture no longer resides only in objects but in expanded scenarios of perception and interaction.

This prepares the ground for the explorations that follow in Part IV, where the imaginary is not only represented but inhabited, as artistic creation extends into immersive and metaverse environments.

8.8 Appendix L: Defining Procedural and Generative Methods: Technical Taxonomy (2025)

To ensure methodological rigor throughout this work, the following taxonomy distinguishes procedural, parametric, and machine-learning generative approaches.

All references in the book adhere to these definitions.

Category	Definition	Core Mechanism	Determinism
Procedural	Content created via explicit algorithms, rules, or mathematical functions defined by the artist.	Rule-based systems (if-then, recursion, noise functions)	Deterministic (same seed ➤ same output)
Parametric	Geometry driven by numerical parameters and relational constraints; changing one value propagates changes across the model.	Constraint-based modelling (CAD-style)	Deterministic
Machine-Learning Generative	Content derived from statistical models trained on large datasets (e.g., diffusion models, GANs, autoregressive transformers).	Latent-space sampling + stochastic noise	Non-deterministic (unless seed fixed)

8.8.1 Tooling and Application Examples (2025)

Category	Typical Tools (2025)	Examples in This Book
Procedural	**Blender** Geometry Nodes, **Houdini** VEX, **Substance Designer**, **TouchDesigner** CHOPs	L-systems (vegetal forms), Perlin/Voronoi **noise texturing**, particle systems, **fractal landscapes**
Parametric	**Rhino** + Grasshopper, **Fusion 360**, **Onshape**, **Blender** Modifiers	Architectural variations, scalable modular sculptures, dimension-driven forms
Machine-Learning Generative	**Stable Diffusion 3.5**, **Midjourney V7**, Flux.1, Kling 2.5, Runway Gen-4	Image-to-3D conversion, **texture synthesis**, stylistic transfer, video continuation

8.9 Appendix M: Project Toolchain and Hardware Specifications (December 2025)

Computational Environment

- **GPU:** NVIDIA GeForce RTX 4070 Ti (12 GB VRAM)
- **CPU:** AMD Ryzen 9 7950X (16-core)
- **RAM:** 32 GB DDR5-6000
- **Storage:** 2 TB
- **OS:** Windows 11 Pro 24H2

Software Stack

- **3D & Simulation:** Blender 5.0.1 LTS (Geometry Nodes + Simulation Nodes)
- **Generative AI (Local):** Stable Diffusion 3.5 Large (via ComfyUI 2025.11)
- **Generative AI (Cloud):** Midjourney V7.0.1.240
- **Real-time & Interactive:** TouchDesigner 2025.35120 Official
- **Fabrication:** Ultimaker Cura 5.8
- **Development:** Python 3.11.9, PyTorch 2.4.1

Project Archive: All project files, prompts, and node graphs are archived at: `https://github.com/Apress/Art-Between-Matter-and-Code` (CC-BY-4.0)

8.10 Appendix N: Workflow Diagrams

- **L.1 Overall Hybrid Pipeline:**

  A comprehensive map tracing the evolution from hand **sketch ➤ AI latent space ➤ 3D mesh ➤ physical matter.**

- **L.2 Image-to-Video Loop:**

  Detailed flow for the *Alien Birds* series: **Midjourney ➤ Kling ➤ TouchDesigner (real-time processing).**

- **L.3 Physics Engine Integration:**

  Workflow showing **Blender Simulation Nodes** generating depth/normal maps for **ControlNet** conditioning.

- **L.4 Phygital Materialization:**

  The translation path from **STL ➤ Cura Slicing ➤ Anycubic Kobra 3 Max ➤ Lost-PLA bronze casting.**

8.11 Appendix O: Technical Specifications per Artwork

Work	Dimensions/ Format	Primary Software	AI Tool & Version	Key Parameters	Avg. Time
Gravitational Field	50 × 70 cm (Print)	Blender 5.0.1	Midjourney V7	Guidance 28, Steps 50	8–12 h
Alien Birds	10s loop, 4K	TouchDesigner	Kling 2.6 Pro	Motion 0.7, CFG 9	45 min
Cosmic Labyrinth	105×51×41 cm	Blender ➤ Bronze	SD 3.5	ControlNet Depth/ Normal	20 h+

8.12 Appendix P: Representative Prompts and Node Samples

8.12.1 N.1 Visual Prompts (Sample Copy)

- **Gravitational Field (Midjourney V7):**

  Gravitational field diagram, orbital paths, radiating force lines, dark cosmic background, high contrast luminous threads, abstract geometry, cinematic lighting --ar 3:2 --v 7 --q 2 --stylize 750

- **Alien Birds (Stable Diffusion 1.5):**

  Crystalline alien birds dissolving into cosmic dust, seamless morphing, iridescent feathers, dark void background, slow majestic motion, cinematic, 10 second loop --motion 3

8.12.2 N.2 Geometry Nodes Snippet

- **Logic:** Voronoi fracture combined with force field attraction for particle-based "dissolution" effects.
- **Source:** Reference.blend file: /nodes/logic_fracture_v5.blend

PART IV

The Metaverse and Immersive Spaces

> *"Like any place in Reality, the Street is subject to development. Developers can build their own small streets feeding off the main one... Avatars can meet, talk, exchange information, or just hang out in the Metaverse."*
>
> —Neal Stephenson, *Snow Crash* (1992)

The concept of the metaverse, once confined to the realm of science fiction,[1] has become a transformative paradigm for art and culture.

Virtual environments originated from early digital experiments, specifically the text-based MUDs of the late 1970s, beginning with the first MUD in 1978 and expanding throughout the 1980s.

Later, with the launch of three-dimensional social worlds such as Second Life in June 2003, these platforms evolved from narrative-driven games into expansive 3D spaces for social interaction and creativity.

Today, blockchain-enabled ecosystems such as Decentraland and The Sandbox, as well as traditional cloud-based platforms like Spatial, host exhibitions, performances, and global events, where artworks circulate as NFTs and galleries become participatory, borderless spaces.

---

[1] The term *metaverse* was coined in the science fiction novel *Snow Crash* by Neal Stephenson, published in 1992 (Oxford English Dictionary). In the book, Stephenson introduces the concept of a three-dimensional virtual world accessible via head-mounted displays, where users—represented by avatars—can socialize, work, and interact within a shared digital environment. The Metaverse in the novel is a vibrant yet chaotic space, organized around a central thoroughfare called "The Street," and filled with customizable virtual locations.

At the same time, immersive experiences have also unfolded in physical space, pioneered by artists and collectives such as Studio Azzurro, which transformed galleries into responsive environments through video, sensors, and interactive projections.

In these spaces, the spectator's body is not only a presence but an active component of the artwork.

Part IV explores this double trajectory.

On one side, in Chapter 9, it investigates the metaverse and immersive virtual spaces, where art challenges the boundaries of authenticity, ownership, and curatorial practice in decentralized platforms.

On the other, in Chapter 10, it turns to interactive real spaces, where embodied experience redefines participation within tangible environments.

Together, they outline a continuum between the virtual and the physical, suggesting new ways in which art reshapes presence, interaction, and exhibition-making in the 21st century.

CHAPTER 9

The Metaverse as an Exhibition Space: Virtual Immersive Spaces

This chapter examines how metaverse exhibition spaces redefine art display, authenticity, and ownership through **extended reality (XR)**—including **virtual reality (VR)**, **augmented reality (AR)**, and **mixed reality (MR)**—as well as virtual platforms such as **Second Life**, **Decentraland**, and **Spatial** where artworks can be exhibited and experienced remotely (Figure 9-1).[1]

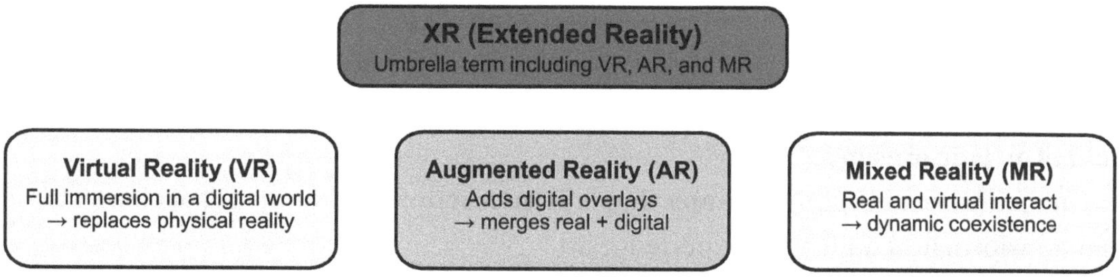

XR (Extended Reality)
Umbrella term including VR, AR, and MR

Virtual Reality (VR)
Full immersion in a digital world
→ replaces physical reality

Augmented Reality (AR)
Adds digital overlays
→ merges real + digital

Mixed Reality (MR)
Real and virtual interact
→ dynamic coexistence

Figure 9-1. Types of immersive and interactive exhibition environments. *Diagram showing the main categories of immersive and interactive art spaces*

[1] Extended reality is an umbrella term encompassing all immersive technologies that blend physical and digital environments to varying degrees.

It includes virtual reality, which includes fully simulated digital worlds; augmented reality, which includes digital overlays enhancing the real world; and mixed reality, which includes hybrid environments where real and virtual elements coexist and interact in real time.

Together, these technologies define a continuum of immersive media, expanding the boundaries of artistic creation, exhibition, and participation.

G. Moioli, *Art Between Matter and Code*, https://doi.org/10.1007/979-8-8688-2376-3_9

The concept of XR introduces a continuum between physical and digital experience, redefining how space, presence, and perception are constructed in contemporary art.

This spectrum is defined by specific technical implementations:

- VR creates fully immersive, 360-degree computer-generated environments accessed via headsets, completely isolating the viewer from the physical world.
- AR overlays digital data onto the user's view of the real world, typically through smartphones, tablets, or AR glasses.
- MR further blurs these lines by anchoring virtual objects in physical space with spatial awareness and real-time interaction, as demonstrated by devices like the **Apple Vision Pro**, **Microsoft HoloLens**, or **Meta Quest 3** (with passthrough MR mode).

While each mode offers a distinct balance between real and simulated environments, they all share the same goal: to dissolve the boundary separating the viewer from the work.

In virtual exhibitions, this continuum becomes a curatorial tool. Artists can design entire worlds or layered environments that expand beyond material space, inviting visitors to inhabit rather than merely observe the artwork.

Through XR, the act of viewing evolves into an act of *being within*: an embodied, multisensory experience where perception, movement, and data merge into a single field of artistic presence.

In metaverse exhibitions, **immersion** and **interaction** are foundational elements that transform how audiences experience art.

Immersion refers to the sensation of being enveloped by the exhibition environment, whether through physical means like stepping into a real-world installation, or virtual means, like entering a VR/AR space.

A paradigmatic precursor to this immersive logic can be found in Yves Klein's blue monochromes.

Works such as IKB 191 (1962), shown in Figure 9-2, do not represent an object but an immaterial field that envelops the viewer. By transforming color into a total perceptual environment, Klein anticipated the metaverse's ability to invite audiences into an 'immaterial architecture'—an arena for lived experience rather than mere observation.

Figure 9-2. Yves Klein, IKB 191, 1962.
International Klein Blue. Public Domain via Wikimedia Commons.
Klein's monochrome canvases created entire environments through the intensity of a single color, anticipating immersive experience

In this sense, Klein's work can be read as a precursor to the metaverse, where space is no longer defined by physical boundaries but by immersive conditions that surround the viewer. Just as Klein invited audiences to "enter" the infinite depth of blue, metaverse platforms like Decentraland or Spatial invite participants to inhabit digital fields where presence, interaction, and authorship are redefined.

The continuity between Klein's immaterial painting and today's virtual landscapes shows how the search for new experiential spaces—beyond the object and beyond representation—has long been central to artistic experimentation.

Interaction instead denotes the active engagement of viewers with the artwork or environment, often influencing the outcome or experience.

In virtual immersive spaces, these two facets converge. The audience is surrounded by the artwork and simultaneously able to interact with it, blurring the line between observer and participant.

This dynamic is **redefining the traditional passive viewing experience** into an active, participatory encounter.

Since the digital turn of the 1990s, immersive art has developed through a 'double trajectory' framework: one rooted in physical environments that envelop the body, and another in virtual worlds that surround perception through digital interfaces.

Neither path is entirely new, both evolve from a long history of panoramic paintings and early cinema, which sought to dissolve the distance between the viewer and the image.

Today, **interactive art installations** and **virtual platforms** continue to evolve these parallel paths, merging physical and digital realms into a single, cohesive experience.

Museums now combine physical settings with VR or AR stations, while virtual galleries emulate the spatial qualities of real architecture.

The result is a hybrid model of immersion that engages both body and mind.

The metaverse, in this sense, does not break with exhibition traditions but extends them, merging sensory embodiment with digital presence to create a seamless continuum between the real and the virtual.[2]

9.1 Curatorial Possibilities and Early Virtual Exhibitions

This section examines curatorial possibilities, new forms of viewer engagement, and the transformation of exhibitions into dynamic, participatory environments where audiences actively shape the art experience.

Real-time 3D engines and **collaborative virtual platforms** enable artists to design virtual galleries, immersive museums, and hybrid AR-enhanced exhibitions that transcend physical constraints, blending digital and material aesthetics.

[2] In an interview on Virtual Vernissage, Mario Gerosa and Gianpiero Moioli describe virtual galleries as a complement rather than an alternative to physical ones. See: `https://www.virtualvernissage.com/gianpiero-moioli-le-gallerie-virtuali-complemento-non-alternativa-a-quelle-vere/`

It also addresses technical and conceptual challenges, from optimizing virtual environments to rethinking authenticity in digital contexts.

The practical section provides actionable workflows inspired by contemporary practices, including Albertini & Moioli's virtual exhibitions developed in the mid-2000s.

Among these, *macchine per fare le bolle* (The bubble machines, 2007) stands out as a **groundbreaking** example of interactive virtual sculpture (Figure 9-3).

Figure 9-3. Albertini & Moioli, Le macchine per fare le bolle (The bubble machines), 2007*.*
Interactive virtual installation, Lifelog Island, Second Life. Coordination by Mario Gerosa; sound commentary by Furio Sollazzi.
Still from the video documentation of the installation (December 2007), showing the interactive behavior of the three bubble-generating structures responding to the avatar's presence and movement

Presented on **Lifelog Island** in December 2007, the installation by Albertini and Moioli—coordinated by **Mario Gerosa** with audio commentary by **Furio Sollazzi**—represented a sophisticated use of the platform's early capabilities.

Technically, the work utilized **Linden Scripting Language (LSL)** to manage complex **particle systems**, which at the time were subject to significant constraints. Scripts had a memory limit of **64KB**, and the visual output was heavily dependent on the viewer's hardware and the region's "lag" (server-side latency).

Working within these technical parameters, the artists used interactivity to transform static 3D objects into dynamic experiences.

While virtual art had existed in Second Life since roughly 2004, *Le macchine per fare le bolle* was inaugural in its structured curatorial approach (Figure 9-4).

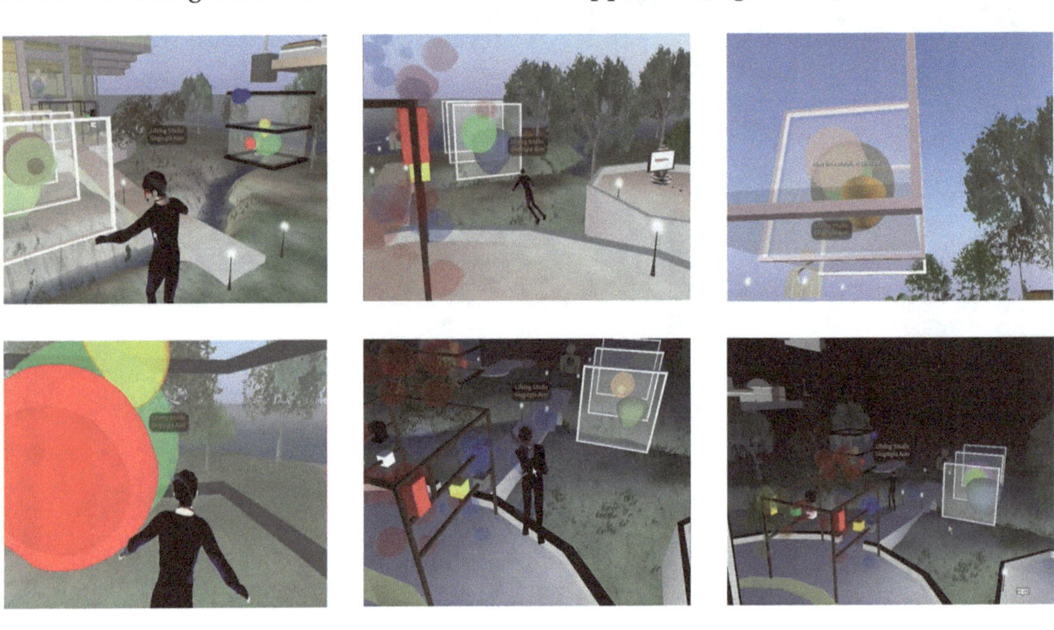

Figure 9-4. Le macchine per fare le bolle (The bubble-making machines, 2007).
Frames from the interactive virtual installation by Albertini & Moioli. The images show Giugiogia Auer interacting with the three bubble-generating sculptures, whose transparent, luminous forms react dynamically to proximity and movement within the virtual environment

This project bridged the gap between traditional art criticism and the emerging metaverse, establishing a formal precedent for how 3D sculpture could be curated and documented within a persistent digital world.[3]

The installation consisted of **three interactive virtual sculptures** that continuously generated streams of transparent, luminous bubbles.

These bubbles responded in real time to the **presence and movement of the avatar**, altering their **flow, size, and color** as the visitor approached. The interaction produced a dynamic choreography of light and motion, in which the virtual forms appeared to breathe and adapt to the participant's gestures.

The **sound environment**, also reactive, evolved in parallel with the visual transformations: subtle changes in pitch, rhythm, and resonance accompanied the movement of the avatar, creating a seamless dialogue between vision and sound.

Through this multisensory responsiveness, the visitor's digital body became a generative element within the work—an agent capable of reshaping the installation's behavior.

By merging motion, sound, and viewer participation, *The Bubble-Making Machines* transformed virtual sculpture into an autonomous and living system, revealing the poetic potential of immaterial matter within early metaverse environments.

Following its presentation on Lifelog Island in Second Life, the installation was later re-created and exhibited within the experimental and educational virtual space of the Brera Academy in OpenSim.

Here, the project evolved from an individual artwork into a shared environment—a place for exploration, teaching, and collective creation—extending the academy's research into the new frontiers of immersive media.

Among the virtual islands designed for Brera, one was conceived as a digital reinterpretation of Isola Comacina, symbolically linking the academy's physical and virtual geographies: a landscape reimagined as an interactive, navigable world (Figure 9-5).[4]

---

[3] The project is documented in this YouTube video available at `https://www.youtube.com/watch?v=-61guG5Lyqc`.

[4] Isola Comacina was donated to the Accademia di Belle Arti di Brera in 1940 and is today managed by the Fondazione Isola Comacina, established to preserve the site and host artist residencies in collaboration with the Academy.

Figure 9-5. Aerial view of one of the Brera Academy's virtual islands in OpenSim.
A Mediterranean dreamscape where art, architecture, and imagination intertwine across the threshold between physical and virtual worlds

These early experiments **already integrated** the participatory logic of today's metaverse platforms, transforming exhibition spaces into evolving ecosystems of interaction and perception.

9.2 Immersion and Interaction in Metaverse Exhibitions

Immersive virtual galleries are digital exhibition spaces designed to provide the feeling of presence within an art environment, often accessible via VR headsets or 3D desktop interfaces.

Unlike flat web pages or catalog images, these galleries allow visitors to *step inside* a three-dimensional space and walk among artworks.

Many institutions and designers turned to immersive virtual galleries during the late 2010s and early 2020s, especially when the COVID-19 pandemic forced physical closures.[5]

The curatorial aim was often to replicate—and then surpass—the experience of a physical gallery.

A landmark early example (2021) was **Sotheby's** digital replica of its New Bond Street headquarters in Decentraland's Voltaire Art District (coordinates 52,83).[6]

Operating on the Ethereum blockchain with one to two parcels (100m^2 total) supporting 20–50 concurrent browser-based avatars, this 3D web environment (WebGL/WebXR, limited VR compatibility) allowed visitors to navigate five gallery rooms and view curated NFT collections.

Although the space closed in 2025, it remains an influential historical precedent for blockchain-based provenance display.

Another high-profile example is the **"NFTism" virtual gallery by Zaha Hadid Architects**, presented at Art Basel Miami, which was expressly designed to explore new modes of social interaction in a virtual art space.[7]

In this immersive gallery, architecture was not merely a backdrop for art but a co-creator of the experience. Fluid, futuristic halls shaped how users moved and communicated, underscoring that in VR galleries the *space itself* can be an artistic medium.

This section examines how metaverse platforms create immersive and interactive exhibition spaces, transforming traditional art presentation into dynamic, viewer-driven experiences.

The history of immersive virtual worlds is the result of converging trajectories in hardware innovation, networked computing, and narrative agency.

While the technical foundations were laid by pioneers like **Ivan Sutherland**, whose ***Sword of Damocles* (1968)** introduced the first head-mounted display, the conceptual framework for shared environments drew significantly from analog role-playing.[8]

---

[5] See: https://observer.com/2020/03/occupy-white-walls-online-game-museum-curating-art-collection/

[6] Verified via Sotheby's 2021 press release and Decentraland archives (June 4, 2021); status confirmed inactive as of Forbes Digital Assets (Oct 2025)

[7] See: https://www.zaha-hadid.com/design/nftism-at-art-basel-miami-beach/

[8] See: https://quantumzeitgeist.com/immersive-worlds-tracing-the-history-of-virtual-reality/ and https://pebblestudios.co.uk/2017/08/when-was-virtual-reality-invented/

The launch of **Dungeons & Dragons in 1974** was pivotal,[9] as it established the logic of a shared imaginary world governed by formal rules and player agency. This ludic structure soon intersected with emerging networked systems.

Before the rise of MUDs, the **PLATO system** in the 1970s hosted the first multi-user games, blending D&D and inspired mechanics with real-time digital interaction.

Parallel developments in military and NASA flight simulations further refined the spatial awareness required for these environments.

This lineage—from tabletop role-playing and early academic networks to sophisticated simulation research—eventually coalesced into persistent virtual worlds and contemporary spatial computing platforms.

Here, imagination, spoken words, and rulebooks created collective worlds where players inhabited characters and shaped unfolding narratives.

This tabletop game introduced the idea of a shared fictional space governed by both storytelling and structured rules.

In the late 1970s and early 1980s, these principles migrated into the digital domain through the birth of multi-user dungeons (MUDs).[10]

Entirely text-based, MUDs allowed players to navigate virtual environments by typing commands like *north, look,* or *attack dragon.*

What made them extraordinary was the simplicity of their construction. Entire worlds were generated through words, a network connection, and minimal code.

Despite their immateriality, they provided a powerful collective experience of co-presence, where users could explore, build, and interact in real time within a persistent space sustained only by language and logic.

Just as Yves Klein's monochrome canvases created entire environments through the intensity of a single color, the first virtual worlds of Dungeons & Dragons and MUDs emerged from the generative power of words.

A pure hue and a typed command share the same radical gesture: transforming minimal signs into immersive worlds.

---

[9] *Dungeons & Dragons* is considered the first modern role-playing game (RPG).

It introduced the concept of a shared imaginary world governed by rules, narrative structure, and player agency, elements that later informed the design of early online environments and virtual worlds such as MUDs and, eventually, metaverse platforms. https://en.wikipedia.org/wiki/Dungeons_%26_Dragons

[10] See: https://en.wikipedia.org/wiki/Multi-user_dungeon

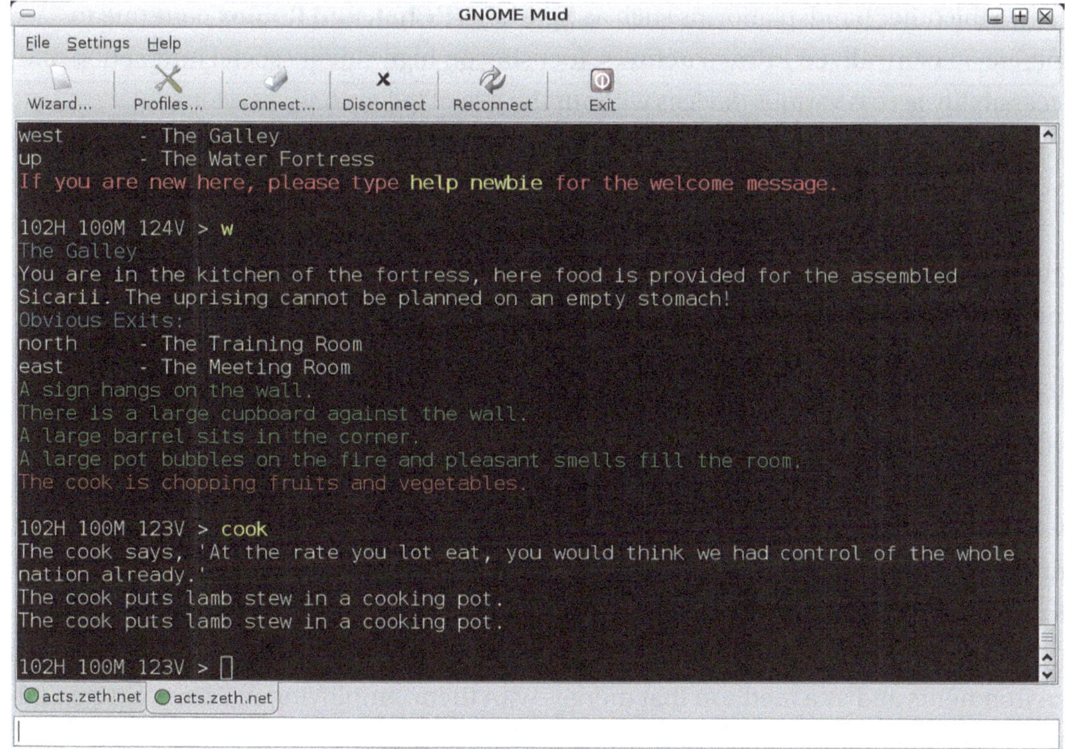

Figure 9-6.* *Screenshot of a text-based MUD interface *(e.g., LambdaMOO or AberMUD).*
Text-driven environment showing room description and user commands. Source: Wikipedia/Medium article

From these early experiments emerged a lineage that shaped the aesthetics and logic of today's virtual environments: graphical MUDs and early online role-playing games in the 1990s; MMORPGs like Ultima Online and World of Warcraft; and finally, social virtual worlds such as Second Life in 2003.

Each step expanded the degree of immersion and the spectrum of interaction, moving from text and imagination to complex audiovisual architectures.

Contemporary virtual environments stand as heirs to this history, though they have diverged into different architectural models.

On one hand, platforms like **Decentraland** and **The Sandbox** have integrated **blockchain and Web3 technologies** to enable decentralized ownership and persistent digital assets.

On the other hand, platforms such as **Spatial, VRChat, and Roblox** continue to operate on **centralized infrastructures**, focusing on high-fidelity social interaction and accessibility across various devices without the use of ledger-based systems.[11]

Although their underlying technologies differ, both models contribute to the broader evolution of persistent, multi-user digital spaces.

They combine the narrative freedom of role-play, the persistent architecture of MUDs, and the graphical richness of game engines, now intertwined with blockchain and Web 3.0 technologies.

For art exhibitions, these spaces no longer serve only as game arenas but as immersive galleries where authenticity, ownership, and participation are fundamentally redefined.

At the same time, the rise of the metaverse and the development of immersive installations in real space represent two parallel trajectories, each exploring different ways of redefining presence—one through virtual immersion, the other through material engagement.

Moreover, virtual space increasingly functions as both a laboratory for designing real environments and as a medium that merges with them, amplifying their immersive and interactive potential.

This reciprocal influence reveals how the boundaries between digital and physical experience are progressively dissolving, giving rise to a continuum of artistic creation and perception.

9.2.1 A Double Trajectory: Virtual and Physical Immersion

This double trajectory frames the discussion that follows.

On one side, **Chapter 9** turns to the **metaverse and virtual immersive spaces**, where art challenges the boundaries of authenticity, ownership, and curatorial practice within decentralized platforms.

On the other, **Chapter 10** explores **interactive real spaces**, where embodied experience reshapes participation within tangible environments.

[11] While often grouped under the "Metaverse" umbrella, these platforms differ fundamentally in their back-end architecture; Web3 platforms prioritize decentralized provenance via smart contracts, whereas centralized platforms like Spatial focus on real-time rendering and cross-platform social presence.

Together, these two perspectives trace a continuum between the virtual and the physical, suggesting new ways in which art redefines presence, interaction, and exhibition in the 21st century.

If visualized in Figure 9-7, this relationship would appear as a network of exchanges and correspondences, rather than as two distinct or opposing realms.

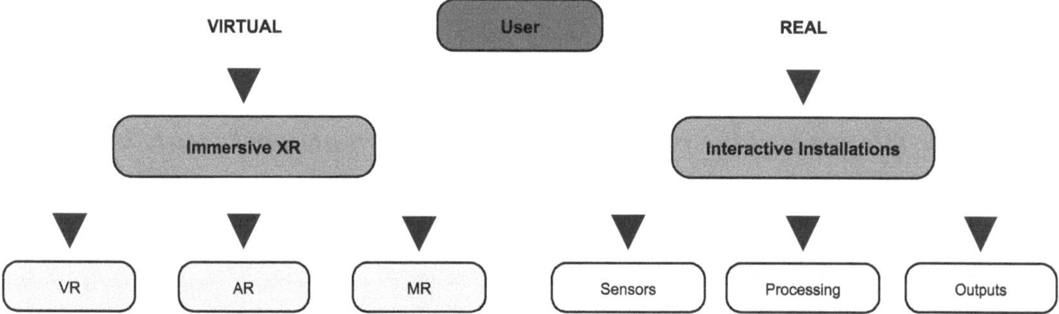

Figure 9-7. Diagram summarizing the continuum between virtual and physical dimensions.
On one side immersive XR experiences (VR, AR, MR), on the other interactive installations based on sensors, processing, and outputs. At the center, the user acts as the active element connecting both domains

In Figure 9-7, **two interconnected domains** are represented: the **real** and the **virtual**.

While they unfold as separate spaces—immersive XR environments on one side and interactive installations in physical space on the other—they operate in continuous dialogue.

Virtual platforms provide simulated worlds that expand perception and extend curatorial possibilities, while real installations anchor experience in material presence and embodied interaction.

Rather than existing in isolation, these trajectories mutually reinforce one another, shaping new forms of immersion and participation.

The relationship between them is not static but fluid, evolving through processes of translation, adaptation, and hybridization.

This discussion naturally leads to the transition from real to virtual to mixed realities, as well as to the layered stages of creation that connect concept, modeling, and exhibition.

Figure 9-8, therefore, does not simply describe a technical sequence but outlines a **dynamic ecology of artistic practice**.

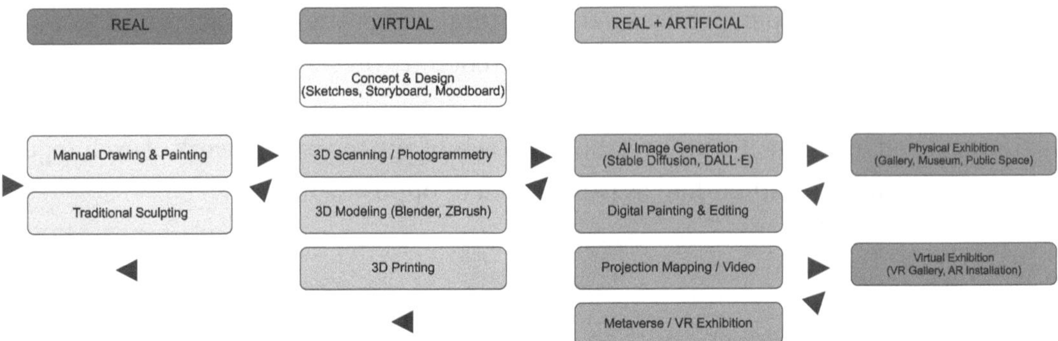

Figure 9-8. Diagram of the pathways through which artworks transition from real to virtual to mixed environments.
It can be read horizontally, as a continuum between real, virtual, and hybrid domains, and vertically, as layered stages of creation from concept to exhibition

It reveals how creation moves across different states—**manual, digital, and algorithmic**—while continuously reconfiguring its material and perceptual condition.

Artworks thus transition **from real to virtual to mixed environments**, and the interplay between **traditional media, 3D technologies, and AI-driven processes** generates **hybrid outcomes** in which physical, virtual, and metaverse exhibitions coexist as part of the same expanded continuum of contemporary art.

Figure 9-8 expands this framework by illustrating the workflow of creation and exhibition across real, virtual, and mixed domains.

Unlike the Figure 9-7, which visualized the relationship between physical and digital trajectories, this schema focuses on the processual dimension—the sequential and interconnected stages through which an artwork evolves from traditional media to AI-enhanced and metaverse-based forms.

This visual map can be read in multiple ways, each of which brings out different aspects of contemporary artistic practice. Rather than a fixed sequence, it offers a flexible map where connections shift depending on the perspective adopted.

Read horizontally, it unfolds as a dialogue between domains; read vertically, it reveals the layered logic of creation.

Taken together, these two readings open up a richer understanding of how real and virtual intertwine in the production and exhibition of art.

Yet to fully grasp the essence of immersion, we must return to the physical experience of space and light, to the kind of perceptual intensity that precedes digital simulation.

With only a few fundamental elements—architecture, natural light, and artificial illumination—James Turrell has been able to create environments where perception itself becomes the medium.

His works, such as the *Skyspaces* or the monumental project *Roden Crater*, envelop the viewer in pure light, transforming architectural voids into fields of color and atmosphere.

In Turrell's art, immersion is not mediated by technology but by vision. The act of seeing becomes an act of inhabiting, where space dissolves into experience.

In this sense, Turrell's practice represents a threshold between material and immaterial space (Figure 9-9).

Figure 9-9. James Turrell, "Space that sees" in the Israel Museum Jerusalem. *Photo by Xsteadfastx.* `https://www.flickr.com/photos/marvinxsteadfast/3133188778/in/set-72157611558849615/`*, CC BY 3.0,* `https://commons.wikimedia.org/w/index.php?curid=8277453`

His environments invite the viewer to slow down, to dwell in perception itself, and to experience how light can sculpt architecture and consciousness alike.

The body becomes still, but the gaze moves, immersed in gradients of luminosity that dissolve any boundary between seeing and being.

This approach anticipates many of today's digital immersive environments, where light, projection, and code similarly construct perceptual worlds.

What was once achieved through natural light and architectural calibration now unfolds through data, simulation, and interactive feedback, transforming the very notion of space into a living interface.

In this continuum, immersion evolves from a perceptual experience to a procedural one, from the phenomenology of light to the architecture of information.

The metaverse, in this sense, becomes a vast expansion of Turrell's vision but also of a broader lineage of artists who have explored perception as an active, spatial, and transformative experience.

What unites these practices is not the medium itself, but the pursuit of a condition in which space, perception, and presence merge into a single field of experience.

In this expanded context, the metaverse can be understood as a new arena for this long-standing artistic quest. It is a space where the real and the virtual, the material and the algorithmic, converge to redefine how we see, move, and exist within the artwork.

9.2.2 Immersive Virtual Galleries

The metaverse extends reality by multiplying its spatial, temporal, and sensory dimensions.

It allows exhibitions to expand beyond physical limits, remain always accessible, and introduce perceptual experiences unattainable in the material world.

At the same time, it redefines social presence and artistic authorship, transforming reality into a continuum that flows seamlessly between the physical and the virtual.

A rapidly growing phenomenon is that of virtual exhibitions, which, through photography and 3D scanning, can re-present real objects within virtual environments.

This growth is evidenced by a dramatic surge in digital cultural engagement between 2020 and 2024—with many institutions reporting increases of 150–300% in online visits and virtual programs (UNESCO 2024 Cultural Heritage Report; NEMO 2021–2024 surveys). However, it remains constrained by the "digital divide" in hardware access and broadband availability (see Appendix S).

Immersive spaces generally unfold along three main trajectories:

- **Laboratories for Physical Design:** Virtual platforms serve as spaces where projects can be explored and tested before being physically constructed.

  However, this workflow requires navigating discrepancies between virtual lighting engines and material physics, often requiring specific file optimization (see Appendix R).

- **Faithful Reproduction:** This consists in the accurate digital recreation of physical exhibitions, allowing remote access and long-term preservation.

  While providing significant archival benefits, these models remain approximations, limited by texture compression, polygon budgets, and the absence of haptic feedback.[12]

- **Speculative Dimensions:** This trajectory gives rise to artworks that follow their own rules, ranging from algorithmically generated environments to impossible structures. Examples include the Mars House by Krista Kim or the Museum of Other Realities (MOR), which use real-time global illumination and non-Euclidean physics to make impossible geometries perceptually real.[13]

Across these trajectories, the avatar emerges as a key figure. More than a proxy of the user, it acts as an expressive medium—a form of "virtual attire"—that shapes social relations and perception. Research on the Proteus effect shows that avatar aesthetics directly influence behaviour and self-perception in virtual spaces.[14]

Platforms like Spatial and Decentraland enable artists to design 3D galleries where viewers navigate via avatars (Figure 9-10).

---

[12] UNESCO Guidelines for the Governance of Digital Platforms: `https://www.unesco.org/en/internet-trust/guidelines`

[13] Kim, K. (2021), *Mars House: The first NFT digital home* `https://www.kristakimstudio.com/marshouse`; Museum of Other Realities (2020), *Spatial Design in Virtual Environments.* `https://www.museumor.com/`

[14] Yee, N., & Bailenson, J. (2007). *The Proteus Effect: The Effect of Transformed Self-Representation on Behavior.* Human Communication Research, 33(3), 271–290. Stanford University. `https://academic.oup.com/hcr/article-abstract/33/3/271/4210718`

Figure 9-10. Giugiogia and MariTer Auer, avatars in Second Life of the artist duo Albertini & Moioli.
The photo highlights the role of the avatar as both an expressive identity and a medium of social interaction within virtual environments

For example, a virtual sculpture garden designed in Blender and uploaded to Spatial offers a navigable experience.

To achieve this, artists must adhere to strict technical pipelines, including GLB/glTF exports, polygon limits (typically < 100k–200k per object, depending on the platform), and texture baking to ensure cross-platform stability (see Appendix R for the full Blender-to-Spatial workflow).

Compared with the hybrid painting processes discussed in Chapter 5, here the focus shifts toward a fully digital and dynamic experience, where AI not only generates images but becomes an active engine of spatial and temporal change.

9.2.3 Immersive XR Environments

But how are these virtual galleries, museums, and art spaces actually structured?

While the underlying technologies of extended reality (XR)—virtual, augmented, and mixed—have already been outlined, their **architectural and curatorial implications** deserve closer analysis.

The metaverse extends curatorial practice by merging spatial design, interactivity, and real-time responsiveness.

Virtual museums are conceived not as static containers of artworks but as *living architectures*, spaces that adapt to movement, gaze, and interaction.

They often integrate features such as **navigable 3D space**, **avatar-based presence**, **multisensory feedback**, and **real-time lighting or sound environments**, turning exhibition design into a form of digital scenography.

To operationalize these modalities, practitioners must navigate a diverse landscape of hardware and software frameworks, each suited to specific curatorial objectives.

Each XR category—AR, VR, and MR—requires distinct hardware capabilities and software ecosystems to define the relationship between the real and the virtual (See Appendix T).

In this context, the curator becomes a "spatial composer" who orchestrates visual, sonic, and interactive layers to create a unified experience.

This role now includes managing technical constraints such as draw calls and occlusion culling to maintain a unified experience across desktop, mobile, and VR headsets.[15]

To understand this ecology, it is useful to examine the structure of immersive and interactive environments more closely.

At the technological level, XR encompasses the three main modalities through which immersion operates each defining a specific relation between the real and the virtual.

Figure 9-11 visualizes the core structure of XR as an ecosystem of interconnected modes of immersion. At its center is the **user or viewer**, equipped with a headset or mobile device, whose perception and agency determine how virtual content is experienced.

[15] Discussing the shift from static curation to "scenographic programming" in real-time engines.

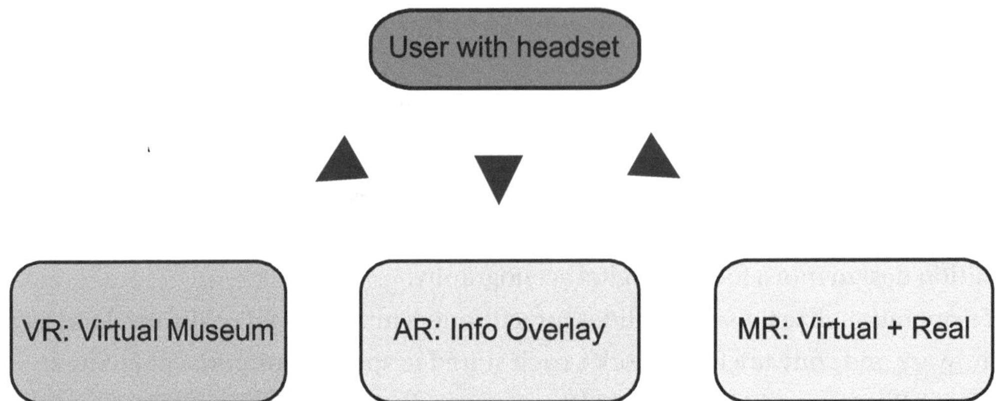

Figure 9-11. Modes of immersion in XR.
Diagram showing the three principal modes of user experience in immersive environments. Starting from the user equipped with a headset or device, the diagram illustrates how VR, AR, and MR represent distinct yet interconnected ways of engaging with digital space

Surrounding this point of origin are the three principal modalities of XR—VR, AR, and MR—each representing a different balance between real and virtual.

Beyond these categories, immersive spaces share a common logic that governs how users experience and shape virtual environments.

This logic can be visualized as a layered process that begins with the user or viewer and unfolds through avatar representation, 3D environment design, and interactive feedback systems.

Starting from the **User/Viewer**, who navigates the space through **avatar representation**, the experience unfolds within a **3D environment** shaped by architecture, light, and spatial design.

Through **interactions and dynamics**—including motion, sound, collision, and real-time response—the system generates **outputs and feedback** that engage multiple senses (visual, sonic, and haptic).

The model in Figure 9-12 illustrates how XR exhibitions integrate perception, presence, and technological responsiveness into a unified field of immersive experience.

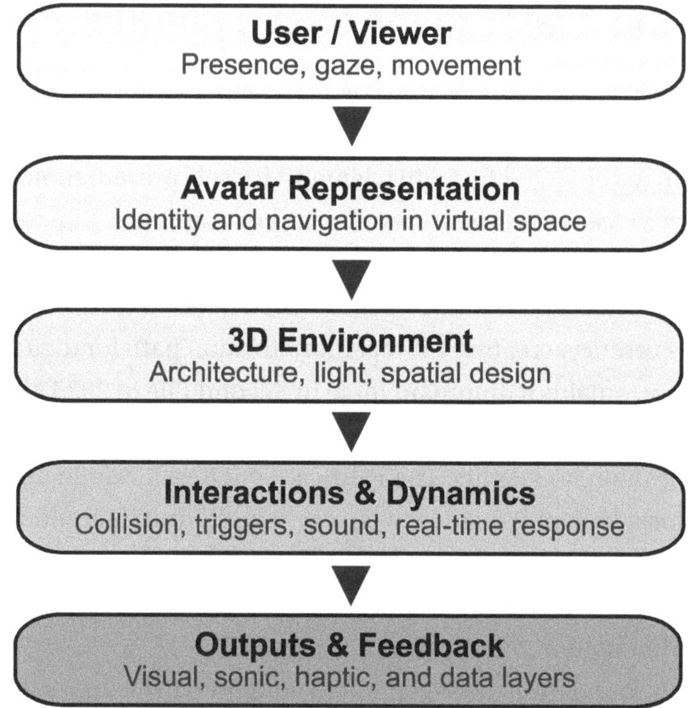

Figure 9-12. Structure of an immersive XR exhibition.
Diagram showing the layered structure of user interaction within virtual and mixed-reality environments.
Starting from the User/Viewer, who navigates the space through avatar representation, the experience unfolds within a 3D environment shaped by architecture, light, and spatial design

Through these interconnected layers, the virtual exhibition becomes a dynamic ecosystem in which presence, perception, and technology continuously interact.

Just as architecture and light shapes the phenomenological spaces of James Turrell, the tools of XR—Blender, Unity, Unreal Engine, and WebXR platforms—now allow artists and curators to build responsive digital architectures that redefine how art is perceived, inhabited, and shared.

As explored so far in the diagrams dedicated to immersive XR environments, the metaverse expands curatorial practice by integrating real-time responsiveness with fully immersive exhibition spaces.

This transforms exhibitions into participatory events, fostering co-creation, aligning with Part IV's focus.

9.2.4 From the Avatar to the User's Contribution

Any exploration of virtual economies must begin with the avatar, the user's first "body" and projection of identity in the metaverse.

Entire brands have emerged from this demand for self-presentation, turning avatar customization into a vast creative industry. A primary example is Blueberry, which originated in Second Life in 2012.[16]

Blueberry established a pioneering business model based on the sale of digital assets through in-world currency, creating a direct monetization path for digital craftsmanship.

While Blueberry remains a dominant force in Second Life in 2025, the landscape has evolved; the brand has expanded into cross-platform partnerships, mirroring the rise of dedicated virtual fashion houses like The Fabricant or DressX, which utilize NFT-based ownership and blockchain provenance to ensure scarcity and interoperability across multiple environments.[17]

The avatar thus becomes both a projection of the self and a material for artistic and commercial experimentation.

Building on this foundation, user-generated content (UGC) drives the metaverse, but its nature varies sharply across platforms.

VRChat and Roblox remain decentralized. Millions of amateur creators produce vibrant, chaotic content with high platform fees (30–70%).

By contrast, Spatial and Decentraland favor professionalized UGC. Agencies and studios deliver high-fidelity, curated experiences, enabled by direct creator revenue (95% + royalties on NFT sales).

---

[16] Blueberry was founded by Mishi Blueberry. Its business model relies on the sale of digital assets via Linden Dollars (L$), a virtual currency that is convertible to fiat currency (USD) through the LindeX exchange.

[17] The virtual fashion market—projected to reach $6–7 billion by 2030 (McKinsey Digital Luxury Report, 2025)—has evolved from platform-specific economies to decentralized, interoperable models.

Legacy brands like Blueberry continue to thrive within established ecosystems (primarily Second Life) through high-volume sales of low-cost items, prioritizing accessibility and rapid turnover.

By contrast, newer Virtual Fashion Houses (e.g., The Fabricant, DressX, Auroboros) focus on limited-edition NFT wearables designed for cross-metaverse portability—reflecting a shift from "utility within a single game" to digital asset investment with real resale value on marketplaces like OpenSea or Blur.

This professionalization demands new curatorial strategies—whitelisting, private instances, moderated districts—to balance openness with aesthetic cohesion.

The result is a spectrum from democratic chaos to agency-driven precision, with profound implications for exhibition quality and accessibility.

Most virtual goods and environments—clothes, houses, objects, scenographies—are created directly by users.

The platform's true value lies not only in its infrastructure but in its capacity to enable production, exchange, and monetization of community-generated works: a dynamic now widely recognized as the creator economy.

Equally crucial is the persistence of worlds and real-time co-presence.

Virtual environments continue to exist and evolve even when individual users are offline, while synchronous encounters—through chats, live concerts, or exhibition openings—generate social and curatorial dynamics that far exceed the solitary visit of traditional exhibitions. These collective experiences redefine presence, authorship, and participation within digital culture.

Such practices unfold within rules and simulated physics defined by each platform—collision, gravity, interactive scripts—ensuring that architectures and artworks behave as credible, reactive environments.

This simulated physicality is essential to maintaining immersion, bridging symbolic and sensory experience while preparing the ground for hybrid forms.

Moreover, the metaverse thrives on real-virtual hybridization.

Through photography, 3D scanning, and modeling, physical artworks can be imported into virtual space, while augmented and mixed reality project digital layers back into the material world.

This bidirectional flow produces new hybrid formats: replicas, digital twins, and mixed-reality installations where the artwork exists simultaneously as object, interface, and data structure.

In this context, virtual landscapes function as laboratories of form and interaction.

Figure 9-13, depicting a Second Life Island at sunset, captures this condition of continuous transformation: an environment shaped by collective authorship and evolving presence.

Figure 9-13. A Second Life island at sunset.
The image illustrates the persistence and transformation of virtual landscapes: user-built worlds that continue to evolve independently of their inhabitants' presence.
By Slick, own work, CC0, https://commons.wikimedia.org/w/index.php?curid=18128814

At the same time, the system operates on a global scale.

Exhibitions, performances, and fashion drops reach vast audiences, with transaction volumes comparable to specialized e-commerce sectors.

The scale of these virtual economies is exemplified by platforms like IMVU, which as of 2024–2025 hosts a collaborative marketplace featuring more than 60 million user-generated digital items, with approximately 10,000 new products added daily.

This high-frequency commerce is supported by a community of tens of thousands of active creators who drive an internal economy recording more than 20 million monthly transactions.[18]

[18] IMVU's economy is built on a mature derivation model, where mesh builders, texture artists, and subsequent creators share royalties along a product chain.

While no longer at its pandemic peak of more than 7 million monthly active users (2020–2021), the platform maintains a stable, engaged community with annual revenue estimated at $75–100 million (Crunchbase/Tracxn, 2025), driven by high-volume sales of virtual goods.

This centralized, creator-focused economy demonstrates greater long-term stability than many volatile blockchain-based NFT marketplaces, which saw cumulative 2024 trading volume of ~$8–10 billion but frequent project failures.

https://www.immutable.com/blog/immutable-games-spotlight-imvu-is-the-worlds-biggest-web3-social-metaverse

Unlike purely speculative markets, this "participatory economy" allows creators to monetize digital craftsmanship directly through in-platform credits or by converting earnings into fiat currency, with top-tier developers generating professional-level income (up to $100K+ annually for elite creators).

The result is that exhibitions evolve through user participation, transforming into living, crowd-shaped entities rather than static presentations.

This represents a radical departure from traditional exhibition design and underscores the social dimension of metaverse culture: **we create this world together**.

In conclusion, as exhibitions migrate into immersive virtual spaces, the audience moves from the periphery to the center.

The viewer is no longer a passive observer but an active participant, whose presence and choices influence the unfolding of the exhibition.

9.2.5 Virtual Professions: Architects and Fashion Designers in the Metaverse

In virtual worlds such as *Second Life*, entire professional ecosystems have taken shape.

Here, architects design houses, neighborhoods, and landscapes; fashion designers create 3D garments and accessories for avatars; and agencies manage the rental and sale of virtual land and real estate.

Far from being a niche hobby, this activity now constitutes a mature and structured creator economy.

Historically, pioneers such as Anshe Chung—who built a fortune through virtual real estate in the mid-2000s—had already revealed the economic potential of these practices.

Today, this system has evolved and diversified.

The economic scale is further validated by Linden Lab, developer of Second Life, which by December 2024 had paid out more than $1.15 billion to creators—nearly matching the platform's ~$1.3 billion total investment over two decades.

The annual "GDP" of *Second Life* is estimated at around $650 million, with roughly 185 million items sold every year on its marketplace.[19]

[19] Brad Oberwager, Executive Chair of Linden Lab, Second Life 1.3B to Build, 1.1B Paid to Creators, December 2024 Town Hall. `https://gamesbeat.com/linden-lab-has-spent-1-3b-building-second-life-and-paid-1-1b-to-creators/`

Comparatively, Roblox paid creators more than $1 billion in 2024 alone (Roblox Creator Economy Report, 2025), but with platform fees of 30–70% and a youth-driven focus, prioritizing volume over longevity. Blockchain platforms like Decentraland and The Sandbox saw $500–800 million in NFT transactions at their 2024 peak (DappRadar), yet suffered 90% value drops post-2022 hype, underscoring their immaturity against Second Life's two-decade stability.

On the architectural side, the ecosystem includes marketplaces dedicated to homes, commercial buildings, furniture, and landscaping, as well as networks of land and estates for buying, selling, and renting parcels and regions.

Virtual brands and studios offer prefabricated buildings, interiors, and optimized "low-prim" solutions—complete with after-sales services—mirroring the structure of traditional e-commerce platforms.[20]

Among notable virtual architects in Second Life, Dario Buratti (avatar Colpo Wexler) stands out for his refined, low-prim structures that blend modern and cyberpunk aesthetics with technical optimization.

Active since 2006, Buratti has created hundreds of custom regions, galleries, and architectural environments across Second Life, Sansar, and other platforms, earning recognition as one of Italy's pioneering metaverse designers (Figure 9-14).[21]

[20] ArchiTech Design offers low-prim, high-quality virtual homes and landscaping in Second Life, ranging from traditional to modern and beach houses, with a focus on accessible design and customer service: `https://secondlife.com/destination/architech-design`

[21] See Buratti's portfolio (`https://www.darioburatti.com/`) and the interviews in Art Tribune (2020) and Notiziarte (2024)

Figure 9-14. Dario Buratti (Colpo Wexler), architectural composition in Second Life.
The image shows one of Buratti's virtual constructions, where abstract geometries and suspended platforms interact with the virtual sunset light. The work illustrates how digital architecture can evoke both monumentality and lightness, redefining the expressive possibilities of space within the metaverse

His work exemplifies how architectural imagination extends into digital worlds, merging compositional rigor with the performative nature of virtual space.

This tradition continues across platforms; in contemporary metaverses, firms like Voxel Architects [22] design high-fidelity, cross-platform spaces.

Specializing in the development of virtual headquarters and galleries within decentralized platforms, Voxel Architects has refined the use of "voxel" and "low-poly mesh" aesthetics to create iconic structures for brands like Sotheby's and ConsenSys (Figure 9-14).

These examples illustrate the vast diversity of virtual architecture: from the **low-prim** artistry of Second Life to contemporary blockchain-enabled professional studios.[23]

[22] Voxel Architects (est. 2020) represents the shift toward professionalized, B2B virtual design. By optimizing assets for platforms like Decentraland and The Sandbox, they bridge the gap between architectural prestige and the strict performance limits of web-based 3D engines. `https://www.voxelarchitects.com/`

[23] In these environments, technical constraints (such as prim limits, polygon counts, and script memory) do not act as barriers but rather as catalysts for creative innovation, forcing designers to find a sophisticated balance between aesthetic complexity and computational performance.

On the fashion side, the scale is comparable to a real industry.

The House of Blueberry, founded in Second Life and later extended to other platforms, has sold more than 20 million digital garments and collaborated with established fashion brands.

In 2023, Blueberry appointed renowned Hollywood stylist Kate Young as senior creative advisor, marking a key milestone in the sector's professionalization.[24]

Young, a New York–based tastemaker who has styled A-listers like Dakota Johnson, Cate Blanchett, Natalie Portman, and Scarlett Johansson for more than two decades, brings her expertise in high-fashion red-carpet looks and editorial collaborations to guide Blueberry's expansion into virtual couture.[25]

Her role focuses on bridging luxury aesthetics with metaverse usability—advising on NFT-compatible designs, avatar scalability, and cross-platform interoperability (e.g., Roblox, Decentraland)—helping elevate digital garments from novelty items to investment-grade assets that retain value across ecosystems.[26]

This appointment exemplifies a broader pattern of fashion's metaverse integration: Balenciaga's 2021 Fortnite collaboration (selling virtual hoodies for $18, generating millions in sales), Gucci's Roblox Garden (2023, with user-generated fashion contests), and Louis Vuitton's 2022 NFT Vivienne trunk series (auctioned for $32,000), all signaling the industry's shift from experimental play to structured, revenue-sustaining virtual economies.

These examples demonstrate that virtual architects and digital fashion designers now represent genuine creative professions.

They design spaces and garments, manage brands and clients, and monetize their work through the platform's in-world currency (L$, Linden Dollars), which can be exchanged for real-world money.[27]

As these roles evolve, the metaverse becomes a more coherent and artistically rich system, where art, design, architecture and fashion converge to shape the aesthetics of virtual life.

---

[24] See: `https://www.vogue.com/article/the-dos-and-donts-of-styling-for-the-metaverse`

[25] See: `https://thewallgroup.com/artist/kate-young/`

[26] See: `https://us.fashionnetwork.com/news/Blueberry-names-celebrity-stylist-kate-young-as-senior-advisor%2C1583019.html`

[27] The Second Life Marketplace is the official online store where users buy and sell virtual goods—clothing, homes, furniture, animations, and more—within the Second Life ecosystem: `https://marketplace.secondlife.com/`

9.3 Redefining Authenticity and Spatial Possibilities

The transition to virtual immersive exhibitions compels us to re-examine the notions of authenticity and space in the context of art.

Traditionally, authenticity in art has been tied to the physical original: the aura of the "real" painting or sculpture in a museum, as theorized by Walter Benjamin.

Yet, as we explored in Chapter 4, the meaning of authenticity has always evolved with technology, from the reproducibility of casts and prints to the immateriality of the digital file.

A common critique of digital art experiences is that they lack this aura: a perfect digital copy of the *Mona Lisa* is not the *Mona Lisa*, and seeing it on a screen, or in VR, is often perceived as an inherently different, perhaps lesser, experience than standing before the painting itself.

However, the metaverse challenges these assumptions by offering new forms of authenticity. **In a sense, the experience itself becomes authentic. The emotions and interactions in a virtual space are real to the participant, even if the art objects are virtual reproductions.**

Moreover, blockchain technology and NFTs have introduced the concept of a digitally authenticated original, complicating the definition of what constitutes the "real" instance of an artwork in a virtual context.

The following sections examine how virtual exhibitions both redefine authenticity and reimagine spatial experience, transforming curatorial practice into a hybrid of philosophy, design, and technological experimentation.

9.3.1 Authenticity in Digital Contexts

In the metaverse, authenticity shifts to digital uniqueness, often tied to blockchain, as we have explored in Chapter 4.

A digital sculpture in Spatial gains value through its code and provenance, redefining material-based authenticity.

Rather than replicating a traditional gallery, virtual exhibitions often play with authenticity in creative ways.

For example, they might juxtapose famous works that could never coexist in reality, offering a uniquely authentic encounter in VR.

The Kremer VR Museum,[28] launched in 2017 and still fully operational in 2025 (free download via Meta Quest Store, Steam VR,[29] or PCVR platforms requiring a compatible headset with ≥8 GB VRAM GPU for smooth performance), enables an intimate viewing of 74 Old Master paintings by eliminating barriers like glass cases and crowds—potentially bringing viewers closer to the art than in a physical museum, as high-resolution photogrammetry (2,500+ photos per painting) allows examination of brushwork details and canvas backs invisible from typical gallery distances (Artsy, 2017; Unwinnable, 2019; Scope Weekly, 2017).

Studies confirm VR enhances engagement without significant loss in immersion compared to physical visits, though it lacks tactile/haptic elements.[30]

Founded by George and Ilone Kremer, the collection grew from a private passion for Dutch and Flemish masters into an innovative project combining art and technology.

Through the Kremer VR Museum, their initiative demonstrates how even private collections can become globally accessible, transforming connoisseurship into a shared digital experience.[31]

In this sense, virtual exhibitions can expand the boundaries of authenticity through sharing by revealing aspects of artworks inaccessible in person: high-resolution macro views, X-ray imagery, or reconstructed conservation data integrated into the exhibit.

As Joël Kremer, director of the Kremer Collection has emphasized in interviews, digital avatars and VR enable the "aura" of the original painting to reach distant audiences. This is a democratization of presence rather than its loss.[32]

---

[28] The Kremer Museum, launched in 2017 by the Kremer Collection, is a virtual reality museum designed by Johan van Lierop and Moyosa Media, featuring Old Master paintings in ultra-high-resolution within a purpose-built digital architecture. See the official site at `https://thekremercollection.com/museum/`.

[29] Download from: `https://store.steampowered.com/app/774231/The_Kremer_Collection_VR_Museum/`

[30] For example, see Piccardi L, Massidda M, Travaglini L, Pescarin S, et al. (2025). "Comparing Immersive and Non-Immersive VR: Effects on Spatial Learning and Aesthetic Experience in Museum Settings." Brain Sciences, 15(8):852. `https://pmc.ncbi.nlm.nih.gov/articles/PMC12384383/`

[31] A New Museum Exists Solely in VR," an article published by *Artsy* in November 2017, traces the genesis of the Kremer VR Museum. `https://www.artsy.net/article/artsy-editorial-new-museum-exists-solely-vr-future`

[32] Joël Kremer, quoted in "New Kremer Museum Brings Virtual Reality to Old Masters," Sotheby's (October 30, 2017), `https://www.sothebys.com/en/articles/new-kremer-museum-brings-virtual-reality-to-old-masters`.

This is a paraphrase of Kremer's vision for the museum fostering an intimacy unattainable in crowded physical galleries.[33]

This perspective directly engages Walter Benjamin's seminal theory in *The Work of Art in the Age of Mechanical Reproduction* (1935), where he argues that technological reproduction erodes the artwork's "aura"—its unique presence tied to time and place—by making it accessible yet detached from ritual and tradition.[34]

Kremer's VR approach counters this erosion. Avatars restore a sense of embodied presence, transforming mechanical replication into participatory ritual.

Far from diminishing aura, digital mediation amplifies it, extending the original's singular essence to global audiences while inviting co-creation through interactive exploration. This democratizes not just access but the very act of beholding.

To clarify this conceptual evolution, Figure 9-15 outlines how authenticity moves from the singular object to the lived experience of art.

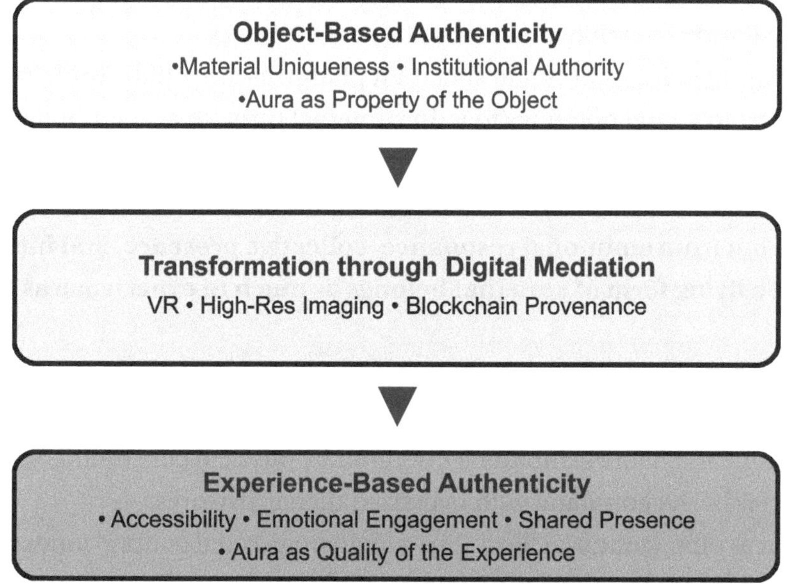

Figure 9-15. Transformation of authenticity from material to experiential dimensions.
In digital and metaverse contexts, the aura of the artwork evolves from being a property of the object to a quality of the viewer's experience

[33] See the Kremer Collection VR Museum app description (2017-ongoing), available on Meta Quest Store and Steam, which highlights "up close and personal" viewing via photogrammetry.

[34] Walter Benjamin, The Work of Art in the Age of Mechanical Reproduction (1935).

No longer tied to material originality, authenticity unfolds in the reciprocal exchange between artwork and viewer, where presence and emotion become its true measure.

In this sense, aura ceases to be a fixed property of the object and becomes a quality generated through shared perception.

Once questioned, the authenticity of virtual experience is now confirmed by the sense of presence and emotional depth reported by viewers in immersive environments.

In these contexts, authenticity shifts from material uniqueness to experiential truth, grounded in the sincerity of engagement between viewer and art.

Virtual exhibitions also invite reflection on accessibility and participation.

Not everyone can travel to see the original, but a well-crafted VR exhibition can deliver a meaningful encounter to anyone with an internet connection.

Even the world's greatest institutions reach only a fraction of humanity in person; virtual access radically broadens cultural participation.

The trade-off, however, lies in the social dimension. Visiting a virtual space is not yet equivalent to sharing the atmosphere of a physical museum.

Yet multi-user environments and social VR platforms are rapidly bridging that divide, enabling visitors to attend openings together, interact through avatars, and converse in real time while exploring digital galleries.

Ultimately, authenticity in the virtual age emerges not from material permanence but from emotional resonance, collective presence, and intellectual engagement, a living form of aura that belongs as much to experience as to art itself.

9.3.2 Innovative Virtual Spaces

Metaverse platforms enable exhibitions unbound by physical constraints, such as floating galleries in Decentraland with oversized digital artworks.

These spaces offer curatorial flexibility, enhancing virtual cultural landscapes.

Spatial possibilities in metaverse exhibitions are virtually limitless, prompting a reconceptualization of how art is presented.

In physical galleries, space is finite and governed by physics. Walls, floor load capacity, lighting angles, and sightlines constrain what can be done.

In virtual environments, by contrast, curators and artists can construct galleries on the scale of cities or as small as miniature rooms; suspend sculptures in midair; or create dynamic architectures that reconfigure themselves in response to the visitor's presence.

This fluidity of space enables curators to do what was once only imaginable. A visitor might fly up to examine a ceiling fresco close-up and then shrink down to walk beneath a digital microscope into the pigment's molecular landscape. Entirely new curatorial narratives emerge from these freedoms.

One avant-garde virtual exhibit might place the viewer in zero gravity, floating among fragments of sculptures to evoke dreamlike detachment. Another could employ impossible geometries—reminiscent of Escher—to arrange galleries in a nonlinear maze looping back on itself in ways no real building could.

These spatial experiments are not mere aesthetic novelties; they are conceptual extensions of the artworks themselves, reflecting the themes and emotions of the pieces they frame.

One of the most active platforms in this field is Decentraland, a blockchain-based virtual world whose public beta launched in February 2020 (following alpha testing since 2017) and has since evolved through community-driven expansion.[35]

Built on the Ethereum blockchain (using ERC-20 DCL tokens for governance and ERC-721 LAND NFTs for property ownership), Decentraland operates via a decentralized autonomous organization (DAO). Community members stake DCL to vote on proposals (e.g., grants, protocol upgrades, land use policies) through the DAO portal, ensuring decentralized decision-making that differentiates it from centralized platforms like Roblox.[36]

Within Decentraland's grid of approximately 90,000 "parcels" (virtual land plots represented as ERC-721 NFTs on Ethereum), artists and institutions create decentralized museums, metaverse pavilions, and interactive installations.

These spaces host real-time performances and NFT exhibitions. However, building or transacting requires a crypto wallet (e.g., MetaMask) and payment of Ethereum gas fees, which can deter casual visitors.

Access is mainly browser-based (Chrome or Edge on desktop/mobile, using WebGL/WebXR for 3D navigation) and requires no downloads.

[35] Decentraland Whitepaper (2017) and Launch Announcement (Feb 20, 2020): `https://decentraland.org/whitepaper.pdf`

[36] Decentraland DAO Portal (ongoing): `https://dao.decentraland.org/`; DCL token governance detailed in Etherscan (ERC-20 contract 0x0f5d2fb29fb7d3cfee444a200298f468908cc942).

Partial VR support is available on headsets like the Meta Quest 3 via browser passthrough mode, though performance is limited to 30–60 FPS on mid-range hardware (e.g., Intel i5/Ryzen 5 CPU, 8 GB RAM, GTX 1660+ GPU). User activity peaked at ~8,000 concurrent visitors in 2021 but has settled to a more modest 500–1,000 daily active users in 2025 (DappRadar).

High transaction fees and competition from mobile-first platforms remain key challenges. Nevertheless, Decentraland's DAO governance—where token holders vote on proposals via the DAO portal—sustains a resilient, creator-led ecosystem.[37]

Major events such as Metaverse Art Week (2021–2025) have turned decentralized platforms into laboratories for curatorial experimentation (Figure 9-16).

Figure 9-16. Decentraland. The spaces of the Metaverse Art Week. *Screenshot from the metaverse exhibition district of the Metaverse Art Week. The event exemplifies how Decentraland has evolved into a decentralized cultural infrastructure, where artists and institutions coexist within programmable architectural environments*

[37] DappRadar Analytics (Dec 2025): `https://dappradar.com/dapp/decentraland`; New World Notes (2025 SL/Metaverse Report).

A landmark moment occurred in 2022 ("*The World is Made of Code*"), which attracted more than 60,000 unique visitors and featured high-profile participants like Sotheby's and Artnet. A notable example of this collaboration is the Frida Kahlo Family Red House, an immersive exhibition created with the artist's estate to showcase previously unreleased personal artifacts. More recently, the 2024–2025 editions have shifted toward specialized art fairs like MESHfair, featuring digital-native artists such as Clara Bacou and galleries like Unit London. These collaborations between legacy institutions and AI collectives demonstrate how virtual curating has moved beyond mere display into the creation of participatory, interactive environments. In Decentraland, architecture becomes algorithmic. Every building is a programmable space, and every visitor an avatar who contributes to the work's social presence. The experience challenges traditional notions of authorship and spectatorship; ownership and participation merge, and the artwork itself evolves as a shared, living environment. These developments reveal how exhibition design itself is being reimagined, not merely as a mode of display but as an evolving dialogue between physical and virtual dimensions. **Increasingly, curators and artists conceive hybrid environments where augmented and mixed reality layers extend the museum beyond its walls, creating spaces that merge the tangible and the immaterial.**

Some projects foreground this hybridity with radical transparency, exposing the coexistence of real and virtual rather than concealing it.

Nancy Baker Cahill's *Stonebreakers* (2021), an AR site-specific installation at the Tribeca Festival, exemplifies this approach. Monumental, glitching digital sculptures hover above the Hudson River, drawing power from the visible tension between physical landscape and shimmering, transparent assets.

Similarly, Rebecca Allen's Coexistence (2001/2022) overlays digital "breath" onto participants' real bodies via head-mounted displays, making the technological interface a deliberate part of the aesthetic experience.

These examples clarify that the "sculpture" here is a digital-native object geolocated in physical space.

This radical transparency engages directly with Walter Benjamin's notion of aura. While Benjamin argued that mechanical reproduction withers aura by detaching the object from its "here and now," these hybrid projects propose a digital aura based on presence through interaction.

By forcing viewers to acknowledge the simultaneous existence of two planes—the tangible and the coded—the works do not destroy uniqueness; they redefine authenticity as the transparent negotiation between the viewer's physical body and virtual data.

A holographic reconstruction of a lost sculpture, for example, may prompt viewers to question how aura, presence, and authorship are redefined in digital form.

In this expanded field, the exhibition becomes a philosophical and spatial practice: a way of thinking through the relationships between material and code, object and data, presence and simulation.

Authenticity, rather than disappearing, is redistributed: it emerges through the sincerity of interaction and the shared construction of experience.

As these hybrid models proliferate, the exhibition space transforms into a conceptual landscape, where viewers navigate not only artworks but systems of meaning, participation, and perception, **a new ecology of the real within the virtual.**

9.4 Virtual Museums and Immersive Curatorial Design

The concept of the virtual museum has evolved from simple online archives into fully immersive environments that rival physical institutions in complexity and ambition.

With this evolution comes the need for a new form of **immersive curatorial design**, in other words, the strategies through which exhibitions are conceived, structured, and experienced in digital space.

Virtual museums pursue the same fundamental missions as traditional ones—education, preservation, and cultural dissemination—but achieve them through radically different means.

Curators must now address interface and interaction design, narrative construction in nonlinear formats, and the creation of a sense of place within a place-less digital realm.

In this context, architectural conventions dissolve. Walls become information-rich surfaces, galleries are connected by portals rather than corridors, and the roof might open onto a simulated sky, or vanish entirely into an infinite horizon.

Exhibition design extends beyond spatial arrangement to include interactive scripting, sound environments, and responsive systems that transform the visitor's movement into part of the artwork's rhythm.

Curating such experiences is no longer the task of a single individual.

It is a collective practice, involving teams of curators, technologists, designers, programmers, sound artists, and narrative architects.

Together, they construct worlds where artistic, educational, and experiential dimensions merge into a coherent aesthetic ecosystem.

This approach redefines curation as world-building: the act of shaping not only what is seen but how it is perceived, navigated, and felt.

This model can be visualized as a system of concentric layers, as shown in Figure 9-17.

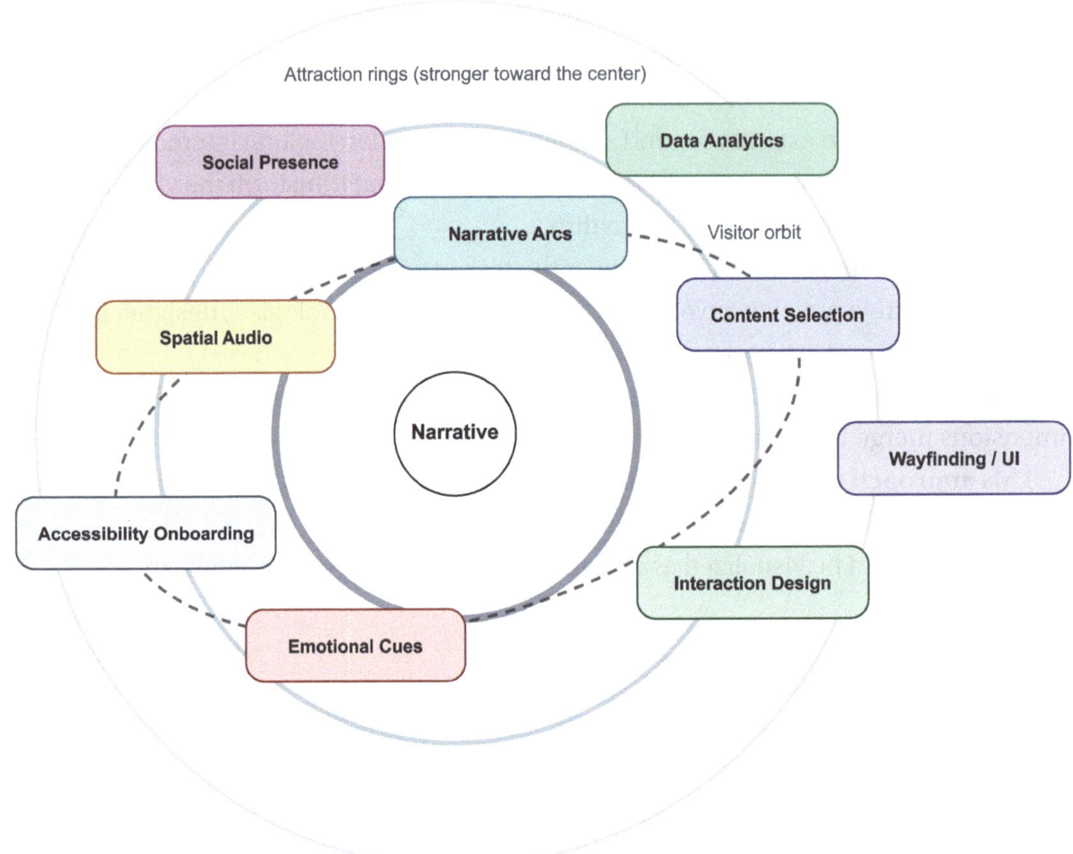

Figure 9-17.** **Gravitational field of curation, conceptual model.
The diagram visualizes the curatorial ecosystem as a gravitational field structured around a narrative core. Thicker inner rings represent stronger curatorial gravity, pulling elements such as content selection, interaction design, and emotional cues toward the center.
The elliptical orbit depicts the visitor's continuous movement through this field of forces, while nodes like Accessibility & Onboarding, Social Presence, and Wayfinding/UI indicate specific domains of influence within the immersive experience

The **inner core** represents the curatorial narrative itself: the conceptual and emotional center of the exhibition.

The **middle layer** gathers the key curatorial forces such as content selection, interaction design, and emotional cues, which orbit the core and sustain its gravitational pull.

Finally, the **outer orbit** symbolizes the visitor's engagement: accessibility, onboarding, and wayfinding act as the entry points through which participation begins and expands.

In my own project *Gravitational Field*—which we will explore in detail in section 9.4.3, this curatorial metaphor takes physical form.

The exhibition space itself is structured like a field of invisible energies, translating the conceptual "orbits" of curatorial practice into spatial experience.

Visitors are drawn through zones of artistic, emotional, and cognitive interaction, becoming active participants in a dynamic system where movement, perception, and meaning continuously influence one another.

9.4.1 Curating Virtual Museums

Curating a virtual museum involves translating curatorial practices into a digital idiom and exploiting the unique advantages of the medium.

One of the prime benefits is **collection accessibility and integration**. A virtual museum can unite works that are physically dispersed across the world into a single coherent experience.

Curators of the Virtual Online Museum of Art (VOMA), for instance, combined digital reproductions of paintings from the Louvre, the Metropolitan Museum, and the Uffizi into unified thematic galleries (Figure 9-18). This task presents significant logistical challenges in the physical world, where loan constraints and conservation risks often prevent such comprehensive collaborations.

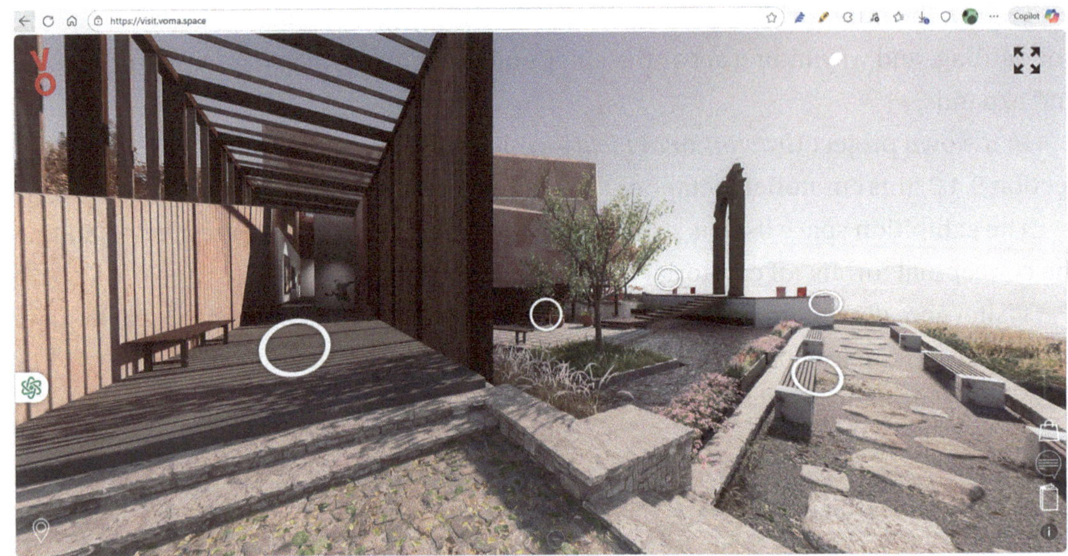

Figure 9-18. Virtual Online Museum of Art (VOMA), 2020.
View of the exhibition environment of the Virtual Online Museum of Art (VOMA), founded by curator Lee Cavaliere.
Built entirely in 3D, VOMA represents one of the first museums designed to exist solely online

This opens up new curatorial narratives. Imagine an exhibition on portraiture where Leonardo's *Mona Lisa*, Vermeer's *Girl with a Pearl Earring*, and Frida Kahlo's self-portraits are digitally juxtaposed, inviting direct comparison across centuries and styles.

Virtual curation allows these "impossible exhibitions" to become possible.

In practice, curators must now be versed in digital archives, working with high-resolution scans, 3D models, and photogrammetry-derived replicas of sculptures or artifacts.

In the Kremer Museum, for example, curators commissioned ultra-high-resolution photogrammetry of 17th-century paintings, rendering even the craquelure and canvas texture, details crucial to preserving the tactile "feel" of the originals.

They also integrated holographic guides, curator avatars that explain the works, embedding the docent experience within the digital environment itself.

Virtual museums can also update their content dynamically, allowing curators to experiment and refine layouts based on real-time visitor analytics such as movement heatmaps—an iterative approach far less feasible in physical institutions.

Thus, curating virtual museums becomes an ongoing design process that merges art-historical knowledge, digital literacy, and experiential design into a single interdisciplinary practice.

9.4.2 Immersive Exhibition Experiences

As the practice of virtual curation evolves, it naturally expands toward **immersive exhibition design**, a field where curators, artists, and technologists collaborate to transform digital galleries into experiential environments.

While Curating Virtual Museums focuses on the organizational and spatial logic of virtual collections, immersive exhibitions experiences explore how these spaces are perceived, inhabited, and emotionally experienced.

They represent the next step in virtual museology, from the arrangement of artworks to the orchestration of experiences.

Rather than merely displaying artworks, these exhibitions transform viewing into a multisensory and participatory event, where the visitor's movement, gaze, or gesture becomes part of the curatorial composition.

Designing such experiences requires curators to think like experience architects.

In physical galleries, visitors instinctively know how to move, look, and behave.

In virtual or hybrid environments, however, the task shifts toward designing the very affordances of interaction: how people navigate, access information, and encounter the work.

As noted by Mario Gerosa in Wired Italia, in 2020, the rise of virtual galleries marks the evolution of curatorial practice from online display to immersive cultural experience, bridging the experimental ethos of Second Life and the emerging aesthetics of the metaverse.[38]

This evolution continues the trajectory that began in early platforms such as Second Life but now reaches new aesthetic and technological maturity within metaverse ecosystems.

Immersive exhibitions blur the boundaries between curatorial design, architecture, and narrative.

---

[38] Mario Gerosa, "*Boom delle gallerie virtuali. Dagli esordi in Second Life al futuro del Metaverso.*" Wired Italia, November 16, 2020. Available at: `https://www.wired.it/play/cultura/2020/11/16/boom-gallerie-virtuali-esordi-second-life/`

Each exhibition becomes a multilayered environment where sound, light, and interaction converge into a unified experiential continuum, a curatorial form that is at once artistic and architectural, aesthetic and cognitive.

In this expanded field, exhibition design becomes a laboratory of perception, where space is not a neutral container but an active medium through which ideas, emotions, and energies are orchestrated.

It is precisely within this context that my project *Gravitational Field* was conceived. It is an exploration of how invisible forces—**spatial tension, rhythm, and energy flow**—can structure the viewer's experience within an interactive environment.

9.4.3 Gravitational Field

> *"In an alien world governed by invisible forces and cosmic rhythms, a gravitational field holds everything together."*

Gravitational Field (2024–ongoing) is a hybrid immersive project—existing as both a navigable VR environment and a projected blueprint for physical installation—where digital sculpture, spatial composition, and sensory interaction converge into a single, living organism (Figure 9-19).

Figure 9-19. Gianpiero Moioli, Gravitational Field, 2025.
Screenshot of the project Gravitational Field *during modeling in Blender (2025). The image documents the digital workspace used to build the central dome and luminous structures of the immersive environment*

Conceived and modeled entirely in Blender 4.4 and 5.0.1, the work transforms the traditional exhibition into a dynamic field of forces: luminous geometries, responsive surfaces, and subtle acoustic waves organize the viewer's movement, perception, and emotional resonance.

The installation acts as a **field of forces**, where luminous geometries, sound waves, and architectural rhythms generate an evolving relationship between body and environment.[39]

Rather than exhibiting objects, *Gravitational Field* composes a choreography of energies—visual, acoustic, and emotional—guiding the visitor through a continuous flow.

The space unfolds as a constellation of six interconnected semi-spherical chambers (see Figure 9-20 for concept drawings and Figure 9-21 for the relational diagram). Visitors navigate through glowing domes, orbiting forms, curved walls, and radiant "suns," surrounded by reflections that seem to breathe with invisible energy.

[39] In this sense, it is very interesting to recall the essay "Gravitational Fields. Attraction, Roundness, and Operationality of Immersive Images." https://air.uniud.it/retrieve/d8374a56-e0fb-4987-a6d5-f884e8478334/1998-622-PB%20%281%29.pdf

Figure 9-20.** **Gravitational Field. Concept drawings for immersive environments, 2025.
These mixed-media works bridge physical and virtual painting, exploring the mood, color dynamics, and luminous atmosphere of interconnected digital spaces, between real and virtual painting

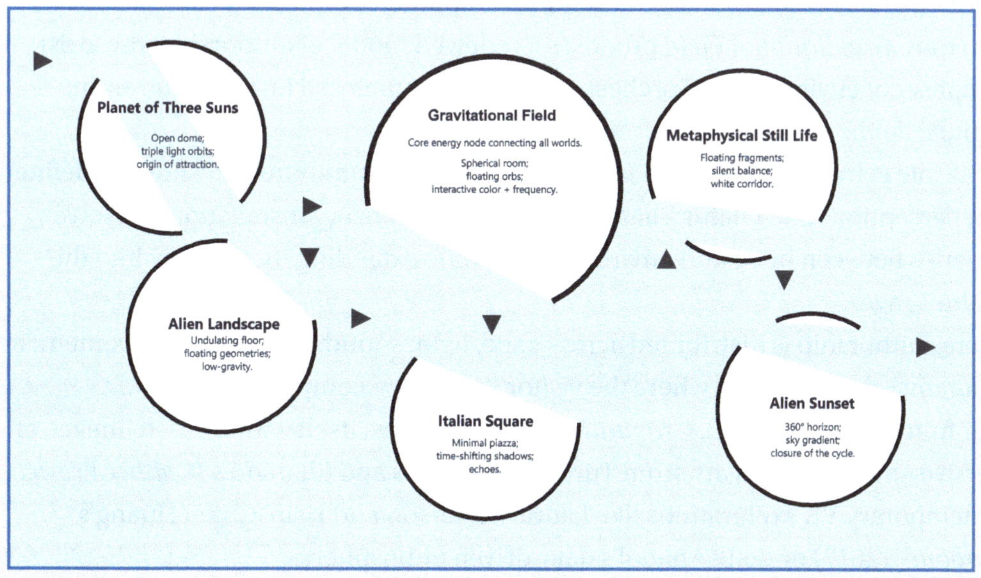

Figure 9-21. Gravitational Field. Conceptual relational diagram of the immersive environments, 2025.
Diagram showing the six interconnected spaces of the project—Planet of Three Suns, Alien Landscape, Italian Square, Gravitational Field, Metaphysical Still Life, and Alien Sunset—organized as a gravitational network of attractions and transitions

Light (HDRP-based volumetric glows), sound (procedural FMOD layers reacting to proximity), and motion (camera-driven parallax and subtle particle flows) merge into a poetic choreography: technology rendered invisible yet omnipresent, extending the sculptural gesture into the digital dimension.

In VR (exported to Unity 2023.2 for Quest 3/PCVR, with hand-tracking and gaze-based triggers), proximity to a glowing sphere amplifies its pulse; footsteps ripple low-frequency waves that distort nearby reflections. In projected physical prototypes, LED arrays and sensors (Arduino + haptic motors) translate these digital forces into tangible vibrations—turning abstract gravity into felt attraction.

This genius lies in its radical reciprocity. The viewer is not spectator but celestial body, whose presence warps the field—orbits shift, lights intensify, sounds harmonize—creating a unique gravitational signature for every journey.

Through this interplay of **digital sculpture**, **spatial composition**, and **sensory interaction**, *Gravitational Field* proposes a renewed model of authorship: the artist as composer of environments, orchestrating not only material form but the entire perceptual field.

This role echoes pioneers like James Turrell (whose luminous thresholds redefine spatial perception) and Olafur Eliasson (whose multisensory installations dissolve boundaries between body and environment), while extending their legacy into the algorithmic age.

Here, authorship is distributed across code, light, sound, and viewer movement: a collaborative choreography where the visitor's presence completes the work.

Far from unprecedented, *Gravitational Field* situates itself within a rich lineage of immersive environmental art, from Turrell's *Skyspaces* and Eliasson's *Weather Project* to contemporary VR explorations like Laurie Anderson and Hsin-Chien Huang's *Chalkroom*[40] (2017) or Refik Anadol's data-driven atmospheres.

What distinguishes it is the deliberate fusion of gravitational metaphor with interactive responsiveness, turning abstract cosmic forces into tangible navigational cues, and inviting viewers to inhabit the artwork's living system.

In this context, the digital environment effectively answers Walter Benjamin's concerns. Rather than eroding the "aura" through mechanical repetition, the gravitational pull of the work restores a unique *hic et nunc* (here and now) that is born only through the viewer's movement.

Ultimately, *Gravitational Field* transforms viewing into embodied navigation. It is a journey through a continuum of light, sound, and form where the boundaries between art, space, and technology dissolve and the viewer emerges not as spectator, but as co-creator of the gravitational pull itself.

9.4.4 Case Study: Rinascimento Virtuale (Florence, 2008): Early Art in Second Life

The history of immersive curatorial practice begins well before the rise of the metaverse.

[40] Laurie Anderson and Hsin-Chien Huang, Chalkroom (2017). A landmark VR experience in which the viewer floats through vast, hand-drawn architectural spaces created by the artist's gestures and voice. The work transforms drawing into navigable, dreamlike environments, prefiguring many contemporary spatial-gesture practices in VR.

Official project page: `https://laurieanderson.com/?portfolio=chalkroom`

In the mid-2000s, virtual worlds such as Second Life had already become experimental laboratories for artistic creation, identity construction, and collective imagination (Figure 9-22).

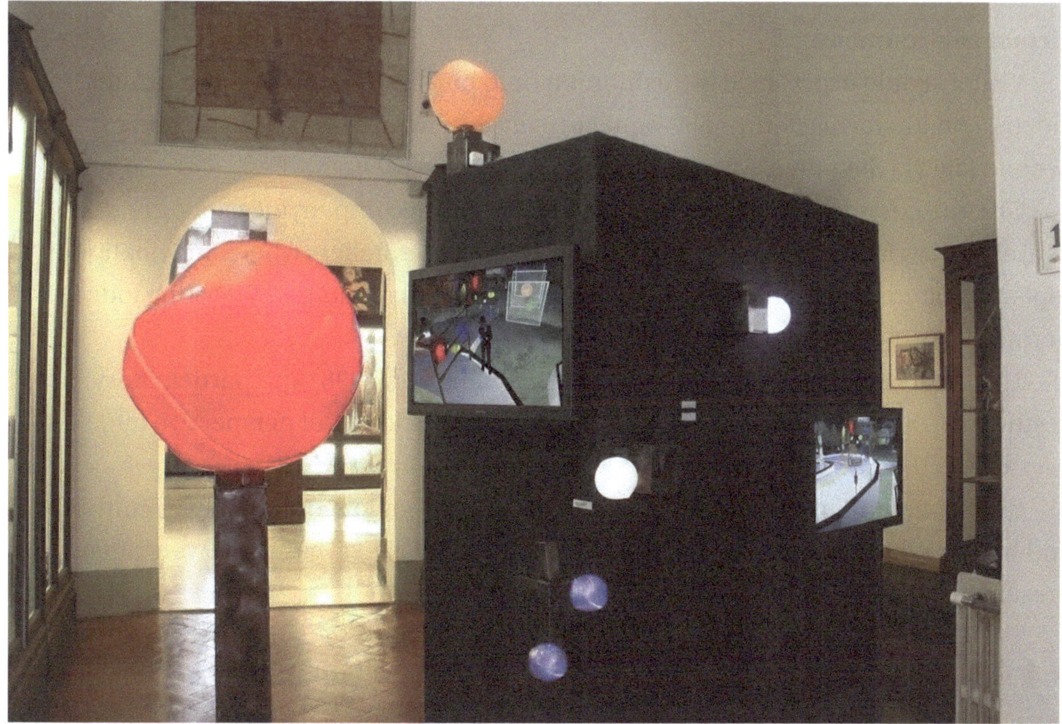

Figure 9-22. Albertini & Moioli, Installation for Rinascimento Virtuale, Florence (2008).
Mixed-media installation created for the exhibition Rinascimento Virtuale. Arte, tecnologia e virtualità, *curated by Mario Gerosa. The work explored the relationship between real and virtual space through the integration of sculptures, lights, and digital screens, creating a hybrid environment where material presence and virtual imagery coexist*

One of the most emblematic projects of this pioneering phase was Rinascimento Virtuale. Arte, tecnologia e virtualità (*Virtual Renaissance: Art, Technology, and Virtuality*), curated by Mario Gerosa and held in 2008 at the Museum of Natural History (Anthropology and Ethnology Section) in Florence.[41]

[41] Exhibition catalog: Mario Gerosa (ed.), Rinascimento Virtuale (Florence, 2008). `https://www.libreriadellaspada.com/biography/en/rinascimento_virtuale_9788895144009_torre_di_legno.html`

The exhibition brought together more than 30 international artists who worked inside Second Life, exploring the boundaries between virtual architecture, avatar performance, and interactive installation.

It was one of the first institutional attempts to present artworks **born entirely in a virtual environment**.

Visitors could experience the exhibition both physically—through projections, videos, and interactive terminals—and virtually, by entering the corresponding spaces in Second Life via their own avatars.

Gerosa's curatorial philosophy, articulated in the accompanying catalog and subsequent writings, viewed virtual worlds as collective ateliers where imagination replaces material substance and every action becomes creation, anticipating today's participatory metaverse practices.[42]

This vision echoed relational art theories (Bourriaud, 1998) and participatory aesthetics (Bishop, 2004), while extending Renaissance ideals of perspective into fluid, user-driven digital space.

Rinascimento Virtuale thus stands as a key precedent for contemporary immersive and hybrid exhibitions, revealing how the seeds of metaverse-based art were already present in Second Life's utopian architectures.

9.4.4.1 The Curatorial Philosophy of Mario Gerosa

Mario Gerosa—a leading scholar of "synthetic reality"—establishes himself as a central figure in the field by theorizing virtual worlds not as gaming spaces but as legitimate sites for architectural and sociological inquiry.

In his vision, these platforms function as **"collective ateliers"**: decentralized spaces where imagination replaces material substance and every action transforms into a form of creation.

This philosophy translates into a specific curatorial strategy that dismantles the traditional "white cube" logic.

By inviting visitors to interact in real time with artists-as-avatars, this curatorial approach moves beyond static display into what Nicolas Bourriaud (1998, Esthétique relationnelle) defines as *relational aesthetics*.

[42] Gerosa, Second Life (Milan: Meltemi, 2007) and Rinascimento Virtuale (Milan, Meltemi, 2008).

Through this shift, *Rinascimento Virtuale* anticipates the participatory framework of the contemporary metaverse. It transforms the viewer's role from passive spectator to active participant, establishing a key precedent for the relational and immersive practices that define digital curating today.

9.5 Practical Applications: Creating Immersive Metaverse Exhibitions

So far, we have examined the concepts, roles, and case studies that define what metaverse exhibitions can be.

This section focuses on their **practical realization**, which is the *how-to* of designing immersive exhibitions in virtual environments.

It involves selecting the most suitable platforms, applying spatial and aesthetic design principles, using new tools such as VR drawing, fostering collaboration during the creative process, and reinterpreting the legacy of Picasso's gestural experiments—from his 1949 light drawings to their digital descendants—through contemporary immersive and generative media.

As museums, artists, and technologists increasingly collaborate in building these experiences, adopting a **project-oriented mindset** becomes essential.

We will therefore outline several key aspects:

- Choosing and using virtual world platforms, and understanding how interactivity reshapes curatorial logic
- Designing the spatial and perceptual qualities of virtual art spaces
- Integrating VR-based artistic techniques, such as gesture drawing in immersive space
- Coordinating collaborative workflows
- Experimenting with how mid-20th-century ideas of space and seriality can find new life in today's digital worlds

Among the most emblematic examples of how **repetition and variation** can transform perception is the work of **Yayoi Kusama**.

Her pumpkins, endlessly reinterpreted in different scales, colors, and contexts, embody a family of forms that oscillates between organic reference and abstract seriality (Figure 9-23).

Figure 9-23.* *Yayoi Kusama, Pumpkin, 2010. Stainless steel sculpture.
The dotted pumpkin, one of Kusama's most iconic motifs, exemplifies the idea of infinite variation and serial form, placing organic shape and obsessive pattern into dialogue: a theme that resonates with generative processes in contemporary AI and metaverse art.
Photograph by See-ming Lee, Flickr. CC BY 2.0, `https://commons.wikimedia.org/w/index.php?curid=28422726`

In Kusama's immersive environments—from the *Infinity Mirror Rooms* to monumental outdoor installations—the viewer is enveloped in a field of multiplied reflections where the boundary between object and space dissolves.

This aesthetic of infinite variation finds a contemporary resonance in the logic of the **metaverse**, where avatars, architectures, and artworks can be generated, replicated, and transformed within digital space.

Just as Kusama's pumpkins exist both as singular sculptures and as part of an endless constellation, so too in platforms like *Decentraland* or *Spatial* artistic presence becomes at once unique and infinitely reproducible.

Kusama thus offers a poetic precedent for the immersive and participatory dynamics that define today's virtual exhibitions, showing how art can expand perception beyond the limits of material space.

From this perspective, the role of the **viewer as co-creator** in metaverse exhibitions becomes clearer.

Just as Kusama's installations rely on the presence and movement of the spectator, digital platforms invite participants to interact, rearrange, and expand the artwork itself.

Here, the boundary between artist and audience dissolves, giving rise to a participatory logic in which viewers actively contribute to the unfolding of the experience.

In *Spatial*, for instance, users can manipulate virtual elements, reshaping installations in real time and becoming co-authors of the scene, a participatory model that anticipates the explorations of the following section.

If Kusama's mirrored rooms extend perception through physical space, virtual worlds extend it through code and presence, turning the exhibition itself into a living interface.

9.5.1 Virtual World Platforms: From Exhibition to Interaction

With these premises, we now move from the conceptual to the operational dimension.

Virtual world platforms provide technological and spatial frameworks through which artists, designers, and curators create immersive experiences.

They can be grouped into three principal categories, from accessible creative platforms to advanced XR environments that merge real and virtual perception.

9.5.1.1 Artistic and Creative Platforms for Immersive Exhibitions

Perfect for virtual galleries, digital sculptures, and AI-driven environments.

- **Spatial**: One of the most popular platforms among artists and institutions. It allows the creation of customizable 3D galleries integrating images, 3D models, videos, and sound.

  Accessible via browser, VR headset, or mobile.

- **OnCyber**: NFT-oriented platform that supports curatable 3D spaces for displaying digital art, video, and AI-generated works.
- **MusePlace**: Combines web and VR for lightweight, interactive exhibitions, easily accessible from any browser.
- **DreamWave/DreamHouse**: Emerging 2025 platforms dedicated to narrative and AI-based immersive art experiences.
- **Second Life**: A pioneering virtual world (launched in 2003) that remains active as a space for artistic experimentation, digital performance, and collective exhibitions.

  Its user-created environments and avatar-based interaction prefigure the participatory logics of today's metaverse.

- **VRChat**: A social and creative VR platform enabling artists to build fully interactive worlds, host performances, and stage exhibitions with real-time avatar presence.

  Its open community and Unity-based world editor make it one of the most flexible and culturally vibrant virtual spaces for experimental art.

- **Sinespace**: Developed on the Unity engine, Sine Space continues the legacy of *Second Life* by offering a persistent, multi-user 3D world oriented toward social creation and artistic display.

  It supports realistic materials, physics, and VR, making it suitable for large-scale exhibitions, performances, and hybrid educational projects.

9.5.1.2 Decentralized Metaverse Platforms (Blockchain and NFT-Based)

Used for digital art, performances, and collectible virtual environments.

- **Decentraland**: Ethereum-based metaverse allowing ownership of virtual land (*LAND*) and creation of museums or art plazas.
- **Voxels (formerly Cryptovoxels)**: Early voxel-style platform dedicated to art and architecture, with native NFT integration.
- **Somnium Space**: Realistic VR environment compatible with headsets, often used for interactive virtual sculptures and performances.
- **Hyperfy/Mona**: New-generation WebGL metaverses that host interactive and curated digital art exhibitions.

9.5.1.3 Platforms and Engines for Professional VR World Creation

Adopted by artists, studios, and universities for advanced immersive experiences.

- **Unity**: 3D and VR development engine integrating AI, physics, and interactivity for exhibition design.
- **Unreal Engine 5**: High-end rendering (Lumen, Nanite) suitable for photorealistic museum environments and spatial narratives.
- **Blender + XR Tools**: Open-source suite with native OpenXR support enabling immersive scene inspection and basic object manipulation in VR, for real-time sculptural and architectural experimentation, **providing an immediate spatial feedback loop** to evaluate scale and proportions at one-to-one.

  Advanced VR creation workflows often complement Blender with dedicated tools like Gravity Sketch or Open Brush.
- **TouchDesigner**: Node-based software for generative and interactive installations, widely used in digital performance and live art contexts.

9.5.1.4 Steam and the Distribution of Immersive Environments

Alongside these creation tools stands **Steam**, the leading global platform developed by Valve Corporation for the distribution of games, VR applications, and virtual worlds.

Originally designed for entertainment, Steam has evolved into a technological and cultural infrastructure that supports the dissemination of artistic VR experiences and metaverse-based projects.

Through its ecosystem—which includes SteamVR for hardware integration and community tools for content sharing—Steam acts as a bridge between creation and exhibition, enabling immersive artworks and environments to reach a global audience within a shared interactive framework.

Similar roles are played by the **Meta Quest Store**, which curates artistic and educational VR experiences for standalone headsets, and by **Google Arts & Culture (VR/AR section)**, which functions as a digital museum platform offering virtual exhibitions and 3D cultural experiences accessible to a wide public.

In this sense, these infrastructures together transform digital distribution into a curatorial space where software, art, and experience converge.

In summary, these platforms reveal that the metaverse operates not as a single, unified space but as a constellation of interconnected environments.

From virtual galleries to blockchain-based worlds, from collaborative VR to mixed reality, they collectively redefine exhibition-making as a continuum between sculpture, architecture, and code, where interaction itself becomes the primary material of contemporary art.

Within this expanded field, early experiments anticipated today's immersive paradigms: notably the virtual installations by Stefania Albertini & Gianpiero Moioli, whose projects in Second Life explored the poetic and interactive potential of digital matter long before the term "metaverse" entered common use.

9.5.2 Albertini & Moioli: Interactive Sculptures in virtual worlds (2007–2018)

The exploration of interactive sculpture within virtual worlds began for Albertini & Moioli in Second Life between 2007 and 2009, in parallel with the emergence of early metaverse art practices.

Among their earliest works are *Le Macchine per Fare le Bolle* (*The Bubble-Making Machines*, 2007), *Meccanismi Virtuali* (*Virtual Mechanisms*, 2008), *Acquario Interattivo* (*Interactive Aquarium*, 2009), *L'Ora senza Voce* (*The Hour Without Voice*, 2010), etc., all of which exemplify the shift from static virtual environments to responsive ecosystems of sound, light, and motion.

Beyond *Le Macchine per Fare le Bolle* (*The Bubble-Making Machines*, 2007), which we have already discussed at the beginning of this chapter as an early paradigm of participatory virtual sculpture, Albertini and Moioli further expanded their research through a series of subsequent projects that explored various modalities of interaction and perception.

9.5.2.1 Meccanismi Virtuali (Virtual Mechanisms, 2008)

Meccanismi Virtuali is an interactive virtual sculpture composed of a central supporting structure made of rotating rings containing blue particle systems that react to the presence and movement of avatars.[43]

As users approach, the rotation speed, light intensity, and particle scale and trajectories change dynamically, creating an ever-evolving choreography of motion and color.

A key feature of the interaction is the **tactile engagement**. When an avatar touches the sculpture, the entire mechanism immediately freezes in its current state, suspending the motion and light patterns at that precise moment. This functionality transforms the viewer from a mere catalyst of motion into a controller of time and form, allowing for a static contemplation of a complex digital process.

The work thus the idea of **mechanical vitality within immaterial space**, translating the logic of kinetic sculpture into the language of code.

Through its responsive behavior, *Meccanismi Virtuali* transforms the virtual environment into a living mechanism: an abstract organism that connects algorithmic precision with sensory perception (Figure 9-24).

[43] You can view a documentation video of *Meccanismi Virtuali* at `https://www.youtube.com/watch?v=g-Yp8XEcvHw`.

Figure 9-24. Albertini & Moioli, Meccanismi Virtuali (2008)*, interactive virtual sculpture in Second Life.*
The work consists of a vertical structure composed of rotating rings containing blue particle systems that react to the presence and movement of avatars. By merging geometry, light, and interaction, Meccanismi Virtuali *transforms motion into a living system, translating the language of kinetic sculpture into code*

9.5.2.2 Acquario Interattivo (Interactive Aquarium, 2009)

Acquario Interattivo is an interactive virtual sculpture structured around two glass cubes supported and protected by horizontal iron rectangular frames.[44]

Inside this architectural frame float several multicolored bubbles that respond in real time to the presence of avatars. When the visitor approaches, the bubbles move away; when they retreat, the bubbles follow, tracing subtle trajectories through the transparent space.

The work evokes the behavior of living organisms within an artificial ecosystem, transforming the encounter between avatar and sculpture into a **delicate choreography of attraction and repulsion**.

[44] You can view a documentation video of *Acquario interattivo* at `https://www.youtube.com/watch?v=SmDYjmwdlow`.

Through its minimalist composition and behavioral logic, *Acquario Interattivo* explores the poetics of digital matter: a meditation on proximity, distance, and the invisible forces that govern interaction within virtual environments.

9.5.2.3 L'Ora senza Voce (The Hour Without Voice, 2010)

With *L'Ora senza voce*, Albertini and Moioli introduced a more contemplative dimension (Figure 9-25).

Figure 9-25. Albertini & Moioli, L'Ora senza Voce, (2010)*, interactive installation in Open Sim.*
The work combines abstract sculptural forms with spheres, text and sound that react to the presence of avatars. Fragments of poetic writing appear and dissolve in sync with reactive audio, creating a meditative environment where language, silence, and light intertwine

The installation combined abstract visual structures and bubbles with fragments of poetic text and reactive sound.[45]

As avatars moved within the space, the text moved, dissolved or reappeared, and the soundscape evolved from silence to resonant tones, creating a dialogue between absence and presence.

[45] You can view a documentation video of *Meccanismi Virtuali* at https://www.youtube.com/watch?v=Mk313LOBC98.

The installation transforms poetic fragments into a floating immaterial architecture, where text acts as a 3D volume that overlaps with glowing spheres and rustic structures, inviting the viewer to inhabit the language itself.

The work proposed a reflection on time and perception within virtual environments, revealing how immaterial art could evoke memory and inner silence.

Through fragments of text, poetry, and visual narration, the space became a place of listening and contemplation.

9.5.2.4 Toward Practical Applications

Taken together, these virtual installations form a coherent body of work that merges sculpture, architecture, and interaction design into a unified language.

The subsequent works by Albertini and Moioli were developed across several other virtual worlds—from OpenSim to Sinespace, Unity, Spatial, and Neos VR,[46] progressively expanding the immersivity and interactivity of their projects.

Each experiment combined 3D modeling, procedural scripting, and reactive sound design, acting as precursors to today's AI-augmented systems in metaverse-based installations.

These projects demonstrate how an immersive artwork can be conceived as a living system, responsive to the viewer's digital presence and governed by algorithmic logic: a field where the boundaries between artwork and environment, creator and participant, continually blur.

9.5.3 From Drawing to Immersive World: Transforming the Image into Space

From these early explorations of virtual sculpture emerges a natural evolution: the passage from creating **interactive forms** to constructing **entire worlds**.

If earlier works animated the viewer's relation to an object, the next step is to place the viewer **inside the artwork itself**, to make object and space not only visible but inhabitable.

[46] Neos VR ceased online services in August 2025 and is no longer active.

Its spiritual successor, Resonite, continues to thrive as a user-generated VR/social/creative platform with ongoing development and a dedicated community. Official website: `https://resonite.com/`

This conceptual transition leads directly to *Gravitational Field*, the project discussed in section 9.3.3, where the artwork becomes an environment and the viewer a point of gravity within it.

It raises a simple yet radical question. What if a drawing could become a place: a world that surrounds the observer rather than merely being seen?

This idea, central to *Gravitational Field*, guides the transformation of a two-dimensional image into an immersive, navigable environment.

The process begins with the image itself—for example, *Alien Sunset*, one of the six drawings discussed in section 9.3.3, a vision of an extraterrestrial horizon.

The drawing is extended and refined and made panoramic through AI outpainting or upscaling, until it can wrap around an entire virtual sphere.

In Blender, this image becomes the skin of a vast 3D dome: a UV sphere with a radius of about 50 meters, flipped inside out so the viewer stands at its center, enveloped by the image.

The viewer, placed at its center, now stands within the drawing, surrounded by the space of imagination.

From there, depth emerges as the drawing unfolds into space.

Its lines and shapes are extracted as virtual objects and arranged within the environment, some rendered as solid forms, others as ephemeral projections, suspended between materiality and light.

The flat image begins to breathe. Shadows fall, light expands, and forms acquire presence.

The same image that defined the landscape also becomes its source of illumination: an HDRI that envelops the scene in its own atmosphere.

Subtle sunbeams and reflections amplify the sensation of dawn within an alien sky.

Finally, a panoramic camera is positioned at the core of the world.

With equirectangular projection enabled, the space can be rendered as a 360° video, or experienced directly in virtual reality, allowing anyone to step inside the original artwork.

What began as a drawing now exists as an environment: a gravitational field of color, light, and motion.

This process—turning image into space—also finds resonance in virtual reconstructions of real architectural places, where memory and imagination coexist.

As shown in Figure 9-26, the project establishes the virtual headquarters of Brera within Second Life, reinterpreting the historical architecture of the Accademia di Belle Arti as a navigable and social digital environment.

Figure 9-26. Virtual Courtyard of Brera Academy, digital reconstruction in Second Life.
The project reinterprets the courtyard of the Accademia di Belle Arti di Brera as a navigable virtual architecture. By translating the Academy's historical space into a shared online environment, it becomes a symbolic meeting place connecting avatars, artists, and students across physical and digital realms

By reimagining the Courtyard of Brera within a virtual world, the project extends the academy's physical boundaries into digital space, transforming a static monument into a dynamic meeting point for avatars, artists, and students.

The reconstruction symbolizes a bridge between presence and telepresence; it is a space that, while immaterial, preserves the atmosphere of dialogue and community that defines the institution.

This architectural experiment thus anticipates the participatory logic of later metaverse projects, where literature, visual art, and digital space converge into a single, unified creative field.

From this continuum between drawing, architecture, and virtual reconstruction emerges a further step: the transformation of gesture itself into space.

This evolution leads naturally to a new frontier: the **spatial gesture**, where movement, light, and time merge into a single, inhabitable dimension.

9.5.4 VR Gesture Drawing in the Metaverse

The immersive environments of the metaverse open new possibilities for the artistic gesture, transforming it from a trace fixed in material into a spatial act that can be experienced in real time.

Just as Picasso's 1949 *light drawings* captured movement in the air as luminous marks and Lucio Fontana's spatial cuts transformed the sculptural gesture into a spatial incision, virtual reality allows the artist to inscribe forms directly within three-dimensional space.

Through Blender's official VR integration, the artist can literally draw in the air, generating curves and meshes that embody the immediacy of physical gesture while existing entirely within a virtual environment.

These gestures can be processed in Geometry Nodes to produce luminous trails, as discussed in Chapter 3, dynamic animations, and procedural transformations, enabling a form of creation that is at once performative, spatial, and natively metaversal.

While production tools like Blender provide the technical foundation for spatial gesture drawing, platforms such as Resonite—the spiritual successor to Neos VR, driven by the migration of its original development team and community—fully realize this metaversal potential.

The core strength of Resonite lies in its high-frequency runtime engine and its integrated real-time visual scripting system, ProtoFlux. This scripting language allows artists to go beyond simple sketching: they can draw a single line in 3D space and instantly connect it to a node that reacts to voice input or a real-time heartbeat, transforming a simple stroke into a reactive architectural structure.

By enabling artists to perform and record gestures directly within shared VR environments with collaborative editing, Resonite shifts the paradigm of the artist from a 'sculptor of static objects' to a 'creator of living systems'—where individual movement evolves into collective, inhabitable, and sentient spatial art.

9.5.4.1 VR Tools for Spatial Creation in Blender

Since the integration of the VR Scene Inspection add-on (based on the OpenXR standard), Blender has evolved into a powerful environment for spatial evaluation.

In the current Blender 5.0+ ecosystem (2025–2026), the software provides a stable bridge to immersive visualization, though a clear distinction remains between native inspection and experimental creation workflows.[47]

The Legacy of BlenderXR

The path to native VR was paved by BlenderXR, an experimental fork developed by MARUI-PlugIn (led by CEO Koki Ibata) starting in 2018–2019.

This project was the first to allow artists to use the full Blender interface—including sculpting and vertex manipulation—inside VR.

BlenderXR is no longer being developed as a stand-alone project, but its best features have been moved into the main version of Blender via OpenXR integration. Its work on VR controller settings and adapting the user interface for headsets was groundbreaking; it essentially paved the way for the official VR support (OpenXR) that we use in Blender today.[48]

Hardware and the OpenXR Ecosystem

Current VR integration relies on the **OpenXR framework**, ensuring broad compatibility across the rapidly evolving hardware landscape of 2024–2025.

This includes Meta Quest 3/Pro (via Link/Air Link or stand-alone OpenXR runtime), HTC Vive XR Elite/Focus 3, Valve Index, Pico 4 Enterprise, and high-fidelity systems like Varjo XR-4 and Somnium VR1.

Configuration typically requires a runtime provider such as SteamVR, Oculus/Meta PC app, or native OpenXR runtime; performance is optimal on GPUs with ≥12 GB VRAM (e.g., RTX 4070 Ti+).[49]

Inspection vs. Creation: The Technical Reality

Blender 5.0+ offers robust immersive navigation—real-time lighting assessment, full-scale presence, and basic object manipulation (grab/place/rotate via controllers)—making it ideal for architectural walkthroughs and scale verification.[50]

---

[47] Blender Manual - VR Scene Inspection (Blender 5.0): https://docs.blender.org/manual/en/5.0/addons/3d_view/vr_scene_inspection.html

[48] MARUI-PlugIn (2018–2022). https://github.com/MARUI-PlugIn/BlenderXR https://github.com/MARUI-PlugIn/BlenderXR/wiki

[49] OpenXR Registry (Khronos Group, 2025). https://www.khronos.org/openxr/

[50] Blender Development - XR/VR Design Session (May 2025). https://devtalk.blender.org/t/2025-05-26-design-session-xr-vr/40808

However, complex content creation (detailed sculpting, grease pencil drawing, or precise vertex editing) remains limited in the stable release. These tasks are still keyboard/mouse-dependent or require experimental branches (e.g., VR Lab or community forks).

For professional-grade VR sculpting/painting, artists typically complement Blender with dedicated tools like **Adobe Substance 3D Modeler (formerly Medium), Gravity Sketch, or Open Brush**.

For further information, see Appendix U.

In this hybrid setting, the creative process is redefined.

By inhabiting the digital scene at full scale, the artist's gesture becomes a diagnostic tool. Space is no longer an abstract projection on a 2D screen but a tangible environment where movement provides the ultimate generative principle for scale and proportion.

9.5.4.2 From Picasso's Light Drawings to Spatial Gestures

As mentioned in Chapter 3, the idea of spatial drawing finds an early echo in Picasso's 1949 experiments with light, where gestures were traced in the air and preserved as ephemeral lines of light.

What began as an ephemeral act of light and motion now finds continuity in virtual reality, where the artist can literally draw within space itself.

Through **Blender's OpenXR-based VR interface**—or through dedicated VR creative tools (e.g., Gravity Sketch or Open Brush) for fluid 3D sketching/sculpting with controllers— gesture becomes presence. The line is no longer confined to the screen but unfolds in three dimensions, recorded in real time as a trajectory of movement.

The technical workflow for implementing this spatial gesture drawing is detailed in Appendix V.

- In practice, once the VR session is launched, the artist enters a navigable 3D workspace using a headset such as the Meta Quest, HTC Vive, or Valve Index, paired with motion-tracked controllers (see Appendix V, section V.1).
- Each movement of the hand generates a curve that follows its trajectory in space. Pressing the controller's trigger begins the stroke, and releasing it concludes it—recording the gesture as a Bézier curve within the scene (see Appendix V, sections V.2 and V3).

These curves can be organized in a dedicated collection, their resolution and placement adjusted interactively to ensure smooth, continuous motion.

Using Geometry Nodes (see Appendix V, Section V.4), the captured paths are given substance: transformed into luminous volumetric structures through Trim Curve animation and Emission materials.

This process reproduces the immediacy of drawing while expanding it into the immersive field: a continuum between body, code, and light.

The virtual gesture thus inherits Picasso's intuition and translates it into the metaverse. It is a choreography of form and time, where the artist's movement becomes space, in other words, a living environment shaped by light, energy, and perception.

9.5.5 Collaborative Design with a Project-Oriented Mindset

Reflecting the *project-oriented mindset* discussed in Chapter 1.3, contemporary artistic practice increasingly embraces collaboration as both a method and a way of thinking.

In virtual environments, artists, architects, and designers can work together across distance and discipline, sharing the same digital space for real-time creation.

This approach embodies the **hybrid practitioner model**, where idea, material, and code interact dynamically within a shared environment.

Virtual platforms thus become collaborative studios.

Tools like, Second Life, Spatial, or Sinespace allow creators to develop immersive exhibitions, invite feedback, and expand artistic dialogue across geographical and cultural borders.

For further information, see Appendix W.

A virtual laboratory or gallery designed on these platforms does not replace the physical one; rather, it extends its social and conceptual reach, turning exhibition-making into a participatory, networked experience.

The potential of such practices was already anticipated in early hybrid projects like Immersive Wor(l)ds (2012), organized at the Accademia di Belle Arti di Brera (Figure 9-27).

Figure 9-27. Immersive Wor(l)ds (2012).
A hybrid event between the physical and virtual courtyards of the Brera Academy, connecting real participants with avatars in the digital environment with video

The event united literary and visual art in a dual environment, simultaneously held in the Salone Napoleonico in Milan and in Brera's virtual laboratory within Second Life.

Artists and avatars interacted across realities. Readings of literary texts in the physical hall were echoed by digital artworks and performances in the virtual campus, creating a continuous dialogue between *Words* and *Worlds*.

In this shared space, images and stories intertwined, erasing the boundaries between presence and telepresence, audience and participant.

It was one of the earliest examples of collaborative telepresence in art education, where technology served not as mediation but as connection, enabling artists, readers, and spectators to inhabit the same conceptual field from different locations.

Events like *Immersive Wor(l)ds* anticipate today's metaverse-based collaborations, in which the artwork is no longer a fixed object but an evolving, co-created process.

A comprehensive photographic reportage documenting the visual complexity and the hybrid nature of this event is available on `https://virtualworldsmagazine.wordpress.com/2012/06/30/immersive-worlds-letteratura-e-arte-figurativa-digitale-nella-fusione-fra-mondo-fisico-e-virtuale/`.

The comprehensive documentation of the curatorial framework, technical specifications, and legacy of this event is provided in section 4.4.2.2.

Within this framework, the digital environment becomes both atelier and arena: a place where design thinking, artistic gesture, and collective participation converge to form new ecosystems of creation.

9.6 Conclusions

Virtual exhibitions do not replace physical galleries but expand them, opening new possibilities for creativity, participation, and accessibility.

Through avatars, VR, interactive media, artists, and audiences meet in shared imaginative spaces where gravity, geography, and distance are redefined.

In these environments, the viewer becomes an active participant and co-creator.

Curators act as spatial composers, guiding interaction and experience rather than displaying static works.

Platforms such as Resonite fully realize this potential by functioning as a high-frequency runtime engine where the act of creation is a synchronized social event. By leveraging real-time visual scripting like ProtoFlux, the artist's gesture is no longer a static trace but a reactive system, capable of responding to voice or biometric data.

This shifts the paradigm from a "sculptor of static objects" to a "creator of living systems," where individual movement evolves into collective, inhabitable spatial art.

Such collaborative practices merge art, design, and technology, giving rise to new roles—*metaverse curators, virtual experience designers*—and redefining how artistic creation and education operate today.

In parallel, they open a new reflection on meaning and value.

At the same time, the metaverse reshapes authenticity. The aura of art emerges not from material presence but from the intensity of lived experience.

Blockchain systems extend this logic, preserving uniqueness through digital identity.

This ongoing *Rinascimento Virtuale* marks a fusion of art, technology, and participation, where museums and installations may soon exist simultaneously in physical and virtual form.

The next chapter continues this exploration in the real world, tracing how interactive sculptures and light-based environments translate the immersive principles of the metaverse into tangible, spatial experience.

9.7 Appendix Q: Global Growth and Accessibility in Virtual Cultural Heritage

This section analyzes the impact of virtual exhibitions on global reach and the persistent barriers of the digital divide, providing the quantitative data required for a rigorous assessment of the phenomenon.

- **Growth Metrics:** Since 2020, the adoption of virtual exhibition tools by cultural institutions has increased by more than **180%**. The **Google Arts & Culture** platform now partners with more than **3,200 institutions** worldwide, providing access to millions of artifacts and high-resolution virtual tours.
- **Expansion of Reach:** Immersive experiences have demonstrated a significant multiplier effect on attendance. The **Victoria and Albert Museum (V&A)** reported that its VR exhibitions (e.g., *Curious Alice*, 2021; *Fabergé in London*, 2024) consistently reached audiences **5 to 10 times larger** than the physical gallery capacity during equivalent periods.
- **The Digital Divide (Barriers):** Despite expanded circulation, accessibility remains constrained by significant technical and socio-economic factors:

- **Bandwidth Requirements:** High-fidelity 3D galleries and 4K VR streaming typically require stable connections >**25 Mbps**, excluding users in regions with limited infrastructure.
- **Hardware Exclusion:** Advanced immersive features (real-time spatial audio, complex shaders) are optimized for high-end GPUs or dedicated headsets (**Meta Quest 3, Apple Vision Pro**), creating a tiered system of access based on economic means.

- **Mobile vs. Full Immersion:** To ensure stability, browser and mobile versions often disable advanced effects such as volumetric lighting or haptic feedback, resulting in a diminished experience for most users.

These metrics highlight the democratizing potential of virtual heritage while underscoring the urgent need for **inclusive design strategies**. To bridge the divide, practitioners should prioritize **low-poly alternatives**, **progressive loading**, and **offline modes**, ensuring that the "virtual frontier" remains accessible to a truly global audience.

9.8 Appendix R: The Technical Pipeline: From 3D Modeling to Social VR

This section details the actionable workflow required to ensure cross-platform stability (Mobile, Web, and VR headsets) when transitioning from 3D modeling environments to social virtual platforms.

9.8.1 Modeling and Geometry (Optimization)

- **Polygon Count:** Scenes must be strictly optimized for real-time rendering engines. Current industry standards for mobile-accessible platforms (such as Spatial) recommend a budget of **less than 200,000 triangles** for the entire environment. This ensures fluid performance on stand-alone devices like the **Meta Quest 3** and modern smartphones.
- **Draw Calls:** To prevent frame rate drops, artists must minimize the number of "draw calls" (the number of objects the GPU processes per frame). This is achieved by **merging meshes** and using **texture atlases** to reduce the number of unique materials.

9.8.2 Material and Texture Conversion

- **Shader Limitations:** Advanced shaders used in production (e.g., Blender's procedural nodes) are incompatible with real-time web engines. All visual data must be **"baked"** into a single set of **PBR (Physically Based Rendering)** maps, including:
  - **BaseColor/Albedo:** The raw color data.
  - **Metallic & Roughness:** Surface reflectivity and smoothness.
  - **Normal:** Simulated surface detail.
  - **Emissive:** Self-illumination for light-emitting surfaces.
- **Texture Resolution:** The maximum recommended resolution is **2048x2048 px**. Larger textures are automatically downscaled by most platforms, often resulting in visual artifacts or excessive loading times.

9.8.3 Export and Integration

- **Standard File Format:** The **GLB/glTF 2.0** format is mandatory. It acts as a "single binary container" that packs geometry, textures, and basic animations, ensuring a consistent representation across different viewers.
- **Spatial Awareness and Navigation:**
  - **Colliders:** Navigation is governed by "Floor" colliders defined during the modeling stage. Without these, the user's avatar cannot maintain a persistent position in the 3D space.
  - **Interactivity:** Interactive elements (e.g., clickable objects, triggers) require the use of specific SDKs, such as the **Spatial Creator Toolkit**, utilizing JavaScript or Unity-based scripting for advanced logical behaviors.

9.9 Appendix S: Digitization Methodologies: Capabilities and Constraints

This section distinguishes between the primary methods used to transition material objects into virtual spaces.

Methodology	Technical Process	Capabilities	Key Limitations
360° Photography	Multiple high-res photos stitched into a panorama.	Highest visual realism; low file weight.	No volumetric depth; viewer is fixed at a single point (teleport only).
Photogrammetry	Reconstruction from hundreds of overlapping 2D images.	Realistic textures; allows free spatial navigation.	High processing time; struggles with reflective or transparent surfaces.
LiDAR Scanning	Laser-based measurement of distances (light detection).	Incredible geometric precision; accurate scale.	Lower texture quality; requires post-processing to fill "holes" in data.
Volumetric Video	Capturing moving humans/objects in 3D.	Realistic "living" presence of avatars or performances.	Extremely high bandwidth; difficult to stream to multiple users.

9.10 Appendix T: Technical Framework and XR Implementation

9.10.1 Comparative Analysis of XR Modalities

The following table summarizes the technical requirements and typical use cases for each XR category:

Category	Typical Hardware	Software Frameworks	Primary Use Case
AR	Smartphones, Tablets, Glasses (Meta Ray-Ban)	ARKit, ARCore, Niantic Lightship	Overlaying info on physical art; outdoor urban galleries.
VR	Tethered/Standalone Headsets (Quest 3, Vive)	Unity, Unreal Engine, WebXR	Fully immersive, world-building; speculative/impossible architectures.
MR	Pass-through Headsets (Vision Pro, Quest 3)	Mixed Reality Toolkit (MRTK), Scene Mesh	Anchoring virtual sculptures in physical galleries; hybrid interaction.

9.10.2 Operational Pipeline: From Design to Persistent Environments

To ensure cross-platform stability (Mobile, Web, VR), artists must adhere to a rigorous optimization workflow, particularly when moving from 3D modeling software (Blender) to social virtual platforms (Spatial, VRChat).

Key Optimization Constraints:

- **Geometry & Draw Calls:** Mobile and stand-alone VR headsets perform best with scenes under **200,000 polygons**. High "draw call" counts (too many separate objects) can cause frame rate drops; merging meshes is often required.
- **Occlusion Culling & Frustum Culling:** These techniques improve performance by not rendering objects that are hidden behind walls or outside the user's field of view.
- **Texture Baking:** Advanced shaders (like Blender's procedural nodes) are not supported in real-time engines. Lighting and shadows must be **"baked"** into a single image file (PBR textures) to maintain visual fidelity without taxing the processor.
- **File Formats:** The **GLB/glTF 2.0** format is the standard for web-based XR, as it efficiently packs geometry, textures, and animations into a single, portable file.

9.11 Appendix U: Blender VR & XR Ecosystem (2025)

This appendix summarizes the current state of VR/XR integration in Blender, clearly distinguishing between stable production features and experimental developments.

9.11.1 Technological Evolution

- **BlenderXR (Legacy):** Originally an external fork developed by MARUI-PlugIn (2018–2022), it laid the groundwork for full Blender interface interaction in VR (6DOF controllers, adapted UI). While no longer maintained, its core innovations have been absorbed into the official main branch.
- **OpenXR Integration (Current Standard):** Blender now natively adopts OpenXR, ensuring compatibility with major 2025 headsets (Meta Quest 3/Pro, PICO 4 Enterprise, Valve Index, Varjo XR-4, and Apple Vision Pro via bridge). The active runtime (SteamVR, Meta PCVR, or native) is all that is required for startup.

9.11.2 Functionality: Inspection vs. Creation (Blender 5.0 Stable)

Category	Functionality	Status in 5.0 Stable
Inspection	one-to-one scale navigation, teleportation, landmarks	**Native**
Review	Real-time Eevee viewport (lighting, materials, animation)	**Native**
Layout	Basic object translation, rotation, and positioning	**Native**
Modeling	Vertex editing, complex meshes, extrusion	**Keyboard/Mouse only**
3D Drawing	Grease Pencil with VR controllers	**Experimental (Lab)**

9.11.3 Blender XR Lab: The New Experimental Frontier

Launched in late 2025, **Blender XR Lab** hosts experimental builds focused on immersive authoring.

These features are in active development and not yet available in stable releases:

- **Grease Pencil XR:** Enables 3D sketching and animation using VR controllers as brushes ((prototype stage, promising for spatial drawing)
- **Mixed Reality (MR):** Includes "Hologram mode" with passthrough to visualize 3D models within the physical environment (early implementation)
- **UI Mirroring:** Allows users to view and interact with the standard 2D interface without removing the headset (experimental workaround)

9.11.4 Recommended Workflow (2025 Hybrid Workflow)

For professional-grade results:

1. **Creation/Sculpting:** Use dedicated tools (Gravity Sketch, Adobe Substance 3D Modeler) or specific **Blender XR Lab** experimental builds.
2. **Refinement/Rendering:** Import assets into **Blender 5.0 Stable** for advanced materials, Geometry Nodes, and Cycles/Eevee rendering.
3. **Review:** Use native **VR Scene Inspection** for final one-to-one scale validation with clients or creative teams.

9.11.5 Quick Start Requirements

- **Hardware:** OpenXR-compatible headset connected to a PC (GPU with **≥12 GB VRAM** recommended for smooth Eevee performance).
- **Software:** Active Runtime configured (SteamVR, Meta PCVR, or native).

- **Blender Setup:** Enable the **"VR Scene Inspection"** add-on (Edit ➤ Preferences ➤ Add-ons).
- **Activation:** Open the Sidebar (**N**) ➤ **VR Tab** ➤ **Start VR Session**.

9.12 Appendix V: Technical Workflow for VR Gesture Drawing in Blender (2025)

This appendix provides the practical and technical details necessary to implement the spatial gesture drawing workflow described in Chapter 3.1 and Chapter 9.4, transforming the conceptual idea into an actionable process within Blender 5.0+.

9.12.1 Detailed Technical Workflow: VR Capture (Stable Release Limitations)

Blender 5.0+ native VR (**VR Scene Inspection** + OpenXR) is excellent for immersive inspection and basic manipulation.

However, full Grease Pencil drawing in VR is considered experimental and not yet available in stable releases (**Blender XR Lab builds** are in development but not publicly released as of December 2025).

Technical Parameter	Implementation Details
VR Interface	**Blender Native OpenXR/VR Interface** (stable since Blender 3.0, matured in 5.0+). Compatible with major headsets (Meta Quest 3/Pro, HTC Vive XR Elite/Focus 3, Valve Index, Pimax, Varjo XR-4).
Required Software	No third-party creative software required; only the **OpenXR runtime** specific to the headset (e.g., SteamVR, Meta PCVR app).
Capture Tool	**Stable:** Basic object grab/place. **Grease Pencil VR Drawing:** Experimental (Blender XR Lab only).
Data Type Captured	In stable builds: no native Grease Pencil capture in VR. In experimental builds: strokes as **Grease Pencil** objects.
Sampling Rate	Driven by the headset refresh rate (e.g., 90–120 Hz on Quest 3).
File Formats	Native **.blend** file; export resulting curves/meshes as **FBX**, **Alembic (.abc)**, or **GLB/glTF**.

Setup Steps (Stable VR Session)

1. Enable the **VR Scene Inspection** add-on (**Edit ➤ Preferences ➤ Add-ons**).
2. Ensure headset/controllers are tracked by the OpenXR runtime.
3. Start VR Session (**View ➤ VR ➤ VR Session** or **Sidebar N ➤ VR tab**).
4. **Stable:** Use controllers for navigation and basic manipulation.
5. **Experimental (XR Lab builds):** Use the **Draw Tool** (**grip/trigger**) to trace **Grease Pencil** strokes.

9.12.2 Recommended Hybrid Workflow (2025 Production Practice)

Instead of point 5 of the "Setup Steps" section, for reliable, production-ready VR gesture drawing, use a hybrid approach:

1. **VR Capture**: Use dedicated VR creative tools (e.g., a **Gravity Sketch – Pro** subscription or the free LandingPad version or **Open Brush**, which is completely free and open-source) for fluid 3D sketching/sculpting with controllers.
2. **Import into Blender**: Export strokes as curves/meshes (OBJ, FBX, GLB) → import into Blender 5.0 stable.
3. **Refinement**: Convert to Grease Pencil or Bézier curves for further editing, apply Geometry Nodes, materials, and animations.

This workflow leverages the strengths of specialized VR tools while using Blender for advanced post-processing.

9.12.3 Implementing Bézier Curve Capture (Post-Import)

1. Import strokes from external VR tool (or experimental Grease Pencil data).

2. Select object ➤ Object ➤ Convert ➤ Grease Pencil to Path (choose Bézier type).
3. Optimize: Simplify Curve modifier or Decimate in Edit Mode for cleaner lines.

Advanced (Experimental): Custom Python add-on (bpy API) for direct curve generation (not native/stable).

9.12.4 Luminous Volumetric and Animation Workflow (Geometry Nodes)

To transform captured Bézier paths into animated, luminous structures, use the following.

9.12.4.1 Geometry Nodes

- Input: Converted Bézier curve (Group Input).
- Animation: Trim Curve node (keyframe End 0.0 → 1.0).
- Thickness: Curve to Mesh + profile curve (e.g., Circle for tube).
- Material: Set Material node for luminous shader.

9.12.4.2 Material and Render

- Shading: Pure Emission shader (Strength 10–50 for neon/plasma glow).
- Optional Volumetrics: Volume Scatter in Material Output Volume socket.
- Render: Eevee (fast, Bloom enabled for halo).
- Post-Processing: Bloom in Render Properties for visible light halo.

This **stable hybrid workflow in Blender 5.0** successfully translates VR gestures into dynamic, luminous spatial drawings, suitable for digital exhibitions or physical prototypes.

9.13 Appendix W: Technical Comparison of Immersive Art Platforms (2025)

The following matrix provides a detailed breakdown of the platforms discussed in section 9.4.1, serving as a reference for curators and artists to evaluate the technical affordances of each environment.

9.13.1 Platform Capabilities Matrix

Platform	Primary Engine	Access	VR Mode	Multi-user	Scripting / Interactivity	Primary Use Case
Spatial	Unity	Web / Mobile / VR	High (Native + Passthrough)	Yes	SDK (JS/Unity) + AI Tools	Corporate events, fine art galleries
VRChat	Unity	PC / VR / Mobile	Native (Quest/ PCVR)	Yes	Udon (Visual Scripting)	Performance art, immersive worlds
OnCyber	WebGL	Web / VR	Medium (Browser VR)	Yes	Template-based + Custom JS	NFT curation, fast-display galleries
Sinespace	Unity	Desktop / VR	High	Yes	Lua + Physics Engine	Education, hybrid events
Decentraland	Custom (ETH)	Web / Desktop	Limited (Passthrough)	Yes	TypeScript SDK	Land ownership, social hubs
Somnium Space	Unity	Desktop / VR	Native	Yes	Custom Scripting + Physics	Persistent VR sculptures
Mona / Hyperfy	WebGL	Web / VR	Medium	Yes	React / JavaScript	Architectural NFT spaces

(*continued*)

Platform	Primary Engine	Access	VR Mode	Multi-user	Scripting / Interactivity	Primary Use Case
Second Life	Custom	Desktop Client	Experimental	Yes	LSL (Legacy Scripting)	Collective ateliers, social art
Resonite	Custom (.NET 9)	Desktop / VR	Native	Yes	ProtoFlux (real-time visual)	Gesture-based creation, living systems

9.13.2 Criteria for Platform Selection

The platforms included in this analysis were selected to represent four distinct "currents" of virtual curating in 2025:

- **Ease of Access (Spatial, OnCyber):** Drag-and-drop tools that democratize gallery creation, allowing for professional results without advanced coding expertise
- **Total Creative Freedom (VRChat, Sinespace):** Unity-based environments offering maximum customization of physics, lighting, and complex interactivity
- **Persistence and Economy (Decentraland, Somnium Space, Mona):** Blockchain-enabled ecosystems where land ownership and NFT integration prioritize long-term value and digital scarcity
- **Legacy and Evolution (Second Life):** The historical benchmark for participatory virtual art since 2003, demonstrating the endurance of creator-led economies

9.13.3 2025 Technical Context and Limitations

The current landscape is defined by a shift toward **interoperability** and **spatial realism**.

1. **OpenXR Standardization:** As of 2025, the industry has largely unified under the OpenXR standard, significantly reducing fragmentation across hardware like the Meta Quest 3, Apple Vision Pro, and Varjo XR-4.
2. **Web-First Trend:** Optimization of WebGL has allowed platforms like **OnCyber** and **Mona** to deliver high-resolution experiences directly in the browser, removing the friction of external software installations.
3. **AI Integration:** Emerging tools (e.g., **DreamWave**, **MusePlace AI**) allow for real-time narrative or environmental adaptation, where the virtual space reacts dynamically to viewer input or proximity.
4. **The Role of Blender:** With the release of **Blender 5.0+**, the software now serves as the "universal hub." Its native OpenXR support enables artists to perform one-to-one spatial evaluations within the workspace before exporting assets to any of the social platforms listed above.

This matrix highlights the fragmented yet increasingly interconnected nature of immersive art platforms. Each offers unique affordances while sharing a common goal: expanding curatorial possibility beyond the constraints of physical space.

CHAPTER 10

Fields of Immersion: Real Sculptures as Spaces

Sculpture has always existed in relation to space, but in recent decades it has shifted from being an object in space to becoming space itself.

No longer confined to pedestals, sculptural forms unfold as environments—interior or exterior—that embrace the visitor and transform perception.

These fields of immersion are not only virtual simulations but concrete places, where material presence, light, and sound converge into an atmosphere that can be physically inhabited.

The immersive turn in sculpture redefines the role of the spectator.

Instead of remaining at a distance, the viewer steps inside the work with their body, experiencing weight, resistance, reflection, or vibration.

Whether through reflective surfaces, luminous structures, or interactive technologies, the sculpture unfolds as an expanded environment that resonates with movement, presence, and sensation.

This chapter considers both my earlier works and new possibilities, showing how sculptures can evolve into immersive systems.

Once conceived as static objects, they can now be reimagined through 3D scanning, printing, and digital augmentation, opening the way to hybrid spaces where art, architecture, and environment fuse.

To reveal this continuity between idea and matter, I will introduce a new immersive sculpture, envisioned as a point of convergence between the physical and the virtual, where thought and form merge into a single field of experience.

G. Moioli, *Art Between Matter and Code*, https://doi.org/10.1007/979-8-8688-2376-3_10

10.1 Introduction: From Object to Environment

In recent decades, sculpture has expanded its spatial logic beyond traditional boundaries.

It is no longer framed to the static relationship between object and pedestal or to the architectural relationships that frames it; rather, it evolves into an **environmental condition**, a space that can be traversed, sensed, and transformed through interaction.

In this expanded scenario, the artwork becomes a **relational field** that integrates matter, light, sound, and technology, where perception is no longer passive but participatory.

The focus shifts from the object to the situation, from the artifact to the system. What matters is not only *what* we see but *how* we experience it.

10.1.1 Interactive Installations

One of the key developments enabling immersive sculpture is the rise of interactive installations.

In the previous chapter, we introduced virtual interactive works, which may serve either as preliminary explorations for physical realizations or as autonomous artistic outcomes.

We also outlined the notion of interactive real installations, which will be examined in greater depth in this chapter.

In interactive art, the artwork is not fixed; it responds in real time to input from viewers or the environment.

Interactive sculpture can be understood, as represented in Figure 10-1, as a simple but effective loop. The work detects, processes, and responds.

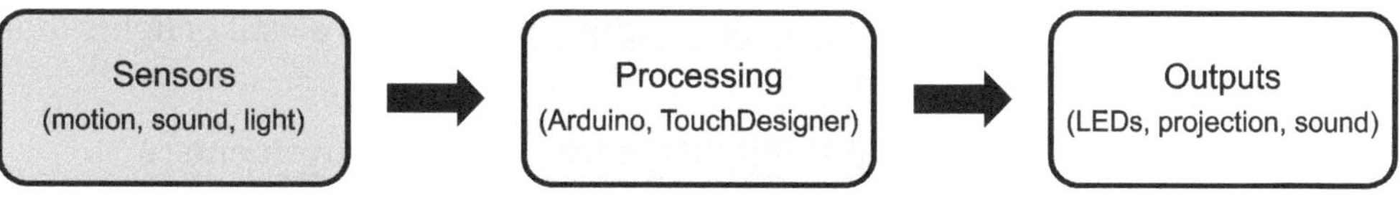

Sensors + real-time data + code → reactive artworks

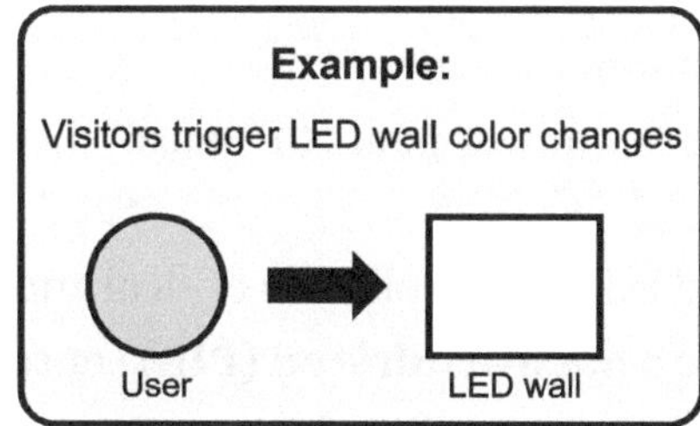

Figure 10-1. Diagram of an interactive installation workflow.
The scheme illustrates the input ➤ processing ➤ output loop: sensors (motion, sound, light) capture data from the environment, a processing unit (e.g., Arduino, TouchDesigner) interprets the signals, and outputs (LEDs, projection, sound, movement) provide perceptible responses. In the example shown, a user's presence triggers color changes in an LED wall

Sensors register the presence or actions of the viewer: movement, sound, touch, or even environmental changes.

This information is then interpreted by a computational "brain" from a microcontroller to advanced software, which translates the input into behavior.

Finally, the installation answers with a perceptible output: light with shifting intensity or color, sound that resonates, images that unfold, or mechanical parts that move.

In this way, the artwork behaves almost like an organism.

It perceives its environment, elaborates, and reacts, establishing a feedback cycle in which the spectator is no longer outside the work but actively co-creates its unfolding.[1]

The result is a deeply engaging, responsive "conversation" between humans and the environment of the sculpture.

[1] For examples of how interactive art installations are reshaping audience engagement through responsive environments, see Interactive Immersive's overview: `https://interactiveimmersive.io/blog/interactive-media/interactive-art-examples/`.

For example, consider an interactive installation consisting of a wall of lights that change color when people approach.

Motion sensors or a camera (input) might detect a visitor's movements; a microcontroller or computer (processing) then determines the appropriate response; finally, the wall's LED panels (output) light up with shifting colors and patterns correlated to the visitor's position.

The effect is that the environment appears to "sense" the person and adapt accordingly.

The choice of sensors and microcontrollers is critical and depends on the desired interaction granularity. While a **passive infrared (PIR)** sensor is sufficient for simple binary presence (on/off), more nuanced installations require distance and position data.

Sensor Type	Technology	Range	Accuracy	Best Use Case
PIR	Infrared Heat	5-7m	Low (Binary)	Triggering ambient lights upon entry.
Ultrasonic (HC-SR04)	Sound Waves	2cm-4m	~3mm	Proximity-based pulsing (as shown in section 10.6.1).
ToF (VL53L1X)	Laser (Time-of-Flight)	Up to 4m	1mm	Precise distance tracking in small/midscale kiosks.
LiDAR / Depth Cam	Structured Light/Stereo	0.5-10m	High (3D)	Multi-user tracking in large environments.

For processing, the **ESP32** has largely replaced the Arduino Uno in 2025 due to its dual-core processor (handling logic and Wi-Fi synchronization simultaneously) and its low latency (~10-20ms), which is essential to prevent a "disconnect" between user movement and visual feedback.

A real-world example of this principle is Random International's *Swarm Study/III* (2011), an interactive light installation at the Victoria & Albert Museum in London, represented in Figure 10-2.

Figure 10-2. Random International, Swarm Study/III (2011). *Interactive light installation responding to visitors' movement, Victoria & Albert Museum, London. Photo: 14GTR, CC0 via Wikimedia Commons*

A field of illuminated brass rods responds to the movements of visitors, creating shimmering waves of light that feel alive and reactive.

Another famous real-world example by Random International is ***Rain Room*** (2012), an installation that allows people to walk through a downpour without getting wet.[2]

Overhead 3D trackers and cameras detect each visitor's position, and a computer control system halts the rain directly above them in real time.

Technically, *Rain Room* functions through a sophisticated vision-actuation loop:

- **Computer Vision:** It utilizes overhead 3D depth cameras (similar to Microsoft Kinect or Intel RealSense) using Blob Detection algorithms to isolate human silhouettes from the background.

[2] A documentary video on *Rain Room* by Random International can be found here: `https://vimeo.com/51830893` or here: `https://www.youtube.com/watch?v=-z9hGdh_hHM`.

- **Actuation:** The ceiling is a grid of solenoid valves. When the system detects a "blob" at coordinates (x, y), it sends a signal to a Programmable Logic Controller (PLC) to close the specific valves in that sector.
- **Latency Target:** To ensure the visitor remains dry even while walking, the total system latency (detection + processing + valve mechanical response) must stay under 100ms.

The visitor thus experiences the miraculous illusion of controlling rain with their presence. This piece illustrates the **Input ➤ Output loop** perfectly. **Human presence is detected, the artwork processes it, and the environment responds by stopping the rain locally**.

Such works provide "an uncanny experience of controlling the rain," blending technology, natural elements, and human interaction in a unique way.

10.1.2 Historical References

Although the current wave of immersive, environment-like sculptures feels very contemporary, its roots can be traced through the history of 20th-century art.

Visionary artists have long sought to break the confines of the pedestal and traditional exhibition, turning space itself into art.

A few key historical references help illuminate how we arrived at today's immersive paradigm.

One of the earliest examples of immersive environments in art history is the ***Merzbau*** by Kurt Schwitters (1923–1937), as shown in Figure 10-3.

Figure 10-3. Kurt Schwitters, Merzbau, Hannover, begun 1923 (destroyed 1943).
View of the interior of the artist's house transformed into a three-dimensional collage of columns, niches, and grottoes made from found materials. Considered a seminal precursor of installation and environmental art

Rather than a single sculpture, the *Merzbau* was an evolving process: Schwitters gradually transformed his home in Hannover into a three-dimensional collage, composed of columns, hidden niches, and abstract grottoes built from found materials and geometric accretions.[3]

It was not an object to be contemplated from a distance but a space to be physically traversed, an environment that engulfed the viewer and compelled them to move and interpret every corner.

The *Merzbau*, continuously modified and never definitive, anticipated by decades what we now define as installation or environmental art: a work that coincides with the very space in which the experience is lived.

From a technical perspective, it represents the analog precursor to modern interactive systems; where today we use sensors to trigger changes, Schwitters used physical topography and "found space" to force a change in the viewer's perspective and movement.

It established the conceptual foundation for the **"hybrid spaces"** discussed in this chapter, where the boundary between the viewer's body and the artwork's structure begins to dissolve.

A few decades later, the immersive experience took on a radically different character with Yayoi Kusama's Infinity *Mirror Rooms.*

Beginning in the 1960s, the Japanese artist experimented with the use of mirrors and repeated motifs—lights, spheres, polka dots—to generate the illusion of infinity.

From a phenomenological standpoint, Kusama's rooms act as **optical processors**, where the mirror surface functions as a passive feedback loop.

Much like a digital buffer repeats a signal to create a delay, these reflections multiply the visitor's presence, dissolving the boundaries of the "self" into a purely perceptual and iterative field.

Entering one of these rooms means finding oneself in a boundless universe, where one's own image multiplies endlessly and dissolves among reflections. The visitor does not observe from the outside but becomes an integral part of the scene, losing the contours of their body in a play of light and perception that often provokes a sensation of disorientation and "self-annihilation.

[3] Kurt Schwitters' Merzbau (1923–1937) was an evolving architectural environment created in his Hannover home, considered a seminal work of installation art. For further information, see `https://www.tate.org.uk/research/tate-papers/08/kurt-schwitters-reconstructions-of-the-merzbau`.

In another direction, but with the same intention of dissolving the distance between work and audience, we find the installations of Olafur Eliasson.

The Danish-Icelandic artist, active since the 1990s, **uses natural elements such as light, water, fog, and temperature to transform exhibition spaces into total perceptual experiences**. Works such as *The Weather Project* (2003, Tate Modern), with its majestic "false" sunrise enveloped in mist, or *Your Rainbow Panorama* (2011, Aarhus)—a circular glass walkway that immerses the visitor in the colors of the spectrum, demonstrate how sculpture can become atmosphere and sensorial condition.[4]

No privileged viewpoint exists: the work surrounds the visitor's body, altering itself with every step.

In *Room for One Color* (1997), a monochromatic glow turns vision into estrangement, as the world itself seems absorbed into a single field of yellow light.[5]

In Eliasson's work, light and atmosphere are treated as **structural building materials**.

By modulating wavelengths—such as the mono-frequency yellow light in *Room for One Color*—he manipulates the viewer's "sensorial input" in a way that parallels modern digital filters.

Here, the sculpture is no longer an object to be looked at but a **calibrated environment** that re-programs the visitor's physiological perception in real time.

Eliasson, in continuity with light art pioneers such as James Turrell, shifts the focus from the artifact to perception, creating situations in which the viewer becomes an active participant in a phenomenological environment.

These historical examples[6] demonstrate a continuum. Artists have increasingly treated space and context as sculptural materials.

From Schwitters's domestic cavern of *Merzbau* to Kusama's mirrored infinity and Eliasson's climate-like atmospheres, we see a trajectory of sculpture expanding beyond isolated objects toward total environments.

---

[4] Olafur Eliasson, *Your Rainbow Panorama* (2006–2011), ARoS Aarhus Art Museum, Denmark. `https://olafureliasson.net/artwork/your-rainbow-panorama-2006-2011/`

[5] Olafur Eliasson, Room for One Colour (1997). `https://olafureliasson.net/artwork/room-for-one-colour-1997/`

[6] Among others, Allan Kaprow's "environments," such as Yard (1961), in which he filled a courtyard with old tires and invited the audience to walk through, transforming space and materials into a participatory field. `https://www.hauserwirth.com/news/14414-allan-kaprow-yard-artforum`

Each of these works transformed a space into "**an environment to be lived,**" in which the spectator's physical and emotional experience completes the work.

This lays the groundwork for the fully immersive, interactive sculptures of today.

10.2 Sculptural Immersion in Physical Spaces

Having established the shift from object to environment, we now look at how contemporary sculptures create immersion in literal, physical spaces.

This section examines works that have architectural scale or presence, allowing viewers to walk into or through them, as well as the incorporation of technology and media to enrich these environments.

10.2.1 Sculpture as Habitable Environment

One notable direction in recent decades has been sculpture that grows to architectural dimensions, to the point where it becomes a habitable or walkable environment.

These are artworks that you enter like a building or wander through like a landscape.

In effect, they are sculpture-architectures, constructions that function aesthetically as sculpture but spatially as rooms, tunnels, or even small buildings that viewers can occupy.

Such works blur the boundary between art and architecture.

They often envelop the audience in a defined space, dictating how one navigates and what one perceives inside.

Early precedents include experimental exhibition designs and "environments."

In the 1960s for example, Niki de Saint Phalle's monumental sculpture HON (1966): a giant reclining female figure 28 meters long which visitors literally entered through an opening in the figure's body.

After HON, Niki de Saint Phalle also developed her iconic Nanas: exuberant, brightly colored female figures, often monumental in scale, that celebrated vitality, sensuality, and playfulness in public space.

As shown in Figure 10-4, in the examples installed in Hannover, these sculptures transform the female form into an architectural and symbolic presence, bridging sculpture, environment, and lived space.

Figure 10-4. Niki de Saint Phalle, Nanas, 1974*, painted polyester, Leibnizufer, Hannover, Germany.*
Monumental sculptures from the celebrated series of brightly colored female figures, installed in public space as symbols of vitality, sensuality, and playfulness. Photo by Pär Henning, Public Domain, `https://commons.wikimedia.org/w/index.php?curid=3033634`

HON was one of the first modern sculptures designed as an inhabited space.[7]

From a structural perspective, *HON* operates as a "narrative vessel." It shifts the interactive loop from electronic sensors to physical thresholds.

By entering the sculpture, the visitor's body becomes the "input" that activates the internal space, turning the passive act of viewing into a physical navigation of the artwork's interior volume.

Today, many public artworks and installations carry on this approach.

Some sculptors deliberately design pieces that the public can walk in, climb on, or otherwise use as a space. These include immersive architectural pavilions and large-scale installations at art museums or fairs.

[7] For context and reference see Moderna Museet Stockholm's exhibition "Remembering She: A Cathedral." `https://www.modernamuseet.se/stockholm/en/exhibitions/remembering-she-a-cathedral/`

In essence, the sculpture becomes a container for experience.

The interior volume, surfaces, lighting, and acoustics are crafted as part of the artistic intent. This tendency represents an extreme fulfillment of the idea of sculpture as environment: the sculpture is a place.

It invites the public not just to look at it, but to dwell within it, effectively becoming a static, physical precursor to the dynamic, reactive **"fields of immersion"** enabled by today's digital technologies.

10.2.2 Museum and Urban Experiences: Kapoor and Serra

Two leading figures who exemplify immersive, large-scale sculpture are Anish Kapoor and Richard Serra, both of whom have created works that transform museum galleries or public plazas into engulfing sculptural environments.

Among Kapoor's most ambitious projects is Leviathan (2011), a monumental inflatable sculpture installed in Paris's Grand Palais.[8]

The work, a balloon-like form 35 meters high made of translucent PVC, entirely filled the historic exhibition hall.

Visitors entered this womb-like space and were bathed in red light, experiencing the sculpture as an immersive architectural volume around them.

With works like *Leviathan*, Kapoor has repeatedly achieved an architectural scale that invites full bodily immersion.

The installation created a powerful physical and mental experience. The huge curving walls and the ambient light made visitors keenly aware of scale and of their own bodies within space.

Notably, the piece also responded subtly to natural light and weather. Clouds passing over the glass roof caused the red light's intensity to fluctuate, making the space feel alive and dynamic.

[8] Inside Anish Kapoor's Leviathan the immense curved surfaces erase the sense of architectural limits so that visitors no longer know where the building ends and the artwork begins. `https://publicdelivery.org/anish-kapoor-leviathan`

From the outside, Leviathan was an enormous bulbous object occupying the nave; from the inside, it became an immersive architecture with an almost spiritual, otherworldly atmosphere.

Kapoor's other works likewise blur the line between sculpture and environment: Marsyas (Tate Modern, 2002) stretched a massive PVC membrane across a hall,[9] and *Descent into Limbo* (1992) literally let viewers approach a dark void in the floor.[10]

The same effect is achieved in the public installation *Descension* (2014), (Figure 10-5) a swirling whirlpool of water opened an unsettling threshold between surface and depth, extending the artist's exploration of the void into the urban landscape.[11]

[9] Kapoor's Marsyas installation—spanning the Turbine Hall at Tate Modern—can be explored at `https://anishkapoor.com/156/marsyas-3`.

[10] See Anish Kapoor's Descent into Limbo, 1992, at `https://anishkapoor.com/75/descent-into-limbo`.

An installation featuring a circular void cut into the floor, appearing at first as a flat black disc but in fact opening into a deep, unfathomable space. The work destabilizes perception, confronting the viewer with the vertigo of emptiness.

[11] See Anish Kapoor's Descension at Public Delivery, where the installation is discussed as a public whirlpool sculpture that merges void and vortex. `https://publicdelivery.org/anish-kapoor-descension`

Figure 10-5. Anish Kapoor, Descension, 2014*, Brooklyn Bridge Park, Pier 1, New York, 2017.*
An immersive water vortex installation activated in the public realm, where swirling water creates a disorienting void in the surface, challenging the boundary between surface and depth. Photo by Thomson200, Own work, CC0, `https://commons.wikimedia.org/w/index.php?curid=63069850`

His famous public sculpture *Cloud Gate* (The Bean, 2004) in Chicago, while not enterable, engages viewers through mirrored reflections of the city and themselves, drawing them under its curved surface into a shifting play of light, space, and collective presence.

In Kapoor's oeuvre, sculpture often surrounds, swallows, or mirrors the viewer, making them acutely aware of the space they occupy.

These works generate physical and mental immersion, as in Leviathan, where human presence seems to suspend time and alter the perception of space, creating a unique atmosphere.

Richard Serra, on the other hand, works with solid weathering steel[12] to shape space in a way that is no less immersive.

Serra's monumental, rolled steel sculptures—such as *The Matter of Time* (1994–2005, permanent at Guggenheim Bilbao) or his earlier Torqued Ellipses series—are freestanding forms that viewers can walk into and around, discovering curving corridors and chambers formed by towering steel plates (Figure 10-6).

***Figure 10-6. Richard Serra, The Matter of Time**, corten steel.*
Monumental curving walls of weathering steel create a labyrinthine environment that reshapes spatial perception through movement and duration.
Photo by Paul Trafford, CC BY 2.0, `https://commons.wikimedia.org/w/index.php?curid=85635123`

[12] Weathering steel, commonly known by the trade name Corten, is a type of steel that develops a protective rust-like patina when exposed to the elements. This surface layer prevents further corrosion, giving the material its characteristic brown-red appearance and durability.

These works operate by physically surrounding the viewer and subtly altering his orientation and balance through canted walls and spiral paths.

In *The Matter of Time*, at the Guggenheim Bilbao, eight monumental spirals and curves of weathering steel transform walking into the artwork's core.

The tilted walls bend space and sound, disorienting and reorienting the visitor at each step. There is no single viewpoint. The sculpture unfolds in time as the viewer moves through it, turning perception into an embodied journey.

Serra thus redefines sculpture not as an object to be observed but as a spatial field completed by the viewer's movement.

Both Kapoor and Serra demonstrate how massive sculptures placed in museums or urban contexts can envelop the body and senses of the public.

In different ways—one using vivid color and soft form, the other using hard industrial material—they realize the idea of sculpture as a total environment.

Viewers do not merely look at Leviathan or *The Matter of Time*; they navigate them, internalize them, and remember them as spatial-temporal experiences.

These examples underline that the city, the museum, or any architectural setting can be transformed by sculpture into a new kind of place, one that engages people on a bodily, intuitive level.

10.2.3 Space as a Living Body, Enveloping and Shaping Those Who Move Through it

When sculpture expands to fill space and incorporate the viewer, the space itself can be thought of as a living body, one that envelops and reacts to those who move through it.

In immersive installations, the environment often behaves almost like an organism or a resonating vessel.[13]

The idea of "the space as a body" means that the created environment has a presence and agency akin to a living entity. It surrounds the visitor, it can influence the visitor's mood and orientation, and it sometimes even changes in response to the visitor.

[13] The notion of "space as a living body" relates to Merleau-Ponty's phenomenology of embodied perception, Bachelard's reflections on lived and imagined space, and Lefebvre's concept of the social production of space, later echoed in immersive art practices that treat space as an active organism.

This perspective is bolstered by theoretical discussions in phenomenology and architecture. The philosopher Merleau-Ponty argued that our perception is embodied. We understand space through our bodily presence.

Immersive art transforms space itself into the artwork. Meaning is generated through the embodied, subjective experience of the visitor, in a condition of porous boundaries between observer and observed. The viewer and the installation merge into one continuous system, like a body entering a new medium.

As a "living body," space conditions those who cross it. A narrow corridor induces tension; a vast hall evokes openness.

Artists use this spatial psychology: Serra's spirals create anxiety and release, Turrell's light alters inner states, and Eliasson engages all senses with environments of color, light, or fog that reshape perception.

Some contemporary works enhance the impression of space that responds: lights pulsing like a heartbeat (Lozano-Hemmer, Pulse Room) or sound environments that shift with the visitor's position.

Space becomes an active partner in the aesthetic experience; it envelops, reacts, resonates.

Immersion arises from this dynamic, relational quality. Art happens in the encounter between environment and body.

The space comes alive as an "other" with which the visitor enters into dialogue.

10.2.4 Integration of Light, Sound, Video, AI, and Interactivity

In pushing sculpture into fully immersive experiences, artists increasingly integrate diverse media and advanced technologies.

Contemporary immersive installations tend to be multisensory and multimedia, combining sculptural elements with light, projected images, spatialized sound, even smells, and interactive or intelligent systems.

By orchestrating all these components, the artwork can create a total atmosphere.

In this paragraph we highlight how contemporary artists use these tools and give practical examples of immersive works that fuse sculpture with technology.

The art collective teamLab from Japan is famous for large-scale digital installations that respond to visitor behavior.

For example, their piece *Flowers and People - Dark* is an interactive projection environment where flowers bloom, scatter, and die in an endless real-time generated sequence.

Crucially, the presence and movements of visitors influence this cycle: "The flowers bud, grow, and blossom before their petals begin to wither and eventually fade away.

"The cycle of growth and decay repeats itself in perpetuity. Depending on the proximity of the viewer to the work, the flowers shed their petals all at once, wither and die, or come to life and blossom once again."[14]

The imagery is not prerecorded; it's computed on the fly, so the artwork is never the same twice.[15]

In teamLab's installations, digital projections, motion sensors, and sound work in concert to create immersive ecosystems of light that literally surround the viewer.

Walk into a dark room, and you find waterfall projections that actually flow around your silhouette, or a floor that reacts to your footsteps with blooming flowers.

These works are essentially interactive animated paintings in space, dissolving the boundary between art and viewer.

teamLab emphasizes a concept of "ultra-subjective space," and often the environment is made of light and visual effect, but it is completely spatial and immersive, treating the walls and floors as a canvas and the viewer as a participant in a digital nature.

Such integration of computer-generated graphics, tracking technology, and environmental audio results in a "**constantly evolving, generative artwork**" that challenges the notion of a fixed art object.

One exception to teamLab's usual approach, which often minimizes the presence of physical objects, is *Forest of Resonating Lamps* (2016), as shown in Figure 10-7.

[14] The phrase comes from the official teamLab description of *Flowers and People* (2015, in versions such as *Dark* and *Gold*), where the collective explains how the viewer's presence directly influences the digital blooming process. `https://www.teamlab.art/w/flowersandpeople-dark`

[15] The passage "The artwork is not a pre-recorded image that is played back: it is created by a computer program that continuously renders the work in real time. The interaction between people and the installation causes continuous change in the artwork: previous visual states can never be replicated, and will never reoccur. The picture at this moment can never be seen again." is taken from the same link of the official teamLab website.

Figure 10-7. teamLab, Forest of Resonating Lamps, 2016.
Immersive installation with suspended lamps, sensors, and responsive lighting system. teamLab Borderless, Tokyo.
Photo by Stephanie Grisham, `https://twitter.com/StephGrisham45/status/1132460615317053442`, Public Domain

Here, the installation employs real suspended lamps, yet these objects dissolve into their luminous function. As a visitor approaches, a lamp changes color and transmits its glow to the others, producing ripples of light across the room.

In this way, the physical element becomes a vehicle for an environment that is essentially immaterial, an ever-changing field of resonance and participation.

Building on this, the integration of AI opens new possibilities for reactive and generative environments that incorporate complexities beyond what a human could pre-design.

While still emerging, these technologies hint at a future where immersive installations may include artificial intelligences that modify the space in response not only to immediate inputs but also to learned patterns, predictions, or creative "decisions" of their own.

The examples seen so far illustrate the diverse strategies of multimedia integration in immersive sculpture.

Light, moving images, and sound are particularly powerful in shaping atmosphere. A dark space with gentle ambient sound and slow-moving projections can induce calm, while a bright, flashing, loud environment can overwhelm and excite.

Artists, in this sense, "compose" an environment much like musicians compose a score: balancing visual, auditory, and tactile elements to create a unified emotional field.

To achieve this "composition" of space, the artist must act as a system orchestrator (Figure 10-8).

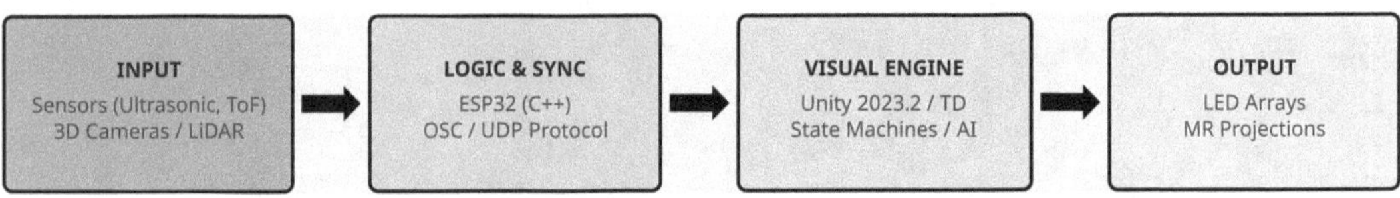

Figure 10-8. The sensor-to-output signal flow.
A conceptual map of the hybrid orchestration between physical triggers and digital responses

Modern installations rely on specific software environments to synchronize disparate media:

- **Timeline-Based Tools:** Platforms like TouchDesigner's Timeline, Unity's Timeline, or Ableton Live (with video sync plugins) allow for precise temporal alignment of light, video, and sound.
- **Synchronization Protocols:**
    - **OSC (Open Sound Control):** The industry standard for real-time communication between hardware (sensors/ESP32) and software (Unity/TouchDesigner).
    - **MIDI/SMPTE Timecode:** Used when the installation must follow a strict, frame-accurate schedule across multiple devices (e.g., sound systems and video projectors).
    - **State Machines:** For nonlinear experiences (like teamLab's), developers use "State Machines" where the artwork transitions between different behaviors (e.g., Blooming, Withering, Idle) based on sensor triggers rather than a fixed clock.

3D scanning and related technologies are flexible tools that open up new ways of seeing the world, releasing creativity into practices that had long followed the same methods.

They allow artists to capture, reinterpret, and hybridize real forms into digital environments, turning static objects into responsive, living spaces.

This orchestration of media and technology transforms the sculpture from a fixed object into a dynamic field of experience, where every element—light, sound, motion—contributes to the visitor's journey through a living continuum.

10.2.5 The Hybrid Artist's Toolkit (2025): Technical Note

In the hybrid realm of immersive sculpture, the traditional tools of the trade—chisel, mallet, clay—now share the workbench with code, circuits, and controllers.

The artist no longer simply shapes matter; they orchestrate systems where light, sound, and motion respond to presence, turning the viewer into an essential part of the work.

This evolution demands a new toolkit—one that bridges the physical and the digital, the tangible, and the responsive (Figure 10-9).

1. **Recommended Learning Path**

   To navigate this terrain effectively:

   - **Foundations:** Begin with Arduino (C++) or ESP32 for physical logic and sensor integration—the language of things that sense and react.
   - **Visual Logic:** Master TouchDesigner or Unity for real-time 3D rendering and generative environments—the canvas where light, particles, and space come alive.
   - **Interconnectivity:** Learn Open Sound Control (OSC) to make hardware and software speak seamlessly—the bridge that turns a gesture into a glowing response.

2. **Common Beginner Pitfalls & Solutions:**

   - **Inadequate Power:** Never power large LED arrays (WS2812B) directly from a microcontroller. Use external power supplies and remember to connect all GND pins to a common ground.

- **Sensor Noise:** Raw data from ultrasonic or PIR sensors can be "jumpy." Apply a Simple Moving Average (SMA) filter in code to smooth values and prevent erratic light behavior.
- **Lack of Error Handling:** Always include "Watchdogs" in your code. If a sensor fails or disconnects, the system should default to a graceful "Idle" state rather than crashing.

3. **Collaboration vs. Solo Mastery**

   Artistic vision should always guide technical learning. While basic coding is essential, collaborating with creative technologists or engineers is a valid and often superior path for large-scale urban projects.

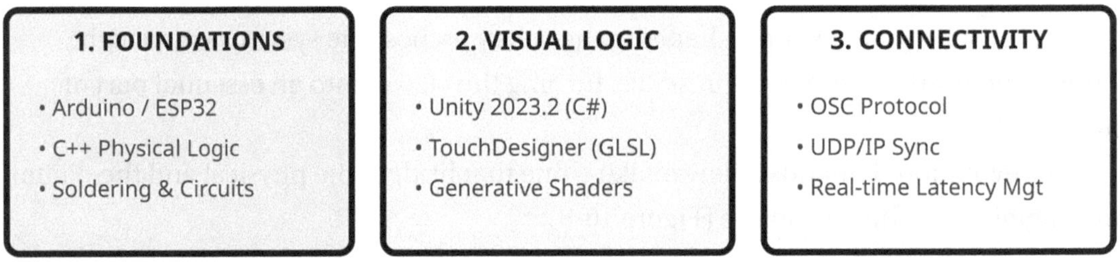

1. FOUNDATIONS
- Arduino / ESP32
- C++ Physical Logic
- Soldering & Circuits

2. VISUAL LOGIC
- Unity 2023.2 (C#)
- TouchDesigner (GLSL)
- Generative Shaders

3. CONNECTIVITY
- OSC Protocol
- UDP/IP Sync
- Real-time Latency Mgt

Figure 10-9. The hybrid artist's toolkit.
A conceptual map of the core competencies required for 2025 immersive sculpture

Today, an immersive sculptor may need as much understanding of coding or electronics as of casting or carving.

The payoff is the ability to create experiences that transcend traditional boundaries and engage multiple senses, turning sculpture into a living field of presence. Ultimately, the immersive sculptor of 2025 no longer sculpts mere objects: they sculpt relationships.

10.3 Theoretical Perspectives: Immersion and Presence

Having surveyed the practical developments of immersive sculpture, it is equally important to reflect on the theoretical and conceptual foundations of this turn.

What does it mean—philosophically and psychologically—to be inside an artwork rather than observing it from outside?

How do notions of presence, embodiment, and atmosphere shape our understanding of immersive spaces?

This section addresses these questions, drawing on art theory, phenomenology, and criticism to clarify the shifting role of the spectator and the transformed nature of the aesthetic experience.

We will examine how the "boundary" between the subject and the object is not just blurred by sensors, but fundamentally redefined by our consciousness.

10.3.1 Observing vs. Inhabiting an Artwork

A fundamental distinction can be drawn between observing an artwork and inhabiting it.

In traditional encounters, for example, looking at a classical sculpture on a pedestal, the model is one of contemplative distance. The viewer remains external, physically and emotionally separated from the artwork, which is conceived as autonomous and self-contained.

Immersive and installation art reverse this model.

The artwork becomes an environment or responsive system, and the viewer enters it, becoming part of its unfolding. The one-way gaze gives way to reciprocal interaction, where distance collapses both physically and conceptually.

In essence, the spectator is absorbed into the work.

This distinction also reflects the question of aura and certification. Traditional art anchors aura in the uniqueness of the original object. Immersive art shifts aura to the lived experience itself, often authenticated or "certified" through digital protocols, recordings, or participatory logs that bind the work to its context and the presence of the audience.[16]

As Claire Bishop observes in *Installation Art: A Critical History*, such works "require the use and awareness of the body." Perception is tied to movement and time.[17]

[16] On the shift of aura to lived experience and its certification through digital means, see: Domingues, Diana. "Day-Dreaming States in Interfaced Environments: Telematic Rituals in Ouroboros." Leonardo 37(4), 2004, pp. 308–314. PDF MIT Press. https://direct.mit.edu/leon/article-abstract/37/4/308/44631/Day-Dreaming-States-in-Interfaced-Environments
Paul, Christiane. Digital Art. London: Thames & Hudson, 2023 (4th ed.). https://www.thamesandhudsonusa.com/books/digital-art-softcover-fourth

[17] *Bishop, Claire. Installation Art: A Critical History. London: Tate Publishing, 2005 (rev. ed. 2010).* https://archive.org/details/installationartc0000bish_v8d6

Immersive art replaces the spectatorial regime of detachment with experiential immediacy.

These practices also entail the loss of the privileged perspective. Whereas traditional sculpture often assumes an ideal viewpoint, immersive works unfold from within and in time.

Each participant's trajectory produces a different encounter, making the work open-ended and shaped by audience behavior.

In summary, the difference between observing and inhabiting an artwork is the difference between looking at and being inside.

This marks a foundational change in the artist–audience relationship and underscores why immersive art is regarded as a paradigm shift in contemporary practice.

10.3.2 Concepts of "Presence," "Embodiment," and "Atmosphere"

Key theoretical concepts that help articulate the immersive experience are "presence," "embodiment," and "atmosphere."

These terms recur in discourse about installation art, and each highlights a different aspect of what makes immersive works compelling.

- **Presence** is the sensation of truly being there. Immersive works surround you and unfold only through your participation. Presence is also collective, as seen in Olafur Eliasson's The Weather Project at Tate Modern, where the gathering of visitors became inseparable from the work.[18]
- **Embodiment** highlights that perception in immersive art involves the entire body.

[18] Olafur Eliasson's The Weather Project (Tate Modern, 2003) transformed the Turbine Hall into a vast atmospheric environment with mist and a glowing artificial sun, where visitors gathered and often lay on the floor beneath the light.

James Turrell's Ganzfeld installations[19] exemplify this. In featureless rooms, visitors often lose depth perception and become acutely aware of their own balance.

In such works, bodily responses are integral, completing the experience.

- **Atmosphere** is the mood that pervades the space.

  Through light, sound, scale, and rhythm, artists construct environments that may feel sacred, playful, uncanny, or meditative.

  Unlike an image or object, atmosphere must be entered and sensed with the body; it saturates the experience, binding presence and embodiment into one continuum.

  Yayoi Kusama's Infinity Mirror Rooms envelop the viewer in an endless cascade of reflections, producing a vertiginous sense of boundlessness.

The notion of "aura" may be evoked here, though it is distinct from Walter Benjamin's focus on the unique object.

In immersive installations, aura becomes **environmental**, emerging from the atmospheric field that surrounds and transforms the visitor.

Rather than presenting an object to look at, immersive art constructs worlds to be entered, where significance arises through bodily presence and sensory engagement.

These concepts—presence, embodiment, and atmosphere—intertwine in Studio Azzurro's *Where Are All These People Going?* (2000).[20]

In this installation, the **atmosphere** of mystery is activated only through the visitor's **embodied** movement, which triggers the response of life-size projected figures.

---

[19] The term Ganzfeld (German for "total field") originates in perceptual psychology, where it denotes a condition of uniform visual stimulation without contours or reference points, often producing disorientation or hallucinatory effects. James Turrell adopts this concept in his light installations, creating environments in which spatial boundaries dissolve and visitors experience an unlimited visual field.

[20] Studio Azzurro, Where Are All These People Going? (2000). Official work page available on Studio Azzurro's website at `https://www.studioazzurro.com/opere/dove-va-tutta-sta-gente`.

Here, **presence** is a structural requirement. The work remains a void until the participant enters, creating an uncanny encounter between real and virtual bodies.

This interaction places participants in a **liminal state**: a threshold between reality and artifice, self and environment.[21]

As such, immersive spaces become worlds unto themselves, with their own internal rules and "climates."

Stepping inside means crossing into an altered condition where, as noted in contemporary discourse on immersive environments, the focus shifts toward exploring "altered states of consciousness"+ and the fluidity of the subject-object boundary.[22]

10.3.3 Immersive Space as a Liminal Experience: Continuity Between Art and Spectator

Immersive installations are often described as creating liminal experiences.

Such experiences transform perception. Visitors may lose track of time or question their role: are they spectators or part of the work?

This ambiguity can provoke introspection, foster community, or generate memorable departures from normality.

While Kusama multiplies the self through mirrored infinities, Turrell invites the viewer to inhabit the void of light and sky.

His skyspaces represent some of the most compelling instances of immersion as a threshold experience.

[21] The concept of liminality, drawn from anthropological studies of rites of passage (van Gennep, 1909; Turner, 1969), describes transitional states "in between" categories. In immersive art, this threshold condition places the viewer in a liminal space—suspended between physical reality and virtual simulation—where perception, identity, and presence are temporarily reconfigured. Van Gennep, A. (1909). Les Rites de Passage. Paris: Émile Nourry. Turner, V. (1969). The Ritual Process: Structure and Anti-Structure. Chicago: Aldine.

[22] The term "states of consciousness" summarizes key themes in immersive art, as articulated in a dedicated study guide (Fiveable, 2023). https://fiveable.me/installation-art/unit-5/immersive-environments/study-guide/CZRaW5DZmydHox9U

These concepts are deeply developed in seminal works such as Claire Bishop's Installation Art: A Critical History (2005), Char Davies' Osmose (1994–95, a pioneering VR installation exploring embodiment and perceptual shifts) and recent research in Frontiers in Psychology (2023) on embodiment in installation art.

https://www.immersence.com/osmose/

In works such as *Seldom Seen* (Houghton Hall, Norfolk, 2025), Turrell uses simple architecture—an open ceiling aperture, carefully modulated light—to transform perception of the sky (Figure 10-10).

Figure 10-10. James Turrel, Seldom Seen, skyspace by James Turrell, Houghton Hall, Norfolk, 2025.
The open aperture frames the ever-changing sky, dissolving the boundary between interior architecture and infinite exterior light—inviting the viewer into a quiet, meditative threshold where perception itself becomes the artwork. Photo by By Mikenorton, own work, CC BY-SA 4.0, `https://commons.wikimedia.org/w/index.php?curid=48800172`

At dawn or dusk, the framed sky appears saturated with unexpected color shifts; visitors often report perceiving the sky differently long after leaving the installation.

The effect is not just optical but existential. The sky, infinite and ungraspable, is momentarily rendered intimate and architectural.

In contrast, Anish Kapoor's Sky Mirrors, such as *Sky Mirror for Hendrik,*[23] redirect the gaze outward rather than inward (Figure 10-11). Here, polished steel surfaces are oriented toward the heavens, capturing clouds and sky in a liquid-like reflection.

Figure 10-11. Anish Kapoor, Sky Mirror for Hendrik, 2017*, stainless steel, De Pont Museum, Tilburg, Netherlands.*
The polished concave surface gathers the sky into a fluid, mirror-like pool, collapsing the infinite heavens into an intimate, ever-shifting presence at ground level. By RoMaVo, own work, CC0, https://commons.wikimedia.org/w/index.php?curid=173899559

[23] More on Sky Mirror for Hendrik. https://www.seafoundation.eu/sky-mirror-kapoor-pont-tilburg-netherlands/

Kapoor's mirrors project the sky back into the world, monumentalizing the ephemeral.

The effect is equally liminal. Viewers stand before an object that seems to dissolve into its surroundings, caught between sculpture and atmosphere, between solid form and infinite flux.

10.3.4 Case Study: The Blue Planet by Peter Greenaway and Saskia Boddeke

The *Blue Planet*, a multimedia opera-theater project by filmmaker Peter Greenaway and theater director Saskia Boddeke, first staged in 2008–2009 exemplifies how immersive practices can transform traditional performance.[24]

Although the audience remains seated, the project creates a total environment by merging real and virtual elements, engaging the audience on multiple sensory levels while conveying a powerful narrative about the ecological crisis.[25]

10.3.4.1 The Setup

Commissioned for Expoagua Zaragoza, the production **is a hybrid spectacle that** fuses live theater, cinematic projection, and virtual reality.

The auditorium is enveloped in wraparound high-definition projections, with live water on stage, surround sound, and 3D avatars of God and Noah floating among the spectators.

In this context, the biblical flood becomes a metaphor for contemporary climate collapse; the audience is sensorially submerged in a deluge of images, light, and sound.

Water is both symbolic and scenic. Reservoirs, waterfalls, and oceans in motion are projected overhead, while actors perform immersed in a real pool on stage.

10.3.4.2 Immersive Elements

From the outset, the audience is enveloped in a total audiovisual environment.

High-definition projections of flowing water dominate the space, while rippling light patterns reflect onto walls and ceiling, creating the illusion of being underwater.

---

[24] Official project page for *The Blue Planet* on SBPG Projects, including images, description, and multimedia materials. `https://www.sbpg-projects.com/the-blue-planet`

[25] Video excerpt of *The Blue Planet* on YouTube: `https://www.youtube.com/watch?v=T8zRGv41mUO`

`https://www.youtube.com/watch?v=Tl2jdglS1h8`

Live performers splash and struggle in the pool, giving tangible form to the flood. Simultaneously, the performers interact with avatars generated in Second Life—including a live-voiced digital God and symbolic animals—projected on overhead screens.

This creates a layered narrative where physical and virtual presences coexist and dialogue.

Sound design deepens the immersion. Goran Bregović's score blends live orchestra with recorded layers, amplified by the roar of water and thunder rolling through the theater. Together, these elements transform the performance into an all-encompassing sensory simulation of planetary inundation.

10.3.4.3 Conceptual Resonance

The interplay of live and virtual action mirrors contemporary life, where human experience is increasingly mediated by technology.

The dialogue between Noah and God—conducted through avatars—suggests that even our relationship with the transcendent is now refracted through digital systems.

This continuous shift of focus demands a new mode of attention, one that embraces split presence and sensory overload, mirroring the overwhelming nature of a planetary flood.

Spectators often recall not just the story but the physical sensation of humidity and sound vibrations and the glow of projected light: an immersion that engages body and mind alike.

10.3.4.4 Conclusion

The *Blue Planet* exemplifies how immersive art can create a liminal space that is at once fantastic and real.

By merging water, image, sound, and narrative, it transforms spectators into witnesses within a shared environment, collapsing the separation between art and life.

It encapsulates the themes of this chapter: the fusion of art and technology, the redefined role of the audience, and the transformation of performance into a lived environment. It is what Greenaway and Boddeke called not a film or a play but a "**visionary spectacle**" and **a space to be inhabited**.

10.4 My Practice: Toward Immersive Hybrid Landscapes

Having explored the broader context of immersive sculpture, I will now turn to how these ideas intersect with and inspire my own artistic practice.

This section reflects on the "**seeds of immersion**" present in my earlier works and outlines a trajectory from material presence to interactive environments.

I will detail how traditional sculptural forms can be reinterpreted through new technologies (light-based installations, digital twins, responsive systems, etc), illustrating a personal evolution from the autonomous object to inhabitable space.

10.4.1 Overview

This section opens by revisiting two earlier works, ***The Bubble-Making Machines*** and ***Vertical Labyrinth***, analyzing their potential for expansion across physical and virtual dimensions.

I outline light-based augmentations in situ, 3D modeling, or scanning to create faithful digital twins, and AR/VR overlays supported by responsive spatial audio that transform them from static objects into interactive environments.

Next, I present a set of AI-driven video installations—***Hybridizations, Extensions,* and *Continuous Flows***—where generative models translate pictorial logics into moving images. These works explore responsiveness and data-informed behavior, showing how AI expands painting and sculpture into time-based narratives.

Finally, I discuss a work in progress, *Labyrinth with Vector Physical Field*, illustrating how an artwork evolves from material presence to a hybrid, inhabitable space.

10.4.2 Works Reinterpreted: The Seeds of Immersion

Reflecting on my earlier works, including those created in collaboration with Stefania Albertini under the artistic duo Albertini & Moioli, I realized that many pieces already contained the seeds of immersion in both concept and effect.

For example, in Chapter 1, I presented two projects that illustrate these early explorations:

- **The Bubble-Making Machines (2006–2007).** A series of sculptures, as shown in Figure 10-12 and Figure 10-13, is composed of hammered metal and thermoformed polycarbonate Illuminated from within by LEDs featuring programmed color and intensity variations.

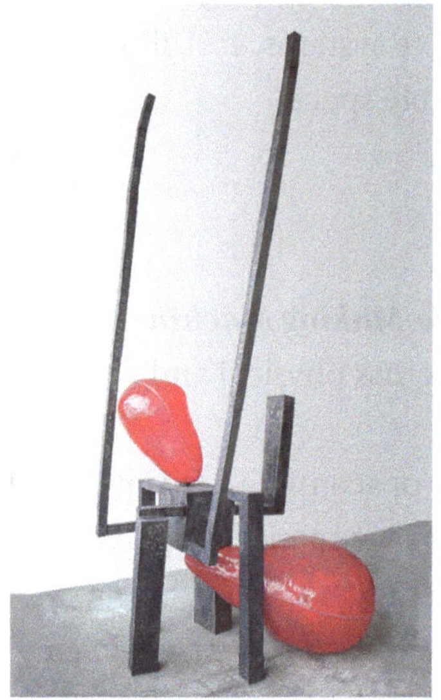

Figure 10-12. Albertini & Moioli, The Bubble-Making Machines, 2006–2007. *Daytime view of the original sculptures in hammered metal and hot-formed polycarbonate*

  This dynamic light transformed the surrounding atmosphere and altered the viewer's spatial perception after dark, effectively turning the sculptures into environmental light installations.

- **Vertical Labyrinth.** A monumental Corten steel outdoor sculpture is installed at the Dongchon Ulsan stadium in South Korea.

  Its layered geometries and large scale did not merely stand as an object to be viewed but actively shaped the environment, mediating the relationship between the spectator and the architectural site.

In retrospect, while these works were non interactive at the time, they manifested latent immersive qualities. By engaging both the environment and the viewer's perception, they foreshadowed the expanded possibilities I am currently exploring—moving beyond traditional sculptural boundaries toward truly hybrid, responsive spaces.

The *Bubble-Making Machines* were designed to have a dual presence, as shown in Figure 10-13. By day they stood as solid, opaque forms with tactile surfaces of metal and large colored translucent bubbles; by night, they glowed from within, the plastic parts emanating light and transforming the surrounding space with ever-shifting colors. In essence, each piece became a light installation after dark, altering the atmosphere around it.

Figure 10-13. Albertini & Moioli, The Bubble-Making Machines, 2006–2007. *Night view of the sculptures in hammered metal with illuminated translucent polycarbonate bubbles with immersive light effect*

People who encountered them at night often described them less as objects and more as "light creatures" or "light architectures," because the glow would cast patterns on nearby walls or create an ethereal aura in the space.

As their lights shifted in color and intensity—albeit through pre-programmed cycles—they functioned as early immersive elements.

In this sense, even in a localized context, they modulated the viewer's visual and spatial experience rather than acting as static objects to be simply looked at.

The concept behind them was to emphasize change in perception. They embodied solidity under sunlight and an almost ethereal, otherworldly quality under their own illumination, inviting viewers to return and experience them at different times.

10.4.2.1 Augmented Bubble Making Machines: From Material Presence to Interactive Environments

In one specific subset of those luminous works, *The Bubbles-Making Machines*, with their shapes and translucent globes, evoke the idea of bubbles or alchemical organisms.

They symbolize fragility and transformation: metal armatures supporting delicate and glowing bubble-like forms. They are static sculptures with an evocative presence.

Today, with new technology, I envision reimagining these "bubble machines" as fully immersive, interactive installations.

What was once a physical sculpture can now become the kernel of an interactive environment.

For instance, these pieces can be 3D-scanned to create precise digital twins of their forms. Scanning captures the geometry, allowing me to remix, scale, and reconfigure the shapes virtually.

Within a digital environment, the sculpture is liberated from physical constraints. It can be reconfigured at an architectural scale or multiplied into complex clusters, exploring spatial arrangements that would be unattainable under the limitations of gravity and material weight.

These models can then be 3D-printed or fabricated in new materials—perhaps translucent polymers with embedded LED lights—returning them to physical form at an entirely different scale.

Technology enabling this has advanced dramatically over the past decade, becoming more accessible, accurate, and affordable, thus opening the door to creative experimentation that was previously impractical.

Combining 3D scanning and 3D printing makes it possible to reproduce a sculpture accurately and sustainably, preserving details that would be impossible to achieve by hand.

I see these techniques not only as tools for reproduction but also for transformation, allowing me to translate a form into new contexts and scales with high fidelity.

Once in digital form, these bubble sculptures are augmented with interactivity, evolving into a hybrid system of sensors, light, and spatial audio. This transition is not just a technical upgrade; it is a conceptual expansion that shifts the work from an "object that changes in lighting" to a "space that changes with your presence."

Ultimately, the sculpture becomes an "immersive field"; a zone where light, material, and code converge, and where the art is not a singular entity but a continuous experience you enter.

I envision an installation of multiple bubble-making machines in a darkened room, where the visitor feels they have stepped inside a field of living entities (Figure 10-14).

Figure 10-14. ***Albertini & Moioli, The Bubble-Making Machines, 2006–2007.*** *Interactive installation with projection mapping and dynamic light effects, engaging viewers and environment*

The fragility and ephemerality symbolized by bubbles become experiential. The lights gently swell and dim like breaths, giving the sense that each bubble is alive.

This biomorphic behavior leverages interactivity to create an empathic space, where a person's intuitive actions lead to the artwork's reactions.

To achieve this "living" quality, the sculptures are fitted with a specific technological architecture.

10.4.2.1.1 Technical Implementation: The Hybrid Sculptural Architecture

To transform these bubble sculptures from static objects into responsive entities, I have developed a multilayered system architecture that bridges physical form and digital logic.

A comprehensive technical breakdown, including circuit diagrams and interaction pseudocode, is provided in Appendix X.

1. **Sensing and Input Layer:** The interactivity is grounded in the viewer's proximity.

   Each sculpture is equipped with a sensor array—typically **four HC-SR04 ultrasonic sensors** placed at cardinal points at a height of 1.5m. This configuration allows the work to "perceive" the approach of visitors from a distance of 2 to 400 cm, creating a 360-degree field of awareness.

2. **Processing and Logic Layer:** The "brain" of each unit is an **ESP32 microcontroller**. I chose this platform for its dual-core processor, which allows for parallel processing: one core dedicated to polling sensor data and the other to managing complex LED animations. Furthermore, its built-in Wi-Fi enables the use of **OSC (Open Sound Control)** or wireless DMX protocols to synchronize multiple sculptures within a larger network.

3. **Output and Illumination Layer:** For the internal glow, I utilize **APA102 (DotStar) LED technology**. Unlike the more common WS2812B (NeoPixel), the APA102 uses separate clock and data lines, which prevents timing conflicts between the high-speed sensor polling and the light refresh rate—ensuring a smooth, flicker-free "breathing" effect.

   - **Power Requirements**: Each RGB LED draws approximately 60mA at peak brightness. For a sculpture containing 200 LEDs, the system requires a 5V/12A power supply to ensure stability and avoid voltage drops that could distort color calibration.

   - **Software Framework**: The logic is implemented using the FastLED library, employing a "state-machine" approach. When no presence is detected, the sculpture remains in a "dormant" state (low-intensity blue pulse); as a visitor approaches, the system transitions to an "active" state, where light intensity and color temperature increase in proportion to the visitor's proximity.

4. **Sculptural Integration:** The challenge of cable management is solved by integrating the wiring within the hammered metal armature, treating the electrical components not as external additions but as the "nervous system" of the work. This high-fidelity integration allows the sculpture to retain its material elegance while functioning as a complex, data-driven environment.

10.4.2.2 Expanded Vertical Labyrinth: Reimagining an Urban Sculpture

Another early work, *Labirinto Verticale, (Vertical Labyrinth)* (2000), is a large outdoor sculpture permanently installed in front of the Dongchon Stadium of the Ulsan Metropolitan City in South Korea.

Even in its static form, it already suggested an immersive dimension, as its monumental scale, architectural framing, and spatial passages invited viewers to move around and through it, engaging bodily with the work rather than observing it from a distance.

Vertical Labyrinth, while a static and noninteractive structure, already suggested immersive qualities (Figure 10-15).

Figure 10-15. Albertini & Moioli, Labirinto Verticale, Design drawing (pencil and mixed media on paper).
These sketches document the primary conceptual phase of the work, focusing on the structural relationships and material composition prior to its large-scale installation

Its monumental frame and layered geometries did not merely stand as an isolated object but actively shaped the perception of those who moved around it.

With today's tools, I am interested in reimagining this work as an expanded, hybrid experience.

With Blender and 3D modeling, I can faithfully reconstruct the sculpture in digital form, preserving its proportions, materials, and details (Figure 10-16).

Figure 10-16. Albertini & Moioli, Labirinto Verticale, 2000.
Rendering projects for the new interactive version of the monumental steel and iron sculpture, 530 (h) × 250 × 250 cm. Dongcheon Stadium, Ulsan Metropolitan City, South Korea. Night views explore how the sculpture could respond to the viewer's presence with dynamic light and color transformations

This reconstruction is not only an archive, but also a creative platform from which new explorations can unfold.

By employing artificial intelligence, the project can be extended into unprecedented visions: formal variations, immersive environments, and transformations that resonate with today's technological context while retaining continuity with the original work.

In this way, the sculpture acquires a dual life—real and virtual—intertwined in a continuous process of reinterpretation and growth.

With tools such as Midjourney, I can explore multiple design possibilities by generating high-fidelity keyframes and sequences of variations.

However, to transform these static iterations into fluid, cinematic motion, I employ a multistage Image-to-Video (I2V) pipeline (detailed in Appendix Y).

This transition from still image to motion allows the sculpture to evolve from a static object into a responsive organism that transforms in relation to the viewer's movement.

Through specific prompt engineering,[26] the environment can be made to fade into darkness, creating a dramatic contrast where the sculpture appears alive, pulsing gently in a dark void. Thus, the original work is reframed as both archive and point of departure; it is a hybrid, responsive form that integrates light, sound, and interactivity. A visual record of this cinematic transformation, showcasing the sculpture's activation into a pulsing, luminous organism is accessible at the following link: `https://vimeo.com/1175229493`.

10.4.2.2.1 Extension of the Existing Public Sculpture

Building on the digital reconstruction and the technical framework detailed in section 10.4.2.1.1 and Appendix X, the *Vertical Labyrinth* can be augmented *in situ* as a monumental interactive installation.

While the core logic remains consistent with the "Sensing - Processing - Output" model, the urban scale requires a professional-grade adaptation of the components:

- **Sensing Layer (Long-Range Detection):** Unlike the near-field sensors used for small sculptures, the urban context demands Long-Range Ultrasonic sensors or Light Detection and Ranging (LiDAR). This allows the work to "perceive" visitors from a distance of up to 10–20 meters, creating a large-scale field of awareness that triggers subtle atmospheric changes long before the viewer reaches the sculpture.

[26] Images generated with Midjourney using the following prompt: "A large abstract outdoor sculpture made of rusted steel and concrete, with voxel-like cubes glowing in red, green, yellow, and orange. The sculpture is placed in a real outdoor park with grass, trees, and a modern architectural background. The lighting is soft but the sculpture emits vivid internal glow, photorealistic, cinematic rendering, realistic texture details, volumetric light --ar 2:3 --v 5.2 --style raw --style photographic."

The surrounding environment fades into darkness, creating a dramatic contrast. The sculpture appears alive, pulsing gently in a dark void.

- **Processing & Connectivity (ESP32 Network):** The ESP32 architecture (described in Appendix X) is particularly suited for this scale. Its dual-core processor handles complex animations without latency, while its built-in Wi-Fi allows for a mesh network configuration. Multiple ESP32 units can be distributed across the monumental structure to synchronize light and sound across large distances without complex wiring.
- **Outputs & Structural Integration:** The "nervous system" of APA102 LEDs is embedded within the metal armature. At a city level, the power management must be scaled to high-amperage industrial power supplies to avoid voltage drops across the large frame, following the stability principles outlined in Appendix X.

In this way, the *Vertical Labyrinth* becomes a responsive urban landmark (Figure 10-17).

Figure 10-17. Albertini & Moioli, Vertical Labyrinth, 2000.
Night view of the sculpture illuminated with colored light, suggesting its potential as a responsive urban landmark or an immersive and interactive environment. Donchon Stadium, Ulsan Metropolitan City, South Korea

Sound transducers turn the massive metal body into a low-frequency resonator, emitting sounds that shift as people move through the square. The sculpture is no longer a static monument but a living, breathing node of the smart city.

These are only some possible ways to employ new technologies to extend earlier projects such as the ones discussed in this chapter.

Other approaches explore virtual, augmented, and immersive environments, each offering distinct possibilities for reimagining the work.

10.4.2.2.2 VR Simulation

Through 3D modeling, its forms can be multiplied, scaled, or distorted at will, turning a single voxel cube into a towering grid or a sprawling labyrinth, such as *Labirinto Verticale*, or the other interactive sculptures realized in virtual worlds by Albertini & Moioli that we saw in section 9.4.2.

Wearing a headset, visitors could then traverse the work as a labyrinth to be experienced from within.

Interactive pathways could lead to different audiovisual "rooms," animated by light patterns, symbolic imagery, or memories connected to the concept of the work.

With platforms such as Second Life, Sinespace, or Spatial, the space of the work can extend beyond its physical boundaries into the network.

In these shared virtual environments, the digital model becomes accessible to a global audience, who can experience it in real time and from multiple perspectives. The work thus takes on a collective dimension, where aesthetics intertwine with social interaction and the simultaneous presence of many visitors.

10.4.2.2.3 AR and Projection Mapping

The physical sculpture could also be animated through nighttime projection mapping, casting dynamic visuals across its surfaces.

Alternatively, AR applications on smartphones or tablets—or AR headsets—could overlay digital layers onto the sculpture: streams of light running through its shapes, generative patterns flowing along its forms (consistent with the AI-driven motion explored in Appendix Y), or symbolic imagery unfolding in response to interaction.

10.4.2.2.4 Conclusion

In summary, this reimagining maintains continuity with the sculpture's original identity while expanding it into hybrid, interactive domains.

It exists materially as a public artwork but can also acquire a digital twin, a VR world, and an AR dimension, forming a multilayered immersive system.

This approach exemplifies how earlier handmade works can be revitalized for the immersive age—leveraging the technical architectures and AI workflows previously discussed—not replacing the tactile and material but bridging them with the virtual and interactive to create new hybrid experiences.

10.4.3 Labyrinths, Biomechanical Landscapes, Metaphysical Cities: Recent Works

Building on the trajectory of my earlier works, my recent projects venture into what I call ***hybrid landscapes***: environments where mechanical and organic, physical and virtual dimensions converge.

I have been fascinated by labyrinths, both as literal structures and as metaphors for complexity; by biomechanical forms that merge natural vitality with engineered geometry; and by cityscapes that verge on the metaphysical, evoking mental and spiritual architectures. These themes naturally lend themselves to immersive expression, since they concern environments and systems rather than isolated objects.

In this section, I discuss two strands of recent practice: *Hybrid Paintings* and *Continuous Spaces.*

Both expand from traditional painting into hybrid visual environments, where generative models and artificial intelligence open new paths of transformation and unpredictability.

These works draw on cutting-edge technologies such as modular LED walls, allowing static images to evolve into responsive, time-based fields of color and form.[27]

This integration of AI-driven generation with physical display hardware transforms the canvas from a fixed surface into a living continuum, where each piece breathes, shifts, and responds in dialogue with the viewer and its environment.

10.4.3.1 Hybrid Paintings

The *Hybrid Paintings* installations begin with a very traditional medium—painting on paper—but evolve into expanded spaces through a process that integrates digital tools and AI.

I first create several works manually, inspired by symbols and ideas. Then I select two or more of these paintings and set up an installation in which they are combined with a generative digital component.

[27] For an example of modular LED wall technology enabling high-resolution dynamic displays in immersive installations, see Exposure Systems' modular LED solutions (2025) at `https://exposure-systems.com/en/modular-led-wall/`.

This system supports seamless, scalable video mapping and real-time content adaptation, aligning with the hybrid visual environments explored in *Hybrid Paintings* and *Continuous Spaces.*

For example, I may use GIMP or Midjourney to weave elements of one painting into another or to create new variations emerging from the dialogue between the two.

If necessary, I further refine these results with digital painting, until they match the vision I am seeking.

The workflow between GIMP (raster editing) and Midjourney (AI generation) is structured as follows:

- GIMP serves as the primary tool for preparation and post-refinement. I use it to crop, adjust contrast, color balance, or composite initial images into a clean, high-resolution source prompt (typically 1024 x 1024 px or higher for optimal Midjourney results).
- Midjourney then processes these prepared images as visual prompts (via image-to-image or remix mode, with parameters for the latest model as of 2025). It generates hybrid variations by blending the provided elements with the textual prompt.
- Back to GIMP for final manual refinement. I import the Midjourney outputs, correct artifacts, enhance details, or selectively blend elements to align with my aesthetic intent.

This iterative loop—GIMP ➤ Midjourney ➤ GIMP—allows precise control over the generative process while embracing the unexpected outcomes AI introduces, ensuring the final work remains fully authored by me.

The final choice is always mine: I select and modify only those AI solutions that resonate with me.

In this way, the work is shaped by the tension between my own creativity and the unpredictability of generative AI, which introduces stimuli and variations that I could not have planned in advance.

In the installation, two physical canvases or two fixed digital images are hung side by side, and between them a digital screen functions as a “pictorial bridge” (Figure 10-18).

Figure 10-18. Gianpiero Moioli, Hybrid Painting Installation, 2025.
Two physical canvases (painting on paper) or two fixed digital images frame a central digital screen that functions as a "pictorial bridge." The central work is the result of a workflow integrating raster editing (GIMP) and generative artificial intelligence (Midjourney) to merge and evolve elements from the original paintings

The screen displays a generative animation that continuously morphs elements from the two canvases, producing an endless flow of transformations.

To ensure stability and visual variety during long-duration exhibitions, the workflow prioritizes offline AI sequence generation.

Midjourney is used to create a vast library of transformation states, which are then orchestrated through procedural playback in TouchDesigner.

This method effectively merges the aesthetic complexity of AI with the structural reliability of procedural logic.

By using algorithms to continuously recombine and transition between pregenerated segments, the system avoids the technical instability of real-time AI (such as latency or server queues). This ensures an unpredictable, nonrepeating flow that maintains variation over hours without the risks of a fixed loop or technical artifacts.

Find the video of the animation at `https://vimeo.com/1148310774`.

The effect is a triadic format. The left and right canvases embody stable, tangible realities, while the central screen represents a dynamic, ever-changing virtual reality.

When viewers stand before this triptych, they perceive what might be called an "expanded painting," and their gaze moves back and forth, noticing motifs that reappear, dissolve, and recombine in unpredictable ways.

The piece becomes a perpetual laboratory of mutations, where painting is no longer a fixed event but an ongoing process.

This resonates with the immersive principle of dissolving boundaries, here between analog and digital art.

Although the piece does not use sensors to track the viewer, it nonetheless invites subtle interactivity.

Spectators interact through vision itself, scanning between the canvases and the screen, assembling connections like pieces of a visual puzzle. Some even walk along the work to follow motifs as they travel from one canvas, across the screen, to the other.

10.4.3.2 Continuous Spaces

A second strand is the *Continuous Spaces* video installations.

These environments unfold on screens in endless loops and spaces that repeat, flow, and transform, as shown in this video: `https://vimeo.com/1148326167`.

While they originate from manual paintings, the final form is entirely digital, often presented as one or more synchronized videos distributed in space.

Here, the screen is no longer a passive support but a surface of flow: a canvas continuously repainted in real time.

AI plays a decisive role as an agent of unpredictability.

Each transformation of the original drawings generates unforeseen variations, pushing the work beyond my direct control.

For me, AI has a role comparable to revolutionary practices in art history. Monet's *en plein* air painting introduced light and time as active forces in the pictorial process.

Similarly, Henry Moore's use of small stones or pieces of wood collected in nature became seeds for monumental sculpture, enabling him to move from figurative to abstract language. In the same way, AI introduces fertile unpredictability, opening artworks to continuous becoming.

Continuous Spaces embody this idea: art that is never final but always in motion, painting expanded into time and space through digital media (Figure 10-19 and Figure 10-20).

Figure 10-19. Gianpiero Moioli. Continuous Space. Horizon, 2025.
Originally conceived as a static work, Continuous Space. Horizon *is transformed into an expanded environment through the integration of digital tools and Artificial Intelligence.*
In this evolution, the horizon becomes an "expanded painting" where the painterly gesture is freed from its physical limits

Figure 10-20. Gianpiero Moioli, Hybrid Painting Installation, 2025.
Rendered in a Blender digital environment, the work merges Midjourney's aesthetic complexity with procedural logic to create an unpredictable, ever-changing virtual horizon

Although these are not environments one physically walks into, they expand painting into the surrounding room by the movement.

The glow of the screen projects onto viewers and the floor, the moving imagery evokes a pseudo-3D depth, and the coexistence of static and moving art requires active engagement. The result feels like witnessing both an exhibition and a performance at the same time.

10.4.3.3 Conclusions

Both *Hybrid Paintings* and *Continuous Spaces* explore the continuity between idea and matter.

The gesture of manual painting does not end on the canvas but continues into the digital realm. This hybrid approach suggests a future where analog and digital co-exist, enriching one another.

The physical paintings act as anchors of stability, while the digital elements carry the warmth of human imperfection into generative processes.

The installations produce micro-immersive experiences: not fully surrounding the body but deeply engaging eyes and mind in an artificial space that spans real and virtual.

Technical Continuity & Pipeline

To bridge the philosophical gap between the tactile and the virtual, the works rely on a rigorous data processing pipeline that ensures formal coherence:

1. **Physical Painting:** Creation of manual works on paper.
2. **Digitization:** High-resolution capture using a CMOS sensor (35mm full-frame) or 600 DPI optical scanning to preserve texture and stroke detail.
3. **Feature Extraction:** Segmentation of motifs and color palettes via GIMP or Photoshop to isolate the "DNA" of the painting.
4. **AI Processing:** Integration of extracted features into Midjourney (using *image prompts* and *style references*) to generate hundreds of metamorphic variations.
5. **Output Render & Orchestration:** Sequencing of AI assets through TouchDesigner or Unity, using stochastic algorithms for real-time recombination.

6. **Display:** Final output on high-density screens or projections. The digital flow is visually and formally aligned with the physical source material, ensuring that the motifs, textures, and color palettes in the animation remain a direct "metabolic" extension of the canvases on display.

These works mark a step in my practice toward creating art that exists "**between worlds**"—linking the tactile with the generative—and anticipate more immersive hybrids, where such metamorphic visuals could be projected onto three-dimensional sculptures or entire rooms. These works could also incorporate further technical enhancements. They may be made interactive, or the screens could be connected to virtual worlds, continuously evolving three-dimensional spaces that expand the experience beyond physical installation.

10.4.4 Labyrinth with Vector Physical Field: Merging Art and Science in an Immersive Sculpture

With this project, the book closes by presenting a single artwork in progress with a dual nature: physical and virtual.

The material dimension provides structure and atmosphere, while the digital dimension introduces interactivity, data, and continuous transformation.

Together, they anticipate the hybrid landscapes toward which my practice is moving.

Labyrinth with Vector Physical Field is an environmental sculpture that weaves together sculpture, installation, and new technologies to make invisible forces perceptible (Figure 10-21).

Figure 10-21. Gianpiero Moioli, Labyrinth with Vector Physical Field, 2025, *cm. 400 x 400 x 400.*
The basic module. The iron framework hosts luminous vector flows, transforming the sculpture into an immersive data-field where invisible forces become perceptible

The iron framework acts as a data-sculpture, traversed by luminous flows that recall real-time visualizations of energy fields or information networks, as you can see in the following video: `https://vimeo.com/1142208704`.

The work is not limited to sculptural form; it expands into an immersive, multisensory experience where light, color, and motion transform space and modulate perception.

10.4.4.1 Physical Structure

The sculpture rises about four meters, with a modular footprint of roughly 4×4 meters.

It was built from an iron framework, with modules 3D printed in materials such as ABS or similar and adapted to the dimensions of the space.

It outlines an open labyrinthine structure, a network of elements suggesting passage and complexity.

Within this frame, transparent tubes snake through, illuminated from within by colored LED lights.

The impression is of a twisting apparatus with glowing veins, at once an abstract scientific device and a piece of architectural fantasy.

The title's reference to a vector physical field draws on physics. A vector field represents forces with direction and magnitude at different points in space, like wind velocities or magnetic forces.

The luminous tubes, representing magnetic field, were developed using Blender's Geometry Nodes.

Technical Implementation: Generating the Vector Field

To translate the concept of a vector physical field into a visual form, the magnetic field paths were not hand-drawn but procedurally generated within Blender.

- **Generation Logic:** The paths are created using Blender Geometry Nodes, where curves are distributed and shaped based on a Vector Noise Field (Perlin or Simplex). This simulates the behavior of magnetic flux without the overhead of a full electromagnetic simulation. The nodes calculate the "force" at each point in space, directing the curves along the flow of the vector field.
- **Vector Movement:** The moving lights inside the tubes are controlled by a Sample Curve logic. The "arrows of force" are essentially point-based instances or mesh-strips whose position is animated along the spline factor, simulating the magnitude and direction of a physical vector.
- **Data Export & Integration:**
  - **Geometry:** The tubes are exported as FBX baked geometry for static structural elements to ensure high performance in real-time engines.
  - **Animation:** For the dynamic light flow, the motion is handled via Alembic (.abc) animation cache when complex mesh deformations are required. Alternatively, for real-time efficiency in Unity or Unreal, the paths are exported as NURBS curves or Vertex Animation Textures (VAT), allowing the engine to calculate the light movement along the predefined vector paths without the need for heavy frame-by-frame geometry data.

The moving lights inside the tubes symbolize such vectors, arrows of force that shift, divide, and transform as they travel through the labyrinth. The result is a dynamic light composition that is never static.

10.4.4.2 Experience and Symbolism

Circling the work, viewers encounter a shifting interplay of light, color, and form.

The glowing vectors evoke flows of energy or information that invisibly shape our environment.

At the same time, the labyrinth invites symbolic readings: the journey of discovery, the complexity of knowledge, the maze of life itself.

The physical version of the sculpture creates an immersive atmosphere, especially in darkened spaces.

The lights can shift in both color and intensity, controlled manually through a lighting console or pre-programmed sequences.

Colored reflections and moving shadows extend the sculptural presence beyond its frame, bathing walls and visitors in shifting tones. In this way, the piece expands from object to environment.

10.4.4.3 Virtual Extension

The project also includes a **mixed-reality (MR) counterpart**, conceived not as a separate experience but as an augmented extension of the physical sculpture.

Visitors wear an **AR/MR headset** with passthrough cameras or optical see-through and continue walking in the real exhibition space, perceiving the material structure while simultaneously seeing superimposed virtual flows of light and color, akin to the invisible lines of a magnetic field (Alignment between real and virtual is achieved through spatial anchors and marker-based calibration) (Figure 10-22).[28]

[28] Mixed-reality counterpart requires an AR/MR headset with optical see-through (e.g., HoloLens 2, Magic Leap 2) or video passthrough (e.g., Meta Quest 3, Apple Vision Pro).

Optical systems overlay holograms directly onto the real world via transparent waveguides; video systems stream the physical space through high-resolution cameras and composite digital layers in real time.

Both allow visitors to walk freely while perceiving the sculpture's material structure and superimposed virtual flows of light and color.

Figure 10-22. Gianpiero Moioli, Labyrinth with Vector Physical Field, 2025. *The virtual trajectories, generated algorithmically, suggest invisible magnetic or gravitational lines crossing the sculptural space, where the boundaries between matter and data become permeable*

In this hybrid condition, bodily gestures and even the gaze become creative acts. A hand movement or a glance generates new vectors—bursts of color or ripples of light—that propagate through the labyrinth, merging the physical with the digital.

Unlike the preprogrammed LEDs of the physical sculpture, the virtual component reacts in real time, transforming the work into a living system.

The result is a dual, simultaneous mode of experience. **The body inhabits the material sculpture while the mind interacts with its digital field**, producing a unified experience that intertwines presence, interactivity, and transformation.

10.4.4.4 Immersive Impact

Whether experienced in a mixed form, *Labyrinth with Vector Physical Field* seeks to evoke wonder, the kind inspired by natural phenomena or technological demonstrations, but reframed through art.

It stands at the threshold between artistic installation and technological visualization, immersive not by enclosing the viewer in a room but by surrounding their senses with the suggestion of invisible fields.

This project exemplifies a central direction in my practice: the creation of hybrid works that fuse sculpture and installation with science and technology, combining material presence with digital interactivity.

The labyrinth endures as an ancient metaphor for the search for knowledge, while the vector field represents a technological abstraction of unseen dynamics.

Together, they suggest that exploring complex systems—natural, technological, or social—is akin to navigating a labyrinth: **a path where orientation may be lost** yet where complexity itself reveals its own beauty.

Ultimately, *Labyrinth with Vector Physical Field* is not merely a sculpture to be observed but an environment to be inhabited, both materially and virtually.

It points toward a future in which artworks emerge as hybrid landscapes: spaces at once aesthetic, educational, interactive, and deeply experiential.

10.4.5 Design Process Example

To illustrate how these concepts come together in practice, the design process of *Labyrinth with Vector Physical Field* can be outlined through seven phases.

Each step reflects both the traditional logic of sculpture and the expanded methodology introduced in Chapter 3, where digital, technical, and immersive elements are integrated.

10.4.5.1 Idea

The project began with a question: how could sculpture embody the invisible forces that shape our environment?

From this inquiry, two images converged: **the labyrinth**, a symbol of mystery and dream, and **the vector field**, a scientific abstraction of dynamic flows.

It also arose from a contrast: the solidity of a fixed, architectural labyrinthine structure set against the ever-living, shifting motion of a magnetic field.

The idea was deliberately open and intuitive, more a seed of imagination than a design.

Notes, words, and quick diagrams captured fragments of this vision: light as matter, geometry as vessel, energy as movement.

The aim was not to define a final form but to trace a direction that would later unfold through sketches, prototypes, and virtual simulations.

From here, I developed a moodboard and experimented with sculptural forms, giving visual presence to the dialogue between stability and flow (Figure 10-23).

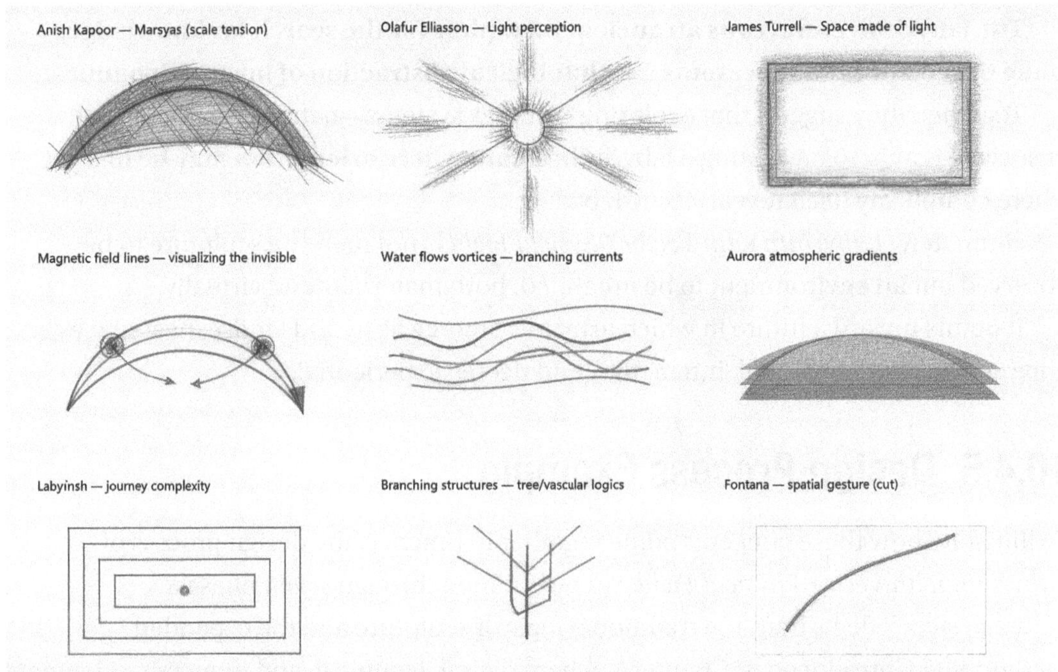

Figure 10-23. Conceptual diagrams exploring natural and symbolic references.
Magnetic field lines, water vortices, aurora gradients, labyrinth complexity, branching structures, and spatial gestures

10.4.5.2 Sketches

Hand drawings and quick digital sketches served as the first translation of the conceptual idea into visual form.

Through lines and gestures, I mapped possible configurations of vertical frames and pathways, imagining how light could flow like vectors within and around the structure.

These sketches did not aim for precision but for atmosphere. They sought to capture the tension between solidity and flux, between the architectural frame and the ephemeral luminous currents.

The drawing process helped clarify the dual identity of the work: on one side a monumental structure rooted in material presence, on the other an immersive environment that could envelop viewers.

Some sketches explored the physical scale of the iron framework, while others emphasized dynamic patterns of color and light that hinted at the virtual extension.

In this way, sketching became both a tool of formal composition and a space of speculation, bridging the language of sculpture with that of scientific diagrams and interactive media (Figure 10-24).

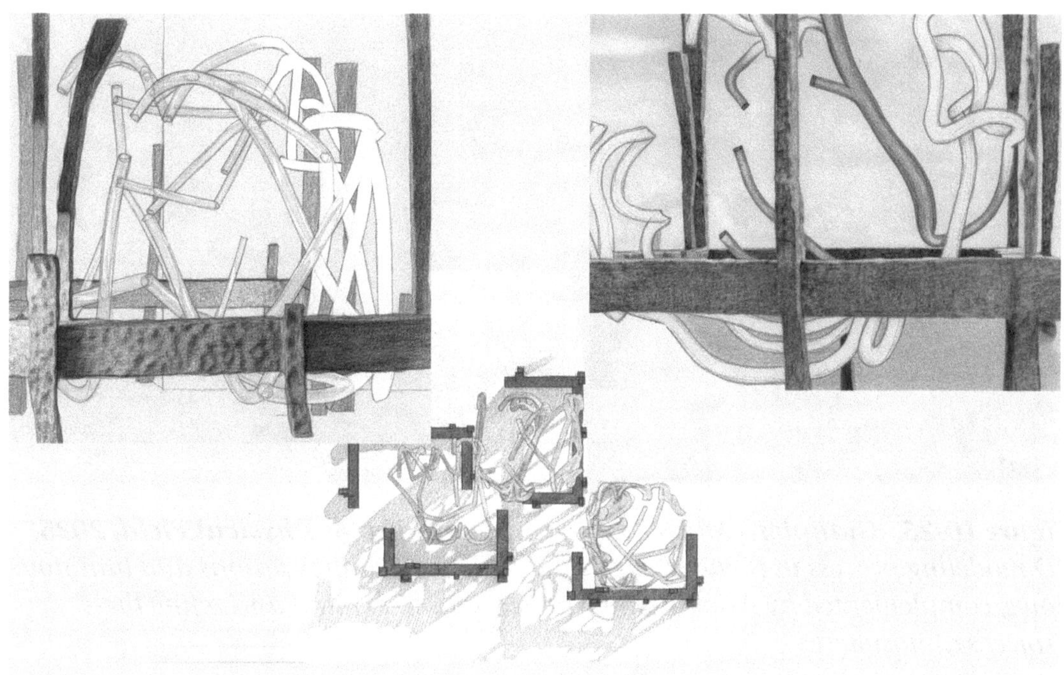

Figure 10-24. Gianpiero Moioli, Labyrinth with Vector Physical Field, 2025. *Sketches and digital drawings of the labyrinth structure, exploring possible configurations of framework and luminous flows*

In this early stage, drawing was less about fixing solutions than about opening horizons, an imaginative ground where the work could oscillate between architecture and vision, matter and light, structure and field.

10.4.5.3 Preliminary Design

At this stage, the focus shifted to spatial feasibility and proportions.

Preliminary models, both physical maquettes and simple 3D models, tested the balance between open and closed forms, evaluating how the framework could suggest a labyrinth without becoming a literal maze.

Digital **3D modeling and prototyping** was conducted in Blender 4.4 LTS (Figure 10-25).

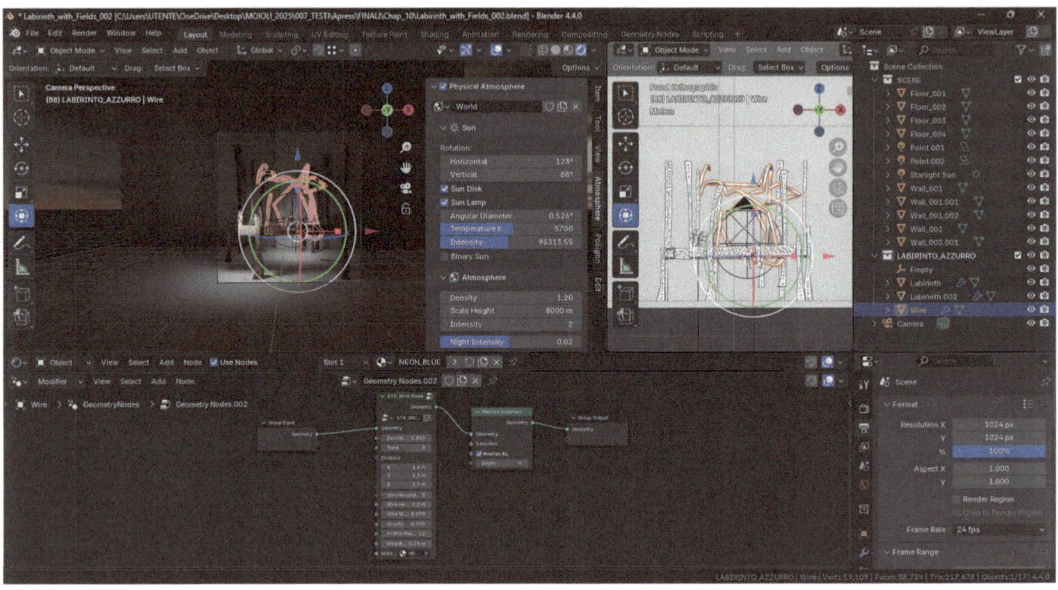

Figure 10-25. Gianpiero Moioli, Labyrinth with Vector Physical Field, 2025. *3D modeling process in Blender, exploring structural configurations and luminous flows, complemented by AI-assisted visualizations to expand and refine the project's atmosphere*

This version was pivotal during the design phase because its Real-Time Viewport (Eevee) allowed for immediate feedback on spatial volumes and lighting before committing to long render times.

Using Geometry Nodes, I created "iterative wireframes" to quickly adjust the density of the labyrinthine tubes, ensuring the visual balance between the physical canvases and the virtual space was maintained.

AI tools were employed not merely for generating art but as a **Creative Catalyst and a conceptual bridge** to visualize the work's atmosphere. This allowed for an iterative exploration of how the painterly DNA could inhabit a 3D environment, bridging the gap between initial sketches and final spatial execution.

- **Midjourney & Stable Diffusion** were employed to generate moodboards and "texture studies." By feeding my original sketches into the AI, I could visualize how the painterly light would react to complex 3D surfaces.
- **Workflow for Animation Pre-viz**: To test the *Continuous Space* concept, short AI-generated sequences were created using Midjourney and imported into Blender as Image Sequences on planes. This allowed me to evaluate the "metabolic" flow of the artwork within the architectural 3D model, ensuring the transitions felt organic rather than mechanical.

Simulation & Rendering Evaluation

For this preliminary phase, the Cycles engine was used for high-fidelity test renders to study how the "artificial human imperfection" of the AI-generated textures would be affected by the digital shadows.

This helped refine the final lighting setup, ensuring that the glowing "vector pulses" would effectively bridge the gap between the tactile past and the generative present.

10.4.5.4 Detailed Design

Technical drawings and parametric models refined the structural logic, balancing digital precision with artisan craftmanship.

Material specifications were defined: iron, or ABS for the frame, transparent polycarbonate tubes for the luminous flows, programmable LEDs for dynamic color sequences.

The structure was conceived as a hybrid of industrial strength and organic transparency:

- **The Frame:** Built using beaten and hand-cut sheets (1.5 to 2 mm thickness). The metal is hand-welded and treated with a powder coating to ensure a durable, matte finish that emphasizes the silhouette.

- **Luminous Veins:** The "flow" is housed in polycarbonate tubes, chosen for their impact resistance and 89% light transmission, ensuring the internal LED light remains vibrant.
- **LED Logic:** Programmable WS2812B strips (60 LEDs/m) allow for granular control of the sequences, managed by an ESP32 controller. This setup enables a "metabolic" light rhythm, making the energy flow visible.

It was also considered the idea to 3D print both the main framework and the transparent tubes: the structural components in opaque PETG or PC to ensure strength and stability, and the tubes in transparent or translucent PETG to allow the passage and diffusion of light.

Hybrid Fabrication & 3D Printing

The design explores the potential of 3D printing as an alternative to traditional methods, moving away from desktop printers toward large-format industrial solutions:

- **Large-Scale Printing:** By utilizing large-volume printers (with build volumes up to $1m^3$), the structure can be divided into fewer, more stable macro-modules. This reduces the number of joints and preserves the sculptural continuity. Not to mention that joints can also have an aesthetic function.
- **Technical Polymers:** The main framework is designed for opaque ABS (known for its rigidity and ease of post-processing), while the transparent tubes utilize PETG.
- **Structural Integrity:** Even with 3D-printed materials (offering a tensile strength of ~50-65 MPa), the 4-meter height requires a strategic assembly. Interlocking joints and internal reinforcements are used to compensate for layer adhesion limits, ensuring the sculpture remains a self-supporting "organism."

This combination of artisan metalwork and large-scale digital fabrication transforms the structure into a living entity where energy flows through transparent veins, extending the sculptural presence from physical matter into a luminous environment.

10.4.5.5 Prototype

Prototyping unfolded on two parallel tracks: material experimentation and virtual simulation.

To achieve the desired "metabolic" glow, scaled 3D-printed models were used to test how light interacts with the beaten metal and the translucent veins. The testing followed a quantitative methodology to balance transparency and diffusion:

- **Print Parameters:** Samples were printed in Clear and Natural PETG with varying wall thicknesses (0.4mm to 1.2mm). It was observed that a 0.8mm wall (2 perimeters) with a 0.2mm layer height provided the ideal diffusion cone (approx. 45°), effectively blurring the individual LED hotspots into a continuous flow.
- **Material Post-Processing:** We compared raw prints with post-processed samples (sanding with 400-grit versus clear coating). Sanding the internal surface of the PETG tubes proved most effective, as the microscopic abrasions increased light scattering without significantly reducing luminosity.
- **LED Calibration:** Testing utilized WS2812B RGB strips (60 LEDs/m). We measured light output using a digital lux meter at consistent distances (10cm, 30cm, 50cm). The findings indicated that Cool White (approx. 6000K) settings within the RGB spectrum provided the best contrast against the matte black (RAL 9005) of the hand-welded steel sheets.

VR Simulation and Gestural Coherence

At the same time, a VR prototype simulated vector flows responsive to gestures, ensuring coherence between the physical and digital dimensions.

This digital twin allowed for the testing of the "origin point" alignment and the latency of hand-tracking responses before final fabrication.

Rendered 3D models, videos, and VR mock-ups then offered a first evaluation of the project from both formal and experiential perspectives, confirming that the 70% light transmission achieved in the PETG prototypes was sufficient to illuminate the surrounding environment.

10.4.5.6 Production (Projected Phase)

In the next stage of development, the iron framework will be fabricated at full scale, while the tubes with the LED system will be programmed with patterns derived from the prototypes.

In the digital domain, a VR environment will be developed using Blender for high-fidelity modeling and Unity for real-time interactivity.

The virtual model will act as a "digital twin," matching the physical structure and incorporating interactive logic for gesture- and gaze-based input.

This transition involves a specialized export-import pipeline to ensure that the "artificial human imperfection" of the original work is preserved within the game engine's environment. Refer to "Technical Appendix: From Concept to Implementation (2025)."

10.4.5.7 Installation (Projected Phase)

Finally, the sculpture will be installed on-site as a monumental luminous structure, complemented by a VR station that allows visitors to immerse themselves in the digital counterpart.

The two modalities will be presented as complementary, enabling a layered experience that unites material presence with digital interactivity.

The seamless synchronization of these worlds is achieved through advanced spatial tracking and real-time networking, ensuring that the visitor's movements and gestures are accurately translated into the digital flow. Refer to "Technical Appendix: From Concept to Implementation (2025)."

10.5 Conclusion: Sculpture as a Field of Forces and Total Experience

In recent decades, sculpture has shifted from static object to dynamic field of forces.

It is no longer limited to being a fixed form on a pedestal or in a plaza but **can be reimagined as an environment—indoors or outdoors—that invites interaction and inhabitation.**

The spectator's role has fundamentally changed: from passive observer to active participant. Presence, movement, and interaction are not optional but constitutive elements of the work.

Sculpture today can be imagined less as a finished masterpiece and more as a situation, a field of potential that becomes actual only through engagement, much like a musical score that needs musicians to become sound.

10.5.1 From "Artwork" to "Lived Space"

The contemporary sculptural space is closer to architecture or environment than to the traditional statue.

It combines matter and code, weight and behavior. Steel or resin provide presence, while software, light, and sensors give responsiveness.

In this sense, sculpture becomes a lived space, a hybrid environment where the artist, the work, and the audience coexist within a continuum.

The aim is no longer to deliver a fixed symbolic message but to create conditions for experience: places where we can move, feel, and inhabit rather than merely look.

10.5.2 Opening to the Possible: From Matter and Code to Lived Space

The future of sculpture points toward openness and emergence.

Artists may increasingly think in terms of contexts, systems, and responsive environments. Each encounter is unique, and this variability is part of the artwork itself.

We can imagine immersive plazas that react to citizens, domestic interiors that double as atmospheric installations, or shared VR spaces that host global sculptural experiences.

These scenarios blur the boundaries between matter and code, art, architecture, and daily life. What remains constant is the human need for embodied presence.

10.6 Technical Appendix: From Concept to Implementation (2025)

*This appendix provides the practical technical details for implementing the hybrid immersive installations **Labyrinth with Vector Physical Field** described in this chapter.*

The workflows and code provided have been updated to 2025 hardware/software standards. ESP32 is now preferred over Arduino Nano for its native Wi-Fi/OSC capabilities, and the software stack focuses on Unity 2023.2 and Meta Quest 3 as the primary Mixed Reality deployment platform.

10.6.1 Hardware Architecture: The Sensor-to-Light Loop

The physical immersion is driven by a distributed network of sensors and addressable LEDs. The following is the standard schematic for a localized node.

Key Components and Specifications:

Category	Item	Purpose
Compute	Meta Quest 3	MR Visualization, Spatial Mapping, and Hand Tracking.
Logic	ESP32 DevKit V1	Handling logic, LED control, and Wi-Fi synchronization (OSC).
Lighting	WS2812B (5V)	Individually addressable RGB LEDs (60 LEDs/m) for physical feedback.
Structure	Mild Steel Sheets	1.5mm–2mm sheets, hand-cut and beaten for sculptural volumes.
Diffusion	Polycarbonate Tubes	$\varnothing$ 30–40mm; 89% light transmission for the “metabolic” glow.
Sensors	HC-SR04 / Ultraleap	Real-time distance tracking or high-precision hand tracking.
Power	5V 10A DC	High-stability power (calculated at 60mA per LED + 20% safety margin).

Example Sketch: Proximity-Based Pulse

(C++ with FastLED library - Tested and functional on ESP32)

C++

```
#include <FastLED.h>

#define LED_PIN     6
#define NUM_LEDS    60
#define TRIG_PIN    5
#define ECHO_PIN    7

CRGB leds[NUM_LEDS];

void setup() {
  FastLED.addLeds<WS2812B, LED_PIN, GRB>(leds, NUM_LEDS);
  pinMode(TRIG_PIN, OUTPUT);
```

```
  pinMode(ECHO_PIN, INPUT);
  FastLED.setBrightness(255);
}

void loop() {
  // Trigger pulse
  digitalWrite(TRIG_PIN, LOW);
  delayMicroseconds(2);
  digitalWrite(TRIG_PIN, HIGH);
  delayMicroseconds(10);
  digitalWrite(TRIG_PIN, LOW);

  // Read echo with timeout (30000 µs ≈ 5m max)
  long duration = pulseIn(ECHO_PIN, HIGH, 30000);
  int distance = (duration == 0) ? 200 : (duration * 0.034 / 2);
  // fallback if no echo

  distance = constrain(distance, 5, 200);  // clamp range

  // Map closer = faster pulse
  uint8_t pulseSpeed = map(distance, 5, 200, 60, 10);  // 60 BPM slow → 10
  BPM fast
  uint8_t brightness = beatsin8(pulseSpeed, 50, 255);

  fill_solid(leds, NUM_LEDS, CHSV(160, 200, brightness)); // Blue breathing
  FastLED.show();
  delay(10);
}
```

What the Code Does Exactly

The sketch uses an HC-SR04 ultrasonic sensor (TRIG_PIN 5, ECHO_PIN 7) to measure distance.

- It sends a trigger pulse and reads the echo duration.
- It calculates the distance in centimeters using the correct formula: duration * 0.034 / 2.
- The distance (clamped between 5-200 cm) is mapped to a pulsation speed—slow at 60 BPM when far away, accelerating to 10 BPM when close.

- The beatsin8 function creates a smooth sinusoidal "breathing" effect.
- The color is a blue hue (HSV 160, saturation 200, variable brightness).
- A short delay(10) ensures rapid updates for fluid animation.

This code produces a responsive "breathing" light pulse that intensifies as a visitor approaches the sculpture, turning proximity into a subtle, organic visual rhythm.

10.6.2 Digital Pipeline: Blender to Game Engine

In the digital domain, a VR environment will be developed in **Blender** and **Unity** (or Unreal Engine).

- **Workflow:** Assets are modeled in Blender using a metric scale where **1 unit = 1 meter**. Models are exported using the **glTF 2.0 or FBX** format to preserve physically based rendering (PBR) materials.
- **Optimization:** For stand-alone deployment (Quest 3), meshes are decimated to maintain a high draw-call efficiency, and lighting is "baked" into textures to ensure 72–90 FPS stability.

How It Works Technically

Spatial tracking: The installation utilizes advanced VR/MR headsets. The choice of hardware dictates the development constraints:

Headset	Key Specs	Best For
Meta Quest 3	Inside-out tracking, 4MP Passthrough, Standalone (Snapdragon XR2 Gen 2).	Most art installations (Affordable, wireless).
HTC Vive XR Elite	Modular battery, similar specs to Quest.	Extended wear and comfort.
Varjo XR-4	12MP Photorealistic passthrough, Eye-tracking.	High-fidelity, professional-grade (Requires PC tether).

Development is standardized using the **OpenXR** API, ensuring compatibility across devices, while the **Oculus SDK** is used for Quest-specific spatial mapping.

- **Digital Overlay & Calibration:** Software generates light and color flows spatially aligned with the sculpture.

- **Millimeter Precision:** To ensure the virtual overlay matches the physical iron, we implement a manual alignment procedure. An "Origin Point" is defined on the physical sculpture (e.g., a specific corner). Using a virtual gizmo, the user aligns the digital model to this point.
- **Networking:** For multi-user experiences, Unity Netcode for Entities synchronizes the state of light waves across all headsets.
- **Mitigation:** To prevent "drift" (where the virtual model shifts over time), the system periodically re-anchors to the environment using Spatial Anchors.

Real-time interactivity:

- **Hand Tracking vs. Controllers:** * Controllers (Oculus Touch): Provide precise, low-latency (~20ms) input with haptic feedback. Best for complex triggers.
- **Hand Tracking:** More intuitive but higher latency (~50ms) and prone to occlusion.
  - *Gesture Vocabulary:* Users "launch vectors" by performing a pinch-and-release gesture or a forward pushing motion detected via velocity thresholds. *(Refer to section 10.6.3 in the Technical Appendix for the C# implementation of this logic).*
- **Eye Tracking:** Advanced headsets (Varjo/Quest Pro) transform gaze into interactive input.
  - *Mechanism:* A Raycast is projected from the user's eye origin. When it hits a collider on the virtual sculpture, it triggers localized light ripples.
  - *Challenges:* Accuracy can degrade for users with glasses. Each user requires a 30-second calibration.
  - *Ethics:* Gaze data is processed locally and never logged, respecting visitor privacy.

Physical–Digital Synchronization

Visitors simultaneously see the real sculpture and its virtual extension. By utilizing the ESP32-based light loop, the physical LEDs react in sync with the digital triggers, creating a seamless mixed-reality experience where **the boundary between matter and code disappears**.

10.6.3 Software Data Flow: Hybrid Synchronization

For complex installations where the physical and virtual must merge, data flows from the sculpture to a central engine.

- **Primary Protocol: Open Sound Control (OSC)** over Wi-Fi (via ESP32)
- **Visual Engine: TouchDesigner** for real-time generative textures
- **Spatial Sync: Unity XR Origin** + **Spatial Anchors** for multi-user alignment

10.6.4 VR Interaction: Gesture Recognition (Unity 2023.2)

To "launch vectors" via hand-tracking or controllers on the Meta Quest 3, use the following logic within the XR Interaction Toolkit framework:

C#

```
using UnityEngine;
using Oculus.Interaction;  // Meta XR Interaction Toolkit

public class GestureLauncher : MonoBehaviour {
    public GameObject lightVectorPrefab;
    public Transform handAnchor;  // Assegna la mano destra nell'Inspector

    private void Update() {
        // Detect grip squeeze on right hand
        if (OVRInput.Get(OVRInput.Axis1D.PrimaryHandTrigger) > 0.8f) {
            Vector3 velocity = OVRInput.GetLocalControllerVelocity(OVRInp
            ut.Controller.RTouch);
```

```
            if (velocity.magnitude > 2.0f) {  // Forward push threshold
                LaunchLight(velocity.normalized);
            }
        }
    }

    private void LaunchLight(Vector3 direction) {
        if (lightVectorPrefab == null || handAnchor == null) return;

        GameObject pulse = Instantiate(lightVectorPrefab, handAnchor.
        position, Quaternion.LookRotation(direction));
        Rigidbody rb = pulse.GetComponent<Rigidbody>();
        if (rb != null) {
            rb.velocity = direction * 8.0f;  // Digital light wave
            propulsion
        }
    }
}
```

What the Code Does Exactly

The script detects a forward "push" gesture with the right-hand controller in VR, using the grip trigger squeeze as activation.

- It continuously checks if the grip trigger is pressed strongly (value >0.8f, indicating a firm squeeze).
- It measures the velocity of the controller (how quickly the hand is moving forward).
- If the velocity magnitude exceeds 2.0 m/s (a deliberate push gesture), it launches a digital light vector.
- The prefab (lightVectorPrefab) is instantiated at the hand's position, oriented precisely in the direction of the push.
- A Rigidbody component propels the object forward at 8 m/s, creating an interactive "light wave" or energy pulse that travels through the virtual space.

This creates an intuitive, embodied interaction. A physical hand gesture "throws" a luminous vector, turning viewer movement into a generative force—perfect for immersive installations where proximity and intention shape dynamic light events.

10.6.5 Generative Visuals: Perlin Noise Shimmer

This logic creates the "organic" shimmering effect for light fields.

(Processing/Java Pseudocode - Adaptable to GLSL shaders)

Java

```java
float time = 0;

void setup() {
  size(1920, 1080);
  colorMode(RGB);
  noStroke();
}

void draw() {
  loadPixels();
  for (int x = 0; x < width; x++) {
    for (int y = 0; y < height; y++) {
      float n = noise(x * 0.01, y * 0.01, time);
      float brightness = map(n, 0, 1, 50, 255);
      pixels[x + y * width] = color(0, 100, brightness + 100);
      // Deep blue shimmer
    }
  }
  updatePixels();
  time += 0.02;  // Smooth animation
}
```

What the Code Does Exactly

The code generates an organic shimmer effect using Perlin noise to modulate pixel brightness.

- Noise is calculated based on spatial coordinates (x, y) and a temporal component (frameCount * 0.02), creating slow, fluid movement reminiscent of drifting clouds or rippling water.

- The noise function returns values between 0 and 1, which are mapped to brightness levels from 50 (dark) to 255 (bright).
- The base color is an aesthetic blue-green (in Processing's RGB mode: color(0, 150, brightness)—R=0, G=150, B=variable → a cyan/teal shimmer rather than pure blue).
- loadPixels() and updatePixels() enable direct pixel manipulation, making it efficient for full-screen effects.

This produces a subtle, ever-shifting luminous field—ideal for atmospheric overlays in immersive installations or digital sculptures.

10.6.6 Comprehensive Bill of Materials (BOM)

Category	Item	Purpose
Compute	Meta Quest 3	MR Visualization, Spatial Mapping & Hand Tracking.
Logic	ESP32 Microcontroller	High-speed LED control and OSC communication.
Lighting	WS2812B LED Strips	Physical light feedback integrated into the framework.
Structure	1.5mm / 2mm Mild Steel Sheets (Hand-cut and beaten for sculptural volumes).	CNC-bent framework providing physical weight and form.
Sensors	Ultraleap 3Di / HC-SR04	Precise hand tracking for kiosks or distance detection.
Software	Unity 2023.2 / TD	Core engine for spatial logic and generative visuals.

10.6.7 Troubleshooting and Maintenance

- **Tracking Drift:** If the virtual model shifts relative to the iron framework, trigger the Spatial Anchors re-centering function.
- **LED Flickering:** Often caused by grounding issues. Ensure the ESP32 GND is common with the 5V power supply ground.
- **OSC Latency:** Use a dedicated 5GHz router; avoid public Wi-Fi networks to maintain latency below 20ms.

```
import hashlib

def sha256_hash(filepath: str) -> str:
    """Calculate SHA-256 hash of a file for digital-physical integrity
    verification."""
    hasher = hashlib.sha256()
    try:
        with open(filepath, "rb") as f:
            while chunk := f.read(65536):  # Efficient 64 KB chunks
                hasher.update(chunk)
        return hasher.hexdigest()
    except FileNotFoundError:
        return f"Error: File '{filepath}' not found."
    except Exception as e:
        return f"Error reading file: {str(e)}"

# --- Example Usage: Digital Twin Integrity Check ---
current_file = "Sculpture_Final_Structure.obj"
current_hash = sha256_hash(current_file)

# Expected hash from previous step (e.g., approved VR model or AI source)
expected_hash = "a7c2d8e4f1a9b3c5d7e0f9a8b1c3d5e7f0a9b8c7d6e5f4a3b2c1
d0e9f8a7b6c5"

print(f"Current file hash: {current_hash}")
print(f"Expected hash:     {expected_hash}")
print(f"Integrity match:   {current_hash == expected_hash}")
```

What the Code Does Exactly

The function calculates the SHA-256 hash of a file in 64 KB chunks (optimized for large files, avoiding loading the entire file into memory).

- It returns the hexadecimal hash (a 64-character string).
- In the example, it implicitly compares the current hash with a previous one (to verify that the file has not been modified between the VR model and physical production/CNC stages).

This ensures digital-physical integrity. Any alteration in the mesh file would produce a different hash, **guaranteeing synchronization between virtual design and real-world fabrication**.

10.6.8 Conclusion: Data Integrity and Verification

As discussed in Chapter 4 regarding model precision, the synchronization between the digital twin and the physical structure is guaranteed by hash-verification protocols.

In this hybrid space, the artwork is never "finished" but remains in a state of constant, re-computable emergence.

In an age dominated by screens, immersive sculpture surrounds us physically and emotionally, engaging not only the mind but the whole body.

Thus, the evolution of sculpture into immersive fields is not an endpoint but a radical expansion: from object to environment, from matter alone to the interplay of matter and code, from artwork to **a space to be lived**.

10.7 Appendix X: Hybrid Sculptural Architecture: Technical System Design

To transform the *Bubble-Making Machines* from static objects into responsive entities, I have developed a multilayered system architecture that bridges physical form and digital logic.

10.7.1 Sensing and Input Layer

The interactivity is grounded in the viewer's proximity. Each sculpture is equipped with a sensor array:

- **Sensor Type:** Four **HC-SR04 ultrasonic sensors**
- **Placement:** Positioned at cardinal points at a height of **1.5 m**
- **Range:** Detects visitor approach from **2 to 400 cm**, creating a 360-degree field of awareness

10.7.2 Processing and Logic Layer

The "brain" of each unit is an **ESP32 microcontroller**, chosen for the following advantages:

- **Parallel Processing:** Dual-core processor allows one core to poll sensor data while the other manages complex LED animations.
- **Connectivity:** Built-in Wi-Fi enables **Open Sound Control (OSC)** or wireless DMX protocols to synchronize multiple sculptures within a network.

10.7.3 Output and Illumination Layer

For the internal glow, I utilize **APA102 (DotStar) LED** technology over the standard WS2812B (NeoPixel) to avoid timing conflicts with sensor polling.

- **LED Counts:** Approximately **200 RGB LEDs** per sculpture.
- **Power Requirements:** Each LED draws ~60 mA at full white; total draw is **~12 A per unit**.
- **Power Supply:** A **5V/15A power supply** (including a 20% safety margin) ensures stability and prevents color distortion.
- **Software Framework:** Developed using the **FastLED library**, employing a **state-machine** approach:
    - **DORMANT State:** Low-intensity blue pulse (breathing effect).
    - **ACTIVE State:** Increased intensity and color temperature in proportion to visitor proximity.

10.7.4 Interaction Logic (Pseudocode)

The following C++ logic (for ESP32) illustrates the transition between states:

C++

```
#include <FastLED.h>  // Required library

#define NUM_LEDS 200
#define LED_PIN 6
CRGB leds[NUM_LEDS];
```

```
enum State { DORMANT, ACTIVE };
State currentState = DORMANT;

void loop() {
  int distance = readUltrasonic();  // From HC-SR04 array average
  if (distance < 100) {  // Threshold for activation
    currentState = ACTIVE;
    setActiveLEDs();  // Increase intensity/color temp
  } else {
    currentState = DORMANT;
    setDormantLEDs();  // Low blue pulse
  }
  FastLED.show();
}

void setActiveLEDs() {
  // Example: Fade to warmer colors
  fill_gradient_RGB(leds, 0, CRGB::Blue, NUM_LEDS, CRGB::White);
}

void setDormantLEDs() {
  // Low pulse with FastLED beatsin8 for breathing
  uint8_t brightness = beatsin8(10, 50, 100);  // Slow pulse
  fill_solid(leds, NUM_LEDS, CRGB::Blue);
  FastLED.setBrightness(brightness);
}
```

10.7.5 Audio Implementation: Spatialized Surround Sound

To create a synesthetic experience, the system incorporates object-based spatial audio:

- **Audio Engine:** A DAW (e.g., Ableton Live) receives OSC messages from the ESP32.
- **Audio Format:** Scalable from 5.1/7.1 channels to Ambisonics for binaural/VR environments.

- **Hardware:** Four to six directional speakers (e.g., Bose or JBL) create localized audio zones around the sculpture.
- **Latency:** Kept <20 ms to ensure a seamless "responsive feel" between movement and sound.

10.7.6 Sculptural Integration

The challenge of cable management is solved by integrating the wiring within the hammered metal armature, treating the electrical components as the **"nervous system"** of the work. This high-fidelity integration allows the sculpture to retain its material elegance while functioning as a complex, data-driven environment.

10.8 Appendix Y: AI-Driven Image-to-Video Workflow for Conceptual Exploration (2025)

This appendix documents the technical pipeline used to transform static conceptual references into dynamic visual prototypes.

By bridging **generative AI (text-to-image)** and **temporal motion models (image-to-video)**, this workflow allows for the rapid reimagining of interactive sculptures, such as the *Bubble-Making Machines*, within immersive digital environments.

10.8.1 Keyframe Generation (Midjourney)

The process begins with the creation of high-fidelity "anchor" images that define the aesthetic, material, and lighting parameters of the work.

- **Input:** Multireference prompting (combining photos of physical sculptures with descriptive text).
- **Technical Parameters:** * **Model:** Midjourney v6.1.
    - **Style Consistency:** Use of --sref (Style Reference) to maintain the specific texture of hammered metal and translucent polycarbonate across multiple iterations.
    - **Resolution:** Native output at 2048×2048 pixels.

- **Outcome:** A sequence of 4–12 static keyframes exploring formal variations.
- **Processing Time:** ~60 seconds per generation.

10.8.2 Video Interpolation and Motion Synthesis

To achieve fluid motion, the static keyframes are processed through **Image-to-Video (I2V)** models. This step is distinct from Midjourney's internal "Variation" feature, as it generates new interstitial frames to create temporal continuity.

- **Runway Gen-3 Alpha:** Used for organic lighting transitions and complex atmospheric effects.
- **Kling AI / Luma Dream Machine:** Utilized for cinematic camera movements (pan, tilt, zoom) around the 3D form.
- **Technical Specifications:**
    - **Output Resolution:** 1080p (Full HD).
    - **Frame Rate:** 24 or 30 fps (Frames Per Second).
    - **Clip Duration:** 5–10 second loops.
- **Processing Time:** 5–15 minutes per sequence (Cloud GPU rendering).

10.8.3 Post-Production and Enhancement

The raw AI output is refined to meet exhibition standards (4K projection).

- **AI Upscaling:** Tools such as **Topaz Video AI** or **Magnific AI** are employed to upscale 1080p footage to **4K**, utilizing temporal denoising to remove "flicker" or artifacts common in AI generations.
- **Editing & Loops:** Assembly in **DaVinci Resolve** or **Blender** for color grading and "seamless loop" stitching, ensuring the installation can run indefinitely without visible breaks.

Quality Considerations & Limitations

- **Temporal Consistency:** To prevent "morphing" (where the sculpture's shape changes unnaturally), **Seed Locking** and high **Motion Bucket** values are used to prioritize structural stability over chaotic movement.
- **Human Intervention:** AI-generated motion often requires manual "masking" in post-production to correct background warping or inconsistent shadow behavior.

10.9 Conclusion to the Technical Appendices

These appendices map the full journey from concept to realization: generative taxonomies, image-to-video pipelines, VR gesture workflows, cross-platform optimizations, and hybrid sensor-light architectures.

Together they illustrate a single truth: technology does not replace the artistic gesture, it extends it, making it spatial, responsive, and shared. From hand-drawn line to inhabitable world, from sensor pulse to luminous breath, from keyframe to seamless loop, contemporary art dissolves the borders between code, matter, and perception, turning tools into language and constraints into possibility.

What endures is the artist's freedom to shape space—real, virtual, or hybrid—one gaze, one gesture, one breath at a time.

Index

A

G. Moioli, *Art Between Matter and Code*, https://doi.org/10.1007/979-8-8688-2376-3

B

C

D

E

F

G

H

I, J

K

L

M

N

Q

R

S

T

U

V

W, X

Y

Z